Fodor's 9th Edition

Austria

KT-528-333

Fodor's Travel Publications • New York, Toronto, London, Sydney, Auckland

www.fodors.com

CONTENTS

MAPS

Circled letters in text correspond to letters on the photographs. For more information on the sights pictured, turn to the indicated page number Ⓐ on each photograph.

DESTINATION
AUSTRIA

Thanks to Richard Rodgers and Oscar Hammerstein, Wolfgang Amadeus Mozart, Johann Strauss, and many other great composers, you're likely to approach Austria with a song in your heart. Craggy, snowcapped peaks, dense forests, clear blue lakes, and unobtrusive man-made delights such as the charmingly onion-domed parish church of Seefeld ensure that you never stop humming. In fact this historically rich, culturally wealthy, geographically diverse country packs enough spectacle within its borders to perpetuate the song long after you've returned home.

VIENNA

Ⓑ 108

Along broad, sweeping boulevards like the Ringstrasse, which evoke the imperial era of Strauss, Metternich, and emperor Franz Josef, Vienna seems to move in the measured three quarter time of its famous waltzes. But while Vienna's outward face is a study in carefully balanced rhythms, constraint and license play a constant game of peekaboo all over the city. The monuments are at once solid and overbearingly opulent; compared to the magisterial presence of the Ⓕ**Parliament** building, its marble trim is as frothy as the *Schlag* served with Sachertorte at the Ⓓ**Hotel Sacher.** In contrast to the unrestrained riot of gilt inside the grand Ⓔ**Schönbrunn Palace**—the ruling Habsburgs' summer retreat in the heyday of the Austro-Hungarian empire and now a much-treasured museum—the acres of surrounding woods and luxuriant gardens are marshalled into a set piece of Baroque symmetry. Propriety and order rule even at the Fasching balls that mark the season of Mardi Gras and at the Ⓑ**Christkindlmarkt,** the Yuletide bazaar. Coffee-drink-

Ⓒ 92

ing is a ritual that every duti-
ful Viennese observes daily at
©**Café Hawelka** and the
city's other coffeehouses—of
which Vienna is said to have more than Switzerland has banks—
as gossip is shared, newspapers are read, and a little business is conducted. Ironically, soaring above this orderly city is
the Ⓐ**Stephansdom,** an asymmetrical, gargoyle-strewn
hodgepodge of a cathedral. It originates from no one historic
period, but it embodies the spirit of Vienna.

VIENNA

Pomp, circumstance, and no small amount of innovation pervade Vienna's 90 museums and its hundreds of churches and other landmarks. The city's vast holdings range from the Brueghels, Rembrandts, Vermeers, and other treasures in the Kunsthistorisches Museum

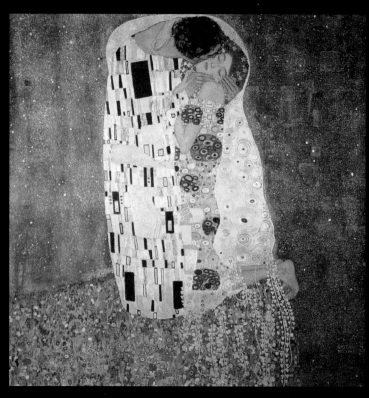

to the rare manuscripts that are lovingly showcased amid splendid frescoes in the magnificent National Library. The ①**Schönbrunn Palace** remains the prime bastion of Habsburgian opulence, most splendidly in the Grand Salon, where the Congress of Vienna celebrated the defeat of Napoléon. In the imperial Hofburg palace and its famed ⑥**Spanische Reitschule,** better known as the Spanish

Riding School, Lipizzaner stallions still prance to a measured cadence, just as they did when pulling emperor Franz Josef's royal carriage. And the Ⓚ**Karlskirche,** fronted by a row of massive pillars, is a magical vision of Baroque ornament, especially when illuminated at night. Nearly two centuries after it was built, a spate of visionary artists emerged from Vienna. Known as Secessionists, because the group had seceded from the conservative national arts academy, they were led by Gustav Klimt, who shocked turn-of-the-century Vienna with luxuriously nontraditional paintings such as *The Kiss,* now on view at the Ⓗ**Belvedere Palace.** His artistic bravado was soon emulated by legions of other painters of the Jugendstil school.

In our own age that honor has been bestowed on Friedensreich Hundertwasser, whose Ⓙ**Hundertwasserhaus** has, hands-down, become the city's most outrageous, antitraditional structure and one of its most popular attractions.

Ⓙ⟩ 44

Ⓚ⟩ 75

9

VIENNA

70

Vienna is the birthplace of some of the world's most beautiful music, from Beethoven's *Pastoral* Symphony to Johann Strauss the Younger's "Blue Danube" Waltz. Every traveler soon discovers that these and other ineffable strains are heard non-stop all over Vienna today. Monuments commemorating the musical geniuses who have lived here pepper the city. Check out the bust of Mozart in Ⓛ**Figarohaus,** one of the composer's many Viennese residences, where he wrote some of his most famous works. Pay your respects at Ⓟ**Pasqualatihaus,** where Beethoven lived while he composed *Fidelio,* his only opera. Tip your hat to the merrily gilded statue of Johann Strauss II in the ⓐ**Stadtpark.** Chances are that somewhere nearby an orchestra or an opera company or a church organist will be performing the works of these great men. To hear beloved operettas you can head for the venue that premiered *Die Fledermaus*

Ⓜ 101

© 59

(P) 52

and *The Merry Widow,* Theatre an der Wien. Amble into the Gothic interior of the Ⓞ**Augustinerkirche** any Sunday morning and you may have the pleasure of hearing its mighty organ accompany a high-mass oratorio by Mozart or Haydn. The city is also home to two of the world's greatest symphony orchestras, the Vienna Philharmonic, which makes its home in the world-renowned Ⓜ**Musikverein,** and the Vienna Symphony, which performs there and in another major venue, the Konzerthaus; not to mention a top opera house, the Staatsoper. Unfortunately, a seat at the Philharmonic's famous New Year's Eve concert at the Musikverein is hard to come by. So is a ticket to the annual Ⓝ**Opernball** at the Staatsoper. If you do manage to snag one and if you are one of those romantic souls

for whom the mere mention of Vienna conjures up images of hand-kissing, deep bows, and white-tied men twirling white-gloved women across the floor, you may think you've died and ascended into heaven—to the accompaniment of a waltz, of course.

© 37

VIENNA WOODS

Ⓐ 128   Ⓑ 136

The Viennese take their leisure seriously. Fortunately, they live in a city surrounded by enticing places to hike, plunge into natural thermal baths, sip a glass of Riesling wine, and otherwise find pleasure in their idle hours. The Wienerwald, as the Vienna Woods are known, marches right from the city's outskirts south to the Alps and across rolling hills sprinkled with dense woods, vineyards, and the occasional palace. The only dark patch in this otherwise blessed terrain is Ⓐ**Mayerling,** where emperor Franz Josef built a Carmelite convent on the site where Rudolf, his only son, and Marie Vetsera met an untimely end (lovers' pact or political intrigue—to this day, no one really knows). Of more interest to Viennese out for an idyllic getaway is ©**Gumpoldskirchen,** the tiny village with the big reputation for producing one of Europe's most famous

white wines. Tempting as it may be to linger over a glass or two at one of its vintners' houses, press on into the romantic countryside north and west of Vienna: the vines are even thicker in the Wine District, the Ⓑ**Weinviertel,** and the forests even denser in the Forest District, the Waldviertel.

Ⓐ 148

Respite from hustle and bustle is the draw of this rural region on the Hungarian border. Here the largest city is picturesque Graz, the *puszta* (steppe) seems to go on forever, Gypsy songs still fill the evening air, church steeples remain the highest structures in charming villages such as little Ⓑ**Murau,** and vineyards run right

EASTERN AUSTRIA

up to the walls of medieval settlements such as ©Ⓓ**Rust.** Near this town, on Ⓐ**Lake Neusiedl,** sometimes called the Viennese Sea because of its vastness, exotic sightings can be a surprise: windsurfers, for instance, often find themselves sharing the water with storks, who come to feed along the lake's reedy shores from their nests atop chimneys in the village—signifying good luck for locals and bringing glee to travelers.

Ⓑ 174

© 151

Ⓓ 151

DANUBE VALLEY

Ⓐ 211

Ⓑ 216

The famously blue Danube courses through Austria on its way from the Black Forest to the Black Sea, past medieval abbeys, fanciful Baroque monasteries, verdant pastures, and compact riverside villages. Although its hue is now somewhat less than azure, the waterway remains one of the most important in Europe, and to traverse its scenic length is to immerse yourself in a dose of heady history and culture—and, of course, to enjoy some pleasant scenery in the process. The storybook market town of Ⓐ**Steyr** is where Anton Bruckner composed his Sixth Symphony. For 10 years he was organist at nearby Ⓔ**St. Florian Abbey,** where he is buried, and his organ still fills the high-ceilinged church with rich, sorrowful notes. Richard the Lion-Hearted's spirit also pervades the region; he was once imprisoned in a castle whose ruins loom over Dürnstein, a village so quaint it seems designed by a stage director. Ⓒ**Krems,** founded more than 1,000 years ago, is another delightful spot, where wine is the main business of the day. For nonpareil splendor, head

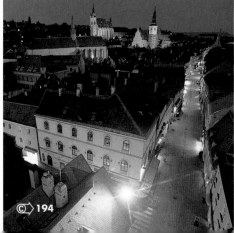

Ⓒ 194

Ⓓ 214

to the vast Benedictine abbey at Ⓑ**Göttweig** or world-famous Ⓓ**Melk Abbey,** best appreciated when the setting sun lights the twin towers cradling its Baroque dome. The magnificent library inside was the real-life setting of Umberto Eco's novel *The Name of the Rose.*

Ⓔ 210

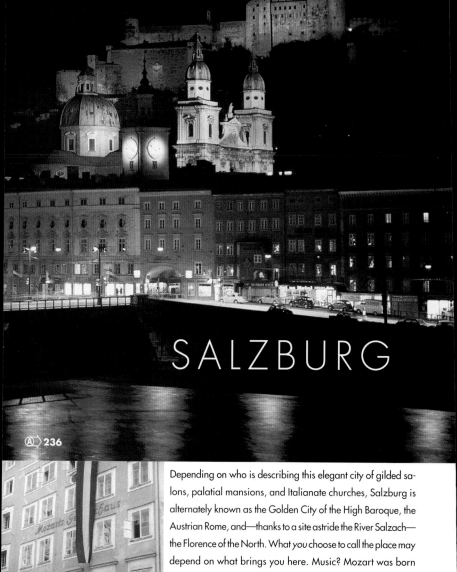

SALZBURG

Ⓐ 236

Depending on who is describing this elegant city of gilded salons, palatial mansions, and Italianate churches, Salzburg is alternately known as the Golden City of the High Baroque, the Austrian Rome, and—thanks to a site astride the River Salzach—the Florence of the North. What *you* choose to call the place may depend on what brings you here. Music? Mozart was born here in 1756 on the third floor of a house now cherished as Ⓑ**Mozarts Geburtshaus.** He penned many a masterpiece in his family home, now known as the Mozart Wohnhaus. His operas and sym-

Ⓑ 231

Ⓒ 234

phonies still ripple through the city, often from the august venue known as the Festspielhaus, most particularly during the city's acclaimed, celebrity-packed, summer music festival. Art? Explore artists' workshops along narrow, medieval Steingasse. Or zero in on Baroque churches and cloistered abbeys and on Rococo palaces such as ©**Schloss Leopoldskron** or, high atop a hill, Ⓐ Ⓔ **Fortress Hohensalzburg,** the brooding medieval fortress that towers over the river Salzach, the lavish state rooms inside belied by its grim facade. Drama? If the city's setting amid Alpine peaks and glacial lakes doesn't provide enough, you can attend the annual performances of *Jedermann* (*Everyman*) in the city square and take in a show at the famed Ⓕ**Marionettentheater.** Of course you need not come to Salzburg with a goal any more ambitious than to take a pleasant walk in a park such as the Ⓓ**Mirabell Gardens.** You may even glimpse an opera diva as you stroll.

The name, which translates into the unappealing "salt estates," doesn't begin to do justice to the scenery in Austria's Lake District. Think of *The Sound of Music,* which was filmed here on the home turf of the musically inclined von Trapp family, and you will easily envision the region's scenic pleasures. It's little wonder that Ⓑ**Hallstatt,** nestled between the dark waters of the Hallstätter See and the granite needles of the Dachstein range, is touted as Austria's prettiest lakeside village. More difficult by far is choosing the region's prettiest lake. Some would accord that honor to the clear blue Wolfgangsee, with the popular

S A L Z K A M M E R G U T

Ⓐ▷ **270**

Ⓑ▷ **268**

© 269

©**St. Wolfgang** vacation village on its shores, and others would nominate the breeze-rippled Traunsee, reflecting Ⓓ**Schloss Orth** in its surface. At Ⓐ**Bad Aussee** the only spectacle likely to divert your attention from the ever-present vista of lake and mountains is that of the unusually costumed citizenry getting into the swing of a summer festival. For natural beauty, Gosau takes best-in-show, for here the great Dachstein massif is mirrored in a fjordlike lake—a panorama so magical it inspired Richard Wagner when he composed *Parsifal*. Hidden within these mountain peaks are the eerily lit ice caves at ©**Dachstein.** You can also explore other caverns that have for centuries been mined for, yes, salt.

Ⓓ 266

EASTERN ALPS

Prettiest, tallest, and most gemütlich. This relatively small parcel of mountainous terrain between Salzburg and the Italian border elicits a barrage of superlatives, and rightly so. Here craggy peaks soar above 10,000 feet, challenging hikers, skiers, climbers, and other run-of-the-mill daredevils. The deep valleys are carpeted with wheat, and you don't have to look far to spot the white edelweiss, immortalized in one of Rodgers and Hammerstein's loveliest melodies (don't worry about picking a few flowers for souvenirs—they are cultivated here precisely for this purpose). The Ⓐ**Grossglockner High**

Ⓒ 316

Ⓑ 312

Alpine Highway, the most spectacular pass through the Alps, produces a thrill a minute, or at least a breathtaking glimpse of a fearsome glacier or a mountain peak every few hundred yards. A word of caution: If you approach the pass from the south you may never get any farther than lovely Ⓓ**Heiligenblut**—so perfect an embodiment of Alpine quaintness that it feels more like a movie set than like real life. Whether or not you succumb to the charm of its folklore, you can't help but be impressed by how perfectly the slender belfry of its Ⓑ**Church of St. Vincent** parish church echoes the soaring peak of the Grossglockner rising behind it. Climbers flock here to conquer the neighboring peaks. Skiers head instead to nearby Schladming, Filzmoos, and St. Johann im Pongau, smaller resorts that dwarf many a major stateside star. After a bracing day on the slopes of one of these, or perhaps the Ⓒ**Kitzsteinhorn,** you may want to check out Badgastein —and check into one of the town's luxurious hotel spas.

Ⓓ 311

INNSBRUCK
AND TIROL

Ⓐ > 357

With the Alps playing the stellar role, Nature steals every scene in the Tirol. Yet this is also a region richly graced with cosmopolitan cities, historic monuments, and the soothing balm of age-old faith. Proof of human endeavor is in ample supply. Innsbruck's famous tower, the Ⓒ**Stadtturm,** was built in the 15th century, in the reign of Maximilian I, when the city was the regal, magnificent seat of the Holy Roman Empire. The emperor's marble tomb in the Ⓑ**Hofkirche** is one of Innsbruck's many marvels, as is the

Ⓑ > 340

Ⓒ > 338

Goldenes Dachl, the legendary "Golden Roof" mansion, topped by gilded tiles at the behest of Duke Friedrich (who soon earned himself the nickname Friedl the Penniless). Maximilian's rule was an era of peace and prosperity for the Tirol, and the heritage is still in evidence, in tidy mountain burgs like Ⓐ**Going** and in religious traditions like Ⓓ**Schemenlaufen,** the Shrove

Ⓔ〉364

Tuesday procession. When the mountains call, you can do no better than make your way to the top of the Ötztal Alps near Ⓔ**Obergurgl,** Austria's highest village, surrounded nearly year-round by glaciers. Or make the trip to Ⓕ**St. Christoph,** founded as an inn for stranded travelers in the 15th century and now a refuge for skiing enthusiasts in search of pristine runs to test their mettle and comfortable inns where they can sleep off their exertions under a duvet as fluffy as the Austrian snow.

In Austria the sun shines most steadily on Carinthia, the warmly inviting southern province dubbed the Austrian Riviera. Here, in a felicitous coalescence of green valleys, crystalline lakes, wooded hills, and pastel towns, the nation's dreamlike charms seem most concentrated. Everyone adores the jaunty resort town of Ⓑ**Velden,** whose lakeside promenade is lined with 19th-cen-

CARINTHIA

Ⓐ〉287

tury mansions and illuminated by gas lamps that cast a glow over the glimmering Wörther See. Another favorite spot is quaint Maria Wörth, a peninsula village, where Baroque churches and crooked alleys are a backdrop for the waterside gaiety of beaches and pleasure boating. In nearby Spittal, at the elegant, amazingly preserved Renaissance-style Ⓐ**Schloss Porcia**, an arcaded courtyard serves as the sublime setting for concerts and plays on summer evenings—gentle entertainment worthy of this gentle corner of the world.

Ⓑ〉284

VORARLBERG

Ⓐ▷ 380

The Alps' formidably rocky ©**Arlberg Range** once isolated this region from the rest of Austria and from the modern world. The great engineering feat of the Arlberg Tunnel has made the area more accessible, yet it remains a little separate. Bridging the distance, classical opera is usually on tap, performed on a floating stage over the Bodensee, at the city's summer music festival, the Ⓐ**Bregenzer Festspiele.** And when it comes to first-class winter chic, Ⓑ**Lech** has some of the finest slopes around, drawing jet-setters with that timeless commodity, untrammeled powder.

Ⓑ▷ 389

©▷ 386

GREAT ITINERARIES

Vienna to Vorarlberg

14 days

Although it is one of Europe's smallest countries, Austria manages to pack within its border as many mountains, lakes, and picturesque cities as countries five times its size. This itinerary allows you to travel the country end-to-end within two weeks, feeling a bit like a Habsburg emperor as you tour the top sights.

VIENNA

3 days. Austria's glorious past is evident everywhere, but especially where this tour begins, in Ⓐ Vienna. Get to know the city by trolley with a sightseeing tour of the Ringstrasse. Take in the Kunsthistoriches Museum (the incredible detail of the famous Brueghel paintings

could keep you fascinated for hours, even if you're not an art aficionado), walk along Kärntnerstrasse to magnificent St. Stephen's Cathedral, and spend an afternoon in one of the city's cozy coffeehouses. Devote a half day to Schönbrunn Palace, and set aside an evening for a visit to a jovial Heuriger wine tavern. ☞ Chapters 1 and 2.

DANUBE RIVER FROM VIENNA TO LINZ

1 day. To zoom from Vienna to Linz by autobahn would be to miss out on one of Austria's most treasured sights, the blue Danube. To tour some quaint wine villages, follow the "Austrian Romantic Road" (Rte. 3), along the north bank of the river, instead of the speedier A1 autobahn. Cross to the south side of the Danube to the breathtaking Baroque abbey at Melk and along the way visit the 1,000-year-old town of Krems

and picture-perfect Dürnstein, in the heart of the Wachau wine region. ☞ Chapter 4.

LINZ

2 days. Fast-forward into Austria's future with a stop in progressive Linz, the country's third largest city. Linz is a busy port on the Danube and an important center for trade and business. Techno geeks will enjoy the recently opened Ars Electronica Center; other visitors will enjoy the beautifully restored medieval courtyards of the Altstadt (old town). For great views, ride the city's Pöstlingbergbahn, the world's steepest mountain railway, or opt for a Danube steamer cruise to Enns. ☞ Chapter 4.

SALZKAMMERGUT

2 days. For Austria in all its Hollywood splendor, head to the idyllic Salzkammergut, better known as the Lake District, where The Sound of Music was filmed. The town of Bad Ischl—famous for its operetta festival and pastries—makes a good base. Travel south to Ebensee on Rte. 145 toward Hallstatt, one of Austria's most photographed lakeside villages. Return to Bad Ischl, then head west to St. Wolfgang and St. Gilgen for swimming and sailing. More adventurous souls will follow A1/E55 to

the Hallein salt mines and then to Europe's largest ice cave, in Werfen.
☞ *Chapters 6 and 8.*

SALZBURG

2 days. This is a city made for pedestrians, with an abundance of churches, palaces, mansions, and—as befits the birthplace of Mozart—music festivals. Stroll through the old city center, with its wrought-iron shop signs, tour the medieval Fortress Hohensalzburg, and relax in the Mirabell Gardens (where the von Trapp children "Do-Re-Mi"-ed). Children of all ages will adore the famed ⑧Marionettentheater.
☞ *Chapter 5.*

INNSBRUCK AND TIROL

2 days. Tour Innsbruck's treasures—including the famous ©Golden Roof mansion and the Hofburg—but do as the Tiroleans do and spend time reveling in the high mountain majesty. After all, Innsbruck is the only major city in the Alps. For a splendid panorama, take the Hungerburgbahn (cable railway) to the Hafelekar, high above the Inn Valley. For a trip through the quaint

villages around Innsbruck, ride the Stubaitalbahn, a charming old-time train, to Neustift, or head by bus to the Stubai Glacier for year-round skiing.
☞ *Chapter 9.*

BREGENZ

2 days. Taking the Arlberg Pass (or the much more scenic Silvretta High Alpine Highway), head to the city of Bregenz, capital of Vorarlberg. Bregenz owes as much of its character to neighboring Switzerland and Germany as to Austria and is most appealing in summer, when sun-worshipers crowd the shores of Lake Constance to enjoy an opera festival set on the world's largest outdoor floating stage. Take a lake excursion and explore Bregenz's medieval Oberstadt (upper town). Trains can easily connect you to Zurich or Munich, or you can head south to Italy via the Brenner Pass from Innsbruck.
☞ *Chapter 10.*

By Public Transportation
There is frequent train service between the major cities. Side trips into the countryside are possible by bus or train. Trains leave every half hour from the Westbahnhof in Vienna, arriving in Linz in

about 2 hours. From Linz, it is 2½ hours to the Salzburg Hauptbahnhof, and another 2 hours to the Innsbruck terminal, then another 2½ hours to Bregenz. For a more romantic kickoff, travel by a DDSG/Blue Danube Schiffahrt riverboat from Vienna to Linz (departs Vienna daily at 7 AM).

Mountain Magic
9 days

This is a tour for romantic dreamers—a trip where Alpine glory is all around you: meadows and forests set against a backdrop of towering craggy peaks, and gentle wooded rambles that lead to clear mountain lakes and storybook castles. The emphasis here is on letting go of your worries and allowing the natural beauty of the countryside to work its magic.

BAD ISCHL/ST. WOLFGANG

2 days. The villages and lakes of the Salzkammergut region extend south from Salzburg like a string of pearls. Base yourself in Bad Ischl, a first-class spa in the heart of the Lake District. From there, head 16 km (10 mi) west to St. Wolfgang, one of the most photo-friendly villages in Austria. For the most scenic surroundings, park in nearby Strobl and hop one of the lake ferries to the pedestrian-only village, where you can relax with a coffee on the terrace of the famous Weisses Rössl (White Horse Inn), marvel at the 16th-century Michael Pacher altarpiece in the parish church, and take the railway up the 5,800-ft Schaftberg peak for heavenly vistas.
☞ *Chapter 6.*

UPPER AUSTRIA
(OBERÖSTERREICH)

Linz

GERMANY

A8

Salzburg

Mondsee

St. Wolfgang

Strobl

Bad Ischl

Gosau am
Dachstein

Altaussee
Bad Aussee

Ellmau   Going

Rattenberg **A12**   Soll   **312**   **Kitzbühel**   Werfen

Alpbach

Krimmler   **161**

Falls   Zell

am See   **311**   **A10**

Hallstatt   **146**

Innsbruck

TIROL

350 km/219 mi.

209 km/131 mi.

SALZ-
BURG

Heiligenblut

CARINTHIA
(KÄRNTEN)

EAST

TIROL

108   **107**

Schloss
Hochosterwitz

Millstadt

Spittal   **A10**

Maria
Wörth   **83**

Velden

A2

Pörtschach

Klagenfurt

HALLSTATT

1 day. Set on fjordlike
ⒹHallstättersee, this jewel is
an optical illusion perched
between water and moun-
tain—a tight grouping of
terraced fishermen's cottages
and churches, offering, at first
glance, no apparent reason
why it doesn't tumble into the
lake. On a sunny day the
views of the lake and village,
considered the oldest settlement in Austria, are spectacular, and on a misty morning
they are even more so.
Consider a canoe outing, or
tour the Hallstatt salt mine,
the oldest in the world.
☞ Chapter 6.

WERFEN

1 day. Take in the birds-of-
prey show at the formidable
Burg Hohenwerfen castle,
built in the 11th century, tour
the Eisriesenwelt ("World of
the Ice Giants")—the largest
collection of ice caves in
Europe—and cap the day
with dinner at Obauer, one of
Austria's finest restaurants.
☞ Chapter 8.

ZELL AM SEE

1 day. Some 50 km (30 mi)
from Werfen, the charming
lake resort of Zell am See is
nestled under the 6,000-ft

Schmittenhöhe mountain.
Ride the cable car from the
center of town for a bird's-eye
view, then take the narrow-
gauge Pinzgauer railroad
through the Salzach river
valley to famous Krimmler
Falls.
☞ Chapter 8.

HEILIGENBLUT

1 day. Head skyward over
the dizzying Hoch
glockner High Alpine Highway (open May–October) to
one of Austria's loveliest
villages, Heiligenblut, which
fans out across the upper
Möll Valley with fabulous
views of the Grossglockner,
at 12,470 ft the highest
mountain in Austria.
☞ Chapter 8.

KITZBÜHEL/GOING

1 day. Travel to the glamorous resort town of
ⒺKitzbühel for a bit of
window shopping and
celebrity spotting, then

continue to Going, Ellmau,
and Söll along Rte. 312.
These villages have superb
restaurants and hotels, but the
real reason to overnight here
is to admire the view of the
rugged "Wild Emperor," one
of the most beautiful mountains in the Alps.
☞ Chapter 9.

RATTENBERG/ALPBACH

2 days. In these two charming villages, you might think
you've been transported back
in time, if it weren't for all the
tourists roaming the ancient
streets. Rattenberg has
colorful medieval facades,

Ⓔ 359

Ⓓ 269

famous glassware, and a delightful Inn River promenade, and the narrow, flower-bedecked streets of tiny Alpbach are set within one of Tirol's most bucolic valleys. Take the Wiedersbergerhorn Gondola to the top of the mountain for a panorama, then hike back to town. End your trip in Innsbruck, 32 km (20 mi) west.
☞ Chapter 9.

By Public Transportation
Although it is much simpler to travel this route by car, it can also be undertaken using public transportation (note that many trains do not run on Sunday). Trains link Salzburg, Bad Ischl, and Hallstatt; travel to St. Wolfgang by post bus. From Hallstatt, hop the train to Bad Aussee and on to Irdning, where you may have to change trains to Bischofshofen before reaching Zell am See. Travel to and from Heiligenblut by bus. Trains will take you to Kitzbühel but not to Going, so bus it from Kitz, and then continue by bus to the train station in Wörgl, which is on the main line to Innsbruck. This line includes a stop in Rattenberg, but the bus is the only way to get to Alpbach.

The Lake Districts
7 days

Although separated by only a few hours' drive, the two most famous lake districts of Austria have distinctly different personalities. The Salzkammergut is the Alps at their most brilliant—after all, The Sound of Music was filmed here. The area is also rich in Habsburg history, first as the source of wealth in the form of "white gold," or salt, and later as the imperial playground, after Emperor Franz Josef I made his official summer residence here in 1854. Today the region is still the playground of the wealthy, who come to luxuriate in royal-class spas. In contrast, the lake district of sunny Carinthia, known as Austria's Riviera, is all about summer fun: swimming,

fishing, boating, and soaking up rays along the shores of the country's warmest lakes.

MONDSEE
1 day. Mondsee (Moon Lake) makes a good starting point in the Salzkammergut due to easy access from the A1 autobahn. You'll want to see St. Michael's parish church, made famous as the wedding chapel in The Sound of Music. Even if the thought of icy-cold lake water makes your toes turn blue, give swimming here a try, as Mondsee is one of the warmest lakes in the region.
☞ Chapter 6.

GOSAU AM DACHSTEIN
1 day. Today leave your bathing suit packed, but lace up your hiking boots. Richard Wagner was inspired by the spectacular view of the Dachstein massif range, reflected in a sparkling, fjord-like mountain lake of the Vorderer Gosausee. Two more (less ideally situated) lakes can be reached on foot in two hours. Take the gondola up to the Gablonzer Hütte for a refreshment, then hike back to Gosau.
☞ Chapter 6.

BAD AUSSEE
1 day. A year-round favorite, Bad Aussee is girded by steep mountains that keep the village cool in midsummer and snowy all winter. Only card-carrying polar bears will want to swim here in the icy, spring-fed lakes. Others will take to the heated pools of

the spa complex and explore the charming village of Altaussee.
☞ Chapter 6.

MILLSTATT
2 days. 160 km (96 mi) from Bad Aussee, Millstatt is a comfortable resort across the lake from Spittal an der Drau, a gateway to the Carinthia lakes region. Austrians flock to Millstatt for its International Music Weeks in July and August. After some bathing and boating, explore the superb Renaissance-era Schloss Porcia in Spittal.
☞ Chapter 7.

KLAGENFURT
2 days. After nosing around this lakeside resort, head north on Rte. 83 to ⓕSchloss Hochosterwitz, the model for Walt Disney's Snow White castle. Return to Klagenfurt, then follow the north bank of the Wörthersee to elegant Pörtschach, beloved for its promenade, beach, and some of the warmest waters in Austria. Nearby are chic, lively Velden, known for its upscale shopping and casino, and the relentlessly picturesque village of Maria Wörth. Both can be reached on a boat tour.
☞ Chapter 7.

By Public Transportation
With the notable exception of one town, Gosau am Dachstein, it is possible to make this trip using a combination of train and bus. Bus service is regularly offered throughout the Salzkammergut. From Bad Aussee you will have to backtrack to Salzburg for trains to Carinthia. Trains connect Salzburg, Spittal, and Klagenfurt, but it is more convenient to make short hops by bus.

ⓕ 297

FODOR'S
CHOICE

Even with so many special places in Austria, Fodor's writers and editors have their favorites. Here are a few that stand out.

MOMENTS

Ⓐ **Mirabell Gardens, Salzburg, after the first snow.** A mantle of white makes this fairy-tale setting even more magical. ☞ p. 237

Ⓒ **Hiking along the Danube, the Wachau.** Pack a bag with water, bread, cheese, cold cuts, and fresh fruit, and spend a day crossing streams, traversing vineyards, meeting the odd deer or fox, or kindred walker, or farmer. ☞ p. 189

Ⓓ **The Spanish Riding School, Vienna.** Where else can you see horses dance a minuet to Mozart? ☞ p. 63

New Year's Day concert in the Musikverein, Vienna. You've seen it on television, but now you're *here* in the Golden Hall—its gilt bare-breasted ladies supporting the balconies, the walls festooned with floral displays—sharing in the excitement. ☞ p. 101

Hallstatt on a misty morning, Salzkammergut. At "the world's prettiest lakeside village," the surrounding mountains often disappear into the mist, leaving the unforgettable shadowy outline of the church and town buildings hugging the lakeshore. ☞ p. 268

PLACES

Ⓘ **Gosau am Dachstein, Salzkammergut.** This vista is so breathtaking it inspired some of Wagner's greatest music. ☞ p. 267

Ⓗ **Prater, Vienna.** No visit to Vienna is complete without a ride on this famous amusement park's 200-ft-high Ferris wheel. ☞ p. 45

Ⓑ **Schönbrunn Palace, Vienna.** Mythically grand, this Habsburgian extravaganza wows one and all with its gilt and grandeur. ☞ p. 80

Ⓖ **St. Florian, Upper Austria.** This abbey, where composer Anton Bruckner was organist, is impressive for its size alone. ☞ p. 210

Ⓕ **Stephansdom, Vienna.** Time seems to have stood still at St. Stephen's Cathedral in the best possible way. ☞ p. 48

Steyr, Upper Austria. Wonderfully colorful decorative facades address the main square, brooded over by the castle above. The ensemble is worthy of Hollywood. ☞ p. 211

Grossglockner Highway, Eastern Alps. This engineering masterpiece challenges the driver but brings, one after another, glorious panoramas of snowswept Alpine horizons and lush meadows. ☞ p. 313

DINING

Landhaus Bacher, Mautern. One of the culinary gems of the Danube Valley, this is the domain of the consistently innovative Lisl Wagner-Bacher. *$$$$* ☞ p. 215

Maria Loretto, Klagenfurt. At this lakeside villa, a view of the Wörther See accompanies some of Carinthia's best seafood. *$$$$* ☞ p. 281

Steirereck, Vienna. In Austria's top restaurant, a cheerfully blazing fire, gleaming sandstone walls, and candlelight create the perfect setting for the chef's contemporary Viennese cuisine. *$$$$* ☞ p. 82

Schratt, Bad Ischl. The enchanting, secluded villa where Katharina "Kati" Schratt, the mistress of Emperior Franz Josef, once lived is one of the best places to dine in the area. Save room for a Guglhupf cake, Franz Josef's favorite, which comes warm out of the oven. *$$$$* ☞ p. 265

Loibnerhof, Unterloiben. In fine weather, tables are spread in the fragrant apple orchard. *$$$* ☞ p. 196

Zum Eulenspiegel, Salzburg. Wonderful nooks and crannies, mullioned windows, gleaming dark-paneled walls, and candlelight make for an unforgettable evening. *$$$* ☞ p. 241

Ⓔ **Artner, Vienna.** Spectacular wines and goat cheese from the Artner Winery in the Carnuntum region east of Vienna are highlighted in this upscale eatery. *$$–$$$* ☞ p. 86

Das Bräu, Lofer. Cowbells, harnesses and stirrups hang from ancient wooden beams in this rustic spot tended by one of Austria's up-and-coming chefs. *$$$* ☞ p. 358

Ⓙ **Café Central, Vienna.** Nothing embodies Viennese café society like this grand coffeehouse. Trotsky supposedly plotted the Russian Revolution here, using the alias Bronstein. *$$* ☞ p. 92

LODGING

Österreichischer Hof, Salzburg. With a staggering Old City view, this grande dame goes out of its way to provide beauty and comfort in each exquisite room. *$$$$* ☞ p. 245

Palais Schwarzenberg, Vienna. Built in the early 1700s, the magnificent palace retains a sense of history while offering sumptuously appointed rooms and that ultimate luxury—a private park in the middle of Vienna. *$$$$* ☞ p. 96

Schloss Obermayerhofen, Bad Waltersdorf. Museum-worthy tapestries and antiques decorate the ancient rooms here. *$$$$* ☞ p. 159

Bad Blumau, Blumau. Designed by Friedensreich Hundertwasser, this phenomenal spa hotel is a brilliant patchwork of checks, turrets, and multi-colored ceramic pillars. *$$$$* ☞ p. 159

Faust Schlössl, Aschach. It's said that the Devil built this golden hilltop castle in a single night for Dr. Faustus—and haunts it still. *$$* ☞ p. 209

Gasthof Zauner, Hallstatt. Carved headboards and balconies embellish this picture-perfect chalet. *$$–$$$* ☞ p. 269

Weisses Kreuz, Innsbruck. Mozart was once a guest at this hotel in the heart of the old city. *$$* ☞ p. 346

1 VIENNA

Magnificent, magnetic, and magical, Vienna beguiles one and all with Old World charm and courtly grace. It is a place where head waiters still bow as if saluting a Habsburg prince and Lipizzaner stallions dance intricate minuets to the strains of Mozart—a city that waltzes and works in three-quarter time. Like a well-bred grande dame, Vienna doesn't hurry, and neither should you. Saunter through its stately streets—peopled by the spirits of Beethoven and Strauss, Metternich, and Freud—marvel at its Baroque palaces, and dream an afternoon away at a cozy *Kaffeehaus*.

Updated by
Bonnie Dodson

T HE CITIZENS OF VIENNA, it has been said, properly waltz only from the waist down, whirling around the crowded dance floor while holding their upper bodies ramrod straight. The sight can be breathtaking in its sweep and splendor, and its elegant coupling of free-wheeling exuberance and rigid formality—of license and constraint—is quintessentially Viennese. The town palaces all over the inner city—built mostly during the 18th century—present in stone and stucco a similar artful synthesis of license and constraint. They make Vienna a Baroque city that is, at its best, an architectural waltz.

Visitors who tour Vienna today can easily feel they're doing so in three-quarter time. As they explore churches filled with statues of golden saints and pink-cheeked cherubs, wander through treasure-packed museums, or while away an afternoon in one of those multitudinous meccas of mocha (the inevitable cafés), they can begin to feel lapped in lashings of rich, delicious, whipped cream—the beloved *Schlagobers* that garnishes most Viennese pastries. The ambience of the city is predominantly ornate and fluffy: white horses dancing to elegant music; snow frosting the opulent draperies of Empress Maria Theresa's monument, set in the formal patterns of "her" lovely square; a gilded Johann Strauss, playing gracefully among a grove of green trees; lavish decorations, discreetly filling the interior courtyards of town houses that present a dignified face to the outside world; grim Greek legends transformed by the voluptuous music of Richard Strauss; the tangible, geometric impasto of Klimt's paintings; the stately pavane of a mechanical clock. All these will create in the visitor the sensation of a metropolis that likes to be visited and admired—and which indeed is well worth admiring and visiting.

For many centuries, this has been the case. One of the great capitals of Europe, Vienna was for centuries home to the Habsburg rulers of the Austro-Hungarian Empire. Today the empire is long gone, but many reminders of the city's imperial heyday remain, carefully preserved by the tradition-loving Viennese. When it comes to the arts, the glories of the past are particularly evergreen, thanks to the cultural legacy created by the many artistic geniuses nourished here.

From the late 18th century on, Vienna's culture—particularly its musical forte—was famous throughout Europe. Haydn, Mozart, Beethoven, Schubert, Brahms, Strauss, Mahler, and Bruckner all lived in the city, producing music that is still played in concert halls all over the world. And at the tail end of the 19th century the city's artists and architects—Gustav Klimt, Egon Schiele, Oskar Kokoschka, Josef Hoffmann, Otto Wagner, and Adolf Loos among them—brought about an unprecedented artistic revolution, a revolution that swept away the past and set the stage for the radically experimental art of the 20th century. "Form follows function," the artists of the late-19th-century Jugendstil proclaimed. Their echo is still heard in the city's contemporary arts and crafts galleries—even in the glinting, space-needle-like object that hovers over the north end of Vienna. It's actually the city waste incinerator, designed by the late, great artist Friedensreich Hundertwasser.

At the close of World War I the Austro-Hungarian Empire was dismembered, and Vienna lost its cherished status as the seat of imperial power. Its influence was much reduced, and its population began to decline (unlike what happened in Europe's other great cities), falling from around 2 million to the current 1.7 million. Today, however, the city's future looks brighter, for with the collapse of the Iron Curtain, Vienna may eventually regain its traditional status as the hub of Central Europe.

For many first-time visitors, the city's one major disappointment concerns the Danube River. The inner city, it turns out, lies not on the river's main course but on one of its narrow offshoots, known as the Danube Canal. As a result, the sweeping river views expected by most newcomers fail to materialize.

For this, the Romans are to blame, for when Vienna was founded as a Roman military encampment around AD 100, the walled garrison was built not on the Danube's main stream but rather on the largest of the river's eastern branches, where it could be bordered by water on three sides. The wide, present-day Danube did not take shape until the late 19th century, when, to prevent flooding, its various branches were rerouted and merged.

The Romans maintained their camp for some 300 years (the emperor Marcus Aurelius is thought to have died in Vindobona, as it was called, in 180) finally abandoning the site around 400. The settlement survived the Roman withdrawal, however, and by the 13th century development was sufficient to require new city walls to the south. According to legend, the walls were financed by the English: in 1192 the local duke kidnapped King Richard I (the Lion-Hearted), en route home from the Third Crusade, and held him prisoner in Dürnstein, upriver, for two years until he was expensively ransomed by his mother, Eleanor of Aquitaine.

Vienna's third set of walls dates from 1544, when the existing walls were improved and extended. The new fortifications were built by the Habsburg dynasty, which ruled the Austro-Hungarian Empire for an astonishing 640 years, beginning with Rudolf I in 1273 and ending with Karl I in 1918. The walls stood until 1857, when Emperor Franz Josef finally decreed that they be demolished and replaced by the famous tree-lined Ringstrasse (Ring Street).

During medieval times the city's growth was relatively slow, and its heyday as a European capital did not begin until 1683, after a huge force of invading Turks laid siege to the city for two months, to be finally routed by an army of Habsburg allies. Among the supplies that the fleeing Turks left behind were sacks filled with coffee beans. It was these beans, so the story goes, that gave a local entrepreneur the idea of opening the first public coffeehouse; they remain a Viennese institution to this day.

The passing of the Turkish threat produced a Viennese building boom, and the Baroque style was the architectural order of the day. Flamboyant, triumphant, joyous, and extravagantly ostentatious, the new art form— imported from Italy—transformed the city into a vast theater in the 17th and 18th centuries. Life became a dream—the gorgeous dream of the Baroque, with its gilded madonnas and cherubs; its soaring, twisted columns; its painted heavens on the ceilings; its graceful domes. In the 19th century, a reaction set in—the Biedermeier epoch, when middle-class industriousness and sober family values led to a new style. Then came the Strauss era—that lighthearted period that conjures up imperial balls, "Wine, Women, and Song," heel-clicking, and hand-kissing. Today, visitors will find that all these eras have left their mark on Vienna, making it a city possessed of a special grace. It is this grace that gives Vienna the cohesive architectural character that sets the city so memorably apart from its great rivals—London, Paris, and Rome.

Pleasures and Pastimes

Café Society

It used to be said that there were more cafés and coffeehouses in Vienna than there were banks in Switzerland. Whether or not this can still be claimed, the true flavor of Vienna can't be savored without visiting some of its meccas of mocha. Every afternoon at 4, the coffee-and-pastry ritual of *Kaffeejause* takes place from one end of the city to the other. Regulars take their *Stammtisch* (usual table) and sit until they go home for dinner. They come to gossip, read the papers, negotiate business, play cards, meet a spouse (or someone else's), or—who knows?—just have a cup of coffee. Whatever the reason, the Viennese use cafés and coffeehouses as club, pub, bistro, and even a home away from home. (Old-timers recall the old joke: "Pardon me, would you mind watching my seat for a while so I can go out for a cup of coffee?")

In fact, to savor the atmosphere of the coffeehouse, you must allow time. There is no need to worry about outstaying one's welcome, even over a single small cup of coffee—so set aside a morning or afternoon, and take along this book. For historical overtones, head for the Café Central— Lev Bronstein, otherwise known as Leon Trotsky, liked to play chess here. For Old World charm, check out the opulent Café Landtmann, which was Freud's favorite meeting place, or the elegant Café Sacher (famous for its Sachertorte); for the smoky art scene, go to the Café Hawelka. Wherever you end up, never ask for a plain cup of coffee; at the very least, order a mocha *mit Obers* (with whipped cream) from the *Herr Ober,* or any of many other delightful variations (☞ Cafés *in* Dining, *below*).

The Heurige

It is a memorable experience to sit at the edge of a vineyard on the Kahlenberg with a tankard of young white wine and listen to the *Schrammel* quartet playing sentimental Viennese songs. The wine taverns, called *Heurige* (the single appellation is *Heuriger*) for the new wine that they serve, are very much a part of and typical of the city (although not unique to Vienna). Heurige sprang up in 1784 when Joseph II decreed that owners of vineyards could open their own private wine taverns. The Viennese discovered that it was cheaper to go out to the wine than to bring it inside the city walls where taxes were levied. The Heuriger owner is supposed to be licensed to serve only the produce of his own vineyard, a rule long more honored in the breach than in the observance (it would take a sensitive palate indeed to differentiate between the various vineyards).

These taverns (☞ Heurige *in* Dining, *below*) in the wine-growing districts on the outskirts of the city (in such villages as Neustift am Walde, Sievering, Nussdorf, and Grinzing) vary from the simple front room of a vintner's house to ornate establishments. The true Heuriger is open for only a few weeks a year to allow the vintner to sell tax-free a certain quantity of his production for consumption on his own premises. The commercial establishments keep to a somewhat more regular season but still sell wine only from their own vines.

The choice is usually between a "new" and an "old" white (or red) wine, but you can also ask for a milder or sharper wine according to your taste. Most Heurige are happy to let you sample the wines before you order. You can also order a *Gespritzter,* half wine and half soda water. The waitress brings the wine, usually in a ¼-liter mug or liter carafe, but you get your own food from the buffet. The wine tastes as mild as lemonade, but it packs a punch. If it isn't of good quality, you will know by a raging headache the next day.

Jugendstil Jewels

From 1897 to 1907, the Vienna Secession movement gave rise to one of the most spectacular manifestations of the pan-European style known as Art Nouveau. Viennese took to calling the look *Jugendstil,* or the "young style." In such dazzling edifices as Otto Wagner's Wienzeile majolica-adorned mansion and Adolf Loos's Looshaus, Jugendstil architects rebelled against the prevailing 19th-century historicism that had created so many imitation Renaissance town houses and faux Grecian temples. Josef Maria Olbrich, Josef Hoffman, and Otto Schönthal took William Morris's Arts and Crafts movement, added dashes of Charles Rennie Mackintosh and flat-surface Germanic geometry, and came up with a luxurious style that shocked turn-of-the-century Viennese (and infuriated Emperor Franz Josef). Many artists united to form the Vienna Secession—whose most famous member was painter Gustav Klimt—and the Wiener Werkstätte, which transformed the objects of daily life with a sleek modern look. Today, Jugendstil buildings are among the most fascinating structures in Vienna. The shrine of the movement is the world-famous Secession Building—the work of Josef Maria Olbrich—the cynosure of all eyes on the Friedrichstrasse.

Museums and Marvels

You could spend months just perusing Vienna's 90 museums. Subjects range alphabetically from art to wine, and in between are found such oddities as bricks and burials, such marvels as carriages and clocks, and such memorials as Mozart and martyrs. If your time is short, the one museum not to be overlooked is the Kunsthistorisches Museum, Vienna's famous art museum. This is one of the great museums of the world, with masterworks by Titian, Rembrandt, Vermeer, and Velásquez, and an outstanding collection of Brueghels.

Given a little more time, the Schatzkammer, or Imperial Treasury, is well worth a visit, for its opulent bounty of crown jewels, regal attire, and other trappings of court life. The sparkling new Silberkammer, a museum of court silver and tableware, is fascinating for its "behind-the-scenes" views of state banquets and other elegant representational affairs. The best-known museums tend to crowd up in late-morning and mid-afternoon hours; you can beat the mobs by going earlier or around the noon hour, at least to the larger museums that are open without a noontime break.

The Sound—and Sights—of Music

What closer association to Vienna is there but music? Boasting one of the world's greatest concert venues (Musikverein), two of the world's greatest symphony orchestras (Vienna Philharmonic and Vienna Symphony), and one of the top opera houses (Staatsoper), it's no wonder that music and the related politics are subjects of daily conversation. During July and August—just in time for tourists—the city hosts the Vienna Summer of Music, with numerous special events and concerts.

For the music-loving tourist who is excited by the prospect of treading in the footprints of the mighty, seeing where masterpieces were committed to paper or standing where a long-loved work was either praised or damned at its first performance, Vienna is tops: the city is saturated with musical history. There is the apartment where Mozart wrote his last three symphonies, the house where Schubert was born, and, just a tram ride away, the path that inspired Beethoven's *Pastoral* Symphony. Just below, you'll find a handy list of these musical landmarks.

Of course, there is also music to delight as well as inspire. The statue of Johann Strauss II in the Stadtpark tells all. To see him, violin tucked under his chin, is to imagine those infectious waltzes, "Wine, Women, and Song," "Voices of Spring," and best of all, the "Emperor." But quite possibly you will not need to imagine them. Chances are, somewhere in the environs, an orchestra will be playing them. Head for the Theatre an der Wien to hear great operetta (*Die Fledermaus* and *The Merry Widow* both premiered here) or to the Volksoper. While the traditional classics are the main fare for the conservative, traditional Viennese, acceptance of modern music is growing, as are the audiences for pop and jazz.

Musicians' residences abound, and many are open as museums. The most famous are Mozart's Figarohaus and Beethoven's Pasqualatihaus, which are discussed in the Exploring sections below. Vienna has many other music landmarks scattered over the city—here's a sample: **Schubert**—a native of the city, unlike most of Vienna's other famous composers—was born at Nussdorferstrasse 54 (☎ 01/317–3601, U-Bahn: U2/Schotten-ring, then Streetcar 37 or 38 to Canisiusgasse), in the Ninth District, and died in the Fourth District at Kettenbrückengasse 6 (☎ 01/581-6730, U-Bahn: U4/Kettenbrückengasse). **Joseph Haydn's house,** which includes a Brahms memorial room, is at Haydngasse 19 (☎ 01/596–1307, U-Bahn: U4/Pilgramgasse or U3/Zieglergasse) in the Sixth District. **Beethoven's Heiligenstadt residence,** where at age 32 he wrote the "Heiligenstadt Tes-tament," an anguished cry of pain and protest against his ever-increas-ing deafness, is at Probusgasse 6 in the 19th District (☎ 01/370–5408, U-Bahn: U4/Heiligenstadt, then Bus 38A to Wählamt). All the above houses contain commemorative museums. Admission is AS25; a block of 10 AS25 tickets for city museums costs AS160. All are open Tuesday–Sunday 9–12:15 and 1–4:30. The home of the most popular composer of all, waltz king **Johann Strauss the Younger,** can be visited at Praterstrasse 54 (☎ 01/214–0121, U-Bahn: U4/Nestroypl.), in the Second District; he lived here when he composed "The Blue Danube Waltz" in 1867.

Stepping Out in Three-Quarter Time

Ever since the 19th-century Congress of Vienna—when pundits laughed "*Elle danse, mais elle ne marche pas*" (the city "dances, but it never gets anything done")—Viennese extravagance and gaiety have been world fa-mous. Fasching, the season of Prince Carnival, was given over to court balls, opera balls, masked balls, chambermaids' and bakers' balls, and a hundred other gatherings, many held within the glittering interiors of Baroque theaters and palaces. Presiding over the dazzling evening gowns and gilt-encrusted uniforms, towering headdresses, flirtatious fans, *cham-bres séparées,* "Wine, Women, and Song," *Die Fledermaus,* "Blue Danube," hand-kissing and gay abandon, was the baton of the waltz emperor, Jo-hann Strauss. White-gloved women and men in white tie would glide over marble floors to his heavenly melodies. They still do. Now, as in the days of Franz Josef, Vienna's old three-quarter-time rhythm strikes up anew each year during Carnival, from New Year's Eve until Mardi Gras.

During January and February, as many as 40 balls may be held in a sin-gle evening, the most famous—some say too famous—being the Opern-ball. This event transforms the Vienna Opera House into the world's most beautiful ballroom (and transfixes all of Austria when shown live on national television). For a price, theoretically, anyone can attend, but corporate interests often buy up most of the tickets. The invitation to the Opernball reads, "*Frack mit Dekorationen,*" which means that it's time to dust off your Legion of Honor medal and women mustn't wear white (reserved for debutantes). Remember that you must dance the *Linkswalzer*—the counterclockwise, left-turning waltz that is the only correct way to dance in Vienna. After your gala evening, finish off the morning with a *Kater Frühstuck*—a hangover breakfast—of goulash soup. For a rundown on the major balls that the public can attend during the winter season, *see* Nightlife *in* Nightlife and the Arts, *below.*

EXPLORING VIENNA

To the Viennese, the most prestigious address of Vienna's 23 *Bezirke,* or districts, is the First District (the inner city, bounded by the Ringstrasse and the Danube Canal). The Second through Ninth districts surround the inner city (starting with the Second District across the Danube Canal and running clockwise); the 10th through 23rd districts form a second concentric ring of suburbs. The vast majority of sightseeing attractions are to be found in the First District. For hard-core sightseers who wish to supplement the key attractions that follow, the tourist office (☞ Contacts and Resources *in* Vienna A to Z, *below*) has a booklet, "Vienna from A–Z" (AS70), that gives short descriptions of some 250 sights around the city, all numbered and keyed to a fold-out map at the back, as well as to numbered wall plaques on the buildings themselves. Note that the nearest U-Bahn (subway) stop to most city attractions described below is included at the end of the service information (☞ Subway system map *in* Getting Around *in* Vienna A to Z, *below*). The more important churches have coin-operated (AS10) tape machines that give an excellent commentary in English on the history and architecture of the church.

Vienna is a city to explore and discover on foot. The description of the city on the following pages is divided into eight areas: seven that explore the architectural riches of central Vienna and an eighth that describes Schönbrunn Palace and its gardens. Above all, *look up* as you tour Vienna: some of the most fascinating architectural and ornamental bits are on upper stories or atop the city's buildings.

Numbers in the text correspond to numbers in the margin and on the Vienna, Hofburg, and Schönbrunn Palace and Park maps.

Great Itineraries

IF YOU HAVE 1 DAY

Touring Vienna in a single day is a proposition as strenuous as it is unlikely, but those with more ambition than time should first get a quick view of the lay of the city by taking a streetcar ride around the Ringstrasse, the wide boulevard that encloses the heart of the city. Then spend the time until early afternoon exploring the city center, starting at Vienna's cathedral, the **Stephansdom** ①, followed by a stroll along the Graben and Kärntnerstrasse, the two main pedestrian shopping streets in the center. About 1 PM, head for **Schönbrunn Palace** (74) to spend the afternoon touring the magnificent royal residence, or visit the **Kunsthistoriches Museum** ㊽, one of the great art museums of the world. After the museum closes at 6 PM, relax over coffee at a café; then spend a musical evening at a concert, opera, or operetta or a convivial evening at a Heuriger, one of the wine restaurants for which Vienna is also famous.

IF YOU HAVE 3 DAYS

Given three days, day one can be a little less hectic, and in any case, you'll want more time for the city center. Rather than going on the do-it-yourself streetcar ride around the Ringstrasse, take an organized sightseeing tour, which will describe the highlights. Plan to spend a full afternoon at **Schönbrunn Palace** (74). Reserve the second day for art, tackling the exciting **Kunsthistoriches Museum** ㊽ before lunch and the magnificent collection of Old Master drawings of the **Albertina Museum** (65) and the impressive **Belvedere Palace** (71). For a contrasting step into modern art in the afternoon—don't miss Klimt's legendary *The Kiss* at the Belvedere. Do as the Viennese do, and fill in any gaps with stops at cafés, reserving evenings for relaxing over music or wine. On the third day, head for the world-famous **Spanische Reitschule** ㉗ and watch the Lipizzaners prance through morning training. While you're in the neighborhood, view the sparkling court jewels in the Imperial Treasury, the **Schatzkammer** ㊲, and the glitzy **Silberkammer** ㉜, the museum of court silver and tableware, and take in one of Vienna's most spectacular Baroque settings, the glorious Grand Hall of the **Hofbibliothek** ㉚. For a total contrast, head out to the Prater amusement park (☞ The Inner City, *below*) in late afternoon for a ride on the giant Ferris wheel and end the day in a wine restaurant on the outskirts, perhaps in Sievering or Nussdorf.

Spend your first three days as outlined in the itinerary above. Then begin your fourth day getting better acquainted with the First District—the heart of the city. Treasures here range from Roman ruins to the residences of Mozart and Beethoven, the **Figarohaus** ⑥ and the **Pasqualatihaus** ⑯; then, slightly afield, the **Freud Apartment** ㊽ (in the Ninth District) or the oddball **Hundertwasserhaus** (in the Third, ☞ The Inner City, *below*). Put it all in contemporary perspective with a backstage tour of the magnificent **Staatsoper** ㊻, the opera house. For a country break on the fifth day, take a tour of the **Vienna Woods** (☞ Chapter 2) or the Danube Valley, particularly the glorious **Wachau district** (☞ Chapter 4), where vineyards sweep down to the river's edge. On the sixth day, fill in some of the blanks with a stroll around the **Naschmarkt** (☞ Pomp and Circumstance, *below*) food-market district, taking in the nearby **Secession Building** ㊽ with Gustav Klimt's famous Beethoven Frieze. Don't overlook the superb Jugendstil buildings on the north side of the market. If you're still game for museums, head for any one of the less usual offerings, such as the Jewish Museum, the Musical Instruments Museum, or the Ephesus Museum, in the **Hofburg** (☞ An Imperial City, *below*), or visit the city's historical museum, **Historisches Museum der Stadt Wien** ㉧; by now, you'll have acquired a good concept of the city and its background, so the exhibits will make more sense. Cap the day by visiting the **Kaisergruft** ㊽ in the Kapuzinerkirche to view the tomb of the Habsburgs responsible for so much of Vienna.

The Inner City: Historic Heart of Vienna

A good way to break the ice on your introduction to Vienna is to get a general picture of its layout as presented to the cruising bird or airplane pilot. There are several beautiful vantage points from which you can look down and over the city—including the terrace of the Upper Belvedere Palace—but the city's preeminent lookout point, offering fine views in all directions, is from the Stephansdom, reached by toiling up the 345 steps of Alt Steffl (Old Stephen, its south tower) to the observation platform. The young and agile will make it up in 8 to 10 minutes; the slower-paced will make it in closer to 20. An elevator, and no exertion, will present you with much the same view from the terrace. From atop, you can see that St. Stephen's is the veritable hub of the city's wheel.

Most of Vienna lies roughly within an arc of a circle, with the straight line of the Danube Canal as its chord. Its heart, the Innere Stadt (Inner City) or First District—in medieval times, the entire city of Vienna—is bounded by the Ringstrasse (Ring), which forms almost a circle, with a narrow arc cut off by the Danube Canal, diverted from the main river just above Vienna and flowing through the city to rejoin the parent stream just below it. The city spreads out from the Stephansdom, accented by the series of magnificent buildings erected—beginning in the 1870s, when Vienna reached the zenith of its imperial prosperity—around the Ringstrasse: the Opera House, the Art History Museum and the Museum of Natural History, the "New Wing" of the Hofburg, the House of Parliament, the Rathaus, the University, and the Votivkirche. For more than eight centuries, the enormous bulk of the cathedral has remained the nucleus around which the city has grown. The bird's-eye view can be left until the last day of your visit, when the city's landmarks will be more familiar. First day or last, the vistas are memorable, especially if you catch them as the cathedral's famous *Pummerin* (Boomer) bell is tolling.

A Good Walk

Stephansplatz, in the heart of the city, is the logical starting point from which to track down Vienna's past and present, as well as any acquaintance (natives believe that if you wait long enough at this intersection of eight streets you'll run into anyone you're searching for). Although it's now in what is mainly a pedestrian zone, **Stephansdom** ①, the mighty cathedral, marks the point from which distances to and from Vienna are measured. Visit the cathedral (it's quite impossible to view all its treasures, so just soak up its reflective Gothic spirit) and consider climbing its 345-step Alt Steffl tower or descending into its Habsburg crypt. Vienna of the Middle Ages is encapsulated in the streets in back of St. Stephen's Cathedral. You could easily spend half a day or more just prowling the narrow streets and passageways—Wollzeile, Bäckerstrasse, Blutgasse—typical remnants of an early era.

Wander up the Wollzeile, cutting through the narrow Essiggasse and right into the Bäckerstrasse, to the **Universitätskirche** ② or Jesuitenkirche, a lovely Jesuit church. Note the contrasting Academy of Science diagonally opposite (Beethoven premiered his *Battle* Symphony in its Ceremonial Hall). Follow the Sonnenfelsgasse, ducking through one of the tiny alleys on the right to reach the Bäckerstrasse; turn right at Gutenbergplatz into the Köllnerhofgasse, right again into tiny Grashofgasse, and go through the gate into the surprising **Heiligenkreuzerhof** ③, a peaceful oasis (unless a handicrafts market is taking place). Through the square, enter the Schönlaterngasse (Beautiful Lantern Street) to admire the house fronts— film companies at times block this street to take shots of the picturesque atmosphere—on your way to the **Dominikanerkirche** ④, the Dominican church with its marvelous Baroque interior. Head east two blocks to that repository of Jugendstil treasures, the **Museum für Angewandte Kunst** ⑤, then head north along the Stubenring to enjoy the architectural contrast of the **Postsparkasse** ⑥ and former War Ministry, facing each other. Retrace your steps, following Postgasse into **Fleischmarkt** ⑦. Nearby Hoher Markt, reached by taking Rotenturmstrasse west to Lichtensteg or Bauernmarkt, was part of the early Roman encampment, witness the Roman ruins under **Hoher Markt** ⑧. The extension of Fleischmarkt ends in a set of stairs leading up past the eccentric Kornhäusal Tower. Up the stairs to the right on Ruprechtsplatz is **Ruprechtskirche** ⑨, St. Rupert's Church, allegedly the city's oldest. Take Sterngasse down the steps, turn left into Marc Aurel-Strasse and right into Salvatorgasse to discover the lacework **Maria am Gestade** ⑩, Maria on the Banks, which once sat above a small river, now underground.

TIMING

If you're pressed for time and happy with facades rather than what's behind them, this route could take half a day, but if you love to look inside and stop to ponder and explore the myriad narrow alleys, figure at least a day for this walk. During services, wandering around the churches will be limited, but otherwise, you can tackle this walk any time, at your convenience.

Sights to See

④ **Dominikanerkirche** (Dominican Church). The Postgasse, to the east of Schönlaterngasse, introduces an unexpected visitor from Rome: the Dominikanerkirche. Built in the 1630s, some 50 years before the Viennese Baroque building boom, its facade is modeled after any number of Roman churches of the 16th century. The interior illustrates why the Baroque style came to be considered the height of bad taste during the 19th century and still has many detractors today. "Sculpt till you drop" seems to have been the motto here, and the viewer's eye is given no respite. This sort of Roman architectural orgy never really gained a foothold in Vienna, and when the great Viennese architects did pull out all the decorative stops—Hildebrandt's interior at the

42

Vienna

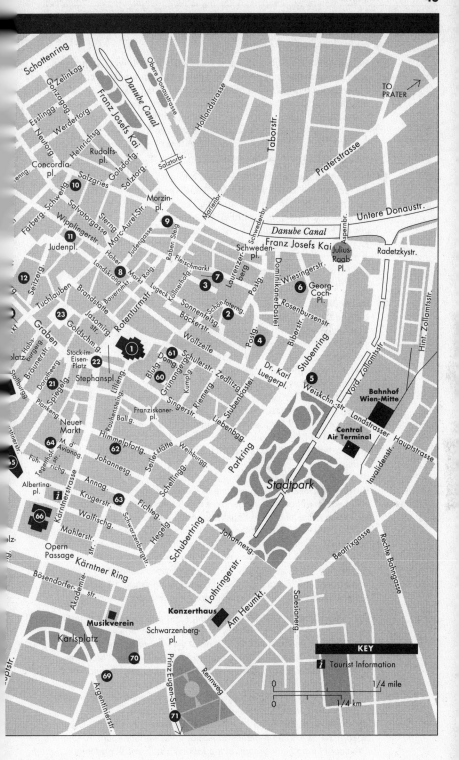

Belvedere Palace, for instance—they did it in a very different style and with far greater success. ✉ *Postg. 4,* ☎ *01/512–7460. U-Bahn: U3 Stubentor/Dr.- Karl-Lueger-Pl.*

❼ Fleischmarkt. Fleischmarkt and the picturesque tiny Griechengasse just beyond the glittering 19th-century Greek Orthodox church are part of the city's oldest core. This corner of the inner city has a medieval feel that is quite genuine; there has been a tavern at Fleischmarkt 11 for some 500 years. The wooden carving on the facade of the current Griechenbeisl restaurant commemorates Max Augustin—best known today from the song "Ach du lieber Augustin"—an itinerant musician who sang here during the plague of 1679.

❸ Heiligenkreuzerhof. Tiny side streets and alleys run off of Sonnenfels-gasse, parallel to Bäckerstrasse. Amid the narrow streets is Heili-genkreuzerhof (Holy Cross Court), one of the city's most peaceful backwaters. This complex of buildings dates from the 17th century but got an 18th-century face-lift. Appropriately, the restraint of the archi-tecture—with only here and there a small outburst of Baroque spirit—gives the courtyard the distinct feeling of a retreat. The square is a favorite site for seasonal markets at Easter and Christmas, and for occasional outdoor art shows.

❽ Hoher Markt. This square was badly damaged during World War II, but the famous Anker Clock at the east end survived the artillery fire. The huge mechanical timepiece took six years (1911–17) to build and still attracts crowds at noon when the full panoply of mechanical fig-ures representing Austrian historical personages parades by. The fig-ures are identified on a plaque to the bottom left of the clock. The graceless buildings erected around the square since 1945 are not aging well and do little to show off the square's lovely Baroque centerpiece, the St. Joseph Fountain (portraying the marriage of Joseph and Mary), designed in 1729 by Joseph Emanuel Fischer von Erlach, son of the great Johann Bernhard Fischer von Erlach. The Hoher Markt does har-bor one wholly unexpected attraction, however: underground Roman ruins.

OFF THE
BEATEN PATH

HUNDERTWASSERHAUS – To see one of Vienna's most amazing buildings, travel eastward from Schwendenplatz or Julius-Raab Platz along Radet-zkystrasse to the junction of Kegelgasse and Löwengasse. Here you'll find the Hundertwasserhaus, a 50-apartment public-housing complex designed by the late Austrian avant-garde artist Friedensreich Hundertwasser. The structure looks as though it was decorated by a crew of mischievous circus clowns wielding giant crayons. The building caused a sensation when it was erected in 1985 and still draws crowds of sightseers. ✉ *Löweng. and Kegelg. U-Bahn: U1 or U4/Schwedenpl., then Streetcar N to Hetzg.*

KRIMINAL MUSEUM (CRIMINAL MUSEUM) – This might be the strangest mu-seum in the city, and it is certainly the most macabre. The vast collection is entirely devoted to murder in Vienna of the most gruesome kind, with the most grisly displays situated, appropriately, in the cellar. Murderers and their victims are depicted in photos and newspaper clippings, and many of the actual instruments used in the killings are displayed, with axes seeming to be the most popular. The Criminal Museum is across the Danube Canal from Schwedenplatz, about a 15-minute walk from Ruprechtskirche, the Hoher Markt, or the Heilegenkreuzerhof. ✉ *Grosse Sperlg. 24,* ☎ *01/214–4678.* 🎫 *AS60.* ☉ *Open Tues.–Sun. 10–5. Streetcar N from Schwedenpl. along Taborstr. to Obere Augartenstr.*

KUNSTHAUS WIEN – Near the Hundertwasserhaus (☞ *above*) you'll find another Hundertwasser project, an art museum, which mounts outstanding international exhibits in addition to showings of the colorful Hundertwasser works. Like the apartment complex nearby, the building itself is pure Hundertwasser, with irregular floors, windows with trees growing out of them, and sudden architectural surprises, a wholly appropriate setting for modern art. ⊠ *Untere Weissgerberstr. 13,* ☎ *01/712–0491–0,* ⊠ *AS90.* ⊙ *Daily 10–7. U-Bahn: U1 or U4/Schwedenpl., then Streetcar N to Radetzkypl.*

🔟 **Maria am Gestade** (St. Mary on the Banks). The middle-Gothic, seven-sided tower of Maria am Gestade, crowned by a delicate cupola, is a sheer joy to the eye and dispels the idea that Gothic must necessarily be austere. Built around 1400 (but much restored in the 17th and 19th centuries), the church incorporated part of the Roman city walls into its foundation; the north wall, as a result, takes a slight but noticeable dogleg to the right halfway down the nave. Like St. Stephen's, Maria am Gestade is rough-hewn Gothic, with a simple but forceful facade. The church is especially beloved, however, because of its unusual details—the pinnacled and saint-bedecked gable that tops the front facade, the stone canopy that hovers protectively over the front door, and (most appealing of all) the intricate openwork lantern atop the south-side bell tower. Appropriately enough in a city famous for its pastry, the lantern lends its tower an engaging suggestion of a sugar caster, while some see an allusion to hands intertwined in prayer. ⊠ *Passauer Pl./Salvatorg. U-Bahn: U1, U3 Stephanspl.*

⑥ **Postsparkasse** (Post Office Savings Bank). The Post Office Savings Bank is one of modern architecture's greatest curiosities. It was designed in 1904 by Otto Wagner, whom many consider the father of 20th-century architecture. In his famous manifesto *Modern Architecture,* Wagner condemned 19th-century revivalist architecture and pleaded for a modern style that honestly expressed modern building methods. Accordingly, the exterior walls of the Post Office Savings Bank are mostly flat and undecorated; visual interest is supplied merely by varying the pattern of the bolts that were used to hold the marble slabs in place on the wall surface during construction. Later architects were to embrace Wagner's beliefs wholeheartedly, although they used different, truly modern building materials: glass and concrete rather than marble. The Post Office Savings Bank was indeed a bold leap into the future, but unfortunately the future took a different path and today the whole appears a bit dated. Go inside for a look at the restored and functioning Kassa-Saal, or central cashier's hall, to see how Wagner carried his concepts over to interior design. ⊠ *Georg-Coch-Pl. 2,* ☎ *01/51400.* ⊙ *Lobby weekdays 8–3.*

OFF THE BEATEN PATH | **PRATER –** Vienna's most famous park and most beloved attraction for children can be found by heading out northeast from the historic city center, across the Danube Canal along Praterstrasse: the famous Prater, the city's foremost amusement park. In 1766, to the dismay of the aristocracy, Emperor Joseph II decreed that the vast expanse of imperial parklands known as the Prater would henceforth be open to the public. East of the inner city between the Danube Canal and the Danube proper, the Prater is a public park to this day, notable for its long promenade (the Hauptallee, more than 4½ km, or 3 mi, in length); its sports facilities (a golf course, a stadium, a racetrack, and a swimming pool, for starters); the landmark giant Ferris wheel (Riesenrad); the traditional, modern amusement-park rides; a number of less-innocent indoor, sex-oriented attractions; a planetarium; and a small but interesting museum devoted to the Prater's long history. If you look carefully, you can discover a handful of children's rides dating from the 1920s and '30s that survived the fire that consumed most of the Volksprater in 1945. The best-known attraction is the 200-ft Ferris wheel that figured so prominently in the 1949 film *The Third Man*. One of three built in Europe at the end of the last century (the others were in England and France but have long since been dismantled), the wheel was badly damaged during World War II and restored shortly thereafter. Its progress is slow and stately (a revolution takes 10 minutes), the views from its cars magnificent, particularly toward dusk. Try to eat at the famous **Schweizerhaus** (⊠ Strasse des 1. Mai 116, ☎ 01/728–0152, closed Nov.–Feb.), which has been serving frosty mugs of beer, roast chicken, and *Stelze* (a huge hunk of crispy roast pork on the bone) for more than 100 years. Its informal setting with wooden plank tables indoors or in the garden in summer adds to the fun. Credit cards are not accepted. ☞ *Park free, Riesenrad AS45.* ☉ *Apr., daily 10 am–11 pm; May–Sept., daily 9 am–midnight; Oct., daily 10–10; Nov.–Feb., daily 10–late afternoon (check with tourist office for exact hours). U-Bahn: U1/Praterstern.*

❺ Museum für Angewandte Kunst (MAK) (Museum of Applied Arts). This fascinating museum contains a large collection of Austrian furniture, porcelain, art objects, and priceless Oriental carpets; the Jugendstil display devoted to Josef Hoffman and his followers at the Wiener Werkstätte is particularly fine. The museum also features a number of changing exhibitions of contemporary works and houses the popular MAK Cafe (☞ Dining, *below*), and the museum shop sells contemporary furniture and other objects (including great bar accessories) designed by young local artists. ⊠ *Stubenring 5,* ☎ *01/711–36–0.* ☞ *Standing exhibits AS30, special exhibits AS90.* ☉ *Tues.–Sun. 10–6, Thurs. 10–9. U-Bahn: U3 Stubentor.*

❾ Ruprechtskirche (St. Ruprecht's Church). Ruprechtsplatz, another of Vienna's time-warp backwaters, lies to the north of the Kornhäusel Tower. The church in the middle, Ruprechtskirche, is the city's oldest. According to legend it was founded in 740; the oldest part of the present structure (the lower half of the tower) dates from the 11th century. Set on the ancient ramparts overlooking the Danube Canal, it is serene and unpretentious. It is usually closed, but sometimes opens for local art shows and summer evening classical concerts. ⊠ *Ruprechtspl. U-Bahn: U1, U4 Schwedenpl.*

Schönlaterngasse (Beautiful Lantern Street). Once part of Vienna's medieval Latin Quarter, Schönlaterngasse is the main artery of an historic neighborhood that has reblossomed in recent years. Thanks in part to government Kultur Schillings—or renovation loans—the quarter has been revamped. Streets are lined with beautiful Baroque town houses (often with colorfully painted facades), now distinct showcases for art galleries, chic shops, and coffeehouses. The most famous house of the quarter is the **Basiliskenhaus** (House of the Basilik, ⊠ Schönlaterng. 7). According to legend, it was first built for a baker; on June 26, 1212, a foul-smelling basilisk (half-rooster, half-toad, with a glance that could kill) took up residence in the courtyard well, poisoning the water. An enterprising apprentice dealt with the problem by climbing down the well armed with a mirror; when the basilisk saw its own reflection, it turned to stone. The petrified creature can still be seen in a niche on the building's facade. Today, modern science accounts for the contamination with a more prosaic explanation: natural-gas seepage. Be sure to take a look in the house's miniature courtyard for a trip back to medieval Vienna (the house itself is private).The picturesque street is named for the ornate wrought-iron wall lantern at Schönlaterngasse 6. Just a few steps from the Basilikenhaus, note the Baroque courtyard at Schönlaterngasse

MOZART, MOZART, MOZART!

WOLFGANG AMADEUS Mozart (1756–91) crammed a prodigious number of compositions into the 35 short years of his life—the mere cataloging of them is the subject of a ponderous work, impressively entitled *Chronologisch-thematisches Verzeichnis sämtlicher Tonwerke Wolfgang Amadeus Mozarts*, the work of one Ludwig von Köchel. This catalogue is filled with incomparable musical riches, and no devotee would want to pass up a trip to his native Austria. Certainly, it's easy to find the places he lived in or visited, all carefully restored or marked by memorial plaques. But a knowledge of his troubled relations with his homeland makes the experience a poignant one.

From the beginning of Wolfgang's precocious career, his father, frustrated in his own musical ambitions at the Archbishopric in Salzburg, looked beyond the boundaries of the Austro-Hungarian Empire to promote the boy's fame. At the age of six, his son was presented to the royal courts of Europe and caused a sensation with his skills as an instrumentalist and impromptu composer.

As he grew up, however, his virtuosity lost its power to amaze and he was forced to make his way as an "ordinary" musician, which then meant finding a position at court. In this he was not much more successful than his father had been, in spite of what would seem to be the decisive advantage of genius. In Salzburg he was never able to rise beyond the level of organist (allowing him, as he noted with sarcastic pride, to sit above the cooks at

table), and his attempts to have his compositions performed were rebuffed.

In disgust, he severed his ties with the Archbishop and tried his luck in Vienna, where despite the popularity of his operas and the admiration of his peers (Joseph Haydn early recognized him as the greatest composer of the time) he was able to obtain only an unpaid appointment as assistant Kapellmeister at St. Stephen's months before his death. By then he had been invited by friends to come to London (where Haydn later made a fortune), and subscriptions had been taken up in Hungary and the Netherlands that would have paid him handsomely. But it was too late. Whatever the truth of the theories still swirling around his untimely death, the fact remains that not only was he not given the state funeral he deserved, but he was buried in an unmarked grave after a hasty, sparsely attended funeral.

If one is inclined to accuse Mozart's fellow countrymen of neglect, they would seem to have made up for it with a vengeance. The visitor to Vienna and Salzburg can hardly ignore the barrage of Mozart candies, wine, beer, coffee mugs, T-shirts, baseball caps—not to mention the gilded statues that make do for a nonexistent monumental tomb. Indeed, he has become a thriving brand-name industry and one of the centerpieces of Austrian tourism.

And Mozart, always one to appreciate a joke, even at his own expense, would surely see the irony in the belated veneration.

— Gary Dodson

8—one of the city's prettiest. A blacksmith's workshop, **Alte Schmiede** (Old Smithy, ✉ Schönlaterng. 9), is now a museum.

★ ❶ **Stephansdom** (St. Stephen's Cathedral). The soaring centerpiece of Vienna, this beloved cathedral enshrines the heart of the city—although it is curious to note that when first built in 1144–47 it actually stood outside the city walls. Vienna can thank a period of hard times for the Mother Church for the distinctive silhouette of the cathedral. Originally the structure was to have had matching 445-ft-high spires, a standard design of the era, but funds ran out, and the north tower to this day remains a happy reminder of what gloriously is not. The lack of symmetry creates an imbalance that makes the cathedral instantly identifiable from its profile alone. The cathedral, like the Staatsoper and some other major buildings, was very heavily damaged in World War II. Since then, it has risen from the fires of destruction like a phoenix, and like the phoenix, it is a symbol of regeneration.

It is difficult now, sitting quietly in the shadowed peace, to tell what was original and what parts of the walls and vaults were reconstructed. No matter: its history-rich atmosphere is dear to all Viennese. That noted, St. Stephen's possesses a fierce presence that is blatantly un-Viennese. It is a stylistic jumble ranging from 13th-century Romanesque to 15th-century Gothic. Like the exterior, St. Stephen's interior lacks the soaring unity of Europe's greatest Gothic cathedrals, with much of its decoration dating from the later Baroque era.

The wealth of decorative sculpture in St. Stephen's can be intimidating to the nonspecialist, so if you wish to explore the cathedral in detail, you may want to buy the admirably complete English-language description sold in the small room marked Dom Shop. One particularly masterly work, however, should be seen by everyone: the stone pulpit attached to the second freestanding pier on the left of the central nave, carved by Anton Pilgram around 1510. The delicacy of its decoration would in itself set the pulpit apart, but even more intriguing are its five sculpted figures. Carved around the outside of the pulpit proper are the four Latin Fathers of the Church (from left to right: St. Augustine, St. Gregory, St. Jerome, and St. Ambrose), and each is given an individual personality so sharply etched as to suggest satire, perhaps of living models. There is no satire suggested by the fifth figure, however; below the pulpit's stairs Pilgram sculpted a fine self-portrait, showing himself peering out a half-open window. Note the toads, lizards, and other creatures climbing the spiral rail alongside the steps up to the pulpit. As you walk among the statues and aisles, remember that many notable events occurred here, including the marriage of Mozart in 1782 and his funeral in December 1791.

St. Stephen's was devastated by fire in the last days of World War II, and the extent of the damage may be seen by leaving the cathedral through the south portal, where a set of prereconstruction photographs commemorates the disaster. Restoration was protracted and difficult, but today the cathedral once again dominates the center of the city. Note the "05" carved into the stone to the right of the outer massive front door. The "0" stands for Österreich, or Austria, and the "5" is for the fifth letter of the alphabet. This translates into OE, the abbreviation for Österreich, and was a covert sign of resistance to the Nazi annexation of Austria. The bird's-eye views from the cathedral's beloved **Alte Steffl** tower will be a highlight for some. The tower is 450 ft high and was built between 1359 and 1433. The climb or elevator ride up is rewarded with vistas that extend to the rising slopes of the Wienerwald. ✉ *Stephanspl.,* ☎ *01/515–520.* ▣ *Each tour AS40, elevator AS40.* ⊙ *Daily 6 AM–10 PM. Guided tours Mon.–Sat. at 10:30 and 3, Sun. at 3; evening tour June–Sept., Sat. at 7; catacombs tour Mon.–Sat. every half hr from 10–11:30*

*and 1:30–4:30, Sun. every half hr from 1:30–4:30; North Tower eleva-
tor to Pummerin bell, Apr.–June and Sept., daily 9–6; July–Aug., daily
9–6:30; Nov.–Mar., daily 8:30–5. U-Bahn: U1, U3 Stephanspl.*

<table>
<tr>
<td>NEED A
BREAK?</td>
<td>If you're in the mood for ice cream, head for Zanoni & Zanoni (✉ Am Lugeck 7, ☎ 01/7979) near St. Stephen's between Rotenturmstrasse and Bäckerstrasse and open 365 days a year. Here you'll have trouble choosing from among 25 or more flavors of smooth, Italian-style gelato, including mango, caramel, and chocolate chip. There are also tables for those who want to rest their feet and enjoy a sundae.</td>
</tr>
</table>

❷ **Universitätskirche** (Jesuit Church). The east end of Bäckerstrasse is punctuated by Dr.-Ignaz-Seipel-Platz, named for the theology professor
who was chancellor of Austria during the 1920s. On the north side is
the Universitätskirche, or Jesuitenkirche, built around 1630. Its flamboyant Baroque interior contains a fine trompe-l'oeil ceiling fresco by
that master of visual trickery Andrea Pozzo, who was imported from
Rome in 1702 for the job. You may hear a Mozart or Haydn mass sung
here in Latin on many Sundays. ✉ *Dr.-Ignaz-Seipl-Pl.,* ☎ *01/512–1335–
0. U-Bahn: U3 Stubentor/Dr.-Karl-Lueger-Pl.*

Bittersweet Vienna: Baroque Gems and Cozy Cafés

As the city developed and expanded, the core quickly outgrew its early
confines. New urban centers sprang up, to be ornamented by government buildings and elegant town residences. Since Vienna was the
beating heart of a vast empire, nothing was spared to make the edifices as exuberant as possible, with utility often a secondary consid-
eration. The best architects of the day were commissioned to create
impressions as well as buildings, and they did their job well. That so
much has survived is a testimony to the solidity both of the designs
and of the structures on which the ornamentation has been overlaid.

Those not fortunate enough to afford town palaces were relegated to
housing that was often less than elegant and confining. Rather than
suffer the discomfitures of a disruptive household environment, the city's
literati and its philosophers and artists took refuge in cafés, which in
effect became their combined salons and offices. To this day, cafés remain an important element of Viennese life. Many residents still have
their *Stammtisch,* or regular table, at which they appear daily. Talk still
prevails—but, increasingly, so do handy cell phones and even laptops.

A Good Walk
Start in the Wipplingerstrasse at the upper (west) end of Hoher Markt
to find touches of both the imperial and the municipal Vienna. On the
east side is the **Altes Rathaus,** which served as the city hall until 1885;
on the west is the **Bohemian Court Chancery** ⑪, once diplomatic headquarters for Bohemia's representation to the Habsburg court. Turn
south into the short Fütterergasse to reach **Judenplatz,** in the Middle
Ages the center of Judaism in Vienna. A clock-watcher's delight is down
at the end of Kurrentgasse in the form of the **Uhrenmuseum** (Clock Museum); around the corner through the Parisgasse to Schulhof, a children's
delight is the **Puppen- und Spielzeug-Museum** (Doll and Toy Museum).
Follow Schulhof into the huge **Am Hof** square, boasting the **Kirche am
Hof** ⑫ and what must be the world's most elegant fire station. The square
hosts an antiques and collectibles market most of the year on Thursday and Friday, plus other ad hoc events. Take the miniscule Irisgasse
from Am Hof into the Naglergasse, noting the mosaic Jugendstil facade
on the pharmacy in the Bognergasse, to your left. Around a bend in the
narrow Naglergasse is the **Freyung,** an irregular square bounded on the

south side by two wonderfully stylish palaces, including **Palais Ferstel** ⑬, now a shopping arcade, and the elegantly restored **Palais Harrach** next door, now an outpost of the Kunsthistoriches Museum. Opposite, the privately run **Kunstforum** art museum mounts varied and outstanding exhibitions. The famous **Kinsky Palace** ⑭ at the beginning of Herrengasse is still partly a private residence. The north side of the Freyung is watched over by the **Schottenkirche** ⑮, a Scottish church that was, in fact, established by Irish monks. The complex also houses a small but worthwhile museum of the order's treasures. Follow Teinfaltstrasse from opposite the Schottenkirche, turning right into Schreyvogelgasse. Climb the ramp on your right past the so-called Dreimäderlhaus at Schreyvogelgasse 10—note the ornate facade of this pre-Biedermeier patrician house—to reach Molker Bastei, where Beethoven lived in the **Pasqualatihaus** ⑯, now housing a museum commemorating the composer. Follow the ring south to Löwelstrasse, turning left into Bankgasse; then turn right into Abraham-a-Santa Clara-Gasse (the tiny street that runs off the Bankgasse) to Minoritenplatz and the **Minoritenkirche** ⑰, the Minorite Church, with its odd, hat-less tower. Inside is a kitschy mosaic *Last Supper*. Landhausgasse will bring you to Herrengasse, and diagonally across the street, in the back corner of the Palais Ferstel, is the **Café Central** ⑱, one of Vienna's hangouts for the famous. As you go south up the Herrengasse, on the left is the odd Hochhaus, a 20th-century building once noted as Vienna's skyscraper. Opposite are elegant Baroque former town palaces, now used as museum and administration buildings by the province of Lower Austria.

TIMING

The actual distances in this walk are relatively short, and you could cover the route in 1½ hours or so. But if you take time to linger in the museums and sample a coffee with whipped cream in the Café Central, you'll develop a much better understanding of the contrasts between old and newer in the city. You could easily spend a day following this walk, if you were to take in all of the museums; note that these, like many of Vienna's museums, are closed on Mondays.

Sights to See

Altes Rathaus (Old City Hall). Opposite the Bohemian Chancery (☞ *below*) stands the Altes Rathaus, dating from the 14th century but displaying 18th-century Baroque motifs on its facade. The interior passageways and courtyards, which are open during the day, house a Gothic chapel (open at odd hours); a much-loved Baroque wall-fountain (Georg Raphael Donner's **Andromeda Fountain** of 1741); and display cases exhibiting maps and photos illustrating the city's history.

Am Hof. Am Hof is one of the city's oldest squares. In the Middle Ages the ruling Babenberg family built their castle on the site of No. 2; hence the name of the square, which means simply "at court." The grand residence hosted such luminaries as Barbarossa and Walter von der Vogelweide, the famous Minnesinger who features in Wagner's *Tannhäuser.* The Baroque **Column of Our Lady** in the center dates from 1667, marking the Catholic victory over the Swedish Protestants in the Thirty Years' War (1618–48). The onetime Civic Armory at the northwest corner has been used as a fire station since 1685 (the high-spirited facade, with its Habsburg eagle, was "Baroqued" in 1731) and today houses the headquarters of Vienna's fire department. The complex includes a firefighting museum (open only on Sunday mornings). Presiding over the east side of the square is the noted Kirche Am Hof (☞ *below*). In Bognergasse to the right of the Kirche Am Hof, around the corner from the imposing Bank Austria headquarters building, at No. 9, is the **Engel Pharmacy**, with a Jugendstil mosaic depicting winged women collecting the elixir of life in outstretched chalices. At the turn of the century the inner city was dotted with storefronts decorated in a similar manner; today this is the sole survivor. Around the bend from the Naglergasse is picturesque Freyung square (☞ *below*).

⑰ Bohemian Court Chancery. One of the architectural jewels of the Inner City can be found at Wipplingerstrasse 7, the former Bohemian Court Chancery, built between 1708 and 1714 by Johann Bernhard Fischer von Erlach. Fischer von Erlach and his contemporary Johann Lukas von Hildebrandt were the reigning architectural geniuses of Baroque Vienna; they designed their churches and palaces during the building boom that followed the defeat of the Turks in 1683. Both had studied architecture in Rome, and both were deeply impressed by the work of the great Italian architect Francesco Borromini, who brought to his designs a wealth and freedom of invention that were looked upon with horror by most contemporary Romans. But for Fischer von Erlach and Hildebrandt, Borromini's ideas were a source of triumphant architectural inspiration, and when they returned to Vienna they produced between them many of the city's most beautiful buildings. Alas, narrow Wipplingerstrasse allows little more than a oblique view of this florid facade. The back side of the building, on Judenplatz, is less elaborate but gives a better idea of the design concept. The building first served as diplomatic and representational offices of Bohemia (now a part of the Czech Republic) to the Vienna-based monarchy and, today, still houses government offices.

⑱ Café Central. Part of the ☞ **Palais Ferstel** complex, the Café Central is one of Vienna's more famous cafés, its full authenticity blemished only by complete restoration in recent years. In its prime (before World War I), the café was "home" to some of the most famous literary figures of the day, who ate, socialized, worked, and even received mail here. The denizens of the Central favored political argument; indeed, their heated discussions became so well known that in October 1917, when Austria's foreign secretary was informed of the outbreak of the Russian Revolution, he dismissed the report with a facetious reference to a well-known local Marxist, the chess-loving (and presumably harmless) "Herr Bronstein from the Café Central." The remark was to become famous all over Austria, for Herr Bronstein had disappeared and was about to resurface in Russia bearing a new name: Leon Trotsky. No matter how crowded the café may become, you can linger as long as you like over a single cup of coffee and a newspaper from the huge international selection provided. Across the street at Herrengasse 17 is the **Café Central Konditorei,** an excellent pastry and confectionery shop associated with the café. ✉ *Herreng. 14,* ☎ *01/533–3763–26. AE, DC, MC, V. Closed Sun. Oct.–Apr. U-Bahn: U3 Herreng.*

The Freyung. Naglergasse, at its curved end, flows into Heidenschuss, which in turn leads down a slight incline from Am Hof to one of Vienna's most prominent squares, the Freyung, meaning "freeing." The square was so named because for many centuries the monks at the adjacent Schottenhof (☞ *below*) possessed the privilege of offering sanctuary for three days. In the center of the square stands the allegorical **Austria Fountain** (1845), notable because its Bavarian designer, one Ludwig Schwanthaler, had the statues cast in Munich and then supposedly filled them with cigars to be smuggled into Vienna for black-market sale. Around the sides of the square are some of Vienna's greatest patrician residences, including the Ferstel, Harrach, and Kinsky palaces (☞ *below*).

Judenplatz. From the 13th to the 15th century, Judenplatz—off Wipplingerstrasse—was the center of Vienna's Jewish ghetto. Today the square's centerpiece is a rectangular block intended as a Holocaust memorial; the architect's concept was a stylized stack of books intended to signify Jewish strivings toward learning. Nearby is a statue of the 18th-century playwright Gotthold Ephraim Lessing, erected after World War II.

⑭ Kinsky Palace. Just one of the architectural treasures that comprise the urban set piece of the Freyung (☞ *above*), the Palais Kinsky is the square's best-known palace, and is one of the most sophisticated pieces of Baroque architecture in the city. It was built between 1713 and 1716 by Hildebrandt, and its only real competition comes a few yards farther on: the Greek temple facade of the Schottenhof (☞ *below*), which is at right angles to the Schottenkirche, up the street from the Kinsky Palace. The palace now houses Wiener Kunst Auktionen, a public auction business offering artworks and antiques. ⊠ *Freyung 4,* ☎ *01/532–4200,* FAX *01/532–42009.* ☉ *Mon.–Fri. 10–6.*

⑫ Kirche Am Hof. On the east side of the Am Hof square, the Kirche Am Hof, or the Church of the Nine Choirs of Angels, is identified by its sprawling Baroque facade, designed by Carlo Carlone in 1662. The somber interior lacks appeal, but the checkerboard marble floor may remind you of Dutch churches. ⊠ *Am Hof 1. U-Bahn: U3 Herreng.*

Kunstforum. The huge gold ball atop the doorway on the Freyung at the corner of Renngasse marks the entrance to the Kunstforum, an extensive art gallery run by Bank Austria featuring outstanding temporary exhibitions. ⊠ *Freyung 8,* ☎ *01/532–0644.* ☜ *AS90.* ☉ *Thurs.–Tues. 10–6, Wed. 10–9. U-Bahn: U3 Herreng.*

⑰ Minoritenkirche (Church of the Minorite Order). The Minoritenplatz is named after its centerpiece, the Minoritenkirche, a Gothic affair with a strange stump of a tower, built mostly in the 14th century. The front is brutally ugly, but the back is a wonderful, if predominantly 19th-century, surprise. The interior contains the city's most imposing piece of kitsch: a large mosaic reproduction of Leonardo da Vinci's *Last Supper,* commissioned by Napoléon in 1806 and later purchased by Emperor Francis I. ⊠ *Minoritenpl. 2A,* ☎ *01/533–4162. U-Bahn: U3 Herreng.*

⑬ Palais Ferstel. At Freyung 2 stands the recently restored Palais Ferstel, which is not a palace at all but a commercial shop-and-office complex designed in 1856 and named for its architect, Heinrich Ferstel. The facade is Italianate in style, harking back, in its 19th-century way, to the Florentine palazzi of the early Renaissance. The interior is unashamedly eclectic: vaguely Romanesque in feel and Gothic in decoration, with here and there a bit of Renaissance or Baroque sculpted detail thrown in for good measure. Such eclecticism is sometimes dismissed as mindlessly derivative, but here the architectural details are so respectfully and inventively combined that the interior becomes a pleasure to explore. The 19th-century stock-exchange rooms upstairs are now gloriously restored and used for conferences and concerts. ⊠ *Freyung 2.*

Palais Harrach. Next door to the Palais Ferstel (☞ *above*) is the newly renovated Palais Harrach, part of which now houses a small but worthwhile gallery of paintings and art objects from the main Kunsthistorisches Museum (which has far more treasures than space in which to display them) as well as special exhibits. ⊠ *Freyung 3,* ☎ *01/523–1753.* ☜ *AS90.* ☉ *During special exhibits, daily 10–6.*

⑯ Pasqualatihaus. Beethoven lived in the Pasqualatihaus while he was composing his only opera, *Fidelio,* as well as his Seventh Symphony and Fourth Piano Concerto. Today his apartment houses a small commemorative museum (in distressingly modern style). After navigating the narrow and twisting stairway, you might well ask how he maintained the jubilant spirit of the works he wrote there. This house is around the corner from the *Third Man* Portal (☞ *below*). ⊠ *8 Mölker Bastei,* ☎ *01/535–8905.* 🎫 *AS25.* ⊙ *Tues.–Sun. 9–12:15 and 1–4:30. U-Bahn: U2 Schottentor.*

☺ **Puppen und Spielzeugmuseum** (Doll and Toy Museum). As appealing as the clockworks of the Uhrenmuseum located just next door is this doll and toy museum, with its collections of dolls, dollhouses, teddy bears, and trains. ⊠ *Schulhof 4,* ☎ *01/535–6860.* 🎫 *AS60.* ⊙ *Tues.– Sun. 10–6. U-Bahn: U1, U3 Stephanspl.*

Schottenhof. Found on the Freyung square (☞ *above*) and designed by Joseph Kornhäusel in a very different style from his Fleischmarkt tower, the Schottenhof is a shaded courtyard. The facade typifies the change that came over Viennese architecture during the Biedermeier era (1815–48). The Viennese, according to the traditional view, were at the time so relieved to be rid of the upheavals of the Napoleonic Wars that they accepted without protest the ironhanded repression of Prince Metternich, chancellor of Austria, and retreated into a cozy and complacent domesticity. Restraint also ruled in architecture, with Baroque license rejected in favor of a new and historically "correct" style that was far more controlled and reserved. Kornhäusel led the way in Vienna; his Schottenhof facade is all sober organization and frank repetition. But in its marriage of strong and delicate forces it still pulls off the great Viennese-waltz trick of successfully merging seemingly antithetical characteristics. *U-Bahn: U2 Schottentor.*

NEED A
BREAK?

In summer, **Wienerwald** restaurant, in the tree-shaded courtyard of the Schottenhof (☞ *above*), is ideal for relaxing over lunch, coffee, or a glass of wine.

⑮ Schottenkirche. From 1758 to 1761, the famous Italian painter Canaletto did paintings of the Freyung square (☞ *above*) looking north toward the Schottenkirche; the pictures hang in the Kunsthistorisches Museum, and the similarity to the view you see about 240 years later is arresting. In fact, a church has stood on the site of the Schottenkirche since 1177; the present edifice dates from the mid-1600s, when it replaced its predecessor, which had collapsed after the architects of the time had built on weakened foundations. The interior, with its ornate ceiling and a decided surplus of cherubs and angels' faces, is in stark contrast to the plain exterior. The adjacent small **Museum im Schottenstift** includes the best of the monastery's artworks, including the celebrated late-Gothic high altar, dating to about 1470. The winged altar is fascinating for its portrayal of the Holy Family in flight into Egypt—with Vienna clearly identifiable in the background. ⊠ *Freyung 6,* ☎ *01/534–98–600.* 🎫 *Church free, museum AS40, special exhibits AS50.* ⊙ *Church Thurs.– Sat. 10–5, Sun. noon–5. U-Bahn: U2 Schottentor.*

Third Man Portal. The doorway at Schreyvogelgasse 8 (up the incline) was made famous in 1949 by the classic film *The Third Man* (☞ Close-up box, *below*); it was here that Orson Welles, as the malevolently knowing Harry Lime, stood hiding in the dark, only to have his smiling face illuminated by a sudden light from the upper-story windows of the house across the alley. The film enjoys a renaissance each summer in the Burg Kino and is fascinating for its portrayal of a postwar Vienna still in ruins. To get here from the nearby and noted Schottenkirche (☞ *above*), follow Teinfaltstrasse one block west to Schreyvogelgasse on the right.

Uhrenmuseum (Clock Museum). Kurrentgasse leads south from the east end of Judenplatz; the beautifully restored 18th-century houses on its east side make this one of the most unpretentiously appealing streets in the city. And at the far end of the street is one of Vienna's most appealing museums: the Uhrenmuseum, or Clock Museum (enter to the

TRACKING DOWN THE THIRD MAN

PROBABLY NOTHING HAS DONE more to create the myth of postwar Vienna than Carol Reed's classic 1949 film, *The Third Man*. The bombed-out ruins of this proud, imperial city created an indelible image of devastation and corruption in the war's aftermath. Vienna was then divided into four sectors, each commanded by one of the victorious American, Russian, French, and British armies. But their attempts at rigid control could not prevent a thriving black market.

In the film, Joseph Cotten plays Holly Martins, a pulp-fiction writer who comes to Vienna in search of his friend Harry Lime (Orson Welles). He makes the mistake of delving too deeply into Lime's affairs, even falling in love with his girlfriend, Anna Schmidt (Alida Valli), with fatal consequences.

Many of the sites where the film was shot still remain and are easily visited. Harry Lime appears for the first time nearly one hour into the film in the doorway of Anna's apartment building at No. 8 Schreyvogelgasse, around the corner from the Mölker-Bastei (a remnant of the old city wall). He then runs to Am Hof, a lovely square lined with Baroque town houses and churches, which appears much closer to Anna's neighborhood than it actually is.

The famous scene between Lime and Martins on the Ferris wheel was filmed on the Riesenrad at the Prater, the huge amusement park across the Danube canal. While the two friends talk in the enclosed compartment, the wheel slowly makes a revolution, with all Vienna spread out below them.

In the memorable chase at the end of the movie, Lime is seen running through the damp, sinister sewers of Vienna, hotly pursued by the authorities. In reality, he would not have been able to use the sewer system as an escape route because the tunnels were too low and didn't connect between the different centers of the city. But a movie creates its own reality. In fact, a more feasible, if less cinematic, possibility of escape was offered by the labyrinth of cellars that still connected many buildings in the city.

Lime's funeral is held at the Zentralfriedhof (Central Cemetery), reachable by the 71 streetcar. This is the final scene of the movie, where Anna Schmidt walks down the stark, wide avenue (dividing sections 69 and 70), refusing to acknowledge the wistful presence of Holly Martins.

After touring sewers and cemeteries, a pick-me-up might be in order. You couldn't do better than to treat yourself to a stop at the Hotel Sacher, used for a scene in the beginning of the movie when Holly Martins is using the telephone in the lobby. The bar in the Sacher was a favorite hangout of director Carol Reed, and when filming finally wrapped, he left a signed note to the bartender, saying: "To the creator of the best Bloody Marys in the whole world."

— Bonnie Dodson

right on the Schulhof side of the building). The museum's three floors display a splendid array of clocks and watches—more than 3,000 timepieces—dating from the 15th century to the present. The ruckus of bells and chimes pealing forth on any hour is impressive, but try to be here at noon for the full cacophony. Right next door is the Puppen und Spielzeugmuseum (☞ *above*). ⊠ *Schulhof 2,* ☎ *01/533–2265.* ⚏ *AS50.* ☉ *Tues.–Sun. 9–4:30. U-Bahn: U1, U3 Stephanspl.*

Vienna's Shop Window:
From Michaelerplatz to the Graben

The compact area bounded roughly by the back side of the Hofburg palace complex, the Kohlmarkt, the Graben, and Kärntnerstrasse belongs to the oldest core of the city. Remains of the Roman city are just below the present-day surface. This was and still is the commercial heart of the city, with shops and markets for various commodities; today, the Kohlmarkt and Graben in particular offer the choicest luxury shops, overflowing into the Graben end of Kärnterstrasse. The area is marvelous for its visual treats, ranging from the squares and varied architecture to shop windows. The evening view down Kohlmarkt from the Graben is an inspiring classic, with the night-lit gilded dome of Michael's Gate to the palace complex as the glittering backdrop.

A Good Walk

Start your walk through this fascinating quarter at **Michaelerplatz** ⑲, one of Vienna's most evocative squares, where the feel of the imperial city remains very strong; the buildings around the perimeter present a synopsis of the city's entire architectural history: medieval church spire, Renaissance church facade, Baroque palace facade, 19th-century apartment house, and 20th-century bank. Look in the Michaelerkirche (St. Michael's Church). Opposite the church is the once-controversial **Looshaus** ⑳, considered a breakthrough in modern architecture (visitors are welcome to view the restored lobby). From Michaelerplatz, take the small passageway to the right of the church; in it on your right is a relief dating from 1480 of Christ on the Mount of Olives. Follow the Stallburggasse through to Dorotheergasse, and turn right to discover the **Dorotheum**, the government-run auction house and the Vienna equivalent of Christie's or Sotheby's. On your right in the Dorotheergasse (toward the Graben) is the enlarged **Jewish Museum** ㉑, which includes a bookstore and café. On the left is the famous Café Hawelka, home to the contemporary art and literature crowd. Turn right in the Graben to come to **Stock-im-Eisen** ㉒; the famous nail-studded tree trunk is encased in the corner of the building with the Bank Austria offices. Opposite and impossible to overlook is the aggressive **Neues Haas-Haus,** an upmarket restaurant and shopping complex. Wander back through the **Graben** for the full effect of this harmonious street and look up to see the ornamentation on the buildings. Pass the **Pestsäule** (Plague Column), which shoots up from the middle of the Graben like a geyser of whipped cream. Just off to the north side is **Peterskirche** ㉓, St. Peter's Church, a Baroque gem almost hidden by its surroundings. At the end of the Graben, turn left into the **Kohlmarkt** ㉔ for the classic view of the domed arch leading to the Hofburg, the imperial palace complex. Even if your feet aren't calling a sit-down strike, finish up at **Demel** ㉕, at Kohlmarkt 14, for some of the best *patisseries* in the world.

TIMING

Inveterate shoppers, window or otherwise, will want to take time to pause before or in many of the elegant shops during this walk, which then could easily take most of a day or even longer. If you're content with facades and general impressions, the exercise could be done in a bit over an hour, but it would be a shame to bypass the narrow side streets. In any case, look into St. Michael's and consider the fascinating Dorotheum, itself easily worth an hour or more.

Sights to See

★ ㉕ **Demel** (✉ Kohlmarkt 14, ☎ 01/535–1717–39), Vienna's best-known pastry shop, offers a dizzying selection, and if you possess a sweet tooth, a visit will be worth every groschen. Chocolate lovers will want to participate in the famous Viennese Sachertorte debate by sampling Demel's version and then comparing it with its rival at the **Café Sacher,** which is in the Hotel Sacher.

Dorotheum. The narrow passageway just to the right of St. Michael's, with its large 15th-century relief depicting Christ on the Mount of Olives, leads into the Stallburggasse. The area is dotted with antiques stores, attracted by the presence of the Dorotheum, the famous Viennese auction house that began as a state-controlled pawnshop in 1707 (affectionately known as "Aunt Dorothy" to its patrons). Merchandise coming up for auction is on display at Dorotheergasse 17. The showrooms—packed with everything from carpets and pianos to cameras and jewelry and postage stamps—are well worth a visit. Some wares are not for auction but for immediate sale. ✉ *Dorotheerg. 17,* ☎ *01/ 515–60–0.* ☉ *Weekdays 8–6, Sat. 9–5. U-Bahn: U1, U3 Stephanspl.*

The Graben. One of Vienna's major crossroads, the Graben, leading west from Stock-im-Eisen-Platz, is a street whose unusual width gives it the presence and weight of a city square. Its shape is due to the Romans, who dug the city's southwestern moat here (Graben literally means "moat" or "ditch") adjacent to the original city walls. The Graben's centerpiece is the effulgently Baroque ☞ **Pestsäule.**

㉑ **Jewish Museum.** The former Eskeles Palace, once an elegant private residence, is now home to the city's Jüdisches Museum der Stadt Wien. Permanent exhibitions tell of the momentous role that Viennese-born Jews played in realms from music to medicine, art to philosophy, both in Vienna—until abruptly halted in 1938—and in the world at large. Changing exhibits add contemporary touches. The museum complex includes a café and bookstore. ✉ *Dorotheerg. 11,* ☎ *01/535–0431.* ▣ *AS70.* ☉ *Sun.–Fri. 10–6, Thurs. 10–8. U-Bahn: U1, U3 Stephanspl.*

㉔ **Kohlmarkt.** The Kohlmarkt, aside from its classic view of the domed entryway to the imperial palace complex of the Hofburg, is best known as Vienna's most elegant shopping street. The shops, not the buildings, are remarkable, although there is an entertaining odd-couple pairing: No. 11 (early 18th century) and No. 9 (early 20th century). The mixture of architectural styles is similar to that of the Graben, but the general atmosphere is low-key, as if the street were consciously deferring to the showstopper dome at the west end. The composers Haydn and Chopin lived in houses on the street, and indeed, the Kohlmarkt lingers in the memory when flashier streets have faded.

★ ⑳ **Looshaus.** In 1911, Adolf Loos, one of the founding fathers of 20th-century modern architecture, built the Looshaus on august Michaelerplatz, facing the Imperial Palace entrance. It was considered nothing less than an architectural declaration of war. After two hundred years of Baroque and neo-Baroque exuberance, the first generation of 20th-century architects had had enough. Loos led the revolt against architectural tradition; *Ornament and Crime* was the title of his famous manifesto, in which he inveighed against the conventional architectural wisdom of the 19th century. Instead, he advocated buildings that were plain, honest, and functional. When he built the Looshaus for Goldman and Salatsch (men's clothiers) in 1911, the city was scandalized. Archduke

Franz Ferdinand, heir to the throne, was so offended that he vowed never again to use the Michaelerplatz entrance to the Imperial Palace. Today the Looshaus has lost its power to shock, and the facade seems quite innocuous; argument now focuses on the postmodern Neues Haas-Haus (☞ *below*) opposite St. Stephen's Cathedral. The recently restored interior of the Looshaus remains a breathtaking surprise; the building now houses a bank, and you can go inside to see the stylish chambers and staircase. ⊠ *Michaelerpl. 3. U-Bahn: U3 Herreng.*

⑲ Michaelerplatz. One of Vienna's most historic squares, this small plaza is now the site of an excavation revealing Roman plus 18th- and 19th-century layers of the past. The excavations are a latter-day distraction from the Michaelerplatz's most noted claim to fame—the eloquent entryway to the palace complex of the Hofburg.

In 1945 American soldiers forced open the doors of the crypt in the **Michaelerkirche** for the first time in 150 years and made a singular discovery. Lying undisturbed over the centuries were the mummified remains of former wealthy parishioners of the church—even the finery and buckled shoes worn at their burial was preserved by the perfect temperatures contained within the crypt. Fascinatingly ghoulish tours are offered hourly, for AS40, given first in German and then in English. Visitors are led down into the shadowy gloom and through a labyrinth of passageways, pausing at several tombs (many of which are open in order to view the remains) with a little explanation of the cause of death given at each site. *U-Bahn: U3 Herreng.*

Neues Haas-Haus. Stock-im-Eisen-Platz is home to central Vienna's most controversial (for the moment, at least) piece of architecture: the Neues Haas-Haus designed by Hans Hollein, one of Austria's best-known living architects. Detractors consider its aggressively contemporary style out of place opposite St. Stephen's, seeing the cathedral's style parodied by being stood on its head; advocates consider the contrast enlivening. Whatever the ultimate verdict, the new restaurant and shopping complex has not been the expected commercial success; its restaurants may be thriving, but its boutiques are not. ⊠ *Stephanspl. 12.* ☉ *Shops weekdays 9–6, Sat. 9–noon.*

Pestsäule (Plague Column). Erected by Emperor Leopold I between 1687 and 1693 in thanks to God for delivering the city from a particularly virulent plague, today the representation looks more like a host of cherubs doing their best to cope with the icing of a wedding cake wilting in the hot sunshine. Staunch Protestants may be shocked to learn that the foul figure of the Pest stands also for the heretic plunging away from the "True Faith" into the depth of hell. But they will have to get used to the fact that the Catholic Church has triumphed over Protestantism in Austria and frequently recalls the fact in stone and on canvas. ⊠ *Graben.*

★ ㉓ Peterskirche (St. Peter's Church). Considered the best example of church Baroque in Vienna—certainly the most theatrical—the Peterskirche was constructed between 1702 and 1708 by Lucas von Hildebrandt. According to legend, the original church on this site was founded in 792 by Charlemagne, a tale immortalized by the relief plaque on the right side of the church. The facade possesses angled towers, graceful tower tops (said to have been inspired by the tents of the Turks during the siege of 1683), and an unusually fine entrance portal. Inside the church, the Baroque decoration is elaborate, with some fine touches (particularly the glass-crowned galleries high on the walls to either side of the altar and the amazing tableau of the martyrdom of St. John Nepomuk), but the lack of light and the years of accumulated dirt create a prevailing gloom, and the much-praised ceiling fres-

coes by J. M. Rottmayr are impossible to make out. Just before Christ-
mastime each year, the basement crypt is filled with a display of nativity scenes. The church is shoehorned into tiny Petersplatz, just off
the Graben. ⊠ *Peterspl. U-Bahn: U1, U3 Stephanspl.*

㉒ Stock-im-Eisen. In the southwest corner of Stock-im-Eisen-Platz, set into
the building on the west side of Kärntnerstrasse, is one of the city's
odder relics: the Stock-im-Eisen, or the "nail-studded stump." Chron-
icles first mention the Stock-im-Eisen in 1533, but it is probably far
older, and for hundreds of years any apprentice metalsmith who came
to Vienna to learn his trade hammered a nail into the tree trunk for
good luck. During World War II, when there was talk of moving the
relic to a museum in Munich, it mysteriously disappeared; it reappeared,
perfectly preserved, after the threat of removal had passed.

An Imperial City: The Hofburg

A walk through the Imperial Palace, known as the **Hofburg,** brings you
back to the days when Vienna was the capital of a mighty empire. You
can still find in Vienna shops vintage postcards and prints that show
the revered and bewhiskered Emperor Franz Josef starting out on a morning drive from his Hofburg palace in his carriage. Today, at the palace—
which faces Kohlmarkt on the opposite side of Michaelerplatz—you
can walk in his very footsteps, gaze at the old tin bath the emperor
kept under his simple iron bedstead, marvel at his bejeweled christen-
ing robe, and, along the way, feast your eyes on great works of art,
impressive armor, and some of the finest Baroque interiors in Europe.

Until 1918 the Hofburg was the home of the Habsburgs, rulers of the
Austro-Hungarian Empire. As a current tourist mecca, it has become
a vast smorgasbord of sightseeing attractions: the Imperial Apartments, two Imperial treasuries, six museums, the National Library, and
the famous Winter Riding School all vie for attention. The entire complex takes a minimum of a full day to explore in detail; if your time is
limited (or if you want to save most of the interior sightseeing for a
rainy day), you should omit the Imperial Apartments and all the museums mentioned below except the new museum of court silver and
tableware, the Silberkammer, and probably the Schatzkammer. An excellent multilingual, full-color booklet describing the palace in detail
is for sale at most ticket counters within the complex; it gives a complete list of attractions and maps out the palace's complicated ground
plan and building history wing by wing.

Vienna took its imperial role seriously, as evidenced by the sprawling
Hofburg complex, today, as then, the seat of government. But this is
generally understated power; while the buildings cover a considerable
area, the treasures lie within, not to be flamboyantly flaunted. Certainly
under Franz Josef II the reign was beneficent—witness the broad
Ringstrasse he ordained and the array of museums and public buildings it hosts. With few exceptions (Vienna City Hall and the Votive
Church), rooflines are kept to an even level, creating an ensemble effect that helps integrate the palace complex and its parks into the urban
landscape without making a domineering statement. Diplomats still bustle in and out of high-level international meetings in the elegant halls.
Horse-drawn carriages still traverse the Ring and the roadway that cuts
through the complex. Ignore the cars and tour buses and you can easily imagine yourself in a Vienna of a hundred or more years ago.

Architecturally, the Hofburg—like St. Stephen's—is far from refined.
It grew up over a period of 700 years (its earliest mention in court documents is from 1279, at the very beginning of Habsburg rule), and its

spasmodic, haphazard growth kept it from attaining any sort of unified identity. But many of the bits and pieces are fine, and one interior (the National Library) is a tour de force.

A Good Walk

When you begin to explore the Hofburg you realize that the palace complex is like a nest of boxes, courtyards opening off courtyards and wings (*Trakte*) spreading far and wide. First tackle **Josefsplatz** ㉖, the remarkable square that interrupts Augustinerstrasse, ornamented by the equestrian statue of Josef II—many consider this Vienna's loveliest square. Indeed, the beautifully restored imperial decor adorning the roof of the buildings forming Josefsplatz is one of the few visual demonstrations of Austria's onetime widespread power and influence. On your right to the north is the **Spanische Reitschule** ㉗, the Spanish Riding School—one emblem of Vienna known throughout the world—where the famous white horses reign. Across Reitschulgasse under the arches are the **Lipizzaner Museum** ㉘ and the Imperial Stables. To the south stands the **Augustinerkirche** ㉙, St. Augustine's Church, where the Habsburg rulers' hearts are preserved in urns. The grand main hall (Prunksaal) of the **Hofbibliothek** ㉚, the National Library, is one of the great Baroque treasures of Europe, a sight not to be missed (enter from the southwest corner of Josefsplatz).

Under the Michaelerplatz dome is the entrance to the **Kaiserappartements** ㉛, hardly the elegance you would normally associate with royalty, but Franz Josef II, the residing emperor from 1848 to 1916, was anything but ostentatious in his personal life. For the representational side, however, go through into the **In der Burg** ㉜ courtyard and look in at the elegant **Silberkammer** ㉝ museum of court silver and tableware. Go through the **Schweizertor** ㉞, the Swiss gate, to the south off In der Burg, to reach the small **Schweizer Hof** ㉟ courtyard with stairs leading to the **Hofburgkapelle** ㊱, the Imperial Chapel where the Vienna Boys Choir makes its regular Sunday appearances. In a back corner of the courtyard is the entrance to the **Schatzkammer** ㊲, the Imperial Treasury, overflowing with jewels, robes, and royal trappings. From In der Burg, the roadway leads under the **Leopold Wing** ㊳ of the complex into the vast park known as **Heldenplatz** ㊴, or Hero's Square. The immediately obvious heroes are the equestrian statues of Archduke Karl and Prince Eugene of Savoy. The Hofburg wing to the south with its concave facade is the **Neue Burg** ㊵, the "new" section of the complex, now housing four specialized museums. Depending on your interests, consider the **Ephesus Museum** ㊶, with Roman antiquities; the **Musical Instruments Collection** ㊷, where you also hear what you see; the impressive **Weapons Collection** ㊸, with tons of steel armor, or the **Ethnological Museum** ㊹, including Montezuma's headdress. Ahead, the **Burgtor** ㊺ gate separates the Hofburg complex from the Ringstrasse. The quiet oasis in back of the Neue Burg is the **Burggarten** ㊻. Catch your breath and marvel that you've seen only a small part of the Hofburg—a large part of it still houses the offices of the Austrian government and cannot be visited by the public.

TIMING
You could spend a day in the Hofburg complex. For most of the smaller museums, figure on anything from an hour upward.

Sights to See

㉙ **Augustinerkirche** (Church of the Augustinian Order). Across Josefsplatz from the Riding School is the entrance to the Augustinerkirche, built during the 14th century and presenting the most unified Gothic interior in the city. But the church is something of a fraud; the interior, it turns out, dates from the late 18th century, not the early 14th. A historical fraud the church may be, but a spiritual fraud it is not. The view from the entrance doorway is stunning: a soaring harmony of vertical piers, ribbed vaults, and hanging chandeliers that makes Vienna's other Gothic interiors look earthbound by comparison. The imposing Baroque organ sounds as fine as it looks, and the Sunday morning high mass sung here—frequently by Mozart or Haydn—can be the highlight of a trip. To the right of the main altar in the small Loreto Chapel stand silver urns containing the hearts of Habsburg rulers. This rather morbid sight is viewable after early mass on Sunday, Monday, or by appointment. ✉ *Josefspl.,* ☎ *01/533–7099–0. U-Bahn: U3 Herreng.*

46 **Burggarten.** The intimate Burggarten in back of the Neue Burg is a quiet oasis that includes a statue of a contemplative Kaiser Franz Josef and an elegant statue of Mozart, moved here from the Albertinaplatz after the war, when the city's charred ruins were being rebuilt. The former greenhouses are now the Schmetterlinghaus (Butterfly House; ☞ *below*) and the Palmenhaus restaurant (☞ Dining, *below*). ✉ *Access from Opernring and Hanuschg./Goethvg. U-Bahn: U2 Babenbergerstr.*

Schmetterlinghaus. The Butterfly House was recently relocated from Schönbrunn Palace to the old Hofburg Palace conservatory. The tropical indoor garden is home to hordes of live butterflies, orchids, and other floral displays. ✉ *Entrance in Burggarten,* ☎ *01/533–8570.* 🎫 *AS65.* ⊙ *Apr.–Oct., daily 10–5; Nov.–Mar., daily 10–4.*

45 **Burgtor.** The failure to complete the ☞ **Hofburg** building program left the old main palace gate stranded in the middle of the Heldenplatz (☞ *below*).

41 **Ephesus Museum.** One of the museums in the Neue Burg (☞ *below*), the Ephesus Museum contains exceptional Roman antiquities unearthed by Austrian archaeologists in Turkey at the turn of the century. 🎫 *Combined ticket with Musical Instrument Collection (*☞ *below) and Weapons Collection (*☞ *below) AS60 (AS100 for special exhibits).* ⊙ *Wed.–Mon. 10–6. U-Bahn: U2 Babenbergerstr.*

44 **Ethnological Museum** (Museum für Völkerkunde). This anthropological museum is entered at the west end pavilion in the Neue Burg (☞ *below*). Montezuma's feathered headdress is a highlight of its collections. 🎫 *AS60.* ⊙ *Jan.–Mar., Wed.–Mon. 10–6; Apr.–Dec., Wed.–Mon. 10–4.*

39 **Heldenplatz.** The long wing with the concave bay on the south side of the square is the youngest section of the palace, called the Neue Burg (☞ *below*). Although the Neue Burg building plans were not completed and the Heldenplatz was left without a discernible shape, the space nevertheless is punctuated by two superb equestrian statues of Archduke Karl and Prince Eugene of Savoy. The older section on the north includes the offices of the federal president.

★ **30** **Hofbibliothek** (formerly Court, now National Library). This is one of the grandest Baroque libraries in the world, in every sense a cathedral of books. Its centerpiece is the spectacular Prunksaal—the Grand Hall of the National Library—which probably contains more book treasures than any comparable collection outside the Vatican. The main entrance to the ornate reading room is in the left corner of Josefsplatz. Designed by Fischer von Erlach the Elder just before his death in 1723 and completed by his son, the Grand Hall is full-blown High Baroque, with trompe-l'oeil ceiling frescoes by Daniel Gran. This floridly Baroque library may not be to everyone's taste, but in the end it is the books themselves that come to the rescue. They are as lovingly displayed as the gilding and the frescoes, and they give the hall a warmth that the rest of the palace decidedly lacks. On the third floor is an intriguing museum of cartographic globes that should not be overlooked. ✉

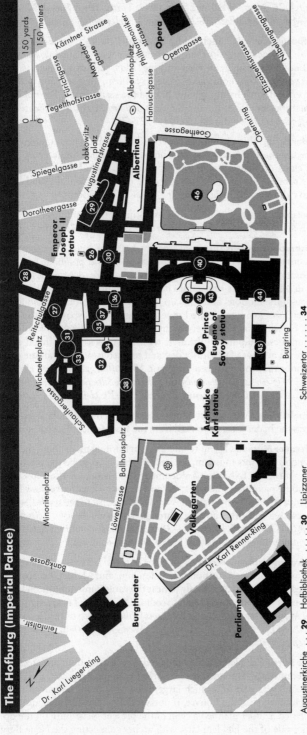

The Hofburg (Imperial Palace)

Opera

Augustinerkirche **29**
Burggarten **46**
Burgtor **45**
Ephesus Museum . . . **41**
Ethnological
  Museum **44**
Heldenplatz **39**

Hofbibliothek **30**
Hofburgkapelle **36**
In der Burg **32**
Josefsplatz **26**
Kaiser
  appartements . . . **31**
Leopold Wing **38**

Lipizzaner
  Museum **28**
Musical Instrument
  Collection **42**
Neue Burg **40**
Schatzkammer **37**
Schweizer Hof **35**

Schweizertor **34**
Silberkammer **33**
Spanische
  Reitschule **27**
Weapons
  Collection **43**

150 yards

150 meters

0

0

Josefspl. 1, at top of stairs inside, ☎ *01/534–100.* ▦ *AS60.* ☉ *May 7–Oct. 26, Mon.–Wed., Fri., Sat. 10–4, Thurs. 10–7, Sun. 10–2; Oct. 27–May 6, Mon.–Sat. 10–2. U-Bahn: U3 Herreng.*

㊱ Hofburgkapelle (Chapel of the Imperial Palace). The Vienna Boys Choir (Wiener Sängerknaben) sings mass at 9:15 on Sunday, Monday, and holidays from September to June. Alas, the arrangement is such that you *hear* the choirboys but don't see them; their soprano and alto voices peal forth from a gallery behind the seating area. For ticket information, ☞ Nightlife and the Arts, *below.* ✉ *Hofburg, Schweizer Hof,* ☎ *01/533–9927,* 🖷 *01/533–9927–75.*

㉜ In der Burg. This prominent courtyard of the Hofburg complex features a statue of Francis II and the noted ☞ **Schweizertor** gateway. Note the **clock** on the far upper wall at the north end of the courtyard: It tells time by the sundial, also gives the time mechanically, and even, above the clock face, indicates the phase of the moon.

㉖ Josefsplatz. Josefsplatz is the most imposing of the Hofburg courtyards, with an equestrian **statue of Emperor Joseph II** (1807) in the center.

㉛ Kaiserappartements (Imperial Apartments). The long, repetitive suite of conventionally luxurious rooms has a sad and poignant feel. The decoration (19th-century imitation of 18th-century rococo) tries to look regal, but much like the empire itself in its latter days it is only going through the motions and ends up looking merely official. Among the few signs of genuine life are Emperor Franz Josef's spartan, iron field bed, on which he slept every night, and Empress Elizabeth's wooden gymnastics equipment (obsessed with her looks, she suffered from anorexia and was fanatically devoted to exercise). Amid all the tired splendor they look decidedly forlorn. ✉ *Hofburg, Schweizer Hof,* ☎ *01/533–7570.* ▦ *AS80, combined ticket with Silberkammer (*☞ *below) AS95, tour AS20 per museum.* ☉ *Daily 9–4:30. U-Bahn: U2 Herreng.*

㊳ Leopold Wing. A long tract of offices known as the Leopold Wing separates the In der Burg courtyard from the vast Heldenplatz (☞ *above*).

㉘ Lipizzaner Museum. If you're interested in learning more about the Lipizzaners, visit this museum, located in what used to be the old imperial pharmacy. Exhibitions document the history of the Lipizzans, including paintings, photographs, and videos giving an overview from the 16th century to the present. A highlight is a visit to the stables, where you can see the horses up close, through a glass window. ✉ *Reitschulg. 2,* ☎ *01/533–78–11,* 🖷 *01/533–38–53.* ▦ *AS70; combined ticket with morning training session AS140.* ☉ *Daily 9–6.*

㊷ Musical Instrument Collection. This Neue Burg (☞ *below*) museum houses pianos that belonged to Brahms, Schumann, and Mahler. An acoustic guided tour allows you actually to hear the various instruments on headphones as you move from room to room. ▦ *Combined ticket with Ephesus Museum (*☞ *below) and Weapons Collection (*☞ *below) museums AS60 (AS100 for special exhibits).* ☉ *Wed.–Mon. 10–6. U-Bahn: U2 Babenbergerstr.*

㊵ Neue Burg. The Neue Burg stands today as a symbol of architectural overconfidence. Designed for Emperor Franz Josef in 1869, this "new château" was part of a much larger scheme that was meant to make the Hofburg rival the Louvre, if not Versailles. The German architect Gottfried Semper planned a twin of the present Neue Burg on the opposite side of the Heldenplatz, with arches connecting the Neue Burg and its twin with the other pair of twins on the Ringstrasse, the Kunsthistorisches Museum (Museum of Art History), and the Naturhistorisches Museum (Museum of Natural History). But World War I intervened, and with the empire's collapse the Neue Burg became merely the last in a long series of failed attempts to bring architectural order to the Hofburg. (From its main balcony, in April 1938, Adolf Hitler, telling a huge cheering crowd below of his plan for the new German empire, declared that Vienna "is a pearl! I am going to put it into a setting of which it is worthy!") Today, visitors flock to the Neue Burg because it houses no fewer than four specialty museums: the ☞ **Ephesus Museum, Musical Instruments Collection, Ethnological Museum,** and **Weapons Collection.** ✉ *Heldenpl.*, 🕾 *01/525240.*

③⑦ Schatzkammer (Imperial Treasury). The entrance to the Schatzkammer, with its 1,000 years of treasures, is tucked away at ground level behind the staircase to the Hofburgkapelle. The elegant display is a welcome antidote to the monotony of the Imperial Apartments, for the entire Treasury was completely renovated in 1983–87, and the crowns and relics and vestments fairly glow in their new surroundings. Here you'll find such marvels as the Holy Lance—reputedly the lance that pierced Jesus' side—the Imperial Crown (a sacred symbol of sovereignty once stolen on Hitler's orders), and the Saber of Charlemagne. Don't miss the Burgundian Treasure, connected with that most romantic of medieval orders of chivalry, the Order of the Golden Fleece. ✉ *Schweizer Hof*, 🕾 *01/533–7931.* 🎟 *AS100.* ☉ *Wed.–Mon. 10–6. U-Bahn: U2 Herreng.*

③⑤ Schweizer Hof. This courtyard was named after the Swiss Guards who were once stationed here. In the southeast corner (at the top of the steps) is the entrance to the Hofburgkapelle (☞ *above*).

③④ Schweizertor (Swiss Gate). Dating from 1552 and decorated with some of the earliest classical motifs in the city, the Schweizertor leads from In der Burg through to the oldest section of the palace, a small courtyard known as the Schweizer Hof (☞ *above*). The gateway is painted maroon, black, and gold; it gives a fine Renaissance flourish to its building facade.

③③ Silberkammer (Museum of Court Silver and Tableware). The large courtyard on the far side of the Michaelertor rotunda is known as In der Burg; here on the west side is the entrance to the sparkling new Silberkammer. There's far more than forks and finger bowls here; stunning decorative pieces vie with glittering silver and gold for attention. Highlights include Franz Josef's vermeil banqueting service, the Jardinière given to Empress Elizabeth by Queen Victoria, and gifts from Marie-Antoinette to her brother, Josef II. The presentation of full table settings gives an idea of court life both as a daily routine and on festive occasions. ✉ *Hofburg, Michaelertrakt*, 🕾 *01/533–7570.* 🎟 *AS80, combined ticket with Kaiserappartements (☞ above) AS95.* ☉ *Daily 9–4:30.*

★ ②⑦ Spanische Reitschule (Spanish Riding School). Located between Augustinerstrasse and the Josefsplatz is the world-famous Spanish Riding School, a favorite for centuries, and no wonder: who can resist the sight of the stark-white Lipizzan horses going through their masterful paces? For the last 300 years they have been perfecting their *haute école* riding demonstrations to the sound of Baroque music in a ballroom that seems to be a crystal-chandeliered stable. The breed was started in 1580, and the horses proved themselves in battle as well as in the complicated "dances" for which they are famous. The interior of the riding school, the 1735 work of Fischer von Erlach the Younger, is itself an attraction—surely Europe's most elegant sports arena—and if the prancing horses begin to pall, move up to the top balcony and examine the ceiling. The school's popularity is hardly surprising, and tickets to some performances must be ordered in writing many weeks in advance. Information offices have a brochure with the detailed schedule (performances are usually March–December, with the school on vacation in July and August). Generally the full, 80-minute show takes place Sunday at 10:45 AM plus selected Wednesdays at 7 PM.

Morning training sessions (without music), held Tuesday–Saturday, with a few in February and August on Mondays as well, are usually open to the public. Tickets can be bought *only* at the door for these morning training sessions at the Josefsplatz entrance, and the line starts forming between 9 and 9:30 for the opening at 10. Note, however, there are classical dressage training sessions on Saturday mornings that are accompanied by music—these tickets are available only by reservation through ticket agencies (a list of these agencies is included in a free leaflet about the Spanish Riding School available from the Austrian National Tourist Office). Note that ticket agencies (legally) add a commission of 22%–25% to the face price of the ticket. For Sunday and Wednesday performance ticket orders, write to **Spanische Reitschule** (✉ Hofburg, A–1010 Vienna). Pick up reserved tickets at the office under the Michaelerplatz rotunda dome. ✉ *Michaelerpl. 1, Hofburg,* ☎ *01/ 533–9031–0,* FAX *01/535–0186.* ☞ *AS250–AS900, standing room AS200, morning training sessions AS100; Sat. classical dressage sessions with music, AS250, available only through travel agencies.* ☉ *Mar.– June and Sept.–mid-Dec. Closed tour wks.*

㊸ **Weapons Collection.** Rivaling the armory in Graz as one of the most extensive arms-and-armor collections in the world is this Neue Burg (☞ *above*) museum. Enter at the triumphal arch set into the middle of the curved portion of the facade. ☞ *Combined ticket with Ephesus Museum (☞ above) and Musical Instrument Collection (☞ above) AS60 (AS100 for special exhibits).* ☉ *Wed.–Mon. 10–6. U-Bahn: U2 Babenbergerstr.*

The Ringstrasse and Its Environs

Along with the Hofburg, the Ringstrasse comprises Vienna's major urban set piece. This grand series of thoroughfares bounds the heart of Vienna, the Innere Stadt (Inner City), or First District. It follows the lines of what were, until an imperial decree ordered their leveling in 1857, the defenses of the city. By the 1870s, Vienna had reached the zenith of her imperial prosperity, and this found ultimate expression in the series of magnificent buildings erected around the Ringstrasse—the Opera House, the Kunsthistoriches Museum, the Natural History Museum, and the Rathaus, University, and Votivkirche.

A Good Walk

Is there a best way to explore the Ring? You can walk it from one end to the other—from where it begins at the Danube Canal to where it returns to the canal after its curving flight. Or, you can explore it whenever you happen to cross it on other missions. While it is a pleasant sequence of boulevards, seeing its succession of rather pompous buildings all in one walk can be overpowering. Or, you can obtain the best of both options by following this suggested itinerary, which leavens the bombast of the Ring with some of Vienna's most fascinating sights.

Immediately across the Ringstrasse from the Hofburg are twin buildings, both museums. To the west is the **Naturhistorisches Museum** ㊼; to the east, the **Kunsthistorisches Museum** ㊽, the art museum packed with world-famous treasures. Allow ample time for exploration here. Not far away is the new **Museumsquartier** ㊾, a museum complex that includes the modern art collections of the Museum Moderner Kunst. Farther west of the museum square is the compact **Spittelberg Quarter** ㊿ of tiny streets between Burggasse and Sibensterngasse, often site of handicraft and seasonal fairs. The **Volksgarten** ㊾ on the inside of the Ringstrasse to the north of the museum square numbers a café and rose garden among its attractions; look also for the small memorial to Franz Josef's wife, Empress Elizabeth, in the back corner. Tackle the Ringstrasse buildings by starting with the **Justizpalast** ⑤ (Central Law Courts), moving along to **Parliament** ㉒, the **Rathaus** ㊌ (City Hall), the **Burgtheater** ㊗ opposite on the inside of the Ring, then the **Universität** ㊏ (the main building of Vienna's university) beyond, again on the outside of the Ring. Next to the university stands the neo-Gothic **Votivkirche** ㊐. If you still have time and energy, walk farther along the Ring to discover the **Börse** ㊙ (Stock Exchange) at the corner of the Ring and Wipplingerstrasse. The outside end of Hohenstaufengasse leads into Liechtensteinstrasse, which will bring you to Berggasse. Turn right to reach No. 19, the **Freud Apartment** ㊘, now a museum and research facility.

TIMING

If you can, plan for Vienna's Louvre—the Kunsthistorisches Museum—early in the day before the crowds arrive, although the size of crowds depends greatly on whatever special shows the museum may be exhibiting. As for the main sights off the Ringstrasse, you could easily lump together visits to the Freud Apartment and the Museum of Modern Art, figuring on about a half day for the two combined.

Sights to See

㊙ **Börse** (Vienna Stock Exchange). This imposing rose-brick building with a pillared portico was constructed 1874–77 and was designed by Theophil Hansen, who also designed the Academy of Fine Arts. Besides the stock exchange, the building also houses a couple of shops and the unusual flower-shop restaurant Hansen (☞ Dining, *below*). The stock exchange is not open to the public. ⊠ *Strauchg. 1–3.*

㊗ **Burgtheater** (National Theater). One of the most important theaters in the German-speaking world, the Burgtheater was built between 1874 and 1888 in the Italian Renaissance style, replacing the old court theater at Michaelerplatz. Emperor Franz Josef's mistress, Katherina Schratt, was once a star performer here, and famous Austrian and German actors still stride this stage. The opulent interior, with its 60-ft relief *Worshippers of Bacchus* by Rudolf Wyer and foyer ceiling frescoes by Ernst and Gustav Klimt make it well worth a visit. For information about performances here, *see* Theater *in* Nightlife and the Arts, *below.* ⊠ *Dr. Karl-Lueger-Ring 2,* ☎ *01/51444.* 🎫 *AS50.* ☉ *Guided tours Tues., Thurs.–Sat. at 9 and 3; Sun. at 11 and 3.*

㊘ **Freud Apartment.** Not far from the historic Hofburg district, beyond the Votivkirche at the Schottenring along the Ringstrasse, you can skip over several centuries and visit that outstanding symbol of 20th-century Vienna: Sigmund Freud's apartment at Berggasse 19 (Apartment 6, one flight up; ring the bell and push the door simultaneously); this was his residence from 1891 to 1938. The five-room collection of memorabilia is mostly a photographic record of Freud's life, with some documents, publications, and a portion of his collection of antiquities also on display. The waiting-room furniture is authentic, but the consulting room and study furniture (including the famous couch) can be seen only in photographs. ⊠ *Bergg. 19,* ☎ *01/319–1596.* 🎫 *AS60.* ☉ *July–Sept., daily 9–6; Oct.–June, daily 9–4. U-Bahn: U2 Schottentor.*

㊑ **Justizpalast** (Central Law Courts). Alexander Wielemans designed this monumental building in the Italian Renaissance style from 1875–81. The main hall is nearly 70 ft high, and is topped by a glass ceiling. At the end of World War II, this area was the center of the Austrian resistance movement, known as the "O5." The "0" stands for Österreich, or Austria, and the "5" is for the fifth letter of the alphabet, which translates into Ö, or OE, the abbreviation for Österreich. Between 1945 and 1955 it served as the headquarters for the Allied military leadership. The Justizpalast is not open to the public. ⊠ *Schmerlingpl. 10–11.*

★ ④⑧ **Kunsthistorisches Museum** (Museum of Fine Art). However short your stay in Vienna, you will surely want to pay a visit to one of the greatest art collections in the world, that of the Kunsthistorisches Museum. For this is no dry-as-dust museum illustrating the history of art, as its name implies. Rather its collections of Old Master paintings reveal the royal taste and style of many members of the mighty House of Habsburg, who during the 16th and 17th centuries ruled over the greater part of the Western world. Today you can enjoy what this great ruling house assiduously (and in most cases, selectively) brought together through the centuries. The collection stands in the same class with those of the Louvre, the Prado, and the Vatican. It is most famous for the largest collection of paintings under one roof by the Netherlandish 16th-century master Pieter Brueghel the Elder—just seeing his sublime *Hunters in the Snow* is worth a trip to Vienna, many art historians will tell you. Brueghel's depictions of peasant scenes, often set in magnificent landscapes, distill the poetry and magic of the 16th century as few other paintings do. Room RX is the Brueghel shrine—on its walls, in addition to *Hunters in the Snow,* hang *Children's Games,* the *Tower of Babel,* the *Peasant Wedding,* the *Nest-Robber,* and eight other priceless canvases by the artist. But there are also hundreds of other celebrated Old Master paintings here, most assembled by the Habsburgs over many centuries. Even a cursory description would run on for pages, but a brief selection of the museum's most important works will give you an idea of the riches to be enjoyed. The large-scale works concentrated in the main galleries shouldn't distract you from the equal share of masterworks in the more intimate side wings.

The Flemish wing also includes Rogier van der Weyden's *Triptych Crucifixion,* Holbein's *Portrait of Jane Seymour, Queen of England,* a fine series of Rembrandt portraits, and Vermeer's peerless *Allegory of the Art of Painting.* The grand style of the 17th century is represented by Rubens's towering altarpieces and his *Nude of Hélène Fourment.* In the Italian wing are works by Titian, including his *Portrait of Isabella d'Este,* whose fiercely intelligent eyes make you realize why she was the first lady of the Renaissance, and Giorgione's *The Three Philosophers,* an enigmatic composition in uniquely radiant Venetian coloring. A short list of other highlights include Raphael's *Madonna in the Meadow,* Correggio's *Jupiter Embracing Io,* Parmigianino's *Cupid Cutting a Bow,* Guercino's *Return of the Prodigal Son,* and Caravaggio's *Madonna of the Rosary.* One level down is the remarkable, less-visited *Kunstkammer,* displaying priceless objects created for the Habsburg emperors. These include curiosities made of gold, silver, and crystal (including Cellini's famous salt cellar), and more exotic materials, such as ivory, horn, and gemstones. In addition, there are rooms devoted to Egyptian antiquities, Greek and Roman art, sculpture (ranging from masterworks by Tilmann Riemenschneider to Italian Mannerist bronzes, which the Habsburgs collected by the roomful) and the decorative arts, and numerous other collections. ⊠ *Maria-Theresien-Pl.,* ☎ *01/525240.* 🖾 *AS120.* ☉ *Tues.–Sun. 10–6; extended hours for picture galleries, Thurs. until 9 PM.*

④⑨ **Museumsquartier** (Museum Quarter). Scheduled to open in summer 2001, this vast culture center, which claims to be the largest of its kind in the world, will be housed in what was once the Imperial Court Stables. The 250-year-old Baroque complex designed by Fischer von Erlach is ideally situated near the Hofburg Palace in the heart of the city. Four museums are planned. The **Leopold Musuem** will contain the famous Egon Schiele collection. The **Museum moderner Kunst Stiftung Ludwig**, or modern art museum, formerly housed in the Palais Lichtenstein, will house the national collection of 20th-century art, ranging from Gustav Klimt to Nam June Paik and including the contemporary Austrian masterpieces of the Ludwig collection. The **Kunsthalle** will be used for special exhibits, and the **ZOOM Kinder Museum** will cater to children. The annual Wiener Festwochen (theater-arts festival) and the International Tanzwochen (dance festival) will be held in the former Winter Riding Hall. In addition to all this there will be an architecture center for contemporary design, a theater where the annual Viennale Film Festival will be held, and shops, cafés, and art galleries. ⊠ *Museumspl. 1–5,* ☎ *01/523–5881.* ⊞ *Not determined at press time.* ☉ *Not determined at press time. U-Bahn: U2 Babenbergerstrasse/U2, U3 Volkstheater.*

47 **Naturhistorisches Museum** (Natural History Museum). The formal museum complex just outside the Ring has two elements—to the east is the celebrated Kunsthistorisches Museum (☞ *above*), to the west is the Naturhistorisches Museum, or Natural History Museum. This is the home of, among other artifacts, the famous Venus of Willendorf, a tiny statuette thought to be some 20,000 years old and symbol of the Iron Age Hallstatt civilization. The reconstructed dinosaur skeletons understandably draw the greatest attention. ⊠ *Maria-Theresien-Pl.,* ☎ *01/521–77–0.* ⊞ *AS30.* ☉ *Wed. 9–9, Thurs.–Mon. 9–6:30. U-Bahn: U2, U3 Volkstheater.*

52 **Parliament.** This sprawling building reminiscent of an ancient Greek temple is the seat of Austria's elected representative assembly. An embracing, heroic ramp on either side of the main structure is lined with carved marble figures of ancient Greek and Roman historians. Its centerpiece is the **Pallas-Athene-Brunnen** (fountain), designed by Theophil Hansen, which is crowned by the goddess of wisdom and surrounded by water-nymphs symbolizing the executive and legislative powers governing the country. ⊠ *Dr. Karl-Renner-Ring 1,* ☎ *01/401–100.* ⊞ *AS40.* ☉ *Guided tours Fri. at 11, 1 and 2.*

55 **Rathaus** (City Hall). Designed by Friedrich Schmidt and resembling a Gothic fantasy castle with its many spires and turrets, the Rathaus was actually built between 1872 and 1883. The facade holds a lavish display of standard-bearers brandishing the coat of arms of the city of Vienna and the monarchy. Guided tours include the banqueting hall and various committee rooms. A palatial park adorns the front of the building and it is usually brimming with activity. In winter it is the scene of the *Christkindlmarkt,* the most famous Christmas market in Vienna, and in summer, concerts are performed here. ⊠ *Rathauspl. 1,* ☎ *01/4000–0.* ⊞ *Free.* ☉ *Guided tours Mon., Wed., Fri., at 1, five person minimum.*

Ringstrasse. Late in 1857, Emperor Franz Josef issued a decree announcing the most ambitious piece of urban redevelopment Vienna had ever seen. The inner city's centuries-old walls were to be torn down, and the *glacis*—the wide expanse of open field that acted as a protective buffer between inner city and outer suburbs—was to be filled in. In their place was to rise a wide, tree-lined boulevard, upon which would stand an imposing collection of new buildings that would reflect Vienna's special status as the political, economic, and cultural heart of the Austro-Hungarian Empire. During the 50 years of building that followed, many factors combined to produce the Ringstrasse as it now stands, but the most important was the gradual rise of liberalism after the failed Revolution of 1848. By the latter half of the Ringstrasse era, support for constitutional government, democracy, and equality—all the concepts that liberalism traditionally equates with progress—was steadily increasing. As the Ringstrasse went up, it became the definitive symbol of this liberal progress; as Carl E. Schorske put it in his *Fin-de-Siècle Vienna*, it celebrated "the triumph of constitutional *Recht* (right) over imperial *Macht* (might), of secular culture over religious faith. Not palaces, garrisons, and churches, but centers of constitutional government and higher culture dominated the Ring."

The highest concentration of public building occurred in the area around the Volksgarten, where are clustered (moving from south to north, from Burgring to Schottenring) the **Kunsthistorisches Museum,** the **Naturhistorisches Museum,** the **Justizpalast** (Central Law Courts), the **Parliament,** the **Rathaus** (City Hall), the **Burgtheater** (National Theater), the **Universität** (University of Vienna), the **Votivkirche** (Votive Church), and slightly farther along, the **Börse** (Stock Exchange) on Schottenring (for all of these sights, see either *above* or *below*). As an ensemble, the collection is astonishing in its architectural presumption: It is nothing less than an attempt to assimilate and summarize the entire architectural history of Europe. As critics were quick to notice, however, the complex suffers from a serious organizational flaw: most of the buildings lack effective context. Rather than being the focal points of an organized overall plan, they are plunked haphazardly down on an avenue that is itself too wide to possess a unified, visually comprehensible character.

To some, the monumentality of the Ringstrasse is overbearing; others, however, find the architectural panorama exhilarating, and growth of the trees over 100 years has served to put the buildings into different perspective. There is no question but that the tree-lined boulevard with its broad sidewalks gives the city a unique ribbon of green and certainly the distinction that the emperor sought.

50 **Spittelberg Quarter.** The Spittelberg quarter, one block northwest of Maria-Theresien-Platz off the Burggasse, offers a fair visual idea of the Vienna which existed outside of the city walls a century ago. Most buildings have been replaced, but the engaging 18th-century survivors at Burggasse 11 and 13 are adorned with religious and secular decorative sculpture, the latter with a niche statue of St. Joseph, the former with cherubic work-and-play bas-reliefs. For several blocks around—walk down Gutenberggasse and back up Spittelberggasse—the 18th-century houses have been beautifully restored. The sequence from Spittelberggasse 5 to 19 is an especially fine array of Viennese plain and fancy. Around holiday times, particularly Easter and Christmas, the Spittelberg quarter, known for arts and handicrafts, hosts seasonal markets offering unusual and interesting items.

56 **Universität** (University of Vienna). After that of Prague, Vienna's is the oldest university in the German-speaking world. It was founded in 1365 by Duke Rudolf IV and reorganized during the reign of Maria Theresa. The main section of the university is a massive block in Italian Renaissance style designed by Heinrich Ferstel and built between 1873 and 1884.

Thirty-eight statues representing important men of letters decorate the front of the building, while the rear, which encompasses the library (with nearly 2 million volumes), is adorned with *sgraffito*. In the courtyard is the *Kastaliabrunnen,* the fountain for the guardians of spring, designed by Edmund Hellmer in 1904. ⊠ *Dr. Karl-Lueger-Ring/Universitätstr.*

㊿ Volksgarten. Just opposite the Hofburg is a green oasis with a beautifully planted rose garden, a 19th-century Greek temple, and a rather wistful white marble monument to Empress Elizabeth—Franz Josef's Bavarian wife, who died of a dagger wound inflicted by an Italian anarchist in Geneva in 1898. If not overrun with latter-day hippies, these can offer appropriate spots to sit for a few minutes while contemplating Vienna's most ambitious piece of 19th-century city planning: the famous Ringstrasse.

㊗ Votivkirche (Votive Church). When Emperor Franz Josef was a young man, he was strolling along the Mölker Bastei, now one of the few remaining portions of the the the old wall that once surrounded the city, when he was taken unawares and stabbed in the neck by an Italian tailor. The assassination attempt was unsuccessful, and Franz Josef ordered that a church be built in thanks for his survival. He wanted it to be exactly at the spot he was gazing at when he was struck down. The neo-Gothic church was built of gray limestone with two openwork turrets between 1856 and 1879. ⊠ *Rooseveltpl.,* ☎ *01/406–1192–13.* ☉ *Tours by prior arrangement.*

Monarchs and Mozart: From St. Stephen's to the Opera House

The cramped, ancient quarter behind St. Stephen's Cathedral offers a fascinating contrast to the luxurious expanses of the Ringstrasse and more recent parts of Vienna. This was—and still is—concentrated residential territory in the heart of the city. Mozart lived here; later, Prince Eugene and others built elegant town palaces as the smaller buildings were replaced. Streets—now mostly reserved for pedestrians—are narrow, and tiny alleyways abound. Facades open into courtyards that once housed the carriages and horses. The magnificent State Opera House shares with St. Stephen's the honor of being one of the city's most familiar and beloved landmarks.

A Good Walk

To pass through these streets is to take a short journey through history and art. In the process—as you visit former haunts of Mozart, kings, and emperors—you can be easily impressed with a clear sense of how Vienna's glittering Habsburg centuries unfolded. Start from St. Stephen's Cathedral by walking down Singerstrasse to Blutgasse and turn left into the **Blutgasse District** ⑥⓪—a neighborhood redolent of the 18th century. At the north end in Domgasse is the so-called **Figarohaus** ⑥①, now a memorial museum, the house in which Wolfgang Amadeus Mozart lived when he wrote the opera *The Marriage of Figaro.* Follow Domgasse east to Grünangergasse, which will bring you to Franziskanerplatz and the Gothic-Renaissance Franziskanerkirche (Franciscan Church). Follow the ancient Ballgasse to Rauhensteingasse, turning left onto **Himmelpfortgasse**—"The Gates of Heaven Street." Prince Eugene of Savoy had his town palace here at No. 8, now the **Finanzministerium** ⑥②, living here when he wasn't enjoying his other residence, the Belvedere Palace. Continue down Himmelpfortgasse to Seilerstätte to visit a new museum devoted to the wonders of music, the **Haus der Musik** ⑥③. Then turn into Annagasse with its beautiful houses, which brings you back to the main shopping street, **Kärnterstrasse,** where you can find everything from Austrian jade to the latest Jill Sander turnouts. Turn left, walking north two blocks, and take the short Donnergasse to reach **Neuer Markt** square and the Providence Fountain. At the southwest corner of the square is the **Kaisergruft** ⑥ in the Kapuzinerkirche (Capuchin Church), the burial vault for rows of once-ruling Habsburgs. Tegetthofstrasse south will bring you to Albertinaplatz, the square noted for the obvious war memorial and even more for the **Albertina Museum** ⑥, one of the world's great collections of Old Master drawings and prints. The southeast side of the square is bounded by the famous **Staatsoper** ⑥, the State Opera House; check for tour possibilities or, better, book tickets for a great *Der Rosenkavalier.*

TIMING

A simple walk of this route could take you a full half day, assuming you stop occasionally to survey the scene and take it all in. The restyled Figarohaus is worth a visit, but note the odd closing hours and schedule your visit accordingly. The Kaisergruft in the Kapuzinerkirche is impressive for its shadows of past glories, but there are crowds, and you may have to wait to get in; the best times are early morning and around lunchtime. Tours of the State Opera House take place in the afternoons; check the schedule posted outside one of the doors on the arcaded Kärntnerstrasse side. Figure about an hour each for the various visits and tours.

Sights to See

⑥ **Albertina Museum.** Some of the greatest Old Master drawings—including Dürer's legendary *Praying Hands*—are housed in this unassuming building, home to the world's largest collection of drawings, sketches, engravings, and etchings. Dürer leads the list, but there are many other highlights, including works by Rembrandt, Michelangelo, and Correggio. In fact, the holdings are so vast that only a limited number can be shown at one time, and some drawings are so delicate that they can be shown only in facsimile. The building is undergoing restoration and is scheduled to reopen in September 2002. For the past several years the collection was housed in the Akademiehof near the Secession, but that is now closed as well while everything is being reassembled. ⊠ *Augustinerstr. 1,* ☎ *01/534–830 or 01/534–820.* ⊙ *Closed for renovation until fall 2002; Tues.–Sun. 10–5 when reopen.*

⑥ **Blutgasse District.** The small block bounded by Singerstrasse, Grünangergasse, and Blutgasse is known as the Blutgasse District. Nobody knows for certain how the gruesome name—*Blut* is German for "blood"—originated, although one legend has it that Knights Templar were slaughtered here when their order was abolished in 1312, although in later years the narrow street was known in those unpaved days as Mud Lane. Today the block is a splendid example of city renovation and restoration, with cafés, small shops, and galleries tucked into the corners. You can look inside the courtyards to see the open galleries that connect various apartments on the upper floors, the finest example being at Blutgasse 3. At the corner of Singerstrasse sits the 18th-century **Neupauer-Breuner Palace,** with its monumental entranceway and inventively delicate windows. Opposite at Singerstrasse 17 is the **Rottal Palace,** attributed to Hildebrandt, with its wealth of classical wall motifs. For contrast, turn up the narrow Blutgasse, with its simple 18th-century facades.

⑥ **Figarohaus.** One of Mozart's 11 rented Viennese residences, the Figarohaus has its entrance at Domgasse 5, on the tiny alley behind St. Stephen's (although the facade on Schulerstrasse is far more imposing). It was in this house that Mozart wrote *The Marriage of Figaro* and the six quartets dedicated to Joseph Haydn (who once called on Mozart here, saying to Leopold, Mozart's father, ". . . your son is the greatest composer that I know in person or by name"). The apartment he occupied now contains a small commemorative museum—"created," alas, by an architect more interested in graphic blandishment than a sense of history; you'll have to use your imagination to picture how Mozart lived and worked here. ⊠ *Domg. 5,* ☎ *01/513–6294.* ☑ *AS25.* ☉ *Tues.– Sun. 9–6. U-Bahn: U1, U3 Stephanspl.*

62 **Finanzministerium** (Ministry of Finance). The architectural jewel of Himmelpfortgasse, this imposing abode—designed by Fischer von Erlach in 1697 and later expanded by Hildebrandt—was originally the town palace of Prince Eugene of Savoy. As you study the Finanzministerium, you'll realize its Baroque details are among the most inventively conceived and beautifully executed in the city; all the decorative motifs are so softly carved that they appear to have been freshly squeezed from a pastry tube. The Viennese are lovers of the Baroque in both their architecture and their pastry, and here the two passions seem visibly merged. Such Baroque elegance may seem inappropriate for a finance ministry, but the contrast between place and purpose could hardly be more Viennese. ⊠ *Himmelpfortg. 8.*

63 **Haus der Musik** (House of Music). It would be easy to spend an entire day at this new, ultra-high-tech museum housed on several floors of an early 19th-century palace near Schwarzenbergplatz. Pride of place goes to the special rooms dedicated to each of the great Viennese composers—Haydn, Mozart, Beethoven, Strauss, and Mahler—complete with music samples and manuscripts. Other exhibits trace the evolution of sound (from primitive noises to the music of the masters) and illustrate the mechanics of the human ear (measure your own frequency threshold). There are also dozens of interactive computer games. You can even record your own CD with a variety of everyday sounds. ⊠ *Seilerstätte 30,* ☎ *01/51648.* ☑ *AS110.* ☉ *Daily 10–10. Restaurant, café. U-Bahn: U1, U2, U4 Karlsplatz, then Streetcar D to Schwartzenbergplatz.*

NEED A BREAK? Take a break at a landmark café in one of the most charming squares in Vienna, between Himmelpfortgasse and Singerstrasse. The **Kleines Cafe** (⊠ Franziskanerpl. 3), open daily, is more for coffee, cocktails, and light snacks than for pastries, and few places are more delightful to sit in and relax on a warm afternoon or evening. In summer, tables are set outside on the intimate cobblestone square where the only sounds are the tinkling fountain and the occasional chiming of bells from the ancient Franciscan monastery next door. Before heading on, be sure to take a short stroll up Ballgasse, the tiny 18th-century street opposite the café.

Himmelpfortgasse. The maze of tiny streets including Ballgasse, Rauhensteingasse, and Himmelpfortgasse (literally, "Gates of Heaven Street") masterfully conjures up the Vienna of the 19th century. The most impressive house on the street is the Ministry of Finance (☞ *above*). The back side of the Steffl department store on Rauhensteingasse now marks the site of the house in which Mozart died in 1791. There's a commemorative plaque that once identified the streetside site together with a small memorial corner devoted to Mozart memorabilia that can be found on the fifth floor of the store.

64 **Kaisergruft** (Imperial Burial Vault). In the basement of the Kapuzinerkirche, or Capuchin Church (on the southwest corner of the Neuer Markt), is one of the more intriguing sights in Vienna: the Kaisergruft, or Imperial Burial Vault. The crypts contain the partial remains of some 140 Habsburgs (the hearts are in the Augustinerkirche and the entrails in St. Stephen's) plus one non-Habsburg governess ("She was always with us in life," said Maria Theresa, "why not in death?"). Perhaps this is the wrong way to approach the Habsburgs in Vienna, starting with their tombs, but it does give you a chance to get their names in sequence as they lie in rows, their coffins ranging from the simplest explosions of funerary conceit—with decorations of skulls and other morbid symbols—to the lovely and distinguished tomb of Maria Theresa and her husband. Designed while the couple still lived, their monument shows the empress in bed with her husband—awaking to the Last Judgment as if it were just another weekday morning, while the remains of her son (the ascetic Josef II) lie in a simple casket at the foot of the bed as if he were the family dog. ⊠ *Neuer Markt/Tegetthoffstr. 2,* ☎ *01/512–6853–12.* ▣ *AS40.* ☉ *Daily 9:30–4. U-Bahn: U1, U3 Stephansplatz.*

Kärntnerstrasse. The Kärntnerstrasse remains Vienna's leading central shopping street. These days Kärntnerstrasse is much maligned. Too commercial, too crowded, too many tasteless signs, too much gaudy neon—the complaints go on and on. Nevertheless, when the daytime tourist crowds dissolve, the Viennese arrive regularly for their evening promenade, and it is easy to see why. Vulgar the street may be, but it is also alive and vital, possessing an energy that the more tasteful Graben and the impeccable Kohlmarkt lack. For the sightseer beginning to suffer from an excess of art history, classic buildings, and museums, a Kärntnerstrasse window-shopping respite will be welcome.

㊅ **Staatsoper** (State Opera House). The famous Vienna Staatsoper on the Ring vies with the cathedral for the honor of marking the emotional heart of the city—it is a focus for Viennese life and one of the chief symbols of resurgence after the cataclysm of World War II. Its directorship is one of the top jobs in Austria, almost as important as that of president, and one that comes in for even more public attention. Everyone thinks they could do it just as well, and since the huge salary comes out of taxes, they feel they have every right to criticize, often and loudly. The first of the Ringstrasse projects to be completed (in 1869), the opera house suffered disastrous bomb damage in the last days of World War II (only the outer walls, the front facade, and the main staircase area behind it survived). The auditorium is plain when compared to the red and gold eruptions of London's Covent Garden or some of the Italian opera houses, but it has an elegant individuality that shows to best advantage when the stage and auditorium are turned into a ballroom for the great Opera Ball.

The construction of the Opera House is the stuff of legend. When the foundation was laid, the plans for the Opernring were not yet complete, and in the end the avenue turned out to be several feet higher than originally planned. As a result, the Opera House lacked the commanding prospect that its architects, Eduard van der Nüll and August Sicard von Sicardsburg, had intended, and even Emperor Franz Josef pronounced the building a bit low to the ground. For the sensitive van der Nüll (and here the story becomes a bit suspect), failing his beloved emperor was the last straw. In disgrace and despair, he committed suicide. Sicardsburg died of grief shortly thereafter. And the emperor, horrified at the deaths his innocuous remark had caused, limited all his future artistic pronouncements to a single immutable formula: *Es war sehr schön, es hat mich sehr gefreut* ("It was very nice, it pleased me very much").

Renovation could not avoid a postwar look, for the cost of fully restoring the 19th-century interior decor was prohibitive. The original basic design was followed in the 1945–55 reconstruction, meaning that sight lines from some of the front boxes are poor at best. These disappointments hardly detract from the fact that this is one of the world's half dozen greatest opera houses, and experiencing a performance here can be the highlight of a trip to Vienna. Tours of the Opera House are given regularly, but starting times vary according to opera rehearsals; the current schedule is posted at the east-side entrance under the arcade on the Kärntnerstrasse marked GUIDED TOURS, where the tours begin. Alongside under the arcade is an information office that also sells tickets to the main opera and the Volksoper. ⊠ *Opernring 2,* ☎

01/514–44–2613. 🎫 *Tour AS60.* 🕐 *Tours Oct.–Apr. at 9, 2 and 3 when there are no rehearsals, May–Sept., 6 tours daily, but call for times. U-Bahn: U1, U2, U4 Karlspl.*

Pomp and Circumstance: South of the Ring to the Belvedere

City planning in the late 1800s and early 1900s clearly was essential to manage the growth of the burgeoning imperial capital. The elegant Ringstrasse alone was not a sufficient showcase, and anyway, it focused on public rather than private buildings. The city fathers as well as private individuals commissioned the architect Otto Wagner to plan and undertake a series of projects. The area around Karlsplatz and the fascinating open food market remains a classic example of unified design. Not all of Wagner's concept for Karlsplatz was realized, but enough remains to be convincing and to convey the impression of what might have been. The unity concept predates Wagner's time in the former garden setting of Belvedere Palace, one of Europe's greatest architectural triumphs.

A Good Walk

The often overlooked **Academy of Fine Arts** ⑥⑦ is an appropriate starting point for this walk, as it puts into perspective the artistic arguments taking place around the turn of the century. While the Academy represented the conservative viewpoint, a group of modernist revolutionaries broke away and founded the Secessionist movement, with its culmination in the gold-crowned **Secession Building** ⑥⑧. Now housing changing exhibits and Gustav Klimt's provocative *Beethoven Frieze,* the museum stands appropriately close to the Academy; from the Academy, take Makartgasse south one block. The famous **Naschmarkt** open food market starts diagonally south from the Secession; follow the rows of stalls southwest. Pay attention to the northwest side of the Linke Wienzeile, to the Theater an der Wien at the intersection with Millöckergasse (Mozart and Beethoven personally premiered some of their finest works at this opera house–theater) and to the **Otto Wagner Houses.** Head back north through the Naschmarkt; at the top end, cross Wiedner Hauptstrasse to your right into the park complex that forms Karlsplatz, creating a setting for the classic **Karlskirche** ⑥⑨. Around **Karlsplatz,** note the Technical University on the south side, and the Otto Wagner subway station buildings on the north. Across Lothringer Strasse on the north side are the Künstlerhaus art exhibit hall and the Musikverein. The out-of-place and rather undistinguished modern building to the left of Karlskirche houses the worthwhile **Historisches Museum der Stadt Wien** ⑦⓪. Cut through Symphonikerstrasse (a passageway through the modern complex) and take Brucknerstrasse to **Schwarzenbergplatz.** The Jugendstil edifice on your left is the French Embassy; ahead is the Russian War Memorial. On a rise behind the memorial sits Palais Schwarzenberg, a jewel of a onetime summer palace and now a luxury hotel. Follow Prinz Eugen-Strasse up to the entrance of the **Belvedere Palace** ⑦① complex on your left. Besides the palace itself are other structures and, off to the east side, a remarkable botanical garden. After viewing the palace and the grounds, you can exit the complex from the lower building, Untere Belvedere, into Rennweg, which will steer you back to Schwarzenbergplatz.

TIMING

The first part of this walk, taking in the Academy of Fine Arts and the Secession, plus the Naschmarkt and Karlsplatz, can be accomplished in an easy half day. The Museum of the City of Vienna is good for a couple of hours, more if you understand some German. Give the Belvedere Palace and grounds as much time as you can. Organized tours breeze in and out—without so much as a glance at the outstanding modern art museum—in a half hour or so, not even scratching the surface of this fascinating complex. If you can, budget up to a half day here, but plan to arrive fairly early in the morning or afternoon before the busloads descend. Bus tourists aren't taken to the Lower Belvedere, so you'll have that and the formal gardens to yourself.

Sights to See

67 Academy of Fine Arts. An outsize statue of the German author Schiller announces the Academy of Fine Arts on Schillerplatz. (Turn around and note his more famous contemporary, Goethe, pompously seated in an overstuffed chair, facing him from across the Ring.) The Academy was founded in 1692, but the present Renaissance Revival building dates from the late 19th century. The idea was conservatism and traditional values, even in the face of a growing movement that scorned formal rules. It was here in 1907 and 1908 that aspiring artist Adolf Hitler was refused acceptance on grounds of insufficient talent. The Academy includes a museum focusing on Old Masters. The collection is mainly of interest to specialists, but Hieronymus Bosch's famous *Last Judgment* triptych hangs here—an imaginative, if gruesome, speculation on the hereafter. ⊠ *Schillerpl. 3,* ☎ *01/588–16–225.* ☜ *AS50.* ☉ *Tues. and Thurs.–Fri. 10–2, Wed. 10–1 and 3–6, weekends 9–1. U-Bahn: U1, U2, U4 Karlspl.*

OFF THE BEATEN PATH

AM STEINHOF CHURCH – Otto Wagner's most exalted piece of Jugendstil architecture is not in the inner city but in the suburbs to the west: the Am Steinhof Church, designed in 1904 during his Secessionist phase. You can reach the church by taking the U4 subway line, which is adjacent to the Otto Wagner Houses (☞ *below*). On the grounds of the Vienna City Psychiatric Hospital, Wagner's design unites mundane functional details (rounded edges on the pews to prevent injury to the patients and a slightly sloped tile floor to facilitate cleaning) with a soaring, airy dome and glittering Jugendstil decoration (stained glass by Koloman Moser). The church is open once a week for guided tours (in German). English tours can be arranged in advance at AS40 per person *if* it's a group of ten people. If there are only two of you, then you still must pay the total price for ten. You may come during the week to walk around the church on your own, but you must call first for an appointment. The church may be closed in 2001 for renovations. ⊠ *Baumgartner Höhe 1,* ☎ *01/910–60–20–031.* ☜ *Free.* ☉ *Sat. 3–4. U-Bahn: U4/Unter-St.-Veit, then Bus 47A to Psychiatrisches Krankenhaus; or U2/Volkstheater, then Bus 48A.*

★ **71 Belvedere Palace.** Baroque architect Lucas von Hildebrandt's most important Viennese work is wedged between Rennweg (entry at No. 6A) and Prinz Eugen-Strasse (entry at No. 27): the Belvedere Palace. In fact the Belvedere is two palaces with extensive gardens between. Built outside the city fortifications between 1714 and 1722, the complex originally served as the summer palace of Prince Eugene of Savoy; much later it became the home of Archduke Franz Ferdinand, whose assassination in 1914 precipitated World War I. Though the lower palace is impressive in its own right, it is the much larger upper palace, used for state receptions, banquets, and balls, that is Hildebrandt's acknowledged masterpiece. The usual tourist entrance for the Upper Belvedere is the gate on Prinz-Eugen-Strasse; for the Lower Belvedere, use the Rennweg gate—but for the most impressive view of the upper palace, approach it from the south garden closest to the South Rail Station. The upper palace displays a remarkable wealth of architectural invention in its facade, avoiding the main design problem common to all palaces because of their excessive size: monotony on the one hand and pomposity on the other. Hildebrandt's decoration here approaches the rococo, that final style of the Baroque era when traditional classical motifs all but disappeared in a whirlwind of seductive asymmetric fancy. The main interiors of the palace go even further: columns are transformed into muscle-bound giants, pilasters grow torsos, capitals sprout great piles of symbolic imperial paraphernalia, and the ceilings are set aswirl with ornately molded stucco. The result is the finest rococo interior in the city.

Today both the upper and lower palaces of the Belvedere are noted museums devoted to Austrian painting. The **Österreichisches Barockmuseum** (Austrian Museum of Baroque Art) in the lower palace at Rennweg 6a displays Austrian art of the 18th century (including the original figures from Georg Raphael Donner's Providence Fountain in the Neuer Markt)—and what better building to house it? Next to the Baroque Museum (outside the west end) is the converted Orangerie, devoted to works of the medieval period.

The main attraction in the upper palace's **Österreichische Galerie** (Austrian Gallery) is the legendary collection of 19th- and 20th-century Austrian paintings, centering on the work of Vienna's three preeminent early 20th-century artists: Gustav Klimt, Egon Schiele, and Oskar Kokoschka. Klimt was the oldest, and by the time he helped found the Secession movement he had forged a highly idiosyncratic painting style that combined realistic and decorative elements in a way that was completely revolutionary. *The Kiss*—his greatest painting and one of the icons of modern art—is here on display. Schiele and Kokoschka went even further, rejecting the decorative appeal of Klimt's glittering abstract designs and producing works that completely ignored conventional ideas of beauty. Today they are considered the fathers of modern art in Vienna. Modern music, too, has roots in the Belvedere complex: the composer Anton Bruckner lived and died here in 1896 in a small garden house now marked by a commemorative plaque. ✉ *Prinz-Eugen-Str. 27,* ☎ *01/795–57–100.* ⊠ *AS90 to all Belvedere museums.* ⊘ *Tues.–Sun. 10–5. U-Bahn: U1, U2, U4 Karlspl., then Streetcar D to Belvedereg.*

⑦⓪ Historisches Museum der Stadt Wien (Museum of Viennese History). Housed in an incongruously modern building at the east end of the regal Karlsplatz, this museum possesses a dazzling array of Viennese historical artifacts and treasures: models, maps, documents, photographs, antiquities, stained glass, paintings, sculpture, crafts, and reconstructed rooms. Paintings include Klimts and Schieles, and there's a life-size portrait of the composer Alban Berg painted by his contemporary Arnold Schönberg. Alas, display information and designations in the museum are in German only, and there's no guidebook in English. ✉ *Karlspl.,* ☎ *01/505–8747–0.* ⊠ *AS50.* ⊘ *Tues.–Sun. 9–4:30. U-Bahn: U1, U2, U4 Karlspl.*

★ **⑥⑨ Karlskirche.** Dominating the Karlsplatz is one of Vienna's greatest buildings, the Karlskirche, dedicated to St. Charles Borromeo. At first glance, the church seems like a fantastic vision—one blink and you half expect the building to vanish. For before you is a giant Baroque church framed by enormous freestanding columns, mates to Rome's famous Trajan's Column. These columns may be out of keeping with the building as a whole, but were conceived with at least two functions in mind: one was to portray scenes from the life of the patron saint, carved in imitation of Trajan's triumphs, and thus help to emphasize the imperial nature of the building; and the other was to symbolize the Pillars of Hercules, suggesting the right of the Habsburgs to their Spanish dominions, which the emperor had been forced to renounce. Whatever the reason, the end result is an architectural tour de force.

The Karlskirche was built in the early 18th century on what was then the bank of the River Wien and is now the southeast corner of the park complex. The church had its beginnings in a disaster. In 1713 Vienna was hit by a brutal plague outbreak, and Emperor Charles VI made a vow: if the plague abated, he would build a church dedicated to his namesake, St. Charles Borromeo, the 16th-century Italian bishop who was famous for his ministrations to Milanese plague victims. In 1715 construction began, using an ambitious design by Johann Bernhard Fischer von Erlach that combined architectural elements from ancient Greece (the columned entrance porch), ancient Rome (the Trajanesque columns), contemporary Rome (the Baroque dome), and contemporary Vienna (the Baroque towers at either end). When it was finished, the church received a decidedly mixed press. History, incidentally, delivered a negative verdict: in its day the Karlskirche spawned no imitations, and it went on to become one of European architecture's most famous curiosities. Notwithstanding, seen lit at night, the building is magical in its setting.

The main interior of the church utilizes only the area under the dome and is surprisingly conventional given the unorthodox facade. The space and architectural detailing are typical High Baroque; the fine vault frescoes, by J. M. Rottmayr, depict St. Charles Borromeo imploring the Holy Trinity to end the plague. ✉ *Karlspl.*, ☎ *01/504–61–87.* ☉ *Weekdays 7:30–7, Sat. 8–7, Sun. 9–7. U-Bahn: U1, U2, U4 Karlspl.*

Karlsplatz. Like the space now occupied by the Naschmarkt, Karlsplatz was formed when the River Wien was covered over at the turn of the century. At the time, Wagner expressed his frustration with the result—too large a space for a formal square and too small a space for an informal park—and the awkwardness persists to this day. The buildings surrounding the Karlsplatz, however, are quite sure of themselves: the area is dominated by the classic **Karlskirche** (☞ *above*), made less dramatic by the unfortunate reflecting pool with its Henry Moore sculpture, wholly out of place, in front. On the south side of the Resselpark, that part of Karlsplatz named for the inventor of the ship's screw propeller, stands the **Technical University** (1816–18). In a house that occupied the space closest to the church, Italian composer Antonio Vivaldi died in 1741; a plaque marks the spot. On the north side, across the heavily traveled roadway, are the **Künstlerhaus** (the exhibition hall in which the Secessionists refused to exhibit, built in 1881 and still in use) and the **Musikverein** (☞ Music *in* Nightlife and the Arts, *below*). The latter, finished in 1869, is now home to the Vienna Philharmonic. The downstairs lobby and the two halls upstairs have been gloriously restored and glow with fresh gilding. The main hall has what may be the world's finest acoustics; this is the site of the annual, globally televised New Year's Day concert.

Some of Otto Wagner's finest Secessionist work can be seen two blocks east on the northern edge of Karlsplatz. In 1893 Wagner was appointed architectural supervisor of the new Vienna City Railway, and the matched pair of small pavilions he designed for the Karlsplatz **train station** in 1898 are among the city's most ingratiating buildings. Their structural framework is frankly exposed (in keeping with Wagner's belief in architectural honesty), but they are also lovingly decorated (in keeping with the Viennese fondness for architectural finery). The result is Jugendstil at its very best, melding plain and fancy with grace and insouciance. The pavilion to the southwest is utilized as a small, specialized museum. In the course of redesigning Karlsplatz, it was Wagner, incidentally, who proposed moving the fruit and vegetable market to what is now the Naschmarkt (☞ *below*).

Naschmarkt. The area between Linke and Rechte Wienzeile has for 80 years been home to the Naschmarkt, Vienna's main outdoor produce market, certainly one of Europe's—if not the world's—great open-air markets, where packed rows of polished and stacked fruits and vegetables compete for visual appeal with braces of fresh pheasant in season; the nostrils, meanwhile, are accosted by spice fragrances redolent of Asia or the Middle East. It's open Monday to Saturday 6:30–6:30 (many stalls close two hours earlier in winter months). *U-Bahn: U1, U2, U4 Karlsplatz.*

NEED A BREAK?   Who can resist exploring the Naschmarkt without picking up a snack as you go along? A host of Turkish stands offer tantalizing *Döner* sandwiches—thinly sliced lamb with onions and a yogurt sauce in a freshly baked roll. If you're in the mood for Italian *tramezzini*—crustless sandwiches filled with tuna and olives or buffalo mozzarella and tomato—head for **Expressi** on the Linke Wienzeile side about midway through the market. You can find a *Stehkaffee* (literally, "stand-up coffee")—limited seats but high tables on which to lean—at the **Anker** pastry and bakery shops.

Otto Wagner Houses. The Ringstrasse-style apartment houses that line the Wienzeile are an attractive, if generally somewhat standard, lot, but two stand out: **Linke Wienzeile 38 and 40**—the latter better known as the "Majolica House"—designed (1898–99) by the grand old man of Viennese fin-de-siècle architecture, Otto Wagner, during his Secessionist phase. A good example of what Wagner was rebelling against can be seen next door, at **Linke Wienzeile 42,** where decorative enthusiasm has blossomed into Baroque Revival hysteria. Wagner had come to believe that this sort of display was nothing but empty pretense and sham; modern apartment houses, he wrote in his pioneering text *Modern Architecture,* are entirely different from 18th-century town palaces, and architects should not pretend otherwise. Accordingly, he banished classical decoration and introduced a new architectural simplicity, with flat exterior walls and plain, regular window treatments meant to reflect the orderly layout of the apartments behind them. There the simplicity ended. For exterior decoration, he turned to his younger Secessionist cohorts Joseph Olbrich and Koloman Moser, who designed the ornate Jugendstil patterns of red majolica-tile roses (No. 40) and gold stucco medallions (No. 38) that gloriously brighten the facades of the adjacent houses—so much so that their Baroque-period neighbor is ignored. The houses are privately owned.

Schwarzenbergplatz. A remarkable urban ensemble, the Schwarzenbergplatz comprises some notable sights. The center of the lower square off the Ring is marked by an oversize equestrian Prince Schwarzenberg—he was a 19th-century field marshal for the imperial forces. Admire the overall effect of the square and see if you can guess which building is the newest; it's the one on the northeast corner (No. 3) at Lothringer Strasse, an exacting reproduction of a building destroyed by war damage in 1945 and dating only to the 1980s. The military monument occupying the south end of the square behind the fountain is the **Russian War Memorial,** set up at the end of World War II by the Soviets; the Viennese, remembering the Soviet occupation, call its unknown soldier the "unknown plunderer." South of the memorial is the stately **Schwarzenberg Palace,** designed as a summer residence by Johann Lukas von Hildebrandt in 1697, completed by Fischer von Erlach father and son, and now (in part) a luxury hotel (☞ Dining and Lodging, *below*). The delightful formal gardens wedged between Prinz Eugen-Strasse and the Belvedere gardens can be enjoyed from the hotel restaurant's veranda.

★ ⑥⑧   **Secession Building.** If the Academy of Fine Arts represents the conservative attitude toward the arts in the late 1800s, then its antithesis can be found in the building immediately behind it to the southeast: the Secession Pavilion. Restored in the mid-1980s after years of neglect, the Secession building is one of Vienna's preeminent symbols of artistic rebellion.

Rather than looking to the architecture of the past, like the revivalist Ringstrasse, it looked to a new antihistoricist future. It was, in its day, a riveting trumpet-blast of a building and is today considered by many to be Europe's first example of full-blown 20th-century architecture.

The Secession began in 1897, when 20 dissatisfied Viennese artists, headed by Gustav Klimt, "seceded" from the Künstlerhausgenossenschaft, the conservative artists' society associated with the Academy of Fine Arts. The movement promoted the radically new kind of art known as Jugendstil, which found its inspiration in both the organic, fluid designs of Art Nouveau and the related but more geometric designs of the English Arts and Crafts movement. (The Secessionists founded an Arts and Crafts workshop of their own, the famous Wiener Werkstätte, in an effort to embrace the applied arts.) The Secession building was the movement's exhibition hall, designed by the architect Joseph Olbrich and completed in 1898. The lower story, crowned by the entrance motto *Der Zeit Ihre Kunst, Der Kunst Ihre Freiheit* ("To Every Age Its Art, To Art Its Freedom"), is classic Jugendstil: the restrained but assured decoration (by Koloman Moser) beautifully complements the facade's pristine flat expanses of cream-color wall. Above the entrance motto sits the building's most famous feature, the gilded openwork dome that the Viennese were quick to christen "the golden cabbage" (Olbrich wanted it to be seen as a dome of laurel, a subtle classical reference meant to celebrate the triumph of art). The plain white interior—"shining and chaste," in Olbrich's words—was also revolutionary; its most unusual feature was movable walls, allowing the galleries to be reshaped and redesigned for every show. One early show, in 1902, was an exhibition devoted to art celebrating the genius of Beethoven; Gustav Klimt's *Beethoven Frieze,* painted for the occasion, has now been restored and is permanently installed in the building's basement. ⊠ *Friedrichstr. 12,* ☎ *01/587–5307–0.* ⌨ *AS90.* ☉ *Tues.–Sun. 10–6, Thurs. 10–8. U-Bahn: U1, U2, U4 Karlsplatz.*

OFF THE
BEATEN PATH

ZENTRALFRIEDHOF – Taking a streetcar out of Schwarzenbergplatz, music lovers will want to make a pilgrimage to the **Zentralfriedhof** (Central Cemetery, ⊠ 11th District on Simmeringer Hauptstr.), which contains the graves of most of Vienna's great composers: Ludwig van Beethoven, Franz Schubert, Johannes Brahms, the Johann Strausses (father and son), and Arnold Schönberg, among others. The monument to Wolfgang Amadeus Mozart is a memorial only; the approximate location of his unmarked grave can be seen at the now deconsecrated St. Marx-Friedhof at Leberstrasse 6–8. *Streetcar 71 to St. Marxer Friedhof, or on to Zentralfriedhof Haupttor/2*

Splendors of the Habsburgs: A Visit to Schönbrunn Palace

The glories of imperial Austria are nowhere brought together more convincingly than in the Schönbrunn Palace (Schloss Schönbrunn) complex. Brilliant "Maria Theresa yellow"—she, in fact, caused Schöbrunn to be built—is everywhere in evidence. Imperial elegance flows unbroken throughout the grounds and the setting, and the impression even today is interrupted only by tourists. This is one of Austria's primary tourist sites, although sadly, few stay long enough to discover the real Schönbrunn (including the little maiden with the water jar, after whom the complex is named). While the assorted outbuildings might seem eclectic, they served as centers of entertainment when the court moved to Schönbrunn in the summer, accounting for the zoo, the priceless theater, the fake Roman ruins, the greenhouses, and the walkways. In Schönbrunn you step back three hundred years into the heart of a powerful and growing empire and follow it through to defeat and demise in 1917.

A Good Walk

The usual start for exploring the Schönbrunn complex is the main palace. There's nothing wrong with that approach, but as a variation, consider first climbing to the **Gloriette** ⑫ on the hill overlooking the site, for a bird's-eye view to put the rest in perspective (take the stairs to the Gloriette roof for the ultimate experience). While at the Gloriette, take a few steps west to discover the **Tiroler House** ⑬ and follow the zigzag path downhill to the palace; note the picture-book views of the main building through the woods. Try to take the full tour of the **Schönbrunn Palace** ⑭ rather than the shorter, truncated version. Check whether the ground-floor back rooms (*Berglzimmer*) are open to viewing. After the palace guided tour, take your own walk around the grounds. The Schöner Brunnen, the namesake fountain, is hidden in the woods to the southeast; continue along to discover the convincing (but fake) Roman Ruins. At the other side of the complex to the west are the excellent **Tiergarten** ⑮ (zoo), and the **Palmenhaus** ⑯ (tropical greenhouse). Closer to the main entrance, both the **Wagenburg** ⑱ (carriage museum) and Schlosstheater (palace theater) are frequently overlooked treasures. Before heading back to the city center, visit the **Hofpavillon** ⑲, the private subway station built for Emperor Franz Josef, located to the west across Schönbrunner Schlossstrasse.

TIMING

If you're really pressed for time, the shorter guided tour will give you a fleeting impression of the palace itself, but try to budget at least half a day to take the full tour and include the extra rooms and grounds as well. The 20-minute hike up to the Gloriette is a bit strenuous but worthwhile, and there's now a café as reward at the top. The zoo is worth as much time as you can spare, and figure on at least a half hour to an hour each for the other museums. Tour buses begin to unload for the main building about mid-morning; start early or utilize the noon lull to avoid the worst crowds. The other museums and buildings in the complex are far less crowded.

Sights to See

⑫ **Gloriette.** At the crest of the hill, topping off the Schönbrunn Palace grounds, sits a Baroque masterstroke: Johann Ferdinand von Hohenberg's incomparable Gloriette, now restored to its original splendor. Perfectly scaled for its setting, the Gloriette—a palatial pavilion that once offered royal guests a place to rest and relax on their tours of the palace grounds and that now houses an equally welcome café—holds the whole vast garden composition together and at the same time crowns the ensemble with a brilliant architectural tiara. This was a favorite spot of Maria Theresa's, though in later years she grew so fat it took six men to carry her in her palanquin to the summit.

⑲ **Hofpavillon.** The most unusual interior of the palace complex, the restored imperial subway station known as the Hofpavillon is just outside the palace grounds (at the northwest corner, a few yards east of the Hietzing subway station). Designed by Otto Wagner in conjunction with Joseph Olbrich and Leopold Bauer, the Hofpavillon was built in 1899 for the exclusive use of Emperor Franz Josef and his entourage. Exclusive it was: the emperor used the station only once. The exterior, with its proud architectural crown, is Wagner at his best, and the lustrous interior is one of the finest examples of Jugendstil decoration in the city. ⊠ *Schönbrunner Schloss-Str., next to Hietzing subway station,* ☎ *01/877–1571.* ⊠ *AS25.* ☉ *Tues.–Sun. 1–4:30. U-Bahn: U4 Hietzing.*

⑯ **Palmenhaus.** On the grounds to the west of Schönbrunn Palace is a huge greenhouse filled with exotic trees and plants. ⊠ *Nearest entrance Hietzing,* ☎ *01/877–5087–406.* ⊠ *AS45.* ☉ *May–Sept., daily 9:30–6 (last admission at 5:30); Oct.–Apr., daily 9:30–5 (last admission at 4:30).*

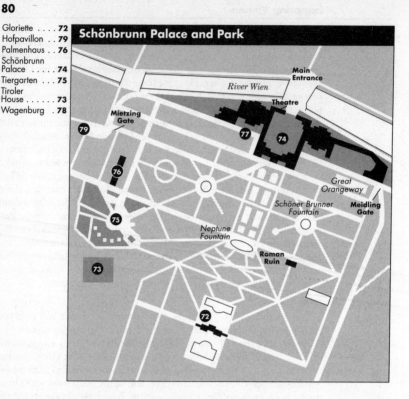

Schönbrunn Palace and Park

★ **74** **Schönbrunn Palace.** Designed by Johann Bernhard Fischer von Erlach in 1696, Schönbrunn Palace, the huge Habsburg summer residence, lies well within the city limits, just a few subway stops west of Karlsplatz on line U4. The vast and elegantly planted gardens are open daily from dawn till dusk, and multilingual guided tours of the palace interior are offered daily. A visit inside the palace is not included in most general city sightseeing tours, which offer either a mercilessly tempting drive past or else an impossibly short half hour or so to explore. The four-hour commercial sightseeing-bus tours of Schönbrunn offered by tour operators cost several times what you'd pay if you tackled the easy excursion yourself; their advantage is that they get you there and back with less effort. Go on your own if you want time to wander the magnificent grounds.

The most impressive approach to the palace and its gardens is through the front gate, located on Schönbrunner Schloss-Strasse halfway between the Schönbrunn and Hietzing subway stations. The vast main courtyard is ruled by a formal design of impeccable order and rigorous symmetry: wing nods at wing, facade mirrors facade, and every part stylistically complements every other. The courtyard, however, turns out to be a mere appetizer; the feast lies beyond. The breathtaking view that unfolds on the other side of the palace is one of the finest set pieces in all Europe and one of the supreme achievements of Baroque planning. Formal *allées* (garden promenades) shoot off diagonally, the one on the right toward the zoo, the one on the left toward a rock-mounted obelisk and a fine false Roman ruin. But these, and the woods beyond, are merely a frame for the astonishing composition in the center: the sculpted fountain; the carefully planted screen of trees behind; the sudden, almost vertical rise of the grass-covered hill beyond, with the ☞ **Gloriette** on top.

Within the palace, the magisterial state salons are quite up to the splendor of the gardens, but note the contrast between these chambers and the far more modest rooms in which the rulers—particularly Franz Josef—lived and spent most of their time. Of the 1,400 rooms, 40 are open to the public on the regular tour, and 2 are of special note: the Hall of Mirrors, where the six-year-old Mozart performed for Empress Maria Theresa in 1762 (and where he met six-year-old Marie Antoinette for the first time, developing a little crush on her), and the Grand Gallery, where the Congress of Vienna (1815) danced at night after carving up Napoléon's collapsed empire during the day. Ask about viewing the ground-floor living quarters (*Berglzimmer*), where the walls are fascinatingly painted with palm trees, exotic animals, and tropical views. As you go through the palace, take an occasional glance out the windows; you'll be rewarded by a better impression of the beautiful patterns of the formal gardens, punctuated by hedgerows and fountains. These window vistas were enjoyed by rulers from Maria Theresa and Napoléon to Franz Josef. ⊠ *Schönbrunner Schloss-Str.,* ☎ *01/81113.* ☞ *Grand tour of palace interior (40 rooms) AS145, self-guided grand tour (40 rooms) AS120, self-guided imperial tour (20 rooms) AS80.* ☉ *Apr.–Oct., daily 8:30–5; Nov.–Mar., daily 8:30–4:30. U-Bahn: U4 Schönbrunn.*

Schönbrunn Palace Park. The palace grounds boast a bevy of splendid divertissements, including a grand zoo (☞ Tiergarten, *below*) and a carriage museum (☞ Wagenburg, *below*). Climb to the Gloriette for a panoramic view out over the city as well as of the palace complex. If you're exploring on your own, seek out the intriguing Roman ruin, now used as a backdrop for outdoor summer opera. The marble *schöner Brunnen* ("beautiful fountain"), with the young girl pouring water from an urn, is nearby. The fountain gave the name to the palace complex. ☉ *May–Oct., daily 9–dusk. U-Bahn: U4 Schönbrunn.*

✪ ㉕ **Tiergarten.** Claimed to be the world's oldest, the zoo has retained its original Baroque decor and, today, has acquired world-class recognition under director Helmut Pechlaner. New settings have been created for both animals and public; in one case, the public looks out into a new, natural display area from one of the Baroque former animal houses. The zoo is constantly adding new attractions and undergoing renovations, so there's plenty to see. ☎ *01/877–9294–0.* ☞ *AS95.* ☉ *Nov.–Jan., daily 9–4:30; Feb., daily 9–5; Mar. and Oct., daily 9–5:30; Apr., daily 9–6; May–Sept., daily 9–6:30. U-Bahn: U4.*

㉓ **Tiroler House.** This charming building to the west of the Gloriette was a favorite retreat of Empress Elizabeth; it now includes a small restaurant (open according to season and weather).

✪ ㉘ **Wagenburg** (Carriage Museum). Most of the carriages are still roadworthy and, indeed, Schönbrunn dusted off the gilt-and-black royal funeral carriage that you see here for the burial ceremony of Empress Zita in 1989. ⊠ *Wagenburg,* ☎ *01/877–3244.* ☞ *AS60.* ☉ *Nov.–Mar., Tues.–Sun. 10–4; Apr.–Oct., daily 9–6. U-Bahn: U4 Schönbrunn.*

DINING

Ever since joining the European Union a few years ago, Austria has undergone a culinary revolution, and nowhere is this more evident than in Vienna. It has emerged from its provincial stagnation with flying colors and now offers its share of world-class restaurants, and they're not only limited to the luxury establishments.

In a first-class restaurant in Vienna you will pay as much as in most other major Western European capitals. But you can still find good food at refreshingly low prices in the simpler restaurants, particularly at neighborhood *Gasthäuser* in the suburbs. If you eat your main meal at noon (as the Viennese do), you can take advantage of the luncheon specials. Be aware that the basket of bread put on your table is not free. Most of the older-style Viennese restaurants charge AS9–AS13 for each roll that is eaten, but more and more establishments are beginning to charge a per person cover charge—anywhere from AS15 to AS35—which includes all the bread you want, plus usually an herb spread and butter.

Vienna's restaurant fare ranges from Arabic to Yugoslav, with strong doses of Chinese, Italian, and Japanese. Assuming you've come for what makes Vienna unique, our listings focus not on exotic spots but on places where you'll meet the Viennese and experience Vienna.

Many restaurants are closed one or two days a week (often weekends), and most serve meals only 11:30–2 and 6–10. An increasing number now serve after-theater dinners, but reserve in advance. The paperback book *Wien wie es isst* (in German; from almost any bookstore) gives up-to-date information on the restaurant, café, and bar scene. For an overview on the highlights of Austrian cuisine, *see* Dining *in* Smart Travel Tips. Note that U-Bahn stations are listed for restaurants located outside the general city center.

CATEGORY	COST*
$$$$	over AS650 (€47)
$$$	AS350–AS650 (€25–€47)
$$	AS175–AS350 (€13–€24)
$	under AS175 (€13)

per person for a typical three-course meal, including a small glass of house wine or beer, service (usually 10%), sales tax (10%), and additional small tip (5%)

Restaurants

$$$$ ✕ **Imperial.** This exquisite restaurant in the Imperial hotel (☞ Lodging, *below*) ranks with the top eateries in the city, and as soon as you're seated in the intimate, wood-paneled room you know you're in for a treat. Chef Stefan Hierzer is from Styria, and you'll find many Styrian specialties on the menu. The cream of potato soup with white truffle oil is especially delicious, and other good choices include Styrian beef with *Krautfleckerl*—little pasta squares with slivers of cabbage in a *Kürbiskernöl* (pumpkin-seed oil) sauce—or turbot with caviar, artichokes, yellow peppers, and snow peas. Service is friendly and attentive without being intrusive. ☒ *Kärntner Ring 16,* ☎ *01/501–10–356,* ꜰꜰᴀ𝚇 *01/50110–410. AE, DC, MC, V. No lunch.*

$$$$ ✕ **Korso.** For many, this is Vienna's top restaurant, and chef Reinhard
   ★   Gerer is known throughout Austria for his creative touch. The setting for such gastronomic excellence is appropriate, with gleaming wood-panel walls, beveled glass, and tables set with fine linen, sparkling Riedel crystal, and fresh flowers. Specialties include *Felchen,* a delicate white fish served with glass noodles, or lobster with white beans, arugula, and black polenta. If money is no object, have the chef prepare a special tasting menu, with a different wine to accompany each course. ☒ *Mahlerstr. 2,* ☎ *01/515–16–546,* ꜰᴀ𝚇 *01/515–16–550. Reservations essential. Jacket and tie. AE, DC, MC, V. Closed 3 wks in Aug. No lunch Sat.*

$$$$ ✕ **Steirereck.** This is generally conceded to be the most famous restau-
   ★   rant in Austria, and it consistently ranks high on critics' lists. You can choose from three elegant settings: the intimate Kaminstüberl (ask for Tables 30–33), with its Renaissance-style fireplace, sandstone walls, and decorative columns; the sunny, plant-filled Winter Garden; or modern, light, spacious rooms with French Impressionist reproductions on the

walls. Extra touches include a bread trolley overflowing with freshly baked breads and, at the end of the meal, an outstanding selection of cheeses from Steirereck's own cheese cellar. Fish choices are plentiful and may include delicate smoked catfish, turbot in an avocado crust, or char with mashed potatoes on a bed of white garlic sauce. Also good is the quail in red wine sauce with zucchini cannelloni or lamb with crepes and spinach cooked simply with garlic and olive oil. ⊠ *Rasumofskyg. 2, A–1030,* ☎ *01/713–3168,* FAX *01/713–5168–2. Reservations essential. Jacket and tie. AE, DC, MC, V. Closed weekends*

$$$$ ✕ **Zu den Drei Husaren.** One of Vienna's oldest restaurants, the "Three
★ Hussars" has triumphantly regained its reputation as a gourmet temple over the last few years, and the friendly staff will put you at ease while you settle in for a relaxing, luxurious evening. The menu offers traditional Viennese cuisine as well as a superb veal cutlet with pesto fettuccine or guinea fowl with stuffed morel mushrooms. Even if dessert is not your thing, you shouldn't pass up such exquisite delights as *Husarenpfannkuchen,* the house crepes. The only caveat is that the enticing but unpriced evening hors d'oeuvre trolley can send your bill soaring. ⊠ *Weihburgg. 4,* ☎ *01/512–1092–0,* FAX *01/512–1092–18. Reservations essential. Jacket and tie. AE, DC, MC, V. Closed mid-July–mid-Aug.*

$$$–$$$$ ✕ **Bauer.** Not far from St. Stephen's on a little street lined with Renaissance and Baroque town houses, this 17th-century house beckons with a pretty bay window. Inside, dusky rose walls and a subtle, contemporary design welcome you, along with a variety of freshly baked breads and a light herbed spread brought to your table while you're perusing the seasonal menu. Highlights include an unusual but deliciously light cream of chestnut soup adorned with shaved truffles, fillet of *Zander* (pike perch) in a sesame crust, or a delicious steak with homemade potato chips. A selection of little cookies and chocolates served on an elegant silver-tiered tray is the perfect choice for a light dessert. ⊠ *Sonnenfelsg. 17,* ☎ *01/512–9871. Reservations essential. AE. Closed Sun. and Mon. No lunch Sat.*

$$$ ✕ **Do & Co.** The spectacular setting at the top of the modern Neues Haas-Haus building smack in the middle of Stephansplatz would make this worthwhile for the view alone, but the food is also excellent and varied, often with a nouvelle-Asian touch. Choices include fresh grilled tuna and crispy frites or a create-your-own wok meal, which you can build from a vast selection of meat, seafood, and vegetables. In the evenings, book a table by the window so you can see the sunset over the spires of St. Stephen's, and in warm weather, ask well in advance for a table outside on the balcony. ⊠ *Stephanspl. 12,* ☎ *01/535–3969,* FAX *01/535–3959. Reservations essential. V.*

$$$ ✕ **Griechenbeisl.** An inn has been on this site since 1457, next to the glittering gold Greek Orthodox church, in one of the prettiest areas in the city. Now housed within the half-timbered walls is a old-fashioned kitchen that serves traditional, delicious Viennese dishes, such as thick and hearty goulash soup, Wiener schnitzel, and *Apfelstrudel.* In summer tables are set up in the charming small square in front of the restaurant. ⊠ *Fleischmarkt 11,* ☎ *01/533–1941. AE, DC, MC, V.*

$$$ ✕ **Neu Wien.** As the name says, this is a taste of the new Vienna. The
★ vaulted interior is enlivened by cheeky modern art, and service is friendly and efficient. The eclectic menu changes frequently, but look for the herbed goat-cheese salad with basil oil dressing; *Zanderfilet,* a crispy pike perch with a cream beet sauce; or veal with tagliatelle in a truffle sauce. Top it all off with a bottle of smooth Vranac from Montenegro. ⊠ *Bäckerstr. 5,* ☎ *01/513–0666. MC, V. Closed weekends in summer. No lunch.*

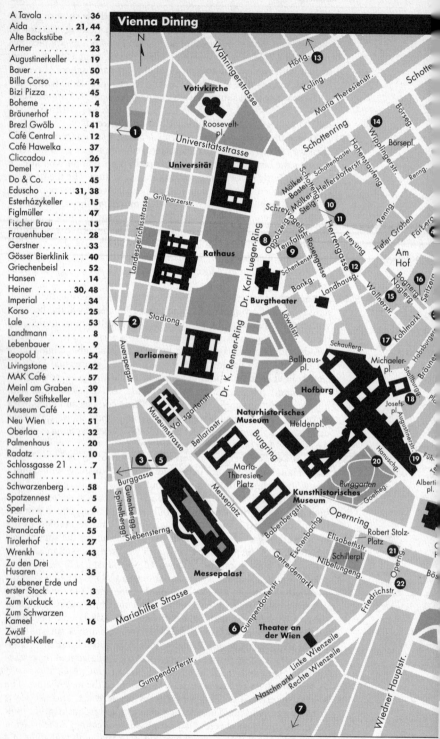

Vienna Dining

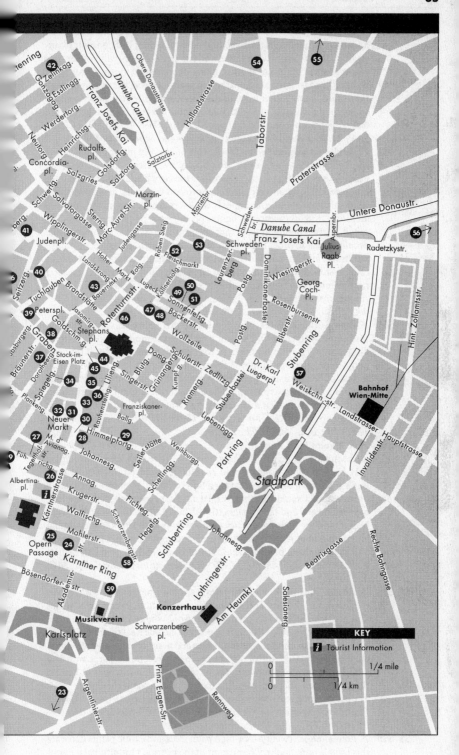

Untere Donaustr.

Danube Canal

Franz Josefs Kai

Stadtpark

Bahnhof Wien-Mitte

Neuer Markt

Stephans pl.

Karlsplatz

Konzerthaus

Musikverein

Opern Passage

Kärntner Ring

Albertina-pl.

Schwarzenberg-pl.

KEY

ℹ Tourist Information

0   1/4 mile
0   1/4 km

$$$ ✕ **Schnattl.** If you're not outdoors in the idyllic courtyard, the setting could be described as cool postmodern: The main room has now acquired a warmer patina but is relatively unadorned, letting you concentrate instead on the attractively set tables and excellent cuisine (which offers occasional surprises such as medallions of mountain ram). Traditional dishes like roast pork are transformed with such touches as a light mustard sauce, lamb with a trace of rosemary, with offerings dependent on season and availability of fresh ingredients. The real bargain here is the daily AS80 lunch special. ⊠ *Langeg. 40,* ☎ *01/405–3400. AE, DC. Closed Sun., 2 wks around Easter, and late Aug.–mid-Sept. No lunch Sat.*

$$$ ✕ **Zu ebener Erde und erster Stock.** This mint-green historic cottage near
★ the Volkstheater was named after a play by Nestroy and means "the ground level and first floor." Upstairs is the cozy Biedermeier room with crocheted pillows and old family photos on the walls, and downstairs is an informal room that appeals to diners who want a light, pretheater meal. *Kürbis* (pumpkin) figures prominently on the menu, from the salted, roasted pumpkin seeds that are brought for you to nibble on while deciding what to order to the pumpkin cream soup to the delicious pumpkin risotto and branzino in rosemary broth. The thyme gnocchi and beef roulade stuffed with mozzarella and eggplant is also wonderful. For dessert try the light *Topfenknödel* with plums. ⊠ *Burgg. 13,* ☎ *01/523–6254. Reservations essential. AE, V. Closed Sat. lunch, Sun.–Mon., and 1st 3 wks of Aug. No lunch Sat. U-Bahn: U2, U3/Volkstheater.*

$$$ ✕ **Zum Kuckuck.** Once you step inside this intimate, vaulted-ceiling restaurant, you enter Old Vienna and leave the modern world behind. Tables are set with pink linen, pewter candlesticks, and fresh flowers, and old prints from Emperor Franz Josef's time adorn the walls. Sip a glass of *Sekt* (Austria sparkling wine) with blood-orange juice while perusing the extensive menu. The kitchen offers good, honest cooking, from beef rouladen marinated in red wine to duck in a honey–green peppercorn sauce. ⊠ *Himmelpfortg. 15,* ☎ *01/512–8470,* ℻ *01/774– 1855. AE, DC, MC, V. Closed Sun.*

$$–$$$ ✕ **A Tavola.** Ever since this casual, trendy Italian restaurant opened, it's been hard to get a table. As soon as you're seated, a basket of heavenly breads (olive, tomato, and rosemary) is placed in front of you, but it's still hard to resist ordering a bowl of thick, chunky tomato soup or an arugula salad for a starter. Pasta dishes are a specialty, including the unusual and tasty spaghetti with curry, black olives, and chicken breast, and the meltingly delicious angel hair with smoked mozzarella and pumpkin puree. Risotto with grilled scampi is another good choice, and there's also a plentiful selection of beef, chicken, and fish dishes. ⊠ *Weihburgg. 3–5,* ☎ *01/512–7955. Reservations essential. DC, MC, V. Closed Sun.*

$$–$$$ ✕ **Artner.** This sleek, modern restaurant has one of the most innova-
★ tive menus in the city and showcases, in addition, exceptional wines and goat cheese from its own 350-year-old winery in the Carnuntum region east of Vienna. Delicious appetizers include a salad of field greens and grilled goat cheese, and recommended main courses are free-range chicken with basil risotto, or pike perch in a zucchini crust. Lamb and veal dishes are also tempting. This is one of the few kitchens in Vienna that stay open all afternoon. It's located just around the corner from Taubstummengasse, one subway stop from Karlsplatz on the U1. ⊠ *Florag. 6 (entrance on Neumanng.),* ☎ *01/503–5033,* ℻ *01/503– 5034. AE, DC, MC, V. No lunch weekends.*

$$–$$$ ✕ **Palmenhaus.** Twenty-foot-high palm trees and exotic plants decorate this large, contemporary restaurant in the historic Hofburg Palace conservatory, at the back of the Burggarten and next to the Schmetterling-haus (Butterfly House). Seafood is the focus here, and it's temptingly featured in soups and risottos or simply grilled with lemon. There's a blackboard that lists daily fish specials, and several vegetarian dishes are also offered, such as pumpkin gnocchi. The Palmenhaus is also worth a stop for coffee and pastry. In fine weather tables are set outside on the terrace overlooking the park. ✉ *Burggarten (entrance through Goetheg. Gate after 8 PM)*, ☎ *01/533–1033. Reservations essential. DC, V, MC.*

$$ ✕ **Boheme.** This charming restaurant in the 18th-century Spittelberg area is a favorite hangout of opera singers, and autograph pictures of some of the opera-loving owner's more famous patrons line the walls. Opera arias play in the background, and the ambience is casual and relaxed. Start with a tasty salad of field greens and fried zucchini in a yogurt dressing or the simple sliced tomatoes with olives and fresh mozzarella; then go on to pork medallions with potato cakes in a mushroom cream sauce or the more traditional roast duck with dumplings and *Rotkraut* (red cabbage). ✉ *Spittelbergg. 19*, ☎ *01/523–3173. AE, DC, MC, V. Closed Sun. No lunch. U-Bahn: U2, U3/Volkstheater.*

$$ ✕ **Figlmüller.** Known for its gargantuan Wiener schnitzel, which is so large it overflows the plate, Figlmüller is always packed. Guests share the benches, the long tables, and the experience. Food choices are limited, and everything is à la carte. There are two entrances; one is off the passageway from Stephansdom. Try to get a table in the small enclosed "greenhouse" in the passageway entry. ✉ *Wollzeile 5*, ☎ *01/ 512–6177. V. Closed Aug.*

$$ ✕ **Gösser Bierklinik.** This charming Old World house, which dates back four centuries, has several dining rooms, including one for nonsmokers. The Wiener schnitzel here is first class and larger than the plate it's served on. Another good choice is the *Käsespätzle,* little pasta dumplings with melted cheese and topped with crispy fried onions, and the bountiful Greek salad. They also have a salad bar. The beer, of course, is Austrian, from the Gösser brewery in Styria. There's a menu in English, but it lists only about half of what's offered on the German one. ✉ *Steindlg. 4*, ☎ *01/535–6897. DC, MC, V. Closed Sun.*

$$ ✕ **Hansen.** Housed downstairs in the Börse (Vienna Stock Exchange)
★ and named for the building's 19th-century architect, Theophil Hansen, this unique restaurant is also an exotic, upscale flower market. The decor is modern and elegant, with close-set tables covered in white linen. The restaurant is at one end of the flower shop, so diners can see shoppers browsing for everything from a single rose to $2,000 lemon trees. The menu highlights Mediterranean-inspired dishes such as scampi risotto or spaghettini with oven-dried tomatoes in a black-olive cream sauce. There are also Austrian dishes done with a fresh slant. Lunch is the main event here, though you can also come for breakfast or a pretheater dinner. ✉ *Wipplingerstr. 34*, ☎ *01/532–0542. Reservations essential. AE, DC, MC, V. Closed Sun. and after 9 PM weekdays. No dinner Sat..*

$$ ✕ **Lale.** Vienna has a substantial Turkish population, and this modern, inviting restaurant in the heart of the Schwedenplatz area serves some of the best Turkish cuisine in the city. Specialties include *Huhnerspiess,* chunks of tender grilled chicken breast on a skewer, or the *Iskender kebab,* slivers of tender lamb served with yogurt and tomato sauce. Don't miss the tasty selection of *meze* (appetizers) temptingly arrayed in the front counter. A perfect choice for a takeout lunch is the vegetarian sandwich—a mouthwatering combination of grilled eggplant, feta, spinach, and hummus in a soft, freshly baked bun. ✉ *Franz-Josef-Kai 29*, ☎ *01/535–2736. No credit cards.*

$$ ✕ **Lebenbauer.** Located in the shadow of the Freyung, this long-standing vegetarian restaurant even has a nonsmoking room, rare in this part of Europe. The menu offers both vegetarian and whole-grain items, and there's a lot to choose from. Specialties include *Hirsegröstl*, a millet hash with pumpkin seeds in an oyster mushroom sauce, and gluten-free pasta with smoked salmon and shrimp in a dill cream sauce. There are also several free-range chicken and fish entrées, all lightly prepared. ✉ *Teinfaltstr. 3,* ☎ *01/533–5556–0. AE, DC, MC, V. Closed Sun. and 1st 2 wks of Aug. No dinner Sat.*

$$ ✕ **Leopold.** This modern, convivial restaurant (across the Danube Canal from Schwedenplatz) takes its name from the church of St. Leopold next door. Walls are a deep ochre and decorated with local artists' paintings. The eclectic menu offers several vegetarian choices and updated variations of Austrian cuisine, such as beef with hash browns and creamed green beans. The warm hazelnut cake doused with caramel chocolate sauce is sublime. ✉ *Grosse Pfarrg. 11,* ☎ *01/214–2170. AE, DC, MC, V. No lunch except Sun. brunch. U-Bahn: U1, U4/Schwedenpl.; Tram N/Obere Augarten.*

$$ ✕ **Livingstone.** If you're homesick for a hamburger and fries, this is the place to go. Buns are homemade, and the Austrian beef is of the finest quality. But if the tropical-colonial setting straight out of a 1940s Bogart movie makes you want to try something more adventurous, you won't be disappointed. The open kitchen allows you to glimpse some of the exotic food being prepared, such as pasta with smoked tofu, tiger shrimp, squash, and green chili peppers in a garlic-ginger sesame oil sauce. ✉ *Zelinkag. 4,* ☎ *01/533–3393–12. AE, DC, V. No lunch.*

$$ ✕ **MAK Cafe.** In the Museum für Angewandte Kunst (☞ Exploring Vienna, *above*), also known as MAK, this is one of the "scene" places in Vienna. The dining room is huge and spare with an impossibly high ceiling. The menu changes frequently and includes lots of vegetarian and pasta items. One staple is the delicious pierogi stuffed with either potatoes or minced beef. In summer sit outside in the shaded inner courtyard. ✉ *Stubenring 3–5,* ☎ *01/714–0121. No credit cards. Closed Mon.*

$$ ✕ **Schlossgasse 21.** There are four different settings in this popular restaurant in the old Margareten area. The cavernous main room is for casual diners; the Hofstöckl offers a more elegant, intimate ambience; the designer cafe, Caudro, is where the *Schickimicki* (yuppie) crowd meets; and the lovely garden courtyard entices everyone in fine weather. The food here is varied and delicious. You can make a meal of the *Bauernsalat*—farmer's salad with field greens, Styrian sheep's cheese, and white beans in a Kürbiskernöl (pumpkin seed oil) dressing—and main courses offer everything from Tandoori burgers to Tex-Mex to exotic Asian dishes. ✉ *Schlossg. 21,* ☎ *01/544–0767. V. No lunch Oct.–Apr. or on weekends. U-Bahn: U4/Pilgrimg.*

$$ ✕ **Strandcafé.** If you want to have a good meal along the banks of the Alte Donau, or Old Danube, this is the place to go. Tables are set on a wooden pier directly on the water, affording prime views of passing sailboats. The specialty of the house is the huge portion of meaty spareribs, served on a butcher's block, but you can also choose from a variety of Viennese dishes, including the delicious *Huhnerschnitzel* (golden-fried chicken breast) and crispy french fries. This café is in the 22nd District, a suburban residential area across the river from the modern city center, so you'll want to use the U-Bahn to get here. ✉ *Florian-Berndl-G. 20,* ☎ *01/203–6747. Reservations essential. No credit cards. U-Bahn: U1/Alte Donau.*

$$ ✕ **Wrenkh.** The menu here is vegetarian and eclectic, and dishes are made from the freshest ingredients. Start with the miso soup and then go on to wild-rice risotto with mushrooms or Greek fried rice with vegetables, sheep's cheese, and olives. The minimalist-style café section offers lunch specials at a great value, while the more elegant adjacent room is perfect for a nice, relaxed lunch or dinner. There is also a no-smoking room. ✉ *Bauernmarkt 10,* ☎ *01/533–1526. AE, DC, MC, V.*

$ ✕ **Brezl Gwölb.** Housed in a medieval pretzel factory between Am Hof and Judenplatz, this snug restaurant fills up fast at night. Try the scrumptious *Tyroler G'röstl,* home-fried potatoes, ham, onions and cheese served in a blackened skillet, or the *Käsenockerl,* spätzle in a pungent cheese sauce. Try to get a table downstairs in the real medieval cellar, which looks like a stage set from *Phantom of the Opera.* ⊠ *Ledererhof 9,* ☎ *01/533–8811. AE, DC, MC, V.*

$ ✕ **Fischer Bräu.** This is known as Vienna's number one brewery restau-
★ rant, and though it's located in the 19th District, it's worth the effort to get here. Several varieties of their own fresh beer are featured, and the menu, though extensive, is nothing fancy. You can choose from stuffed baked potatoes, salads, or Wiener schnitzel—huge and served with a side order of potato salad. Especially scrumptious is the golden-fried *Hühnerschnitzel* (chicken breast). The beer garden with its twinkling lights strung through the trees is packed on summer evenings, so come early to get a table. Every Sunday there is a popular jazz brunch, with live music. ⊠ *Billrothstr. 17,* ☎ *01/369–5949. No credit cards. No lunch, except Sun. brunch. U-Bahn: U2/Schottentor; Tram 37, 38.*

$ ✕ **Spatzennest.** This is simple, hearty Viennese cooking at its best, lo-cated on a quaint, cobblestone pedestrian street straight out of a 1930s Hollywood movie set in Old Vienna. Tasty dishes include Wiener schnitzel, roast chicken, and pillowy fried spätzle with slivers of ham and melted cheese. It's especially delightful in summer, when tables are set outside. It can be smoky indoors. ⊠ *Ulrichspl. 1 ,* ☎ *01/526–1659. MC. Closed Fri.–Sat. U-Bahn: U2, U3/Volkstheater*

Munch on the Run

If you don't have time for a leisurely lunch, or you'd rather save your money for a splurge at dinner, here's a sampling of the best places in the city center to grab a quick, inexpensive, and tasty bite to eat. In the lower level of the Ringstrasse Galerie shopping mall, the gourmet su-permarket **Billa Corso** (⊠ Kärntner Ring 9–13, ☎ 01/512–6625, closed Sun.) has a good salad bar, and will prepare the sandwich of your choice at the deli counter. (The Ringstrasse Galerie is in two similar build-ings, so make sure you're in the one on the Kärtner Ring.) The best pizza by-the-slice can be found near St. Stephen's at **Bizi Pizza** (⊠ Rotenturmstr. 4, ☎ 01/513–3705). Open daily, **Cliccadou** (⊠ Kärntnerstr. 20, ☎ 01/ 513–4394) has baguette sandwiches, marzipan croissants, chocolate-chip cookies and brownies to go along with a cup of excellent coffee. Next to the produce section on the ground floor of Vienna's premier gourmet grocery store, **Meinl am Graben** (⊠ Graben 19, ☎ 01/532–3334, closed Sun.) is a smart, stand-up café where you can choose from a selection of soups, sandwiches, or antipasti (don't confuse it with the full-service restaurant upstairs). Near the Freyung, the epicurean deli **Radatz** (⊠ Schotteng. 3a, ☎ 01/533–8163, closed Sun.) offers sand-wiches made-to-order from a vast selection of mouthwatering meats and cheeses. Around the corner from Am Hof, **Zum Schwarzen Kameel** (⊠ Bognerg. 5, ☎ 01/533–8967, closed Sun.) serves elegant little open-faced sandwiches and baby quiches in their stand-up section.

A sure way to spike a lively discussion among the Viennese is to ask which *Würstelstand* serves the most delicious grilled sausages. Here are three that are generally acknowledged to be the best: **Ehrenreich's** (⊠ Naschmarkt, on the Linke Wienzeile side across from Piccini, under the clock, closed Sun.) serves scrumptious *Käsekrainer,* beef sausages oozing with melted cheese, alongside a *Semmel* (soft roll) and mild, sweet mustard. Behind the Opera House, **Oper** (⊠ Corner of Philharmonikerstr./Hanuschg.) en-tices passersby with its plump, sizzling *Bratwurst.* **Würstelstand am Hoher Markt** (⊠ Hoher Markt, corner of Marc-Aurel Str.), serves Amer-ican-style hot dogs and is open daily from 7 AM to 5 AM.

Wine Taverns

In-town wine restaurants cannot properly be called *Heurige*, since they are not run by the vintner, so the term is *Weinkeller* (wine restaurant, or cellar). Many of them extend a number of levels underground, particularly in the older part of the city. Mainly open in the evening, they are intended primarily for drinking, though you can always get something to eat from a buffet, and increasingly, full dinners are available. As at their country cousins, wine is served by the mug. Some of the better wine restaurants follow; no credit cards are accepted except where noted.

$$ ✕ **Augustinerkeller.** This ground-floor Keller is open at noontime as
★ well as in the evening. The spit-roasted chicken is excellent, as is the filling *Stelze* (roast knuckle of pork). For dessert, try the *Apfelstrudel*, moist and warm from the oven. There's kitschy live music at night. ✉ *Augustinerstr. 1/Albertinapl.,* ☏ *01/533–1026. AE, DC, MC, V.*

$$ ✕ **Esterházykeller.** This maze of rooms offers some of the best Keller wines in town plus a typical Vienna menu noontime and evenings, as well as a hot and cold buffet, but the atmosphere may be too smoky for some. ✉ *Haarhof 1,* ☏ *01/533–3482. No credit cards. No lunch weekends. Closed weekends in summer.*

$$ ✕ **Melker Stiftskeller.** Down and down you go, into one of the friendli-
★ est Keller in town, where Stelze is a popular feature, along with outstanding wines by the glass or, rather, mug. ✉ *Schotteng. 3,* ☏ *01/533–5530. DC, MC, V. Closed Sun.–Mon. No lunch.*

$ ✕ **Zwölf Apostel-Keller.** You pass a huge wood statue of St. Peter on the way downstairs to the two underground floors in this deep-down cellar in the oldest part of Vienna. The young crowd comes for the good wines and the atmosphere, and there's buffet food as well. ✉ *Sonnenfelsg. 3,* ☏ *01/512–6777. AE, DC, MC, V. No lunch.*

Heurige

Few cities the size of Vienna boast wine produced within their city limits, and even fewer offer wines ranging from good to outstanding. But in various suburban villages—once well outside the center but now parts of the urban complex—the fringes of the city have spawned characteristic wine taverns and restaurants, sometimes in the vineyards themselves. Summer and fall are the seasons for visiting the Heurige, though often the more elegant and expensive establishments, called *Noble-Heurige*, stay open year-round. Heurige are concentrated in several outskirts of Vienna: Stammersdorf, Grinzing, Sievering, Nussdorf, Neustift, and a corner of Ottakring. Perchtoldsdorf, just outside Vienna, is also well known for its wine taverns.

$$ ✕ **Haslinger.** In Sievering, Haslinger offers good wines and a small but tasty buffet. The atmosphere is plain but honest, both inside and outdoors in the small, typical vine-covered garden in summer. ✉ *Agnesg. 3,* ☏ *01/440–1347. No credit cards. Closed Mon. U-bahn: U4/Heiligenstadt; Bus 39A/Sievering.*

$$ ✕ **Mayer am Pfarrplatz.** Heiligenstadt is home to this legendary *Heuriger* in Beethoven's former abode. The atmosphere in the collection of rooms is genuine, the à la carte offerings and buffet more than abundant, and the house wines excellent. You'll even find some Viennese among the tourists. ✉ *Heiligenstädter Pfarrpl. 2,* ☏ *01/370–1287. AE, DC, MC, V. No lunch weekdays or Sat. Tram D/Nussdorf from the Ring.*

$$ ✕ **Robert Helm.** Located across the Danube in Stammersdorf, this is a place for good wines, a small but complete buffet including desserts from the house kitchen, and a wonderfully inviting tree-shaded garden. Call to confirm that it is open; it sometimes closes for irregular periods. ✉ *Stammersdorfer Str. 121, A–1210,* ☏ *01/292–1244. No* *credit cards. Closed Sun. and Mon. U-Bahn: U2, U4/Schottenring; Tram 31/Stammersdorf.*

$$ ✕ **Schreiberhaus.** In Neustift am Walde, the Schreiberhaus has one of
★ the prettiest terraced gardens in the city, with picnic tables stretching straight up into the vineyards. The buffet offers a delicious array of dishes, such as spit-roasted chicken, salmon pasta, and a huge selection of tempting grilled vegetables and salads. The golden Traminer wine is excellent. ⊠ *Rathstr. 54, A–1190,* ☎ *01/440–3844. AE, DC, MC, V. U-Bahn: U4, U6/Spittelau; Bus 35A/Neustift am Walde.*

$$ ✕ **Schübel-Auer.** In Nussdorf seek out the Schübel-Auer for its series of atmospheric rooms and good wines. Known for its home-style cooking, it also offers vegetarian dishes and has several varieties of Austrian cheese. ⊠ *Kahlenbergerstr. 22, A–1190,* ☎ *01/372222. No credit cards. Closed Sun. No lunch. Tram: D/Nussdorf from the Ring.*

$$ ✕ **Wieninger.** Wine and food are both top-notch here, and the charming, tree-shaded inner courtyard and series of typical vintner's rooms are perfect for whiling away an evening. Wieninger's bottled wines are ranked among the country's best. It's located across the Danube in Stammersdorf, one of Vienna's oldest Heurige areas. ⊠ *Stammersdorfer Str. 78, A–1210,* ☎ *01/292–4106. No credit cards. Closed Mon. and Dec.–Feb. No lunch except Sun. U-Bahn: U2, U4/Schottenring; Tram 31/Stammersdorf.*

$$ ✕ **Zimmermann.** East of the Grinzing village center, Zimmermann has excellent wines, an enchanting tree-shaded garden, and an endless collection of small paneled rooms and vaulted cellars. You can order from the menu or choose from the tempting buffet. This well-known *Heuriger* attracts the occasional celebrity, including fashion model Claudia Schiffer. ⊠ *Armbrusterg. 5/Grinzinger Str., A–1190,* ☎ *01/ 370–2211. AE, DC, MC, V. Closed Sun. No lunch. U-Bahn: U2/Schottentor; Tram 38/Grinzing.*

$$ ✕ **Zum Martin Sepp.** The Grinzing district today suffers from mass tourism, with very few exceptions, but at Martin Sepp at least the wine, food, service, and ambience are all good. ⊠ *Cobenzlg. 34, A–1190,* ☎ *01/320–7618. DC, V. U-Bahn: U2/Schottentor; Tram 38/Grinzing.*

Cafés

One of the quintessential Viennese institutions, the coffeehouse, or café, is club, pub, and bistro all rolled into one. For decades, a substantial part of Austrian social life has revolved around them (though now less than in the past) as Austrians by and large are rather reluctant to invite strangers to their homes and prefer to meet them in the friendly, but noncommittal, atmosphere of a café.

To savor the atmosphere of the coffeehouses, take time; set aside an afternoon, a morning, or at least a couple of hours, and settle down in one of your choice. Read or catch up on your letter writing: there is no need to worry about outstaying one's welcome, even over a single small cup of coffee, better identified as a *kleiner Schwarzer* (black) or *kleiner Brauner* (with milk). (Of course, in some of the more opulent coffeehouses, this cup of coffee can cost as much as a meal.)

Coffee is not just coffee in Austria. It comes in many forms and under many names. Morning coffee is generally *Melange* (half coffee, half milk) or, with a little milk, a *Brauner.* The usual after-dinner drink is *Mokka,* very black, and most Austrians like it heavily sweetened. Restaurants that serve Balkan food offer *Türkischer,* or Turkish coffee, a strong, thick brew. Most delightful are the coffee-and-whipped-cream concoctions, universally cherished as *Kaffee mit Schlag,* a taste that is easily acquired and a menace to all but the very thin. The coffee may be either hot or cold. A customer who wants more whipped cream than coffee asks for a *Doppelschlag*. Hot black coffee in a glass with one knob of whipped cream is an *Einspänner* (literally, "one-horse coach"). Then you can go to town on a *Mazagran*, black coffee with ice and a tot of rum, or *Eiskaffee*, cold coffee with ice cream, whipped cream, and biscuits. Or you can simply order a *Portion Kaffee* and have an honest pot of coffee and jug of hot milk.

The typical Viennese café, with polished brass or marble-topped tables, bentwood chairs, supplies of newspapers, and tables outside in good weather, is a fixed institution, of which there are literally hundreds. All cafés serve pastries and light snacks in addition to beverages. Many offer a menu or fixed lunch at noon, but be aware that some can get rather expensive. No credit cards are accepted unless noted.

Of course, when tourists think of Viennese cafés, Demel (☞ Exploring Vienna, *above*) and Café Sacher leap to mind, but they are hardly typical. When you want a quick (but excellent) coffee and dessert, look for an **Aida** café; they are scattered throughout the city. **Eduscho** is a coffee chain located throughout the city, offering a selection of coffee for a fraction of what you'd pay in a cafe, though there's no place to sit.

Here's a sampling of the best of the traditional cafés: **Alte Backstube** (⊠ Langeg. 34, ☎ 01/406–1101), in a gorgeous Baroque house—with a café in front and restaurant in back—was once a bakery and is now a museum as well. **Bräunerhof** (⊠ Stallburgg. 2, ☎ 01/512–3893) has music
★ on some afternoons. **Café Central** (⊠ Herreng. 14/in Palais Ferstel, ☎ 01/533–3763–26) is where Trotsky played chess. **Frauenhuber** (⊠ Himmelpfortg. 6, ☎ 01/512–4323) has its original turn-of-the-century interior and a good choice of desserts. **Landtmann** (⊠ Dr.-Karl-Lueger-Ring 4, ☎ 01/532–0621) is an elegant turn-of-the-century café, reputed to have been a favorite of Freud's. In fine weather you can sit outside on the front terrace, to take in glorious views of the city. **Museum** (⊠ Friedrichstr. 6, ☎ 01/586–5202), with its original interior by the architect Adolf Loos, draws a mixed crowd and has lots of newspapers. **Schwarzenberg** (⊠ Kärntner Ring 17, ☎ 01/512–8998–13), with piano music in late afternoons, is highly popular, particularly its sidewalk tables in summer. **Tirolerhof** (⊠ Tegetthoffstr. 8/Albertinapl., ☎ 01/512–7833), with ample papers and excellent desserts, is popular with students.
Café Hawelka (⊠ Dorotheerg. 12, ☎ 01/512–8230) deserves special mention; whole books have been written at and about this shabby gathering place—its international clientele ranges from artists to politicians. Hawelka is jammed any time of day, so you share a table (and the very smoky atmosphere). In a city noted for fine coffee, Hawelka's is superb, even more so when accompanied by a freshly baked *Buchterln* (sweet roll, evenings only).

Pastry Shops

Viennese pastries are said to be the best in the world. In all shops you can buy them to enjoy on the premises, usually with coffee, as well as to take out. A 200-year-old institution is **Demel** (☞ Exploring Vienna, *above*). **Gerstner** (⊠ Kärntnerstr. 11–15, ☎ 01/512–4963–77) is in the heart of the bustling Kärntnerstrasse and is one of the more modern Viennese cafés. Popular here is the Brueghel torte, a marzipan pastry especially concocted for their branch in the Kunsthistorisches Museum. **Heiner** (⊠ Kärntnerstr. 21–23, ☎ 01/512–6863–0; ⊠ Wollzeile 9, ☎ 01/512–2343) is dazzling for its crystal chandeliers as well as for its pastries. **Oberlaa** (⊠ Neuer Markt 16, ☎ 01/513–2936) has irresistible confections, cakes, and bonbons, as well as light lunches and salad plates, served outdoors in summer. **Sperl** (✉ Gumpendorferstr. 11, ☎ 01/586–4158), founded in 1880, was voted the best café in Vienna in 1998 because of its superb coffee and all-around Old Viennese ambiance.

LODGING

In Vienna's best hotels the staff seems to anticipate your wishes almost before you express them. Such service, of course, has its price, and if you wish, you can stay in Vienna in profound luxury. For those with more modest requirements, ample rooms are available in less expensive but entirely adequate hotels. Pensions, mainly bed-and-breakfast establishments often managed by the owner, generally represent good value. A number of student dormitories are run as hotels in summer, offering about the most reasonable quarters of all. And several apartment-hotels accommodate those who want longer stays.

When you have only a short time to spend in Vienna, you will probably choose to stay in the inner city (the First District, or 1010 postal code) or fairly close to it, within walking distance of the most important sights, restaurants, and shops. Although most of the hotels there are in the more expensive categories, excellent and reasonable accommodations can be found in the Sixth, Seventh, and Eighth districts and put you close to the major museums. You'll also find a group of moderate ($$) and inexpensive ($) hotels in the Mariahilferstrasse–Westbahnhof area, within easy reach of the city center by subway.

For the high season, Easter–September, and around the Christmas–New Year holidays, make reservations a month or more in advance. Vienna is continually the site of some international convention or other, and the city fills up quickly.

Our hotel categories correspond more or less to the official Austrian rating system, with five stars the equivalent of our very expensive ($$$$) category. Color television is usual in the top two categories; breakfast is included with all *except* the highest category. Air-conditioning is rare except in the larger, newer chain hotels. These seem constantly to be hosting conventions or seminar groups, making service somewhat less personal, but there are exceptions, as noted.

CATEGORY	COST*
$$$$	over AS3,000 (€220)
$$$	AS1,800–AS3,000 (€130–€220)
$$	AS1,000–AS1,800 (€72–€129)
$	under AS1,000 (€72)

All prices are for two persons in a standard double room, including local taxes (usually 10%), service (15%), and breakfast (except in most $$$$ hotels).

🕾 *following the text of a review is your signal that the property has a Web site, where you will find details and, usually, images; for a link, visit www.fodors.com/urls.*

$$$$ 🏨 **Bristol.** This hotel has one of the finest locations in Europe, on the Ring next to the Opera House. The accent here is on tradition, from the brocaded walls to the Biedermeier period furnishings in the public rooms and some of the bedrooms. The house dates from 1892, and during the 1945–55 occupation it was the U.S. military headquarters. The view is better from rooms on the Kärntnerstrasse or the Ring, and some rooms have balconies facing the Opera. Sometimes the hotel offers special rates at great value. The Bristol also houses the acclaimed Korso restaurant (☞ *Dining, above*). ✉ *Kärntner Ring 1, A–1010,* ☎ *01/515–16–0,* ℻ *01/515–16–550. 141 rooms. 2 restaurants, bar, health club. AE, DC, MC, V.* 🕾

94

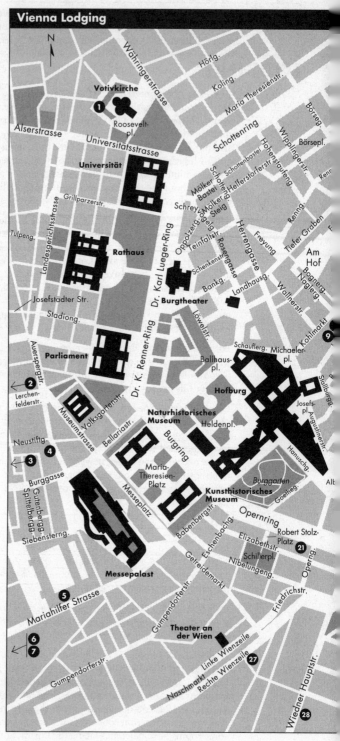

Vienna Lodging

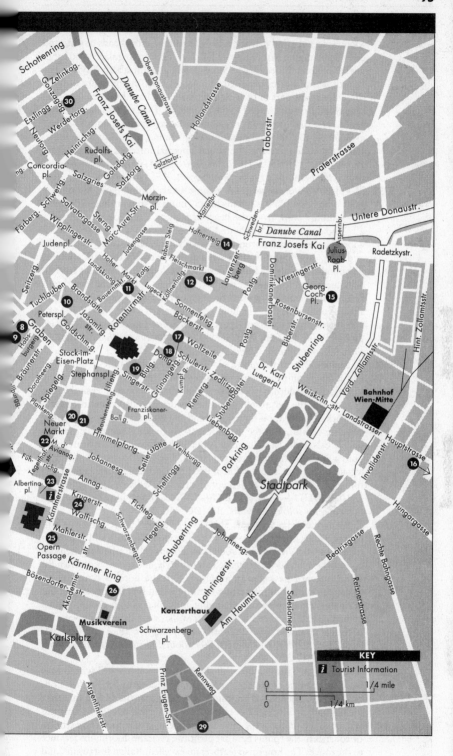

$$$$ 🏨 **Imperial.** The hotel is as much a palace today as when it was formally opened in 1873 by Emperor Franz Josef. The emphasis is on Old Vienna elegance and privacy, which accounts for the heads of state and celebrities staying here. Michael Jackson checks in regularly, and other guests have included Bruce Springsteen and Elizabeth Taylor. The beautiful rooms are furnished in antique style, though only the first three floors are part of the original house and have high ceilings; subsequent floors were added in the late 1930s. Don't overlook, as if you could, the grand marble staircase and ornate reception rooms. The hotel also houses the Imperial restaurant (☞ *Dining, above*) and the Imperial Café, which features the famed Imperial torte. ⊠ *Kärntner Ring 16, A–1010,* ☎ *01/501–10–0,* FAX *01/501–10–410. 128 rooms. Restaurant, café, piano bar, no-smoking rooms. AE, DC, MC, V.* 🏨

$$$$
★ 🏨 **Palais Schwarzenberg.** Set against a vast formal park, the palace, built in the early 1700s, seems like a country estate, though it's just a few minutes' walk from the heart of the city. Each room is individually and luxuriously appointed, with the family's original artwork adorning the walls. Bathrooms are sleekly done, with heated towel racks and long, deep bathtubs. One wing at the far end of the park contains ultramodern suites by Italian designer Paolo Piva. You don't have to be a guest here to come for a drink, coffee, or light lunch, served outside on the terrace in summer or beside a roaring fireplace in the main sitting-room in winter. The hotel restaurant is in a lovely glassed-in terrace overlooking the formal gardens. ⊠ *Schwarzenbergpl. 9, A–1030,* ☎ *01/798–4515–600,* FAX *01/798–4714. 44 rooms with bath. Restaurant, bar, pool, free parking. AE, DC, MC, V.* 🏨

$$$$
★ 🏨 **Sacher.** One of the grand old hotels, the Sacher dates from 1876, and it has retained its sense of history over the years while providing luxurious, modern-day comfort. The corridors are a veritable art gallery, and the exquisitely furnished bedrooms also contain original artwork. The location directly behind the Opera House could hardly be more central, and the ratio of staff to guests is more than two to one. Meals in the Red Room or Anna Sacher Room are first-rate, with both a Continental and Viennese menu. The Café Sacher, of course, is legendary. British director Carol Reed filmed some of his classic 1949 film *The Third Man* in the reception area. ⊠ *Philharmonikerstr. 4, A–1010,* ☎ *01/514–56–0,* FAX *01/514–57–810. 108 rooms. 2 restaurants, bar, café, no-smoking rooms. AE, DC, MC, V.* 🏨

$$$ 🏨 **Biedermeier im Sünnhof.** This jewel of a hotel is tucked into a renovated 1820s house that even with all modern facilities still conveys a feeling of Old Vienna. The rooms are compact but efficient, the public areas tastefully done in the Biedermeier style, and the service is friendly. The courtyard passageway around which the hotel is built has attracted a number of interesting boutiques and handicrafts shops, but at times there is an excess of coming and going as tour groups are accommodated. It's about a 20-minute walk or a 6-minute subway ride to the center of the city. ⊠ *Landstrasser Hauptstr. 28, A–1030,* ☎ *01/ 716–71–0,* FAX *01/716–71–503. 204 rooms. Restaurant, bar, parking (fee). AE, DC, MC, V.* 🏨

$$$ 🏨 **Das Triest.** This is a little off the beaten track but still within easy walking distance of the city center. Totally redone by Sir Terence Conran, it's now Vienna's chicest hotel, giving guests the feeling that they are onboard an ultrasleek ocean liner—a bit surprising, considering this was once the stable of the old Vienna-Trieste posthouse. The extra little touches in the rooms here are plentiful; even the doorknobs feel nice to the touch. The hotel also features an excellent Italian restaurant, and breakfast is included in the room rate. ⊠ *Wiedner Hauptstr. 12, A– 1010,* ☎ *01/589–180,* FAX *01/589–1818. 73 rooms. Restaurant, bar, café, health club. AE, DC, MC, V.* 🏨

$$$ ⊞ **Europa.** Renovated from top to bottom, this 1957-vintage hotel offers modern, rather charmless rooms with all the amenities. The selling point here is the great location. Rooms on the Neuer Markt side are quieter than those on Kärntnerstrasse. ⊠ *Neuer Markt 3, A–1010,* ☎ *01/515–94–0,* ℻ *01/513–8138. 113 rooms. Restaurant, bar, café. AE, DC, MC, V.* ✏

$$$ ⊞ **König von Ungarn.** In a 16th-century house in the shadow of St. Stephen's Cathedral, this hotel began catering to court nobility in 1815. (Mozart lived in the house next door when he wrote *The Marriage of Figaro.*) A superb redesign turned it into a modern hotel, and you could hardly hope for a happier result. The hotel radiates charm—rooms (some with Styrian wood-paneled walls) are furnished with country antiques and have walk-in closets and double sinks in the sparkling bathrooms. The two suites are two-storied. The inviting atrium bar beckons you in to sit and have a drink. Insist on written confirmation of bookings. ⊠ *Schulerstr. 10, A–1010,* ☎ ℻ *01/515–84–0. 32 rooms. Restaurant, bar. DC, MC, V.*

$$$ ⊞ **Wandl.** The restored facade identifies a 300-year-old house that has been in family hands as a hotel since 1854. You couldn't find a better location, tucked behind St. Peter's Church, just off the Graben. The hallways are punctuated by cheerful, bright openings along the glassed-in inner court. The rooms are modern, but some are a bit plain and charmless, despite parquet flooring and red accents. Ask for one of the rooms done in period furniture, with decorated ceilings and gilt mirrors; they're palatial, if slightly overdone. ⊠ *Peterspl. 9, A–1010,* ☎ *01/534–55–0,* ℻ *01/534–55–77. 138 rooms. Bar. AE, DC, MC, V.* ✏

$$–$$$ ⊞ **Kummer.** In the heart of the shopping district and with an imposing, Georgian-style exterior, this old hotel has an equally noble lobby with a grand, sweeping staircase. Each comfortably furnished room is different, and the ones facing the busy Mariahilferstrasse have soundproof windows. Some rooms have an alcove sitting area. The hotel is also close to the Westbahnhof and major museums. ⊠ *Mariahilferstr. 71a, A–1060,* ☎ *01/58895,* ℻ *01/587–8133. 100 rooms. Restaurant, bar. AE, DC, MC, V.* ✏

$$–$$$ ⊞ **Regina.** This dignified old hotel with grand reception rooms sits regally on the edge of the Altstadt, commanding a view of Sigmund Freud Park. It's near the Votivkirche, and about a 10-minute walk from the center. The high-ceilinged rooms are quiet, spacious and attractively decorated with contemporary furniture, and most have charming sitting areas. Freud, who lived nearby, used to eat breakfast in the hotel's café every morning. Buffet breakfast is included. ⊠ *Rooseveltpl. 15, A–1090* ☎ *01/404–460,* ℻ *01/408–8392. 125 rooms. Restaurant. AE, DC, MC, V.* ✏

$$–$$$ ⊞ **Royal.** Just around the corner from St. Stephen's and Kärntnerstrasse, this modern hotel is on the site of a former pilgrim hostel from the early 16th century. It was destroyed in World War II and rebuilt in 1960. Rooms are contemporary and pleasantly decorated, though despite the prime location none has a view. The hotel's Italian restaurant, Firenze Enoteca, is favored by opera singers, including Pavarotti. In summer the restaurant also operates on the rooftop terrace with a spectacular view of the Graben and St. Stephen's. ⊠ *Singerstr. 3, A–1010,* ☎ *01/51568–0,* ℻ *01/513–9698. 77 rooms. 2 restaurants. AE, DC, MC, V.* ✏

$$ ⊞ **Altstadt.** This small hotel was once a patrician home, and it's a gem.
★ Rooms are large with all the modern comforts, though they retain an antique feel. The English-style lounge has a fireplace and plump floral sofas. Upper rooms have views out over the city roofline. The management is personable and helpful. You're one streetcar stop or a pleasant walk from the main museums. ⊠ *Kircheng. 41, A–1070,* ☎ *01/526–3399–0,* ℻ *01/523–4901. 25 rooms. Bar. AE, DC, MC, V.* ✏

$$ ⊞ **Austria.** This older house, tucked away on a tiny cul-de-sac, offers the ultimate in quiet and is only five minutes' walk from the heart of the city. The high-ceiling rooms are pleasing in their combination of dark wood and lighter walls; the decor is mixed, with Oriental carpets on many floors. Rooms without full bath are a bit cheaper. There is a nice courtyard terrace that is perfect for sipping coffee after a day of sightseeing. You'll feel at home here, and the staff will help you find your way around town or get opera or concert tickets. ⊠ *Wolfeng. 3 (Fleischmarkt), A–1010,* ☎ *01/515–23–0,* FAX *01/515–23–505. 46 rooms, 42 with bath. AE, DC, MC, V.* 🐾

$$ ⊞ **Fürstenhof.** This turn-of-the-century building, directly across from the Westbahnhof, describes its large rooms as "old-fashioned comfortable," and you reach them via a marvelous hydraulic elevator. Furnishings are a mixed bag. The side rooms are quieter than those in front. Rooms without bath are less expensive. A very nice breakfast is included in the price. ⊠ *Neubaugürtel 4, A–1010,* ☎ *01/523–3267,* FAX *01/523–3267–26. 58 rooms, 39 with bath. AE, DC, MC, V.* 🐾

$$ ⊞ **Kärntnerhof.** Behind the "Maria Theresa yellow" facade of this elegant 100-year-old house on a quiet cul-de-sac lies one of the friendliest small hotels in the center of the city. Take the gorgeously restored Biedermeier elevator to the guest rooms upstairs, which contain reproduction antiques and modern baths. The staff is adept at getting theater and concert tickets for "sold-out" performances and happily puts together special outing programs for guests. Pets are welcome here. ⊠ *Grashofg. 4, A–1010,* ☎ *01/512–1923–0,* FAX *01/513–2228–33. 43 rooms. Parking (fee). AE, DC, MC, V.* 🐾

$$ ⊞ **Museum.** Located in a beautiful Belle Epoque mansion just a five-
★   minute walk from the Kunsthistorisches Museum, Natural History Museum, and the new Museumsquartier, this elegant pension offers good-sized rooms with large, comfortably modern bathrooms. There is also a pretty, sunny sitting room with deep, stuffed sofas and wing-back chairs, perfect for curling up with a good book. This is a popular place, so book ahead. ⊠ *Museumstr. 3, A–1070,* ☎ *01/523–44–260,* FAX *01/523–44–2630. 15 rooms. AE, DC, MC, V.*

$$ ⊞ **Neuer Markt.** You're in the heart of the city at this attractive pastel-yellow pension, situated in a lofty position at the head of the pretty square bearing the same name. Rooms are modern and comfortable, and the staff is very friendly and helpful, making you feel right at home. ⊠ *Seilerg. 9, A–1010,* ☎ *01/512–2316,* FAX *01/513–9105. 37 rooms. AE, DC, MC, V.*

$$ ⊞ **Pension Aviano.** Tucked away in a corner of the Neuer Markt, this small pension is close to the Opera House. Rooms are cheerful and quiet, and the two junior suites have a charming turret where you can sit and gaze out over the rooftops of Vienna. In summer, breakfast tables are set outside on the balcony overlooking the inner courtyard. ⊠ *Marco d'Avianog. 1, A–1010,* ☎ *01/512–8330,* FAX *01/512–8330–6. 17 rooms. DC, MC, V.*

$$ ⊞ **Pension Christina.** This quiet pension, just steps from Schwedenplatz and the Danube Canal, offers mainly smallish modern rooms, warmly decorated with attractive dark-wood furniture set off against beige walls. ⊠ *Hafnersteig 7, A–1010,* ☎ *01/533–2961–0,* FAX *01/533–2961–11. 33 rooms. MC, V.*

$$ ⊞ **Pension City.** You'll be on historic ground here: in 1791 the playwright Franz Grillparzer was born in the house that then stood here; a bust and plaques in the entryway commemorate him. On the second floor of the present 100-year-old house, about three minutes away from St. Stephen's Cathedral, the rooms are outfitted in a successful mix of modern and 19th-century antique furniture against white walls. The baths are small but complete. ⊠ *Bauernmarkt 10, A–1010,* ☎ *01/533–9521,* FAX *01/535–5216. 19 rooms. AE, DC, MC, V.*

$$ 🏨 **Pension Domizil.** Located around the corner from the house where Mozart wrote *The Marriage of Figaro,* the Domizil offers quiet, well-equipped rooms decorated with rather bland contemporary furniture. The staff is pleasant, and you're right in the middle of a series of charming Old World cobblestone streets near St. Stephen's. ⊠ *Schulerstr. 14,* ☎ *01/513-3199–0,* FAX *01/512-3484. 40 rooms. AE, DC, MC, V.*

$$ 🏨 **Pension Nossek.** This family-run establishment on the upper floors
★ of a 19th-century office and apartment building lies at the heart of the pedestrian and shopping area. The rooms have high ceilings and are eclectically but comfortably furnished; those on the front have a magnificent view of the Graben. Do as the many regular guests do: book early. ⊠ *Graben 17, A–1010,* ☎ *01/533-7041–0,* FAX *01/535-3646. 27 rooms, 25 with bath. No credit cards.*

$$ 🏨 **Pension Pertschy.** Housed in a former town palace just off the Graben, this pension is as central as you can get. A massive arched portal leads to a yellow courtyard, around which the house is built. A few rooms contain lovely old ceramic stoves (just for show). Most rooms are spacious, and each one is comfortable, though overall the furniture is a bit kitschy. Baths are satisfactory. Use the elevator, but don't overlook the palatial grand staircase. ⊠ *Habsburgerg. 5, A–1010,* ☎ *01/534-49–0,* FAX *01/534-49–49. 43 rooms. DC, MC, V.*

$$ 🏨 **Zur Wiener Staatsoper.** A great deal of loving care has gone into this family-owned hotel near the State Opera, reputed to be one of the Viennese settings in John Irving's *The Hotel New Hampshire.* The florid facade, with oversize torsos supporting its upper bays, is pure 19th-century Ringstrasse style. Rooms are small but have high ceilings and are charmingly decorated with pretty fabrics and wallpaper. ⊠ *Krugerstr. 11, A–1010,* ☎ *01/513-1274–0,* FAX *01/513-1274–15. 22 rooms. AE, MC, V.*

$–$$ 🏨 **Drei Kronen.** This nice, pastel peach hotel is across the street from the colorful Naschmarkt, Vienna's largest and most famous outdoor market. Rooms are modern and a bit dull, but perfectly adequate, and have cable TV. You'll be within walking distance of the city center. ⊠ *Schleifmühlg. 25, A–1040,* ☎ *01/587-3289,* FAX *01/587-8284–11, 41 rooms. AE, DC, MC, V.*

$ 🏨 **Pension Grun.** A minimum stay of three nights is required here, but if you're staying that long you can't beat the five-minute walk to the city center. It's around the corner from the happening Schwedenplatz area and the Bermuda Triangle, where a lot of the most fun bars and nightclubs are located. Rooms are spacious, baths are across the hall, and there's a comfortable sitting room. ⊠ *Gonzagag. 1, 3rd floor, Suite 19, A–1010,* ☎ *01/533-2506. 3 rooms without bath. No credit cards.*

$ 🏨 **Pension Reimer.** Friendly and comfortable, this hotel is in a prime location just off Mariahilferstrasse. The modern rooms have high ceilings and large windows, and the atmosphere throughout is cheerful. Breakfast is included. ⊠ *Kircheng. 18, A–1070,* ☎ *01/523-6162,* FAX *01/524-3782. 14 rooms. MC, V.*

$ 🏨 **Pension Riedl.** Across the square from the Postsparkasse, the 19th-century postal savings bank designed by Otto Wagner, this small establishment offers modern, pleasant rooms with cable TV. As an added touch, breakfast is delivered to your room. Cheerful owner Maria Felser is happy to arrange concert tickets and tours. ⊠ *Georg–Coch-Pl. 3/4/10, A–1010,* ☎ *01/512-7919,* FAX *01/512-79198. 8 rooms. DC, MC, V. Closed first 2 wks of Feb.*

$ 🏨 **Pension Wild.** This friendly, family-run pension on several floors of
★ an older apartment house draws a relaxed, younger crowd to one of the best values in town. Rooms are simple but modern, with light-wood

furniture and pine-paneled ceilings. Each wing has a kitchenette. The breakfast room–TV lounge is bright and attractive, and you're close to the major museums. ⊠ *Langeg. 1, A–1080,* ☎ *01/406–5174,* 𝔽𝔸𝕏 *01/402–2168. 14 rooms. Sauna, exercise room. AE, DC, MC, V.*

Seasonal Hotels

Student residences, which operate as hotels July–September, can provide excellent bargains in the inexpensive ($) category. They have single or double rooms, all (unless noted) with bath. You can book by calling any of the **Rosenhotels** (☎ 01/911–4910, 𝔽𝔸𝕏 01/910–0269) or central booking for the student residence hotels of the **Albertina group** (☎ 01/512–74930, 𝔽𝔸𝕏 01/512–1968). Unless otherwise noted, credit cards are accepted.

▦ **Academia.** Among this group, this is a fairly luxurious choice. ⊠ *Pfeilg. 3a, A–1080,* ☎ *01/40176,* 𝔽𝔸𝕏 *01/40176–20. 300 rooms. Restaurant, bar.*

▦ **Accordia.** Belonging to the Albertina group, this is the newest of the seasonal hotels and is fairly close to the center. ⊠ *Grosse Schiffg. 12, A–1020,* ☎ *01/212–1668,* 𝔽𝔸𝕏 *01/212–1668–697. 90 rooms.*

▦ **Ambiente.** This accommodation is an Albertina member near the U.S. embassy, a quiet location. ⊠ *Boltzmanng. 10, A–1090,* ☎ *01/310–3130,* 𝔽𝔸𝕏 *01/310–3130–33. 43 rooms.*

▦ **Avis.** This option even features its own restaurant and bar. ⊠ *Pfeilg. 4, A–1080,* ☎ *01/40174 or 01/40176–55,* 𝔽𝔸𝕏 *01/40176–20. 72 rooms. Restaurant, bar. AE, MC, V.*

▦ **Haus Technik.** An Albertina member, this place is fairly close to the center. ⊠ *Schäfferg. 2, A–1040,* ☎ *01/587–6560,* 𝔽𝔸𝕏 *01/586–8505. 99 rooms. Restaurant.*

▦ **Rosenhotel Burgenland 3.** For weary travelers, the restaurant is a boon but tips the house into the $$ category. ⊠ *Bürgerspitalg. 19, A–1060,* ☎ *01/597–9475,* 𝔽𝔸𝕏 *01/597–9475–9. 120 rooms. Restaurant, bar. AE, MC, V.*

▦ **Studentenheim der Musikhochschule.** This choice offers the most central location of any of the seasonal hotels, in the heart of the city. ⊠ *Johannesg. 8, A–1010,* ☎ *01/514–84–0,* 𝔽𝔸𝕏 *01/514–84–49. 85 rooms, some with bath.*

NIGHTLIFE AND THE ARTS

The Arts

Dance

Under new directors, the **ballet evenings** that are on the Staatsoper and Volksoper schedule (☎ 01/514–44–0) are now much improved and finally up to international standards. Vienna also has theaters offering contemporary dance, representing Austria's up-and-coming choreographers and theater artists. Check out **Szene Wien** (⊠ Hauffg. 26, A–1110, ☎ 01/749–3341, 𝔽𝔸𝕏 01/749–2206) and **dietheater Wien** (⊠ Karlspl. 5, A–1010, ☎ 01/587–0504–0, 𝔽𝔸𝕏 01/587–8774) for their seasonal programs.

Film

Vienna has a thriving film culture, with viewers seeking original rather than German-dubbed versions. Look for films in English at **Artis** (⊠ corner of Shulterg./Jordang., near the Hoher Markt, A–1010, ☎ 01/535–6570); at the **Burg** (⊠ Opernring 19, A–1010, ☎ 01/587–8406)—in summer, Carol Reed's Vienna-based classic *The Third Man,* with

Orson Welles, is a regular feature; also try the **Haydn** (✉ Mariahilferstr. 57, A–1060, ☎ 01/587–2262); and sometimes the **Votiv-Kino** (✉ Währinger Str. 12, A–1090, ☎ 01/317–3571).

The film schedule in the daily newspaper *Der Standard* lists foreign-language films (*Fremdsprachige Filme*) separately. In film listings, *OmU* means original language with German subtitles.

The **Filmmuseum** in the Albertina shows original-version classics with a heavy focus on English-language films and organizes retrospectives of the works of artists, directors, and producers. The monthly program is posted outside. If you aren't a member, you must purchase a guest membership (AS60 per day). The theater is closed July, August, and September. ✉ *Augustinerstr. 1,* ☎ *01/533–7054.* ◩ *AS110 (incl. AS60 guest membership), AS50 with AS150 yearly membership.*

Galleries
A host of smaller galleries centers on the Singerstrasse and Grünangergasse, although there are many more scattered about the city.

Music
Vienna is one of the main music centers of the world. Contemporary music gets its hearing, but it's the hometown standards—the works of Beethoven, Brahms, Haydn, Mozart, and Schubert—that draw the Viennese public. A monthly program, put out by the city tourist board and available at any travel agency or hotel, gives a general overview of what's going on in opera, concerts, jazz, theater, and galleries, and similar information is posted on billboards and fat advertising columns around the city.

Vienna is home to four full symphony orchestras: the great Vienna Philharmonic, the outstanding Vienna Symphony, the broadcasting service's ORF Symphony Orchestra, and the Niederösterreichische Tonkünstler. There are also hundreds of smaller groups, from world-renowned trios to chamber orchestras.

The most important concert halls are in the buildings of the Gesellschaft der Musikfreunde, called the **Musikverein** (✉ Dumbastr. 3; ticket office at Karlspl. 6, ☎ 01/505–8190, ⨋ 01/505–9409, ✍), which contains the Grosser Musikvereinssaal and the Brahmssaal, and the **Konzerthaus** (✉ Lothringerstr. 20, ☎ 01/712–4686; 01/712–1211 ticket window, ⨋ 01/712–2872, ✍), which houses the Grosser Konzerthaussaal, Mozartsaal, and Schubertsaal halls.

Concerts are also given in the small **Figarosaal** of Palais Palffy (✉ Josefspl. 6, ☎ 01/512–5681–0), the **Radio Kulturhaus** (✉ Argentinierstr. 30A, ☎ 01/501–70–377), and the **Bösendorfersaal** (✉ Graf Starhemberg-G. 14, ☎ 01/504–6651, ⨋ 01/504–6651–39). Students of the **music school** regularly give class recitals in the school's concert halls during the academic year; look for announcements posted outside for dates and times (✉ Seilerstätte 26 and Johannesg. 8, ☎ 01/588–06–0).

Although the **Vienna Festival** (☎ 01/589–22–11), held mid-May to mid-June, wraps up the primary season, the summer musical scene is bright, with something scheduled every day. Outdoor symphony concerts are performed weekly in the vast arcaded courtyard of the Rathaus (entrance on Friedrich Schmidt-Pl.). You can catch musical events in the Volksgarten and in the St. Augustine, St. Michael's, Minorite, and University churches; at Schönbrunn Palace they're outside in the courtyard as well as part of an evening guided tour.

Mozart concerts are performed in 18th-century costume and powdered wigs in the large hall, or Mozartsaal, of the Konzerthaus (☞ *above*); operetta concerts are held in the Musikverein (☞ *above*), and the Hofburg and Palais Ferstel. There are no set dates, so inquire through hotels and travel and ticket agencies for availabilities. Note, however, that some of these concerts, including intermission lasting possibly an hour, are rather expensive affairs put on for tourists and are occasionally of disappointing quality.

Church music, the mass sung in Latin, can be heard Sunday mornings during the main season at St. Stephen's; in the Franciscan church, St. Michael's; the Universitätskirche; and, above all, in the Augustinerkirche. The Friday and Saturday newspapers carry details. St. Stephen's also has organ concerts most Wednesday evenings from early May to late November.

The **Vienna Boys Choir** (Wiener Sängerknaben) sings mass at 9:15 AM in the Hofburgkapelle (✉ Hofburg, Schweizer Hof, ☏ 01/533–9927, FAX 01/533–9927–75) from mid-September to late June. Written requests for seats should be made at least eight weeks in advance (✉ Hofmusikkapelle Hofburg, A–1010 Vienna). You will be sent a reservation card, which you exchange at the box office (in the Hofburg courtyard) for your tickets. Tickets are also sold at ticket agencies and at the box office (open daily 11:30–1 and 3–5). Each person is allowed two tickets only. General seating costs AS70, prime seats in the front of the church AS380. It's important to note that only the 10 side balcony seats allow a view of the choir; those who purchase floor seats, standing room, or center balcony will not be able to see the boys. On Sunday at 8:45 AM all unclaimed pre-ordered tickets are sold. If you've missed the Vienna Boys Choir at the Sunday mass, you may be able to hear them in a more popular program in the Konzerthaus.

TICKETS

Most theaters now reserve tickets by telephone against a credit card; you pick up your ticket at the box office with no surcharge. The same applies to concert tickets. Ticket agencies (☞ Contacts and Resources *in* Vienna A to Z, *below*) charge a minimum 22% markup and generally deal in the more expensive seats. Expect to pay (or tip) a hotel porter or concierge at least as much as a ticket-agency markup for hard-to-get tickets. Tickets to musicals and some events including the Vienna Festival are available at the **"Salettl" gazebo** kiosk alongside the Opera House on the Kärntnerstrasse. Tickets to that night's musicals are reduced by half after 2 PM.

Opera and Operetta

The **Staatsoper** (State Opera House, ✉ Opernring 2, ☏ 01/514–440, ✍), one of the world's great opera houses, has been the scene of countless musical triumphs and a center of unending controversies over how it should be run and by whom. (When Lorin Maazel was unceremoniously dumped as head of the Opera not many years ago, he pointed out that the house had done the same thing to Gustav Mahler a few decades earlier.) A performance takes place virtually every night September–June, drawing on the vast repertoire of the house, with emphasis on Mozart and Verdi works. (Opera here is nearly always performed in the original language, even Russian.) Guided tours of the Opera House are held year-round. The opera in Vienna is a dress-up event, and even designer jeans are not acceptable. Evening dress and black tie, though not compulsory, are recommended for first-night performances and in the better seats.

Opera and operetta are also performed at the **Volksoper** (✉ Währingerstr. 78, ☏ 01/514–440, ✍), outside the city center at Währingerstrasse and Währinger Gürtel (third stop on Streetcar 41, 42, or 43, which run from "downstairs" at Schottentor, U2, on the Ring). Prices here are significantly lower than in the Staatsoper, and performances can be every bit as rewarding. Operas are sung here in German.

You'll find musicals and operetta also at the **Raimundtheater** (⊠ Wallg. 18, ☎ 01/599–77–0), **Ronacher** (⊠ Seilerstätte/Himmelpfortg., ☎ 01/514–110), and the **Theater an der Wien** (⊠ Linke Wienzeile 6, ☎ 01/588–30–0). Opera and operetta are performed on an irregular schedule at the **Kammeroper** (⊠ Fleischmarkt 24, ☎ 01/512–01–000).

In summer, light opera or operetta performances by the Kammeroper ensemble are given in the exquisite **Schlosstheater** at Schönbrunn. Send a fax to 01/51201–00–30 for details.

TICKETS

Tickets to the **state theaters** (Staatsoper, Volksoper, Burgtheater, and Akademietheater) can be charged against your credit card. You can order them by phoning up to a month before the performance (☎ 01/513–1513) or buy them in person up to a month in advance at the Theaterkassen, the **central box office**. ⊠ *Theaterkassen, back of Opera, Hanuschg. 3, in courtyard.* ⊙ *Weekdays 8–6, Sat. 9–2, Sun. and holidays 9–noon.*

You can get information and tickets for the **Staatsoper and Volksoper** at the ticket office for those theaters. ⊠ *Goetheg. 1,* ☎ *01/514–44–2958; weekends phone 01/514–4478–10.* ⊙ *Weekdays 10–6.*

You can write ahead for tickets as well. The nearest **Austrian National Tourist Office** can give you a schedule of performances and a ticket order form. Send the form (no payment is required) to the ticket office (⊠ Kartenvorverkauf Bundestheaterverband, Goetheg. 1, A–1010 Vienna), which will mail you a reservation card; when you get to Vienna, take the card to the main box office to pick up and pay for your tickets.

Theater

Vienna's **Burgtheater** (⊠ Dr.-Karl-Lueger-Ring 2, A–1010 Vienna; ☞ State Theaters, *above,* for ticket details) is one of the leading German-language theaters of the world. The repertoire has recently begun mixing German classics with more modern and controversial pieces. The Burg's smaller house, the **Akademietheater** (⊠ Lisztstr. 1), draws on much the same group of actors for classical and modern plays. Both houses are closed during July and August.

The **Kammerspiele** (⊠ Rotenturmstr. 20, ☎ 01/42700–304) does modern plays. The **Theater in der Josefstadt** (⊠ Josefstädterstr. 26, ☎ 01/42700–306) stages classical and modern works year-round in the house once run by the great producer and teacher Max Reinhardt. The **Volkstheater** (⊠ Neustiftg. 1, ☎ 01/523–3501–0) presents dramas, comedies, and folk plays.

For theater in English (mainly standard plays), head for **Vienna's English Theater** (⊠ Josefsg. 12, ☎ 01/402–1260). Another option is the equally good **International Theater** (⊠ Porzellang. 8, ☎ 01/319–6272).

Nightlife

Balls

The gala Vienna evening you've always dreamed about can become a reality: among the many **balls** given during the Carnival season, several welcome the public—at a wide range of prices, from about AS700 to AS3,000 per person. Dates change every year, but most balls are held in January and February. Some of the more popular balls are the Blumen Ball (Florists' Ball), Kaffeesieder Ball (Coffee Brewers' Ball), Bon-

bon Ball (Confection Ball), and the most famous and expensive of them all, the Opernball (Opera Ball). You can book tickets with a Eurocheck or through hotel concierges (for more information call ☎ 01/211140, FAX 01/216–8492).

For a background on these festive events, *see* Stepping Out in Three-Quarter Time *in* Pleasures and Pastimes, *above.*

Bars and Lounges

Vienna has blossomed in recent years with delightful and sophisticated bars. Happy hour is popular, but note that here it means two drinks per person for the price of one—not half-price drinks. Here's a sampling of the best bars in the First District. In the "Bermuda Triangle" area near St. Ruprecht's you'll find **First Floor** (⊠ Corner of Seitenstetteng./Rabensteig., ☎ 01/533–7866), which is actually up one floor from ground level. The **Kruger Bar** (⊠ Krugerstr. 5, ☎ 01/512–2455), off Kärntnerstrasse near the Opera, has an English gentlemen's club atmosphere in a former 1950s cinema. Near the Börse (Vienna Stock Exchange) is the **Planter's Club** (⊠ Zelinkag. 4, ☎ 01/533–3393–16), offering a nice selection of rums in an exotic, tropical colonial atmosphere. Let the outdoor glass elevator at the Steffl department store whisk you up to the **Skybar** (⊠ Kärtnerstr. 19, ☎ 01/513–1712) for soft piano music to go along with the stunning view. The best place to sample wines from all over Austria is the intimate **Vis à Vis** (⊠ Wollzeile 5, ☎ 01/512–9350, closed weekends), located in the passageway by St. Stephen's.

Cabaret

Cabaret has a long tradition in Vienna. To get much from any of it, you'll need good German with a smattering of Viennese vernacular as well, plus some knowledge of local affairs. **Simpl** (⊠ Wollzeile 36, A–1010, ☎ 01/512–4742) continues earning its reputation for barbed political wit but has had to give way to some newcomers at **Kabarett Niedermair** (⊠ Lenaug. 1A, A–1080, ☎ 01/408–4492).

Casinos

Try your luck at the casino **Cercle Wien** (⊠ Kärntnerstr. 41, ☎ 01/512–4836), in a former town palace redone in dark-wood paneling and millions of twinkling lights. Games include roulette and blackjack. You'll need your passport for entry identification.

Disco

The disco scene is big in Vienna, and the crowd seems to follow the leader from one "in" spot to the next. A few continually draw full houses.

Try **Atrium** (⊠ Schwarzenbergpl. 10, ☎ 01/505–3594); **Queen Anne,** still very much "in" (⊠ Johannesg. 12, ☎ 01/512–0203); and **U–4,** popular with a mixed group, early thirties and younger (⊠ Schönbrunnerstr. 222, ☎ 01/815–8307).

Irish Pubs

After Austria joined the European Union several years ago, Irish pubs started popping up all over the place, and most are open all day. Along with British and Irish expatriates you can find a substantial Viennese crowd. Live Irish music is offered some nights at **Bockshorn** (⊠ Naglerg. 7 [entrance on Körblerg.], ☎ 01/532–9438). Offering light dishes to go along with Guinness on tap is **Flanagan's** (⊠ Schwarzenbergstr. 1–3, ☎ 01/513–7378). The place to go in the Margareten area for Murphy's Red Irish beer, Harp on tap, and Irish stew is **Little Stage Irish Pub** (⊠ Ramperstorfferg. 66/corner of Bräuhausg., A–1050, ☎ 01/544–2690). You can eat fish-and-chips in a book-lined "library" at the popular **Molly Darcy's** (⊠ Teinfaltstr. 6, ☎ 01/533–2311).

Jazz Clubs

Vienna has good jazz, though places where it can be heard tend to come and go. Nothing gets going before 9 PM. Live groups appear almost nightly at **Jazzland** (⊠ Franz-Josefs-Kai 29, ☎ 01/533–2575) and **Der Neue Engel** (⊠ Rabensteig 5, ☎ 01/535–4105).

Nightclubs

Vienna has no real nightclub tradition, although there are a number of clubs in town. Most of the ones with floor shows are horribly expensive and not very good; some are outright tourist traps. One where you run the least risk is the upscale **Moulin Rouge** (⊠ Walfischg. 11, ☎ 01/512–2130). The leading spots for dancing are the **Eden Bar,** which always has a live band and is for the well-heeled, mature crowd (⊠ Lilieng. 2, ☎ 01/512–7450); **Havana** for lively salsa and a younger crowd (⊠ Mahlerstr. 11, ☎ 01/513–2075); and **Volksgarten** (⊠ Volksgarten, Burgring 2, ☎ 01/532–0907), where a mixed younger set comes, particularly in summer for outdoor dancing.

OUTDOOR ACTIVITIES AND SPORTS

Participant Sports

Bicycling

Look for the special pathways either in red brick or marked with a stylized cyclist in yellow. Note and observe the special traffic signals at some intersections. You can take a bike on the subway (except during rush hours) for half fare, but only in cars with a "bike" shield on the door, and only on stairs or elevators with the "bike" shield, not on escalators. The city tourist office has a brochure in German with useful cycling maps, plus a leaflet, "See Vienna by Bike," with tips in English. At most bookstores you can purchase a cycling map of Vienna put out by a local cycling organization known as ARGUS (⊠ Frankenbergg. 11, ☎ 01/505–8435). You can rent a bike starting at about AS60 per hour, leaving your passport or other identification as a deposit.

Rent a bike year-round at the Westbahnhof, Wien Nord (Praterstern), or Floridsdorf rail stations. Or pick up a bike at one of the following: **Radverleih Hochschaubahn** (☎ 12/729–5888), mid-March–October, in the Prater amusement park, by the Hochschaubahn, slightly right after the Ferris wheel; **Radverleih Praterstern,** April–October, at street level under the Praterstern North rail station.

Pedal Power (⊠ Ausstellungsstr. 3, A–1020, ☎ 01/729–7234, FAX 01/729–7235) offers guided bike tours of Vienna and the surrounding vicinity in English from April to October, including the main sights of the city, or tours to the outlying vineyards for a glass of wine. It's also possible to rent a bike and do your own exploring. Rentals cost AS60 per hour; three-hour guided tours cost AS280 (AS230 for students); a five-hour bike rental on your own is AS300; for a full day, AS395.

Boating

Both the Alte Donau (Old Danube), a series of lakes to the north of the main stream, and the Neue Donau, on the north side of the Donauinsel (the artificial island in the river), offer good waters for paddleboats, rowboats, kayaks, sailboats, and Windsurfers. The Danube itself is somewhat too fast-moving for anything but kayaks.

Rent boats from **Auzinger Boote** (⊠ Laberlweg 19–22, ☎ 01/23–57–88), **Eppel** (⊠ Wagramer Str. 48, ☎ 01/263–3530), **Karl Hofbauer** (⊠ Obere Alte Donau 185; ☎ 01/238–2853), and **Newrkla** (⊠ Obere Alte Donau,

☎ 01/272–1664). For details about sailing and sailing events, check with
Haus des Sports (✉ Prinz-Eugen-Str. 12, ☎ 01/505–3742–0).

Golf

The top in-town golf course is at **Freudenau** in the Prater (☎ 01/728–
9564–0, FAX 01/728–9564–20). But this 18-hole, par-70 course is so popular from March to November, even with the Monday to Friday AS800
fee, that you'll probably need to be invited or have an introduction from
a member to play. It's closed Saturday and Sunday. You can also try
Süssenbrunn (✉ Weingartenallee, ☎ 01/25072), located 15 minutes
from the city center in the 22nd District. Süssenbrun is an 18-hole, par-
72 course open to the public.

There are other alternatives, but these, too, are generally overbooked.
Weekdays, of course, will be best for any of the courses, particularly
those farthest from Vienna. Try one of the following: **Golf and Country Club Brunn,** an 18-hole, par-72 course about 10 km (6 mi) to the
southwest (✉ Rennweg 50, Brunn am Gebirge, ☎ 02236/33711, FAX
02236/33863); **Colony Club Gutenhof,** 10 km (6 mi) to the southeast,
with two courses of 18 holes, par-73 each, at Himberg (✉ Gutenhof,
☎ 02235/87055–0); **Golfclub Schloss Ebreichsdorf,** 27 km (17 mi)
south of Vienna, an 18-hole, par-72 course (✉ Schlossallee 1, Ebreichsdorf, ☎ 02254/3888–0); **Golfclub Am Wienerberg,** a 9-hole, par-
35 course on the south side of Vienna, open March–November (✉
Gutheil Schoder-G. 9, ☎ 01/66123–0); or **Golfclub Hainburg,** 50 km
(31 mi) east of Vienna, with 18 holes, par-72 (✉ Auf der Heide 762,
Hainburg, ☎ 02165/62628, FAX 02165/65331).

Health and Fitness Clubs

Try **Fitness Center Harris** (✉ Niebelungeng. 7, ☎ 01/587–3710), or
Zimmermann Fitness (✉ Ringstrasse Galerie/Kärtner Ring, ☎ 01/
512–1020).

Ice-Skating

The **Wiener Eislaufverein** (✉ Lothringer Str. 22, behind InterContinental
Hotel, ☎ 01/713–6353–0) has outdoor skating with skate rentals, Oc-
tober–March. Weekends are crowded. For indoor skating, check the
Wiener Stadthalle (✉ Vogelweidpl. 14, ☎ 01/981–00–0).

Jogging

Jogging paths run alongside the Danube Canal, and runners also frequent the Stadtpark and the tree-lined route along the Ring, particularly the Parkring stretch. Farther afield, in the Second District, the Prater
Hauptallee, 4 km (2½ mi) from Praterstern to the Lusthaus, is a favorite.

Riding

Splendid bridle paths crisscross the Prater park. To hire a mount, contact the **Reitclub Donau** (✉ Hafenzufahrtstr. 63, ☎ 01/728–9716) or
Reitclub Prater/Reitschule Sylvia Kühnert (✉ Dammhaufen 62, ☎ 01/
728–1335).

Skiing

A nearby slope, **Hohe Wand,** west of the city in the 14th District, offers limited skiing, with a ski lift and man-made snow when the heavens refuse. Take Bus 49B from the Hütteldorf stop of the U4 subway.
Serious Viennese skiers (that includes nearly everybody) will take a train
or bus out to nearby Niederösterreich (Lower Austria), with the area
around the **Semmering** (☞ Chapter 3), about an hour from the city,
one of the favorite locations for a quick outing.

Swimming

Vienna has at least one pool for each of its 23 districts; most are indoor pools, but some locations have an outdoor pool as well. An in-

door favorite is **Rogner's** (✉ Strohbachg. 7–9, ☎ 01/587–0844–0), complete with water slide.

For a less formal environment, head for the swimming areas of the Alte Donau or the Donauinsel (☞ Boating, *above*). The pools and the Alte Donau (paid admission) will be filled on hot summer weekends, so the Donauinsel can be a surer bet. Some beach areas are shallow and suitable for children, but the Donauinsel has no lifeguards, though there are rescue stations for emergencies. Changing areas are few, lockers nonexistent, so don't take valuables. And don't be tempted to jump into the Danube Canal; the water is definitely not for swimming, nor is the Danube itself, because of heavy undertows and a powerful current.

The city has information on all places to swim; contact the **Magistratesabteilung 44** (✉ ☎ 01/601120). Ask for someone who speaks English to give directions to reach the following:

Donauinsel Nord is a huge free recreation area with a children's section and nude bathing. **Donauinsel Süd** is free and offers good swimming and boating and a nude bathing area. It's harder to get to and less crowded than other areas, and food facilities are limited. **Gänse-häufel** is a bathing island in the Alte Donau with paid admission, lockers, changing rooms, children's wading pools, topless and nude areas, and restaurants; on sunny weekends, it's likely to be full by 11 AM or earlier. **Krapfenwaldbad** is an outdoor park-pool tucked among the trees on the edge of the Vienna Woods, full of Vienna's beautiful people and singles. Get there early on a sunny Sunday or you won't get in. **Stadionbad** is an enormous sports complex popular with the younger crowd; go early. For the fun of it, ride the miniature railway (*Liliput-bahn*) from behind the Ferris wheel in the Prater amusement park to the Stadion station and walk the rest of the way.

Tennis

Though Vienna has plenty of courts, they'll be booked solid. Try anyway; your hotel may have good connections. Top businesspeople and political leaders head to **Tennis Point Vienna** (✉ Nottendorferg./Baumg., ☎ 01/799–9997) for the 10 indoor courts, squash, sauna, and an outstanding fitness studio; a bar and an excellent and remarkably reasonable restaurant are here as well. **Vereinigte Tennisanlagen** (✉ Prater Hauptallee 121, ☎ 01/728–1811) has courts in other locations as well. Or you can try **Tennisplätze Arsenal** (✉ Arsenalstr. 1, by Südbahnhof, ☎ 01/799–0101; ✉ Faradayg. 4, ☎ 01/798–7265; ✉ Gudrunstr. 31, ☎ 01/602–1521), which has 57 sand courts; **Union Tennis Club Schönbrunn** (✉ Schönbrunner Schloss-Str. 52, ☎ 01/521–52–2129); or **Wiener Eislaufverein** (✉ Lothringer Str. 22, behind Inter-Continental Hotel, ☎ 01/713–6353–0).

Spectator Sports

Football (Soccer)

Matches are played mainly in the **Ernst–Happel–Stadion** (stadium) in the Prater (✉ Meiereistr. 7, ☎ 01/728–0854). Indoor soccer takes place in the **Stadthalle** (✉ Vogelweidpl. 14, ☎ 01/981–00–01). Tickets can usually be bought at the gate, but the better seats are available through ticket agencies (☞ Contacts and Resources *in* Vienna A to Z, *below*).

Horse Racing

Two **racetracks** (flat and sulky racing) are in the Prater, the **Galopprennen** (✉ Freudenau, ☎ 01/728–9535, FAX 01/728–9587) and the **Trabrennen** (✉ Krieau, ☎ 01/728–0046, FAX 01/728–0046–20). The season runs April–November. The highlight is the Derby, which usually takes place in June.

Tennis

Professional matches are played in the Prater or in the Stadthalle (☞ Football [Soccer], *above*). Ticket agencies will have details.

SHOPPING

Shopping Districts

The Kärntnerstrasse, Graben, and Kohlmarkt pedestrian areas in the **Inner City** claim to have the best shops in Vienna, and for some items, such as jewelry, some of the best anywhere, although you must expect high prices. The side streets within this area have developed their own character, with shops offering antiques, art, clocks, jewelry, and period furniture. **Ringstrasse Galerie,** the indoor shopping plaza at Kärntner Ring 5–7, brings a number of shops together in a modern complex, although many of these stores have other, larger outlets elsewhere in the city. Outside the center, concentrations of stores are on **Mariahilferstrasse,** straddling the Sixth and Seventh districts; **Landstrasser Hauptstrasse** in the Third District; and, still farther out, **Favoritenstrasse** in the 10th District. A collection of attractive small boutiques can be found in the **Palais Ferstel** passage at Freyung 2 in the First District. A modest group of smaller shops has sprung up in the **Sonnhof** passage between Landstrasser Hauptstrasse 28 and Ungargasse 13 in the Third District. The **Spittelberg** market, on the Spittelberggasse between Burggasse and Siebensterngasse in the Seventh District, has drawn small galleries and handicrafts shops and is particularly popular in the weeks before Christmas and Easter. Christmas is the time also for the tinselly **Christkindlmarkt** on Rathausplatz in front of City Hall; in protest over its commercialization, smaller markets specializing in handicrafts have sprung up on such traditional spots as Am Hof and the Freyung (First District), also the venue for other seasonal markets.

Vienna's **Naschmarkt** (between Linke and Rechte Wienzeile, starting at Getreidemarkt) is one of Europe's great and most colorful food and produce markets. Stalls open at 5 or 6 AM, and the pace is lively until 5 or 6 PM. Saturday is the big day, when farmers come into the city to sell at the back end of the market, but shops close around 3 PM. It's closed Sunday.

ANTIQUES

You will find the best antiques shops located in the First District, many clustered close to the Dorotheum auction house, in the Dorotheergasse, Stallburggasse, Plankengasse, and Spiegelgasse. You'll also find interesting shops in the Josefstadt (Eighth) district, with prices considerably lower than those in the center of town. Wander up Florianigasse and back down Josefstädterstrasse, being sure not to overlook the narrow side streets.

D&S Antiquitäten (⊠ Dorotheerg. 12, ☎ 01/512–1011) specializes in old Viennese clocks. For Art Deco, look to **Galerie bei der Albertina** (⊠ Lobkowitzpl. 1, ☎ 01/513–1416). Look in at **Glasgalerie Kovacek** (⊠ Spiegelg. 12, ☎ 01/512–9954) to see a remarkable collection of glass paperweights and other glass objects. You'll find paintings and furniture in many shops in this area, including **Kunst Salon Kovacek** (⊠ Stallburgg. 2, ☎ 01/512–8358). **Peter Feldbacher** (⊠ Annag. 6, ☎ 01/512–2408) has items ranging from glass to ceramics to furniture.

Auctions

The **Dorotheum** (⊠ Dorotheerg. 17, ☎ 01/515–60–0) is a state institution dating from 1707, when Emperor Josef I determined that he didn't want his people being exploited by pawnbrokers. The place is intriguing, with goods ranging from furs to furniture auctioned almost daily. Information on how to bid is available in English. Some items are for immediate cash sale. Also check out **Palais Kinsky** (✉ Freyung 4, ☎ 01/532–4200) for paintings and antiques.

Flea Markets

Every Saturday (except holidays), rain or shine, from about 7:30 AM to 4 or 5, the **Flohmarkt** in back of the Naschmarkt, stretching along the Linke Wienzeile from the Kettenbrückengasse U4 subway station, offers a staggering collection of stuff ranging from serious antiques to plain junk. Haggle over prices. On Thursdays and Fridays from late spring to mid-fall, an outdoor combination arts-and-crafts, collectibles, and flea market takes place on **Am Hof.** On Saturday and Sunday in summer from about 10 to 6, an outdoor **art and antiques market** springs up along the Danube Canal, stretching from the Schwedenbrücke to beyond the Salztorbrücke. Lots of books are sold, some in English, plus generally better goods and collectibles than at the Saturday flea market. Bargain over prices.

Department Stores

The **Steffl** department store (✉ Kärntnerstr. 19) is moderately upscale without being overly expensive. The larger department stores are concentrated in Mariahilferstrasse.By far the best is **Peek & Cloppenburg** (✉ Mariahilferstr. 26–30), definitely upscale; outstanding gourmet shops and restaurants are in the basement. Farther up the street you will find slightly cheaper goods at **Gerngross** (✉ Mariahilferstr. and Kircheng.) and cheaper still at **Stafa** (✉ Mariahilferstr. 120).

Specialty Stores

BOOKS

Several good stores whose stock includes books in English are on the Graben and Kärntnerstrasse in the First District. The perfect place for maps and books on art and architecture (some in English) is **Georg Prachner** (✉ Kärtnerstr. 30, ☎ 01/512–8549). For more bookstores specializing in English-language books, *see* Contacts and Resources *in* Vienna A to Z, *below.*

CERAMICS AND PORCELAIN

Ceramics can be found at **Berger** (✉ Weihburgg. 17, ☎ 01/512–1434). Gmunden primitive country ceramics are at **Pawlata** (✉ Kärntnerstr. 14, ☎ 01/512–1764). More country ceramics can be found at **Plessgott** (✉ Kärntner Durchgang, ☎ 01/512–5824). Check out Viennese porcelain patterns at **Augarten** (✉ Graben/Stock-im-Eisen-Pl. 3, ☎ 01/512–1494–0), **Albin Denk** (✉ Graben 13, ☎ 01/512–4439), and **Rosenthal** (✉ Kärntnerstr. 16, ☎ 01/512–3994).

CRYSTAL AND GLASS

Select famous Vienna glassware at **Bakalowits** (✉ Spiegelg. 3, ☎ 01/512–6351–0). **Lobmeyr** (✉ Kärntnerstr. 26, ☎ 01/512–0508–0), another glassware vendor, also has a small museum of its creations upstairs; the firm supplied the crystal chandeliers for the Metropolitan Opera in New York City, a gift from Austria.

Exquisite Riedl crystal is available from **Albin Denk** (✉ Graben 13, ☎ 01/512–4439), **Berndorf** (✉ Wollzeile 12, ☎ 01/512–2944), and **Rasper & Söhne** (✉ Graben 15, ☎ 01/534–33–0).

GIFT ITEMS

Niederösterreichisches Heimatwerk (☞ Women's Clothing, *below*) has handmade folk objects and textiles.

Österreichische Werkstätten (✉ Kärntnerstr. 6, ☎ 01/512–2418) offers outstanding and unusual handmade handicrafts, gifts, and quality souvenirs ranging from jewelry to textiles.

Souvenir in der Hofburg (✉ Hofburgpassage 1 and 7, ☎ 01/533–5053) is another source of more traditional gift items.

110

Vienna Shopping

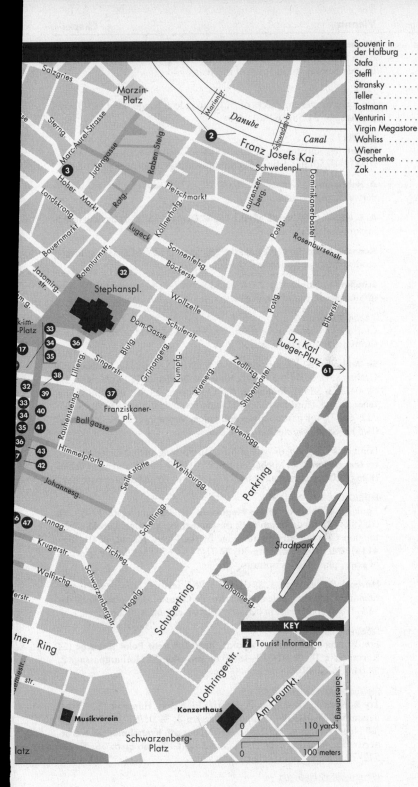

Wiener Geschenke (✉ Reitschulg. 4/Michaelerpl., ☎ 01/533–7078) has a nice selection of quality gift and traditional souvenir items and is open Sunday during part of the year.

JADE

Discover interesting pieces of Austrian jade at **Burgenland** (✉ Opernpassage, ☎ 01/587–6266).

JEWELRY

Haban (✉ Kärntnerstr. 2, ☎ 01/512–6730–0; ✉ Kärntnerstr. 17, ☎ 01/512–6750) has a fine selection of watches and jewelry.

A. Heldwein (✉ Graben 13, ☎ 01/512–5781) sells elegant jewelry, silverware, and watches.

A. E. Köchert (✉ Neuer Markt 15, ☎ 01/512–5828–0) has outstanding original creations.

Eleonora Kunz (✉ Neuer Markt 13, ☎ 01/512–7112) sells stunning modern pieces for men and women.

Schullin (✉ Kohlmarkt 7, ☎ 01/533–9007–0) has some of the most original work found anywhere.

MEN'S CLOTHING

Clothing in Vienna is far from cheap but is of good quality. The best shops are in the First District:

Sir Anthony (✉ Kärntnerstr. 21–23, ☎ 01/512–6835), **E. Braun** (✉ Graben 8, ☎ 01/512–5505–0), **House of Gentlemen** (✉ Kohlmarkt 12, ☎ 01/533–3258), **Malowan** (✉ Opernring 23, ☎ 01/587–6296), **Teller,** in the Third District (✉ Landstrasser Hauptstr. 88–90, ☎ 01/712–6397), for particularly good value, **Venturini** (✉ Spiegelg. 9, ☎ 01/512–8845) for custom-made shirts.

For men's *Trachten,* or typical Austrian clothing, including lederhosen, try **Loden-Plankl** (✉ Michaelerpl. 6, ☎ 01/533–8032), and go to **Collins Hüte** (✉ Opernpassage, ☎ 01/587–1305) to get the appropriate hat.

MUSIC

Look for CDs at the **Virgin Megastore** (✉ Mariahilferstr. 37–39, ☎ 01/588370), if you haven't got the same thing at home. **Carola** is best for pop CDs (✉ Albertinapassage by the Opera House, ☎ 01/586–4114). **EMI** (✉ Kärntnerstr. 30, ☎ 01/512–3675) has a wide selection of pops, plus classics upstairs.

Havlicek (✉ Herreng. 5, ☎ 01/533–1964) features classics and is particularly knowledgeable and helpful. **da Caruso** (✉ Operng. 4, ☎ 01/513–1326) specializes in classics, with an emphasis on opera.

NEEDLEWORK

For Vienna's famous petit point, head for **Petit Point Kovacec** (✉ Kärntnerstr. 16, ☎ 01/512–4886) or **Stransky** (✉ Hofburgpassage 2, ☎ 01/533–6098).

SHOES AND LEATHER GOODS

Try **R. Horn** (✉ Bränerstr. 7, ☎ 01/513–8294), **Humanic** (✉ Kärntnerstr. 51, ☎ 01/512–5892; ✉ Singerstr. 2, ☎ 01/512–9101), **Nigst** (✉ Neuer Markt 4, ☎ 01/512–4303), **Popp & Kretschmer** (✉ Kärntnerstr. 51, ☎ 01/512–6421–0), and **Zak** (✉ Kärntnerstr. 36, ☎ 01/512–7257).

WOMEN'S CLOTHING

The couturier to Vienna is **Adlmüller** (✉ Kärntnerstr. 41, ☎ 01/512–6650–0). Check also **Flamm** (✉ Neuer Markt 12, ☎ 01/512–2889), E. Braun, or Malowan (☞ Men's Clothing, *above*). You'll find modern young styling at **Maldone** (✉ Kärntnerstr. 4, ☎ 01/512–2761; ✉ Graben 29, ☎ 01/533–6091; ✉ Hoher Markt 8, ☎ 01/533–2555).

Check out the selection of dirndls and women's *Trachten,* the typical Austrian costume with white blouse, print skirt, and apron, at **Lanz** (✉ Kärntnerstr. 10, ☎ 01/512–2456), **Loden-Plankl** (☞ Men's Clothing, *above*), **Niederösterreichisches Heimatwerk** (✉ Herreng. 6, ☎ 01/533–3495), **Resi Hammerer** (✉ Kärntnerstr. 29–31, ☎ 01/512–6952), and **Tostmann** (✉ Schotteng. 3a, ☎ 01/533–5331, ℻ 01/533–5331–31).

VIENNA A TO Z

Arriving and Departing

By Boat

If you arrive in Vienna via the Danube, the **Blue Danube Steamship Company/DDSG** will leave you at Praterlände near Mexikoplatz (✉ Friedrichstr. 7, ☎ 01/588–800). The Praterlände stop is a two-block taxi ride or hike from the Vorgartenstrasse U1/subway station, or you can take a taxi directly into town.

By Bus

International long-distance bus service (Bratislava, Brno) and most postal and railroad buses arrive at the **Wien Mitte** central bus station (✉ Landstrasser Hauptstr. 1b, ☎ 01/711–07–3850 or 01/711–01), across from the Hilton Hotel on the Stadtpark.

By Car

Vienna is 300 km (187 mi) east of Salzburg, 200 km (125 mi) north of Graz. Main routes leading into the city are the A1 Westautobahn from Germany, Salzburg, and Linz and the A2 Südautobahn from Graz and points south.

On highways from points south or west or from the airport, ZENTRUM signs clearly mark the route to the center of Vienna. From there, however, finding your way to your hotel can be no mean trick, for traffic planners have installed a devious scheme prohibiting through traffic in the city core (the First District) and scooting cars out again via a network of exasperating one-way streets. In the city itself a car is a burden, though very useful for trips outside town.

By Plane

Vienna's airport (☎ 01/7007–0 for flight information) is at Schwechat, about 19 km (12 mi) southeast of the city. **Austrian Airlines** (☎ 01/1789), and **Lauda Air** (☎ 01/7000–777) fly into Schwechat from North America.

BETWEEN THE AIRPORT AND CITY CENTER

Buses leave the airport frequently for the **city air terminal** (✉ Am Stadtpark, ☎ 01/5800–33369, or 01/2300), by the Hilton. The cheapest way into town is the S7 **train** (called the *Schnellbahn*), which shuttles every half hour between the airport and the Landstrasse/Wien–Mitte (city center) and Wien–Nord (north Vienna) stations; the fare is AS38 and it takes about 35 minutes. Follow the picture signs of a train to the basement of the airport. Your ticket is also good for an immediate transfer to your destination within the city on the streetcar, bus, or U-Bahn. **Buses** also run every hour (every half hour on weekends and holidays Apr.–Sept.) from the airport to the Westbahnhof (West Train Station) and the Südbahnhof (South Train Station). Be sure you get on the right bus! The one-way fare for all buses is AS70. A **taxi** from the airport to downtown Vienna costs about AS350–AS500; agree on a price in advance. Cabs (legally) do not meter this drive, as airport fares are more or less fixed (legally again) at about double the meter fare. The cheapest cab service to the airport is **C+K Airport Service** (☎ 01/1731, FAX 01/689–6969), charging a set price of AS270, plus usually a AS30 tip. C+K will also meet your plane at no extra charge if you let them know your flight information in advance.

By Train

Trains from Germany, Switzerland, and western Austria arrive at the **Westbahnhof** (West Station), on Europaplatz, where Mariahilferstrasse crosses the Gürtel. If you're coming from Italy or Hungary, you'll generally arrive at the **Südbahnhof** (South Station, ✉ Wiedner Gürtel 1). The current stations for trains to and from Prague and Warsaw are **Wien Nord** (North Station, ✉ Praterstern) and **Franz-Josef Bahnhof** (✉ Julius-Tandler-Pl.). **Central train information** (☎ 01/1717) will have details and taped schedule information (in German) for trains to and from the west (☎ 01/1552) or for trains to and from the south (☎ 01/1553).

Getting Around

Vienna is divided into 23 numbered districts. Taxi drivers may need to know which district you seek, as well as the street address. The district number is coded into the postal code with the second and third digits; thus A–1010 (the "01") is the First District, A–1030 is the Third, A–1110 is the 11th, and so on. Some sources and maps still give the district numbers, either in Roman or Arabic numerals, as Vienna X or Vienna 10.

Vienna is a city to tackle on foot. With the exception of the Schönbrunn and Belvedere palaces and the Prater amusement park, most sights are concentrated in the center, the First District (A–1010), much of which is a pedestrian zone anyway.

By Bus and Streetcar

Vienna's public transportation system is fast, clean, safe, and easy to use. Get public transport maps at a tourist office or at the transport-information offices (*Wiener Verkehrsbetriebe*), underground at Karlsplatz, Stephansplatz, and Praterstern. You can transfer on the same ticket between subway, streetcar, bus, and long stretches of the fast suburban railway, *Schnellbahn* (*S-Bahn*). Buy single tickets for AS22 from dispensers on the streetcar or bus; you'll need exact change. The ticket machines at subway stations (*VOR-Fahrkarten*) give change and dispense 24-hour, 72-hour, and eight-day tickets, as well as single tickets separately and in blocks of two and five. At *Tabak-Trafik* (cigarette shops/newsstands) or the underground *Wiener Verkehrsbetriebe* offices you can get a block of five tickets for AS95, each ticket good for one uninterrupted trip in more or less the same general direction with unlimited transfers. Or you can get a three-day ticket for AS150, good on all lines for 72 hours from the time you validate the ticket; there's also a 24-hour ticket for AS60. If you're staying longer, get an eight-day ticket (AS300), which can be used on eight separate days or by any number of persons (up to eight) at any one time. Prices may go up in 2001. Children under 6 travel free on Vienna's public transport system; children under 15 travel free on Sundays, public holidays, and during Vienna school holidays. Public transportation is on the honor system, but if you're caught without a punched ticket, the fine is AS560, payable immediately. **Tabak-Trafik Almassy** (✉ Stephanspl. 4, to the right behind cathedral, ☎ 01/512–5909) is open every day from 8 AM to 7 PM and has tickets as well as film and other items.

Ask at tourist offices or your hotel about a **Vienna-Card**; costing AS210, the card combines 72 hours' use of public transportation and discounts at certain museums and shops.

The first streetcars run from about 5:15 AM. From then on, service (barring gridlock on the streets) is regular and reliable, and most lines operate until about midnight. Where streetcars don't run, buses do; route maps and schedules are posted at each bus or subway stop.

Should you miss the last streetcar or bus, special night buses with an N designation operate at half-hour intervals over several key routes; the starting (and transfer) points are the Opera House and Schwedenplatz. The night-owl buses take a special fare of AS25, tickets available on the bus; normal tickets, your 72-hour, and Vienna-Card are not valid.

Within the heart of the city, bus lines 1A, 2A, and 3A are useful crosstown routes. These carry a reduced fare of AS8.50 per trip if you have bought the *Kurzstrecke* ticket (AS38), good for four trips or up to four people on one trip (with no transfer). The *Kurzstrecke* tickets are also valid for two stops on the subway or shorter distances on the streetcar lines.

By Car
Traffic congestion within Vienna has gotten out of hand, and driving to in-town destinations generally takes longer than public transportation. City planners' solutions have been to make driving as difficult as possible, with one-way streets and other tricks, and a car in town is far more of a burden than a pleasure. Drivers not familiar with the city literally need a navigator. The entire First and Sixth through Ninth districts are limited-parking zones and require that a *Parkschein,* a paid-parking chit available at most newsstands and tobacconists, be displayed on the dash during the day. Parkscheine cost AS6 for 30 minutes, AS12 for 1 hour, and AS18 for 90 minutes. You can park 10 minutes free of charge, but you must get a "gratis" sticker to put in your windshield. You can also park free in the First District on Saturday and Sunday, but not overnight. Overnight street parking in the First and Sixth through Ninth districts is restricted to residents with special permits; all other cars are subject to expensive ticketing or even towing, so in these districts be sure you have off-street garage parking.

By Horse Cab
A *Fiaker,* or horse cab, will trot you around to whatever destination you specify, but this is an expensive way to see the city. A short tour of the inner city takes about 20 minutes and costs AS500; a longer one including the Ringstrasse takes about 40 minutes and costs AS800, for the whole Fiaker. The carriages accommodate four (five if someone sits next to the coachman). Starting points are Heldenplatz in front of the Hofburg, Stephansplatz beside the cathedral, and across from the Albertina, all in the First District. For longer trips, or any variation of the regular route, agree on the price first.

By Subway
Five subway (*U-Bahn*) lines, whose stations are prominently marked with blue *U* signs, crisscross the city. Karlsplatz and Stephansplatz are the main transfer points between lines. The last subway (U4) runs at about 12:30 AM.

By Taxi
Taxis in Vienna are relatively inexpensive. The initial charge is AS26 for as many as four people daytime, AS27 nighttime, weekends, and holidays. A small extra charge is added for radio cabs ordered by phone and for each piece of luggage that must go into the trunk, and a charge is added for waiting beyond a reasonable limit. It's customary to round up the fare to cover the tip. Service is usually prompt, but when you hit rush hour, the weather is bad, or you need to keep to an exact schedule, call ahead and order a taxi for a specific time. If

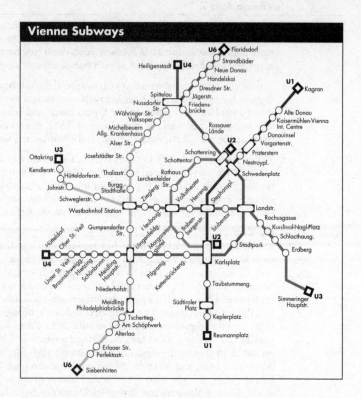

your destination is the airport, ask for a reduced-rate taxi. For the cheapest taxi to the airport, *see* Between the Airport and City Center, *above*.

For a chauffeured limousine call **Göth** (☎ 01/713–7196), **Mazur** (☎ 01/604–2233), or **Peter Urban** (☎ 01/713–5255).

Contacts and Resources

Car Rentals

Rental cars can be arranged at the airport or in town. Major firms include:

Avis (✉ Airport, ☎ 01/7007–32700; ✉ Opernring 5, ☎ 01/587–6241), **Budget** (✉ Airport, ☎ 01/7007–32711; ✉ Hilton Hotel, Am Stadtpark, ☎ 01/714–6565–0), **Europcar** (✉ Airport, ☎ 01/7007–33316; ✉ Erdberg Park & Ride, ☎ 01/799–6176), **Hertz** (✉ Kärntner Ring 17, ☎ 01/512–8677).

Buchbinder (✉ Schlachthausg. 38, ☎ 01/717–50–0) is a local firm with particularly favorable rates and clean cars.

Doctors and Dentists

If you need a doctor and speak no German, ask your hotel, or in an emergency, phone your consulate.

Embassies

Canadian Embassy (✉ Laurenzerberg 2, on the 3rd floor of Hauptpost building complex, ☎ 01/531–38–01). **U.K. Embassy and Consulate** (✉ Jauresg. 10, ☎ 01/71613–5151). **U.S. Embassy** (✉ Boltzmanng. 16, ☎ 01/313–39). **U.S. Consulate** (✉ Gartenbaupromenade, Parkring 12A, Marriott building, ☎ 01/313–39).

Emergencies

The emergency numbers are ☎ 133 for the **police,** ☎ 144 for an **ambulance,** and ☎ 122 for the **fire department.**

English-Language Bookstores and Video Rentals

The leading sources of books in English are **Big Ben Bookstore** (✉ Serviteng. 4a, ☎ 01/319–6412), **British Bookstore** (✉ Weihburgg. 24–26, ☎ 01/512–1945–0), and **Shakespeare & Co.** (✉ Sterng. 2, ☎ 01/535–5053). **Alphaville** (✉ Schleifmühlg. 5, ☎ 01/585–1966) rents videotapes and DVDs.

Guided Tours

EXCURSIONS

All three bus tour operators (☞ Orientation Tours, *below*) offer short trips outside of the city. Check their offerings and compare packages and prices to be sure you get what you want. Your hotel will have brochures.

ORIENTATION TOURS

When you're pressed for time, a good way to see the highlights of Vienna is via a sightseeing bus tour, which gives you a once-over-lightly of the heart of the city and allows a closer look at Schönbrunn and Belvedere palaces. You can cover almost the same territory on your own by taking either Streetcar 1 or 2 around the Ring and then walking through the heart of the city (☞ Self-Guided Tours, *below*). For tours, contact one of the following: **Cityrama Sightseeing** (✉ Börseg. 1, ☎ 01/534–13–12, ℻ 01/534–13–16) or **Vienna Sightseeing Tours** (✉ Stelzhammerg. 4/11, ☎ 01/712–4683-0, ℻ 01/714–1141).

Vienna Sightseeing Tours and CityTouring Vienna run 1¼-hour "get acquainted" tours daily. Both have tours of about three hours (AS400), including brief visits to Schönbrunn and Belvedere palace grounds. If you want to see the Schönbrunn interior, you'll have to pay a separate entrance fee, with some operators offering a 30-minute or one-hour stop, or in some cases leaving you to find your way back to the center of town yourself. All three firms offer a number of other tours as well (your hotel will have detailed programs) and provide hotel pickup for most tours.

For a wide range of interesting guided tours, including informative walks through the old Jewish Quarter and a *Third Man* tour from the classic film starring Orson Welles, contact **Vienna Walks and Talks** (✉ Wiethestr. 69/1, A–1220, ☎ 01/774–8901, ℻ 01/774–8933).

STREETCAR TOURS

From early May through September, a 1929 vintage streetcar leaves each Saturday at 11:30 AM and 2 PM and Sunday, Monday, and holidays at 9:30 and 11:30 AM and 2 PM from the Otto Wagner Pavilion at Karlsplatz for a guided tour. For AS200 (AS180 if you have the Vienna-Card), you'll go around the Ring, out past the big Ferris wheel in the Prater and past Schönbrunn and Belvedere palaces in the course of the two-hour trip. Prices may go up in 2001. The old-timer trips are popular, so get tickets in advance at the **transport-information office** underground at Karlsplatz, weekdays 7 AM–6 PM, weekends and holidays 8:30–4 (☎ 01/7909–44026).

PERSONAL GUIDES

Guided walking tours (in English) are a great way to see the city highlights. Tour topics range from "Unknown Underground Vienna" to "1,000 Years of Jewish Tradition" and "Vienna Around Sigmund Freud." Tours take about 1½ hours, are held in any weather provided at least three people turn up, and cost AS150–AS200, plus any entry fees. No reservations are needed. Get a list of the guided-tour possibilities at the **city information office** (✉ Kärntnerstr. 38). Ask for the monthly brochure "Walks in Vienna," which details the tours, days, times, and starting points. You can also arrange to have your own privately guided tour for AS1,375 for a half day.

SELF-GUIDED TOURS

Get a copy of "Vienna Downtown Walking Tours" by Henriette Mandl from any bookshop. The six tours take you through the highlights of central Vienna with excellent commentary and some entertaining anecdotes that most of your Viennese acquaintances won't know. The booklet "Vienna from A–Z" (in English, AS70; available at bookshops and city information offices) explains the numbered plaques attached to all major buildings.

Late-Night Pharmacies

In each area of the city one pharmacy stays open 24 hours; if a pharmacy is closed, a sign on the door will tell you the address of the nearest one that is open. Call 01/1550 for names and addresses (in German) of the pharmacies open that night.

Lost and Found

If you've lost something valuable, check with the police at the **Fundangelegenheiten** (Lost and Found; ✉ Wasag. 22, ☎ 01/580–0356–56). If your loss occurred on a train coming in from Salzburg, check the **Reisegepäck** (☎ 01/5800–31061) at the Westbahnhof, from Villach or the south, check the **Reisegepäck** (☎ 01/5800–31051) at the Südbahnhof. Losses on the subway system or streetcars can be checked by calling the **Fundstelle U-Bahn** (☎ 01/7909–43500).

Ticket Agencies

American Express (✉ Kärntnerstr. 21–23, 1010, ☎ 01/515–40–0, FAX 01/515–40–777), **Cosmos** (✉ Kärntner Ring 17, A–1010, ☎ 01/515–33–0, FAX 01/513–4147), or **Vienna Ticket Service/Cityrama** (✉ Börseg. 1, A–1010, ☎ 01/534170, FAX 01/534–1726).

Travel Agencies

American Express (✉ Kärntnerstr. 21–23, ☎ 01/515–40–0, FAX 01/515–40–70), **Carlson/Wagonlit** (✉ Millennium Tower 94/Handelskai, A–1200, ☎ 01/240600, FAX 01/24060–65), **Cosmos** (✉ Kärntner Ring 15, ☎ 01/515–33–0, FAX 01/513–4147), and **Österreichisches Verkehrsbüro** (✉ Friedrichstr. 7, opposite the Secession Building, ☎ 01/588–00–0, FAX 01/588–000–280).

Visitor Information

The main center for information (walk-ins only) is the **Vienna City Tourist Office** (✉ Am Albertinapl. 1, A–1010, ☎ 01/211–13–222, FAX 01/216–84–92), open daily 9–7 and centrally located between the Hofburg and Kärntnerstrasse.

If you need a room, go to **Information-Zimmernachweis,** operated by the Verkehrsbüro in the Westbahnhof (☎ 01/892–3392) and in the Südbahnhof (☎ 01/505–3132). At the airport, the **information and room-reservation office** in the arrivals hall is open daily 8:30 AM–9 PM.

If you're driving into Vienna, get information or book rooms at **Tourist Information** at the end of the Westautobahn (exit Autobahnausfahrt Wien-West) at **Wientalstrasse/Auhof Raststätte** (☎ 01/979–1271), or from April to September at the end of the Südautobahn at Triesterstrasse 149 (☎ 01/616–0071 or 01/616–0070).

2 SIDE TRIPS FROM VIENNA

FROM THE VIENNA WOODS TO THE WEINVIERTEL

Is it the sun or the soil? The dreamy castle-capped peaks? Whatever the lure, the idyllic regions outside Vienna have always offered perfectly pastoral escapes for the Viennese. Rich in scenic splendor, this countryside is also saturated with musical history: here Beethoven was inspired to write his *Pastoral* Symphony, Johann Strauss set the Vienna Woods to music, and a glass of intoxicating Retzer Wein urged Richard Strauss to compose the "Rosenkavalier Waltz." From the elegant spa of Baden to mysterious Mayerling, this region is a day-tripper's delight.

Updated by
Bonnie Dodson

T HE VIENNESE ARE UNDENIABLY LUCKY. Few populaces enjoy such glorious—and easily accessible—options for day-tripping. Stressed-out city residents in droves tie their bicycles to the roof racks of their Mercedes on Saturdays and Sundays; vacationers in Vienna can share in the natives' obvious pleasure in the city's environs any day of the week. For many the first destination is, of course, the Wienerwald, the deservedly fabled Vienna Woods—a large range of rolling, densely wooded hills extending from Vienna's doorstep to the outposts of the Alps in the south (and not a natural park or forest, as you think from listening to Strauss or the tourist blurbs). This region is crisscrossed by country roads and hiking paths, dotted with forest lodges and inns, and solidifies every now and then into quaint little villages and market towns.

In addition to such natural pleasures, the regions outside of Vienna offer something for everyone. History and mystery? Turning south to May-erling leads you to the site where in 1889 the successor to the Austrian throne presumably took his own life after shooting his secret love—a mystery still unresolved. For scenic beauty, you can opt to head north-east, into wonderfully encompassing woods and gently rolling hills sprinkled with elegant summer palaces. To the north, you can have one long, liquid, adventure by exploring the Weinstrasse (Wine Road), along which vast expanses of vineyard produce excellent, mainly white wines. Here, you'll find Gumpoldskirchen, one of Austria's most famous wine-producing villages and the home of one of Europe's pleasantest white wines. Vintners' houses line its main street, with gates leading into the vine-covered courtyard-gardens where the Heuriger (wine of the last vintage) is served at wooden tables, sometimes to the tune of merry or not-so-merry melodies played by an accordionist. Another choice is to follow the trail of the defensive castles that protected the land from invaders from the north, or you can even trace the early days of Masonic lore in Austria—both Haydn and Mozart were members of what was then a secret and forbidden brotherhood. For a contrast, head to the elegant spa town of Baden, where Beethoven passed 15 summers and composed large sections of the Ninth Symphony.

These subregions of Lower Austria (which derives its name from the fact that for centuries it was the "lower"—in the sense of the Danube's course—part of the archduchy of Austria) are simple, mainly agricultural, country areas. People live close to the earth, and on any sunny weekend from March through October you'll find whole families out working the fields. This isn't to suggest that fun is forgotten; just as often, you'll stumble across a dressy parade with the local brass band done up in lederhosen and feathered hats. Sundays here are still generally days of rest, with many families venturing to morning mass, then retiring to the local Gasthaus to discuss weather and politics. Whatever destination you choose in this area, however, the lakes are waiting, the biking paths are open, and the lovely countryside cafés beckon.

Pleasures and Pastimes

Bicycling
The Carnuntum region and the southeast corner of the Weinviertel, a region known as the Marchfeld, offer outstanding cycling, with a number of marked routes. Cycle paths follow the southern bank of the Danube past Carnuntum (Petronell) through Bad Deutsch–Altenburg to Hainburg, and other parts of the region are flat enough to offer fine cycling without exertion. In the Marchfeld, another marked route close to the March river includes the Baroque castles at Marchegg and Schlosshof.

Castles

To take advantage of the fact that the Danube forms a natural line of defense, barons and bailiffs decided centuries ago to fortify bluffs along the river. Castles were the best answer, and a wonderful string of these more or less follows the course of the Thaya river, starting in Weitra and Heidenreichstein close to the Czech border, then eastward to Raabs, Riegersburg, and Hardegg. The 17th- and 18th-century structures vary from turreted hilltop fortresses to more elegant moated bastions, but all were part of a chain against invaders. Several are basically intact, others are restored, and all are impressive relics well worth visiting. Castle concerts have become popular during summer months, when the buildings are open for tours as well.

Dining

With very few exceptions, food in this region, while influenced by Viennese cuisine, is simple. The basics are available in abundance: roast meats, customary schnitzel variations, game in season, fresh vegetables, and standard desserts such as *Palatschinken* (crepes filled with jam or with nuts topped with chocolate sauce). Imaginative cooking is rare; this is not tourist country, and the local population demands little beyond reasonable quality and quantity.

Wines are equally taken for granted, although four of the areas included here are designated as separate wine regions—the Weinviertel, or wine quarter to the north of Vienna; the Kamptal, which divides the Weinviertel from the Waldviertel to the west; the Carnuntum–Petronell region, just below the Danube to the southeast of Vienna; and the Thermen region, south and southwest of the capital. The specialties are mainly white wines, with the standard types, Grüner Veltliner and Rieslings and increasingly Weissburgunder, predominating. Reds are coming more into favor, with lighter reds such as Zweigelt and even rosés to be found in the northern areas, the heavier reds such as Blaufränkisch and St. Laurent and the spicier Gewürztraminer and Müller–Thurgau whites in the south. Most of the vintners work small holdings, so output is limited. The wine market in Poysdorf, center of one of Austria's largest wine regions, offers an opportunity to sample a wide choice of area wares.

Restaurant prices include taxes and a service charge, but it is customary to give the waiter an additional tip of 5%, usually rounding up the bill to the nearest AS5 or AS10.

CATEGORY	COST*
$$$$	over AS350 (€25)
$$$	AS200–AS350 (€14–€25)
$$	AS150–AS200 (€11–€13)
$	under AS150 (€11)

per person for a typical two-course meal, including a small glass of wine or beer but excluding a tip

Hiking and Walking

The celebrated Vienna Woods to the west and southwest of Vienna are crisscrossed by hundreds of easy hiking paths, numbered, color-coded, and marked for destinations. Excellent hiking maps available from most bookstores will give ideas and routes. Paths will take you through woods, past meadows and vineyards, alongside streams and rivers, with an occasional tavern hidden away deep in the woods where you can stop for refreshment or a cold snack. Deer, wild boar, and a host of small animals inhabit these preserves. The area is protected, and development is highly restricted, making it ideal for pleasurable hiking.

Lodging

Accommodations in the countryside around Vienna are pretty basic. This is underdeveloped tourist territory, prime turf for the more adventuresome, with rooms frequently to be found as an adjunct to the local *Gasthaus*. Nearly all are family-run; the younger members will speak at least some school English. You'll probably have to carry your own bags, and elevators to upper floors are scarce. Booking ahead is a good idea, as most places have relatively few rooms, particularly rooms with full bath. Window screens are almost unknown in Austria, as bugs are few, but in farming areas, both flies and occasionally mosquitoes can be a nuisance in the warmer seasons. Since you'll want windows open at night, take along a can of bug spray and you'll sleep more peacefully. The standard country bed covering is a down-filled feather bed, so if you're allergic to feathers or want more warmth, ask for blankets. Even the simpler hotels will be spotless, and almost without exception you'll be offered a tasty breakfast included in the room price, which can range from fresh rolls with cold cuts and cheese and tea or coffee to an ample buffet spread with cereals and fruit as well. Hotel room rates usually include breakfast—although check to be sure.

CATEGORY	COST*
$$$$	over AS1,500 (€110)
$$$	AS1,200–AS1,500 (€87–€110)
$$	AS800–AS1,200 (€58–€86)
$	under AS800 (€58)

All prices are for a standard double room for two, including taxes and service charge.

🐾 *following the text of a review is your signal that the property has a Web site, where you will find details and, usually, images; for a link, visit www.fodors.com/urls.*

Exploring Vienna's Environs

The region surrounding Vienna divides itself logically into four areas. The Vienna Woods, that huge, unspoiled belt of forest green stretching westward south of the Danube, was celebrated by composers Beethoven, Schubert, and Strauss and remains a favorite of the Viennese today. The towns to the south—Mödling, Baden, and Bad Vöslau—mark the east end of the rolling, wooded hills. There the fertile Vienna Basin begins, sweeping east to the low, wooded Leitha Mountains, which shelter the Puszta Plain extending on into Hungary. The northern part of the basin widens into the Danube Valley, forming the Carnuntum agricultural and wine region, with Slovakia to the east.

North of the Danube, two great regions are divided by the Kamp River, with the wooded Waldviertel (or Forest District) to the northwest adjoining the Czech Republic, and the rolling hills of the agricultural Weinviertel (or Wine District) to the northeast, bordering on the Czech Republic and on Slovakia, where the March River flows into the Danube.

Great Itineraries

The four districts surrounding Vienna are compact, and each can be explored in a day or two. To pursue the lives of the famous composers Schubert and Beethoven, take the route to the south, to Mödling and Baden; for Haydn's birthplace, go to the east to Rohrau, then possibly on to Eisenstadt (☞ Chapter 3). To tour a chain of defensive castles, head for the forested Waldviertel. To enjoy rolling hills and vast expanses of vineyards and to sample their output, seek out the Weinviertel to the north.

Numbers in the text correspond to numbers in the margin and on the Baden and Environs and the Waldviertel and Weinviertel maps.

South of the Danube

IF YOU HAVE 1 DAY

To get a taste of the fringes of the Vienna Woods to the capital's south and west, head for **Mödling** ② and **Baden** ⑦. Both are smaller communities with unspoiled 17th-century town centers on a scale easy to assimilate. The route to Baden runs through the band of rolling wooded hills that mark the eastern edge of the Vienna Woods. The hills are skirted by vineyards forming a "wine belt," which also follows the valleys south of Vienna.

IF YOU HAVE 3 DAYS

With more time, you might spend two days in the Vienna Woods area, starting off with two particularly picturesque towns, **Perchtoldsdorf** ① and **Mödling** ②—with perhaps a look at the grand garden of **Schloss Laxenburg** ③—then following the scenic *Weinstrasse* (Wine Road) through the lush vineyard country to the noted wine-producing village of **Gumpoldskirchen** ⑥. Overnight in ☷ **Baden** ⑦; then spend your second day taking in the sights of the fashionable spa town, including its grand Kurpark and Casino. Set out in the afternoon for mysterious ☷ **Mayerling** ⑧. After an evocative dawn and morning there, head for the great abbey at **Heiligenkreuz** ⑨, continuing on to Vienna.

North of the Danube

IF YOU HAVE 1 DAY

The decision will have to be woods or wine, if you're tight on time. If woods, then head for **Waidhofen an der Thaya** ⑳, returning via picturesque **Raabs an der Thaya** ㉑, **Geras** ㉔, and **Horn** ⑪. If wine, start at the bustling shipbuilding city of Korneuburg, then head northward to the border town of **Laa an der Thaya** ㉘ and return via **Poysdorf** ㉙, famous as a wine center.

IF YOU HAVE 3 DAYS

Spend a leisurely two days tracking the castles of the Waldviertel, starting at **Ottenstein** ⑬; moving on to **Zwettl** ⑭, with its magnificent abbey; overnighting at the noted castle-hotel-Masonic museum in ☷ **Rosenau** ⑮; and continuing on to **Weitra** ⑯, with its painted facades, for the start of the defensive castles route. The next mighty castle is at **Heidenreichstein** ⑲; follow the castle route with an overnight in ☷ **Raabs an der Thaya** ㉑ and proceed onward to **Schloss Riegersburg** ㉒ and **Burg Hardegg** ㉓, overlooking the river forming the border with the Czech Republic. A stop in the ancient city of **Retz** ㉗ will give you a taste of the wine country; to end your excursion, head on to **Laa an der Thaya** ㉘ and **Poysdorf** ㉙.

When to Tour Vienna's Environs

Most of the regions around Vienna are best seen in the temperate seasons between mid-March and mid-November. The Waldviertel, however, with its vast stands of great forest, offers picture-book scenery throughout the year. The combination of oaks and evergreens offers a color spectrum ranging from intense early spring green, through the deep green of summer, and into traces of autumn foliage, particularly in the Kamp River valley; in winter, occasional spectacular displays of hoarfrost and snowswept vistas turn the region into a glittering three-dimensional Christmas card.

ON THE ROAD TO BADEN AND MAYERLING

This short, though history-rich tour takes you to Baden through the legendary band of rolling wooded hills of the Vienna Woods that bor-

Baden and Environs

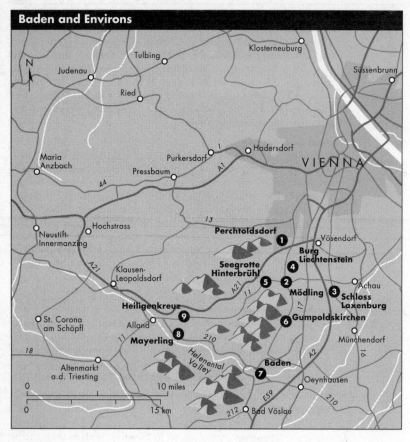

der Vienna on the west. The hills are skirted by vineyards forming a "wine belt," which also follows the valleys south of Vienna. You can visit this area easily in a day's outing, either by car or by public transportation, or you can spend the night in Baden, Mödling, or Alland for a more leisurely tour, visiting Mayerling, Heiligenkreuz, and a few other sights in the area.

Perchtoldsdorf

❶ *12 km (7½ mi) southwest of Vienna center.*

Just over the Vienna city line to the southwest lies Perchtoldsdorf, a charmingly picturesque market town with many wine taverns, a 13th-century Gothic parish church, and the symbol of the town—an imposing stone tower completed in 1511, once forming a piece of the town's defense wall. Familiarly known as Pedersdorf, the town is a favorite excursion spot for the Viennese, who come mainly for the good local wines. Wander around the compact town square to admire the Renaissance houses, some with arcaded courtyards. The Pestsäule (Plague Column) in the center of the square, which gives thanks for rescue from the dread 16th-century plague, was created by the famous Baroque architect Fischer von Erlach and is similar to the Plague Column that adorns the Graben in Vienna (☞ Vienna's Shop Window: From Michaelerplatz to the Graben *in* Chapter 1). The most recent version of *The Three*

Musketeers, starring Chris O'Donnell and Charlie Sheen, was partly filmed here within the old defense walls. Without a car, you can reach Perchtoldsdorf from Vienna by taking the S-Bahn, or train, from the Westbahnbof, to Liesing, and then a short cab ride to the town.

Dining

$$$$ ✕ **Jahreszeiten.** This elegant, formal yet relaxed restaurant is in the capable hands of Günter Winter, whose reputation as a top chef continues to grow. The menu reflects international cuisine with an Austrian flair. You might be offered game and spring lamb in season, or try any of the fish offerings, perhaps sweet-sour shrimp on saffron rice. Finish with *Topfensouffle,* a delicately light cheesecake concoction. Beyond the kitchen, the atmosphere, like the tables, is set to perfection, and the menu is supplemented by wines from an outstanding cellar, international as well as local. ⊠ *Hochstr. 17,* ☎ *01/865–3129. Reservations essential. AE, DC, MC, V. Closed Mon., Easter wk, and late July–early Aug. No lunch Sat. or dinner Sun.*

Mödling

2 *20 km (12½ mi) southwest of Vienna.*

Founded in the 10th century, Mödling has a delightful town center, now a pedestrian zone. Here you can admire centuries-old buildings, most one- or two-story, which give the town an intimate feeling. Composers Beethoven and Schubert appreciated this in the early 1800s; Mödling was one of Beethoven's favored residences outside of Vienna. Note the domineering **St. Othmar Gothic parish church** on a hill overlooking the town proper, a Romanesque 12th-century charnel house (where the bones of the dead were kept), and the town hall, which has a Renaissance loggia. Later eras added Art Nouveau, which mixes happily with the several 16th- and 17th-century buildings.

3 A couple of miles east of Mödling is **Schloss Laxenburg,** a complex consisting of a large Baroque Neues Schloss (New Castle), a small 14th-century Altes Schloss (Old Castle), and an early 19th-century neo-Gothic castle set into the sizable lake. The large park is full of birds and small game, such as roe deer and hare, and is decorated with statues, cascades, imitation temples, and other follies. The park and grounds are a favorite with the Viennese for Sunday outings. The Altes Schloss was built in 1381 by Duke Albrecht III as his summer residence, and several Habsburg emperors spent summers in the Neues Schloss, which now houses the International Institute of Applied Systems Analysis. Opposite is the large Baroque convent of the Charitable Sisters. The castle is currently occupied by a research institute and is generally not open to the public, but the gardens are open daily. ⊠ *Schlosspl. 1,* ☎ *02236/712–26–0.* ⌧ *Garden AS15, boat to castle AS5, tour AS45.* ☉ *Gardens daily 10–5; tours at 11, 2, and 3.*

4 A couple of miles east of Mödling is **Burg Liechtenstein,** an imposing medieval castle perched formidably on a crag overlooking the Vienna Woods. The pale stone walls and turrets have withstood marauding armies and the elements for more than 800 years, but the interior has been largely restored and includes a squires' hall, kitchen, bedchambers, a chapel, and even a medieval toilet. Not to be missed is the Tower Room, with its 13th-century red Italian marble fireplace and carved wooden spiral staircase. The Tower Room was the last refuge in case of an attack, and you can see where boiling water and refuse were poured onto the invaders. In summer, concerts are held in the courtyard. ⊠ *Maria Enzersdorf,* ☎ *02236/44294.* ⌧ *AS60.* ☉ *Apr.–Oct., Tues.–Sun. 9:30–5.*

⟲ ❺ West of Mödling on Route 11 is the **Seegrotte Hinterbrühl,** a fascinating but now somewhat commercialized underground sea, created
years ago when a mine filled up with water. You can take a 45-minute
motorboat trip and look at the reflections through the arched caverns
of the mine. Some of the recent film *The Three Musketeers,* starring
Charlie Sheen and Chris O'Donnell, was filmed here. ⊠ *Grutschg. 2,
Hinterbrühl,* ☎ *02236/26364.* ⌑ *AS55.* ⊙ *Apr.–Oct., daily 9–5;
Nov.–Mar., daily 9–3:30.*

Dining

$$$ ✕ **Hotel-Restaurant Höldrichsmühle.** Höldrichsmühle, where a mill
has turned since the 12th century, is now a famed 200-year-old coun-
try inn. Legend holds that the linden tree and the well found here in-
spired composer Franz Schubert to one of his better-known songs. Stop
at this traditional restaurant for fish, game, or various wild mushroom
dishes in season. ⊠ *Gaadnerstr. 34,* ☎ *02236/26274–0. No credit cards.*

Gumpoldskirchen

❻ *4 km (2½ mi) west of Mödling.*

From Mödling, follow the scenic Weinstrasse (an unnumbered road to
the west of the rail line) through the lush vineyard country to the fa-
mous wine-producing village of Gumpoldskirchen. This tiny village on
the eastern slopes of the last Alpine rocks has lived for wine for two
thousand years, and its white wines enjoy a fame that is widespread.
At one stage, there was more Gumpoldskirchner on the world mar-
kets than the village could ever have produced—a situation reminis-
cent of the medieval glut of pieces of the True Cross. **Vintners' houses**
line the main street, many of them with the typical large wooden gates
that lead to the vine-covered courtyards where the Heuriger (wine of
the latest vintage) is served by the owner and his family at simple wooden
tables with benches. Gumpoldskirchen also has an arcaded Renaissance
town hall, a market fountain made from a Roman sarcophagus, and
the (private) castle of the Teutonic knights, whose descendants still own
some of the best vineyard sites in the area.

Dining

$$ ✕ **Altes Zechhaus.** Perched at the the top of the Old Town, this centuries-old drinking tavern is still going strong. Choose from the tempt-
ing array of salads downstairs and then order a hearty schnitzel,
spit-roasted chicken, or duck, which will be brought to your table pip-
ing hot. Try to get a table upstairs in the wood-beamed Gothic Room,
where plank tables are set against ancient stone walls and mullioned
windows. Be sure to check out their house wine with its bawdy label,
on display in the foyer. ⊠ *Kirchenpl. 1,* ☎ *02252/62247,* ℻ *02252/
63541. AE, DC, MC, V.*

Baden

★ ❼ *7 km (4½ mi) south of Gumpoldskirchen, 32 km (20 mi) southwest of
Vienna.*

The Weinstrasse brings you to the serenely elegant spa town of Baden.
Since antiquity, Baden's sulfuric thermal baths have attracted the ail-
ing and the fashionable from all over the world. When the Romans
came across the springs, they dubbed the town Aquae; the Babenbergs
revived it in the 10th century; and when the Russian czar Peter the Great
visited in 1698, Baden's golden age began. Austrian emperor Franz II
spent 31 successive summers here: every year for 12 years before his
death in 1835, the royal entourage moved from Vienna for the season.
Later in the century, Emperor Franz Josef II was a regular visitor, be-

coming the inspiration for much of the regal trappings the city still flaunts. In Baden, Mozart composed his "Ave Verum"; Beethoven spent 15 summers here and wrote large sections of his Ninth Symphony and *Missa Solemnis* when he lived at Frauengasse 10; Franz Grillparzer wrote his historical dramas here; and Josef Lanner, both Johann Strausses (father and son), Carl Michael Ziehrer, and Karl Millöcker composed and directed many of their waltzes, marches, and operettas.

For many people the primary reason for a visit to Baden is the lovely, sloping **Kurpark** in the center of town, where occasional outdoor public concerts still take place. Operetta is performed under the skies in the Summer Arena (the roof closes if it rains); in winter, it is performed in the Stadttheater. People sit quietly under the old trees or walk through the upper sections of the Kurpark for a view of the town from above. The old Kurhaus, now enlarged and renovated, incorporates a convention hall. ⊠ *Kaiser Franz-Ring.*

The ornate **Casino**—with a bar, restaurant, and gambling rooms—still includes traces of its original 19th-century decor but has been enlarged and overlaid with glitz that rivals that of Las Vegas. ⊠ *Kaiser Franz-Ring 1–3, Kurpark,* ☎ *02252/44496–0.* ☉ *Casino daily from 1 PM, gambling daily from 3 PM.*

Music lovers will want to visit the **Beethoven House** (⊠ Rathausg. 10, ☎ 02252/86800–231). Admission is AS20, and hours are Tuesday–Friday 4–6, weekends 9–11 and 4–6. Children of all ages will enjoy the enchanting **Doll and Toy Museum** (⊠ Erzherzog Rainer-Ring 23, ☎ 02252/41020). Admission is AS20, and the museum is open Tuesday–Friday 4–6, weekends 9–11 and 4–6.

One of the pleasures associated with Baden is getting there. You can reach the city directly from Vienna by bus or, far more fun, interurban streetcar, in about 50 minutes—the bus departs from the Ring directly opposite the Opera House; the blue streetcar departs from the Ring across from the Bristol Hotel. Both drop you in the center of Baden. By car from Vienna, travel south on Route A2, turning west at the junction of Route 305. It is possible, with advance planning, to go on to Mayerling and Heiligenstadt on post office buses (☎ 01/711–01).

Dining and Lodging

$$$$ ✕⊞ **Grand Hotel Sauerhof.** "Maria Theresa yellow" marks this appealing country house, which has elegant rooms in the Old Vienna style.
★ The hotel caters heavily to seminars and group activities, but individual guests are not ignored, and accommodations are very comfortable. It is also possible to go for a day's outing to their Beauty Farm and pamper yourself with the full body treatment. The hotel's Rauhenstein restaurant is excellent (try the veal with a red-wine mushroom sauce, and for dessert, the famous house crepes). ⊠ *Weilburgstr. 11–13, A–2500,* ☎ *02252/41251–0,* FAX *02252/48047. 88 rooms with bath. Restaurant, bar, indoor pool, sauna, tennis court, exercise room. AE, DC, MC, V.*

$$$$ ✕⊞ **Schloss Weikersdorf.** You're in a restored Renaissance castle but just minutes away from the center of Baden. The setting on the edge of a vast public park offers bonuses of a rose garden and boating on the lake. Rooms and baths are luxuriously outfitted. ⊠ *Schlossg. 9–1, A–2500,* ☎ *02252/48301,* FAX *02252/48301–150. 104 rooms with bath. Restaurant, bar, indoor pool, sauna, tennis courts, bowling. AE, DC, MC, V.*

$$$–$$$$ ✕⊞ **Krainerhütte.** This friendly house, in typical Alpine style, with balconies and lots of natural wood, has been family-run since 1876. The location on the outskirts of town is ideal for relaxing or exploring the surrounding woods. Facilities are up-to-date, and the restaurant offers a choice of cozy rooms or an outdoor terrace along with international and Austrian cuisine, with fish and game from the hotel's own reserves. ⊠ *Helenental, A–2500,* ☎ *02252/44511–0,* ⅢX *02252/44514. 60 rooms with bath. Restaurant, indoor pool, sauna, tennis court. AE, DC, MC, V. Closed mid-Jan.–early Feb.*

Mayerling

⑧ *11 km (7 mi) northwest of Baden, 29 km (18 mi) west of Vienna.*

Scenic Route 210 takes you through the quiet Helenental Valley west of Baden to Mayerling, scene of a tragedy that is still passionately discussed and disputed by the Austrian public, press, and historians at the slightest provocation, and still provides a torrid subject for moviemakers and novelists in many other parts of the world. On the snowy evening of January 29, 1889, the 30-year-old Habsburg heir, Crown Prince Rudolf, Emperor Franz Josef's only son, and his 17-year-old mistress, Baroness Marie Vetsera, met a violent and untimely end at the emperor's hunting lodge at Mayerling. Most historians believe it was a suicide pact between two desperate lovers (the Pope had refused an annulment to Rudolf's unhappy marriage to Princess Stephanie of Belgium). There are those, however, who feel Rudolf's pro-Hungarian political leanings might be a key to the tragedy. Given information gleaned from private letters that have recently come to light, it is also possible Rudolf was hopelessly in love with a married woman and killed himself in despair, taking Marie Vetsera with him. In an attempt to suppress the scandal—the full details are not known to this day—the baroness's body, propped up between two uncles, was smuggled back into the city by carriage (she was buried hastily in nearby Heiligenkreuz). The bereaved emperor had the hunting lodge where the suicide took place torn down and replaced with a rather nondescript Carmelite convent. Mayerling remains beautiful, haunted—and remote: the village is infrequently signposted.

Heiligenkreuz

⑨ *4 km (2½ mi) west of Mayerling, 14 km (8¾ mi) west of Mödling.*

Heiligenkreuz, in the heart of the southern section of the Vienna Woods, is a magnificent Cistercian abbey with a famous Romanesque and Gothic church, founded in 1135 by Leopold III. The church itself is lofty and serene, with beautifully carved choir stalls (the Cistercians are a singing order) surmounted by busts of Cistercian saints. The great treasure here is the relic of the cross that Leopold V is said to have brought back from his crusade in 1188. The cloisters are interesting for the Chapel of the Dead, where the brothers lie in state guarded by four gesticulating skeletons holding a candelabra. The chapter house contains the tombs of Babenberg rulers. On a corner of the abbey grounds, you can follow the Baroque stations of the cross along paths lined with chestnut and linden trees. ⊠ *Heiligenkreuz 1,* ☎ *02258/8703.* ⛩ *Abbey free, tour AS65.* ☉ *Tours Mon.–Sat. at 10, 11, 2, 3, and 4; Sun. at 11, 2, 3, and 4 (additional tour at 5 daily in summer).*

From Vienna, reach Heiligenkreuz by taking Route A21 southwest or via bus from Südtirolerplatz.

Dining and Lodging

$$$ ✕Ⅲ **Gasthof Zur Linde.** In the heart of the Vienna Woods, some 24 km (15 mi) northwest of Mayerling, lies the small town of Laaben bei Neulengbach—equally distant (about 22½ km/14 mi northwest of Mayerling) from Mayerling and Heiligenkreuz, in the shadow of the

2,900-ft Schöpfl Mountain. This family-run country inn offers an excellent base from which to explore the countryside. Rooms are modest but complete and comfortable, with rustic decor. The rambling restaurant, with its several wood-beamed rooms, serves standard tasty Austrian fare, with seasonal specialties such as lamb, asparagus, and game. ⊠ *Hauptpl. 28, A–3053 Laaben bei Neulengbach,* ☎ *02774/ 8378–0,* ⨳ *02774/8378–20. 10 rooms with bath. Restaurant. No credit cards. Closed Tues., Wed., mid-Feb.–Mar.*

THE WALDVIERTEL

The "Forest Quarter" north of the Danube and to the northwest of Vienna was long dormant, cut off from neighboring Czechoslovakia by a sealed border until 1990. Today, with the reopening of many crossing points, the Waldviertel has reawakened. Here, gentle hills bearing stands of tall pine and oak are interspersed with small farms and friendly country villages. The region can be seen in a couple of days, longer if you pause to explore the museums, castles, and other attractions. Zwettl and Raabs an der Thaya, where facilities are more modest and much less expensive than those of the major tourism routes, make good bases for discovering this area.

The main rail line from Vienna to Prague passes through the Waldviertel, making the region accessible by train. In addition, post office buses cover the area fairly well and with reasonable frequency. Bus hubs are Horn, Waidhofen, and Zwettl. An express bus service runs between Vienna and Heidenreichstein via Waidhofen an der Thaya.

Kleinwetzdorf

① *52 km (32½ mi) northwest of Vienna.*

The celebrated Austrian field marshal Joseph Wenzel Graf von Radetsky (1766–1858) is buried at **Heldenberg,** near the tiny village of Kleinwetzdorf, in elegant but lugubrious surroundings. The great field marshal was instrumental in defeating Napoléon in 1814, thus saving the Habsburg crown for the young Franz Josef II. Radetzky's tomb, arranged for by a wealthy uniform supplier, is marked by an obelisk set in a park studded with dozens of larger-than-life busts of Austrian royalty and nobility. Follow the marked path to the west back of the park past the memorial to young emperor Franz Josef II to reach the lion-guarded memorial to Radetzky's military campaigns in Italy and Hungary. The whole complex is a slightly eerie phantasmagoria—but historically fascinating. ⊠ *Heldenberg 46,* ☎ *02956/2372.* ⨳ *Free.* ☉ *May–mid-Sept., Mon.–Sat. 9–5, Sun. 10–4.*

The small, 17th-century **Schloss Wetzdorf** has a **Radetzky museum,** although of all the memorials to the field marshal, probably Johann Strauss Sr.'s "Radetzky March" is the best known. Half hidden to the south of the castle is a freestanding arched gate surmounted with wonderful reclining lions. The castle's **Schlosstaverne** (open only on weekends and holidays) offers light snacks and basics such as Wiener schnitzel, coffee, and cooling drinks. The courtyard makes a delightful setting in good weather. ⊠ *Kleinwetzdorf 1,* ☎ *02956/2372.* ⨳ *Tour AS40, parking free.* ☉ *Tour May–Oct. 26, weekends 10–6.*

Dining and Lodging

$$–$$$ ✕⊡ **Restaurant Naderer.** A fine "food-with-a-view" spot, the Naderer
★ is at the top of the hill above Maissau, 14 km (9 mi) northwest of Kleinwetzdorf on Route 4. The cuisine is of a standard that draws guests from as far away as Vienna. The menu features innovative twists on

The Waldviertel and the Weinviertel

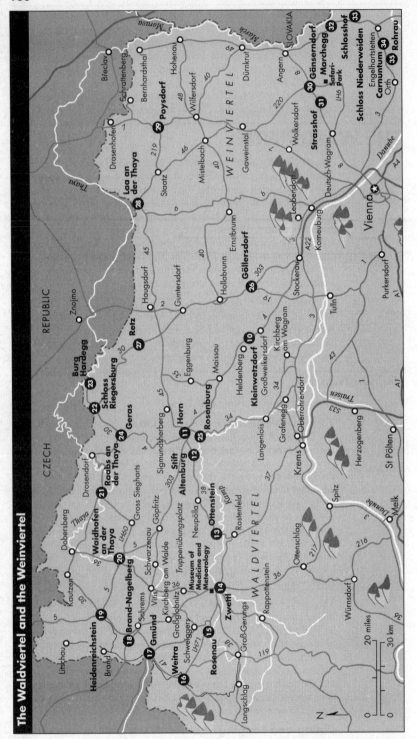

CZECH REPUBLIC

SLOVAKIA

WEINVIERTEL

WALDVIERTEL

Vienna

Břeclav
Schrattenberg
Bernhardsthal
Hohenau
Wilfersdorf
Dürnkrut
Angern
Günserndorf ③⓪
Marchegg ③②
Safari Park
Schlosshof ③③
Niederweiden
Engelhartstetten
Carnuntum ③④ Rohrau ③⑤
Orth
Drösing
Poysdorf ②⑨
Schrick
Staatz
Mistelbach
Gaweinstal
Wolkersdorf
Strasshof
Strasshof ③① Schloss
Laa an der Thaya ②⑧
Znojmo
Haugsdorf
Guntersdorf
Ernstbrunn
Hollabrunn
Göllersdorf ②⑥
Stockerau
Leobendorf
Korneuburg
Retz ②⑦
Burg Hardegg ②③
Schloss Riegersburg ②②
Geras ②④
Sigmundsherberg
Eggenburg
Maissau
Rosenburg
Heldenberg
Kirchberg am Wogram
Kleinwetzdorf ⑩
Großweikersdorf
Tulln
Purkersdorf
Drosendorf
Raabs an der Thaya ②①
Gross Siegharts
Horn ⑪ ②⑤
Stift Altenburg ⑫
Ottenstein ⑬
Rosenburg
Grafenegg
Langenlois
Krems
Spitz
Herzogenberg
St Pölten
Melk
Dobersberg
Waidhofen an der Thaya ②⓪
Schwarzenau
Göpfritz
Kirchberg am Walde
Museum of Medicine and Meteorology
Neupölla
Rastenfeld
Zwettl ⑭
Ottenschlag
Würnsdorf
Heidenreichstein
Litschau
Kautzen
Brand
Schrems
Gmünd ⑰
Brand-Nagelberg ⑱
⑲
Weitra ⑯
Großschönau
Schweiggers
Groß-Gerungs
Rappottenstein
Rosenau ⑮
Langschlag

20 miles
30 km
N

old Austrian favorites, such as the delicious *Wallergröstl*, chunks of mild, local white lake fish mixed with home-fried potatoes and slivers of red and yellow peppers. The cakes from the house kitchens are particularly good. Most of the excellent wines come from the surrounding vineyards. In summer, lunching on the terrace overlooking the valley can be a particularly pleasurable experience. Eight hotel rooms are available for overnights. ⊠ *Am Berg 44, A–3712 Maissau,* ☎ *02958/ 82334. 8 rooms with bath. AE, DC. Closed July, Nov., Thurs. in winter, and one wk. in Feb.*

Horn

⑪ *32 km (20 mi) northwest of Kleinwetzdorf, 81 km (50½ mi) northwest of Vienna.*

Horn lies at the eastern edge of the Waldviertel. Remnants of the impressive fortification walls, with its watchtowers built in 1532 to defend against invading Turks, are still obvious. Wander through the core of the old city, which dates from the 15th century. Note the painted Renaissance facade on the house (1583) at Kirchenplatz 3. **St. Stephen's parish church** on the edge of the cemetery out of the center boasts a Gothic choir and late-Gothic stone chancel. The Baroque **Piarist church,** built in 1660, features a 1777 altar painting by the renowned regional artist Kremser Schmidt. The castle, started in the 1500s and completely rebuilt in the 18th century, sits at the edge of the large, attractive Schlosspark. Horn is host to an international chamber-music festival in summer.

⑫ About 5 km (3 mi) west of Horn, at Altenburg on Route 38, **Stift Altenburg** was built in 1144 and rebuilt in 1645–1740 after its destruction by the Swedes. The library and the frescoed ceilings by the master artist Paul Troger are glorious. ⊠ *Altenburg 1,* ☎ *02982/ 345121,* ℻ *02982/345113.* ▨ *Free, tours AS50.* ☉ *Mar.–Dec. 23, daily 9–12 and 1–5.*

⑬ Almost 35 km (21 mi) west of Altenburg, on Route 38 in Rastenfeld, the castle (⊠ Ottenstein 1, ☎ 02826/254) at **Ottenstein,** now a hotel-restaurant, has a number of impressive reception rooms and parts dating to 1178. Ottenstein defied the invading Swedes in 1645 only to be devastated by the Russians in 1945. Sports enthusiasts will find boating and swimming at the reservoir and golf at Niedergrünbach. The ruined Lichtenfels castle nearby can be explored.

Zwettl

⑭ *49 km (31 mi) west of Horn, 125 km (78 mi) northwest of Vienna.*

Zwettl lies in the heartland of the Forest District. The town center, squeezed between a river bend, is attractive for its gabled houses and colorful pastel facades. The city wall, dating from the Middle Ages, still includes eight defensive towers. But Zwettl is best known for the vast **Stift Zwettl,** a Cistercian abbey dating from 1138, about 2¼ km (1½ mi) west of the town. The Zwettl abbey, perched above the Kamp River, was established as an outpost of the abbey at Heiligenkreuz in the Vienna Woods (☞ Heiligenkreuz, *above*). The imposing south gate in the cloisters remains from the original edifice; the church, with its massive Gothic choir, was completed in 1348. Later renovations added the glorious Baroque touches, with the west wall crowned by a 292-ft tower. An international organ festival is held here annually from the end of June to the end of July. ☎ *02822/550–57.* ▨ *AS50.* ☉ *Tours May–June and Oct., Mon.–Sat. at 10, 11, 2, and 3, Sun. at 11, 2, and 3; July–Sept., additional tour daily at 4. Closed Nov.–Apr.* ✒

About 2 km (1 mi) north of Zwettl on Route 36, at Dürnhof, a fascinating **Museum of Medicine and Meteorology** is housed in a cloister chapel built in 1294. Exhibits follow the development of medicine from earliest times to the present, and the courtyard garden of medicinal herbs adds another dimension to the history. ☎ 02822/53180. ☞ AS40. ☼ May–Oct., Tues.–Sun. 10–6.

Dining and Lodging

$$ ✕ **Stiftstaverne-Restaurant.** Set within the Zwettl abbey, this spacious tavern complex serves good Austrian country fare such as grilled chicken and roast pork with bread dumplings and, occasionally, regional specialties such as Waldviertel potato dumplings. The outstanding beer, fresh from the nearby brewery, is alone worth a stop, as are the wines, which come from the abbey's own cellars. ⊠ *Stift Zwettl,* ☎ *02822/550–36. No credit cards. Closed 1st 2 wks of Feb. and Tues. Nov.–Easter.*

$$ ⊡ **Gasthof Hamerlingsaal.** The cream-color plain facade gives way to a relatively simple but modernized family-run hotel set somewhat to the east of the town center. Rooms are comfortable enough, and the buffet breakfast is ample. ⊠ *Galgenbergstr. 3, A–3910,* ☎ *02822/52344–0,* FAX *02822/52344–85. 24 rooms with bath. AE, DC, MC, V.*

Rosenau

⓯ *8 km (5 mi) west of Zwettl.*

Schloss Rosenau, with its prominent central tower, is an impressive Renaissance structure built in 1590 with later Baroque additions. The castle was ravaged by the Soviets in 1945, then rebuilt as a hotel and museum complex housing the unique **Freimaurer-Museum** (Freemasonry Museum). A secret room once used for lodge ceremonies was discovered during the renovations and is now part of the museum. Displays show the ties of Haydn and Mozart to freemasonry, and many exhibits reflecting the origins of the brotherhood are in English. ☎ *02822/58221.* ☞ *AS50, with tour AS70.* ☼ *Mid-Apr.–Oct., daily 9–5; call for tour times.*

Dining and Lodging

$$$–$$$$ ✕⊡ **Schloss Rosenau.** Set in an elegant castle, this small hotel offers
★ country quiet and modern rooms furnished in period style. The theme of the hotel is the rose, and roses are everywhere, even strewn throughout the rooms, making it a very romantic retreat. The wood-paneled restaurant is one of the best in the area, featuring garlic soup, bread soup, and lamb or game in season. In summer, food seems to taste even better on the sunny outdoor terrace, which overlooks great expanses of grain fields set about a jewel of a tiny castle. ☎ *02822/58221,* FAX *02822/58222–8. 18 rooms with bath. Restaurant, indoor pool, sauna, fishing. AE, DC, MC, V. Closed mid-Dec.–Mar.*

Weitra

★ ⓰ *16 km (11 mi) northwest of Rosenau.*

The small town of Weitra, set along the main road of LH71, is renowned for its stunning, ornate painted house facades (*sgraffiti*) dating from the 17th and 18th centuries. A charming small brewery has been in business here since 1321. And the tradition is well founded: in 1645, 33 Weitra citizens held the right to operate breweries. The 15th-century fortress **Schloss Weitra,** with its Renaissance features, is privately owned, though some rooms are open to the public; the rococo theater, ceremonial hall, the tower, and the extensive Schlosskeller (with an exhibition on beer brewing) are particularly worthwhile. This is the most westerly of the line of castles built to defend against possible invaders from the north. ☎ *02856/3311.* ☞ *AS60.* ☼ *Mid-May–late Oct., Wed.–Sun. 10–5.*

Dining and Lodging

$$ ✕⌑ **Gasthof Waschka.** This is a typical Austrian Gasthaus with plain wooden banquets and a smoky haze in the air. But Hadmar Bräu is fresh on tap, named after Hadmar II, the founder of Weitra, and the specialty of the house is the tasty Waldviertler *Knödelgröstl,* a hefty portion of fried potato dumplings mixed with crispy onions and fried egg. There are rooms upstairs for overnighters. ✉ *Rathauspl. 8, A–3970,* ☎ *02856/2296. 12 rooms with bath. Restaurant, bar, sauna. No credit cards. Closed Wed.*

Gmünd

⑰ *16 km (10 mi) north of Weitra, 55 km (34½ mi) northwest of Horn.*

The town of Gmünd was curiously divided in 1918 when the border with Czechoslovakia was established. The actual line passes through a few houses and backyards, but, now with the barbed-wire defenses removed, the border is a harmless affair. The core of the old town remains in Austria and is worth viewing for the painted facades (sgraffiti) around the main square. Adjacent to the square is the once-moated (private) castle, which dates from the 16th century.

Railroad fans have a field day in Gmünd; the Czechs still use some steam locomotives for switching, and on the Austrian side Gmünd is one of the main points on the delightful narrow-gauge **Waldviertler Schmalspurbahn** (☎ 02852/52588–0), which runs occasional steam excursions plus some regular services. The excursion runs generally include a club car with refreshments.

The **Naturpark Blockheide Gmünd-Eibenstein** wildlife preserve to the northeast of the town center, open free to the public all year, includes a geological open-air museum and a stone marking the 15th meridian east of Greenwich. No one knows the source of the huge granite boulders that adorn the park. ✉ *Schremserstr. 6,* ☎ *02852/52506.*

Northwest of Schrems, a detour west from Route 30, on Route 303, **⑱** leads to **Brand–Nagelberg,** pressed against the Czech border and a center of glassmaking since 1740. Among the operating glassworks that you can visit to see how glass is made and blown is **Glasstudio Zalto** (✉ Neu–Nagelberg 58, ☎ 02859/7217). Another, **Stölzle Kristall** (✉ Hauptstr. 45, Alt–Nagelberg, ☎ 02859/7531–0), has a showroom and factory outlet.

Heidenreichstein

⑲ *9 km (5½ mi) southwest of Gmünd, 51 km (32 mi) northwest of Horn.*

★ The scenic route north from Schrems parallels the narrow-gauge railway to Heidenreichstein, noted for the massive moated **Burg Heidenreichstein,** with its corner towers, which has never been captured by enemy forces since it was built in the 15th century; some of the walls, 10 ft thick, went up in the 13th century. This is one of the most remarkable "water" castles in Austria. Water—or moated—castles were surrounded by a body of water (natural or artificial) for defense purposes, whereas "hill" castles used steep, often rocky and inaccessible slopes for protection. The building is in remarkable condition, the best-preserved of all moated castles in Austria, and some of the rooms are furnished with pieces dating from the 15th and 16th centuries. It is open for tours only. ✉ *Schremserstr. 1,* ☎ *02862/52268.* ⌑ *Tour AS60.* ☉ *Tours mid-Apr.–mid-Oct., Tues.–Sun. at 9, 10, 11, 2, 3, and 4.*

Waidhofen an der Thaya

⑳ *14 km (9 mi) east of Heidenreichstein, 32 km (20 mi) north of Zwettl, 37 km (23 mi) northwest of Horn.*

Route 5 between Heidenreichstein and Waidhofen an der Thaya is particularly scenic. Waidhofen itself is a three-sided, walled defense city typical of those of the 13th century. Fires destroyed much of the early character of the town, but the town square, rebuilt at the end of the 19th century, has a pleasing unity. The town is dominated by its Baroque **parish church,** locally known as the Cathedral of the Thaya Valley; the rococo chapel to Mary includes a Madonna of 1440 and distinguished portraits marking the stations of the cross. Outside the city walls, the **Bürgerspitalkapelle** has a side altar with a Gothic carved-wood relief of the Madonna and child and 13 assistants, dating from about 1500.

Raabs an der Thaya

㉑ *21 km (13 mi) northeast of Waidhofen an der Thaya, 42 km (26 mi) northwest of Horn.*

The Thaya River wanders leisurely through Raabs an der Thaya, an unusually attractive village watched over by 11th-century **Burg Raabs,** perched dramatically on a rock outcropping and reflected in the river below. This was one of the chain of defensive castles through the Waldviertel region. The river is popular for fishing and swimming. The castle is now privately owned.

Dining and Lodging

$$ ✕🏠 **Hotel Thaya.** A friendly, family-run hotel directly on the river, the Thaya offers comfortable, modern, if slightly spartan rooms in the annex. Rooms directly overlooking the river are the favorites. The restaurant prepares such solid local specialties as roast pork and veal. ⊠ *Hauptstr. 14, A–3820,* ☎ *02846/202–0,* 🖷 *02846/8202–20. 25 rooms with bath. Restaurant, bar, beer garden, sauna, exercise room, dance club, parking. V. Closed Feb. and possibly other winter months.*

OFF THE
BEATEN PATH
DROSENDORF – Northeast of Raabs along Route 30 is the border town of Drosendorf, with a castle built in 1100 and a historic center typical of a small walled community. The encircling wall is virtually intact and complete with watchtowers.

En Route   The intriguing ruins of Kollmitz Castle to the southeast of Raabs on the way to Riegersburg can be explored, and a bit farther along are the ruins of Eibenstein Castle, another link in the 16th- and 17th-century defense chain along the border with Bohemia.

Riegersburg

28 km (17½ mi) east of Raabs an der Thaya, 33 km (20½ mi) north of Horn, 18½ km (11½ mi) northwest of Retz.

㉒ The impressive **Schloss Riegersburg** was originally moated before the substantial edifice was given a Baroque makeover in 1731 and again virtually rebuilt after the Russians inflicted heavy damage in 1945. Thankfully, you can now see the elegant public rooms and period furnishings in all their former glory. Note the window variations and the classic figures that ornament the roofline. ☎ *02916/332 or 02916/425.* 🎫 *Tour AS88.* ⊙ *Late Mar.–mid-Nov., daily 9–5; July.–Aug., daily 9–7.*

Hardegg, about 6 km (4 mi) east of Riegersburg on an unnumbered road,
 ㉓ is the smallest village in Austria. It features a wonderfully eclectic **Burg Hard-**

egg, which stands mightily on a rock promontory high above the Thaya River, watching over the Czech Republic. (The river midstream marks the boundary; as recently as 1990 the pedestrian bridge was impassable, the border sealed, and Czech border defenses concealed in the woods opposite.) The earliest parts of the castle date from 1140. The armory and armament collection, chapel, and the museum's exhibits on the emperor Maximilian in Mexico alone are worth a visit. In addition, the kitchen and other working rooms of the castle give a real feeling of the daily life of an earlier era. An English-speaking guide is available for small-group tours. ⊠ *Hardegg,* ☎ *02949/8225.* ⊡ *Castle AS70, tour AS25.* ⊙ *Late Mar.– mid-Nov., daily 9–5; Jul.–Aug., daily 9–7.*

Geras

㉔ *14 km (8½ mi) southwest of Riegersburg, 22 km (14 mi) north of Horn, 23 km (14½ mi) southeast of Raabs an der Thaya.*

Another of the Waldviertel's great abbeys, **Stift Geras,** is situated here. Established in 1120, the impressive complex has had from its beginnings close ties to its agricultural surroundings. The abbey was given a glorious full-blown Baroque treatment in the course of rebuilding following a fire in 1730, including a translucent fresco by the noted Paul Troger in the 18th-century Marble Hall, now often used for concerts. While the abbey still functions as a religious center, the complex is also a noted school for arts and crafts. ⊠ *Hauptstr. 1,* ☎ *02912/345.* ⊡ *AS50.* ⊙ *Tours May–Oct., Tues.–Sun. at 10, 11, 12, 2, 3, and 4.*

Dining and Lodging

$$$ ✕⊡ **Stiftsrestaurant und Hotel "Alter Schüttkasten."** A former granary outbuilding of the abbey has been turned into a modern hotel with all the amenities. Rooms are comfortable; those on the front look out over the fields toward the abbey. The restaurant offers seasonal specialties such as fish and game in addition to pork, beef, and other regional standards. ⊠ *Vorstadt 11, A–2093,* ☎ *02912/332,* ℻ *02912/332–33. 26 rooms with bath. Restaurant, bar, sauna, parking. No credit cards.*

Kamptal

Rosenburg is 23 km (14½ mi) south of Geras, 80 km (50 mi) northwest of Vienna.

㉕ The gloriously scenic Kamp River valley (Kamptal), running from **Rosenburg** in the north some 30 km (19 mi) south roughly to Hadersdorf am Kamp, technically belongs to the Waldviertel, though for the amount of wine produced here, it might as well be a part of the Weinviertel, the Wine District to the east. The river, road, and railroad share the frequently narrow and twisting route that meanders some 25 km (15½ mi) through the valley from Rosenburg south to Langenlois. The villages along the route—Gars am Kamp, Schönberg am Kamp, Zöbing, Strass, and Langenlois—are all known for excellent wines, mainly varietal whites. Strass in particular has become an active center of viticulture, and many vintners offer wine tastings. Castle ruins dot the hilltops above the woods and vineyards; the area has been populated since well before 900 BC. Scattered through the valley are some noted eateries and hotels; the best are reviewed below. Route 34 takes you through more vineyards to Kollersdorf, where Route 3 east will return you to Vienna.

♨ The massive fortress **Rosenburg Forstverwaltung Hoyos** dates from 1200 and dominates the north entrance to the Kamptal Valley. Its features include the original jousting field as a forecourt and impressive reception rooms inside, where armor and other relics of the period are on display. Curious Renaissance balconies and small courtyards are incorporated into the design, although the variety in the 13 towers added in the 15th century is the touch that immediately catches the eye. The first Sunday of the month, falconry demonstrations are performed in medieval costume. ⊠ *Rosenburg am Kamp,* ☏ *02982/2911.* 🎫 *AS65 (includes tour); demonstration AS65; combination ticket AS100.* ☉ *Apr.– mid-Nov., daily 9–5; falconry demonstration Apr.–Nov., daily at 11 and 3; tour begins 1 hr before demonstration.*

Dining

$–$$ ✕ **Bründlmayer.** This country Heuriger in the center of Langenlois offers outstanding wines from one of Austria's top vintners, as well as a tasty hot-and-cold buffet, all in an indoor stone-vaulted setting with a cheery fireplace or outdoors in the Renaissance courtyard. The simple but delicious fare might include *Krautfleckerl,* a cabbage and noodle dish with cheese and lightly-smoked ham. Take the opportunity to taste some of their excellent wines, including the crisp and fruity Grüner Veltliner Alte Reben, made with grapes from old vines. ⊠ *Walterstr. 14, Langenlois,* ☏ *02734/21720. DC, MC, V.* ☉ *Thurs.–Fri. 3– 10, Sat.–Sun. 1–10. Closed Mon.–Wed. and early-Dec.–early Mar.*

THE WEINVIERTEL

Luckily, Austria's Weinviertel (Wine District) has been largely neglected by the "experts," and its deliciously fresh wines form an ideal treasure trove to reward those who enjoy drinking wine and dislike the all-too-frequent nonsense that goes with it. This region takes its name from the rustic and delightful rolling countryside north of Vienna. The Weinviertel is bounded by the Danube on the south, the Thaya River and the reopened Czech border on the north, the March River and Slovakia to the east. No well-defined line separates the Weinviertel from the Waldviertel to the west; the Kamp River valley, officially part of the Waldviertel, is an important wine region. Whether wine, crops, or dairies, this is farming country, its broad expanses of vineyards and farmlands broken by patches of forest and neat villages. A tour by car, just for the scenery, can be made in a day; you may want two or three days to savor the region and its wines—these are generally on the medium-dry side. Don't expect to find here the elegant facilities found elsewhere in Austria; prices are low by any standard, and village restaurants and accommodations are mainly *Gasthäuser* that meet local needs. This means that you'll rub shoulders over a glass of wine or a beer with country folk.

Göllersdorf

㉖   *10 km (6 mi) north of Stockerau West interchange on Rte. 303/E59.*

The rolling hills and agricultural lands of the southwest Weinviertel around Hollabrunn offer little excitement other than panoramas and scenic pleasures, but one exception is **Schloss Schönborn,** about 2 km (1 mi) south of Göllersdorf on Route 303. The castle was laid out in 1712 by that master of Baroque architecture Johann Lukas von Hildebrandt. Today the castle is in private hands, but the harmony of design can be appreciated from the outside. The parish church in Göllersdorf is also a Baroque Hildebrandt design of 1740 overlaid on a Gothic structure dating from the mid-1400s.

Retz

★ **㉗**   *43 km (27 mi) north of Göllersdorf, 70 km (44 mi) north of Vienna.*

Retz, at the northwest corner of the Weinviertel, is a charming town with an impressive rectangular central square formed by buildings dating mainly from the 15th century. Take time to explore Retz's tiny streets leading from the town square; the oldest buildings and the wall and gate-tower defenses survived destruction by Swedish armies in 1645 during the Thirty Years' War. The Dominican church (1295) at the southwest corner of the square also survived, and it is interesting for its long, narrow design. The pastel Biedermeier facades along with the sgraffiti add appeal to the square, which is further marked by the impressive city hall with its massive Gothic tower in the center. The landmark of the town is the pretty **Windmühle,** a Dutch windmill set incongruously in the middle of vineyards on the edge of town. Follow the markers leading up to the summit, where you can sit and rest on benches offering a stunning view of the surrounding countryside.

Retz is best known for its red wines. Here you can tour **Austria's largest wine cellar,** tunneled 65 ft under the town, and at the same time taste wines of the area. Some of the tunnels go back to the 13th century, and at the end of the 15th century each citizen was permitted to deal in wines and was entitled to storage space in the town cellars. Efforts to use the cellars for armaments production during World War II failed because of the 88% humidity. The temperature remains constant at 8°C–10°C (47°F–50°F). Entrance to the cellars is at the Rathauskeller, in the center of town. ⊠ *Hauptpl.,* ☎ *02942/2700.* ⌚ *Tour AS80.* ☉ *Tour daily, May–Oct., 10:30, 2, and 4, Sun., 10:30 and 2; Mar.–Apr., Nov.–Dec., 2; Jan.–Feb. by appt..*

Dining and Lodging

$$$$ ✕⚏ **Althof Retz/Hotel Burghof.** Two hotels are tucked into an ancient estate building just off the town square. Take your choice of the upscale Hotel Burghof or the slightly less expensive Althof, which also serves as a training hotel. Both are done in whites and light wood. Rooms are modern, comfortable, and have all facilities. The restaurant has been less successful, but the standards and regional specialties are fine. The excellent wines naturally come mainly from the area. ⊠ *Althofg. 14, A–2070,* ☎ *02942/3711–0,* ℻ *02942/3711–55. 65 rooms with bath. Restaurant, parking. AE, DC, MC, V.*

Laa an der Thaya

㉘ *39 km (24 mi) east of Retz, 65 km (41 mi) north of Vienna.*

From 1948 until about 1990, Laa an der Thaya was a town isolated by the Cold War, directly bordering what was then Czechoslovakia. Laa is considerably livelier now that the border is open. (As long as you have your passport with you, you can cross into the Czech Republic and return without complication.) The town's huge central square is adorned with a massive neo-Gothic city hall, in stark contrast to the low, colorful buildings that form the square. A good time to visit is mid-September during the Onion Festival, when all varieties of onions are prepared in every imaginable way in food stalls set up throughout the village. If you're traveling from Retz to Laa an der Thaya, retrace your way south on Route 30 to Route 45.

Laa boasts a **Bier Museum,** located in the town fortress, that traces the history of beer (the nearby Hubertus brewery has been in business since 1454) and displays an imposing collection of beer bottles. ☎ *02522/ 2501–29.* ⌚ *AS20.* ☉ *May–Sept., weekends 2–4.*

Dining

$$ ✕ **Restaurant Weiler.** Light woods and country accessories set the tone ★ in this family-run restaurant; in summer, dinner is served in the outdoor garden. Try the delicate cream of garlic soup or the house specialty, game in season. For dessert, the delicious cakes of the house are

temptingly displayed in a showcase. ⊠ *Staatsbahnstr. 60,* ☎ *02522/ 2379. No credit cards. Closed Mon., 2 wks in Feb., and July.*

Poysdorf

㉙ *22 km (13 mi) southeast of Laa an der Thaya, 61 km (38 mi) north of Vienna.*

Poysdorf is considered by many the capital of the Weinviertel. Wine making here goes back to the 14th century. Poysdorf vintages, mainly whites, rank with the best Austria has to offer. Narrow paths known as *Kellergassen* (cellar streets) on the northern outskirts are lined with wine cellars set into and under the hills. A festival in early September marks the annual harvest. At the **wine market** (⊠ Singerstr. 2) in the center of town, you can taste as well as buy; the market is open Monday–Thursday 8–5, Friday 8–6, and weekends 10–noon and 1–6.

The town **Museum** includes a section on viticulture and wine making. ⊠ *Brunner Str. 9,* ☎ *02552/3209.* 🎫 *AS40.* ⊘ *Easter–Oct., Wed.– Mon. 9–noon and 1–5; call to confirm.*

Dining

$$–$$$ ✕ **Zur Linde.** This friendly family-run restaurant with rustic decor 16
  ★   km (10 mi) south of Poysdorf is setting higher standards for such traditional fare as roast pork, stuffed breast of veal, flank steak, and fresh game in season. Desserts are excellent; try the extraordinary *Apfelstrudel* (apple strudel). A major attraction here is the remarkable range of wines from the neighborhood at altogether reasonable prices. ⊠ *Bahnhofstr. 49, Mistelbach,* ☎ *02572/2409. AE, DC, MC, V. Closed Mon., late Jan.–mid-Feb., and late July–mid-Aug. No dinner Sun.*

  $$ ✕ **Gasthaus Schreiber.** Choose the shaded garden under huge trees or the country-rustic decor indoors. The typical Austrian fare—roast pork, stuffed breast of veal, boiled beef, fillet steak with garlic—is commendable, as is the house-made ice cream. The wine card lists more than 60 area labels. ⊠ *Bahnstr. 2,* ☎ *02552/2348. No credit cards. Closed Tues. and late Jan.–Feb. No dinner Mon.*

Gänserndorf

㉚ *41 km (26 mi) south of Poysdorf, 30 km (19 mi) northeast of Vienna.*

☾ Three kilometers (2 miles) south of Gänserndorf, the **Safari-Park und Abenteuerpark** (Safari Park and Adventure Park) allows visitors to drive through re-created natural habitats of live wild animals, many of which (lions and tigers) are hardly indigenous to Austria. The adventure takes five to six hours, allowing time for the petting zoo and the extra animal shows, which start every half hour. For those without a car, a safari bus leaves for the circuit every hour. ⊠ *Siebenbrunner Str.,* ☎ *02282/70261– 0,* FAX *02282/70261–27.* 🎫 *AS193.* ⊘ *Early Apr.–Oct., daily 9:30–4.* ✎

Strasshof

㉛ *3 km (2 mi) southwest of Gänserndorf.*

The area around Gänserndorf includes one of Austria's few gas and oil fields, where operating pumps patiently pull up crude to be piped to the refinery about 20 km (12½ mi) south. Underground, exhausted gas wells serve as natural storage tanks for gas coming to Western Europe from Russia.

☾ The **Eisenbahnmuseum Das Heizhaus,** north of Strasshof, is a fascinating private collection of dozens of steam locomotives and railroad cars stored in a vast engine house. Enthusiasts have painstakingly rebuilt and restored many of the engines; steam locomotives are up and running on the first Sunday of each month. The complex includes transfer table, water towers, and coaling station, and visitors can climb around among many of the locomotives awaiting restoration. ⊠ *Sillerstr. 123,* ☎ *01/603–5301,* FAX *01/602–2196–22.* ☜ *AS70, steam days AS90, including parking and tour.* ☉ *Apr.–Oct. 26, Tues.–Sun. 10–4.* ☜

Dining

$$$$ ✕ **Marchfelderhof.** In nearby Deutsch Wagram, this sprawling complex, with its eclectic series of rooms bounteously decorated with everything from antiques to hunting trophies, has a reputation for excess in the food department as well. The menu's standards—Wiener schnitzel, roast pork, lamb—are more successful than the more expensive efforts at innovation. Deutsch Wagram is 9 km (5½ mi) southwest of Strasshof on Route 8, 17 km (11 mi) northeast of Vienna on Route 8. ⊠ *Bockfliesser Str. 31, Deutsch Wagram,* ☎ *02247/2243–0,* FAX *02247/2236–13. AE, DC, MC, V.*

Marchegg

32   *16 km (10 mi) southeast of Gänserndorf, 43 km (27 mi) east of Vienna.*

The tiny corner of the lower Weinviertel to the southeast of Gänserndorf is known as the Marchfeld, for the fields stretching east to the March River, forming the border with Slovakia. In this region—known as the granary of Austria—two elegant Baroque castles are worth a visit; they have been totally renovated in recent years and given over to changing annual exhibits, concerts, and other public activities. These country estates have lost none of their gracious charm over the centuries.

The northernmost of the pair is the **Jagdschloss Marchegg,** its oldest parts dating to 1268. What you see today is the Baroque overlay added in 1733 to the basic building from the Middle Ages. The castle now houses a hunting and African art museum. To reach Marchegg from Gänserndorf, take Route 8a 6 km (4 mi) east to Route 49, then Route 49 10 km (6 mi) south. ☎ *02285/8224.* ☜ *AS30.* ☉ *Mid-Mar.–Nov., Tues.–Sun. 9–noon and 1–5.*

33   The castle at **Schlosshof** is a true Baroque gem, a product of that master designer and architect Johann Lukas von Hildebrandt, who in 1732 reconstructed the four-sided castle into an elegant U-shape building, opening up the eastern side to a marvelous Baroque formal garden that gives way toward the river. The famed Italian painter Canaletto captured the view before the reconstruction. The castle—once owned by Empress Maria Theresa—is now used for changing annual exhibits, but you can walk the grounds without paying admission. The castle is about 8 km (5 mi) south of Marchegg. ⊠ *Schlosshof,* ☎ *02285/6580.* ☜ *AS70.* ☉ *Early Apr.–Nov. 1, Tues.–Sun. 10–5.*

Carnuntum

34   *32 km (20 mi) east of Vienna.*

The remains of the important legionary Roman fortress Carnuntum, which once numbered 55,000 inhabitants, is in the tiny village of Petronell, reachable by the S7, a local train that departs from Wien Mitte/Landstrasse or Wien-Nord. Though by no means as impressive as Roman ruins in Italy and Spain, Carnuntum still merits a visit, with three amphitheaters (the first one seating 8,000) and the foundations of former residences, baths, and trading centers, some with mosaic floors. The ruins are quite spread out, with the impressive remains of a Roman arch, the **Heidentor** (Pagan's Gate), a good 15 minutes' walk from the main excavations. A pleasant path along the north end of the ruins leads past a dilapidated 17th-century palace once belonging to the counts of Traun, to the remains of a Roman bath. In summer Greek plays are sometimes performed in English at the **main amphitheater** (☎ 02163/ 3400). ⊠ *Petronell,* ☎ *02163/33770.* ☞ *AS50.* ☉ *Apr.–Oct., weekdays 9–5, weekends 9–6.*

Many of the finds from the excavations at Carnuntum are housed 4 km (2½ mi) northeast of Petronell in the village of Bad Deutsch-Altenburg, in the Museum **Carnuntium.** The pride of the collection is a carving of Mithras killing a bull. ⊠ *Badg. 40–46, Petronell,* ☎ *02163/33770.* ☞ *AS60, combination ticket with Carnuntum AS100.* ☉ *Tues.–Sun. 10– 5; closed Dec. 15–Jan. 15.*

③⑤ Just 5 km (3 mi) south of Petronell, in the tiny village of **Rohrau,** is the birthplace of Joseph Haydn. The quaint reed-thatched cottage where in 1732 Haydn, son of the local blacksmith, was born is now a small museum, with a pianoforte he is supposed to have played, as well as letters and other memorabilia. After Haydn had gained worldwide renown, he is said to have returned to his native Rohrau and knelt to kiss the steps of his humble home. ⊠ *Hauptstr. 60, Rohrau,* ☎ *02164/ 2268.* ☞ *AS20.* ☉ *Tues.–Sun. 10–5.*

Also in Rohrau is the cream-and-beige palace, **Schloss Rohrau,** where Haydn's mother worked as a cook for Count Harrach. The palace has one of the best private art collections in Austria, with emphasis on 17th- and 18th-century Spanish and Italian paintings. ⊠ ☎ *02164/2252.* ☞ *AS70.* ☉ *Open Apr.–Oct., Tues.–Sun. 10–5.*

OFF THE   **ARTNER WEINBAU –** Some of the best wines and freshly made *Ziegenkäse*
BEATEN PATH   (goat cheese) in the region can be found in the tiny village of Höflein, 12 km (7½ mi) southwest of Petronell. Artner has been a family business since 1650, and owner Hannes Artner is proud to offer tastings of his wines, including Chardonnay Barrique, cabernet sauvignon, and Blauer Zweigelt Kirchtal. Check for the opening times of the outdoor *Heurige* during selected weeks from May to August, when the new wine is available for tasting. ⊠ *Höflein Hauptstr. 58, Höflein,* ☎ *02162/63142.*

SIDE TRIPS FROM VIENNA A TO Z

Arriving and Departing

By Car

The autobahn A1 traverses the Vienna Woods in the west; the A2 autobahn runs through the edge of the Vienna Woods to the south. The A4 autobahn is a quick way to reach the Carnuntum region. The Waldviertel and Weinviertel are accessed by major highways but not autobahns.

By Train

The main east–west train line cuts through the Vienna Woods; the main north–south line out of Vienna traverses the eastern edge of the Vienna Woods. The main line to Prague and onward runs through the Waldviertel. Train service in the Weinviertel is regular to Mistelbach, irregular after that. The rail line east out of Vienna to the border town of Wolfstal cuts through the Carnuntum region. The line to the north of the Danube to Bratislava runs through the middle of the Marchfeld.

Getting Around

By Bus

Buses are a good possibility for getting around, although if you're not driving, a combination of bus and train is probably a better answer in many cases. Frequent scheduled bus service runs between Vienna and Baden, departing from across from the Opera House in Vienna to the center of Baden. Connections are available to other towns in the area. Bus service runs between Vienna and Carnuntum–Petronell, and on to Hainburg. Service to the Waldviertel is less frequent but is available between Vienna and Horn, Zwettl, Waidhofen, and Raabs an der Thaya. From these points, you can get buses to other parts of the Waldviertel. An express bus service runs between Vienna and Heidenreichstein via Waidhofen an der Thaya. In the Weinviertel, bus service is fairly good between Vienna and Laa an der Thaya and Poysdorf.

By Car

Driving through these regions is by far the best way to see them, since you can wander the byways and stop whenever and wherever you like. To get to the Weinviertel and the Waldviertel, follow signs to Prague, taking Route E461 toward Mistelbach and Poysdorf if you want to go northeast. Or take the A22 toward Stockerau, changing to Route 303 or the E49 in the northwesterly direction of Horn and Retz. If you're going east to Carnuntum, follow signs to the A23 and the airport (Schwechat). And if you're going to Baden and the surrounding villages, take the A2 south in the direction of Graz, getting off in Baden and taking Route 210 west.

By Train

You can get to the Weinviertel from Vienna's Franz Josef Bahnhof, with buses running between the small villages. The main rail line from Vienna to Prague passes through the Waldviertel, making the region accessible by train, but you'll need a bus connection to reach the smaller towns.

The Schnellbahn (suburban train) running from Wien-Mitte (Landstrasser Hauptstrasse) stops at Petronell, with service about once an hour. Carnuntum is about a 10-minute walk from the Petronell station. Trains go on to Hainburg, stopping at Bad Deutsch-Altenburg.

Contacts and Resources

Car Rentals

Cars can be rented from all leading companies at the Vienna airport (☞ Vienna A to Z *in* Chapter 1) or, in Baden, from **Autoverleih Buchbinder** (☎ 02252/48693) or **Autoverleih Schmidt** (☎ 0663/803289).

Emergencies

Police: ☎ 133, **fire:** ☎ 122. For **ambulance** or medical emergency: ☎ 144.

Guided Tours

The Vienna Woods is one of the standard routes offered by the sightseeing-bus tour operators in Vienna, and it usually includes a boat ride through the "underground sea" grotto near Mödling. These short tours give only a quick taste of the region; if you have more time, you'll want to investigate further. For details, check with your hotel or with

Cityrama Sightseeing (☎ 01/534–130) or **Vienna Sightseeing Tours** (☎ 01/712–4683–0).

Visitor Information

Get information in Vienna before you start out, at the **Tourist Office of Lower Austria** (✉ Walfischg. 6, A–1010 Vienna, ☎ 01/513–8022, FAX 01/513–8022–30). There are several helpful regional tourist offices: **March–Donauland** (✉ Hauptpl. 296, A–2404 Petronell/Carnuntum, ☎ 02163/3555, FAX 02163/3556), **Waldviertel** (✉ Hamerlingstr. 2, A–3910 Zwettl, ☎ 02822/54109–0, FAX 02822/54109–36), **Weinviertel** (✉ Liechtensteinstr. 1, A–2170 Poysdorf, ☎ 02552/3515, FAX 02552/ 3715), **Wienerwald** (✉ Hauptpl. 11, A–3002 Purkersdorf, ☎ 02231/ 62176, FAX 02231/65510).

Local tourist offices are generally open weekdays. The offices for the Vienna Woods region are as follows: **Baden** (✉ Brusattipl. 3, ☎ 02252/ 22600–0, FAX 02252/22600–622), **Gumpoldskirchen** (✉ Schrannenpl. 1, ☎ 02252/62421), **Mödling** (✉ Elisabethstr. 2, ☎ 02236/26727, FAX 02236/41632), **Perchtoldsdorf** (✉ Marktpl. 11, ☎ 01/86683–34).

The Waldviertel district has numerous tourist offices: **Gars am Kamp** (✉ Hauptpl. 83, ☎ 02985/2276, FAX 02985/3181), **Gmünd** (✉ Weitraer- str. 44, ☎ 02852/53212, FAX 02852/54713), **Waidhofen an der Thaya** (✉ Hauptstr. 25, ☎ 02842/51500, FAX 02842/51547), **Zwettl** (✉ Land- str. 10, ☎ 02822/52233, FAX 02822/52233).

The Weinviertel region has several tourist centers: **Gänserndorf** (✉ Rathauspl. 1, ☎ 02282/2651–16, FAX 02282/2651–6), **Laa an der Thaya** (✉ Rathaus, ☎ 02522/2501–29), **Poysdorf** (✉ Liechtensteinstr. 1, ☎ 02552/3515, FAX 02552/3715), **Retz** (✉ Hauptpl. 30, ☎ 02942/2700).

3 EASTERN AUSTRIA

BURGENLAND, GRAZ, AND THE STYRIAN WINE COUNTRY

Despite its proximity to vibrant Vienna, Eastern Austria offers rustic pleasures and simple treasures: a stork alighting on the chimney atop a Mother Goose house; the haunting sounds of Gypsy music; heady vistas of lush vineyards; magical castles; and the city of Graz, whose preserved Old City is a time-warp marvel. In Burgenland, discover vast Lake Neusiedl— so shallow you can wade across it—and Eisenstadt, alive with the sound of Joseph Haydn's celebrated music.

Updated by
Bonnie Dodson

NO PART OF THE NATION offers a greater range of scenery than the area loosely defined as Eastern Austria, yet despite its proximity to Vienna it is largely overlooked by foreign tourists. Not that the region lacks for visitors—long a favorite of Austrians, it is now becoming increasingly popular with Hungarians and other Eastern Europeans. Accordingly, most of the visitors are cost-conscious and demand strict value for their money, ensuring that prices will remain lower here than in other parts of the country for some time.

There are no singularly great sights in the region—no Schönbrunn Palace, no Salzburg, no not-to-be-missed five-star attractions; still, the aggregate of worthwhile sights is most impressive. You'll find a largely unspoiled land of lakes, farms, castles, villages, and vineyards. It's also a sports lover's paradise and is rich in history, with a distinguished musical past and—yes—one genuine city, Graz, whose sophistication and beauty may surprise you. In short, this is an ideal destination for experienced travelers who have already explored Vienna, Salzburg, the Tirol, and other better-known parts of Austria.

Eastern Austria, as it is defined here, consists of Burgenland, most of Styria (Steiermark), and a small section of Lower Austria (Niederösterreich)— three distinct provinces with little in common. The geography varies from haunting steppes and the mysterious Lake Neusiedl (Neusiedler See) in the east to the low, forested mountains of the south; the industrial valleys of the center and west; and the more rugged mountains of the north, where Austrian skiing began. Culturally, Eastern Austria is strongly influenced by neighboring Hungary and Slovenia, especially in its earthy and flavorful cuisines. Along with hearty food, the region is noted for its wines, many of which never travel beyond the borders.

We begin with Burgenland, intriguing both for its flatness and for the shallow Lake Neusiedl, with its reed-lined shore forming a natural nature preserve. Storks come in the thousands to feed in the lake, and stork families, in turn, obligingly nest atop nearby chimneys—allegedly bringing luck to the household below (and assuring travelers of some great photos). Off to the east, the lake gives way to the vast Hungarian plain, interrupted by occasional thatch-roof farmhouses and picturesque pole-and-pail wells. Music lovers will want to make the pilgrimage to Eisenstadt, where the great composer Joseph Haydn (1732–1809) was in the employ of Prince Esterházy. The impressive Esterházy Castle stands as it did in Haydn's time, with its spacious theater-auditorium in which Haydn conducted his own operas and orchestral works almost nightly for the prince's entertainment.

The route from Burgenland southwest to Graz achieves an end-around run, circling the eastern tail of the Alps through a territory marked by monumental defensive castles built to ward off invaders from the east. Graz, Austria's second-largest city, boasts one of Europe's best-preserved Renaissance town centers, dating to an era when Graz, not Vienna, was the capital. The compact pedestrian zone that forms the city core sets imaginations on fire, with eye-catching discoveries around every corner. History notwithstanding, the city today is a pulsating metropolis, a surprise even to many Austrians. Styria offers the chance to visit one of Europe's oldest and still-revered religious pilgrimage sites, at Mariazell. The dramatic onward route northward can be accomplished by rail or road; the latter climbs to above 3,000 ft at Annaberg in a series of more than a dozen hairpin turns. The easier route to Vienna via the Semmering Pass achieves the same elevation and also offers some magnificent panoramas, including views of the snowcapped Schneeberg.

Pleasures and Pastimes

Dining

When choosing a restaurant, keep in mind that each province has its own cooking style. In Burgenland, the local Pannonian cooking, strongly influenced by neighboring Hungary, features such spicy dishes as *gulyas* (goulash) flavored with paprika. You'll also find fish from Lake Neusiedl, goose, game, and an abundance of fresh, local vegetables. Styria, bordering on Slovenia (formerly northern Yugoslavia), has a hearty cuisine with Serbian overtones; a typical dish is *Steirisches Brathuhn* (roast chicken turned on a spit). The intensely nutty *Kürbiskernöl* (pumpkin-seed oil) is used in many soup and pasta dishes, as well as in salad dressings. Such Balkan specialties as *cevapcici* (spicy panfried sausages) are also often found on Styrian menus. You are most likely to encounter the more urbane Viennese cooking in Lower Austria, where you can get Wiener schnitzel nearly everywhere.

Many of the restaurants listed in the chapter are actually country inns that provide overnight accommodations as well as meals, as noted in the reviews. Restaurant prices include taxes and a service charge, but it is customary to give the waiter an additional tip of 5%.

CATEGORY	COST*
$$$$	over AS500 (€36)
$$$	AS300–AS500 (€22–€36)
$$	AS200–AS300 (€14–€21)
$	under AS200 (€14)

per person for a typical three-course meal, excluding drinks and additional tip

The Great Outdoors

Eastern Austria is prime **hiking country**, and most tourist regions have marked trails. You'll need a local hiking map (*Wanderkarte*), usually for sale at a town's tourist office—whose staff can also suggest short rambles in the vicinity. Some particularly good places for walks are around Lake Neusiedl and Güssing in Burgenland; in the Mur Valley of Styria, especially the Bärenschützklamm at Mixnitz; around Mariazell; and atop the Schneeberg, Rax, and Semmering in Lower Austria.

For the truly ambitious, several long-distance trails cut through this region, among them the Nordalpen-Weitwanderweg past the Raxalpe to Rust, and the Oststeiermärkischer-Hauptwanderweg from western Austria to Riegersburg. There's no need to carry either food or a tent, because you stay overnight in staffed huts. Camping is strongly discouraged for both safety and environmental reasons.

The *puszta* (steppe) to the east of Lake Neusiedl is known as the Seewinkel, a perfect place for **horseback riding,** and horses (*Pferde*) can be hired in several villages. Ask at the local tourist office. Weekends are particularly popular, so book your steed well in advance.

Lodging

Accommodations in Eastern Austria range from luxury city hotels to mountain and lakeside resorts to castles and romantic country inns, and all are substantially lower in price than those in Vienna or Salzburg. Every town and village also has the simpler *Gasthäuser,* which give good value as long as you don't expect a private bath. Accommodations in private homes are cheaper still. These bargains are usually identified by signs reading ZIMMER FREI (room available) or FRÜHSTÜCKSPENSION (bed-and-breakfast).

The tourist information office (*Fremdenverkehrsverein, Fremdenverkehrsamt,* or *Gästeinformation*) in virtually every town can usually find you a decent place to sleep if you haven't made a reservation (☞ Visitor Information *in* Eastern Austria A to Z, *below*). Hotel room rates include taxes and service, and usually breakfast—although you should always ask about the latter.

CATEGORY	COST*
$$$$	over AS2,200 (€160)
$$$	AS1,400–AS2,200 (€100–€160)
$$	AS1,000–1,400 (€72–€99)
$	under AS1,000 (€72)

*All prices are for a standard double room for two, including taxes and service charge.

🕮 *following the text of a review is your signal that the property has a Web site, where you will find details and, usually, images; for a link, visit www.fodors.com/urls.*

Wines

Eastern Austria vies with Lower Austria as a source of the country's best wines. In both Burgenland and Styria, you can travel between villages along "wine routes" and sample local vintages. Outstanding white wines predominate, although, increasingly, there are excellent reds and rosés as well. Burgenland's vineyards, mostly around Lake Neusiedl, produce wines that tend to be slightly less dry, with perhaps the best examples coming from the village of Rust and the areas around Donnerskirchen, Purbach, and Jois. Some of the sweet dessert wines (*Spätlese,* late harvest, and *Eiswein,* pressed from frozen grapes) are extraordinary, and all Burgenland wines are gaining a reputation for high quality. Many vintners happily share samples of their wares and will provide bread and cheese as accompaniment. In Styria, the wines from south of Graz along the Slovenian border and near Leibnitz are superb, especially the tart, pale orange Schilcher.

Exploring Eastern Austria

The Eastern Austrian countryside has been fought over many times, which in part explains the host of defensive hilltop castles overlooking the flatter outlands to the east. Both conqueror and conquered have left their marks. The topography here, which ranges from the flat puszta of the north to the rolling hills of the south, demonstrates that there's more to Austria than the Alps. Graz is the only real city here; other centers are little more than villages in comparison.

Great Itineraries

Travelers who tackle Eastern Austria usually design their trip around three different destinations—Burgenland, the city of Graz, and the mountain route to Vienna—and the following suggested itineraries highlight these destinations.

Numbers in the text correspond to numbers in the margin and on the Burgenland, Eastern Styria and Lower Austria, and Graz maps.

IF YOU HAVE 1 DAY

Travelers with only a day at their disposal could head for **Eisenstadt** ⑧ and along the west shore of **Lake Neusiedl** to **Rust** ⑥, then return to Vienna via **Wiener Neustadt** ㊷. Other good (but full) one-day excursions are to **Mariazell** ㊳ or to **Puchberg am Schneeberg** ㊶, both reachable from Vienna by car or train.

IF YOU HAVE 3 DAYS

Pick **Eisenstadt** ⑧ as a first stop, spending a half day here, and then move onward to the west shore of **Lake Neusiedl** to **Rust** ⑥ for brief stops before continuing southward to 🏨 **Graz** ⑭ for two overnights,

Burgenland

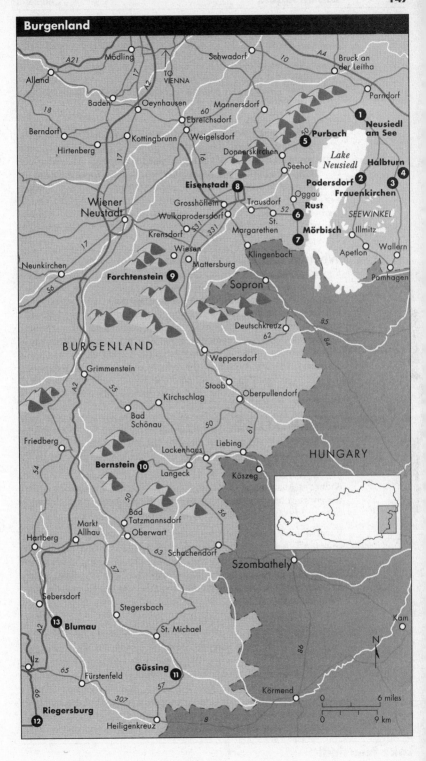

Mödling
Alland
Baden
Oeynhausen
Berndorf
Hirtenberg
Kottingbrunn
Weigelsdorf
Ebreichsdorf
Mannersdorf
Schwadorf
Bruck an der Leitha
Parndorf
1
Neusiedl am See
Purbach **5**
Halbturn
Donnerskirchen
Seehof
Eisenstadt **8**
Podersdorf **2**
4
3
Frauenkirchen
Grosshöflein
Trausdorf
Oggau
Rust
6
Wulkaprodersdorf
St.
Krensdorf
Margarethen
Mörbisch
7
Wiener Neustadt
Wiesen
Mattersburg
Klingenbach
Illmitz
Apetlon
Wallern
Pamhagen
SEEWINKEL
Lake Neusiedl
Neunkirchen
Forchtenstein **9**
Sopron
Deutschkreuz
Grimmenstein
Weppersdorf
Stoob
Kirchschlag
Oberpullendorf
Bad Schönau
Friedberg
Lockenhaus
Liebing
HUNGARY
Bernstein **10**
Langeck
Kőszeg
Bad Tatzmannsdorf
Markt Allhau
Oberwart
Hartberg
Schachendorf
Szombathely
Sebersdorf
13 **Blumau**
Stegersbach
St. Michael
Ilz
Fürstenfeld
Güssing **11**
Riegersburg
12
Heiligenkreuz
Körmend
Kam

BURGENLAND

TO VIENNA

N

0   6 miles
0   9 km

with a day spent exploring the city. From Graz, head northward via **Bruck an der Mur** ㉚, over the pass at **Semmering** ㊵, and **Wiener Neustadt** ㊷ to Vienna.

IF YOU HAVE 5–7 DAYS

A leisurely pursuit of Eastern Austria is highly rewarding. Get better acquainted with the curiously flat puszta on the eastern side of **Lake Neusiedl**; then head back over to the western side and spend your first overnight in ⊡ **Rust** ⑥. The next day head to the historic town of ⊡ **Eisenstadt** ⑧ and follow in the footsteps of famed Baroque-era composer Joseph Haydn and the Esterházy princes. Follow the Burgenland wine route south, and for contrast, spend two nights and a day discovering the delightful Altstadt and bustling metropolis that is ⊡ **Graz** ⑭. Take in the magnificent abbey at **Seckau** ㉜ and the vast **Eisenerz** ㉟ open-pit iron-ore mines, with an overnight in nearby ⊡ **Leoben/Niklasdorf** ㉛ before continuing north for the attractions of Lower Austria. You might consider an overnight at ⊡ **Semmering** ㊵ on the way back to Vienna.

When to Tour Eastern Austria

Spring, summer, and fall are the seasons for Eastern Austria, unless you're a winter sports enthusiast, when downhill skiers head for Lower Austria and the less crowded slopes of Styria. Other than coming across festival goers and, in summer, visitors to the shores of Lake Neusiedl, you'll find relatively few tourists in this region. Graz functions year-round, but its treasures are less touted and crowds are unknown; Christmas in Graz is a visual spectacle, with whole sections of the city turned into a Christmas market. Winter in the area is an enigma: the Semmering mountains mark the eastern tail end of the Alps—north of the divide can be overcast and dreary while the area to the south basks in sunshine.

LAND OF CASTLES

This tour demonstrates that there's more to Austria than the Alps; it travels the length of Burgenland from the flat puszta of the north to the rolling castle-capped hills of the south before turning west to Styria, ending at Austria's second city, Graz. Although it is possible to cover the entire route of about 300 km (185 mi) in a single day, a leisurely pace is, of course, preferable.

Burgenland, a region of castles, fields of grain, and vineyards, is a narrow, fertile belt of agricultural land stretching some 170 km (106 mi) from the Slovak (formerly Czechoslovak) border, along the Hungarian frontier, and south to Slovenia (formerly northern Yugoslavia). Only 65 km (40 mi) across at its widest point, the region narrows to a mere 4 km (2½ mi).

The name Burgenland, meaning land of castles, dates only from 1921; prior to World War I this area was a part of Hungary. Throughout its long history it has been a battleground between east and west. It was part of the ancient Roman province of Pannonia, occupied by Celts, Roman settlers, Ostrogoths, and Slavs. After them came the Bavarians, Hungarians, and Austrians, followed by invading Turks. This legacy of conflict has continued into the late 20th century, with the tensions of the Iron Curtain a stark fact of life until 1989. The opening of the Hungarian border has again brought change and increased Burgenland's appeal to tourists.

Lake Neusiedl

Located in the north part of Burgenland, and one of the region's chief attractions, Lake Neusiedl occupies a strange world. One of the largest lakes in Europe, it is the Continent's only true steppe lake—a bizarre body of warm brackish water. Its sole tributary is far too small to replenish the water lost through evaporation, and there is no outflow at all. Underground springs feed it, but when they fail it dries up, which last happened in the 1860s. At present the water is nowhere more than about 7 ft deep; its many shallower sections make it possible (but dangerous) to wade across the lake. Its depth has varied dramatically, however, at times nearly engulfing the villages on its banks. Most of its 124-square-mi surface area is in Austria, but the southern reaches extend into Hungary.

What really sets Lake Neusiedl apart is the thick belt of tall reeds—in some places more than a mile wide—that almost completely encircles it. This is the habitat of a large variety of birds (more than 250 species) that nest near the water's edge. The lake is also a paradise for anglers, boaters, and windsurfers; other activities include swimming and, along its banks, bicycling.

The flat plains around Lake Neusiedl, with their tiny hamlets and un-spoiled scenery, are perfect for leisurely bicycling. Practically every village has a bike-rental shop (*Fahrradverleih* or *Radverleih*), but demand is so great that it's a good idea to reserve in advance. A bike route en-circles the lake, passing through Hungary on the southern end (you can shorten the route by taking the ferry between Illmitz beach and Mörbisch). This and many other routes are described in a German-language map-brochure called "Radeln in Burgenland," available free at tourist offices.

Neusiedl am See

❶ *51 km (32 mi) southeast of Vienna.*

Neusiedl am See, at the north end of the lake for which it is named, is a pleasant resort town with good facilities. Direct hourly commuter trains from Vienna have made it very popular, so you won't be alone here. To reach the lake itself, follow the main street for three blocks east of the Hauptplatz and turn right on Seestrasse, a mile-long cause-way that leads through the reeds to the lake, where you can rent small boats, swim, or just laze on the beach.

In Neusiedel am See itself, visit the ruins of the 13th-century hill fortress Ruine Tabor, a 15th-century parish church near the town hall, and the **Pannonisches Heimatmuseum** (Museum of Local Pannonian Life). ⊠ *Kalvarienbergstr. 40,* ☎ *02167/8173.* ⛿ *Donation suggested.* ⊙ *May–Oct., Tues.–Sat. 2:30–6:30, Sun. 10–noon and 2:30–6:30.*

Lodging

$$$ ⌖ **Hotel Wende.** This sprawling three-story hotel complex is close to the lake and has many standard amenities, but don't expect the charm of a country inn. The comfortable rooms with balconies are of ade-quate size, and the restaurant is quite well regarded. ⊠ *Seestr. 40, A–7100,* ☎ *02167/8111-0,* 🖷 *02167/8111-649. 105 rooms with bath. Restaurant, bar, indoor pool, sauna, exercise room, bicycles. No credit cards. Closed late Jan.–mid-Feb.*

Podersdorf

❷ *14 km (8½ mi) south of Neusiedl am See.*

The region east of Lake Neusiedl is the beginning of the unusual Hun-garian puszta, the great flat steppe marked with occasional windmills and characteristic wells with long wooden poles for drawing up water— a circular tour of about 70 km (44 mi) by car (or bicycle) would cover nearly everything of interest before returning you to Neusiedl am See. Some of the picturesque houses in Podersdorf have typical thatched roofs, and their chimneys are often adorned in summer with storks nesting after wintering in Egypt. Podersdorf has excellent swimming.

The **Natur und Tierlehrpfad**—a nature trail with cement casts of native bird and animal groupings—and a windmill (open for limited times only) educate tourists. ⊠ *Mühlstr. 26,* ☎ *02177/2227.* ⊠ *AS25.* ☉ *Mid-May–mid-Sept., daily 6 AM–7 PM.*

Dining and Lodging

$$ ✕ **Gasthof zur Dankbarkeit.** The kitchen offers fine local fare as well
★   as creative dishes with occasional Hungarian touches, served in comfortable *Stuben.* The menu changes daily, but you might find chicken-liver pâté, lamb sausages, rabbit, or rack of venison. The courtyard garden makes a delightful setting in summer. The excellent wines come from neighboring vineyards. ⊠ *Hauptstr. 39,* ☎ *02177/2223. DC, V. Closed Dec.–mid-Feb., Mon.–Thurs. mid-Feb.–mid-Apr., Tues.–Wed. mid-Apr.–Nov.*

$$–$$$ ⌂ **Haus Attila.** In this small, simple, family-run lakefront hotel, the balconied rooms overlooking the lake are especially appealing. The Karner family also runs the nearby smaller (and slightly cheaper) **Seewirt** (⊠ Strandpl. 1, ☎ 02177/2415). ⊠ *Strandpl. 8, A–7141,* ☎ *02177/2415,* FAX *02177/2465–30. 34 rooms with bath. Restaurant, sauna. No credit cards. Closed Dec.–Feb.*

En Route Podersdorf marks the beginning of the **Seewinkel,** a flat, marshy area dotted with small lakes and ponds, much of which is a wildlife sanctuary. The national park in **Illmitz** has a noted biological station and a nature trail (☎ 02175/3442). Beyond Illmitz, the road goes through Apetlon to **Pamhagen,** a border hamlet with a small zoo exhibiting animals and birds native to the Hungarian steppes.

Frauenkirchen

❸ *7½ km (4½ mi) east of Podersdorf, 16½ km (10¼ mi) southeast of Neusiedl am See.*

Frauenkirchen is known mainly for its **pilgrimage church,** rebuilt in 1702 after its 14th-century predecessor was destroyed by invading Turks, and again restored following World War II. The Baroque interior has a much-venerated wooden statue of the Virgin, from the 13th century. Note the miniature Mount Calvary depiction alongside the church.

Halbturn

❹ *5 km (3 mi) northwest of Frauenkirchen, 14 km (8½ mi) southeast of Neusiedl am See.*

Halbturn contains the exquisite Baroque **Schloss Halbturn,** an imperial hunting lodge built in 1710 by Lukas von Hildebrandt, the great architect of the period. This restored jewel was once used by Empress Maria Theresa as a summer residence and is noted for its ceiling frescoes. Devastated by Russian troops in the occupation following World War II, then rebuilt in the 1970s, the castle in summer now houses special annual exhibitions. You can stroll through the large, wooded surrounding park anytime, but in late spring when the red and pink chestnut trees are in bloom, the spectacle easily rivals a Monet landscape. In the courtyard, a shop sells excellent wines from the Halbturn vineyards, and a small art museum displays a copy of Gustav Klimt's impressive *Beethoven Frieze,* with the decided advantage over the Vienna original that here you can see the details up close. ⊠ *Schloss Halbturn,* ☎ *02172/8577.* ⊠ *AS60.* ☉ *May–Oct., daily 9–6.*

Purbach

⑤ *13 km (8½ mi) southwest of Neusiedl am See.*

Purbach, like the nearby wine villages of Breitenbrunn and Donner-skirchen, retains traces of its medieval fortifications. Look for the bust of a Turk atop a chimney in the town center; legend has it that when the invaders withdrew in 1532, one hungover, sleepy Turk missed the retreat and, fearing retribution, climbed down a chimney for safety. He was discovered, became an honored citizen, and lived in Purbach happily ever after. The wines of this area, the reds in particular, are outstanding and merit stopping for samples. In late fall and early winter you'll still see bunches of shriveled grapes on the leafless vines; these will be turned into rare Spätlese and still-rarer Eiswein dessert wines.

Dining and Lodging

$$$–$$$$
★ ✕ **Nikolauszeche.** This is one of Burgenland's best restaurants, noted for its elegant country decor in a 15th-century Renaissance house (it is a member of the Romantik Hotels & Restaurants group) as well as for its excellent regional cuisine. Specialties vary with the season, but you might find local goat cheese with olive oil, roast leg of lamb with rosemary and scalloped potatoes, or a pink fillet of young goat with mushroom cream sauce. There is an excellent selection of local wines, including some from the house's own winery. ⊠ *Bodenzeile 3,* ☎ *02683/5514,* 𝔽𝔸𝕏 *02683/5077. AE, DC, MC, V. Closed mid-Dec.–mid-Mar.*

$$–$$$ ✕▦ **Am Spitz.** This country inn, at the end of an attractive row of wine cellars, is known for its local Burgenland and Pannonian cooking. The restaurant is in a former cloister, and the outside garden enjoys an exquisite floral setting, looking down over the lake. The menu changes daily but always features fresh fish, possibly including a spicy Hungarian fish soup, a cassoulet of lake fish in basil cream, and roast veal steak. The somewhat plain and modern associated Gasthof ($$) is pleasant but less gemütlich. ⊠ *Waldsiedlg. 2, A–7083,* ☎ *02683/5519. 14 rooms with bath. Restaurant. No credit cards. Closed Mon.–Tues. and late Dec.–Mar.*

Rust

⑥ *14 km (9 mi) south of Purbach, 28 km (17½ mi) southwest of Neusiedl am See.*

Picturesque Rust is easily the most popular village on the lake for its colorful pastel facades and for lake sports. Tourists flock here in summer to see for themselves the famed sights of storks nesting atop the Renaissance and Baroque houses in the town's well-preserved historic center. Be sure to look for *Steckerl,* a delicious local fish caught from the Neusiedlersee and grilled barbecue-style with spices. It's available in most restaurants, but only in the hot months of summer. If you're heading from Purbach, leave Route 50 at Seehof and follow the local road past Oggau to arrive in Rust.

Visit the restored Gothic **Fischerkirche** (Fishermen's Church) off the west end of the Rathausplatz. Built between the 12th and 16th centuries, it is surrounded by a defensive wall and is noted for its 15th-century frescoes and an organ from 1705. ⊠ *Conradpl. 1,* ☎ *02685/502.* ▦ *AS10, AS20 with tour.* ☉ *Open Apr.–Oct. by arrangement.*

A causeway leads through nearly a mile of reeds to the **Seebad** beach and boat landing, where you can take a sightseeing boat round-trip or to another point on the lake, rent boats, swim, or enjoy a waterside drink or snack at an outdoor table of the Seerestaurant Rust.

Rust is also renowned for its outstanding wines. There are wine-tasting opportunities at the **Weinakademie** (⊠ Hauptstr. 31, ☎ 02685/6853,

FAX 02685/6431). Two of the better family-owned wineries that offer tastings are **Weingut Feiler-Artinger** (✉ Hauptstr. 3, ☎ 02685/237, FAX 02685/6552) and **Ernst Triebaumer** (✉ Raiffeisenstr. 9, ☎ 02685/528).

You can sample the excellent local vintages, along with a light lunch, in a number of friendly cafés, cellars, and the typical *Heurige,* where young wines are served by their makers. A favorite spot is the **Rathauskeller** (✉ Rathauspl. 1), open daily except Wednesday from 11:30 AM. The Ruster Blaufränkisch red wine is particularly good, resembling a well-rounded Burgundy.

Dining and Lodging

$ ✕ **Schandl.** For good, simple food to go along with the excellent wine from the family's winery, join the locals at this popular *Buschenschank* (inn). The buffet offers a selection of sausages, salads, cheese, and pickles, as well as a few hot dishes that change daily. There is a pleasant courtyard for outdoor dining in summer. ✉ *Hauptstr. 20,* ☎ *02685/ 265. No credit cards. Closed Tues. and Nov.–Mar.*

$$$ ✕🏨 **Rusterhof.** A lovingly renovated burgher's house—the town's oldest—at the top of the main square is home to an excellent and imaginative restaurant. Light natural woods and vaulted ceilings set the atmosphere in the series of smaller rooms; in summer there's an outside garden. The menu depends on what's fresh and might include grilled fish or saddle of hare in *Eiswein* sauce. Finish with a rhubarb compote. The complex also includes four very nice apartments for guests. ✉ *Rathauspl. 18, A-7071,* ☎ *02685/6416,* FAX *02685/6416–11. 4 rooms with bath. Restaurant. MC, V. Closed Jan.–Mar.*

$$$ 🏨 **Seehotel.** Set on the very edge of Lake Neusiedl, this rambling, modern complex contrasts strikingly with the bordering historic village. The comfortable guest rooms are contemporary Scandinavian in style; ask for one facing the lake. The kitchen is excellent. Golfers get reduced greens fees at the nearby Donnerskirchen course. ✉ *Am Seekanal 2– 4, A-7071,* ☎ *02685/381–0,* FAX *02685/381–419. 110 rooms with bath. 2 restaurants, bar, indoor pool, sauna, tennis courts, exercise room, squash, beach, boating. AE, DC, MC, V.*

Mörbisch

❼ *5½ km (3½ mi) south of Rust.*

Mörbisch is the last lakeside village before the Hungarian border. Considered by many to be the most attractive settlement on the lake, the town is famous for its low, whitewashed, Magyar-style houses, whose open galleries are colorfully decorated with flowers and bunches of grain. The local vineyards produce some superb white wines, especially the fresh-tasting Welschriesling and the full-bodied Muscat-Ottonel. Here, too, a causeway leads to a beach on the lake, where an international operetta festival is held each summer (☞ Nightlife and the Arts, *below*). A leisurely activity is to tour the countryside in a typical open **horse-drawn wagon.** Operators in several lakeside villages will arrange this, including **Johann Mad** (✉ Ruster Str. 14, ☎ 02685/8250) and **Evi Wenzl** (✉ Weinbergg. 12, ☎ 02685/8401).

Lodging

$$–$$$ 🏨 **Hotel Steiner.** Though in the center of the village, the family-run Steiner is also close to the vineyards and Lake Neusiedl. The somewhat plain modern exterior conceals rustic-style accommodations with all of the conveniences. ✉ *Hauerstr. 1, A-7072,* ☎ *02685/8444–0. 52 rooms with bath. Restaurant, indoor pool, sauna, bicycles. No credit cards. Closed Dec.–Mar.*

Nightlife and the Arts

At the **Mörbisch Lake Festival,** held on Fridays, Saturdays, and Sundays mid-July–August on Burgenland's Lake Neusiedl, operettas are performed outdoors on a floating stage. For information, contact the Mörbisch tourist office or the **festival office** (Seefestspiele Mörbisch) in Schloss Esterházy in Eisenstadt (☎ 02682/66210–0, FAX 02682/6621–14) or, from June through August, in **Mörbisch** itself (☎ 02685/8181–0, FAX 02685/8334).

Eisenstadt

❽ *22 km (14 mi) northwest of Mörbisch, 48 km (30 mi) south of Vienna, 26 km (16¼ mi) west of Wiener Neustadt.*

Burgenland's provincial capital, Eisenstadt, scarcely more than a village, nevertheless has an illustrious history and enough sights to keep you busy for a half, if not a full, day. It is connected to Neusiedl am See by train and to Vienna and places throughout Burgenland by bus. From Rust, take Route 52 west past St. Margarethen and Trausdorf to the capital.

Although the town has existed since at least the 12th century, it was not of any importance until the 17th, when it became the seat of the Esterházys, a princely Hungarian family that traces its roots to Attila the Hun. The original Esterházy made his fortune by marrying a succession of wealthy landowning widows. Esterházy support was largely responsible for the Habsburg reign in Hungary under the Dual Monarchy. At one time, the family controlled a far-flung agro-industrial empire, and it still owns vast forest resources. The composer Joseph Haydn lived in Eisenstadt for some 30 years while in the service of the Esterházys. When Burgenland was ceded to Austria after World War I, its major city, Sopron, elected to remain a part of Hungary, so in 1925 tiny Eisenstadt was made the capital of the new Austrian province.

In addition to what's listed below, Eisenstadt has a few other attractions that its tourist office can tell you about, including the Museum of Austrian Culture, the Diocesan Museum, the Fire Fighters Museum, Haydn's little garden house, and an assortment of churches.

★ **Schloss Esterházy,** the yellow-facaded former palace of the ruling princes, reigns over the town. Built in the Baroque style between 1663 and 1672 on the foundations of a medieval castle, it was later modified and is still owned by the Esterházy family, who lease it to the provincial government for use mostly as offices. Part of the recently mounted exhibition on the Esterházy family is still open; the rooms alone are worth viewing. The lavishly decorated **Haydn Room,** an impressive concert hall where the composer conducted his own works from 1761 until 1790, is still used for presentations of Haydn's works, with musicians often dressed in period garb. It can be seen on guided tours (in English on request) lasting about 30 minutes. The **park** behind the Schloss is pleasant for a stroll or a picnic; in late August it is the site of the Burgenland wine week. The **Schloss-Café Zachs,** opposite the west end of Schloss Esterházy at Glorietteallee 1, is open daily for snacks and refreshments. ✉ *Esterházy Pl.,* ☎ *02682/719–3000.* ✍ *AS60.* ☺ *Open Easter and Apr.–Oct., daily 9–6, guided tour hourly; Nov.–Mar., Mon.–Fri. 9–5, guided tour at 10 and 2.*

At the crest of Esterházystrasse perches the **Bergkirche,** an ornate Baroque church that includes the strange *Kalvarienberg,* an indoor Calvary Hill representing the Way of the Cross with life-size figures placed in cavelike rooms along an elaborate path. At its highest point, the trail reaches the platform of the belfry, offering a view over the town and this section of Burgenland. The magnificent wooden figures were carved and painted by Franciscan monks more than 250 years ago. The main part of the church contains the tomb of Joseph Haydn, who died in 1809 in Vienna. When the body was returned to Eisenstadt for burial 11 years later at the request of Prince Esterházy, it was unaccountably headless. A search for the head ensued, but it was not discovered until 1932. It had been under glass in the possession of the Gesellschaft der Musikfreunde, the main Viennese musical society. Finally, in 1954 Haydn's head was returned to Eisenstadt, to be buried with his body in a crypt inside the church. ⊠ *Josef Haydn Pl. 1,* ☎ *02682/62638.* ▨ *AS30.* ☉ *Apr.–Oct., daily 9–noon and 2–5.*

Wertheimergasse and Unterbergstrasse were boundaries of the Jewish ghetto from 1671 until 1938. During that time, Eisenstadt had a considerable Jewish population; today the **Österreichisches Jüdisches Museum** (Austrian Jewish Museum) recalls the experience of all Austrian Jews throughout history. A fascinating private synagogue in the complex survived the 1938 terror and is incorporated into the museum. ⊠ *Unterbergstr. 6,* ☎ *02682/65145.* ▨ *AS50.* ☉ *Late May–late Oct., Tues.–Sun. 10–5.*

The **Landesmuseum** (Burgenland Provincial Museum) brings the history of the region to life with displays on such diverse subjects as Roman culture and the area's wildlife. There's a memorial room to the composer Franz Liszt, along with more relics of the town's former Jewish community. ⊠ *Museumg. 5,* ☎ *02682/62652-0.* ▨ *AS30.* ☉ *Tues.– Sun. 9–noon and 1–5.*

Joseph Haydn lived in the simple house on Haydn Gasse from 1766 until 1778. Now the **Haydn Museum,** it contains several of the composer's original manuscripts and other memorabilia. The house itself, and especially its flower-filled courtyard with the small back rooms, is unpretentious but quite delightful. ⊠ *Haydn Gasse 21,* ☎ *02682/ 62652-29.* ▨ *AS30.* ☉ *Easter–late Oct., daily 9–noon and 1–5.*

Dining and Lodging

$$ ✕ **Zum Eder.** This sunny atrium restaurant in the center of town offers friendly service and a wide variety of selections. The emphasis here is on light, healthy dishes, including white pork fillet with fresh spinach and a large salad with grilled strips of chicken, and there are several vegetarian items to choose from as well, such as tasty carrot and celery lasagne. ⊠ *Hauptstr. 25,* ☎ *02682/62645. No credit cards.*

$ ✕ **Haydnbräu.** A red-tiled floor against white stucco walls and lots of natural wood provide the right setting for the "First Burgenland Restaurant-Brewery." Indeed, the excellent beer comes directly from polished copper vats behind the bar. The food, too, is good, for either snacks or a main meal; try the beef in spicy beer pepperoni sauce or fried calamari in beer batter. ⊠ *Pfarrg. 22,* ☎ *02682/61561. No credit cards.*

$$ ✕⬚ **Gasthof Ohr.** This personal, family-run hotel and restaurant is about a 10-minute easy walk from the town center. The immaculate rooms are comfortably attractive, done in natural woods and white with color accents; those in the back are quieter. The rustic wood-paneled restaurant offers specialty weeks—goose, game, new asparagus—in addition to Austrian and regional standards such as schnitzel and Hungarian fish soup. In summer, the canopied outdoor dining terrace is a green oasis. Wine comes from the family vineyards. ⊠ *Ruster Str. 51, A–7000,* ☎ *02682/ 62460,* ℻ *02682/624609. 24 rooms with bath. Restaurant. MC, V.*

$$$ ⬚ **Hotel Burgenland.** Considered the province's best, this strikingly contemporary hotel has everything you'd expect in a first-class establishment. It's near the town center, and the large rooms are bright and airy. The restaurants, alas, have been inconsistent, although the glassed-in

winter-garden café offers a pleasant pastel setting for a coffee or snack. ⊠ *Schubertpl. 1, A–7000,* ☎ *02682/696,* ℻ *02682/65531. 88 rooms with bath. 2 restaurants, bar, indoor pool, sauna. AE, DC, MC, V.*

Nightlife and the Arts

Eisenstadt devotes much cultural energy to one of its favorite sons. In the first half of September, it plays host to the annual **Haydn Festival** in the Esterházy Palace. Many of the concerts are by world-famous performers, and admission prices vary with the event. Other concerts featuring the works of Joseph Haydn run from mid-May to early October. Contact the Haydnfestspiele office (☎ 02682/61866–0, ℻ 02682/61805) in Schloss Esterházy (☞ *above*) or the local tourist office. Eisenstadt's **Haydn Quartet,** in 18th-century costumes, plays short matinee concerts of the master's works at 11 AM Tuesday and Friday, from mid-May to late October, at the Esterházy Palace (☎ 02682/63384, ℻ 02682/63384–20); tickets are AS80.

En Route Heading southwest from Eisenstadt brings you to the narrow waist of Burgenland, squeezed between Lower Austria and Hungary. The leading attraction here is Forchtenstein; take Route S31 for 20 km (12½ mi) to Mattersburg, then a local road 3 km (2 mi) west.

Forchtenstein

❾ *23 km (14½ mi) southwest of Eisenstadt.*

In the summer, people throng to the small village of Forchtenstein for its strawberries, but its enduring dominant feature is the medieval hilltop castle, **Burg Forchtenstein.** This formidable fortress was built in the early 14th century, enlarged by the Esterházys around 1635, and twice defended Austria against invading Turks. Captured enemy soldiers were put to work digging the castle's 466-ft-deep well, famous for its echo. As befits a military stronghold, there is a fine collection of weapons in the armory and booty taken from the Turks; there's also an exhibition of stately carriages. ⊠ *Burgpl. 1,* ☎ *02626/81212.* ▨ *AS70.* ☉ *Apr.– Oct., Mar.–Dec. daily 9–12 and 1:30–6; July–Aug. daily 9–6.*

Dining and Lodging

$$$ ✕ **Reisner.** The delicately prepared traditional food served at this popular restaurant attracts people from all over the region. You can eat in the somewhat formal dining room or in a rustic tavern favored by the locals, with the offerings matching the setting. Some typical dishes are trout with a ragout of fresh vegetables; excellent steaks; and, for dessert, rhubarb tart and poppy-seed parfait. ⊠ *Hauptstr. 141,* ☎ *02626/ 63139. No credit cards. Closed Wed.–Thurs. and early Mar.*

$ ▥ **Gasthof Sauerzapf.** This simple country inn on the main road just five minutes west of the castle has recently modernized its rooms. ⊠ *Rosalienstr. 9, A–7212,* ☎ *02626/81217. 14 rooms with bath. Restaurant. No credit cards.*

En Route You can get to Bernstein from Forchtenstein by returning to the highway from Burg Forchtenstein and taking S31 and Route 50 south past Weppersdorf and Stoob, the latter famous for its pottery. The road then goes through Oberpullendorf and close to Lockenhaus, where a renowned music festival is held each summer in the 13th-century castle (☞ Nightlife and the Arts *in* Bernstein, *below*).

Bernstein

❿ *73 km (45 mi) south of Forchtenstein.*

The small village of Bernstein is one of few sources of *Edelserpentin,* a dark green serpentine stone also known as Bernstein jade. Jewelry

THE CASTLE ROAD

IF YOU ARE HEADING SOUTH from Vienna to Graz on the A2 autobahn, the flat plains give way suddenly to steeply wooded hills and rocky gorges, with tantalizing glimpses of proud and seemingly inaccessible castles perched atop craggy promontories. More than a dozen castles along the Schlösserstrasse (Castle Road) have withstood the invading armies of the Huns and Turks to repose today in all their splendor as museums or hotels.

You can begin the tour by dipping into the eastern edge of Styria, leaving the autobahn at the Hartberg exit to visit **Schloss Hartberg,** a castle dating from the 13th century and now a museum, with occasional summer concerts. From Hartberg take Highway 54 south to Kaibing, where there will be signs for St. Johann bei Herberstein and **Schloss Herberstein,** famous for its Florentine-style courtyard and animal and nature park. You can also inspect the castle's weaponry collection and stroll in the Baroque garden. **Schloss Stubenberg,** north along the lakeside drive Stubenbergsee, is a fortresslike structure with an impressive ceramics display and summer concerts. The Allhau exit off the A2 autobahn a short distance north of Hartberg takes you to Highway 50 and Bernstein. This is home of **Burg Bernstein,** now a hotel but once the castle owned by Count Almásy, the character played by Ralph Fiennes in *The English Patient.*

East of Bernstein on Highway 50 is **Lockenhaus** (☎ 02616/2394, FAX 02616/2766), the castle with the most grisly history in Austria. In the 16th century, Countess Elisabeth Bathory was infamous for luring virgin peasant girls to her employ with promises of a dowry after two years' servitude; most girls never made it out alive. Obsessed with retaining her beauty, the depraved countess tortured and killed more than 500 girls, believing that bathing in their blood would keep her young. As a member of the nobility, the countess was never tried for her crimes. The castle is now a very nice hotel, with a medieval restaurant serving simple food like roast chicken and sausages.

Highway 50 south of Bernstein takes you to Stadtschlaining, the home of **Burg Schlaining,** famous for its weaponry collection, chapel, and palatial rooms (closed Monday). Highway 57 south of Highway 50 leads to **Burg Güssing,** not far from the Slovenian and Hungarian borders. After this the Castle Road continues on into Styria, southeast of Graz, with several more noteworthy castles to visit or stay in.

A drive along the Castle Road can take anywhere from four or five hours to a couple of days, depending on how many of the castles you stop to visit—either to tour or to spend the night in. Even if you're in a hurry, it's relatively easy to get off and on the A2 autobahn to visit a castle. The best time to visit this area is between April and October, because most of the castles are closed during the winter months. For more information about the Castle Road, contact the **Büro Die Schlösserstrasse** (✉ Schloss Kornberg, A–8330 Feldbach, ☎ 03152/7419 or 03152/3079, FAX 03152/5824 or 03152/5804).

— Bonnie Dodson

and objets d'art made locally from the town's stone are on display in the **Felsenmuseum** (Stone Museum), located partly within a former mine. ⊠ *Potsch, Hauptpl. 5,* ☎ *03354/6620–0.* ⊡ *AS50.* ☉ *Mar.–Oct., daily 9–noon and 1:30–6; Nov.–Dec., daily 9–noon and 1:30–5.*

Shops in town explain cutting and exhibit stones. A visit to the **Piringer** shop and museum includes a look into the caves from which the Edelserpentin is hewn. ⊠ *Hauptpl. 3 and 7,* ☎ *03354/6504 or 03354/ 6506.* ⊡ *AS15.* ☉ *Mid-Mar.–mid-Dec., daily 9–noon and 1:30–5:30.*

Overlooking the village is **Burg Bernstein,** a 12th-century fortress that was rebuilt in the 17th century. Part of it is now a romantic castle-hotel, but the rest may be visited. ☎ *03354/6382.* ⊡ *AS50.* ☉ *Mar.–Dec. daily 9–12, 1:30–6; July–Aug. daily 9–6.*

<table>
<tr><td>OFF THE
BEATEN PATH</td><td>**SOUTH BURGENLAND OPEN-AIR MUSEUM** – South of Bernstein in Bad Tatzmannsdorf is the Freilichtmuseum (South Burgenland Open-Air Museum), which displays wonderfully restored old barns, farmhouses, and stables from the region, giving a feeling of life as experienced a century or more ago. ⊠ *Josef-Hölzel-Allee 1,* ☎ *03353/8284 or 03353/ 8717.* ⊡ *AS10.* ☉ *Daily 9–5.*</td></tr>
</table>

Dining and Lodging

$ ✕ **Gasthof Heanznhof-Frühwirth.** In this typical Gasthof in the center of town you'll find unusually good regional cooking with strong Hungarian overtones: thick spicy soups, goose, duck, and other game in season. ⊠ *Hauptstr. 59,* ☎ *03354/6503. No credit cards. Closed Jan. and Thurs. Nov.–Mar.*

$$$–$$$$ ▥ **Burg Bernstein.** This medieval castle, built in the 12th century, became a hotel in 1953, with indoor plumbing being the only concession to modern life. It has gained a certain fame of late because it once belonged to Count Almásy, the character portrayed by Ralph Fiennes in *The English Patient.* It's now owned by an offshoot of the family, and you can still find Count Almásy's books on the shelves in the corridors, and his room is preserved the way he left it. The hilltop location gives it a bird's-eye view of the peaceful Tauchen Valley, just west of the village of Bernstein. The rooms, which tend to be large, look much as they must have in the mid-1800s. Meals, prepared by Countess Berger-Almásy herself, are served with regional wines in the Rittersaal, a baronial hall. ⊠ *Schlossweg 1, A–7434,* ☎ *03354/6382,* FAX *03354/6520. 14 rooms with bath. Pool, sauna, fishing, hunting. AE, DC, MC, V. Closed mid-Oct.–Apr.*

Nightlife and the Arts

The **International Chamber Music Festival** (Kammermusikfest) of Lockenhaus, 15 km (9½ mi) east of Bernstein, takes place during the first half of July in a 13th-century castle. World-famous musicians are invited to this intimate festival, and the audience may attend morning rehearsals. Call the local church office (*Pfarramt*) for information, reservations, and accommodations (☎ 02616/2072, FAX 02616/2766).

Güssing

⑪ *54 km (34 mi) south of Bernstein, 13 km (8½ mi) north of Heiligenkreuz, Hungary.*

Güssing is yet another of Burgenland's castle-dominated villages. From Bernstein many travelers arrive via Route 50 past Bad Tatzmannsdorf, then follow Route 57.

The classic 12th-century fortress **Burg Güssing,** perched high on a solitary volcanic outcrop, has wonderful views of the surrounding countryside.

It also has a fine collection of Old Master paintings (including portraits by Lucas Cranach), weapons, and armor, and a Gothic chapel with a rare 17th-century cabinet organ. There is also an exhibition celebrating fairy tales, with rooms devoted to Hansel and Gretel and Snow White. ☎ 03322/43400 or 03322/42491. ▣ *Castle museum and fairy-tale exhibition AS80.* ⏱ *May–Oct., daily 10–6 (last admission at 5).*

If you stop in Güssing to explore its castle, consider also visiting the nearby game park, **Naturpark Raab-Örsg-Goricko,** where a variety of wild animals indigenous to Eastern Austria reside in more than a square mile of open space. Observation posts are scattered throughout, and you should take your time at them—the animals have to come to you. ⊠ *1 km (½ mi) northeast of Güssing,* ☎ *03322/42419–0 or 03322/43026.* ▣ *Free.* ⏱ *Daily dawn–dusk.*

Dining and Lodging

$$ ✕▥ **Gasthof Gibiser.** Its proximity to Hungary has inspired the creative dishes served at this classic, white, villa-style country inn. The Pannonian cuisine combines the best of Austrian and Hungarian culinary traditions to produce such specialties as cabbage soup and steak stuffed with goose liver. For overnight guests there are several quiet rooms plus a few rustic thatch-roof cottages in the garden. ⊠ *Heiligenkreuz 81, A–7561,* ☎ *03325/4216–0,* ▣ *03325/4246–44. 12 rooms with bath, 3 cottages. AE, DC, MC, V. Closed 1st 2 wks of Feb., late Dec., and Mon. in winter.*

Riegersburg

⓬   *57 km (35 mi) southwest of Güssing, 56 km (34¾ mi) east of Graz.*

To arrive at Riegersburg from Güssing, stay on Route 57 to the frontier village of Heiligenkreuz-im-Laftnitztal; then take Route 65 west to Fürstenfeld, leaving Burgenland and crossing into Styria. Continue on to Ilz, and then turn south on Route 66 to Riegersburg. Riegersburg is a quiet agricultural community overshadowed by the massive fortress that perches atop an extraordinary volcanic outcropping. The rock has had its attraction over the centuries; archaeological finds have established that there were settlements here more than 6,000 years ago.

Rising some 600 ft above the valley below is the mighty and well-restored **Schloss Riegersburg,** one of Austria's great defensive bastions. Originally built in the 11th century on the site of Celtic and Roman strongholds, it has never been humbled in battle, not even in 1945, when its German occupants held out against the Russians. The present structure dates from the 17th century and is entered by way of a heavily defended, winding path, so be prepared to climb for 20 to 30 minutes. (Taxis will take travelers with disabilities up; check with the Zehethofer BP filling station in town, or call them at ☎ 03153/8281.) The castle has weapons displays, rooms with period furnishings, and a separate exhibit of witchcraft and magic. Needless to say, the views are magnificent. ☎ *03153/8213–0.* ▣ *Each exhibit AS90, both exhibits AS130.* ⏱ *Apr.–Oct., daily 9–5.*

Adjacent to the Riegersburg Castle you can observe free flight of birds of prey at **Greifvogelwarte Riegersburg** (Birds-of-Prey Keep). At various hours, falcons and eagles are set loose from a stand within the aviary preserve (returning to the keepers' care—and tempting meals, of course). ☎ *03153/7390.* ▣ *AS60.* ⏱ *Mon.–Sat. at 11 and 3; Sun. at 11, 2, and 4, weather permitting.*

Dining and Lodging

$$ ✕▥ **Gasthof Fink Zur Riegersburg.** This venerable, family-run country inn near the foot of the castle is prettily adorned with flower boxes and shutters. Its large, paneled dining room—complete with ceiling beams—is bright and airy, and there's also garden dining in season. The Austrian cuisine is hearty, with such dishes as bratwurst with sauerkraut and dumplings, and roast beef with cornmeal. A fine selection of Styrian wines is offered. ⊠ *Riegersburg 29, A–8333,* ☎ *03153/8216,* 🅵🅰🆇 *03153/7357. 33 rooms with bath. Restaurant. AE, DC, MC, V. Closed Feb.*

Blumau

❸ *60 km (37 mi) northeast of Graz.*

Midway between Vienna and Graz, this tiny hamlet was known until recently as one of the poorest farming communities in the country. Then in the late 1970s an oil company was drilling for gas and found a thermal spring instead. Not realizing its value, they blocked it up, but the people in the area didn't forget about it. It wasn't until the mid-1990s that permission was granted to drill again, and when the volcanic springs were released, the area became a mecca for spa treatments and cures.

Dining and Lodging

$$$$ ✕🏨 **Bad Blumau.** Designed by the late visionary artist, Friedensreich
★ Hundertwasser, this phenomenal spa hotel complex resembles a fantasy by Gaudí—undulating walls covered by a brilliant patchwork of checks, turrets, and mismatched windows, as well as sloping rooftop gardens and multicolored ceramic pillars. Rooms have curved walls, soothing fabrics and oddly angled bathrooms. Take an evening swim (even in winter) in the outdoor thermal pool, whose natural hot springs keep the water at a constant 34°C (92°F). Your days can be filled with a variety of spa treatments, from sound therapy to qi-gong to hay wraps. Anything is possible here. The spa restaurants serve tasty Austrian fare, using produce and meat provided by local farmers. ⊠ *A–8283 Blumau,* ☎ *03383/5100–0,* 🅵🅰🆇 *03383/5100–9100, 271 rooms with bath. 2 restaurants, bar, indoor and outdoor thermal pool, massage therapy center, sauna, boutiques.*

$$$$ ✕🏨 **Schloss Obermayerhofen.** The queen of all the castle hotels along
★ the Castle Drive from Vienna to Graz (☞ Close-up box, *above*) is located just a little over 3 km (2 mi) northwest of Blumau. No expense was spared in providing luxurious modern-day comfort while retaining the ancient feel of the castle, and no two rooms are alike. Some are furnished in French Empire style, and some with gleaming Biedermeier antiques, canopied beds and museum-worthy tapestries. The gourmet restaurant serves such tempting items as salmon tartare on a bed of crispy potato strips or panfried pike perch with white-truffle mashed potatoes. The menu changes frequently. ⊠ *A–8272 Sebersdorf/Bad Waltersdorf,* ☎ *03333/2503,* 🅵🅰🆇 *03333/2503–50, 20 rooms with bath. Restaurant. Jan. 6–Feb.*

GRAZ AND ITS ENVIRONS

200 km (125 mi) southwest of Vienna, 285 km (178 mi) southeast of Salzburg.

Native son Arnold Schwarzenegger hasn't managed to give Graz quite the cultural cachet that Mozart bestowed on Vienna and Salzburg, so this second-largest Austrian city (and capital of the province of Styria) has had to work harder to grab the spotlight. The Styriarte summer music festival has become one of the most prestigious cultural events in the country, and the opera now attracts top companies like the Bolshoi. With its skyline dominated by the squat 16th-century clock tower, this stylish city has a well-preserved medieval center whose Italian Renaissance overlay gives it a Mediterranean feel in contrast to other Austrian cities.

Lying in a somewhat remote corner of the country and often overlooked by tourists, Graz is easily reached from Vienna or Salzburg and provides the urban highlight of an itinerary through southeastern Austria. The name Graz derives from the Slavic *gradec,* meaning "small castle"; there was probably a fortress atop the Schlossberg hill as early as the 9th century. This strategic spot guarded the southern end of the narrow Mur Valley—an important approach to Vienna—from invasion by the Turks. By the 12th century, a town had developed at the foot of the hill, which in time became an imperial city of the ruling Habsburgs. Graz's glory faded in the 17th century when the court moved to Vienna, but the city continued to prosper as a provincial capital, especially under the enlightened 19th-century rule of Archduke Johann.

If you're staying in the city for more than a day, you might want to make a short excursion or two into the countryside. Ask at the information office for the detailed folder in English, "Excursions around Graz," with suggestions as well as travel directions. Three favorite trips—to Stübing bei Graz, Piber, and Bärnbach—can each be done in a few hours.

A Good Walk

On the left bank of the River Mur at the center of the Old City is the **Hauptplatz** ⑭, which was converted from a swampy pastureland to a town square by traveling merchants in 1164. It wasn't until 1550 that the Rathaus (City Hall) was built, but little remains now of the original structure. Modernized over the centuries until it began to look out of place in the Renaissance-style square, its facade was restored to the initial design in 1966. Facing the Rathaus is the impressive Erzherzog Johann Brunnen (Archduke Johann Fountain). Before leaving the Hauptplatz, go to the corner of Sporgasse for a look at the Baroque Luegg Haus, which gets its name from the German phrase *ums Eck lugen,* or "peer around the corner."

Backtrack towards the Rathaus and take the second right from the Hauptplatz onto the narrow, medieval Franziskanergasse. Walk its short length to the Franziskanerplatz and the Franziskanerkirche, a church and Franciscan monastery dating from 1240, with a 14th-century choir, a 16th-century nave, and a 17th-century tower. The area is known as the Kälbernes Viertel, or Butchers Quarter, because in the Middle Ages it was where butchers had their stalls offering meat and sausages for sale. Return to the Hauptplatz and go past the Rathaus on the right side, which is Schmiedgasse, or Blacksmith Lane. A block ahead it is lined with old burgher houses in pretty pastel shades. If you're up for visiting a series of museums, make a detour by going right on Landhausgasse, then an almost immediate left onto Raubergasse to the entrance to the natural-history section of the **Landesmuseum Joanneum** ⑮. The entrance to the applied arts department, displaying works by Lucas Cranach and Pieter Brueghel the Younger, is on Neutorgasse, parallel to but west of Raubergasse.

Go back to Landhausgasse and turn right onto Herrengasse. Across the street to your left at No. 3 is the Gemaltes Haus, a centuries-old ducal residence with lovely frescoes. At the corner of Herrengasse and Stempfergasse, note the Bären Apotheke (Chemist at the Sign of the Bear) for its rococo exterior. Opposite the Apotheke is the **Landhaus** ⑯, the home of the Styrian parliament. Take a moment to enter the arcaded courtyard, which was designed by Italian architect Domenico dell'Allio in Renaissance Lombard style. Adjoining the Landhaus is the **Landeszeughaus** ⑰, once the most important armory of southern Austria. Today it houses more than 30,000 exhibition pieces, mainly from the 16th and 17th centuries. Across the street at Herrengasse 13 is a house where Napoléon supposedly once spent the night.

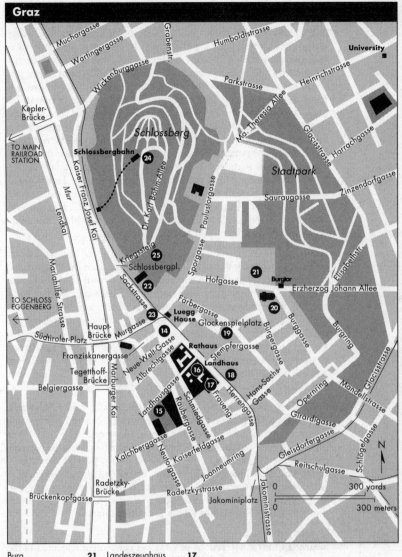

Graz

Continue south on Herrengasse to the **Stadtpfarrkirche** ⑱, a splendid church dating from the early 16th century, worth a visit, and on to Hans-Sachs-Gasse. Exit the church and turn left, then left again onto Schlossergasse (Locksmith Lane), passing Bischofsplatz and going on to **Glockenspielplatz** ⑲, famous for the wood-carved, life-size Styrian couple who dance to the sound of the Glockenspiel (chimes). Just past the square is the Mehlplatz, which is lined with historic houses and has a number of bars. This is popularly known as the Bermuda Triangle, because the university students have such a good time here that they "never come out again." In summer it's perfect for sipping a beer while watching the passing crowd. Go back through Glockenspielplatz and go left on Abraham-a-Santa- Clara-Gasse, then left again onto Bürgergasse. Almost immediately to your right, some steps lead to the late-Gothic **Domkirche** ⑳ and the Mausoleum of Emperor Ferdinand II. Return to the Mausoleum and go through the passageway that leads to Burggasse (not Bürgergasse). Across the street the castle gateway (Burgtor) leads to the Stadtpark, the vast city park, with its fountains, pathways, and park benches offering relaxation.

Just left of the Burgtor on Hofgasse is another grand archway, which is the entrance to the **Burg** ㉑, or old imperial palace, now used for government offices, but worth a trip inside the courtyard to see the Gothic staircase. Exiting the Burg, turn right onto Hofgasse, or Court Lane, and follow it to Sporgasse. Sporgasse (Spur Lane) was where spur makers and weaponry makers of the 14th and 15th centuries lived and worked. Go left on Sporgasse, and if you're still game after passing Luegg Haus from the beginning of the tour, go right onto Sackstrasse to **Herberstein Palace** ㉒, home to a collection of modern Styrian art, and the **Palais Khuenburg** ㉓, which now houses the city museum. Emerging from the Stadtmuseum, go right to Schlossbergplatz.

Schlossbergplatz is the base of the **Schlossberg** ㉔, or Palace Mountain. This is where the fortress guarding Graz was located and where you'll mount the steep steps leading to the famous **Uhrturm** ㉕. This clock tower is the most famous landmark in Graz. Continue following the path upward to the Glockenturm, the bell tower that is part of the original fortress on the Schlossberg. This winds up the end of the walking tour, and if you're too tired to go back on foot to the center of the city, consider taking the Schlossbergbahn, the funicular that carries the weary down to Kaiser-Franz-Josef-Kai at 15-minute intervals.

TIMING

Nearly all tourist attractions in Graz are conveniently located in the compact Altstadt, or Old City quarter, which can easily be explored on foot in an hour or so, not including any stops. With several stops, a walk through the Old City of Graz can take all day. If you're pressed for time, choose which part of the Old City you'd rather see: the lower section, with its churches, historical houses, and museums, or the upper town, with its winding wooded paths, famous clock tower, and the Schlossberg, the lookout point of the city. The best time to visit is between April and October when the weather is at its most inviting, but most tourist attractions are open year-round.

Sights to See

㉑ **Burg.** The scanty remains of this former imperial palace now house government offices. Most of this uninspired structure is from the 19th and 20th centuries, but two noteworthy vestiges of the original 15th-century stronghold remain: the **Burgtor** (palace gate), which opens into the sprawling **Stadtpark** (municipal park); and the unusual 49-step, 26-ft carved stone double-spiral **Gothic staircase** of 1499, in the hexagonal tower at the far end of the first courtyard.

⓴ Domkirche. On the south exterior wall is a badly damaged 15th-century fresco called the *Landplagenbild,* which graphically depicts contemporary local torments—the plague, the locusts, and the Turks. Step inside to see the outstanding high altar made of colored marble, the choir stalls, Raphael Donner's 1741 tomb of Count Cobenzl, and Konrad Laib's *Crucifixion* of 1457. The 15th-century reliquaries on either side of the triumphal arch leading to the choir were originally the hope chests of Paola Gonzaga, daughter of Ludovico II of Mantua. The Baroque **Mausoleum** of Emperor Ferdinand II, who died in 1637, adjoins the cathedral. Its sumptuous interior is partly an early design by native son Fischer von Erlach and his only work to be seen in Graz. ⊠ *Burgg. 3.* ⌨ *Free.* ☉ *May–Sept., Mon.–Sat. 11–noon and 2–3; tour Oct.–Apr., Mon.–Sat. at 11.*

⓳ Glockenspielplatz. Every day at 11 AM and 3 and 6 PM two mullioned windows open in the mechanical clock high above the square, revealing a wooden man adorned in lederhosen, a tankard of beer in his upraised fist, and a dirndl-clad Austrian maiden. An old folk tune plays and they dance on the window ledges before returning to their hidden perch. The musical box was erected in 1903 by the owner of the house. Look into the courtyard at No. 5, which has an impressive 17th-century open staircase. The house at No. 7 has an arcaded Renaissance courtyard.

NEED A BREAK?
Part deli, part café, **Frankowitsch** (⊠ Stempferg. 2–4) is worth a stop just to look at the selection of artistic pastries (which invariably sell out by late afternoon). Choose from a series of rooms, both upstairs and down, where you can nibble on little open-faced sandwiches and sip excellent coffee or a glass of Styrian wine. Make sure you look upstairs at the selection of exquisite chocolates on display. Frankowitsch is closed in the evenings and Sunday.

★ ⓮ Hauptplatz (Main Square). This triangular area was first laid out in 1164 and is used today as a lively open-air produce market. In its center stands the **Erzherzog Johann Brunnen** (Archduke Johann Fountain), dedicated to the popular 19th-century patron whose enlightened policies did much to develop Graz as a cultural and scientific center. The four female figures represent what were Styria's four main rivers; today only the Mur and the Enns are within the province. The **Luegg House,** at the corner of Sporgasse, is noted for its Baroque stucco facade. On the west side of the square are Gothic and Renaissance houses. The late-19th-century **Rathaus** (City Hall) totally dominates the south side. From the Neue-Welt-Gasse and Schmiedgasse you get a superb view of the Hauptplatz.

⓲ Herberstein Palace. This 17th-century former city residence of the ruling princes now houses the **Neue Galerie** (New Gallery). Its collection of paintings and sculpture from the 19th century to the present includes works by Austrian artists such as Egon Schiele, along with the newest in Styrian art. ⊠ *Sackstr. 16,* ☎ *0316/829155.* ⌨ *AS60.* ☉ *Tues.–Sun. 10–6, Thurs. 10–8.*

⓯ Landesmuseum Joanneum. This is the oldest public museum in Austria, founded by Archduke Johann in 1811. Actually, this is part of a large complex of museums—with collections ranging from natural-history exhibits to Old Master paintings—several of which are in other parts of town. The **Alte Galerie** (Old Gallery) is a world-famous collection of art from the Middle Ages through the Baroque period. Among its treasures are works by Pieter Brueghel the Younger and both Hans and Lucas Cranach, the noted *Admont Madonna* wood carving from 1400, and a medieval altarpiece depicting the murder of Thomas à Becket. ⊠ *Alte Galerie and Applied Arts: Neutorg. 45; Natural His-*

tory Museum: Rauberg. 10, ☎ Alte Galerie and Applied Arts: 0316/ 8017–9700; Natural History Museum: 0316/8017–9700. ☒ AS60. ☉ Alte Galerie and Applied Arts: Tues.–Sun. 10–5; Natural History Museum Tues.–Sun. 9–4.

☾ **⑰** **Landeszeughaus.** This provincial arsenal is possibly the most noted attraction in Graz. Virtually unchanged since it was built in 1643, this four-story armory still contains the 16th- and 17th-century weapons intended for use by Styrian mercenaries in fighting off the Turks. Nearly 30,000 items are on display, including more than 3,000 suits of armor (some of which are beautifully engraved), thousands of halberds, swords, firearms, cannons, and mortars. (Pieces from this collection were shown in the United States and Canada in 1992.) Probably the most important collection of its type in the world, it is now being rearranged for better presentation—to turn the displays into a "living exhibition" highlighting unusual items in contrast to the sheer quantity on hand. Call for possible new winter and evening hours. ☒ *Herreng. 16,* ☎ *0316/8017–9810.* ☒ *AS80.* ☉ *Mar.–Oct., Tues.–Sun. 9– 5; Nov.–Dec., Tues.–Sun. 10–3. Closed Jan.–Feb.*

⑯ **Landhaus.** The Styrian provincial parliament house was built between 1557 and 1565 by Domenico dell'Allio in the Renaissance Lombard style. Its arcaded courtyard is magnificently proportioned and features a 16th-century fountain that is an unusually fine example of old Styrian wrought-iron work. ☒ *Herreng. 16.*

㉓ **Palais Khuenburg.** This was the birthplace in 1863 of Archduke Franz Ferdinand, heir to the throne of the Austro-Hungarian Empire. His assassination at Sarajevo in 1914 led directly to the outbreak of World War I. The palace is now home to the **Stadtmuseum** (City Museum), whose exhibits trace the history of Graz and include an old-time pharmacy. The museum may be closed in early 2001 for renovations. Check with the tourist office for possible new opening hours. ☒ *Sackstr. 18,* ☎ *0316/ 822580–0.* ☒ *AS50.* ☉ *Tues. 10–9, Wed.–Sat. 10–6, Sun. 10–1.*

㉔ **Schlossberg** (Palace Mountain). The view from the summit of Graz's midtown mountain takes in all of the city and much of central Styria. A stone staircase beginning at Schlossbergplatz leads to the top, but since it is a 395-ft climb, you may prefer to use the **Schlossbergbahn** funicular railway (Kaiser-Franz-Josef-Kai 38) for AS20. The defensive fortress, whose ramparts were built to prevent the invading Turks from marching up the Mur Valley toward Vienna, remained in place until 1809, when a victorious Napoléon had them dismantled after defeating the Austrians. The town paid a large ransom to preserve two of the castle's towers, but the rest was torn down and is today a well-manicured and very popular park. Atop the Schlossberg and a few steps east of the funicular station is the **Glockenturm** (bell tower), an octagonal structure from 1588 containing Styria's largest bell, the famous 4-ton Liesl. This is also the departure point for guided walking tours of the Schlossberg, conducted daily, every hour from 9 to 5, except in winter. The **Open-Air Theater,** just yards to the north, is built into the old casemates of the castle and has a sliding roof in case of rain. Both opera and theater performances are held here in summer.

NEED A BREAK?   The **Schlossberg Café** (☎ 0316/823050) at the top of the funicular railway, has garden tables with a sweeping view across Graz. Among its specialties are *Germknödel* (a sweet dumpling in poppy-seed sauce) and *Most* (a light nonalcoholic wine).

Schloss Eggenberg. This 17th-century palace is on the very edge of the city and is surrounded by a large deer park. Built around an arcaded courtyard lined with antlers, this fine example of the high Baroque style contains the gorgeous **Prunkräume** (State Apartments) noted for their elaborate stucco decorations and frescoes, as well as three branch museums of the Joanneum. During the summer, candlelit chamber concerts are held here. The **Jagdmuseum** (Hunting Museum), on the first floor, displays antique weapons, paintings, and realistic dioramas. The **Abteilung für Vor- und Frühgeschichte** (Archaeological Museum) has a remarkable collection of Styrian archaeological finds, including the small and rather strange Strettweg Ritual Chariot dating from the 7th century BC. The **Münzensammlung** (Numismatic Museum) is tucked away in a corner on the ground floor. The attractive outdoor café in the park surrounding the castle is the perfect place to fortify yourself before or after visiting the museums. ✉ *Eggenberger Allee 90,* ☎ *0316/583–264–0.* 🎫 *AS80; for grounds only, AS2.* ⊙ *Prunkräume and Jagdmuseum, Mon.–Fri. 10–5, weekends 9–5; Abteilung für Vor- und Frühgeschichte and Münzensammlung, daily 9–5.*

⑱ Stadtpfarrkirche. The city parish church was built early in the 16th century and later received its Baroque facade and 18th-century spire. Tintoretto's *Assumption of the Virgin* decorates the altar. Badly damaged in World War II, the stained-glass windows were replaced in 1953 by a Salzburg artist, Albert Birkle, who portrayed Hitler and Mussolini as malicious spectators at the scourging of Christ (left window behind the high altar, fourth panel from the bottom on the right). Across the street begins a narrow lane named after Johann Bernhard Fischer von Erlach, the great architect of the Austrian Baroque, who was born in one of the houses here in 1666. ✉ *Herreng. 23,* ☎ *0316/829624–0.* ⊙ *7–7.*

㉕ Uhrturm (Clock Tower). This most famous landmark of Graz dates from the 16th century, though the clock mechanism is two centuries younger. The clock has four giant faces that might at first confuse you—until you realize that the *big* hands tell the hour and the *small* hands the minutes. At the time the clock was designed, this was thought to be easier to read at a distance. The 16th-century wooden parapet above the clock was once a post for firefighters, who kept a lookout on the city and sounded the alarm in case of fire.

Dining and Lodging

$$$$ ✗ **Johan.** A flickering torch marks the Renaissance portal entrance to
★ this chic restaurant, set under a low vaulted ceiling and enhanced by dramatic lighting from wall sconces and candles. Start with a selection of fish on a skewer over a bed of mango rice and shiitake mushrooms, then go on to grilled salmon and sauteed greens or veal with a light cheese crust and crisp shoestring potatoes. The homemade mango sherbet with coconut milk is sublime. ✉ *Landhausg. 1,* ☎ *0316/ 821312–0,* 🅵🅰🆇 *0316/815410. Reservations essential. AE, DC, MC, V. Closed Sun.–Mon. No lunch.*

$$$–$$$$ ✗ **Casino-Restaurant.** It's no gamble when you dine in this tony restaurant, even if you have to pass the roulette wheels to reach the elegant, glitzy dining salons. Try the changing multicourse fixed menu or select from regional and international specialties such as *Steinbutt* (turbot) in a nut crust with caviar sauce and gnocchi, or duck breast in a honey herb sauce. Desserts are excellent, especially berry compote with marzipan crust or elderberry sherbet. ✉ *Landhausg. 10,* ☎ *0316/ 821380. Jacket and tie. AE, DC, MC, V. No lunch.*

$$$ ✗ **Hofkeller.** With its dark, wood-panel walls, this popular place looks more like an old burgher cellar than an Italian restaurant. The blackboard menu changes daily, but there's usually a good choice of simple salads to start with, such as arugula with shaved Parmesan, as well as several pasta dishes, including a few vegetarian choices, such as manicotti stuffed with ricotta and spinach. Fish is always featured and is lightly prepared. ⊠ *Hofg. 8,* ☎ *0316/832439. No credit cards. Closed Sun.*

$$–$$$ ✕ **Landhauskeller.** The Landhaus complex (☞ Sights to See, *above*), which houses the provincial parliament and the armory, also includes a favorite traditional restaurant containing a labyrinth of charming, Old World dining rooms set within the ancient arcaded Landhaus itself. Styrian beef is the main event here, but there are lots of other dishes to choose from, such as chicken breast in a sesame crust with herbed, butter noodles or *Käsespätzle,* little pasta dumplings in baked cheese with fried onions. ⊠ *Schmiedg. 9,* ☎ *0316/830276. AE, DC, MC, V. Closed Sun. and late Dec.–mid-Jan.*

$$–$$$ ✕ **Stainzerbauer.** Local residents return again and again to this cozy
★ restaurant, one block south of the cathedral, to eat at their regular tables or, in summer, in the cool courtyard. The popular Styrian specialties may include such hearty dishes as pork ribs on a wooden plank with garlic bread, or *Perlhuhn,* guinea fowl stuffed with spinach and cheese and served with pumpkin pasta. Be sure to try the crispy salad tossed with *Kürbiskernöl* (pumpkin-seed oil) and yogurt dressing. ⊠ *Bürgerg. 4,* ☎ *0316/821106. AE, DC, MC, V. Closed Sun. and holidays.*

$ ✕ **Mangold's Vollwertrestaurant.** Located near Südtirolerplatz, this popular vegetarian restaurant offers a variety of tasty dishes, served cafeteria-style. ⊠ *Griesg. 10,* ☎ *0316/918002. No credit cards. No dinner Sat. Closed Sun.*

$ ✕ **Temmel.** Commanding the prominent corner of Herrengasse and Kaiserfeldgasse is this grand café, offering a selection of pastries, coffee, and light meals. Be sure to leave room for ice cream, which is the best in town. Owner Charly Temmel, a native of Graz, also owns a couple of trendy ice-cream shops in Santa Monica, California. ⊠ *Kaiserfeldg. 1,* ☎ *0316/830436. No credit cards. Closed Sat. evening and Sun.*

$$$$ ✕🖾 **Grand Hotel Wiesler.** With five stars and a supreme location just
★ across the Mur River from the Old City, the Wiesler is the grande dame of Graz hotels. Arnold Schwarzenegger checks in when he's in town, and Alfred Hitchcock was once a guest. It dates from the turn of the century, as evidenced by high ceilings and large spaces, and the decoration is predominantly Art Nouveau. Rooms are subtly fetching with cherry-wood accents, plush carpeting, and striking fabrics. A popular jazz buffet brunch is held every Sunday from October through June, with live music to accompany the sumptuous feast. ⊠ *Grieskai 4–8, A–8020,* ☎ *0316/7066–0,* ℻ *0316/7066–76. 98 rooms with bath. Restaurant, bar, parking (fee). AE, DC, MC, V.*✺

$$$$ 🖾 **Schlossberg.** This robin's-egg-blue town house, tucked up against the foot of the Schlossberg, is owned by a former race car driver who turned it into a hotel in 1982. The owner's wife is an avid art collector, and the tastefully furnished rooms display provincial antiques as well as 18th-century portraits, while the corridors are filled with modern artworks and an interesting variety of old Styrian lamps. The outdoor pool, on a rocky terrace, offers a spectacular view of the city. ⊠ *Kaiser-Franz-Josef-Kai 30, A–8010,* ☎ *0316/8070–0,* ℻ *0316/8070– 160. 55 rooms with bath. Bar, pool, sauna, exercise room, meeting rooms, parking (fee). AE, DC, MC, V.*✺

$$$–$$$$ 🖾 **Erzherzog Johann.** Travelers who prefer a traditionally elegant city hotel will be happy with this Old World establishment in a 16th-century building. Its location, just steps from the Hauptplatz in the Old City, is perfect for tourists. Rooms are furnished charmingly in Biedermeier style and open onto a sunny atrium. ⊠ *Sackstr. 3–5, A– 8010,* ☎ *0316/811616,* ℻ *0316/811515. 62 rooms with bath. Restaurant, bar, café, sauna, parking (fee). AE, DC, MC, V.*✺

$$$ 🖾 **Europa.** This modern hotel is directly across from the main train station, about a 15-minute walk from the Old City. Its thoroughly contemporary design and interiors and ease of access make it popular with both businesspeople and tourists. Rooms are well equipped and quiet. An underground shopping mall connects it directly with the rail station and air terminal. ⊠ *Bahnhofgürtel 89, A–8020,* ☎ *0316/7076– 0,* FAX *0316/7076–666. 114 rooms with bath, 4 suites. Restaurant, bar, café, sauna, parking (fee). AE, DC, MC, V.* 🍽

$$–$$$ ☎ **Mariahilf.** A comfortable old hotel in the center of things, the Mariahilf is just across the river from the Old City. Although the location is fairly busy, the simple, modern rooms are quiet thanks to soundproofing. Those without private bath rate in the $ category. ⊠ *Mariahilferstr. 9, A–8020,* ☎ *0316/713163,* FAX *0316/717652. 44 rooms, 33 with bath. Restaurant. AE, DC, MC, V.*

$$ ☎ **Rosenhotel Steiermark.** An exceptional value, this very modern student accommodation, two blocks northeast of the university, functions as a hotel from early July until early September. Naturally, it attracts a young crowd and has an institutional feel, but if you want a clean room with a private bath at a low price, this is a good choice. ⊠ *Liebigg. 4, A–8010,* ☎ *0316/381–503–0,* FAX *0316/381–503–62. 121 rooms with bath. Restaurant, bar, parking (fee). AE, DC, MC, V. Closed Oct.–June.*

$ ☎ **Strasser.** This friendly budget hotel, just two blocks south of the main train station, offers acceptable accommodations at rock-bottom prices. There is no elevator, the toilets are down the hall, and it is a bit noisy, but the rooms are large, comfortable, and clean, and the restaurant is a good value. ⊠ *Eggenberger Gürtel 11, A–8020,* ☎ *0316/ 713977,* FAX *0316/916856. 40 rooms with bath. Restaurant, parking (fee). No credit cards.*

Nightlife and the Arts

Graz is noted for its avant-garde theater and its opera, concerts, and jazz. The Graz tourist office distributes the quarterly "Graz Guide," with information in English, and the "Graz Stadtanzeiger" ("City Informer"), a free monthly guide in German.

The **Styriarte** festival (late June to mid-July), under the direction of native son Nikolaus Harnoncourt—one of the most famous names in the early music world—gathers outstanding musicians from around the world. Performances take place at Schloss Eggenburg and various halls in Graz. For program details contact the tourist office (☞ Visitor Information *in* Eastern Austria A to Z, *below*) or Styriarte (⊠ Palais Attems, Sackstr. 17, A–8010 Graz, ☎ 0316/825–000, FAX 0316/877–3836, 🍽).

The annual **Styrian Autumn Festival** (Steirische Herbst), a sometimes shocking celebration of the avant-garde in experimental theater, music, opera, dance, jazz, film, video, and other performing arts, is held in Graz in October. Contact Styriarte (☞ *above*) or the tourist office for details.

The 19th-century **Graz Opera House** (⊠ Kaiser-Josef-Pl. 10, ☎ 0316/ 8000, FAX 0316/8008–565), with its resplendent rococo interior, is a famed showcase for young talent and experimental productions as well as more conventional works; it stages three to five performances a week late September–June. Tickets are generally available until shortly before the performances; call for information.

Graz, a major university town, has a lively theater scene known especially for its experimental productions. Its **Schauspielhaus**, built in 1825, is the leading playhouse, and there are smaller theaters scattered around town. Contact the tourist office for current offerings.

Popular **candlelight concerts** are held in the Eggenberg Palace on Monday evenings from mid-July to mid-September at 8 PM. Ask the Graz tourist office for details. During July and August, students and, occasionally, faculty of the **American Institute of Musical Studies** (AIMS)

(☎ 0316/327066, FAX 0316/325574) offer concerts. For information, check with the tourist office or the institute.

Graz's **after-hours scene** is centered on the area around Prokopigasse, Bürgergasse, and Glockenspielplatz. Here you'll find activity until the early morning hours. The crowd moves around, so check with the tourist office for the current "in" spots. The **Casino Graz** (✉ Landhausg. 10, ☎ 0316/832578), at the corner of Landhausgasse and Schmiedgasse in the Old City, is open daily from 3 PM. It offers French and American roulette, blackjack, baccarat, and punto banco. The entrance fee of AS260 gets you AS300 worth of chips. A passport is required, you must be at least 21, and men are expected to wear a jacket and tie.

Shopping

Graz is a smart, stylish city with great shopping. In the streets surrounding Sackstrasse you'll find top designer boutiques and specialty shops. Be on the lookout for traditional skirts, trousers, jackets, and coats of gray and dark green woolen loden cloth; dirndls; modern sportswear and ski equipment; handwoven garments; and objects of wrought iron. The **Heimatwerk** shops at Paulustorgasse 4 and Herrengasse 10 are associated with the local folklore museum and stock a good variety of regional crafts and products. For a wide selection of conventional goods, try the leading department store, **Kastner & Öhler,** at Sackstrasse 7, just off the Hauptplatz.

The English Bookshop (✉ Tummelpl. 7, ☎ 0316/826266–0) is the only English-language bookstore in Graz, offering a great collection of current hardbacks as well was paperbacks and magazines. It's open Monday–Friday from 9–6 and Saturday from 9–noon.

Stübing bei Graz

 15 km (9 mi) northwest of Graz.

The attraction in Stübing bei Graz is the **Austrian Open-Air Museum** (Österreichisches Freilichtmuseum), which covers some 100 acres of hilly woodland. Here is a fascinating collection of about 80 authentic farmhouses, barns, Alpine huts, working water mills, forges, and other rural structures dating from the 16th century through the early 20th century, moved to this site from every province of Austria. Buildings that otherwise would have been lost in the rush to "progress" have been preserved complete with their original furnishings. Most are open to visitors, and in several of them artisans can be seen at work, sometimes in period costume. There is a restaurant and outdoor café by the entrance. You can reach Stübing bei Graz from Graz via Route 67 to Gratkorn, by train (15 minutes) to Stübing and a 2-km (1-mi) walk from there, or by municipal bus (40 minutes) from Lendplatz. ✉ *Stübing bei Graz,* ☎ *03124/53700.* ☑ *AS75.* ☉ *Apr.–Oct., Tues.–Sun. 9–5 (last admission at 4).*

Piber

★ ☺ ㉗ 44 km (27 mi) west of Graz.

The hamlet of Piber on the northeast outskirts of Köflach (take Route 70 to and beyond Köflach) is devoted to raising horses, and from the **Lipizzaner Stud Farm** come the world-famous stallions that perform at the Spanish Riding School in Vienna (☞ An Imperial City: The Hofburg *in* Chapter 1). These snow-white horses trace their lineage back to 1580, when Archduke Karl of Styria established a stud farm at Lipica near Trieste, using stallions from Arabia and mares from Spain. After World War I, when Austria lost Lipica, the farm was transferred to Piber.

Born black, the steeds gradually turn white between the ages of two and seven. To get to Piber from Graz you can drive (take Route 70) or take a bus (75 minutes) or a train (about an hour), with departures every hour or two. Some trains split en route; be sure to board the correct car. Walk or take a taxi the 3 km (2 mi) between Köflach and Piber. ⊠ *Bundesgestüt Piber,* ☎ *03144/3323.* ⊠ *Tour AS100.* ☉ *Mid-Apr.– Oct., 1-hr tour daily at 9, 10:15, 2, and 3:15.*

Bärnbach

33 km (21 mi) west of Graz, 3 km (2 mi) north of Voitsburg.

Bärnbach offers the amazing vision of the **Church of St. Barbara.** Completely redone in 1988 by the contemporary Austrian painter Friedensreich Hundertwasser, its exterior is a fantasy of abstract religious symbols in brilliant colors and shapes.

At the interesting **Stölzle Glass Center,** you can watch glass blowing and purchase original glass articles. ⊠ *Hochregisterstr. 1,* ☎ *03142/ 62950.* ⊠ *AS75.* ☉ *Weekdays 9–5, Sat. 9–1; May–Oct., also Sun. 9– 1. Last admission 1 hr prior to closing.*

THROUGH STYRIA TO VIENNA

The mountainous green heartland of Styria embraces a region where ancient Romans once worked the surrounding mines of what are accurately called the Iron Alps. Here in West Styria, the atmosphere can change abruptly from industrial to tourist and can often combine the two—as at the Erzberg, literally a mountain of iron. The prime destination, however, remains Mariazell. In the past, royalty—not only the Habsburgs but princes of foreign countries as well—went there, not for social pleasures but for religious reasons, for Mariazell has a double personality. It is a summer and winter pleasure resort and a renowned place of pilgrimage. The evening candlelit processions through the village to its famed basilica are beautiful and inspiring.

To tour this region, you can head southwest—after a scenic ride north through the Mur Valley to the historic crossroads of Bruck an der Mur— to Judenburg and possibly Murau and even continue into Salzburg province. Another option is to start toward Judenburg but turn northwest beyond Leoben to the abbey at Admont and then either return to Bruck via Eisenerz or continue north through Upper Austria to Amstetten or via Steyr to Linz on the Danube. Back at Bruck an der Mur, where several highways and rail lines converge, you can head north to Mariazell and then continue on one of the country's most scenic mountain drives (or rail trips) back to the Danube Valley.

Peggau

28 *20 km (12 mi) north of Graz.*

Just north of the industrial town of Peggau (rail stop: Peggau-Deutschfeistritz) is the famous **Lurgrotte,** the largest stalactite and stalagmite cave in Austria. Conducted tours lasting an hour follow a subterranean stream past illuminated sights, and there is a small restaurant at the entrance. To get to Peggau from Graz, head north on Route 67, driving through the heavily forested, narrow Mur Valley toward Bruck an der Mur. (A rail line parallels the road, with trains every hour or two making local stops near the points of interest.) ☎ *03127/2580.* ⊠ *One hr tour AS60, 2-hr tour AS85.* ☉ *Apr.–Oct., daily 9–4.*

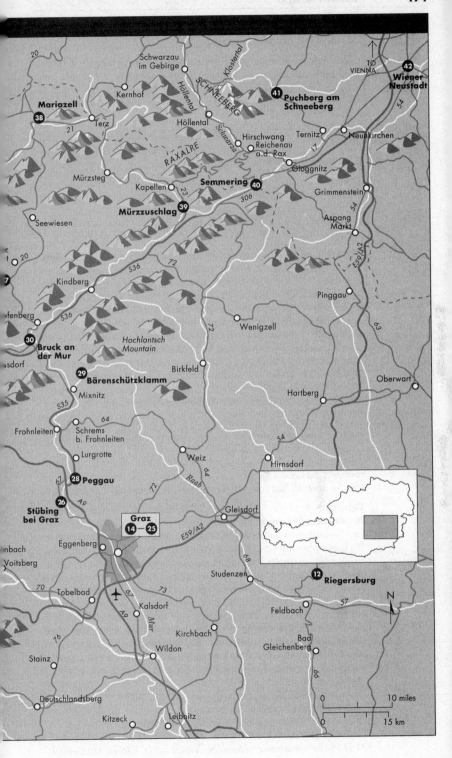

Mixnitz

20 km (12 mi) north of Peggau.

㉙ Mixnitz is the starting point for a rugged 4½-hour hike through the wild **Bärenschützklamm,** a savage gorge that can be negotiated only on steps and ladders but is nevertheless worth visiting for its spectacular foaming waterfalls. Beyond it are peaceful mountain meadows and finally the 5,650-ft mountain.

Bruck an der Mur

㉚ *55 km (34 mi) north of Graz.*

Bruck an der Mur is known primarily as Styria's major traffic junction, a point where four valleys and two rivers converge and where several highways and main rail lines come together. Although most of the busy town is devoted to industry, its compact historic center, dating partially from the 13th century, is well worth a short visit.

The architecturally distinguished main square, **Koloman-Wallisch-Platz,** is four blocks west of the train station. On the square's northeast corner stands the late-15th-century **Kornmesserhaus,** a magnificent example of secular architecture in the late-Gothic style, noted especially for its elaborate loggia and arcades. The filigreed **Eiserner Brunnen** is across the square. This ornamental wrought-iron well housing dating from 1620 is considered to be the best piece of ironwork in Styria, a province noted for its metalwork. The **Rathaus** (Town Hall) facing it is also attractive and houses a small museum of local life (✉ Hauptpl., ☎ 03862/51521–0). On the hill behind the square is the **Pfarrkirche** (Parish Church), built between the 13th and 15th centuries, which has an interesting late-Gothic sacristy door of wrought iron.

Overlooking the town, just two blocks northeast of its center, are the remains of **Burg Landskron,** a 13th-century fortress that once defended the confluence of the Mur and Mürz rivers. Today only its clock tower remains intact, but the view is worth the short climb. The small park surrounding the Landskron ruins, on the Schlossberg hill, makes a wonderful spot for a picnic. Buy your supplies at one of the shops in the streets below.

Dining

$$ ✕ **Wirtshaus Steirereck.** The sign "Griasdi"—Styrian dialect for "Greet-
★ ings"—welcomes guests to this charming, green-shuttered farmhouse. It's located northwest of Bruck an der Mur, but it's well worth the trek to get here, as owner and chef Heinz Reitbauer—son of the owner of the famous Steirereck in Vienna—has created possibly the most unusual restaurant in the country, one-half gourmet restaurant, one-half working farm. There are goats and other farm animals in a fenced enclosure, while indoors the many dining rooms retain the farmhouse-rustic decor of the early part of the 20th century. Especially good is the crispy farm duck for two with light homemade dumplings, *Backhendl* (fried chicken adorably served in a toy-sized feeding trough), Styrian beef, and fresh fish. The restaurant also offers its own microbrewed beer and a good selection of wines by the glass. For more of the restaurant's homey ambience, be sure to look at the quaint rooms upstairs before you leave. To get to Wirtshaus Steirereck, take Route 116 north toward St. Lorenzen, exiting at St. Marein. From there follow signs to Pogusch. ✉ *Pogusch 21, St. Lorenzen,* ☎ *03863/2000,* 𝔽𝔸𝕏 *03863/ 515151. Reservations essential. No credit cards. Closed Mon.–Wed.*

Leoben

③ *16 km (10 mi) southwest of Bruck an der Mur.*

Interesting side trips fan out in several directions from the main junction of Bruck an der Mur. One takes you southwest by car (Route S6), train, or bus to Leoben, the largest town in central Styria and the center of an important mining and heavy-industry region. Most of the attractions are in the charming **Altstadt** (Old City), near the Hauptplatz. Here, six blocks south of the train station, you will find some historic sights, including the **Altes Rathaus** (Old City Hall) of 1568, the **Pestsäule** (Plague Column) of 1717, and the handsome 17th-century **Hacklhaus** with its densely decorated Baroque facade. Walking one block west brings you to the **Museum der Stadt Leoben** (✉ Kirchg. 6, ☎ 03842/4062–227), a municipal museum of local history, industry, art, and nature. Next door is the **Stadtpfarrkirche** (City Parish Church) of 1660; a block to the south is the **Mautturm** (Customs Tower) of 1615, locally called the Schwammerl, because it resembles a mushroom.

Across the Mur River from the Mautturm is the **Maria-am-Wasser Kirche,** a Gothic church with outstanding 15th-century stained-glass windows.

The suburb of Göss, 2 km (1 mi) south, is home of the famous Gösser beer, made in a former monastery founded in 1020. The small **Brau Museum** (Brewing Museum) and the brewery may be toured by prior arrangement on Saturday and Sunday from 9–6 (✉ Brauhausstr., ☎ 03842/2090–0).

Seckau

③ *33 km (20½ mi) southwest of Leoben.*

For 550 years, Seckau was the episcopal center of Styria, and its abbey is well worth a detour. The famed **Seckau Abbey** was founded in 1140 and over the years has been a significant religious center. The original Romanesque style of its church is visible despite later additions, and the complex contains several outstanding features of various periods, from the late-Renaissance mausoleum of Archduke Karl II to the strikingly modern apocalyptic frescoes in the Angels' Chapel by the 20th-century painter Herbert Boeckl. The whole complex of buildings bears rich testimony to the wealth that was lavished upon it—from stained-glass windows to wrought-iron fittings, paintings, and sculptures. The abbey is north of the small industrial town of Knittelfeld, which is southwest of Leoben on Route S6/E7. ☎ 03514/52340. ▣ *Donation requested.* ☉ *Tours Sun. at 11:45 and 2:45, other days and times by appointment.*

Judenburg

③ *15 km (9 mi) southwest of Knittelfeld.*

The ancient and attractive hill town of Judenburg overlooks the steelworks along the Upper Mur River valley. Its origins date to prehistoric times—the famous Strettweg Ritual Chariot (now on display at Schloss Eggenberg in Graz) was found here—but the town's name derives from a medieval colony of Jewish merchants.

From its Hauptplatz rises the lofty **Stadtturm,** a 240-ft-high watchtower built between 1449 and 1520, which you can climb. The tower is open May and June, Friday–Sunday 10–6; July–September, daily 10–6; and October, Friday–Sunday 10–5. The early 16th-century **Pfarrkirche** (parish church) next to the Stadtturm has some excellent sculptures, especially of the Virgin Mary.

The small **Stadtmuseum** (City Museum) around the corner offers dioramas depicting local history and a display of minerals from nearby mines. ⊠ *Kaserng. 27,* ☎ *03572/85053.* ⊡ *Donation requested.* ☉ *Sept.–June, weekdays 9–noon; Jul.–Aug., weekdays 9–3. Open Sun. by arrangement.*

Just across the river from the Stadtmuseum, on Feldgasse, stands the 12th-century **Magdalenenkirche,** a Romanesque church with 14th-century frescoes and medieval stained-glass windows.

Dining and Lodging

$$$ ✕▥ **Schloss Gabelhofen.** Straight out of a fairy tale, this 15th-century
★ castle-hotel comes complete with four squat towers and a wooden drawbridge (over a grassed-in moat). From the vast inner courtyard—now covered by a skylight—Renaissance-era stairways lead to an upper arcaded gallery and the guest rooms. Historic features have been lovingly preserved, but every modern convenience has also been provided. The smartly turned-out bedrooms are large and have contemporary furniture, plump floral sofas, and crimson shutters, while bathrooms are state-of-the-art. Step into the atmospheric dungeon bar and sip a glass of Schilcher Frizzante, the local sunset-colored sparkling wine, before repairing upstairs for dinner in the excellent hotel restaurant. The menu features Styrian specialties as well as fried catfish, beef stroganoff, and vegetarian dishes. To reach Schloss Gabelhofen, take the Judenburg exit from the A1 Autobahn and go in the direction of Judenburg (not Fohnsdorf) for about 1 km. ⊠ *Schlossg. 54, A–8753, Fohnsdorf,* ☎ *03573/5555–0,* ℻ *03573/ 5555–6. 57 rooms with bath. Restaurant, bar. AE, DC, MC, V.* ✎

Outdoor Activities and Sports

GOLF

Golf Club Murtal (☎ ℻ 03512/75213), in Spielberg, 10 km (5 mi) from Judenburg, has 18 holes, and is open April to November. Greens fees are AS480 on weekdays and AS550 on weekends. Guests staying at Schloss Gabelhofen receive a 25% discount.

RIDING

Reit Club Sachendorf (☎ ℻ 03512/82258), close to the golf course in Spielberg (10 km/5 mi from Judenburg), has horses for riding and also offers riding lessons for AS140 an hour, with an English-speaking trainer.

Judenburg plays host to the Formula-1 car race, which takes place on the A-1 racetrack every July. For information on tickets to this world-class event, contact the Steirische Tourismus (☞ Visitor Information *in* Eastern Austria A to Z, *below*).

Murau

★ ㉞ *47 km (29½ mi) west of Judenburg.*

Murau is a stunningly picturesque, well-preserved medieval town where you can see stretches of the ancient town wall; the Pfarrkirche from 1296 with its ancient frescoes and late-Gothic "lantern of the dead" in the churchyard; the dominating Schloss Obermurau, a 13th-century castle that was rebuilt in the 17th century (where summer classical music concerts are now held); and the Altes Rathaus, the Old Town Hall that was once a part of the fortifications. Stroll along the river, looking up at the timbered houses atop the wall, to get the full effect of the town's medieval defensive character. A number of artists reside here, which explains the occasional contemporary works of art in the town (including the eye-catching bottle-glass entrance to the public rest rooms). Another unusual feature of the town is a vending machine dispensing fresh milk. Murau is an excellent base if you're interested in visiting working mills—water, grain, and handweaving. It's also a sports-lover's paradise, with everything from skiing and sleigh rides in winter to mountain biking, hiking, swimming, and fishing in summer.

The **Murau brewery** (✉ Raffaltpl. 17, ☎ 03532/3266–37), with more than 500 years' brewing tradition, has a small museum and a souvenir shop, but stop in the ground-floor Brauhaus restaurant to sample the brews and possibly have a filling meal of Styrian specialties as well. The museum is open Friday from 4–6, or by prior arrangement.

If you ever dreamed of becoming a steam-locomotive engineer (*Lokführer*), Murau is your place. The narrow-gauge **Murtalbahn** (Mur Valley Railroad), which is more than 100 years old and is operated by the Steiermärkische Landesbahnen (Styrian Provincial Railways), gives engine-driving lessons on Monday from early July until late August, ranging from 15 minutes on just a locomotive to longer periods with passenger cars attached; bring your friends, stock the bar car, and hire the local brass band to provide inspiration while you shovel the coal. The steam line also provides regular passenger service on the 37-km (23-mi) stretch between Murau and Tamsweg several days a week from late June to mid-September. ☎ *03532/2233*, ᶠᵃˣ *0316/2231–22.*

This part of Styria is famous for the vast amount of timber it produces, and the **Holz-Museum** (timber museum) gives you an idea of the fascinating ways wood is used. The exhibit encompasses everything from ancient tools to modern furniture, with workshops offered in barrel making or wood sculpture. Each summer several Austrian artists take part in a hands-on carpentry workshop. *St. Ruprecht ob Murau,* ☎ *03534/2202,* ᶠᵃˣ *03534/2204–4.* ⊠ *AS55.* ☼ *Apr. and Oct., daily 10–4; May–Jun., daily 9–4; Jul.–Aug., daily 9–5; Sept., daily 9–4.*

Dining and Lodging

$$–$$$ ✗ **Rahmhube.** High above Murau on the Stolzalpe ("Proud Mountain") is this fine restaurant where you can sample chef Erich Pucher's Austrian nouvelle cuisine. Notable delights include *Seeteufel*—monkfish, with lobster risotto—and flying duck breast in a honey rosemary sauce. Lunch is less pricey, and may include generous portions of *Backhendl*—crispy fried chicken in a basket with potato salad—and *Kärntner Käsnudel,* light-as-a-feather Styrian cheese ravioli, accompanied by a salad of greens, capers, and Tuscan beans. The Rahmhube also has a few bedrooms for overnighters that are in the $ category. ✉ *Stolzalpe 24, A-8852,* ☎ *03532/2508,* ᶠᵃˣ *03532/2508–11. No credit cards. Closed 2 wks in July or Aug.*

$$$ ✗🏠 **Hotel Lercher.** This family-owned hotel with cheery red- and white-★ striped shutters goes back to the time of Maria Theresa. Most rooms, however, have contemporary furnishings, yet still possess a great deal of charm. Care has been taken to anticipate every need, including vanity tables and comfortable sitting areas. Several rooms have skylights, with shades thoughtfully provided, some have balconies, and all have great views of the mountains. The family suite is two-storied and has two baths. The hotel's popular restaurant serves Styrian specialties, such as smoked trout, but it's also famous for its mouthwatering beef or cheese fondue. The staff is exceptionally warm and helpful, and can arrange sleigh rides, hayrides, and summer tobogganing, among other activities. ✉ *Schwarzenbergstr. 10, A–8850,* ☎ *03532/2431,* ᶠᵃˣ *03532/3694. 48 rooms with bath. Restaurant, bar, sauna, massage. AE, DC, MC, V.* 🐾

Eisenerz

★ ㉟ *30 km (18¼ mi) northwest of Leoben.*

The old mining town of Eisenerz is fascinating not only for its own attractions but also for the huge mountain of remarkably pure iron ore next to it. The community huddles around the Gothic parish church of **St. Oswald,** first built in 1282 and fortified as a bastion against the invading Turks in 1532. Its fantastically embellished interior is well worth seeing. West of the parish church stands the famous **Schichtturm,** an old tower whose bell once signaled the change of shifts at the mines.

The 17th-century building now housing the **Eisenerz Stadtmuseum** was converted to an elegant hunting lodge by Emperor Franz Josef; the museum today is devoted to mining and ironworking, as well as to local life and culture. ⊠ *Im Kammerhof,* ☎ *03848/3615.* ⌑ *AS45.* ⊙ *May–Oct., Tues.–Fri. 9–noon and 2–5; Sat. 10–noon and 2–5; Sun. by appt.*

Just south of the town is its reason for being: the rust-colored, towering **Erzberg.** This mountain of iron ore has been worked since ancient times and still yields an ore that is 34% pure iron. Its present height is about 4,800 ft, although it was once much higher. Strip mining has given it a steplike appearance, similar to that of a ziggurat. Guided Schaubergwerke tours lasting about 1½ hours are conducted through the underground workings. It's cool inside no matter what the outside temperature, so take warm clothing. You can also tour the great stepped workings; transportation is via a crawler-truck fitted with seats. The trip takes about an hour. ⊠ *Lower station of cableway, near road from Präbichl,* ☎ *03848/3200.* ⌑ *Schaubergwerke AS120, Tagebau (open mines) AS140, both tours AS230.* ⊙ *Schaubergwerke tour May–Oct., daily at 10, 12:30, and 3; Tagebau tour May–Oct., daily by appointment with ticket office.*

Near Erzberg, southeast on Route 115, is the 6,250-ft **Polster** mountain, which can be ascended by chairlift, offering great panoramic views to the west across the iron mountain.

En Route   Route 115 between Trofaiach and Hieflau to the northwest takes you
★   through the scenic **Erzbach Valley,** with sensational vistas of snowcapped peaks to the southwest. The highway passes through the ancient mining town of **Vordernberg,** where Romans once worked with iron. Northeast of Eisenerz is a hidden mountain lake of great beauty, the **Leopoldsteiner See,** worth the slight detour. Between Hieflau to Admont, Route 112 parallels the spectacular **Gesäuse Ravine,** where the Enns River with its plunging waterfalls surges through limestone formations. The magnificent 7,770-ft Hochtor peak can be seen to the south. This is among the wildest scenery in the Alps, and it's a favorite challenge for rock climbers.

Admont

★ ㊱ *40 km (25 mi) west of Eisenerz.*

The small market town of Admont is dominated by its famous Benedictine abbey, **Stift Admont,** founded in the 11th century but almost entirely rebuilt after a disastrous fire in 1865. Of the earlier structures, only the glorious Baroque **library** survived intact. Fortunately, its treasures were also saved and are on view, including a Bible that belonged to Martin Luther and a New Testament edited by Erasmus. The main building, 236 ft long, contains some 150,000 volumes and is noted for its 18th-century ceiling frescoes by Bartholomeo Altomonte as well as for its statues called *The Four Last Things* (Death, Judgment, Hell, and Heaven). There is also an extensive natural-history museum with lots of insects, an art museum, and a museum of local life. Many travelers visit this abbey from Bruck an der Mur, crossing mountainous country through western Styria, via Routes S6, 113, and A9 almost to Liezen, then east Route 117 east. The total distance is 100 km (62 mi); both trains and a limited bus service operate over the entire route, with changes required. ☎ 03613/2312–601. ✆ AS40. ☼ Apr.–Oct., daily 10–1 and 2–5; Nov.–Mar., by appt. (minimum 15 people).

Thörl

㊲   *15 km (9 mi) north of Bruck an der Mur.*

A popular excursion from Bruck an der Mur takes you north to Mariazell, a historic pilgrimage center. Along the way on Route 20, you'll discover the village of Thörl, dominated by the ruined 15th-century stronghold of **Schloss Schachenstein** (privately owned). Nearby stands a curious roadside chapel with an unusually carved Calvary dating from 1530. Just north is the popular mountain health resort of **Aflenz Kurort,** from which a chairlift ascends the 5,110-ft Bürgeralm. It operates daily during the ski season, but only Friday–Monday and on holidays the rest of the year. The village church, dating partially from the 12th century, is noted for its rustic stonework.

En Route   Headed north on Route 20, you'll climb to over 4,000 ft as the road crosses the **Seeberg Pass,** from which you can see the surrounding mountain ranges of Hochschwab and Veitschalpe. A descent to the valley is followed by another rise to Mariazell.

Mariazell

㊳   *42 km (26¼ mi) north of Thörl.*

An excursion to Mariazell—famed for its pilgrimage church and gingerbread—is an adventure, thanks to the winding road that brings you there. The town has been a place of pilgrimage since 1157, when the Benedictines established a priory here. After Louis I, King of Hungary, attributed his victory over the Turks in 1377 to the intervention of its Virgin, Mariazell's reputation for miracles began to spread. As a year-round resort, Mariazell offers a wide range of sports and recreation; in winter there's a good ski school for beginners and young people.

The impressive **Mariazeller Basilica** stands resolutely over the town square. The present structure replaced the original church during the 14th century and was itself enlarged in the late 17th century by the Italian architect Domenico Sciassia. Its exterior is unusual, with the original Gothic spire and porch flanked by squat, bulbous Baroque towers. Step inside to see the incredibly elaborate plasterwork and paintings. In the **Gnadenkapelle** (Chapel of Miracles), the nave holds the main object of pilgrimage: the 12th-century statue of the Virgin of Mariazell. It stands under a silver baldachin designed in 1727 by the younger Fischer von Erlach and behind a silver grille donated by Empress Maria Theresa, who took her first communion here. Following her example, thousands of youngsters neatly turned out in white are brought annually from all over Austria to Mariazell for their first communion, usually on or around Whitsun. The **high altar** of 1704, by the elder Fischer von Erlach—the leading architect of the Austrian Baroque— is in the east end of the nave. Don't miss seeing the **Schatzkammer** (treasury) for its collection of votive offerings from medieval times to the present. Walls are covered with plaques, many of them illustrated, given in thanks for assorted blessings, including rescues ranging from runaway horses to shipwrecks. ✆ *Basilica free, Schatzkammer 40AS.* ☼ *Schatzkammer May–Oct., Tues.–Sat. 10–3, Sun. 10–4.*

Pay a visit to the **Heimatmuseum** (Regional Museum of Local Life; ⊠ Wienerstrasse 35, ☎ 03382/2366). Bruno Habertheuer's **mechanical Nativity figurines** are at the **stations of the cross** on Calvary Hill (⊠ Kalvarienberg 1). The nativity scene with its 130 moving figures took 18 years to build. Admission to the museum is AS40.

☼ The **Museumtramway,** the world's oldest steam tramway, dating from 1884, operates between Mariazell and the Erlaufsee, for a 20-minute ride of about 3½ km (2 mi) to a lovely lake. For AS150 extra charge, you can accompany the engineer in the cab. ⊠ Bahnhof Mariazell, ☎ 03882/3394, 𝔽𝔸𝕏 03882/3393. ⊡ Round-trip AS50. ☉ July–Sept., weekends only, hourly 10:20–4:30.

The famous narrow-gauge **Mariazellerbahn** rail line ambles over an 84-km (52½ mi) route between Mariazell and St. Pölten, coursing through magnificent valleys and surmounting mountain passes in the process. This remarkable engineering achievement—the line incorporates 21 tunnels and 75 bridges and viaducts—was built in 1907 and electrified in 1911. The cars are modern but the sensation is one of ages long past. About five trains a day traverse the route in each direction. In St. Pölten, the narrow-gauge line connects with the main east–west rail route. For schedules, contact the Austrian Federal Railways system (☎ 03382/2366).

Dining and Lodging

$$$ ✕🏨 **Hotel Feichtegger.** Although this is a five-story modern hotel near the basilica and the cable car, its ambience is one of quiet, understated luxury. The well-equipped guest rooms have balconies. The restaurant serves tasty Austrian fare. ⊠ Wienerstr. 6, A–8630, ☎ 03882/2416–0, 𝔽𝔸𝕏 03382/2416–80. 48 rooms with bath. Restaurant, bar, indoor pool, sauna, exercise room. AE, DC, MC, V. Closed 2 wks in mid-Dec.

$$$ ✕🏨 **Mariazellerhof.** This small, cheerfully modern chalet-style hotel one block west of the basilica is known for its gingerbread snacks; the spicy aroma fills the house. Its comfortable rooms have balconies. ⊠ Grazer Str. 10, A–8630, ☎ 03882/2179–0, 𝔽𝔸𝕏 03882/2179–51. 10 rooms with bath, 4 with shower. Café. DC, MC. Closed last 3 wks of Jan.

Outdoor Activities and Sports

The skiing on 4,150-ft **Bürgeralpe** is quickly reached by the Bürgeralpebahn cable car from a lower station just two blocks north of the basilica. Paths from the upper station fan out in several directions for country walks in summer. ⊠ Wienerstr. 28, ☎ 03882/2555. ⊡ Round-trip AS95. ☉ May–June and Oct., daily 9–5; July–Aug., daily 8:30–5:30; Sept., daily 8:30–5.

Shopping

Parts of town are permeated by the spicy aroma of baking **gingerbread** for which Mariazell is famous, and you'll see the decorated cookies everywhere.

THE MOUNTAIN ROUTE TO VIENNA

The most direct route from Bruck an der Mur northward to Vienna is also in some ways the most interesting. It takes you through the cradle of Austrian skiing, past several popular resorts, and over the scenic Semmering Pass and offers an opportunity to ride a 19th-century steam cogwheel train to the top of the highest mountain in this part of the country, a peak that often remains snowcapped into the summer. It also takes you to Wiener Neustadt, a small, historic city. This area's proximity to Vienna makes day trips or weekend excursions from the capital practical.

Mürzzuschlag

㊴ *37 km (23 mi) northeast of Bruck an der Mur, 92 km (57 mi) north of Graz.*

The resort town of Mürzzuschlag is popular for both winter and summer sports. From Bruck an der Mur, head northeast on S6, past the industrial town of Kapfenberg, and take the exit marked for the resort. It is regarded as the birthplace of Austrian skiing and, in a sense, of the Winter Olympics, since the first Nordic Games were held here in 1904, but the main focus of ski activity has long since moved west to the Tirol.

Mürzzuschlag is popular with the Viennese and preserves its past glories in the excellent **Winter-Sports-Museum,** which displays equipment past and present from around the world. ⊠ *Wienerstr. 79,* ☎ *03852/ 3504.* 🎫 *AS45.* ☉ *Tues.–Sun. 9–noon and 2–5.*

The **Brahms Museum,** Austria's only museum dedicated to composer Johannes Brahms, a German who adopted Austria as his home, is in Mürzzuschlag, where he spent many summers. The museum also hosts a number of chamber-music concerts and recitals. ⊠ *Wienerstr. 4.,* ☎ *03852/3434.* 🎫 *AS40.* ☉ *May–Oct., daily 10–noon and 2–6; Nov.– Apr., Thurs.–Sun. 10–noon and 2–4.*

Semmering

㊵ *14 km (8½ mi) northeast of Mürzzuschlag, 90 km (56¼ mi) southwest of Vienna.*

Climbing along Route 306, high atop the Semmering Pass, at a height of 3,230 ft, lies the boundary between the provinces of Styria and Lower Austria. A bridle path has existed on this mountainous route since at least the 12th century, but the first road was not built until 1728. Today's highway is an engineering wonder, particularly on the Lower Austrian side, where the new road high on concrete stilts leaps over deep valleys; the old road snakes up in a series of switchback curves. The Styrian side is less dramatic, but offers distant Alpine vistas. Given the technologies of the era, the railway—completed in 1854—that crosses the divide is a technical marvel, with its great viaducts and tunnels, and is still the main north–south rail route. At the top is Semmering, the first town in Lower Austria, a resort on a south-facing slope overlooking the pass. Sheltered by pine forests and built on terraces reaching as high as 4,250 ft, Semmering is considered to have a healthy atmosphere and has several spa-type hotels and pensions. In the early 20th century, wealthy Viennese came here for their *Sommerfrische* (summer vacation), and many built grand villas for the purpose, which you can still glimpse from the outside. The Semmering area plus the nearby Rax and Schneeberg regions are immensely popular in winter with Viennese skiers. This is the area in which most Viennese first learn to ski, meaning that there are slopes ranging from gentle to the more challenging, although they are no match for the rugged Alpine stretches of Tirol and Salzburg province.

OFF THE
BEATEN PATH

HÖLLENTAL – A delightful side trip can be made from Semmering into the Höllental (Valley of Hell), an extremely narrow and romantic gorge cut by the Schwarza stream between two high mountains, the Raxalpe and the Schneeberg. From Hirschwang, at the beginning of the valley, you can ride the **Raxbahn cable car** to a plateau on the Raxalpe at 5,075 ft. ☎ *02666/52497.* 🎫 *Round-trip AS185.* ☉ *High season, daily 8–5:30 at ½-hr intervals; other months, daily 9–4:30 at ½-hr intervals.*

Dining and Lodging

$$$ ✕📺 **Panoramahotel Wagner.** The view over the surrounding moun-
tains distinguishes this renovated hotel, which delights in the personal
touch. The kitchen has established itself as the best in the area; try the
lamb or fish. The excellent beer comes from a tiny brewery in the val-
ley below. ⊠ *Hochstr. 267, A–2680,* ☎ *02664/2512–0,* FAX *02664/2512–
61. 26 rooms with bath. Restaurant, sauna. DC, MC. Closed early Nov.–
early Dec. and various wks in May and June.*

$$–$$$ ✕📺 **Belvedere.** Recently renovated, this old Alpine-style mountain inn
is well known for its hearty Austrian food. Though located in town,
it has an outdoor garden for dining in fine weather. Expect to find such
offerings as fresh cream of asparagus soup, pork chops, and roast chicken.
⊠ *Hochstr. 60, A–2680,* ☎ *02664/2270,* FAX *02664/2267–42. 19
rooms with bath. Restaurant, indoor pool, sauna. AE, DC, MC, V.
Closed two wks in May or June.*

$$$–$$$$ 📺 **Hotel Panhans.** This classic and popular mountain-lodge resort is
set near the center of town; it is frequently booked for conventions,
though it also attracts royalty, such as the late King Hussein of Jor-
dan. Built in 1888, the main lodge has retained its characteristic Art
Nouveau ambience. A luxurious modern annex is connected by an en-
closed walkway to the main building; it offers imaginative minisuites
for honeymooners, stargazers (telescopes provided), and those who want
their own open hearth. The elegant Kaiser Karl restaurant is ambitious
but inconsistent and occasionally disappointing; the more relaxed
Wintergarten restaurant is a better choice. Wines are excellent, and the
hotel has its own Vinotek for tastings. ⊠ *Hochstr. 32, A–2680,* ☎ *02664/
8181–0,* FAX *02664/8181–513. 112 rooms with bath. Restaurant, bar,
café, indoor pool, sauna, exercise room, dance club. AE, DC, V.*

Puchberg am Schneeberg

④ *33 km (21 mi) north of Semmering.*

People flock to the quiet mountain resort of Puchberg am Schneeberg
largely to ride to the top of the Schneeberg mountain, Lower Austria's
highest peak. You get to Puchberg via regular trains from Vienna, Wiener
Neustadt, or points south. From Vienna, the railroads have a package
ticket that includes the regular rail connection, the cog railway, and a
chit for lunch at one of the mountaintop restaurants. From Höllental,
continue north into the valley for 18 km (11 mi), passing through the
wildest section, to Schwarzau im Gebirge. Then circle the north slope
of the Schneeberg via the Klostertal to the resort.

☺ The marvelous old narrow-gauge **Puchberg cog-wheel steam train** as-
cends to a plateau near Schneeberg's summit. Although many use the
rail line as a starting point for mountain hiking, the journey itself is an
exciting outing. Allow the better part of a day for this trip, since the
ride takes 1½ hours each way and the trains are none too frequent, some
running on a schedule and others according to demand. This excursion
is very popular; make reservations well in advance—particularly for week-
ends and holidays—at any rail station in Europe. If you don't already
have them, make reservations at Puchberg for the return trip before you
board for the trip up. Bring along a light sweater or jacket even in sum-
mer; it can be both windy and cool at the top. Ordinary walking shoes
are sufficient unless you wander off the main trails, in which case you'll
need hiking boots, along with some mountain experience.

The steam engines, dating from the 1890s, are built at a peculiar angle
to the ground to keep their fireboxes level while climbing. The wooden
cars they haul are of equal vintage, with hard seats. A rest stop is made
at the **Baumgartner Haus,** where you can get refreshments before con-

tinuing up past the timberline and through two tunnels. Near the upper station hut at altitude 5,892 ft is the small **Elizabeth Chapel** and the **Berghaus Hochschneeberg,** a simple lodge with a restaurant and overnight guest facilities. From here, you can walk to the **Kaiserstein** for a panoramic view and to the **Klosterwappen** peak, at 6,811 ft. Real stick-to-your-ribs mountain food, draft beer, and plenty of Gemütlichkeit are served up at the inexpensive **Damböck Haus,** a rustic hut operated by the Austrian Touring Club (*ÖTK*). It's only a 15-minute walk from the upper station of the Puchberg line.

Allow about two to three hours total for these walks. Maps are available at the lodge. The last train down usually leaves at about 4:30 or 5:30 PM; later runs are made if traffic warrants. Eurailpass and Euro Domino card holders may use their passes but must make seat reservations. ⊠ *Schneeberg Bahn, Bahnhof Puchberg,* ☎ *02636/3661–0.* ☒ *Round-trip AS290.* ☉ *Late Apr.–early Nov.*

☽ Don't miss a drive along the **Hohe Wand** (High Wall), a scenic nature park east of Puchberg (from Puchberg, go east past Grünbach to Oberhöflein, where you turn left at the sign for Hohe Wand). The spectacular route has many twists and turns leading to the limestone plateau, and there are several simple country inns along the way that provide good bases for hiking. The 4 km (2.5 mi) road ends at the top at Kleine Kanzel in the west and Herrgottschnitzerhaus in the east, so you must retrace your route down along the Panoramastrasse, unless you're mountain biking, or hiking. Also worth a visit is the **Heimatmuseum** (open Easter to October, Tuesday to Sunday from 9–6, and only on weekends at the same hours the rest of the year), with displays of local artifacts. On weekends there is a charge for entrance to the park of AS20 per car and AS20 per person (which includes admission to the museum), but during the week it's free. The inns on the Hohe Wand offer average Austrian fare, but just past Gaaden on the road to Winzendorf and Wiener Neustadt, is Pizzeria Napoli at Emmerberg No. 7 (closed Monday)—the thin-crust pizzas here are excellent. You can get detailed maps of the Hohe Wand from the Wiener Neustadt tourist office (☞ Visitor Information *in* Eastern Austria A to Z, *below*).

Lodging

$$–$$$ ✕⌂ **Schneeberghof.** Across the street from Puchberg am Schneeberg's
★ tiny train station, this 100-year-old chalet hotel with a modern annex is nestled at the foot of the towering Schneeberg. It's a popular spot for sports lovers, and King Juan Carlos of Spain is a regular guest during hunting season. Rooms are large, with contemporary furnishings and pastel fabrics, and all have balconies. The restaurant, with live folk music on weekends, has a selection of delicious fish and meat dishes, including grilled *Welsfilet* (catfish) and pork medallions in a honey herb sauce. The Schneeberghof also offers a "Teddy Bear" weekend year-round, which provides two nights with half pension at great value. ⊠ *Wiener Neustädterstr. 24, A–2734,* ☎ *02636/3500,* FAX *02636/3233. 74 rooms with bath. Restaurant, sauna, indoor pool, indoor and outdoor tennis courts. AE, DC, MC, V.* ☺

Wiener Neustadt

④ *19 km (12 mi) southeast of Puchberg am Schneeberg, 45 km (28¼ mi) south of Vienna, 38 km (23¾ mi) northeast of Semmering, 27 km (16¼ mi) west of Eisenstadt.*

Although today's Wiener Neustadt is a busy industrial center built on the ashes of its prewar self, enough of its past glories survived World War II's bombings to make a visit worthwhile. The small city was established in 1194 as a fortress to protect Vienna from the Hungarians. During the mid-15th century it was an imperial residence, and in 1752 it became, and still is, the seat of the Austrian Military Academy.

Begin your exploration of the Old City at the **Hauptplatz,** the largely traffic-free main square, which contains several rebuilt medieval houses with Gothic arcades standing opposite the 16th-century **Rathaus** (City Hall).

The mighty **Stadtpfarrkirche** (Town Parish Church), also known as the Liebfrauenkirche, rises imposingly out of the center of Domplatz, or Cathedral Square. Begun in the 13th century, the church had cathedral status from 1468 until 1784, and a number of choirs and chapels were added during that period. Note the ornate entryway on the south side, dating from about 1230. Styles are mixed between Romanesque and Gothic, but the interior is impressive for its unity of columned walls and ribbed ceiling. Look for the painted wooden figures of the Apostles dating from about 1500, a mural of the Last Judgment from about 1300, and the splendid tomb of Cardinal Khlesl with a bust carved in 1630 attributed to the school of Giovanni Bernini, the master of the Italian Baroque.

A narrow lane called the Puchheimgasse leads to the 12th-century **Reckturm,** a defensive tower said to have been built with part of the ransom money paid to free Richard the Lion-Hearted. Down Baumkirchnerring at the corner of Wiener Strasse is the 14th-century **Church of St. Peter-an-der-Sperr,** once a defense cloister, now an exhibition gallery. The greatest treasure in the **Stadtmuseum,** which is in a one-time Jesuit residence on Wiener Strasse, is the Corvinusbecher, an elegant 32-inch-high goblet from 1487 that was a gift from the Hungarian king who conquered the town.

To the east of the Hauptplatz, on Neuklostergasse, is the **Neukloster Church,** part of a Cistercian convent founded in 1250. Behind the high altar in the richly Baroque interior is the tomb of Eleanor of Portugal (died 1467), wife of the emperor Frederick III. Mozart's Requiem was first performed here in 1793.

The massive **Burg** on Grazer Strasse, a castle begun in the 13th century and rebuilt as an imperial residence in the 15th century, was designated the Austrian Military Academy by order of Empress Maria Theresa in 1752. The Nazis took it over in 1938, and its first German commandant was General Erwin Rommel, the Desert Fox. The complex was battered by bombing in 1943 and 1945 but subsequently rebuilt. Enter its grounds through the south gate to visit the famous 15th-century **Church of St. George** (you will need to be escorted by a guard), whose exterior gable is decorated with, among others, 14 Habsburg coats of arms. Beneath the gable is a statue of Friedrich III, curiously inscribed with "A.E.I.O.U.," which some believe stands for the Latin words meaning "Austria will last until the end of the world." Inside the church, under the steps of the high altar, the remains of Emperor Maximilian I are buried.

Dining and Lodging

$$$–$$$$ ✕ **Gelbes Haus.** The 1906 Art Deco "Yellow House," slightly north of the center, offers limited but outstandingly prepared dishes served in tasteful surroundings. Look for consommé with meat-filled strudel, *Tafelspitz* (boiled beef), and breast of duck with goose liver, and, for dessert, figs with apple-cinnamon parfait. The homemade sherbets are also outstanding. The wine selection is broad, by the glass as well as the bottle. ⊠ *Kaiserbrunng. 11,* ☎ *02622/26400. DC, MC, V. Closed Sun.*

$$$ ✕⌖ **Hotel Corvinus.** A modern, unexceptional hotel next to the city park, the Corvinus is the best choice in town. Located two blocks east of the train station and only a few minutes' stroll from the main

square, it caters primarily to business travelers. Rooms are spartan but clean and have all the amenities. The restaurant serves surprisingly sophisticated fare. ✉ *Bahng. 29–33, A–2700,* ☎ *02622/24134,* FAX *02622/24139. 68 rooms with bath. Restaurant, bar, sauna, meeting rooms. AE, DC, MC, V.*

Nightlife and the Arts

The **Wiesen Jazz Festival** attracts top-name performers from America and around the world for a couple of days in early July in Wiesen, Burgenland (12 km/7½ mi, southeast of Wiener Neustadt). For information, contact Landesverband Burgenland Tourismus (☞ Visitor Information *in* Eastern Austria A to Z, *below*).

EASTERN AUSTRIA A TO Z

Arriving and Departing

By Bus

There is good service to Neusiedl am See, Eisenstadt, and Güssing in Burgenland; Mariazell in Styria; and Wiener Neustadt in Lower Austria. Direct express service to Graz is infrequent. Most buses leave Vienna from the Wien Mitte Bus Station on Landstrasser Hauptstrasse, opposite the air terminal and Hilton Hotel, but be sure to check first, since some services to the south may depart from the bus terminal area at Südtirolerplatz, to the west of the Südbahnhof rail station. The major bus services connecting Vienna to towns in Eastern Austria are **Blaguss Reisen** (☎ 01/501–80–0, FAX 01/501–80–299) and **Bundesbus** (☎ 01/71101).

By Car

Two main autobahns traverse this region: the A3 between Vienna and Eisenstadt and the heavily traveled A2 between Vienna and past Wiener Neustadt to Graz and farther south. Northern Burgenland can be reached via the A4 autobahn east out of Vienna.

By Plane

The northern part of Eastern Austria is served by Vienna's international airport at Schwechat, 19 km (12 mi) southeast of the city center (☞ Vienna A to Z *in* Chapter 1).

Graz has its own international airport at Thalerhof, just south of the city, with flights to and from Vienna, Innsbruck, Linz, Munich, Frankfurt, Düsseldorf, and Zürich. Austrian Airlines and its subsidiary Tyrolean Airways, as well as Lufthansa, are the major carriers. Call for information (☎ 0316/2902–0).

By Train

Vienna and Graz are the logical rail arrival or departing points for this part of Austria. The main international north–south route connecting Vienna and northeastern Italy runs through this region and is traversed by EuroCity trains from Munich, Salzburg, Linz, Klagenfurt, and Venice, as well as other cities in neighboring countries. Nearly all long-distance trains going through this region meet at Bruck an der Mur, where connections can be made.

Getting Around

By Bus

Post office and railroad buses cover the area thoroughly, although services are less frequent in less populated areas more distant from city centers. Take trains for the main routes.

By Car

Driving is the best way to explore Eastern Austria, especially if you're visiting the smaller towns and villages or if your time is limited. Route 10 from Vienna to Lake Neusiedl in Burgenland is the preferred scenic alternative to the A4 autobahn. Graz is connected to Vienna by both A2 and a more scenic mountain road, Route S6 over the Semmering Pass to Bruck an der Mur, then south through the Mur Valley. Driving in the Graz city center is not advisable, because there are many narrow, one-way, and pedestrian streets and few places to park.

By Streetcar

In Graz, **streetcars and buses** (☎ 0316/887411 information) are an excellent way of traveling within the city. Single tickets (AS20) can be bought from the driver, and one-day and multiple-ride tickets are also available. All six streetcar routes converge at Jakominiplatz near the south end of the Old City. One fare may combine streetcars and buses as long as you take a direct route to your destination.

By Taxi

In Graz, **taxis** can be ordered by phone (☎ 0316/1718, 0316/2204, 0316/222, or 0316/2801).

By Train

If you're not driving, take trains on the main routes; services are fast and frequent. Trains depart from Vienna's Südbahnhof (South Station) hourly for the one-hour ride to Neusiedl am See. Connections can be made there for Eisenstadt and Pamhagen. There is also express service every two hours from the same station in Vienna to Graz, 2½ hours away, with intermediate stops at Wiener Neustadt, Mürzzuschlag, and Bruck an der Mur, and connections to Puchberg am Schneeberg, Semmering, and points west. Trains for Mariazell depart from Vienna's Westbahnhof (West Station), with a change at St. Pölten. Call for information (☎ 01/1717 departures from Vienna; 0316/1717 Graz's main station).

Contacts and Resources

Bicycling

Bicycling is enormously popular in the flatlands around Lake Neusiedl. Try the following for rentals: in **Illmitz,** Polay (✉ Florianig. 5, ☎ 02175/3161); in **Mörbisch,** Posch (✉ Blumentalg. 9, ☎ 02685/8242); in **Neusiedl am See,** Bahnhof (☎ 02167/8284) and Hotel Wende (✉ Seestr. 40, ☎ 02167/8111–0); in **Podersdorf,** Fahrradverleih Waldherr (✉ Hauptstr. 42, ☎ 02177/2297) and Reichow (✉ Strandg. 9, ☎ 02177/2411); in **Rust,** Schneeberger (✉ Rathauspl. 15, ☎ 02685/6442).

Boating

You can hire boats (*Bootsvermietung* or *Bootsverleih*) around Lake Neusiedl. Expect to pay about AS50 per hour for a rowboat, AS80 for a pedal boat, and AS120 for an electric boat; sailboat prices vary widely. Rent from: **Baumgartner** (✉ Neusiedl am See, ☎ 02167/2782), **Friedrich Lang** (✉ Mörbisch, ☎ 02685/8381), **Knoll** (✉ Podersdorf, ☎ 02177/2431), or **Ruster Freizeitcenter** (✉ Rust, ☎ 02685/595).

Horseback Riding

The area around Lake Neusiedl is ideal for riding. Livery stables on the east side of the lake include two at **Podersdorf,** Frankl (☎ 02177/2251) and **Lang** (☎ 02177/2764). A different adventure is riding Icelandic ponies, possible at the Islandpferdehof zur Villa stables (☎ 02610/42020) in **Neckenmarkt** in south Burgenland.

Skiing

The best place to ski near Vienna is **Semmering** (✉ A–2680, ☎ 03852/4770), FAX 03852/5394). Other good options include the **Bürgeralpe** (✉ Mariazell, A-8630, ☎ 03882/2555) near Mariazell, and the **Schneeberg** (✉ Puchberg am Schneeberg, A–2734, ☎ 02636/3661, FAX 02636/3262), where you can take a train to the summit. Great cross-country skiing can be found in western Styria on the 50-km (31-mi) **Murtal Loipe,** the 30-km (19-mi) **Tauern-Süd-Loipe,** and the 12-km (7½-mi) **Katschtal-Sonnen Loipe,** all near Murau (✉ Murau, A-8850, ☎ FAX 03532/2720). Adults and children can learn to ski at the **Franz Skazel Ski School** (✉ Mariazellerstr. 19, Mürzzuschlag, A–8680, ☎ 03852/2615–2).

Car Rentals

Cars can be rented at all airports and in Graz from **Avis** (✉ Schlögelg. 10, ☎ 0316/812920, FAX 0316/841178, **Buchbinder** (✉ Keplerstr. 93–95, ☎ 0316/717330, FAX 0316/718843), **Budget** (✉ Airport, ☎ 0316/2902–342; ✉ Europl. 12 ☎ 0316/722074, FAX 0316/722076), **Europcar** (✉ Airport, ☎ 0316/296757), and **Hertz** (✉ Andreas-Hofer-Pl. 1, ☎ 0316/825007, FAX 0316/810288).

Emergencies

Police: ☎ 133. **Fire:** ☎ 122. **Ambulance:** ☎ 144. In Graz, **Medical Service:** ☎ 141.

Guided Tours

ORIENTATION TOURS

Relatively few guided tours visit Eastern Austria, and those that do are in German, although English may be available on request. Inquire when booking. General orientation tours depart from Vienna and last one to four days. The one-day tours are usually to Lake Neusiedl and include a boat ride or to the Semmering mountain region with a cable-car ride. Reputable operators include the following: **Cityrama Sightseeing** (✉ Börseg. 1, A–1010 Vienna, ☎ 01/534–130, FAX 01/534–13–28); **Vienna Sightseeing Tours** (✉ Stelzhammerg. 4/11, 1030 Vienna, ☎ 01/712–4683-0, FAX 01/714–1141).

TOURS OF GRAZ

Guided walking sightseeing tours of Graz in English and German are conducted daily at 2:30, April–October, and on Saturdays at 2:30 November–March. The meeting point for these tours is Tourist Information, Herrengasse 16. The cost is AS75. Guided tours of the Schlossberg are conducted daily Easter–October, departing hourly 9–5 from the Glockenturm (Bell Tower) near the upper station of the Schlossberg funicular. The cost is AS30, with a minimum of five people. For more information, contact the city tourist office (☞ Visitor Information, *below*).

Late-Night Pharmacies

To find a **pharmacy** open late in Graz, call ☎ 18.

Travel Agencies

Check in Graz with **Reisebüro Kuoni** (✉ Sackstr. 6, ☎ 0316/824571–0, FAX 0316/824571–6) or **Ruefa** (✉ Opernring 9, ☎ 0316/829775–0, FAX 0316/829775–23).

Visitor Information

The regional tourist information office for Burgenland province is the **Landesverband Burgenland Tourismus** (✉ Schloss Esterházy, A–7000 Eisenstadt, ☎ 02682/63384–23, FAX 02682/63384–32). Lower Austria has a tourist office in Vienna: the **Tourist Office of Lower Austria** (✉ Walfischg. 6, A–1010 Vienna, ☎ 01/513–8022, FAX 01/513–8022–30). For **Styria,** the provincial tourist office is Steirische Tourismus (✉ St. Peter–Hauptstr. 243, A–8042 Graz, ☎ 0316/4003, FAX 0316/4003–10).

For **Graz,** the quarterly *Graz-Guide* brochure, available from the tourist office (✉ Herreng. 16, ☎ 0316/80750), includes a city map and provides information on current events.

There are several helpful local *Fremdenverkehrsämter* (tourist offices). **Bruck an der Mur:** Tourismusverband (✉ An der Postwiese 4, A–8600, ☎ 03862/54722, FAX 03862/54910). **Eisenstadt:** Eisenstadt Tourismus (✉ Schloss Esterházy, A–7000, ☎ 02682/67390, FAX 02682/67391). **Graz:** Grazer Tourismus (✉ Herrreng. 16, A–8010, ☎ 0316/80750, FAX 0316/807555; ✉ Platform 1 of main train station, ☎ 0316/916837). **Mariazell:** Tourismusverband (✉ Hauptpl. 13, A–8630, ☎ 03882/2366, FAX 03882/3945). **Murau:** Information (✉ Am Bahnhof, A–8850, ☎ FAX 03532/2720). **Neusiedl am See:** Tourismusbüro (✉ Hauptpl. 1, A–7100, ☎ 02167/2229, FAX 02167/2637). **Rust:** Gästeinformation (✉ Rathaus, A–7071, ☎ 02685/502, FAX 02685/502–10). **Wiener Neustadt:** Fremdenverkehrsverein (✉ Hauptpl. 1–3, A–2700, ☎ 02622/373–468, FAX 02622/373–498).

4 THE DANUBE VALLEY

A tonic in any season, a trip up the Austrian Danube unveils a parade of storybook-worthy sights: fairy-tale castles-in-air, medieval villages, and Baroque abbeys crowned with "candle-snuffer" cupolas. The Danube itself is a marvel—on a summer day it even takes on the proper shade of Johann Strauss blue. Along its banks, you'll discover the beautiful Wachau Valley and cheery Linz, whose pastry shops produce the best Linzer tortes around.

Updated by
Bonnie Dodson

T
O THE SIGHTSEER, a trip along the Austrian Danube unfolds rather like a treasured picture book of history. Roman ruins (some built by Emperor Claudius), remains of medieval castles-in-air, and Baroque monasteries crowned with "candle-snuffer" cupolas perch precariously above the river, compelling the imagination with their legends and myths. This is where Isa—cousin of the Lorelei—lured sailors to the shoals; where Richard the Lion-Hearted was locked in a dungeon for years; and where the Nibelungs—immortalized by Wagner—caroused operatically in battlemented forts. Once, Roman sailors used to throw coins into the perilous whirlpools around Grein to placate Danubius, the river's tutelary god. Today, thanks to the technology of modern dams, travelers have the luxury of seeing this part of Austria from the tame deck of a comfortable river steamer. In clement weather, the nine-hour trip upriver to Linz is highly rewarding. If you have more time to spare, the voyage onward to Passau may be less dramatic but gives more time to take in the picturesque vineyards and the castles perched like so many eagles' aeries on crags above bends in the river.

Even more of the region's attractions can be discovered if you travel by car or bus. You can explore plunging Gothic streets, climb Romanesque towers, and then linger over a glass of wine in a vaulted Weinkeller. River and countryside form an inspired unity here, with fortress-topped outcroppings giving way to broad pastures that swoop down to the very riverbanks. Many visitors classify this tour as one of Europe's great trips: here you feel you can almost reach out and touch the passing towns and soak up the intimacy unique to this stretch of the valley. In this chapter, we follow the course of the Danube upstream from Vienna as it winds through Lower Austria (Niederösterreich) and a bit of Upper Austria (Oberösterreich) to Linz, past monasteries and industrial towns, the riverside vineyards of the lower Weinviertel, and the fragrant expanses of apricot and apple orchards.

Linz, Austria's third-largest city (and its most underrated), is a key industrial center. It's also a fine town for shopping; the stores are numerous and carry quality merchandise, often at more reasonable prices than in Vienna or the larger resorts. Concerts and operas performed at Linz's modern Brucknerhaus make every bit as good listening as those in Vienna or Salzburg.

It is, however, the Danube itself, originating in Germany's Black Forest and emptying into the Black Sea, that is our focal point: the route that brought the Romans to the area and contributed to its development remains one of Europe's important waterways, with four national capitals on its banks—Vienna, Bratislava, Budapest, and Belgrade. It was not only the Romans who posited "Whoever controls the Danube controls all Europe." The Kuenringer (the robber knights who built many of the hilltop castles) thrived by sacking the baggage caravans of the early Crusaders; later, castles were financed through somewhat more businesslike means—Frederick Barbarossa, leading his army downstream, had to pay a crossing toll at Mauthausen. Subsequently, cities sprang up to serve as ports for the salt, wood, ores, and other cargo transported on the river. Today, modern railroads and highways parallel most of the blue Danube's course.

This is a wonderful trip to take in early spring or in the fall after the grape harvest, when the vineyards turn reddish blue and a bracing chill settles over the Danube—the Empress Maria Theresa would plan her itinerary to arrive in Linz in May, just as the fruit trees were about to bloom. No matter when you come, be sure to try some of those fruits in a Linzer torte (a filling of brandy-flavored apricots, raspberries, or plums under a latticed pastry crust), a treat as satisfyingly rich and copious as the Danube Valley itself.

Pleasures and Pastimes

Abbeys
While castles galore dot the area—ranging from crumbling mountain-top ruins to wonderfully restored edifices replete with gargoyles—the real gems in these environs are the abbeys, majestic relics of an era when bishops were wealthy and as influential as kings. The greatest are Melk, Klosterneuburg, Kremsmünster, St. Florian, and Göttweig, all of which have breathlessly imposing scope and elegance.

Bicycling
The trail along the Danube must be one of the great bicycle routes of the world. For much of the way (the exception being the Korneuburg–Krems stretch) you can bike along either side of the river. Some small hotels will even arrange to pick up you and your bike from the cycle path. You'll find bicycle rentals at most riverside towns and at rail stations. The terrain around Linz is relatively level, and within the city there are 89 km (55 mi) of marked cycle routes. In the areas of Eferding, St. Florian, through the Enns River valley, and around Steyr, the territory, with its gentle hills and special routes, is generally good for cycling.

Dining
Wherever possible, restaurants capitalize on the river view, and alfresco dining overlooking the Danube is one of the region's unsurpassed delights. Simple *Gasthäuser* are everywhere, but better dining is more often found in the country inns. The cuisine is basically Austrian, although desserts are often brilliant local inventions, including the celebrated Linzer torte and Linzer Augen, jam-filled cookies with three "eyes" in the top cookie.

Wine is very much the thing in the lower part of the Weinviertel, particularly in the Wachau region, on the north bank of the Danube. Here you'll find many of Austria's best white wines, slightly dry and with a touch of fruity taste. In some of the smaller villages, you can sample the vintner's successes right in his cellars. Restaurants, from sophisticated and stylish to plain and homey, are often rated by their wine offerings as much as by their chef's creations.

CATEGORY	COST*
$$$$	over AS500 (€36)
$$$	AS300–AS500 (€22–€36)
$$	AS200–AS300 (€14–€21)
$	under AS200 (€14)

per person for a typical three-course meal with a glass of house wine

Hiking
You could hardly ask for better hiking country: From the level ground of the Danube Valley, hills rise on both sides, giving great views when you reach the upper levels. There are *Wanderwege* (marked hiking paths) virtually everywhere; local tourist offices have maps and route details. Around Linz you might retrace the route of the Linz–Budweis horse-drawn tramway, Continental Europe's first railway, or trek from one castle to another. You can hike in the Mühlviertel from Freistadt to Grein and even arrange to get your pack transferred from hotel to hotel.

Lodging
Accommodation options range from castle hotels, where you'll be treated like royalty, to quieter but elegant, usually family-run country inns, to standard city hotels in Linz. The region is compact, so you can easily stay in one place and drive to a nearby locale to try a different restau-

rant. Rates understandably reflect the quality of service and amenities and usually include breakfast, which may range from a fast to a feast.

CATEGORY	COST*
$$$$	over AS1,750 (€127)
$$$	AS1,200–AS1,750 (€87–€127)
$$	AS900–AS1,200 (€65–€86)
$	under AS900 (€65)

All prices are for a standard double room, including tax and service.

✍ *following the text of a review is your signal that the property has a Web site, where you will find details and, usually, images; for a link, visit www.fodors.com/urls.*

Exploring the Danube Valley

Although much of the river is tightly wedged between steep hills rising from a narrow valley, the north and south banks of the Danube present differing vistas. The hills to the north are terraced so that the vineyards can catch the sun; to the south, the orchards, occasional meadows, and shadowed hills are just as visually appealing if less dramatic. Upstream from the Wachau region the valley broadens, giving way to farmlands and the industrial city of Linz straddling the river.

Great Itineraries

The Wachau section of the Danube Valley is a favorite outing for Viennese seeking a pleasant Sunday drive and a glass or two of good wine, but for foreign visitors to treat the region this casually would cause them to miss some of Austria's greatest treasures. Once there, castles and abbeys beckon, picturesque villages beg to be explored, and the vine-covered wine gardens prove nearly irresistible.

Numbers in the text correspond to numbers in the margin and on the Lower Danube Valley, Upper Danube Valley, and Linz maps.

IF YOU HAVE 3 DAYS

Start out early from Vienna, planning for a stop to explore the medieval center of **Krems** ③. The Vinotek Und's eponymous Kloster will give you a good idea of the regions's best wines. From Krems, you can scoot across the river to visit Stift Göttweig at **Göttweig** ㊷ or you can leave it until the return trip. Spend a night in a former cloister, now an elegant hotel, in 🏨 **Dürnstein** ⑤, in the shadow of the ruined castle where Richard the Lion-Hearted was imprisoned. An early-morning climb up to the ruin or a jog along the Danube shoreline will reward you with great views. Take time to explore Dürnstein before heading along the Danube, and crossing to 🏨 **Melk** ㊴, rated one of the greatest abbeys in Europe. This is high Baroque at its most glorious. Follow the river road on to 🏨 **Göttweig** ㊷ and have lunch on the terrace at the abbey. The abbey's Baroque chapel is breathtaking. Continuing eastward, follow the river as closely as possible (signs indicate Zwentendorf and Tulln) to **Klosterneuburg** ㊻, an imposing abbey that was once the seat of the powerful Babenburger kings, and onward to Vienna.

IF YOU HAVE 5 DAYS

A more leisurely schedule would follow the same basic route but permit a visit at either **Burg Kreuzenstein,** near **Korneuburg** ① or **Schloss Grafenegg** near **Haitzendorf** ② before stopping in **Krems** ③ and **Weinkolleg Kloster Und** (☞ Krems, *below*), and overnighting in 🏨 **Dürnstein** ⑤. Spend the morning exploring Dürnstein, including the colorfully restored Baroque Stiftskirche. In the afternoon, discover the wine villages of **Weissenkirchen** ⑥ and **Spitz** ⑦. Plan on two overnights in 🏨 **Linz** ⑪–㉕, to tour the city itself and to fit in a side trip across the river north to the walled city of **Freistadt** ㉖, and then on to **Kefermarkt** ㉗ to view the 42-ft-high intricately carved, wood winged altar dating from 1497. On day four, take in **Kremsmünster** ㉜ and **St. Florian** ㉛; then proceed to ⛴ **Melk** ㊴. The fifth day will be full, but start with the Melk abbey, then the abbey at **Göttweig** ㊷, and move onward to **Klosterneuburg** ㊻.

IF YOU HAVE 7 DAYS

Additional time would allow far better acquaintance with this region. Located to the northwest of the Wachau, the Mühlviertel—the mill region north of Linz—turned out thousands of yards of linen from flax grown in the neighboring fields in the 19th century. You might follow the "textile trail," which takes you to museums tracing this bit of history. On your way along the northern Danube bank, visit the fascinating theater in **Grein** ⑨ and view the curious chancel in the church at **Baumgartenberg** ⑩. From ⛴ **Linz** ⑪–㉕, take trips upriver to **Eferding** ㉘, **Hartkirchen** ㉙, and **Aschach** ㉚, and south to ⛴ **Steyr** ㉞— you might also consider an overnight in this charming medieval city with its vast center square framed in pastel facades. From Steyr, attractive back roads will bring you to the town of **Waidhofen an der Ybbs** ㊲, parts of whose walls date from the Turkish invasion of the 1600s. Rather than trying to pack three abbeys into one day, spread out the pleasures, dining in **Mautern** ㊶ and overnighting in ⛴ **Tulln** ㊹ before heading on to **Klosterneuburg** ㊻ and, finally, returning to Vienna.

When to Tour the Danube Valley

The Wachau—both north and south Danube banks—is packed wall-to-wall with visitors in late April to early May, but of course there's a reason: the apricot and apple trees are in glorious blossom, and bright orange poppies blanket the fields. Others prefer the chilly early to mid-autumn days, when a blue haze curtains the vineyards. Throughout the region, winter is drab. Seasons hardly withstanding, crowds jam the abbey at Melk; you're best off going first thing in the morning, before the tour buses arrive, or at midday, when the throngs have receded.

THE WACHAU, NORTH BANK OF THE DANUBE

Unquestionably the loveliest stretches of the Danube's Austrian course run from the outskirts of Vienna, through the narrow defiles of the Wachau to the Nibelungengau—the region where the mystical race of dwarfs, the Nibelungs, are supposed to have settled, at least for a while. If you're taking the tour by train, take Streetcar D to Vienna's Franz Josefs Bahnhof, for your departure. If you're driving, the trickiest part may be getting out of Vienna. Follow signs to Prague to get across the Danube, but once across, avoid the right-hand exit marked Prague—which leads to the autobahn—and continue ahead, following signs for Prager Strasse and turning left at the traffic light. Prager Strasse (Route 3) heads toward Langenzersdorf and Korneuburg.

Korneuburg

❶ 18 km (11¼ mi) northwest of Vienna.

Until recently, Korneuburg was the center of Austrian shipbuilding, where river passenger ships, barges, and transfer cranes were built to order for Russia, among other customers. Stop for a look at the imposing neo-Gothic city hall (1864), which dominates the central square and towers over the town.

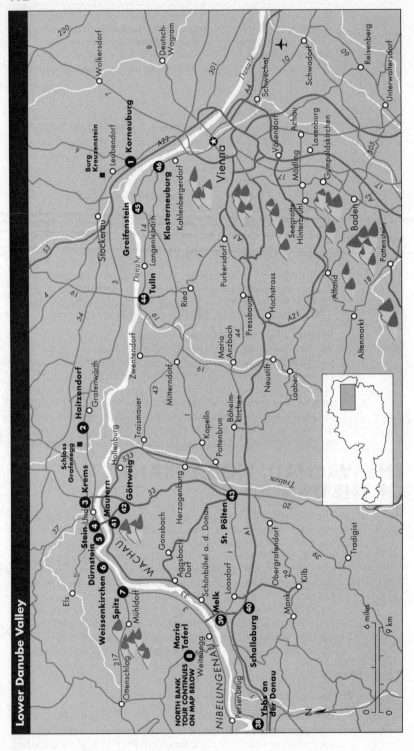

Lower Danube Valley

220

Wolkersdorf

Deutsch-Wagram

8

301

Danube

A4

Schwechat

10

Reisenberg

69

Unterwaltersdorf

Leopoldsdorf

305

Burg Kreuzenstein

① Korneuburg

A22

7

9

Vienna

Vösendorf

Achau

Laxenburg

Mödling

Gumpoldskirchen

46 45 Klosterneuburg

Kahlenbergerdorf

17

Seegrotte Hinterbrühl

Baden

A2

17

Greifenstein

Stockerau

14 Langenlebarn

Perchtoldsdorf

Pottenstein

S3

Danube

Tulln

44

3

Ried

1

Purkersdorf

A1

Hochstrass

18

Altland

Altenmarkt

4

61

34

Zwentendorf

61

Mitterndorf

Maria Anzbach

44

Pressbaum

A21

Laaben

Neustift

② Haitzendorf

Grafenwörth

43

Traismauer

Kapelln

Potenbrun

Böheim-kirchen

Schloss Grafenegg

Hollenburg

Hollenburg

533

1

533

Krems

③ Stein Und ④ Mautern

42 Göttweig

33

Herzogenburg

St. Pölten

43

Traisen

20

⑤

41

Gansbach

WACHAU

Dürnstein

⑥

37

Aggsbach Dorf

Schönbühel a. d. Donau

Loosdorf

1

Obergrafendorf

Kilb

Tradigist

39

Weissenkirchen

Spitz ⑦

Mühldorf

33

Melk

39 40

Mank

29

Els

2

Schallaburg

NIBELUNGENGAU

Maria Taferl

Weißenegg

⑧

Ottenschlag

217

Persenbeug

6 miles

9 km

NORTH BANK TOUR CONTINUES ON MAP BELOW

N

38 Ybbs an der Donau

0

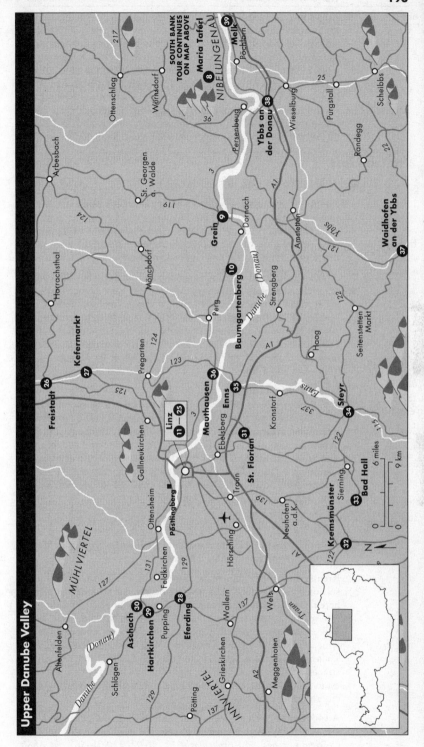

Upper Danube Valley

SOUTH BANK
TOUR CONTINUES
ON MAP ABOVE

NIBELUNGENAU

Maria Taferl **8**

Melk **39**

Pöchlarn

Scheibbs

217

Weinsdorf

Ottenschlag

36

Persenbeug

Wieselburg

Purgstall

25

 Randegg

22

Ybbs an
der Donau **38**

Arbesbach

St. Georgen
a. Walde

611

3

Grein **9**

Dornach

A1

Amstetten

1

Waidhofen
an der Ybbs **37**

Ybbs

121

124

Harrachsthal

Mönchdorf

10

Baumgartenberg

Strengberg

Danube (Donau)

Perg

122

Haag

Seitenstetten
Markt

Kefermarkt

Pregarten

124

123

1

A1

Enns

Mauthausen **36**

35

Kronstorf

Enns

337

Steyr **34**

Freistadt **26**

27

125

3

Linz
11 — 25

Ebelsberg

31

St. Florian

Traun

Neuhofen
a.d.K.

139

122

115

Gallneukirchen

Kremsmünster **32**

33
Bad Hall

Sierning

6 miles

9 km

MÜHLVIERTEL

Ottensheim

Pöstlingberg

Feldkirchen

129

Hörsching

A1

122

127

131

Aschach

Harkirchen **29**

30

Pupping

28
Eferding

Wallern

137

Wels

Traun

Altenfelden

Schlögen

129

Pötting

137

INNVIERTEL

Grieskirchen

A2

Meggenhofen

Danube (Donau)

★ Atop a hillside 3 km (2 mi) beyond Korneuburg along Route 3 sits **Burg Kreuzenstein,** a castle with fairy-tale turrets and towers. Using old elements and Gothic and Romanesque bits and pieces brought to this site of a previously destroyed castle, Count Wilczek built Kreuzenstein from 1879 to 1908 to house his late-Gothic collection of art objects. You'll see rooms full of armaments, the festival and banquet halls, library, chapel, even the kitchens. It is possible to reach Kreuzenstein via the suburban train (S-Bahn) to Leobendorf followed by a ¾-hour hike up to the castle. ✉ *Leobendorf bei Korneuburg,* ☎ *02262/66102.* 🎟 *AS100.* ☉ *Mid-Mar.–mid-Nov., Tues.–Sun. 8–4.*

Haitzendorf

❷ *51 km (38½ mi) west of Korneuburg.*

The tiny farming community of Haitzendorf (to reach it from Korneuburg, take Route 3, 33 km/21 mi past Stockerau, then turn right at Graftenwörth) features a church dating from the 14th century. In early summer, the vast strawberry fields surrounding the town yield a delicious harvest, which you can pick yourself.

A lush meadow and woodland area also surrounds the best-known site,
★ the turreted **Schloss Grafenegg.** The moated Renaissance castle dating from 1533 was stormed by the Swedes in 1645 and rebuilt from 1840 to 1873 in the English Gothic Revival style. Greatly damaged during the 1945–55 occupation, it was extensively restored in the 1980s. Look for such fascinating details as the gargoyle waterspouts, and don't miss the chapel. ☎ *02735/2205–14.* 🎟 *AS70.* ☉ *Mid-Apr.–Oct., Tues.–Sun. 10–5.* 🖾

Dining and Lodging

$$–$$$ ✕🏠 **Schlosstaverne Mörwald.** Beyond the golden facade of this elegant tavern across from Schloss Grafenegg you'll find a friendly and welcoming atmosphere. Rooms are comfortably furnished and done in beiges and reds. The restaurant offers game in season and local cuisine with international touches. The strawberries of early summer taste even better outdoors on the sunny dining terrace. ✉ *A–3485, Haitzendorf,* ☎ *02735/2616–60,* 🖷 *02735/2298–6. 6 rooms. Restaurant. AE, DC, MC, V. Closed Jan.–Feb.*

Krems

★ ❸ *12 km (7 mi) west of Haitzendorf, 80 km (50 mi) northwest of Vienna, 26 km (16¼ mi) north of St. Pölten.*

Krems marks the beginning (when traveling upstream) of the Wachau section of the Danube. The town is closely tied to Austrian history; here the ruling Babenbergs set up a dukedom in 1120, and the earliest Austrian coin was struck in 1130. In the Middle Ages, Krems looked after the iron trade while neighboring Stein traded in salt and wine, and over the years Krems became a center of culture and art. Today the area is the heart of a thriving wine production, and narrow streets, a Renaissance Rathaus, a parish church that is one of the oldest in Lower Austria, and a pedestrian zone make Krems an attractive city to wander through.

A 14th-century former Dominican cloister, farther along the street, now serves as the **Weinstadt Museum Krems,** a wine museum that holds occasional tastings. ✉ *Körnermarkt 13,* ☎ *02732/801–567.* 🎟 *AS50.* ☉ *Mar.–Nov., Tues. 9–6, Wed.–Sun. 1–6.*

Dining and Lodging

$$$ ✕ **Zum Kaiser von Österreich.** At this landmark in the Old City district, you'll find excellent regional cuisine along with an outstanding wine selection (some of these vintages come from the backyard). The inside rooms are bright and pleasant, and the outside tables in summer are even more inviting. Owner-chef Haidinger learned his skills at Bacher, across the Danube in Mautern, so look for fish dishes along with specialties such as potato soup and roast shoulder of lamb with scalloped potatoes. ⊠ *Körnermarkt 9,* ☎ *02732/86001,* 🖷 *02732/ 86001–4. DC, MC, V. Closed Mon.*

$$$ ✕🏨 **Am Förthof.** An inn has existed on the riverside site of this modern hotel for hundreds of years. The rooms are comfortable and balconied; those in front have a view of the Danube and Göttweig abbey across the river—and the sounds of the traffic. The dining room and in summer the inviting courtyard garden offer good regional cuisine; the chef's ambitions occasionally surpass his achievements, but the sumptuous breakfasts are an assured culinary experience. ⊠ *Förthofer Donaulände 8, A–3500,* ☎ *02732/83345 or 02732/81348,* 🖷 *02732/ 83345–40. 20 rooms. Restaurant, pool, sauna. DC, MC, V.*

$–$$ ✕🏨 **Alte Post.** You're allowed to drive into the pedestrian zone to this romantic house in the heart of the Old Town, next to the Steinener Tor (Stone Gate). The rooms are in comfortable country style (full baths are scarce), but the real feature here is dining on regional specialties or sipping a glass of the local wine in the arcaded Renaissance courtyard (the restaurant is closed Wednesday). The staff is particularly friendly, and cyclists are welcome. ⊠ *Obere Landstr. 32, A–3500, Krems,* ☎ *02732/82276–0,* 🖷 *02732/84396. 24 rooms, 8 with bath. Restaurant. No credit cards. Closed Jan.–mid-Mar.*

En Route Between Krems and Stein, in a beautifully restored Capuchin cloister
★ in the tiny town of Und, is the **Weinkolleg Kloster Und.** The building also houses the tourist office and a small wine museum, where you can taste (and buy) more than 100 Austrian wines. ⊠ *Undstr. 6, Krems–Stein,* ☎ *02732/73073–0,* 🖷 *02732/73074–85.* 💳 *AS180 (includes tasting).* ☉ *Daily 11–7. Closed Dec. 23–mid-Mar.*

Stein

4 *5 km (3 mi) east of Krems.*

A frozen-in-time hamlet that has, over the years, become virtually a suburb of the adjacent city of Krems, Stein is dotted with lovely 16th-century houses, many on the hamlet's main street, Steinlanderstrasse. The 14th-century **Minoritenkirche,** just off the main street in the pedestrian zone, now serves as a museum with changing exhibits. A few steps beyond the Minoritenkirche, an imposing square Gothic tower identifies the 15th-century **St. Nicholas parish church,** whose altar painting and ceiling frescoes were done by Kremser Schmidt. The upper part of the Gothic charnel house (1462), squeezed between the church and the hillside, has been converted to housing. Notice, too, the many architecturally interesting houses, among them the former tollhouse, which has rich Renaissance frescoes. Stein was the birthplace of Ludwig Köchel, the cataloger of Mozart's works, still referred to by their Köchel numbers.

Dürnstein

5 *4 km (2½ mi) west of Stein, 90 km (56 mi) northwest of Vienna, 34 km (21¼ mi) northeast of Melk.*

If a beauty contest were held among the towns along the Wachau Danube, chances are Dürnstein would be the winner, hands down—

as you'll see when you arrive along with droves of tourists. The town is small; leave the car at one end and walk the narrow streets.

Set among terraced vineyards, the town is landmarked by its gloriously Baroque **Stiftskirche,** dating from the early 1700s, which sits on a cliff overlooking the river—this cloister church's combination of luminous blue facade and stylish Baroque tower is considered the most beautiful of its kind in Austria. After taking in the Stiftskirche, most visitors head up the hill, climbing 500 ft over the town, to the famous **Richard the Lion-Hearted Castle** where Leopold V held Richard the Lion-Hearted of England, captured on his way back home from the Crusades. In the tower of this castle, Richard was imprisoned (1192–93) until he was rescued by Blondel, the faithful minnesinger. It's said that Blondel was able to locate his imprisoned king when he heard his master's voice completing the verse of a song Blondel was singing aloud. The rather steep 30-minute climb to the ruins will earn you a breathtaking view up and down the Danube Valley and over the hills to the south.

Dining and Lodging

$$$ ✕ **Loibnerhof.** It's hard to imagine a more idyllic setting for a memo-
★   rable meal, especially if the weather is fine and tables are spread invit-
ingly in the fragrant apple orchard. The kitchen offers inventive variations on regional themes: Wachauer fish soup, crispy roast duck, and various grilled fish or lamb specialties. The house is famous for its *Butterschnitzel,* an exquisite variation on the theme of ground meat (this one's panfried veal with a touch of pork). To reach Loibnerhof, look for the Unterloiben exit a mile east of Dürnstein. ⊠ *Unterloiben 7,* ☎ *02732/82890–0,* 𝔽𝔸𝕏 *02732/82890–3. DC, MC, V. Closed Mon.–Tues. and mid-Jan.–mid-Feb.*

$$$$ ✕🔟 **Richard Löwenherz.** The impressive vaulted reception and din-
★   ing rooms of this former convent are beautifully furnished with an-
tiques, reflecting the personal warmth and care of the family management. The inviting open fire, stone floors, and friendly touches make this one of the most romantic of the Romantik Hotels group. Though all rooms are spacious and comfortable, the balconied guest rooms in the newer part of the house are more modern in decor and furnishings. Wander through the grounds and gardens, admiring the crumbling ruined walls left from earlier centuries. A terrace overlooking the Danube offers stunning views. The outstanding restaurant is known for its regional specialties and local wines. ⊠ *A–3601,* ☎ *02711/ 222,* 𝔽𝔸𝕏 *02711/222–18. 40 rooms. Restaurant, bar, pool. AE, DC, MC, V. Closed Nov.–mid-Mar.*

$$$$ ✕🔟 **Schlosshotel Dürnstein.** This 17th-century early Baroque castle, on
★   a rocky terrace with exquisite views over the Danube, offers genuine el-
egance and comfort. The best rooms look onto the river, but all are un-usually bright and attractive. Some rooms are furnished in grand Baroque style, others with country antiques or comfortable modern pieces. Half-board is standard. The kitchen matches the quality of the excellent wines from the area, and the tables set outside on the large stone balcony over-looking the river makes dining here a memorable experience. Even if you don't stay at the hotel, it's worth a stop for a delicious lunch or a leisurely afternoon pastry and coffee. ⊠ *A–3601,* ☎ *02711/212,* 𝔽𝔸𝕏 *02711/351. 37 rooms. Restaurant, bar, indoor and outdoor pools, sauna, exercise room. AE, DC, MC, V. Closed Nov.–Mar.*

$$$ 🔟 **Sänger Blondel.** Behind the yellow facade is a very friendly, tradi-
tional family hotel with elegant country rooms of medium size that have attractive paneling and antique decorations. The staff is partic-ularly helpful and can suggest excursions in the area. The hotel is known for its restaurant, which features local specialties and a wide range of salads and lighter dishes. ⊠ *No. 64, A–3601,* ☎ *02711/253–0,* 𝔽𝔸𝕏

02711/253–7. 16 rooms. Restaurant. MC, V. Closed mid-Nov.–mid-Mar. and 1 wk in early July.

Weissenkirchen

6   *5 km (3 mi) west of Dürnstein, 22 km (14 mi) northeast of Melk.*

Tucked among vineyards, just around a bend in the Danube, is Weissenkirchen, a picturesque town that was fortified against the Turks in 1531. A fire in 1793 laid waste to much of the town, but the 15th-century parish church of **Maria Himmelfahrt**, built on earlier foundations, largely survived. The south nave dates from 1300, the middle nave from 1439, the chapel from 1460. The Madonna on the triumphal arch goes back to the Danube school of about 1520; the Baroque touches date from 1736; and to complete the picture, the rococo organ was installed in 1777.

On the Marktplatz, check out the 15th-century **Wachaumuseum** (Wachau museum), which has a charming Renaissance arcaded courtyard. The building now contains many paintings by Kremser Schmidt. ✉ *Marktpl.,* ☎ *02715/2268.* ☑ *AS30.* ◔ *Apr.–Oct., Tues.–Sun. 10–5.*

Dining and Lodging

$$$ ✕ **Jamek.** Josef Jamek is known for his outstanding wines; his wife, Edeltraud, for what she and her chefs turn out in the kitchen of this fine restaurant, which is also their home. You dine in one of several rooms tastefully decorated with 19th-century touches or outdoors in the shady garden. Creative variations on typical Austrian specialties are emphasized; lamb and game in season are highlights. Wines are from the nearby family vineyards. Jamek is located just west of Weissenkirchen in Joching. ✉ *Joching 45,* ☎ *02715/2235,* 𝖥𝖠𝖷 *02715/2235-22. Reservations essential. DC, MC, V.* ◔ *Mon.–Thurs. 4–11:30, Fri.–Sat. 11:30–11. Closed mid-Dec.–mid-Feb.*

$$ ✕ **Gasthaus Erwin Schwarz.** Natives will tell you this is the best restaurant in the area, offering delicious regional cooking in a former farmhouse and butcher's shop. There is virtually nothing in the village of Nöhagen, which is 7 km (4½ mi) north of Weissenkirchen, yet people come from miles around to dine here. The restaurant raises its own animals, and all produce is grown on the premises. You're in luck if the succulent crispy duck with *Rotkraut* (red cabbage) and dumplings is on the menu. For information on the pleasant drive to this countryside spot, see the En Route below. ✉ *Nöhagen 13,* ☎ *02717/8209. No credit cards. Closed Mon.–Tues., and Mon.–Thurs. Nov.–mid-Apr.*
★

$$$ ⊡ **Raffelsbergerhof.** This lovely Renaissance building (1574), once a shipmaster's house, has been tastefully converted into a hotel with every comfort. The rooms are attractively decorated without being overdone. The family management is particularly friendly, and there's a quiet garden to complement the gemütlich public lounge. ✉ *A–3610,* ☎ *02715/2201,* 𝖥𝖠𝖷 *02715/2201-27. 14 rooms. DC, MC, V. Closed Nov.–Apr.*

En Route   One of the prettiest drives in the Wachau leads from Weissenkirchen to the renowned Gasthaus Erwin Schwarz (☞ *above*) in Nöhagen. From the main entrance to the town of Weissenkirchen, follow the road (Route L7094) north up through the village, veering to your right past the church. Soon the village gives way to a forested incline, after which you'll emerge into a verdant landscape of soft-contoured hills and vineyards and an occasional old farmhouse, passing through Weinzierl on Route L7090 on your way north to Nöhagen. From Nöhagen, take Route L7040 east toward Reichau, then to sleepy, rambling Senftenberg ("Mustard Mountain") with its romantic castle ruin perched above the town. A few kilometers east of Senftenberg, change to Route 218, going northeast to Langenlois. From here there will be signs to Vienna or back to Krems.

Spitz

❼ *5 km (3 mi) southwest of Weissenkirchen, 17 km (10½ mi) northeast of Melk.*

Picturesque Spitz is off the main road and back from the Danube, sitting like a jewel in the surrounding vineyards and hills. One vineyard, the "Thousand Bucket Hill" is so called for the amount of wine it is said to produce in a good year. A number of interesting houses in Spitz go back to the 16th and 17th centuries. The late-Gothic 15th-century **parish church** contains Kremser Schmidt's altar painting of the martyrdom of St. Mauritius. Note the carved wood statues of Christ and the 12 apostles, dating from 1380, on the organ loft. Just beyond Spitz and above the road is the ruin of the **castle Hinterhaus,** to which you can climb.

Lodging

$$$ ⊞ **Burg Oberranna.** About 7 km (4½ mi) beyond the village of Mühldorf, directly west of Spitz, stands this well-preserved castle-hotel, surrounded by a double wall and dry moat. The original structure dates from the early 12th-century, and the St. George chapel possibly even earlier. Some of the charming antiques-filled rooms include a kitchenette and sitting room. This is a great base for hiking and also perfect for those who just want to get away. ⊠ *Ober-Ranna 1, A–3622 Mühldorf,* ☎ *02713/8221,* 𝔽𝔸𝕏 *02713/8366. 11 rooms, 4 suites. Café, kitchenettes. AE, V. Closed Nov.–Apr.*

En Route   The vistas are mainly of the other side of the Danube, looking across at Schönbühel and Melk, as you follow a back road via Jauerling and Maria Laach to Route 3 at Aggsbach. Shortly after Weitenegg the Wachau ends, and you come into the part of the Danube Valley known as the **Nibelungenau,** where the Nibelungs—who inspired the great saga *Nibelungenlied,* source of Wagner's *Ring*—are supposed to have settled for a spell. If you have always thought of the Nibelungs as a mythical race of dwarfs known only to old German legends and Wagner, dismiss that idea. The Nibelungs existed, though not as Wagner describes them, and this area was one of their stomping grounds.

Maria Taferl

❽ *49 km (31 mi) southwest of Spitz, 13 km (8 mi) west of Melk, 7½ km (4¾ mi) northeast of Persenbeug/Ybbs an der Donau.*

Crowning a hill on the north bank is the two-towered **Maria Taferl Basilica,** a pilgrimage church with a spectacular outlook. It's a bit touristy, but the church and the view are worth the side trip.

About 5 km (3 mi) up a back road is **Schloss Artstetten,** a massive square castle with four round defense towers at its corners. This is the burial place of Archduke Franz Ferdinand and his wife, Sophie, whose double assassination in 1914 in Sarajevo was one of the immediate causes of World War I. ⊠ *Artstetten,* ☎ *07413/8302.* ▣ *AS70.* ☉ *Apr.–Oct., daily 9–5:30.*

Lodging

$$$ ⊞ **Krone–Kaiserhof.** Two hotels under the same family management share each other's luxurious facilities. The Krone looks out over the Danube Valley, while the Kaiserhof has views of the nearby Baroque pilgrimage church. Both have rooms done a bit slickly in country style, and the restaurants are popular. An associated guest house ($) is less elegant but also shares facilities. Cyclists staying overnight will be picked up free at Marbach or Klein Pöchlarn landing stations on the Danube. ⊠ *A–3672,* ☎ *07413/6355–0,* 𝔽𝔸𝕏 *07413/6355–83. 72 rooms.*

2 restaurants, bar, café, indoor and outdoor pools, sauna, miniature golf, exercise room. V. Closed Jan.–Feb.

Grein

9 *32 km (20 mi) west of Maria Teferl, 20 km (12 mi) west of Persenbeug/Ybbs an der Donau.*

Set above the Danube, Grein is a picture-book town complete with castle. The river bend below, known for years as the "place where death resides," was one of the most hazardous stretches of river until the reefs were blasted away in the late 1700s. Take time to see the intimate rococo **Stadttheater** in the town hall, built in 1790 and still occasionally used for concerts or plays. ⊠ *Rathaus,* ☎ *07268/7055.* ◻ *AS30.* ⊙ *Apr.–Oct., tours daily at 10, 1:30, and 4.*

Baumgartenberg

10 *11 km (7 mi) west of Grein, 17½ km (11 mi) east of Mauthausen.*

The small village of Baumgartenberg is worth a visit for its ornate Baroque **parish church.** Note the lavish stucco-work and exquisitely carved 17th-century pews—and the unusual chancel supported by a tree trunk. The church is the only reminder of a once-famed Cistercian abbey, founded in 1141 by Otto von Machland, that used to thrive here. Outside the town is the picturesque **castle of Klam,** which used to belong to Swedish playwright August Strindberg; it now contains a small museum.

LINZ

130 km (81¼ mi) east of Salzburg, 185 km (115½ mi) west of Vienna.

The capital of Upper Austria, set where the Traun River flows into the Danube, Linz has a fascinating Old City core and an active cultural life. In 1832 it had a horse-drawn train to Czechoslovakia that functioned as the first rail line on the Continent. Once known as the "Rich Town of the River Markets" because of its importance as a medieval trading post, it is today the center of Austrian steel and chemical production, both started by the Germans in 1938. A city of contrasts, Linz has Austria's largest medieval square and is home to one of the country's most modern multipurpose halls, the Brucknerhaus, which is used for concerts and conventions.

With the city's modern economic success, Linz's attractions for tourists have been generally overlooked. Nevertheless, Linz boasts beautiful old houses on the Hauptplatz; a Baroque cathedral with twin towers and a fine organ over which composer Anton Bruckner once presided; and its "city mountain," the Pöstlingberg, with a unique railway line to the top. Extensive redevelopment, ongoing restoration, and the creation of traffic-free zones continue to transform Linz. The heart of the city—the Altstadt (Old City)—has been turned into a pedestrian zone; either leave the car at your hotel or use the huge new parking garage under the main square in the center of town. Distances are not great, and you can take in the highlights in the course of a two-hour walking tour.

A Good Walk

The center of the Old City is the Hauptplatz, with its pretty pastel town houses. Dominating the square is the **Pillar to the Holy Trinity** ⑪, erected in 1723 in gratitude for Linz's survival after threats of war, fire, and the dreaded plague. Head down Klostergasse to the **Minoritenkirche** ⑫, which is worth a stop to inspect the church's rococo interior before visiting the adjacent **Landhaus** ⑬, a rambling Renaissance building

Linz

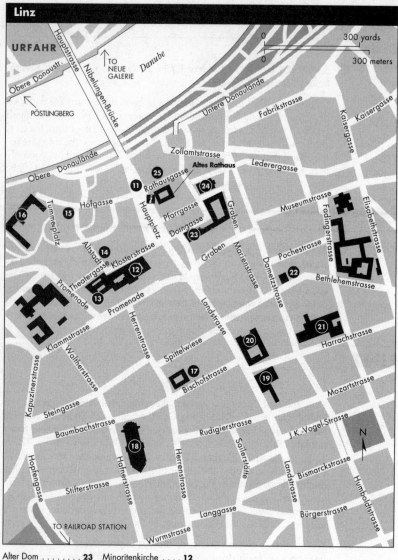

with three inner courtyards. In the arcaded courtyard is the Fountain of the Planets, with Jupiter as the crowning glory.

Turn right on Altstadtgasse, and at Number 17 is the **Mozart Haus** ⑭, where Mozart stayed as a guest of the Count of Thun and composed the Linz Symphony in his spare time. At Number 10 is the **Kremsmünstererhaus** ⑮, with its turrets and onion domes, where Emperor Friedrich III supposedly died in August 1493. Turn left from Altstadtgasse onto Hofgasse (one of the prettiest corners in the city), and climb the quaint narrow street that leads up to the Rudolfstor, one of the entrances to **Linz Castle** ⑯. Since its early days as a prime fortress on the Danube, it has served as a hospital, army barracks, and even a prison, before becoming a provincial museum. The view from the castle promontory is one of the most impressive in Linz. Walk through the castle grounds to the **Martinskirche**, one of the oldest churches in Austria, with its nave dating from 799.

Follow Römerstrasse along the castle walls down to the Promenade, veering right when you get to Herrenstrasse. Where Bichofstrasse meets Herrenstrasse is the **Bischofshof** ⑰, which was built between 1721 and 1726 for the Kremsmünster monastery and is still the seat of the bishop of Linz. The west end of Bishofstrasse angles onto Baumbachstrasse, which is the setting for the **Neuer Dom** ⑱, the massive 19th-century cathedral, which can hold up to 20,000 worshipers. Note the Linz Window depicting the history of Linz before heading back to Herrenstrasse.

Turn right and shortly afterward left onto Rudigerstrasse. Follow this to Landstrasse, where you'll make another left. Two Baroque churches are located here, that of the **Carmelitenkloster** ⑲, modeled after St. Joseph's in Prague, and across the street, the **Ursulinenkirche** ⑳. Between these two churches is Harrachstrasse, which holds another Baroque gem, the **Deutschordenskirche** ㉑, or seminary church, located shortly after you cross Dametzgasse. After you're finished inspecting the high altar by Hildebrandt, backtrack along Harrachstrasse to Dametzstrasse, where you'll turn right. At the corner of Dametzstrasse and Bethlehemstrasse is the **Nordico** ㉒, the city museum, which was originally an early 17th-century town house used by the Kremsmünster monastery for nearly 200 years as a Jesuit training center for young Scandinavian men. Now it houses a collection that ranges from archaeological finds to the Biedermeier era.

Keep going along Dametzstrasse until you reach the Graben, where you turn left and walk for a short while before turning right on Domgasse. Here is the **Alter Dom** ㉓, the old city cathedral where Anton Bruckner played the organ for 12 years, beginning in 1856. From here follow Domgasse around to the **Stadtpfarrkirche** ㉔, near the intersection to Kollegiumgasse. This was originally a Romanesque basilica before being rebuilt in the Baroque style in the mid-17th century. In the entrance hall and approach to the tower staircase you can see Gothic cross-ribbing on the vaulted ceiling.

Go left from the church onto Kollegiumgasse, then left into the Pfarrplatz. From the northwest edge of the square, head down Rathausgasse to Number 5, the last stop on the walking tour, the **Kepler Haus** ㉕, home of astronomer Johannes Kepler. He lived here with his family for 10 years, beginning in 1612. More than a hundred years later, Linz's first printing shop was established here. Rathausgasse leads into the Hauptplatz, which brings you back to the starting point of the tour.

TIMING

Of course the best time to visit Linz is from May to September, but fortunately the main tourist attractions are open year-round. Touring the

Old City takes two to three hours, depending on how many of the sights you stop to visit. If you're pressed for time, head straight for Linz Castle. You'll pass through the loveliest parts of the city, and from the heights of the castle grounds you'll be able to enjoy stupendous views of the Danube.

Numbers in the text correspond to numbers in the margin and on the Linz map.

Sights to See

㉓ Alter Dom (Old Cathedral). Hidden away off the Graben, a narrow side street off of the Taubenmarkt above the Hauptplatz, is this Baroque gem (1669–78), whose striking feature is the single nave together with the side altars. Anton Bruckner was organist here from 1856 to 1868. ⊙ *Daily 7–noon and 3–7.*

Altes Rathaus (Old City Hall). Located at the lower end of the main square, the original 1513 building was mainly destroyed by fire and replaced in 1658–59. Its octagonal corner turret and lunar clock, as well as some vaulted rooms, remain, and you can detect traces of the original Renaissance structure on the Rathausgasse facade. The present exterior dates from 1824. The approach from Rathausgasse 5, opposite the Kepler Haus, leads through a fine arcaded courtyard. On the facade here you'll spot portraits of Emperor Friedrich III, the mayors Hoffmandl and Prunner, the astronomer Johannes Kepler, and the composer Anton Bruckner. ⊠ *Hauptpl.*

⑰ Bischofshof (Bishop's Residence). At the intersection of Herrenstrasse and Bischofstrasse is this impressive mansion, which dates from 1721. Graced by a fine wrought-iron gateway, this remains the city's most important Baroque secular building. The design is by Jakob Prandtauer, the architectural genius responsible for the glorious Melk and St. Florian abbeys.

⑲ Carmelitenkloster. This magnificent Baroque church on Landstrasse was modeled on St. Joseph's in Prague. ⊠ *Langg. 17,* ☎ *0732/770217.* ⊙ *Daily 7–11:45 and 3–5.*

㉑ Deutschordenskirche. This former seminary church from 1723 is a beautiful yellow-and-white Baroque treasure with an elliptical dome designed by Johann Lukas von Hildebrandt, who also designed its high altar. ⊠ *Harrachstr.,* ☎ *no phone.* ⊙ *Daily 8–6.*

Elisabethinenkloster. This church dates from the mid-18th century. Note the unusually dynamic colors in the dome fresco by Altomonte. ⊠ *Bethlehemstr. 23,* ☎ *0732/76760.*

㋡ Märchengrotte (Fairy-tale Grotto) Railroad. Trains run through a colorful imaginary world at the top of the ☞ **Pöstlingberg**. It's entertaining for the rest of the family as well as the kids. ☎ *0732/7801–7506.* ▨ *AS40.* ⊙ *Apr. and mid-Sept.–mid–Nov., daily 10–5; May–mid-Sept., daily 10–6.*

㉕ Kepler Haus. The astronomer Johannes Kepler lived here from 1612 to 1622; Linz's first printing shop was established in this house in 1745. The interior is closed to the public. ⊠ *Rathausgasse 5.*

⑮ Kremsmünstererhaus. Emperor Friedrich III is said to have died here in 1493. The building was done over in Renaissance style in 1578–80, and a story was added in 1616, with two turrets and onion domes. There's a memorial room to the emperor here; his heart is entombed in the Linz parish church, but the rest of him is in St. Stephen's cathedral in Vienna (☞ Chapter 1). The traditional rooms are now home to one of Linz' best restaurants, the Kremsmünsterer Stuben (☞ Dining and Lodging, *below*). ⊠ *Altstadt 10.*

⑬ **Landhaus.** The early Renaissance monastery adjoining the ☞ **Minoritenkirche** is now the Landhaus, with its distinctive tower, seat of the provincial government. Look inside to see the arcaded courtyard with the Planet Fountain and the Hall of Stone on the first floor, above the barrel-vaulted hall on the ground floor; for a more extensive look at the interior, inquire at the local tourist office for their scheduled guided tours. The beautiful Renaissance doorway (1570) is of red marble. ⊠ *Klosterstr. 7.*

⑯ **Linz Castle.** The massive four-story building in Tummelplatz was rebuilt by Friedrich III around 1477, literally on top of a castle that dated from 799. Note the **Friedrichstor** (the Friedrich Gate), with the same *A.E.I.O.U.* monogram also found in Krems, and the two interior courtyards. The castle houses the Upper Austrian provincial museum—weapons, musical instruments, Nativity scenes, Upper Austrian art, and prehistoric and Roman relics. ⊠ *Tummelpl. 10,* ☎ *0732/774419.* ▨ *AS40.* ☉ *Tues.–Fri. 9–5, weekends 10–4.*

⑫ **Minoritenkirche.** Situated at the end of the Klosterstrasse, this church was once part of a monastery. The present building dates from 1752 to 1758 and has a delightful rococo interior with side altar paintings by Kremser Schmidt and the main altar by Bartolomeo Altomonte. ⊠ *Klosterstr. 7,* ☎ *0732/7720–1364.* ▨ *Free.* ☉ *Mon.–Sat. 8–11 AM, Sun. 8–noon.*

⑭ **Mozart Haus.** This three-story Renaissance town house, actually the Thun Palace, has a later Baroque facade and portal. Mozart arrived here in 1783 with his wife to meet an especially impatient patron (Mozart was late by 14 days). As the composer forgot to bring any symphonies along with him, he set about writing one and he completed the sublime Linz Symphony in the space of four days. The palace now houses the local tourist office and private apartments, but the courtyard can be viewed. ⊠ *Altstadt 17.*

Neue Galerie. Across the river in the Urfahr district is one of Austria's best modern art museums. The fine collection is well balanced, featuring mainly contemporary international and Austrian artists. ⊠ *Blütenstr. 15, Urfahr,* ☎ *0732/7070–3600.* ▨ *AS40.* ☉ *May–Oct., Mon.–Wed. and Fri. 10–6, Thurs. 10–10, Sat. 10–1; Nov.–Apr., Fri.–Wed. 10–6, Thurs. 10–10.*

⑱ **Neuer Dom** (New Cathedral). In 1862 the bishop of Linz engaged one of the architects of the Cologne cathedral to develop a design for a cathedral in neo-Gothic French-cathedral style and modestly ordered that its tower not be higher than that of St. Stephen's in Vienna. The result was the massive 400-ft tower, shorter than St. Stephen's by a scant 6½ ft. ⊠ *Baumbachstr.,* ☎ *0732/777885.* ▨ *Free.* ☉ *Mon.–Sat. 7:30–5:30, Sun. 1–5:30.*

㉒ **Nordico.** At the corner of Dametzstrasse and Bethlehemstrasse, you'll find the city museum, dating from 1610. Its collection follows local history from pre-Roman times to the mid-1880s. ⊠ *Bethlehemstr. 7,* ☎ *0732/7070–1900.* ▨ *Free, except for special exhibits.* ☉ *Weekdays 9–6, weekends 2–5.*

⑪ **Pillar to the Holy Trinity.** One of the symbols of Linz is the 65-ft Baroque column in the center of the Hauptplatz square. Completed in 1723 of white Salzburg marble, the memorial offers thanks by an earthly trinity—the provincial estates, city council, and local citizenry—for deliverance from the threats of war (1704), fire (1712), and plague (1713). From March through October there's a flea market here each Saturday (except holidays), from 7 AM to 2 PM.

Pöstlingberg. With a glass of chilled white wine, drink in the grand vista over Linz and the Danube from one of the flower-hung restaurants located at the top of Linz's "city mountain." At the summit is the **Church of Sieben Schmerzen Mariens,** an immense and splendidly opulent twin-towered Baroque pilgrimage church (1748), visible for miles as a Linz landmark. Also on the mountain is the ☞ **Märchengrotte (Fairy-tale Grotto) Railroad.** An electric railway, the **Pöstlingbergbahn,** gives a scenic ride up the mountain. To reach the base station for the railway, take Streetcar 3 across the river to Urfahr, Linz's left bank. Note the railway's unusual switches, necessary because the car-wheel flanges ride the outside of the rails rather than the (usual) inside. When the line was built in 1898, it boasted the steepest incline of any noncog railway in Europe. In summer, the old open-bench cars are used. On a clear day the view at the top takes in a good deal of Upper Austria south of the Danube, with a long chain of the Austrian Alps visible on the horizon. ☎ *0732/7801–7002.* ⊡ *Round-trip AS35, combined ticket with Streetcar Line 3 AS48 (tickets available at Tourist Information).* ☉ *Daily, every 20 min 5:30 AM–8:20 PM.*

㉔ Stadtpfarrkirche. This city parish church dates from 1286 and was rebuilt in Baroque style in 1648. The tomb in the right wall of the chancel contains Friedrich III's heart. The ceiling frescoes are by Altomonte, and the figure of Johann Nepomuk (a local saint) in the chancel is by Georg Raphael Donner, in a setting by Hildebrandt. ⊠ *Domg.* ☉ *Daily 8–6.*

㉑ Ursulinenkirche. The towers at this Baroque church are one of the identifying symbols of Linz. Inside is a blaze of gold and crystal ornament. Note the Madonna figure wearing a hooded Carmelite cloak with huge pockets, used to collect alms for the poor. ☎ *0732/7610–3151.* ☉ *Daily 1–6, towers daily 7:30–6.*

Dining and Lodging

$$$$ ✕ **Kremsmünsterer Stuben.** In a beautifully restored historic house in
★ the heart of the Old City, you'll find an attractive wood-paneled restaurant offering everything from regional specialties to a six-course dinner. You might choose from saddle of hare or fillet of venison as a main course as you relax in the comfortable, traditional ambience of the city's best restaurant. ⊠ *Altstadt 10,* ☎ *0732/782111,* ⅉ⅃⃫ *0732/784130. Reservations essential. Jacket and tie. AE, DC, MC, V. Closed Sun., 2 wks in Jan., and 2 wks in Aug. No lunch Sat. and Mon.*

$$$$ ✕ **Verdi.** Linz's favored dinner restaurant is in Lichtenberg, about 3 km (2 mi) north of the center, off Leonfelder Strasse. The cuisine is regional Austrian, with Italian and French overtones; the name refers to the opulent green-hued decor. Some complain of overemphasis on presentation, but this hardly deters the many regulars. Choose game in season or tender lamb. ⊠ *Pachmayrstr. 137,* ☎ *0732/733005. No credit cards. Closed Sun., Mon., and 3 wks in Jan.*

$$ ✕ **Papa Joe's.** This just might be the most happening place in town, with
★ an incongruous location next to the 18th-century Ursuline Abbey. The tropical-kitsch decor makes you feel like you're going to have a good time from the moment you walk in the door. Choose from a vast selection of salads, ribs, burgers, and steaks, or if you want something more adventurous, try the delicious duck with pumpkin or chicken with mangoes. Portions are huge. ⊠ *Landstr. 31,* ☎ *0732/7746860. AE, DC, MC, V.*

$ ✕ **Glockenspiel.** This atmospheric coffeehouse is in the oldest patrician town house on the Hauptplatz. It is warm and inviting, with a vaulted ceiling, polished-wood decor, and intimate tables that beckon you to sit and enjoy a mélange and fresh pastry. ⊠ *Hauptpl. 18,* ☎ *0732/795399. No credit cards.*

$ ✕ **K & K Hofbäckerei** (Fritz Roth). The tantalizing aroma of freshly baked bread will beckon you to this Old World bakery just off the Hauptplatz. Choose from a variety of tempting breads and pastries, order a cup of coffee, and then take a seat in the cozy adjoining candlelit room. The friendly owner speaks English. ⊠ *Pfarrg. 17,* ☎ *0732/784110. No credit cards. Closed Sun. No dinner.*

$ ★ ✕ **Traxlmayr.** Proud with the patina of age, this is one of Austria's great old-tradition coffeehouses. You can linger all day over a single cup of coffee, reading the papers (*Herald Tribune* included) in their bentwood holders, and then have a light meal. In winter it's extremely smoky, but in summer you can sit outside on the charming terrace and watch passersby. Ask for the specialty, Linzer torte, with your coffee. ⊠ *Promenade 16,* ☎ *0732/773353. No credit cards. Closed Sun.*

$$$$ 🏨 **Schillerpark.** You're close to the south end of the pedestrian zone but still reasonably near the center and the sights in this very modern glass complex. The rooms have clean lines, contemporary furnishings, and some have waterbeds. The buffet breakfast is outstanding and included in the room price. The casino is in the same building. ⊠ *Rainerstr. 2–4, A–4020,* ☎ *0732/6950–0,* ℻ *0732/6950–9. 111 rooms. 2 restaurants, 2 bars, café, no-smoking floor, sauna. AE, DC, MC, V.*

$$$ 🏨 **Drei Mohren.** Directly across from the Landhaus Park and in the very heart of the city center, this modest hotel offers simple yet comfortable quiet rooms and a nice buffet breakfast. The staff is friendly and helpful. ⊠ *Promenade 17, A–4020,* ☎ *0732/772626–0,* ℻ *0732/ 772626–6. 25 rooms. AE, DC, MC, V.*

$$–$$$ ★ 🏨 **Wolfinger.** This charming, traditional hotel in an old building is a favorite of regular guests, in part because of the friendly staff, and its location couldn't be more central. The medium-size rooms have been recently modernized, with comfortable new furniture and bright fabrics. Those in the front are less quiet but give a view of city activities. ⊠ *Hauptpl. 19, A–4020,* ☎ *0732/773291–0,* ℻ *0732/773291–55. 45 rooms. AE, DC, MC, V.*

$$ 🏨 **Zum Schwarzen Bären.** The "Black Bear" is a fine, traditional house near the center of the Old City, a block from the pedestrian zone, and incidentally was the birthplace of the renowned tenor Richard Tauber (1891–1948). The rooms are smallish and plain, and the baths (most with shower) are modern, if compact. ⊠ *Herrenstr. 9–11, A–4020,* ☎ *0732/ 772477–0,* ℻ *0732/772477–47. 35 rooms, 29 with bath. Restaurant, bar, Weinstube. AE, DC, MC, V.*

Nightlife and the Arts

Linz is far livelier than even most Austrians realize. The local population is friendlier than in either Vienna or Salzburg, and much less cliquish. Nor has Linz lagged behind other Austrian cities in developing its own hot section, known as the Bermuda Triangle. Around the narrow streets of the Old City (Klosterstrasse, Altstadt, Hofgasse) are dozens of fascinating small bars and lounges; as you explore, you'll probably meet some Linzers who can direct you to the current "in" location.

THE ARTS

The **Linz opera company** is talented and often willing to mount venturesome works and productions. Most performances are in the Landestheater, with some in the Brucknerhaus.

The tourist office's monthly booklet "Was ist los in Linz und Oberösterreich" ("What's on in Linz and Upper Austria") will give you details of theater and concerts. Two **ticket agencies** are **Linzer Kartenbüro** (⊠ Herrenstr. 4, ☎ 0732/778800) and **Ruefa** (⊠ Landstr. 67, ☎ 0732/ 662681–0, ℻ 0732/662681–33).

Concerts and recitals are held in the **Brucknerhaus,** the modern hall on the bank of the Danube, From mid-September to early October, it's the center of the International Bruckner Festival. In mid-June, the hall hosts the biggest multimedia event in the area, the Ars Electronica, a musical and laser-show spectacle. ⊠ *Untere Donaulände 7,* ☎ *0732/ 7612–0,* FAX *0732/783745.* ⊙ *Box office weekdays 10–6.*

NIGHTLIFE

A good starting point, where both the young and the older will feel comfortable, is the bar **S'Linzerl** (⊠ Hofberg 5), which is open Monday–Saturday 9 PM–3 AM.

The Linz **casino,** with roulette, blackjack, poker, and slot machines, is in the Hotel Schillerpark; the casino complex includes a bar and the Rouge et Noir restaurant. A passport is required for admission. ⊠ *Rainerstr. 2–4,* ☎ *0732/654487–0,* FAX *0732/654487–24.* ⊿ *AS210 (includes 5 AS50 tokens).* ⊙ *Daily 3 PM–3 AM. Closed Nov. 1 and Dec. 24.*

For the young crowd there are several choices for popular late-night clubs. One of the most frequented is **Sassi** (⊠ Spittelwiese 6–12, ☎ 0732/787850), in the Arkade Shopping Mall on the pedestrian Landstrasse, which features behind the bar a pyramid of champagne bottles that can only be reached by stepladder. Open every day from 9 to the wee hours, the modern bar also offers soup, sandwiches, and light pasta dishes. **Monkey Circus** (⊠ Spittelwiese 6–8, entrance on Landstrasse, ☎ 0732/787868) is another hopping establishment, located next door to the Arkade Shopping Mall and open every day from 5 on, with live music on Sunday and Monday at 8.

Shopping

Linz is a good place to shop; prices are generally lower than those in resorts and the larger cities, and selections are varied. The major shops are found in the main square and the adjoining side streets, in the old quarter to the west of the main square, in the pedestrian zone of the Landstrasse and its side streets, and in the Hauptstrasse of Urfahr, over the Nibelungen Bridge across the Danube.

For local handmade items and good-quality souvenirs, try **O. Ö. Heimatwerk** (⊠ Landstr. 31, ☎ 0732/773376–0), where you'll find silver, pewter, ceramics, fabrics, and some clothing. Everything from clothing to china is sold at the **Flea Market,** open March–mid-November, Saturday 7–2, on the Hauptplatz (main square). From mid-November through February the market moves across the river next to the new city hall and runs Saturday from 8 to 2. At the state-run **Dorotheum auction house** (⊠ Fabrikstr. 26, ☎ 0732/773132–0), auctions take place every Wednesday at 1:30.

For antiques head for the Old City, on the side streets around the main square. Try **Otto Buchinger** (⊠ Bethlehemstr. 5, ☎ 0732/770117), **Richard Kirchmayr** (⊠ Bischofstr. 3a, ☎ 0732/797711), **Kunsthandlung Kirchmayr** (⊠ Herrenstr. 23, ☎ 0732/774667), or **Ute Pastl** (⊠ Wischerstr. 26, Urfahr, ☎ 0732/737306).

For jewelry, try **Pfaffenberger** (⊠ Landstr. 42, ☎ 0732/772495) or **Wild** (⊠ Landstr. 49, ☎ 0732/774105–0).

Outdoor Activities and Sports

Buy tickets for sports events at **Kartenbüro Ruefa** (⊠ Landstr. 67, ☎ 0732/662681–0, FAX 0732/662681–33). The office is open weekdays 8:30–noon and 2–6 and Saturday 8:30–noon.

BICYCLING

Cyclists appreciate the relatively level terrain around Linz, and within the city there are 89 km (55 mi) of marked cycle routes. Get the brochure *Cycling in Linz* from the tourist office. You can rent a bike through **Fahrradzentrum B7** (⊠ Oberfelderstr. 12, ☎ 0732/330550) or **LILO Bahnhof** (✉ Coulinstr. 30, ☎ 0732/600703) or at the **Haupt-bahnhof** (✉ Main rail station, Bahnhofstr. 3, ☎ 0732/6909–0).

GOLF

Fairly close to Linz is the 9-hole, par-72 **Golfclub St. Oswald-Freistadt** (✉ Promenade 22, St. Oswald, ☎ 07945/7938). The 18-hole, par-72 **Böhmerwald Golfpark** (✉ Seitelschlag 50, Raiffeisenpl. 1, Ulrichsberg, ☎ 07288/8200) is near Linz. East of Linz is the relatively new 18-hole, par-71 **Linzer Golf Club Mühlviertel** (✉ Am Luftenberg 1a, Luftenberg, ☎ 07237/3893), playable mid-March–November.

ICE-SKATING

Linz is an ice-skating city. From late October to late February, there's outdoor skating at the city rink, daily 2–5, and also Friday–Wednesday 6–9, weekends 9–noon; skating is also available late September to April indoors at the adjoining indoor sports complex, the **Eishalle,** Wednesday 9–noon, Saturday 2–5 and 6–9, and Sunday 10–noon, 2–5, and 6–9. Hockey and skating competitions are also held in the Eishalle. ✉ *Untere Donaulände 11,* ☎ *0732/776508–31.*

SOCCER

Soccer matches are played in Linz in the **Stadion** (✉ Roseggerstr. 41, corner of Ziegeleistr., ☎ 0732/660670 or 0732/660680).

TENNIS

Tennis matches and other sports events are held at the **Stadthalle** (☎ 0732/660680).

WATER SPORTS

The Danube is not suitable for swimming, but alternatives exist. The closest swimming is at **Pleschinger Lake**; to get there, take Tram 1 to Urfahr/Reindlstrasse and Bus 32 to the lake, or Tram No. 3 or 1 to Rudolfstr., then Bus 33 or 33a to the lake. This is a pleasant spot for family swimming, although it tends to be crowded on sunny, warm weekends. The **Kral Waterskiing School** (✉ Talg. 14, at Ottensheimerstr., ☎ 0732/731494) offers waterskiing and other water sports.

EXCURSIONS FROM LINZ

Many travelers find Linz the most practical point of departure for visits to the Mühlviertel and the Gothic and Baroque sights found in the towns of St. Florian, Kremsmünster, and Steyr, although Steyr certainly merits an overnight itself. North of Linz toward Freistadt and the Czech border, the Mühlviertel (a "mill district" now in the agricultural, not industrial, sense) is made up of meadows and gentle wooded hills interspersed with towns whose appearance has changed little since the Middle Ages. To the west of Linz, south of the Danube, lies the Innviertel, named for the Inn River (which forms the border with Germany before it joins the Danube), a region of broad fields and meadows, and enormous woodland tracts, ideal for cycling, hiking, and riding. To the south, the hilly landscape introduces the foothills of the Austrian Alps.

Freistadt

★ ㉖ *41 km (26 mi) northeast of Linz.*

Located in the eastern part of the Mühlviertel, Freistadt developed as a border defense city on the salt route into Bohemia (now the Czech Republic), which accounts for the wall, towers, and gates, still wonderfully preserved today. To get to Freistadt, cross the Danube to Linz-Urfahr and turn right onto Freistädter Strasse (Route 125/E55).

A walk around the wall gives an impression of how a city in the Middle Ages was conceived and defended; it takes about a half hour. Look at the late-Gothic **Linzertor** (the Linz Gate), with its steep, wedge-shape roof, and the **Böhmertor,** on the opposite wall, leading to the Czech Republic. The city's **central square,** aglow with pastel facades, is virtually the same as it was 400 years ago; only the parked cars belie the picture of antiquity. Pause for a local beer; the town's first brewery dates from 1573. The 15th-century parish church of **St. Catherine's** was redone in Baroque style in the 17th century but retains its slender tower, whose unusual balconies have railings on all four sides.

The late-Gothic castle to the northeast of the square now houses the **Mühlviertel Heimathaus** (district museum); the display of painted glass in the chapel and the hand tools in the 163-ft tower are especially interesting. ☎ 07942/72274. ⊠ AS20. ⊙ *Daily 9–noon and 2–5, evening tour on Wed.*

Centering on Freistadt is a historical road called the **Museumstrasse,** which takes you to points of interest from the glory days of the Mühlviertel, when this area was famous for its mills. Among places to stop and visit are historical mills, a former dyeing-works museum, and a leather-working museum. Contact the Mühlviertel Tourist Office in Linz (☞ Visitor Information *in* Danube Valley A to Z, *below*) for information.

A fun excursion for kids and grown-ups alike is the **Pferdeeisenbahn,** which is the Austrian version of an old stagecoach ride. You'll travel by horse-drawn carriage along the back roads, stopping for meals and at a hotel for the night. Contact the Mühlviertel Tourist Office in Linz (☞ Visitor Information *in* Danube Valley A to Z, *below*) for information.

Dining and Lodging

$$ ✕▢ **Zum Goldenen Adler.** Here you'll be in another 600-year-old
★ house; it has been run by the same family since 1807, so tradition runs strong. The medium-size rooms are modern yet full of country charm; hotel service is exceptionally accommodating. The garden contains a piece of the old city wall as background and is a delightful oasis. The restaurant is known for regional specialties such as *Böhmisches Bierfleisch* (beef cooked in beer). The desserts are outstanding. ⊠ *Salzg. 1, A–4240,* ☎ *07942/72112–0,* FAX *07942/72112–44. 37 rooms. Restaurant, bar, pool, sauna, exercise room. AE, DC, MC, V.*

Kefermarkt

㉗ *9 km (5½ mi) south of Freistadt.*

From Freistadt, you can get to Kefermarkt either via marked back roads or by turning east off Route 125/E14. Both towns can be visited on a loop excursion from Linz. The late-Gothic **Church of St. Wolfgang** has one of Austria's great art treasures, a 42-ft-high winged altar intricately carved from linden wood, commissioned by Christoph von Zelking and completed in 1497. So masterly is the carving that it has been ascribed to famous 15th-century sculptors Veit Stoss and Michael Pacher, but most historians now attribute it to Jürg Huber and Martin Kriechbaum. Some figures, such as St. Christopher, are true masterpieces of northern Renaissance sculpture. The church also has some impressive 16th-century frescoes.

Eferding

㉘ *25 km (16 mi) west of Linz.*

Eferding, a centuries-old community with an attractive town square, lies west of Linz. You can easily drive the 25 km (16 mi) on Route 129, but the more adventurous route is via the **LILO** (Linzer Lokalbahn) interurban railway from Coulinstrasse 30 (☎ 0732/654376), near the main rail station.

In Eferding, the double door in the south wall of the 15th-century **Church of St. Hippolyte** is a gem of late-Gothic stonecutting, with the Madonna and Child above flanked by Saints Hippolyte and Agyd. Inside, note the Gothic altar with its five reliefs and the statues of Saints Wolfgang and Martin. Visit the **Spitalskirche** (built in 1325) and note the Gothic frescoes in the Magdalen chapel, which date from about 1430.

Dining and Lodging

$$$$ ✕ **Dannerbauer.** Two kilometers (1 mi) north of Eferding, on the road
★   to Aschach and directly on the Danube, is one of the area's best restaurants. It serves many species of fish—some you probably never heard of—to your taste: poached, grilled, broiled, or fried. Many of the fish come from the river; some are raised in the house ponds, to ensure freshness. There are meat dishes, too, and game in season, and the soups (try the nettle soup) are excellent. The place has a pleasant outlook with lots of windows. ⊠ *Brandstatt bei Eferding,* ☎ *07272/2471. AE, DC. Closed Mon.–Tues. and mid-Jan.–mid-Feb.*

$ 🏠 **Zum Goldenen Kreuz.** The golden facade indicates a typical country-style hotel, simple and with the appealing charm of a family-run establishment. You'll sleep under fluffy feather-bed coverlets. The restaurant is known for its good regional cuisine, and there are occasional specialty weeks. ⊠ *Schmiedstr. 29, A–4070,* ☎ *07272/4247–0,* 🆁 *07272/4249. 21 rooms. Restaurant. AE, DC, MC. Closed Christmas wk.*

Hartkirchen

㉙ *12 km (7 mi) north of Eferding, 26 km (16¼ mi) northwest of Linz.*

The **parish church** at Hartkirchen is worth a visit to see fine Baroque wall and ceiling frescoes, dated 1750, that create the illusion of space and depth. To reach Hartkirchen, take Route 130 north from Eferding to Pupping and continue 3 km (2 mi).

Aschach

㉚ *2 km (1 mi) north of Hartkirchen, 21 km (13¼ mi) northwest of Linz.*

Aschach, a small village that was once a river toll station, is the birthplace of Leonard Paminger, one of the most noted 16th-century Austrian composers. It features several gabled-roof burghers' houses, a castle, and a late-Gothic church that are all well preserved. Less intact is the castle, now semi-ruined, that once belonged to the counts of Harrach, located near the town.

Lodging

$$ 🏠 **Faust Schlössl.** As you enter Aschach you're struck by the glimpse
★   of this golden castle perched high on a hill on the opposite shore of the Danube. Rumor has it that the place is haunted by the Devil, who is said to have built it in a single night for Dr. Faustus. Nowadays the converted castle offers pleasantly decorated rooms with comfortable chairs, good reading lamps, well-designed bathrooms, and great views. Its popular restaurant offers good, traditional Austrian cooking and in nice weather tables are set on the terrace facing stunning views of the river. This is an ideal place to stop if you're biking between Passau and Vienna. ⊠ *Oberlandshaag 2, A–4082 Feldkirchen,* ☎ *07233/ 7402–0,* 🆁 *07233/7402–40. 15 rooms. Restaurant, pool, fishing, bicycles. AE, DC, MC, V. Closed Jan.*

St. Florian

★ ③ *13 km (8 mi) southeast of Linz.*

St. Florian is best known for the great Augustinian abbey, considered among the finest Baroque buildings in Austria. Composer Anton Bruckner (1824–96) was organist here for 10 years and is buried in the abbey. From Linz, you can drive south through Kleinmünchen and Ebelsberg to St. Florian, or for a more romantic approach try the **Florianer Bahn,** a resurrected electric interurban tram line, which runs museum streetcars on Sundays from May through the end of September, 6 km (4 mi) from Pichling to St. Florian (☎ 0732/387778); streetcars depart at 10:44, 2:14, and 3:44.

Guided tours of **Stift St. Florian** (St. Florian Abbey) include a magnificent figural gate encompassing all three stories, a large and elegant staircase leading to the upper floors, the imperial suite, and one of the great masterworks of the Austrian Baroque, Jakob Prandtauer's **Eagle Fountain courtyard,** with its richly sculpted figures. In the splendid **abbey church,** where the ornate decor is somewhat in contrast to Bruckner's music, the Krismann organ (1770–74) is one of the largest and best of its period. Another highlight is the **Altdorfer Gallery,** which contains several masterworks by Albrecht Altdorfer, the leading master of the 16th-century Danube School and ranked with Dürer and Grunewald as one of the greatest northern painters. ✉ *Stiftstr. 1,* ☎ *07224/8902–10,* FAX *07224/8902–60.* ✉ *AS60.* ☉ *1½-hr tour Apr.–Oct., daily at 10, 11, 2, 3, and 4. Call ahead for other bookings.*

Nightlife and the Arts

Summer concerts are held in June and July at the Kremsmünster (☞ *below*) and St. Florian abbeys; for tickets, contact Oberösterreichische Stiftskonzerte (✉ Domgasse 12, ☎ 0732/776127). A **chamber music festival** (☎ 0732/775230) takes place in July at Schloss Tillysburg, 1½ km (1 mi) from St. Florian. In July and August, a series of **concerts** on the Bruckner organ are given on Sunday afternoons at 4:30 in the church (☎ 07224/8903).

Kremsmünster

③ *36 km (22½ mi) south of Linz.*

The vast Benedictine **Stift Kremsmünster** was established in 777 and remains one of the most important abbeys in Austria. Most travelers arrive here by taking Route 139 (or the train) heading southwest from Linz. Inside the church is the Gothic memorial tomb of Gunther, killed by a wild boar, whose father, Tassilo, duke of Bavaria (and nemesis of Charlemagne), vowed to build the abbey on the site. Centuries later, the initial structures were replaced in the grand Baroque manner, including the extraordinary tower. There are magnificent rooms: the Kaisersaal and the frescoed library with more than 100,000 volumes, many of them manuscripts. On one side of the Prälatenhof courtyard are Jakob Prandtauer's elegant fish basins, complete with sculpted saints, holding squirming denizens of the deep, and opposite is the Abteitrakt, whose art collection includes the Tassilo Chalice, from about 765. The seven-story observatory houses an early museum of science. ☎ *07583/275–216.* ✉ *Rooms and art gallery AS45, observatory and tour AS50.* ☉ *Rooms and art-gallery tour (minimum 5 people) Easter–Oct., daily at 10, 11, 2, 3, and 4; Nov.–Easter at 11 and 2. Observatory tour (minimum 5 people) May–June and Sept.–Oct., daily at 10 and 2; July–Aug., daily at 10, 2, and 4.*

Schloss Kremsegg has a collection of rare musical instruments, mostly brass, with plans for a woodwind and folk music section in the future. ⊠ *Kremseggerstr. 59,* ☎ *07583/5247,* FAX *07583/6830.* ⚐ *AS70.* ☉ *Apr.–Oct., daily 9–noon and 1–5. Open in winter by arrangement.*

$$$
★
✕ **Gasthof Moser.** North of Kremsmünster on Highway 139 in the village of Neuhofen, the Moser is known throughout the countryside for its good cooking. Built in 1640, it retains an Old World ambience with its vaulted ceilings, curving, thick white walls, and dark wood. The menu ranges from old standards like turkey cordon bleu to the innovative cannelloni stuffed with *Zanderfilet* (pike perch) on a bed of roast zucchini and tomatoes. ⊠ *Marktpl. 9, A–4501 Neuhofen an der Krems,* ☎ *07227/4229,* FAX *07227/42294. Reservations essential. V. Closed Mon. No Sun. dinner..*

Bad Hall

㉝ *9 km (5½ mi) southeast of Kremsmünster, 36 km (22 mi) south of Linz.*

Bad Hall is a curious relic from earlier days when "taking the cure" was in vogue in Europe. It's still a spa and its saline-iodine waters are prescribed for internal and external application, but you can also enjoy the town for its turn-of-the-century setting. Since those on the cure need amusement between treatments, the town lays on numerous sports offerings—during warm weather, there are especially excellent opportunities for golf and tennis—and an operetta festival in summer.

Dining and Lodging

$$
✕ **Forsthof.** Located between Bad Hall and Steyr in the village of Sierning on Highway 122, this bustling, popular restaurant is reminiscent of a large, venerable farmhouse, with lots of cozy rooms. The kitchen prides itself on good home-style cooking and local specialties might include turkey breast in a paprika sauce or *Pfandl,* a hearty skillet dish of pork fillet with spinach spätzle and cheese gratiné. ⊠ *Neustr. 29, A–4522 Sierning,* ☎ *07259/23190,* FAX *07259/2319–66. AE, DC, MC, V. No dinner Sun.*

$$$$
★
🏨 **Schlosshotel Feyregg.** You'll be in an exclusive setting in this Baroque castle just outside town, once the elegant summer residence of an abbot. The comfortable, spacious guest rooms are a tribute to the Biedermeier style, and the charming, period knickknacks scattered throughout add to the overall feeling of being a guest in a treasured home, not a hotel. Baths are modern and filled with light. The township's golf course is within an easy stroll. This is an ideal base for exploring the monasteries in the area. ⊠ *A–4540,* ☎ *07258/2591. 11 rooms. No credit cards.*

Steyr

★ ㉞ *18 km (11 mi) east of Bad Hall, 40 km (25 mi) south of Linz. If you travel to Steyr from Kremsmünster, follow Route 139 until it joins Route 122 and take the road another 17 km (10½ mi).*

Steyr is one of Austria's best-kept secrets, a stunning Gothic market town that watches over the confluence of the Steyr and Enns rivers. Today the main square is lined with pastel facades, many with Baroque and rococo trim, all complemented by the castle that sits above. The Bummerlhaus at Number 32, in its present form dating from 1497, has a late-Gothic effect. On the Enns side, steps and narrow passageways lead down to the river.

In Steyr you are close to the heart of Bruckner country. He composed his Sixth Symphony in the parish house here, and there is a Bruckner room in the Meserhaus, where he composed his "sonorous music to confound celestial spheres." Schubert also lived here for a time. So many of the houses are worthy of attention that you will need to take your time and explore. Given the quaintness of the town center, you'd hardly guess that in 1894 Steyr had Europe's first electric street lighting.

The **Steyrertalbahn** (☎ 07252/53229–0 or 0664/38122–98), a narrow-gauge vintage railroad, wanders 17 km (10½ mi) from Steyr through the countryside on weekends June–September, and on selected weekends in December.

The **Museum Industrielle Arbeitswelt** (industrial museum), set in former riverside factories, is a reminder of the era when Steyr was a major center of ironmaking and armaments production; hunting arms are still produced here, but the major output is powerful motors for BMW cars, including those assembled in the United States. ⊠ *Wehrgrabeng. 7,* ☎ *07252/77351.* ☎ *AS65.* ☉ *Early Mar.–Dec. 21, Tues.–Sun. 9–5.*

Dining and Lodging

$$$ ✕ **Rahofer.** You'll have to search for this popular restaurant, which is
★ hidden away at the end of one of the passageways off the main square. Inside it's warm and cozy with dark-wood accents and candlelight. The focus here is Italian, from the Tuscan bread and olives that are brought to your table at your arrival to the selection of fresh pastas and lightly prepared meat and fish dishes. Individual pizzas are baked to perfection with a thin, crispy crust and toppings ranging from arugula and shaved Parmesan to tuna and capers. ⊠ *Stadtpl. 9,* ☎ *07252/54606. MC, V. Closed Sun.–Mon.*

$ ✕ **Treffpunkt.** Just off the main square is a narrow passageway going down to the bank of the river, through which you must duck under an ancient archway to reach this old establishment. It's dark and cozy inside, with candlelit tables and odd scraps of artwork on the walls. There's a full cocktail menu, and light dishes are served as well. In summer, tables are set outside on the riverfront terrace, a perfect spot for sipping a cold beer. ⊠ *Goldschmiedg. 3,* ☎ *07252/47237. No credit cards.*

$$$ ✕🏨 **Minichmayr.** From this traditional hotel the view alone—out over the confluence of the Enns and Steyr rivers, up and across to Schloss Lamberg—will make your stay memorable. The rooms don't quite measure up to the charm of the building's exterior and public rooms; your best bet is to ask for one on the river side. The restaurant offers light cuisine, specializing in fresh fish. The grilled trout with almond butter is especially good. The hotel is one of the Romantik Hotel group. ⊠ *Haratzmüllerstr. 1–3, A–4400,* ☎ *07252/53410–0,* ℻ *07252/48202–55. 51 rooms. Restaurant, bar, Weinstube, no-smoking rooms, sauna, exercise room, bicycles. AE, DC, MC, V.*

$$ ✕🏨 **Mader/Zu den Drei Rosen.** In this very old family-run hotel with small but pleasant modern rooms, you're right on the attractive town square. The restaurant offers solid local and traditional fare, with outdoor dining in a delightful garden area within the ancient courtyard. ⊠ *Stadtpl. 36, A–4400,* ☎ *07252/53358–0,* ℻ *07252/53358–6. 61 rooms. Restaurant, Weinstube. AE, DC, MC, V.*

THE WACHAU ALONG THE SOUTH BANK OF THE DANUBE

South of the Danube and east of Linz, the gentle countryside is crossed by rivers that rise in the Alps and eventually feed the Danube. Little evidence remains today, in this prosperous country of small-industry and agriculture, that the area was heavily fought over in the final days of World War II. From 1945 to 1955, the River Enns marked the border between the western (U.S., British, and French) and the eastern (Russian) occupying zones.

Enns

⑤ *20 km (12 mi) southeast of Linz.*

A settlement has existed continuously at Enns since at least AD 50; the Romans set up a major encampment shortly after that date. Contemporary Enns is dominated by the 184-ft square city tower (1565–68) that stands in the town square. A number of Gothic buildings in the center have Renaissance or Baroque facades.

Visit the **Basilika St. Laurenz,** built on the foundations of a far earlier church, west of the town center, to view the glass-encased archaeological discoveries. And outside, look for the Baroque carved-wood Pontius Pilate disguised as a Turk, alongside a bound Christ, on the balcony of the old sanctuary.

Guided tours (☎ 07223/82777) of the town's highlights, starting at the tower, are available for a minimum of three persons daily at 10:30, May–mid-September.

Lodging

$$$ ⊞ **Lauriacum.** You might overlook this plain contemporary building, set as it is among Baroque gems in the center of town, but it's the best place to stay. The bright rooms offer modern comfort, and the quiet garden is a welcoming spot. ⊠ *Wiener Str. 5–7, A–4470,* ☎ *07223/82315,* FAX *07223/82332–29. 30 rooms. Restaurant, bar, café, sauna. MC, V.*

Mauthausen

⑥ *14 km (8½ mi) southeast of Linz, 6 km (4 mi) north of Enns.*

Adolf Hitler had the **Mauthausen Konzentrationslager,** the main concentration camp in Austria, built here along the banks of the Danube in the town of the same name. From Linz, follow signs to Enns and Perg, and then to the EHEMALIGE KZ DENKMAL, the concentration-camp memorial. The pretty town of Mauthausen was selected as the site for a concentration camp because of the granite quarries nearby, which would provide material needed for the grand buildings in Hitler's projected "Führer cities." The grim, gray fortress was opened in August 1938 for male prisoners (including children), and the conditions under which they labored were severe even by SS standards. More than 125,000 lost their lives here before the camp was liberated by the American army in May 1945. The site includes a small museum and memorials, as well as a bookstore. ⊠ *Erinnerungsstr. 1, A–4310,* ☎ *07238/2269 or 07238/3696,* FAX *07238/4889.* ☜ *AS25.* ☉ *Feb.–Mar. and Oct.–Dec. 15, daily 8–4 (last admission 3 PM); Apr.–Sept., daily 8–6 (last admission 5 PM).* ☜

Waidhofen an der Ybbs

⑦ *30 km (18 mi) east of Steyr.*

Waidhofen an der Ybbs is well worth a slight detour from the more traveled routes. This picturesque river town developed early as an industrial center, turning Styrian iron ore into swords, knives, sickles, and scythes. These weapons proved successful in the defense against the invading Turks in 1532; marking the decisive moment of victory, the hands on the north side of the town tower clock remain at 12:45.

In 1871, Baron Rothschild bought the collapsing castle and assigned Friedrich Schmidt, architect of the Vienna's City Hall, to rebuild it in neo-Gothic style. Stroll around the two squares in the Altstadt to see the Gothic and Baroque houses and to the Graben on the edge of the Old City for the delightful Biedermeier houses and churches and chapels. From Enns, take the A1 autobahn or Route 1 east to just before Amstetten, where Route 121 cuts south paralleling the Ybbs River and the branch rail line for about 25 km (16 mi).

Ybbs an der Donau

38 *69 km (43 mi) east of Linz.*

Floods and fires have left their mark on Ybbs an der Donau, but many 16th-century houses remain, their courtyards vine-covered and shaded. The parish church of **St. Laurence** has interesting old tombstones, a gorgeous gilded organ, and a Mount of Olives scene with clay figures dating from 1450. To get to Ybbs an der Donau from Waidhofen an der Ybbs, make your way back to the Danube via Routes 31 and 22 east, then take Route 25 north through the beer-brewing town of Wieselburg.

Melk

★ **39** *22 km (13 mi) east of Ybbs an der Donau, 18 km (11 mi) west of St. Pölten, 33 km (20¼ mi) southwest of Krems.*

The ideal time to approach the magnificent abbey of Melk is mid- to late afternoon, when the sun sets the abbey's ornate Baroque yellow facade aglow. As one heads eastward paralleling the Danube, the abbey, shining on its promontory above the river, comes into view—unquestionably one of the most impressive sights in all Austria. The glories of the abbey tend to overshadow the town—located along Route 1—but the riverside village of Melk itself is worth exploring. A self-guided tour (in English, from the tourist office) will head you toward the highlights and the best spots from which to photograph the abbey.

★ By any standard, **Stift Melk** (Melk Abbey) is a Baroque-era masterpiece. Part palace, part monastery, part opera set, Melk is a magnificent vision thanks greatly to the upward-reaching twin towers, capped with Baroque helmets and cradling a 208-ft-high dome, and a roof bristling with Baroque statuary. Symmetry here beyond the towers and dome would be misplaced, and much of the abbey's charm is due to the way the early architects were forced to fit the building to the rocky outcrop that forms its base. The Benedictine abbey's history actually extends back to the 11th century, as it was established in 1089. The glorious building you see today ia architect Jakob Prandtauer's reconstruction, completed in 1736, in which some earlier elements are incorporated; two years later a great fire nearly totally destroyed the abbey and it had to be rebuilt. A tour of the building includes the main public rooms: a magnificent library, with more than 90,000 books, nearly 2,000 manuscripts, and a superb ceiling fresco by the master Paul Troger; the marble hall, whose windows on three sides enhance the ceiling frescoes; the glorious spiral staircase; and the church of Saints Peter and Paul, an exquisite example of the Baroque style. Call to find out if tours in English will be offered on a specific day. The **Stiftsrestaurant**, which is closed November–April, offers standard fare, but the abbey's excellent wines elevate a simple meal to a lofty experience—particularly on a sunny day on the terrace. ✉ *Abt Berthold Dietmayr-Str. 1,* ☎ *02752/555-232,* 𝔽𝔸𝕏 *02752/555-249.* ▣ *AS85.* ⊙ *Apr. 15– Nov. 15, daily 9–6 (ticket office closes at 5); Nov. 16–Apr. 15, daily 9– 5 (ticket office closes at 4).*

Dining and Lodging

$$–$$$ ✕🏨 **Stadt Melk.** Nestled below the golden abbey in the center of the vil-
★   lage square, this elegant restaurant has been well known ever since the
       Duke and Duchess of Windsor dined here long ago. Though the decor
       is decidedly Biedermeier, the food is nouvelle Austrian, and may include
       duck in a honey glaze or chicken breast stuffed with leeks and accom-
       panied by corn and potato croquettes. There are also 16 rather plain bed-
       rooms upstairs, if you don't feel like driving on. ⊠ *Hauptpl. 1, A–3390,*
       ☎ *02752/52475,* FAX *02752/52475–19. 16 rooms. AE, DC, MC, V.*

$$ 🏨 **Hotel zur Post.** Here in the center of town you're in a typical village
       hotel with the traditional friendliness of family management. The rooms
       are nothing fancy, though comfortable, and the restaurant offers solid,
       standard fare. ⊠ *Linzer Str. 1, A–3390,* ☎ *02752/52345,* FAX *02752/*
       52345–50. 15 rooms. Restaurant. MC, V, Closed Jan.–mid-Feb.

Schallaburg

➍ *6 km (4 mi) south of Melk.*

    From Melk, take a road south marked to Mank to arrive at the restored
    Schloss Schallaburg (dating from 1573), a castle featuring an impos-
    ing two-story arcaded courtyard that is held to be the area's finest ex-
    ample of Renaissance architecture. Its ornate, warm brown terra-cotta
    decoration is unusual. The yard once served as a jousting court. Many
    centuries have left their mark on the castle: inside, the Romanesque
    living quarters give way to an ornate Gothic chapel. The castle now
    houses changing special exhibits. ⊠ *3382 Schloss Schallaburg,* ☎
    02754/6317, FAX *02754/631755.* 🎫 *AS90.* ☉ *End of Mar.–Oct., daily*
    10–5 (last admission 1 hr before closing). ✎

En Route To return to the Wachau from Schallaburg, head back toward Melk and
    take Route 33 along the south bank. This route, attractive any time of
    the year, is spectacular (and thus heavily traveled) in early spring, when
    apricot and apple trees burst into glorious blossom. Among the palette
    of photogenic pleasures is **Schönbühel an der Donau,** whose unbeliev-
    ably picturesque castle, perched on a cliff overlooking the Danube, is
    unfortunately not open to visitors. Past the village of Aggsbachdorf
    you'll spot, on a hill to your right, the romantic ruin of 13th-century Ag-
    gstein Castle, reportedly the lair of pirates who preyed on river traffic.

Mautern

➍ *34 km (21 mi) north east of Melk, 1 km (½ mi) south of Stein.*

    Mautern, opposite Krems, was a Roman encampment mentioned in
    the tales of the Nibelungs. The old houses and the castle are attrac-
    tive, but contemporary Mautern is known for one of Austria's top restau-
    rants (☞ Dining and Lodging, *below*), in an inn run by Lisl Bacher;
    another culinary landmark—also excellent—is run by her sister (☞
    Schickh *in* Göttweig, *below*).

Dining and Lodging

$$$$ ✕🏨 **Landhaus Bacher.** This is one of Austria's best restaurants, ele-
★   gant but entirely lacking in pretension. The innovative style of Lisl Wag-
       ner-Bacher, the top female chef in the country, is constantly changing,
       but lamb and fish dishes are always present. For starters, try the potato
       soup with truffles, served in a huge, hollowed-out potato, or the fresh
       cheese ravioli in an artichoke ragout. Dining in the garden in summer
       enhances the experience. For an added treat, stay overnight in a Laura
       Ashley–decorated bedroom in the 10-room guest house. It's on the river-
       bank opposite Krems. ⊠ *Südtirolerpl. 208,* ☎ *02732/82937–0 or*

02732/85429, FAX 02732/74337. Reservations essential. DC, V. Closed Mon.–Tues. and Jan. 7–end of Feb.

Göttweig

④ *4 km (2½ mi) south of Mautern, 7 km (4½ mi) south of Krems.*

★ You're certain to spot **Stift Göttweig** (Göttweig Abbey) as you come along the riverside road: the vast Benedictine abbey high above the Danube Valley watches over the gateway to the Wachau. To reach it, go along Route 33, turn right onto the highway south (marked to Stift Göttweig and St. Pölten), and turn right again (marked to Stift Göttweig) at the crest of the hill. Göttweig's exterior was redone in the mid-1700s in the classical style, which you'll note from the columns, balcony, and relatively plain side towers. Inside, it is a monument to Baroque art, with marvelous ornate decoration against the gold, brown, and blue. The stained-glass windows behind the high altar date from the mid-1400s. The public rooms of the abbey are splendid, particularly the Kaiserzimmer (Emperor's Rooms), in which Napoléon stayed in 1809, reached via the elegant Emperor's Staircase. ⊠ *Furth bei Göttweig,* ☎ *02732/85581–231.* ☞ *AS50.* ☉ *Daily 10–5; tours (minimum 8 people) Easter–Oct., daily at 10, 11, 2, 3, and 4.*

Dining

$$$ ✕ **Schickh.** This restaurant, tucked away among lovely old trees below
★ the north side of Göttweig Abbey, is worth looking for. Creative ideas out of the kitchen transform seasonal and regional specialties. You might be offered asparagus wrapped in smoked lamb or tender roast baby lamb. In summer you'll dine in the garden, probably rubbing elbows with the knowledgeable Viennese elite. There's a handful of guest rooms available for overnights. ⊠ *Klein-Wien 2, Furth bei Göttweig,* ☎ *02736/7218–0,* FAX *02736/7218–7. Reservations essential. No credit cards. Closed Wed.–Thurs. and mid-Jan.–Mar.*

St. Pölten

④ *18 km (11 mi) south of Göttweig, 65 km (40¼ mi) west of Vienna.*

St. Pölten, Lower Austria's capital to the south of the Danube, is a busy industrial and commercial center, but still worth a detour (20 km (12½ mi) to the south of the main stretch of the Wachau. The old municipal center, now mainly a pedestrian zone, shows a distinctly Baroque face. The originally Romanesque cathedral on Domplatz has a rich Baroque interior; the rococo Franciscan church at the north end of the Rathausplatz has four altar paintings by Kremser Schmidt.

Dining and Lodging

$$$ ✕ **Galerie.** Mellow furnishings lend an old-fashioned grandmotherly atmosphere to this popular restaurant, a favorite with locals. In contrast to the antiques, the kitchen strives—generally successfully—for a nouvelle approach to fine Austrian standards like pork fillet and turkey breast. ⊠ *Fuhrmanng. 1,* ☎ *02742/351305. AE, DC, MC, V. Closed Sun.–Mon. and 2 wks around Easter.*

$$$ ☷ **Metropol.** Slick modern styling marks this modern hotel on the edge of the pedestrian zone at the heart of the Old City. Rooms are comfortable, if rather uniform. ⊠ *Schillerpl. 1, A–3100,* ☎ *02742/70700–0,* FAX *02742/70700–133. 87 rooms. Restaurant, bar, sauna, parking (fee). AE, DC, MC, V.*

OFF THE **HERZOGENBURG –** The great Augustinian monastery of Herzogenburg is
BEATEN PATH 11 km (6½ mi) north of St. Pölten (take Wiener Strasse/Route 1 out of St. Pölten heading east for 12 km, or 8 mi, to Kapelln; then turn left to

Herzogenburg). The present buildings date mainly from the mid-1700s. Fischer von Erlach was among the architects who designed the abbey. The church, dedicated to Saints George and Stephen, is wonderfully Baroque, with exquisitely decorated ceilings. ☎ *02782/83112–0.* 🎫 *AS50.* ⊙ *1-hr tour Apr.–Oct., daily 9–noon and 2–5 on the hr.*

En Route Small rural villages abound on the south bank plain, some quaint, some typical. From St. Pölten, head north on Route S33 or the parallel road, marked to Traismauer, and pick up Route 43 east. If you're ready for back roads (too well marked for you to get lost), cut off to the left to Oberbierbaum and then proceed on to Zwentendorf (there's a fascinating "black" Madonna in the side chapel of the parish church here). If you follow Route 43, it will land you on Route 1 at Mitterndorf; drive east and after 4 km (2½ mi), turn left off Route 1 onto Route 19, marked for Tulln.

Tulln

㊹ *41 km (24½ mi) northeast of St. Pölten, 42 km (26¼ mi) west of Vienna.*

At Tulln, you'll spot a number of charming Baroque touches in the attractive main square. There's an **Egon Schiele Museum** to honor the great modern artist (1890–1918), who was born here; the museum showing a selection of his works is in the onetime district prison, with a reconstruction of the cell in which Schiele—accused of producing "pornography"—was locked up in 1912. ⊠ *Donaulände 28,* ☎ *02272/64570.* 🎫 *AS40, more for special exhibits.* ⊙ *Tues.–Sun. 9–noon and 2–6.*

A former **Minorite cloister** now houses a collection of museums. Among the more interesting are the **Limesmuseum,** which recalls the early Roman settlements in the area, and the **Landesfeuerwehrmuseum,** documenting rural fire fighting. Also look inside the well-preserved, late-Baroque (1750) Minorite church next door. ⊠ *Minoritenpl. 1,* ☎ *02272/61915.* 🎫 *Each museum AS30.* ⊙ *Wed.–Fri. 3–6, Sat. 2–6, Sun. 10–6.*

Dining and Lodging

$$$$ ✕ **Zum Roten Wolf.** In an unpretentious but attractive rustic restaurant
★ (one of Austria's top 20) in Langelebarn, 4 km (2½ mi) east of Tulln, the stylishly elegant table settings complement the consistently outstanding food. Neither preparation nor presentation leaves anything to be desired. Start with artichoke cream soup, followed by duck breast in a ginger curry sauce with juniper berries and rosemary Rösti, or lamb in an olive crust with okra and vegetable lasagne. The service is especially friendly; ask for advice on the wines. You can get here by local train from Vienna; the station is virtually at the door. ⊠ *Bahnstr. 58,* ☎ *02272/62567. Reservations essential. AE, DC, MC, V. Closed Mon.–Tues.*

$$ 🏨 **Zur Rossmühle.** From the abundant greenery of the reception area to the table settings in the dining room, you'll find pleasing little touches in this attractively situated hotel on the town square. The rooms are done in grand old yet brand-new Baroque. Take lunch in the courtyard garden; here, as in the more formal dining room, you'll be offered Austrian standards. ⊠ *Hauptpl. 12–13, A-3430,* ☎ *02272/ 62411,* 🖷 *02272/62411–33. 55 rooms. Restaurant, bar, sauna, horseback riding. AE, DC, MC, V.*

Greifenstein

㊺ *10 km (6½ mi) northeast of Tulln.*

Greifenstein is east of Tulln along Route 14; turn left at St. Andrä-Wördern and stay on the Danube shoreline. Atop the hill at Greifenstein,

yet another **castle** with spectacular views looks up the Danube and
across to Stockerau. Its earliest parts date from 1135, but most of it stems
from a thorough but romantic renovation in 1818. The view is worth
the climb, even when the castle and inexpensive restaurant are closed.
✉ *Kostersitzg. 5*, ☎ *02242/32353.* ⊘ *Mar.–Oct., weekends noon–5.*

Klosterneuburg

   🔴 *13 km (8 mi) northwest of Vienna.*

The great Augustinian abbey **Stift Klosterneuburg** dominates the town.
The structure has changed many times since the abbey was established
in 1114, most recently in 1892, when Friedrich Schmidt, architect of Vienna's City Hall, added neo-Gothic features to its two identifying towers. Klosterneuburg was unusual in that until 1568 it housed both men's
and women's religious orders. In the abbey church, look for the carved-
wood choir loft and oratory and the large 17th-century organ. Among
Klosterneuburg's treasures are the beautifully enameled 1181 Verdun Altar
in the Leopold Chapel, stained-glass windows from the 14th and 15th
centuries, Romanesque candelabra from the 12th century, and gorgeous
ceiling frescoes in the great marble hall. In an adjacent outbuilding
there's a huge wine cask over which people slide. The exercise, called
Fasslrutsch'n, is indulged in during the Leopoldiweinkost, the wine tasting around St. Leopold's Day, November 15. The **Stiftskeller,** with its
atmospheric underground rooms, serves standard Austrian fare and
wine bearing the Klosterneuberg label. ✉ *Stiftspl. 1*, ☎ *02243/411–0.*
⊡ *AS50.* ⊘ *1-hr tour Mon.–Sat. at 9:30, 10:30, 1:30, 2:30, 3:30, 4:30,
Sun. at 11, 2 (English-language); 1;30, 2:30, 3:30, 4:30..*

The new **Sammlung Essl** contemporary art museum, somewhat alarm-
ingly resembling a sports center from the exterior, was designed by Heinz
Tesar and features works created after 1945. The permanent collection
includes works by such regional artists as Hermann Nietsch and Arnulf
Rainer, and changing exhibitions focus on contemporary artists, including Nam June Paik. The emphasis here is on "new," including special
evening concerts highlighting various modern composers' work. To get
to the Sammlung Essl museum, take the U-4 to Heilegenstadt, then transfer to Bus 239 to Klosterneuberg. ✉ *An der Donau–Au 1*, ☎ *0800/232–
800,* ⅲ *02243/370–5022.* ⊡ *AS80.* ⊘ *Tues.–Sun. 10–5, Wed. 10–9.*

OFF THE   **KAHLENBERGERDORF** – Near Klosterneuburg and just off the road tucked
BEATEN PATH under the Leopoldsberg promontory is the charming small vintners' vil-
              lage of Kahlenbergerdorf, an excellent spot to stop and sample the local
              wines. You're just outside the Vienna city limits here, which accounts for
              the crowds (of Viennese, not international tourists) on weekends.

DANUBE VALLEY A TO Z

Arriving and Departing

By Boat

Large riverboats with sleeping accommodations ply the route between
Vienna and Linz and between Passau on the German border and Linz
from late spring to early fall. Smaller day boats go between Vienna and
the Wachau Valley, and there you can change to local boats that crisscross the river between the colorful towns.

For information on boat schedules, contact **Blue Danube Steamship
Company/DDSG** (✉ Friedrichstr. 7, A–1043 Vienna, ☎ 01/588–800,
ⅲ 01/58880–440; ✉ Untere Donaulände 10, A–4010 Linz, ☎ 0732/

783607) or **Fitzcaraldo Donauschiffahrt** (⊠ Ottensheimer Str. 37, A–
4010 Linz, ☎ 0664/140–4568). Danube boat services from Melk to
Krems with stops between within the Wachau region are operated by
Brandner Schiffahrt (⊠ Ufer 50, A–3313 Wallsee, ☎ 07433/2590–0).

By Car
A car is certainly the most comfortable way to see this region, as it conveniently enables you to pursue the byways. The main route along the
north bank is Route 3; along the south bank, there's a choice of autobahn Route A1 or a collection of lesser but good roads.

By Plane
Linz is served mainly by Austrian Airlines, Lufthansa, Swissair, and Tyrolean. Regular flights connect with Vienna, Amsterdam, Berlin, Düsseldorf, Frankfurt, Paris, Stuttgart, and Zürich. The **Linz airport** (☎
07221/600) is in Hörsching, about 12 km (7½ mi) southwest of the
city. Buses run between the airport and the main railroad station according to flight schedules.

By Train
Rail lines parallel the north and south banks of the Danube. Fast services from Vienna run as far as Stockerau; beyond that, service is less
frequent. The main east–west line from Vienna to Linz closely follows
the south bank for much of its route. Fast trains connect German
cities via Passau with Linz.

Getting Around
By Boat
Bridges across the river are few along this stretch, so boats provide essential transportation; service is frequent enough that you can cross
the river, visit a town, catch a bus or the next boat to the next town,
and cross the river farther up- or downstream. You can take a day trip
from Vienna and explore one of the stops, such as Krems, Dürnstein,
or Melk. Boats run from May to late September.

By Bus
If you link them together, bus routes will get you to the main points
in this region and even to the hilltop castles and monasteries, assuming you have the time. If you coordinate your schedule to arrive at a
point by train or boat, you can usually make reasonable bus connections to outlying destinations. You can book bus tours in Vienna (☞
Guided Tours, *below*); in Linz, ask at the municipal bus station (⊠ Bahn-
hofpl. 12, ☎ 0732/6909–0).

By Car
A car is certainly the most hassle-free way to get around. Roads are
good and well marked, and you can switch over to the A1 autobahn,
which parallels the general east–west course of the route (☞ Car
Travel *in* Smart Travel Tips A to Z).

By Train
Every larger town and city in the region can be reached by train, but the
train misses the Wachau Valley along the Danube's south bank. The rail
line on the north side of the river clings to the bank in places; service is
infrequent. You can combine rail and boat transportation along this route,
taking the train upstream and crisscrossing your way back on the river.
From Linz, the delightful **LILO** (Linzer Lokalbahn) interurban line (☎
0732/654376 or 0732/7070–1450) makes the run up to Eferding. A charming narrow-gauge line meanders south to Waidhofen an der Ybbs.

Contacts and Resources

Bicycle Rentals

For details on the scenic Danube river route, ask for the folder "Danube Cycle Track" (in English, from **Tourist Office of Lower Austria**; ✉ Walfischg. 6, A–1010 Vienna, ☎ 01/513–8022, FAX 01/513–8022–30). The brochure "Radfahren" is in German, but lists contact numbers for cycle rentals throughout Upper Austria. You can rent a bike in Linz (☞ Outdoor Activities and Sports *in* Linz, *above*) at the **Freistadt railroad station** (☎ 07942/2319), the **Steyr railroad station** (☎ 07252/595–385), or privately in Kremsmünster at **Tenniscenter Stadlhuber** (☎ 07583/7498–0).

Canoeing

The Danube is fast and tricky, so you're best off sticking to the calmer waters back of the power dams (at Pöchlarn, above Melk, and near Grein). You can rent a canoe at Pöchlarn. You can also canoe on an arm of the Danube near Ottensheim, about 8 km (5 mi) west of Linz. For information call **Ruderverein Donau** (☎ 0732/736250) or **Ruderverein Ister-Sparkasse** (☎ 0732/774888).

Car Rentals

Cars can be rented at the airports in Vienna (☞ Vienna A to Z *in* Chapter 1) or Linz. Linz contacts are as follows:

Avis (✉ Europapl. 7, ☎ 0732/662881), **Buchbinder** (✉ Wienerstr. 166, ☎ 0732/343030), **Hertz** (✉ Bürgerstr. 19, ☎ 0732/784841–0).

Emergencies

Police, ☎ 133. **Fire,** ☎ 122. **Ambulance,** ☎ 144. If you need a doctor and speak no German, ask your hotel how best to obtain assistance.

Fishing

In the streams and lakes of the area around Linz, you can fly-cast for rainbow and brook trout and troll for pike and carp. Check with the town tourist offices about licenses and fishing rights for river trolling and fly-casting in Aggsbach-Markt, Dürnstein, Emmersdorf, Grein, Klein-Pöchlarn, Krems, Mautern, Mauthausen, Persenbeug–Gottsdorf, Pöchlarn, Schönbühel/Aggsbachdorf, Spitz, Waidhofen/Ybbs, and Ybbs.

Guided Tours

Tours out of Vienna take you to Melk and back by bus and boat in eight hours, with a stop at Dürnstein. Bus tours operate year-round except as noted, but the boat runs only April–October. Operators include the following: **Cityrama Sightseeing** (✉ Börseg. 1, ☎ 01/534–13–0, FAX 01/534–13–28), for AS790 and **Vienna Sightseeing Tours** (✉ Stelzhammerg. 4/11, ☎ 01/712–4683–0, FAX 01/714–1141), for AS790.

Hiking

Local tourist offices have maps and route details of the fabulous trails in the area. For information on the Mühlviertel from Freistadt to Grein, call ☎ 0732/735020.

Travel Agencies

In Linz, leading travel agencies include the following: **American Express** (✉ Bürgerstr. 14, ☎ 0732/669013, FAX 0732/655334), **Kuoni** (✉ Hauptpl. 14, ☎ 0732/771301, FAX 0732/775338), and **Oberösterreichisches Landesreisebüro** (✉ Hauptpl. 9, ☎ 0732/771061–0, FAX 0732/771061–49).

Visitor Information

For general information on the area, check with the following district tourist offices:

Tourist Office of Lower Austria (⊠ Walfischg. 6, A–1010 Vienna, ☎ 01/513–8022, FAX 01/513–8022–30). **Upper Austria** (⊠ Schillerstr. 50, A–4010 Linz, ☎ 0732/602210, FAX 0732/600220). **Linz** (⊠ Hauptpl. 5, A–4020 Linz, ☎ 0732/7070–1777, FAX 0732/772873), where you can pick up the latest *Linz City News* in English as well as German. **Mühlviertel** (Mühlviertel Tourist Office, ⊠ Blütenstr. 8, A–4040 Linz, ☎ 0732/735020, FAX 0732/712400, ✍). **Wachau** (⊠ Undstr. 6, A–3500 Krems, ☎ 02732/82676, FAX 02732/70011).

Most towns have a local *Fremdenverkehrsamt* (tourist office): **Bad Hall** (⊠ Kurhaus, A–4540, ☎ 07258/200–0, FAX 07258/200–20). **Dürnstein** (⊠ Parkpl. Ost, A–3601, ☎ 02711/219, FAX 02711/442). **Eferding** (⊠ Stadtpl. 1, A–4070, ☎ 07272/5555–20, FAX 07272/5555–33). **Freistadt** (⊠ Hauptpl. 12, A–4240, ☎ 07942/72974, FAX 07942/73207). **Grein** (⊠ Hauptstr. 3, A–4360, ☎ 07268/2550, FAX 07268/7290). **Klosterneuburg** (⊠ Niedermarkt 4, A–3400, ☎ 02243/32038, FAX 02243/26773). **Krems/Stein** (⊠ Undstr. 6, A–3500, ☎ 02732/82676, FAX 02732/70011). **Melk** (⊠ Babenbergerstr. 1, A–3390, ☎ 02752/52307–410, FAX 02752/52307–490). **Pöchlarn** (⊠ Regensburger Str. 11, A–3380, ☎ 02757/2310–30, FAX 02757/2310–66). **St. Pölten** (⊠ Rathauspl. 1, A–3100, ☎ 02742/353354, FAX 02742/333–2819). **Steyr** (⊠ Stadtpl. 27, A–4400, ☎ 07252/53229–0 or 07252/53229–15, FAX 07252/48154–15). **Tulln** (⊠ Minoritenpl. 2, A–3430, ☎ 02272/65836, FAX 02272/65838). **Waidhofen an der Ybbs** (⊠ Obere Stadtpl. 32, A–3340, ☎ 07442/511–0, FAX 07442/511–259). **Weissenkirchen** (⊠ Gemeinde Weissenkirchen, A–3610, ☎ 02715/2600, FAX 02715/2600).

5 SALZBURG

Mozart, Mozart, Mozart! Birthplace of one of the 18th century's greatest composers, Salzburg is a world-class music mecca that hosts the world's most stirring music festival every summer. Ironically, many who come to this golden city of High Baroque may first hear strains of music from the film that made Salzburg a household name: From Winkler Terrace to Nonnberg Convent, it's hard to go exploring without hearing someone humming "How Do You Solve a Problem Like Maria?"

Updated by
Bonnie Dodson

A LL SALZBURG IS A STAGE," Count Ferdinand Czernin once wrote. "Its beauty, its tradition, its history enshrined in the grey stone of which its buildings are made, its round of music, its crowd of fancy-dressed people, all combine to lift you out of everyday life, to make you forget that somewhere far off, life hides another, drearier, harder, and more unpleasant reality." Shortly after the count's book, *This Salzburg,* was published in 1937, the unpleasant reality arrived; but having survived the Nazis, Salzburg once again became one of Austria's top drawing cards. Art lovers call it the Golden City of High Baroque; historians refer to it as the Florence of the North, or the German Rome; and, of course, being the birthplace of Mozart, music lovers know it as the Festival City—home of the world-famous Salzburger Festspiele (Salzburg Festival).

The setting could not be more perfect. Salzburg lies on both banks of the Salzach River, at the point where it is pinched between two mountains, the Kapuzinerberg on one side, the Mönchsberg on the other. In broader view are many beautiful Alpine peaks. Man's contribution is a trove of buildings worthy of such surroundings. Salzburg's rulers pursued construction on a grand scale ever since Wolf-Dietrich von Raitenau—the "Medici prince-archbishop who preached in stone"—began his regime in the latter part of the 16th century. Astonishingly, they all seem to have shared the same artistic bent, with the result that Salzburg's many fine buildings blend into a harmonious whole. Perhaps nowhere else in the world is there so cohesive a flowering of Baroque architecture.

While Salzburg is a visual pageant of Baroque motifs, music is the aural element that shapes the life of the city. It is heard everywhere: in churches, castles, palaces, and, of course, concert halls. Although the young Mozart was the boy wonder of Europe, Salzburg did him no particular honor in his lifetime, but it is making up for it now. Since 1920, the Salzburg Festival has honored this native son with performances of his works by the world's greatest musicians. To see and hear them, crowds pack the city from mid-July until the end of August. Whether performed in the festival halls (Grosses und Kleines Festspielhaus) or outdoors with opulent Baroque volutes and scrolls of Salzburg's architecture as background, Mozart's music serves as the heartbeat of the city.

Only the tourist who visits Salzburg outside of the festival season will have time to explore its other fascinating attractions. Many visitors love to make the town's acquaintance by visiting all the sights featured in *The Sound of Music,* filmed here in 1964. It's hard to take in the Mirabell Gardens, Winkler's Terrace, the Pferdeschwemme fountain, Nonnberg Convent, the Residenzplatz, and all the other filmed locations without imagining Maria and the von Trapp children trilling "Do-Re-Mi." (Like Mozart, the von Trapp family—who escaped the Third Reich by fleeing their beloved country—were little appreciated at home; Austria was the only place on the planet where the film failed, closing after a single week's showing in Vienna and Salzburg.) Whether it's the melodies of Rodgers and Hammerstein or of Joannes Chrysostomus Wolfgangus Amadeus Theophilus Mozart filling your head, the city of Salzburg is a symphony of both sounds and sights.

Pleasures and Pastimes

A Lot of Night Music

Music in Salzburg is not just *Eine Kleine Nachtmusik,* to mention one of Mozart's most famous compositions. The city's nightlife is livelier than it is reputed to be. Folklore performances are given twice a week during the summer season at the Augustinerbräu. In winter, "in" areas include the "Bermuda Triangle" (Steingasse, Imbergstrasse) and Rudolfskai; young people tend to populate the bars and discos around Gstättengasse. Of course, Salzburg is most renowned for its **Salzburger Festspiele** of music and theater (mid-July–August), and most visitors come during this season. Much of Salzburg's very special charms can, however, best be discovered and enjoyed off-season. For instance, real Mozart connoisseurs come to Salzburg in January for the **Mozart Week** (a 10-day festival held around Mozart's birthday, on January 27). And in general, music lovers face an embarrassment of riches in this most musical of cities, ranging from chamber concerts, held in the Marble Hall of the Mirabell Palace or the Golden Hall of the Fortress, to the numerous concerts organized by the International Mozarteum Foundation from October to June in the Great Hall of the Mozarteum. Salzburg's concerts by the Camerata Academica are now just as much in demand as the subscription series by the Vienna Philharmonic in the Musikverein in Vienna. The **Landestheater** season runs from September to June and presents opera, operetta, plays, and ballet. No music lover should miss the chance to be enchanted and amazed by the skill and artistry of the world-famous **Salzburg Marionette Theater** performing operas by Mozart, Rossini, Johann Strauss, and Offenbach.

Bicycling

As most Salzburgers know, one of the best and most pleasurable ways of getting around the city and the surrounding countryside is by bicycle. Bikes can be rented (☞ Salzburg A to Z, *below*), and the tourist office has maps of the extensive network of cycle paths. The most delightful ride in Salzburg? The **Hellbrunner Allee** from Freisaal to Hellbrunn Palace is a pleasurable run, taking you past Frohnburg Palace and a number of elegant mansions on either side of the tree-lined avenue. The more adventurous can go farther afield, taking the **Salzach cycle path** north to the village of Oberndorf, or south to Golling and Hallein.

Dining

Salzburg has some of the best—and most expensive—restaurants in Austria; even better, the city is plentifully supplied with good eateries, offering not only good, solid Austrian food (not for anyone on a diet), but also peppery Hungarian dishes, spicy Slav specialties, and newerthan-now *neue Küche* (nouvelle cuisine) delights. There are certain dining experiences that are quintessentially Salzburgian, including restaurants perched on the town's peaks that offer "food with a view"—in some cases, it's too bad the food isn't up to the view—or rustic inns that offer "Alpine evenings" with entertainment. A favorite dish is the *Forelle blau getsotten*—trout, presented with its price tag attached; you pay according to the weight of the fish—and don't forget to have a *Mozartball* for dessert. Finally, everyone knows the top place at cocktail time is the gemütlich bar of the Goldener Hirsch, where countesses and opera divas use up every square inch of space from five to seven—and where you can get that rarity in Europe, a genuine martini.

CATEGORY	COST*
$$$$	over AS600 (€44)
$$$	AS400–AS600 (€29–€44)
$$	AS200–AS400 (€15–€28)
$	under AS200 (€15)

per person for a three-course meal, including house wine, 10% service, and VAT, but excluding extra tip

ONE LAST TRAVEL TIP:

Pack an easy way to reach the world.

MCI WORLDCOM · *WORLDPHONE.*

123 456 7891 2345
J.D. SMITH

Wherever you travel, the MCI WorldCom Card℠ is the easiest way to stay in touch. You can use it to call to and from more than 125 countries worldwide. And you can earn bonus miles every time you use your card. So go ahead, travel the world. MCI WorldCom℠ makes it even more rewarding. For additional access codes, visit **www.wcom.com/worldphone.**

MCI WORLDCOM.

EASY TO CALL WORLDWIDE

1. Just dial the WorldPhone® access number of the country you're calling from.

2. Dial or give the operator your MCI WorldCom Card number.

3. Dial or give the number you're calling.

Austria ◆	0800-200-235
Belgium ◆	0800-10012
Czech Republic ◆	00-42-000112
Denmark ◆	8001-0022
Estonia ★	800-800-1122
Finland ◆	08001-102-80
France ◆	0-800-99-0019
Germany	0800-888-8000
Greece ◆	00-800-1211
Hungary ◆	06▼-800-01411
Ireland	1-800-55-1001
Italy ◆	172-1022
Luxembourg	8002-0112
Netherlands ◆	0800-022-91-22
Norway ◆	800-19912
Poland ÷	800-111-21-22
Portugal ÷	800-800-123
Romania ÷	01-800-1800
Russia ◆ ÷	747-3322
Spain	900-99-0014
Sweden ◆	020-795-922
Switzerland ◆	0800-89-0222
Ukraine ÷	8▼10-013
United Kingdom	0800-89-0222
Vatican City	172-1022

◆ Public phones may require deposit of coin or phone card for dial tone. ★ Not available from public pay phones.
▼ Wait for second dial tone. ÷ Limited availability.

EARN FREQUENT FLIER MILES

Limit of one bonus program per customer. All airline program rules and conditions apply. © 2000 WorldCom, Inc. All Rights Reserved.
The names, logos, and taglines identifying WorldCom's products and services are proprietary marks of WorldCom, Inc. or its subsidiaries.
All third party marks are the proprietary marks of their respective owners.

Bureau de change

Cambio

外国為替

In this city, you can find money on almost any street.

NO-FEE FOREIGN EXCHANGE

The Chase Manhattan Bank has over 80 convenient locations near New York City destinations such as:

Times Square
Rockefeller Center
Empire State Building
2 World Trade Center
United Nations Plaza

Exchange any of 75 foreign currencies

THE RIGHT RELATIONSHIP IS EVERYTHING.®

©2000 The Chase Manhattan Corporation. All rights reserved. The Chase Manhattan Bank. Member FDIC.

Lodging

The Old City has a wide variety of hotels and pensions, some in surprising locations and with considerable atmosphere, but everything has its price and there are few bargains. In high season, and particularly during the festival (July and August), some prices soar and rooms are very difficult to find, so try to reserve at least two months in advance. Note that during the high season, rate differences may push a hotel into the next-higher price category. If you don't have a reservation, go to one of the tourist information offices or the accommodations service (*Zimmernachweis*) on the main platform of the railway station. If you're looking for something really cheap (less than AS500 for a double), clean, and comfortable, stay in a private home, though the good ones are all a little way from downtown. The tourist information offices don't list private rooms; try calling Eveline Truhlar of **Bob's Special Tours** (☎ 0662/849511–0), who runs a private-accommodations service.

CATEGORY	LOW SEASON*	HIGH SEASON*
$$$$	over AS3,000	over AS3,500
$$$	AS2,000–AS3,000	AS2,300–AS3,500
$$	AS1,000–AS2,000	AS1,200–AS2,300
$	under AS1,000	under AS1,200

All prices are for a standard double room for two, with bath, including breakfast (except where noted) and VAT. To compute Euro equivalencies, divide AS amount by 13.76.

☜ *following the text of a review is your signal that the property has a Web site; for a link, visit www.fodors.com/urls.*

EXPLORING SALZBURG

The Altstadt, or Old City—a very compact area between the jutting outcrop of the Mönchsberg and the Salzach River—is where most of the major sights are concentrated. The cathedral and interconnecting squares surrounding it form what used to be the religious center, around which the major churches and the old archbishops' residence are arranged. The rest of the Old City belonged to the wealthy burghers: the Getreidegasse, the Alter Markt (old market), the town hall, and the tall, plain burghers' houses (like Mozart's Birthplace). The Mönchsberg cliffs emerge unexpectedly behind the Old City, crowned to the east by the Hohensalzburg Fortress. Across the river, in the small area between the cliffs of the Kapuzinerberg and the riverbank, is Steingasse, a narrow medieval street where working people lived. Northwest of the Kapuzinerberg lie Mirabell Palace and its gardens, now an integral part of the city but formerly a country estate on the outskirts of Salzburg.

It's best to begin by exploring the architectural and cultural riches of the Old City, then go on to the fortress and after that cross the river to inspect the other bank. Ideally, you need two days to do it all. An alternative, if you enjoy exploring churches and castles, is to stop after visiting the Rupertinum and go directly up to the fortress, either on foot or by returning through the cemetery to the funicular railway.

Numbers in the text correspond to numbers in the margin and on the Salzburg map.

Great Itineraries

IF YOU HAVE 1 DAY

It is the tourist who comes to Salzburg outside of the festival season who will have most time to explore its many fascinating attractions. But even for busy festival visitors, making the acquaintance of the town is not too difficult, for most of its sights are conveniently located within a comparatively small area. Of course, if you are doing this spectacular city in just one day, there is a flip-book-fast way to take a course in Salzburg 101: take one of those escorted bus tours through the city. However, much of Salzburg's historic city center is for pedestrians only, and the bus doesn't get you close to some of the best sights—which may explain why there's always an army of bipeds exploring on foot.

Start at the **Mozartplatz** ①—not just to sweeten your tour with a few *Mozart Kugeln,* the omnipresent candy balls of pistachio-flavored marzipan rolled in nougat cream and dipped in dark chocolate—but to make a pit stop at the main tourist information office. Flower-bedecked cafés beckon, but this is no time for a coffee—one of the glories of Europe is just a few steps away: the **Residenz** ③, the veritable center of Baroque Salzburg. Nearby are the **Dom** ④, Salzburg's grand cathedral, and two of the city's most opulent churches, **St. Peter's Abbey** ⑥ and the **Franziskanerkirche** ⑦. You're now ready to take the funicular (it's just behind the cathedral) up to the **Fortress Hohensalzburg** ⑰—the majestic castle atop the Mönchsberg peak that overlooks the city. Enjoy a rest at the Grand Café Winkler, or opt for enjoying some picnic provisions or lunch at the Burgerwehr-Einkehr restaurant. Descend back to the city via the Mönchsberg express elevators, which will deposit you at Gstättengasse 13. Head over to the **Pferdeschwemme** ⑫—the Baroque and royal horse trough that is a somewhat bewildering tribute to the equine race—then over to the **Getreidegasse,** the Old City's main shopping street, for some serious retail therapy and visit **Mozarts Geburtshaus** ⑯. Welcome twilight with a *Kaffee mit Schlag* (coffee with whipped cream) at the famous Café Tomaselli on the charming **Alter Markt** square. Choose from the more than 40 pastries and congratulate yourself: You may not have seen everything in Salzburg, but you've missed few of its top sights.

IF YOU HAVE 3 DAYS

With three days, you can explore the **Old City** and the **Fortress and the New Town** as described in the two walking tours below. Try to catch an evening **concert**—perhaps of Mozart's music—at one of the many music halls in the city (before you arrive in Salzburg, do some advance telephone calls to determine the music schedule of the city for the time you will be there and, if need be, book reservations; if you'll be attending the summer Salzburg Festival, this is a must). For your third day, try one of three options: book a *Sound of Music* tour (☞ Close-up box, *below*) then, in the afternoon, relax and take a ride up the **Untersberg** (☞ Short Side Trips from Salzburg, *below*) or try to arrange an excursion to the beautiful **Salzkammergut** (☞ Chapter 7) and the picture-book towns of Mondsee or St. Wolfgang.

The Old City: In Mozart's Footsteps

To most people, Salzburg today means the city of Mozart. Ever since the film *Amadeus,* Wolfgang Amadeus Mozart has been the 18th-century equivalent of a rock star. Born in Salzburg on January 27, 1756, he crammed a prodigious number of compositions into the 35 short years of his life, many of which he spent in Salzburg (he moved to Vienna in 1781). Start by exploring the Altstadt (Old City), the heart of the Baroque Salzburg Mozart knew. Other Mozart-related sights are included in our second Salzburg tour (☞ The Fortress and the New Town, *below*). Don't forget to take Mozart tapes along for your Walkman.

A Good Walk

In Salzburg, as anywhere else, if you start from the right departure point, you will have a good journey and ultimately arrive at the proper place. For this city, there is no more appropriate center-of-it-all than **Mozart-**

platz ①, the square named to honor the genius who set lovely Salzburg to music. Get in the mood by noticing, near the statue of Mozart, the strolling street violinists, who usually play a Mozart sonata or two. Walk past the Glockenspiel café into the next square, the Residenzplatz, centered by the 40-ft-high Court Fountain, which is often illuminated at night. Take in the famous **Glockenspiel** ② atop the Neubau Palace (chances are the tunes it plays will be by you-know-who); then enter the **Residenz** ③, the opulent Baroque palace of Salzburg's prince-archbishops and Mozart's patrons. From the Residenzplatz, walk through the arches into Domplatz, the majestic cathedral square of the city—in August, set out with seats for the annual presentation of Hofmannsthal's play *Jedermann*. The **Dom** ④ (Salzburg Cathedral) is among the finest Italian-style Baroque structures in Austria. Walk into the Kapitelplatz through the arches across the square and go through two wrought-iron gateways into **St. Peter's Cemetery** ⑤—one of the most historic and beautiful places in Salzburg. Enter the church of **St. Peter's Abbey** ⑥. Above the main entrance the Latin inscription reads: "I am the door—by me if any man enters here, he shall be saved." If it's nearing lunchtime, you may want to stop at the Stiftskeller St. Peter—so legendary a restaurant that the story has it Mephistopheles met Faust here.

As you leave St. Peter's, look up to the right to see the thin Gothic spire of the **Franziskanerkirche** (Franciscan Church) ⑦. Leave the courtyard in this direction, cross the road, and enter the church by the side entrance, which will bring you directly into the Gothic apse crowned by the ornate red-marble altar designed by Fischer von Erlach. Go down the aisle and leave the church by the front entrance, which opens on Sigmund-Haffner-Gasse. Opposite is the rear entrance to Salzburg's museum of 20th-century art, the **Rupertinum** ⑧—its café is a handy spot for a lunch break. Turn left around the corner into **Toscaninihof** ⑨, the square cut into the dramatic Mönchsberg cliff. The wall bearing the harp-shape organ pipes is part of the famed **Festspielhaus** ⑩. The carved steps going up the Mönchsberg are named for Clemens Holzmeister, architect of the festival halls. If you climb them, you get an intimate view of the Salzburg churches at the level of their spires, and if you climb a little farther to the right, you can look down into the open-air festival hall, cut into the cliffs. From Hofstallgasse you can either walk directly up to Herbert-von-Karajan-Platz or, preferably, walk around by Universitätsplatz to take a look at one of Fischer von Erlach's Baroque masterpieces, the **Universitätskirche** ⑪. In Herbert-von-Karajan-Platz is another point at which building and cliff meet: the **Pferdeschwemme** ⑫, a royal horse trough decorated with splendid paintings. To the left is the Neutor, the impressive road tunnel blasted through the Mönchsberg in 1764. Looking back toward Universitätsplatz, you'll see the famous Goldener Adler hotel, its two buildings painted pink and blue. The arcaded Renaissance court on your left houses the **Spielzeugmuseum** ⑬, a delightful toy museum.

Pass by the tiny church of St. Blasius, built in 1350, and follow the road on through the Gstättentor to the **Mönchsberg elevator** ⑭ for a trip up the hill to the Winkler Terrace, Salzburg's most famous outlook. After descending from the heights, turn left into the short street leading to Museumsplatz to explore the **Carolino Augusteum Museum** ⑮. Walk back toward the Blasius church, which stands at the beginning of the Old City's major shopping street, Getreidegasse, hung with numerous signs depicting little wrought-iron cobblers and bakers (few people could actually read centuries ago). Amid the boutiques and Salzburg's own McDonald's (featuring its own elegant sign) is **Mozarts Geburtshaus** ⑯, the celebrated birthplace of the composer. Continue down the street past the Rathaus (town hall), and enter the Alter

Markt, the old marketplace, adorned with historic buildings, including the Café Tomaselli (1703) and the Baroque Hofapotheke (court apothecary, 1591), still kept as it was back then. Finish up with some "I Was Here" photographs at the marble St. Florian's Fountain, and then head back to Mozartplatz.

TIMING

The Old City—the left bank of the Salzach River—contains many of the city's top attractions. Other than exploring by horse-drawn cabs (*Fiakers*), available for rental at Residenzplatz, most of your exploring will be done on foot, since this historic section of town bans cars. The center city is compact and cozy, so you can easily cover it in one day. Note that many churches close at 6 PM, so unless you're catching a concert at one of them, be sure to visit them during the daylight hours. In addition, several of the main attractions, such as the Residenz palace, can only be seen by guided tour; refer to the hours we list and try to plan your day with such tours in mind.

Sights to See

Alter Markt (Old Market). Right in the heart of the Old City is the Alter Markt, the old marketplace and center of secular life in past centuries. The square is lined with 17th-century middle-class houses, colorfully hued in shades of pink, pale blue, and yellow ocher. Look in at the old royal pharmacy, the **Hofapotheke**, whose incredibly ornate black-and-gold rococo interior was built in 1760. Inside, you'll sense a curious apothecarial smell, traced to the shelves lined with old pots and jars (labeled in Latin). These are not just for show: this pharmacy is still operating today. You can even have your blood pressure taken—but preferably not after drinking a *Doppelter Einspänner* (black coffee with whipped cream, served in a glass) in the famous Café Tomaselli just opposite. In warm weather, the café's terrace provides a wonderful spot for watching the world go by as you sip a *Mélange* (another coffee specialty, served with frothy milk or cream), or, during the summer months, rest your feet under the shade of the chestnut trees in the Tomaselli garden at the top end of the square. Next to the coffeehouse, you'll find the **smallest house in Salzburg**, now the site of an optician; note the slanting roof decorated with a dragon gargoyle. In the center of the square, surrounded by flower stalls, is the marble **St. Florian's Fountain**, dedicated in 1734 to the patron saint of firefighters.

⓯ Carolino Augusteum Museum. Here you can see remains of Salzburg's ancient Roman ruins as well as the famous Celtic bronze flagon found earlier this century on the Dürrnberg near Hallein (10 km, or 6 mi, south of Salzburg), and an outstanding collection of old musical instruments. Special exhibitions are mounted throughout the year. ✉ *Museumspl. 1,* ☎ *0662/841134-0,* 𝖥𝖠𝖷 *0662/841134-10.* ☞ *AS40; combined ticket with Spielzeugmuseum and Dom Museum (☞ below) AS60.* ⊙ *July–Sept., Tues.–Sun. 10–6, Thurs. 9–8; Oct.–June, Tues.–Sun. 9–5, Thurs. 9–8.* ✎

★ ❹ Dom (Cathedral). When you walk through the arches leading from Residenzplatz into **Domplatz,** it is easy to see why Max Reinhardt chose it in August of 1920 as the setting for what has become the annual summer production of Hugo von Hofmannsthal's *Jedermann* (*Everyman*). The plaza is a complete, aesthetic concept and one of Salzburg's most beautiful urban set pieces. In the center rises the Virgin's Column, and at one side is the cathedral, considered to be the first early Baroque building north of the Alps, and one of the finest. Its facade is of marble, its towers reach 250 ft into the air, and it holds 10,000 people. There has been a cathedral on this spot since the 8th century, but the present structure dates from the 17th century. Archbishop Wolf-Dietrich took

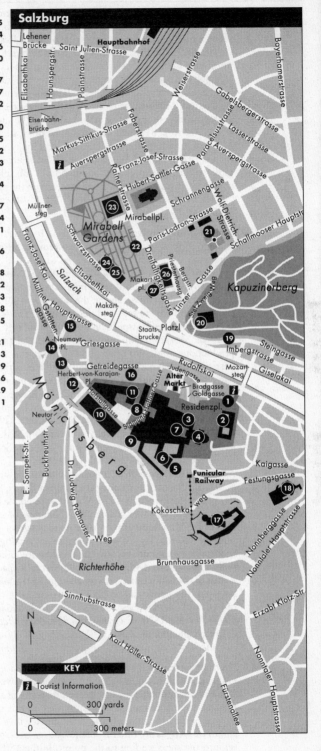

Salzburg

advantage of (some say he initiated) the old Romanesque-Gothic cathedral's destruction by fire in 1598 to demolish the remains and make plans for a huge new structure facing onto the Residenzplatz. His successor, Markus Sittikus, and the new court architect, Santino Solari, built the present Renaissance-style cathedral, which was consecrated with great ceremony in 1628. The simple gray-and-white interior of the church, a peaceful counterpoint to the usual Baroque splendor, dates from a later renovation. Mozart was christened, the day after he was born, at the 13th-century font inside this cathedral, where he later served as organist from 1779 to 1781. Some of his compositions, such as the *Coronation Mass*, were written for the cathedral, and many were performed here for the first time. On Sunday, mass is sung here at 10 AM—the most glorious time to experience the cathedral's full splendor. Many of the church's treasures are in a special museum on the premises. ⊠ *Dompl.,* ☎ *0662/844189,* FAX *0662/840442.* ⊠ *AS40.* ☉ *May 20–Oct. 29, Mon.–Sat. 10–5, Sun. and holidays 1–6.*

➓ Festspielhaus (Festival Hall Complex). To attend the world famous Salzburg Festival, all music lovers head for the Hofstallgasse, the street where the three main festival theaters are located. The street owes its name to the fact that in the 17th century the court stables were located here. Now, in the place of prancing horses, festival visitors promenade along the Hofstallgasse during the intervals of summer performances, showing off their suntans and elegant attire. The festival complex consists of the **Kleines Festspielhaus** (Small Festival Hall, sometimes referred to as the Mozart Stage), built in 1937 and nowadays used mainly for productions of Mozart operas and chamber concerts, and the **Grosses Festspielhaus** (Great Festival Hall), built into the solid rock of the Mönchsberg and opened in 1960, with a maximum stage width of 104 ft and a seating capacity of more than 2,000. In recent seasons the Grosses Festspielhaus, nicknamed the Wagner Stage because of its width, has been the venue for spectacular productions such as *Boris Godunov* and *Der Rosenkavalier.* Stage directors are faced with the greatest challenge in the **Felsenreitschule,** the former Summer Riding School, which—hewn out of the rock of the Mönchsberg during the 17th century—offers a setting more dramatic than anything presented on stage. Max Reinhardt made the first attempt at using the Summer Riding School for Salzburg Festival performances in 1926. With its retractable roof it gives the impression of an open-air theater; the three tiers of arcades cut into the rock of the Mönchsberg linger in the mind of fans of *The Sound of Music* film, for the von Trapps were portrayed as singing "Edelweiss" here, in their last Austrian concert. The theaters are linked by tunnels (partially in marble and with carpeted floors) to a spacious underground garage in the Mönchsberg. If you want to see the inside of the halls, it's best to go to a performance, but guided tours are given and group tours can be booked on request. ⊠ *Hofstallg. 1,* ☎ *0662/849097,* FAX *0662/ 8045–760.* ⊠ *AS70.* ☉ *Group tour Jan.–May, Oct.–Dec. 20, daily at 2; June, Sept., daily at 2 and 3:30; July–Aug., daily at 9.30, 2, and 3:30. Advance booking necessary for groups of more than 10 people.*

➐ Franziskanerkirche (Franciscan Church). The graceful, tall spire of the Franciscan Church stands out from all other towers in Salzburg; the church itself encompasses the greatest diversity of architectural styles. Even in the 8th century, a church existed on this spot but it was destroyed by fire. The new one was consecrated with a Romanesque nave, still to be seen, as are other Romanesque features, such as a stone lion set into the steps leading to the pulpit. In the 15th century the choir was rebuilt in Gothic style, then crowned in the 18th century by an ornate red-marble and gilt altar designed by Austria's most famous Baroque architect, Fischer von Erlach. Mass—frequently one of Mozart's compositions—is celebrated here on Sunday at 9 AM. ⊠ *Franziskan-erg. 5,* ☏ *0662/843629–0.* ☞ *Free.* ⊙ *Daily 6:30 AM–7:30 PM.*

★ **Getreidegasse.** This is the main shopping street in the Old City center. According to historians the historic name means "trade street"—not "grain street," as many people believe. Today it is the address of elegant fashion houses, international shoe chains, and a McDonald's (note its wrought-iron sign—one of many on the street—with classy bronze lettering: like all the other shops, it has conformed with Salzburg's strict Old City conservation laws). Other than coming to shop, visitors flock to this street because at Getreidegasse 9 they'll find **Mozarts Geburtshaus** (☞ *below*). Needless to say, in the summer the street is as densely packed with people as a corncob is with kernels. You can always escape for a while through one of the many arcades—mostly flower-bedecked and opening into delightful little courtyards—that link the Getreidegasse to the river and the Universitätsplatz.

❷ **Glockenspiel** (Carillon). The famous carillon tower is perched on top of the **Residenz Neubau** (New Residence), Prince-Archbishop Wolf-Dietrich's government palace and his first attempt at the Baroque style. The carillon is a later addition, brought from the Netherlands in 1688 and finally put in working order in 1702. The 35 bells play classical tunes (usually by Weber, Haydn, and you-know-who) at 7 AM, 11 AM, and 6 PM—with charm and ingenuity often making up for the occasional musical inaccuracy. From Easter to October, the bells are immediately followed by a resounding retort from the 200-pipe "Bull" organ housed in the Hohensalzburg Fortress. Details about the music selections are listed on a notice board across the square on the corner of the Residenz building. ⊠ *Mozartpl. 1.*

⑭ **Mönchsberg elevator.** Just around the corner from the Pferdeschwemme (☞ *below*), at Neumayr Platz, you'll find the Mönchsberg elevator, which takes you up through solid rock to the **Winkler Terrace,** where you can walk along wooded paths while enjoying spectacular vistas of Salzburg. In summer this can be a marvelous—and quick way—to escape the tiny crowded streets of the Old City. At the top of the Mönchsberg, follow the signs and path south to **Burgerwehr-Einkehr,** a popular café-restaurant open May–mid-October with a magnificent view of the churches and the fortress from its outdoor garden. ⊠ *Gstätteng. 13.* ☞ *Round-trip AS27, one-way AS16.* ⊙ *Open daily 9 AM–11 PM; 9–7 when cafe is closed.*

⑯ **Mozarts Geburtshaus** (Mozart's Birthplace). Pilgrims to the city of Mozart's birth usually make this their first stop. Mozart was born on the third floor of this tall house on January 27, 1756, and the family lived here, when they were not on tour, until 1773 (the child prodigy composed many of his first compositions in these rooms). Mozart's piano and tiny violin are on display, as well as portraits of the family, autograph letters, and manuscripts, all exhibited in cases illuminated by laser to make them easier to read. On the first floor, miniature stage models from various productions of Mozart operas are displayed, and on the second floor a special annual exhibition is mounted, which opens the last week in January and runs until early October. ⊠ *Getreideg. 9,* ☏ *0662/844313.* ☞ *AS70.* ⊙ *Daily 9–6 (last tickets 5:30).* ✑

NEED A
BREAK?
On the ground floor of Mozart's Birthplace, stop in at **Trzesniewski's** (⊠ Getreideg. 9) for a light snack of open sandwiches (18 different spreads on fresh whole-meal bread) and an excellent cup of coffee.

❶ **Mozartplatz** (Mozart Square). In the center of the square stands the statue of Wolfgang Amadeus Mozart, the work of sculptor Ludwig Schwanthaler and unveiled in 1842 in the presence of the composer's two surviving sons. It was the first sign of public recognition the great composer had received from his hometown since his death as a pauper in Vienna in 1791. As you will notice, the Mozart memorial industry has grown considerably since then. In fact, in 1991—the 200th anniversary of Mozart's death—a local sculptor caused an uproar, when, protesting the overcommercialization of Mozart, he had the statue buried under a mountain of 200 supermarket shopping carts. The statue shows a 19th-century stylized view of Mozart, draped in a mantle, holding a page of music and a copybook. A more appropriate bust of the composer, modeled by Viennese sculptor Edmund Heller, is to be found on the Kapuzinerberg. It contains the inscription *Jung gross, spät erkannt, nie erreicht*—"Great while young, belatedly appreciated, never equaled."

⓬ **Pferdeschwemme** (Royal Horse Drinking Trough). At the western end of the Hofstallgasse is the Herbert-von-Karajan-Platz (named after Salzburg's second-greatest son, maestro Herbert von Karajan, the legendary conductor and music director of the Salzburg Festival for many decades). On the Mönchsberg side of the square is the Pferdeschwemme—a royal trough where prize horses used to be cleaned and watered, constructed in 1695; as they underwent this ordeal they could delight in the frescoes of their pin-up fillies on the rear wall. Looking back toward Universitätsplatz, you'll see the famous hotel and restaurant the Goldener Hirsch, its two buildings painted pink and blue. ⊠ *Herbert-von-Karajan-Pl..*

Rathaus (Town Hall). Where the Sigmund-Haffner-Gasse meets the Getreidegasse you will find the Rathaus, a remarkably insignificant building in the Salzburg skyline—apart from its clock, which chimes every quarter hour—no doubt reflecting the historical weakness of the burghers vis-à-vis the church, whose opulent monuments and churches are evident throughout the city. ⊠ *Getreideg. and Sigmund-Haffner-G..*

❸ **Residenz.** Situated at the very heart of Baroque Salzburg, the Residenz overlooks the spacious Residenzplatz and its famous horse fountain. The palace was built between 1600 and 1619 as the home of the prince-archbishops. The *Kaisersaal* (Imperial Hall) and the *Rittersaal* (Knight's Hall), one of the city's most regal concert halls, can be seen along with the rest of the state rooms on a guided tour. Today, the Residenz is often used for official functions, banquets, and exhibitions. In recent seasons, its courtyard has been the lovely setting for opera productions of the Salzburg Festival. The **Residenzgalerie,** an art museum specializing in 17th-century Dutch and Flemish art and 19th-century paintings of Salzburg, is situated on the second floor of the Residenz. ⊠ *Residenzpl. 1,* ☎ *0662/8042–2690; 0662/840451 art collection.* ▧ *AS90 for both museums.* ☉ *Daily 10–5, closed two wks before Easter. Tours by arrangement. Art Collection: Daily 10–5, closed Wed., Oct.–Mar.*

❽ **Rupertinum.** If you are interested in 20th-century art, don't miss the chance to see the outstanding permanent collection of paintings and graphic art on display in this gallery. Take a rest in the museum's excellent café. ⊠ *Wiener-Philharmoniker-G. 9,* ☎ *0662/8042–2336.* ▧ *AS40.* ☉ *Tues., Thurs.–Sun. 10–5, Wed. 10–9; mid-July–Aug., Thurs.–Tues. 10–6, Wed. 10–9.*

❻ **Stift St. Peter** (St. Peter's Abbey). The most sumptuous church in Salzburg, St. Peter's is where Mozart's Mass in C Minor premiered in 1783; his *Requiem* is performed every year on the anniversary of his death. The porch has beautiful Romanesque vaulted arches from the original structure built in the 12th century; the interior was decorated in the characteristically voluptuous late-Baroque style when additions were made in the 1770s. Note the side chapel by the entrance, with the unusual crèche portraying the Flight into Egypt and the Massacre of the Innocents. ⊠ *St. Peter Bezirk,* ☎ *0662/844578–0.* ⬚ *Free.* ☉ *May–Sept., Tues.–Sun. 10:30–5; Oct.–Apr., Wed. and Thurs. 10:30–3:30, Fri.–Sun. 10:30–4.*

⑤ St. Peter's Cemetery. This eerie but intimate cemetery is the oldest Christian graveyard in Salzburg, dating back to 1627. Enclosed on three sides by wrought-iron grilles, Baroque vaults contain chapels belonging to old patrician families of Salzburg. The graveyard is far from mournful: the individual graves are tended with loving care, decorated with candles, fir branches, and flowers—especially pansies (because their name means "thoughts"). In Crypt XXXI is the grave of Santino Solari, architect of the cathedral; in XXXIX that of Sigmund Haffner, a patron for whom Mozart composed a symphony and named a serenade. The final communal crypt contains the body of Mozart's sister, Nannerl, and the torso of Joseph Haydn's brother, Michael (his head is in an urn stored in St. Peter's). ⊠ *St. Peter Bezirk,* ☎ *0662/844578–0.* ⬚ *AS12.* ☉ *Tours May–Sept., daily 10–5 on the hr; Oct.–Apr., daily 10:30–3:30 (check times on notice board).*

⚫ ⑬ Spielzeugmuseum (Toy Museum). On a rainy day this is a delightful diversion for both young and old, with a collection of dolls, teddy bears, model railways, and wooden sailing ships. On some Wednesday and Friday afternoons at 3, special Punch and Judy puppet shows are performed. ⊠ *Bürgerspitalpl. 2,* ☎ *0662/847560.* ⬚ *AS30.* ☉ *July–Sept., Tues.–Sun. 10–6; Oct.–June, Tues.–Sun. 9–5.*

⑨ Toscaninihof (Arturo Toscanini House). The famous Italian maestro Arturo Toscanini conducted some of the Salzburg Festival's most legendary performances during the 1930s. Throughout the summer months the courtyard here is a hive of activity, with sets for the stage of the Kleines Festspielhaus being brought in through the massive iron folding gates.

⑪ Universitätskirche (Kollegienkirche, or Collegiate Church). Consecrated in 1707, this structure is architect Fischer von Erlach's masterpiece of the genre in Salzburg as well as one of the finest examples of Austrian Baroque. The interior has a liberating feeling of space and light, which stage directors have used to great advantage in recent years for Salzburg Festival performances of contemporary music. ⊠ *Universitätspl.,* ☎ *0662/841-327-72.* ⬚ *Free.* ☉ *Mon.–Sat., 9–7, Sun. 10–7 (winter closing hours approximately 3 hrs earlier).*

Wiener Philharmoniker-Gasse. Previously known as Marktgasse (Market Street), the street blooms with an open-air food market every Saturday morning (note that a daily fruit and vegetable market is held on the Universitätsplatz every day). The street was renamed after the world-famous Vienna Philharmonic Orchestra in recognition of the unique contribution it has made annually to the Salzburg Festival, playing for most opera productions and for the majority of orchestral concerts.

The Fortress and the New Town

According to a popular saying in Salzburg, "If you can see the fortress, it's just about to rain; if you can't see it, it's already raining." Fortunately there are plenty of days when spectacular views can be had of Salzburg and the surrounding countryside from the top of the fortress. Looking across the River Salzach, you can pick out the Mirabell Palace and Gardens, the Landestheater, the Mozart Residence and the Mozarteum, the Church of the Holy Trinity, and the Kapuzinerkloster perched on the Kapuzinerberg. Ranging from the "acropolis" of the city—the medieval Fortress Hohensalzburg—to the celebrated Salzburg Mari-

OH, THE HILLS ARE ALIVE . . .

FEW SALZBURGERS WOULD publicly admit it, but *The Sound of Music*, Hollywood's interpretation of the trials and joys of the local von Trapp family, has become their city's most eminent emissary when it comes to international promotion. The year after the movie's release, international tourism to Salzburg jumped 20%, and soon *The Sound of Music* was a Salzburg attraction. The soundtrack and other movie and von Trapp memorabilia are hot-selling items around town.

A May–September **dinner show** in the grand ballroom of the K+K Stieglkeller (✉ Festungsg. 10, ☎ 0662/832029) features Rodgers and Hammerstein songs, folk dancing, a three-course meal, and drinks. Included in the AS520 price tag, the *plat de résistance* is that preposterous but genuinely Andrews–von Trapp combination: schnitzel and noodles. A 10-minute video interview with Maria von Trapp, in which she tells of her courtship with Baron von Trapp, is shown.

Perhaps the most important *Sound* spin-off are the **tours** offered by several companies (☞ Guided Tours *in* Salzburg A to Z, *below*). Besides showing you some of the film's locations (usually very briefly), these four-hour rides have the advantage of giving a very concise tour of the city. The buses generally leave from Mirabellplatz; lumber by the "Do-Re-Mi" staircase at the edge of the beautifully manicured Mirabell Gardens; pass by the hardly visible Aigen train station, where the von Trapps caught the escape train; and then head south to Schloss Anif. This 16th-century water castle, which had a cameo appearance in the opening scenes of the film, is now in private hands and not open to the public.

First official stop for a leg-stretcher is at the gazebo in the manicured park of Schloss Hellbrunn, about 6 km (4 mi) south of Salzburg (☞ Short Side Trips from Salzburg, *below*). This is where Liesl von Trapp sings "I Am Sixteen Going on Seventeen" and where Maria and the Baron woo and coo "Something Good." The simple little structure, which was in fact rebuilt in Hollywood a size larger for choreographic reasons, is the most coveted prize of photographers.

After driving by another private castle with limited visiting rights, Schloss Leopoldskron (used for the scene where Maria and the Baron dance on the balcony during the ball), and the Nonnberg Convent at the foot of the daunting Hohensalzburg fortress (☞ *below*), the bus leaves the city limits for the luscious landscape of the Salzkammergut. These are the hills "alive with music," where Julie Andrews prances about in the opening scenes and forgets all about her fellow nuns. You get a chance for a meditative walk along the shores of the Wolfgangsee in St. Gilgen before the bus heads for the pretty town of Mondsee (☞ Chapter 7). In real life, Maria and Georg von Trapp were married at the Collegiate Church here.

Tour guides are well trained and often have a good sense of humor, with which they gently debunk myths about the movie and its making. Did you know, for example, that all interior scenes were built in the Fox studios, even the superb replica of the convent's halls? And Switzerland was "moved" 160 km (100 mi) eastward so the family could hike over the mountains to freedom (while singing "Edelweiss")? Well, in Hollywood, as in Salzburg and its magical environs, anything is possible.

onette Theater, this part of Salzburg encapsulates the charm of the city. If you want to see the most delightful Mozart landmark in this part of town, the Zauberflötenhäuschen—the mouthful used to describe the little summerhouse where he finished composing *The Magic Flute*—note that you have to set up a special appointment at the Mozarteum.

A Good Walk

Start with Salzburg's number one sight—especially the case at night, when it is spectacularly spotlit—the famed **Fortress Hohensalzburg** ⑰, the 12th-century castle that dominates the town. Take the Mönchsberg elevator or the funicular railway on Festungsgasse, located behind the cathedral near St. Peter's Cemetery. If it's not running, you can walk up the zigzag path that begins a little farther up Festungsgasse; it's steep in parts but gives a better impression of the majestic nature of the fortress. Once you've explored this, the largest medieval fortress in Central Europe, head back to the footpath but, rather than taking the steps back into town, turn right toward the **Nonnberg Convent** ⑱. Explore the church—Maria von Trapp almost found her calling here—then return along the path to the first set of steps, take them down them into Kaigasse, and continue on to Mozartplatz. From here you can cross the Salzach River over the footbridge, Mozartsteg. Cross the road and walk west a minute or two along Imbergstrasse until you see a bookstore on the corner. Here a little street runs into **Steingasse** ⑲—a picturesque medieval street. After exploring this "time machine," walk through the Steintor gate, past the chapel of St. Johann am Imberg to the Hettwer Bastion on the **Kapuzinerberg Hill** ⑳ for a great vista of the city.

Continue up the path to the Kapuziner-Kloster. From here, follow the winding road down past the stations of the cross. Turn right at the bottom of the road into Linzergasse, the New Town's answer to the Getreidegasse. Continue up this street to St. Sebastian's Church on the left. An archway will lead you into the tranquil **St. Sebastian's Cemetery** ㉑—if it looks somewhat familiar that's because this setting inspired the scene at the end of *The Sound of Music,* where the von Trapps are nearly captured. When you leave the cemetery, walk north through a passageway until you reach Paris-Lodron-Strasse. To the left as you walk west down this street is the Loreto Church. At Mirabellplatz, cross the road to the **Mirabell Gardens** ㉒—the Pegasus Fountain (remember "Do-Re-Mi"?) and the Dwarfs' Garden are highlights here.

Take in the adjacent **Mirabell Palace** ㉓ and its noted 18th-century Angel Staircase. Turn left out of the garden park onto busy Schwarzstrasse. Along this road you will find the **Mozarteum** ㉔. Next door is the **Marionettentheater** ㉕—home to those marionettes known around the world. Turn left at the corner, around the Landestheater, and continue onto Makartplatz, dominated at the far end by Fischer von Erlach's **Dreifaltigkeitskirche** ㉖. Across from the Hotel Bristol is the **Mozart Wohnhaus** ㉗, where you can complete your homage to the city's hometown deity.

TIMING

Allow half a day for the fortress, to explore it fully both inside and out. If you don't plan an intermission at one of the restaurants on the Mönchsberg, you can stock up on provisions at Schwaighofer (Kranzlmarkt 3 in the Old City) for a picnic in the beautiful Mirabell Gardens. Call the Mozarteum to see if there will be evening recitals in their two concert halls; hearing the *Linz* Symphony or the *Davidde Penitente* cantata could be a wonderfully fitting conclusion to your day.

Sights to See

㉖ **Dreifaltigkeitskirche** (Church of the Holy Trinity). The Makartplatz is dominated at the top (east) end by Fischer von Erlach's first architectural work in Salzburg, built 1694–1707. It was modeled on a church by Borromini in Rome and prefigures von Ehrlach's Karlskirche in Vienna. Dominated by a lofty, oval-shape dome—which features a painting by Michael Rottmayr—this church was the result of the archbishops' concern that Salzburg's new town was developing in an overly haphazard manner. The Dreifaltigkeitskirche was intended to create a sense of order by introducing a spectacular monument of the Baroque—the signature style of the city—on the Makartplatz. The interior is small but perfectly proportioned, surmounted by its dome, whose trompe-l'oeil fresco seems to open up the church to the sky above. ✉ *Dreifaltigkeitsg. 14,* ☎ *0662/877495.* 🎫 *Free.* ⊙ *Mon.–Sat. 6:30–6:30, Sun. 8–6:30.*

Festungsbahn (funicular railway). This is the easy way up to Fortress Hohensalzburg (☞ *below*); it's located behind St. Peter's Cemetery. ✉ *Festungsg. 4,* ☎ *0662/842682.* 🎫 *Round-trip AS76, one-way AS38.* ⊙ *Every ten min Oct.–Apr., 9–5; May–Sept., 9–9.*

★ ⑰ **Fortress Hohensalzburg.** Founded in 1077, the Fortress Hohensalzburg is Salzburg's acropolis and the largest preserved medieval fortress in Central Europe. Brooding over the city from atop the Festungsberg, it was originally built by Salzburg's Archbishop Gebhard, who had supported the pope in the political struggle against the Holy Roman Emperor. Over the centuries, the archbishops gradually enlarged the castle, using it originally as a residence then as a siege-proof haven against invaders and their own rebellious subjects. The exterior of the fortress may look grim, but inside there are lavish state rooms, such as the glittering **Golden Room,** the **Burgmuseum**—a collection of medieval art—and the **Rainersmuseum,** with its brutish arms and armor. Politics and church are in full force here: there's a torture chamber not far from the exquisite late-Gothic **St. George's Chapel.** In 1502, the fortress acquired the 200-pipe organ, played daily after the carillon in the Neugebäude. It is best to listen to it from a respectful distance, as it is not called the Bull without reason. Everyone will want to climb up the 100 tiny steps to the **Reckturm,** a grand lookout post with a sweeping view of Salzburg and the mountains. Remember that queues to the fortress can be long, so try to come early.

You can either take the funicular railway, the ☞ **Festungsbahn,** up to the fortress (advisable with young children) or walk up the zigzag path that begins just beyond the Stieglkeller on Festungsgasse. Note that you don't need a ticket to walk down the footpath. ✉ *Mönchsberg 34,* ☎ *0662/842430–11.* 🎫 *Fortress AS35, fortress and tour AS70.* ⊙ *Oct.–May., daily 8–6; June–Sept., daily 8–7; 50-min tour Nov.–Mar., daily 10–4:30 every ½ hr; Apr.–June and Sept.–Oct., daily 9:30–5 every ½ hr; July–Aug., daily 9–5:30 every ½ hr.*

⑳ **Kapuzinerberg Hill.** Directly opposite the Mönchsberg on the other side of the river, Kapuzinerberg Hill is crowned by several interesting sights. By ascending a stone staircase near Steingasse 9 you can start your climb up the peak. At the top of the first flight of steps is a tiny chapel, **St. Johann am Imberg,** built in 1681. Farther on is a signpost and gate to the **Hettwer Bastion,** part of the old city walls and offering one of the most spectacular viewpoints in Salzburg. At the summit is the gold-beige **Kapuzinerkloster** (Capuchin Monastery), dating from the time of Prince-Archbishop Wolf-Dietrich. Pope John Paul II stayed here during his visit to Salzburg in 1988. The road downward is called Stefan Zweig Weg, after the great Austrian writer who had a house on the Kapuzinerberg until 1935, when he had to flee Austria. Along the road are set the stations of the cross.

★ ℭ ㉕ **Marionettentheater** (Marionette Theater). This is both the world's. greatest marionette theater and—surprise—a sublime theatrical experience. Many critics have noted that viewers quickly forget the strings controlling the puppets, which assume lifelike dimensions and provide a very real dramatic experience. The Marionettentheater is identified above all with Mozart's operas, which seem particularly suited to the skilled puppetry; a delightful production of *Così fan tutte* captures the humor of the work better than most stage versions. The company is famous for its world tours but is usually in Salzburg around Christmas, during the late-January Mozart Week, at Easter, and from May to September (schedule subject to change). ⊠ *Schwarzstr. 24,* ☎ *0662/ 872406–0,* 🕿 *0662/882141.* 🍴 *AS250–AS500.* ⊙ *Box office Mon.– Sat. 9–1 and 2 hrs before performance; Salzburg season May–Sept., Christmas, Mozart Week (Jan.), Easter.*

★ ℭ ㉒ **Mirabell Gardens.** While there are at least four entrances to the Mirabell Gardens—from the Makartplatz, the Schwarzstrasse, and the Rainerstrasse—you'll want to enter from the Rainerstrasse and head for the Rosenhügel (Rosebush Hill): you'll arrive at the top of the steps where Julie Andrews and her seven charges showed off their singing ability in *The Sound of Music.* This is also an ideal vantage point for admiring the formal gardens and offers one of the best views of Salzburg, as it shows how harmoniously architects of the Baroque period laid out the city. The center of the gardens—one of Europe's most beautiful parks, partly designed by Fischer von Erlach, and grand setting for the Mirabell Palace (☞ *below*)—is dominated by four large groups of statues representing the elements and designed by Ottavio Mosto, who came to live in Salzburg from Padua. A bronze version of the horse Pegasus stands in front of the southern facade of the Mirabell Palace in the center of a circular water basin. The most famous part of the Mirabell Gardens is the **Zwerglgarten** (Dwarfs' Garden), which can be found opposite the Pegasus fountain. Here you'll find 12 statues of dwarves sculpted in marble—the real-life models of which were presented to the bishop by the landgrave of Göttweig. Prince-Archbishop Franz Anton von Harrach had the stone figures made for a theater that was later closed. It's open daily 7 AM–8 PM. The **Baroque Museum** (⊠ Orangeriegarten, ☎ 0662/ 877432), beside the Orangery of the Mirabell Gardens, features a collection of late-17th-century and 18th-century paintings, sketches, and models illustrating an extravagant vision of life. Works by Giordano, Bernini, and Rottmayr are highlights of the collection. The museum is open Tuesday to Saturday, 9 to noon and 2 to 5 and Sunday and holidays 10 to 1; July 23 to August 29, daily from 9 to 5; admission is AS40.

㉓ **Mirabell Palace.** The "Taj Mahal of Salzburg," the Mirabell Palace was built by Prince-Archbishop Wolf-Dietrich for his mistress, Salomé Alt, and their 10 children: It was originally called Altenau in her honor. Over the centuries the Mirabell Palace, now the City Hall, has undergone extensive alteration. Due to the fire that ravaged Salzburg in 1818, nothing remains of the original palace except the Marble Hall upstairs, nowadays used for civil wedding ceremonies, and regarded as the most beautiful registry office in the world (candlelit chamber concerts are also held here in the evenings). The recently restored hall, with its marble floor in strongly contrasting colors and walls of stucco and marble ornamented with elegant gilt scrollwork, looks more splendid than ever.

The only other part of the palace to survive the fire was the magnificent marble staircase, sculpted by Georg Rafael Donner. Staircases of important buildings afforded many Baroque artists ideal opportunities for ingenious and exuberant ornamentation, and Donner produced a particularly charming example of this highly specialized art in Mirabell. The staircase is romantically draped with white marble putti, whose faces and gestures reflect a multitude of emotions, from questioning innocence to jeering mockery. Outdoor concerts are held at the palace and gardens May though August, Sunday mornings and Wednesday evenings. ✉ *Off Makartpl.,* ☎ *0662/8485–86.* 🎫 *Free.* ⊙ *Weekdays 8–6.*

Mozart Audio and Video Museum. In the same building as the Mozart Wohnhaus (Residence) (☞ *below*) is the Mozart Audio and Video Museum, an archive of thousands of Mozart recordings as well as films and video productions, all of which can be listened to or viewed on request. ✉ *Makartpl. 8,* ☎ *0662/883454.* 🎫 *Free.* ⊙ *Mon.–Tues. and Fri. 9–1, Wed.–Thurs. 1–5.*

🦢 **㉗** **Mozart Wohnhaus** (Mozart Residence). The Mozart family moved from their cramped surroundings in the Getreidegasse to this house on the Hannibal Platz, as it was then known, in 1773. Wolfgang Amadeus Mozart lived here until 1780, his sister Nannerl stayed here until she married in 1784 and their father Leopold lived here until his death in 1787. The house is, therefore, now referred to as the Mozart Residence, signifying that it was not only Wolfgang who lived here. During the first Allied bomb attack on Salzburg in October 1944, the house was bombed and partially destroyed. Despite international protest at the time, a six-story office block was built in its place. Now, in an exemplary building and sponsorship project, the office block has been demolished and the house reconstructed. Mozart composed the "Salzburg Symphonies" here, as well as violin concertos, church music and sonatas, and parts of his early operatic masterpieces. Besides an interesting collection of musical instruments, among the exhibits on display are books from Leopold Mozart's library. Autograph manuscripts and letters can be viewed, by prior arrangement only, in the cellar vaults. One room is devoted to more personal details about Mozart—his height, color of his hair, his method of dress, and his numerous travels across Europe. ✉ *Makartpl. 8,* ☎ *0662/874227–40,* FAX *0662/872924.* 🎫 *Mozart residence AS65, combined ticket for Mozart Residence and Birthplace AS110.* ⊙ *Daily 10–6.*

㉔ **Mozarteum.** Two institutions share the address here—the International Mozarteum Foundation, set up in 1870, and the Academy of Music and Performing Arts, founded in 1880. Both are important centers of academic research; the Mozarteum also organizes the annual Mozart Week festival in January and sponsors concerts from October to June in its two recital halls, the Grosser Saal (Great Hall) and the Wiener Saal (Vienna Hall). ✉ *Schwarzstr. 26,* ☎ *0662/88940–21.*

⑱ **Nonnberg Convent.** Situated just below the south side of the Fortress Hohensalzburg—and best visited in tandem with it—this convent was founded around AD 700 by St. Rupert, and his niece St. Erentrudis was the first abbess (in the archway a late-Gothic statue of Erentrudis welcomes the visitor). It is more famous these days as Maria's convent—both the one in *The Sound of Music* and that of the real Maria. She returned to marry her Captain von Trapp here in the Gothic church. Each evening in May at 6:45, the nuns sing a 15-minute service called Maiandacht. Their beautiful voices can be heard also at midnight mass on December 24. Parts of the private quarters for the nuns, which feature some lovely, intricate woodcarving, can be seen by prior arrangement. ✉ *Nonnbergg. 2,* ☎ *0662/841607–0.* ⊙ *Fall–spring, daily 7–5; summer, daily 7–7.*

㉑ **St. Sebastian's Cemetery.** Located in the shadows of St. Sebastian's Church, the Friedhof St. Sebastian is one of the most peaceful spots in Salzburg. Prince-Archbishop Wolf-Dietrich commissioned the cemetery at the end of the 16th century to replace the old cathedral graveyard, which he planned to demolish. It was built in the style of an Italian *campo santo*, with arcades on four sides, and in the center of the square he had an unusual, brightly tiled Mannerist mausoleum built for himself, in which he was interred in 1617. Several famous people are buried in this cemetery, including the physician and philosopher Paracelsus, who settled in Salzburg in the early 16th century (the grave is by the church door); Mozart's wife Constanze; and his father, Leopold (by the central path leading to the mausoleum). If the gate is closed, try going through the church, or enter through the back entrance on Paris-Lodron-Strasse. ⊠ *Linzerg.* ⊙ *Daily 7 AM–7 PM.*

⑲ Steingasse. This narrow medieval street, walled in on one side by the bare cliffs of the Kapuzinerberg, ran along the riverfront before the Salzach was regulated. Nowadays it's a fascinating mixture of artists' workshops, antiques shops, and trendy nightclubs, but with its tall houses the street still manages to convey an idea of how life used to be in the Middle Ages. **Steingasse 9** is the house where Josef Mohr, who wrote the words to the Christmas carol "Silent Night, Holy Night," was born in 1792. The **Steintor** marks the entrance to the oldest section of the street; here on summer afternoons the light can be particularly striking. House Number 23 on the right still has deep, slanted peep-windows for guarding the gate.

Short Side Trips from Salzburg

Gaisberg and Untersberg. Adventurous people might like to ascend two of Salzburg's "house mountains" (so-called because they are so close to the city settlements). You can take the bus to the summit of the Gaisberg, where you'll be rewarded with a spectacular panoramic view of the Alps and the Alpine foreland. In summer the bus leaves from Mirabellplatz at 9 AM and 11 AM, and the journey takes about half an hour. The Untersberg is the mountain Captain von Trapp and Maria climbed as they escaped the Nazis in *The Sound of Music.* In the film they were supposedly fleeing to Switzerland; in reality, the climb up the Untersberg would have brought them almost to the doorstep of Hitler's retreat at the Eagle's Nest above Berchtesgaden. A cable car from St. Leonhard (about 13 km/8 mi south of Salzburg) takes you up 6,020 ft right to the top of the Untersberg, giving you a breathtaking view. In winter you can ski down (you arrive in the village of Fürstenbrunn and taxis or buses take you back to St. Leonhard); in summer there are a number of hiking routes from the summit. ⊠ *Untersbergbahn,* ☎ *06246/72477.* 🎫 *Round-trip AS215.* ⊙ *Mar.–June and Oct. 1–26, daily 9–5; July–Sept., daily 8:30–5:30; Dec. 20–Feb. 28, daily 10–4.*

OFF THE
BEATEN PATH

NEUKIRCHEN/VÖCKLA – In this tiny village about 50 km (30 mi) north of Salzburg is the Freilichtmuseum Stehrerhof, which houses a 400-year-old furnished farmhouse with related exhibits and even a still. From Salzburg go in the direction of Linz on the B1, turning north at Vöcklamarkt. From here follow signs east to Langwies and then to Neukirchen. 🎫 *AS45.* ⊙ *Apr.–Oct., 10–noon and 1–5; July–Oct., 10–5.*

Oberndorf. This little village 21 km (13 mi) north of Salzburg has just one claim to fame; it was here, on Christmas Eve, 1818, that the organist and schoolteacher Franz Gruber composed the Christmas carol "Silent Night, Holy Night" to a lyric by the local priest, Josef Mohr. The church where the masterpiece was created was demolished and replaced in 1937 by a tiny commemorative chapel containing a copy of the original composition (the original is in the Carolino-Augusteum Museum in Salzburg); stained-glass windows representing Gruber and Mohr; and a Nativity scene. About a 10-minute walk from the village center along the riverbank, the local **Heimatmuseum** (⊠ Stille-Nacht-Pl. 7, ☎ 06272/4422), opposite the chapel, documents the history of the carol. The museum is open daily 9–noon and 1–5; admission is AS40.You can get to Oberndorf by the local train (opposite the main train station), by car along the B156 Lamprechtshausener Bundesstrasse, or by bicycle along the River Salzach.

★ ☾ **Schloss Hellbrunn** (Hellbrunn Palace). Just 6½ km (4 mi) south of Salzburg, the Lustschloss Hellbrun was the pleasure palace of the prince-archbishops. It was built in the early 17th century by Santino Solari for Markus Sittikus, after he had imprisoned his uncle, Wolf-Dietrich, in the fortress. The castle has some fascinating rooms, including an octagonal music room and a banquet hall with a trompe-l'oeil ceiling. From the magnificent gardens and tree-lined avenues to the silent ponds, Hellbrunn Park is often described as a jewel of landscape architecture. It became famous far and wide because of its **Wasserspiele**, or trick fountains: in the formal Baroque gardens, some of the exotic and humorous fountains spurt water from strange places at unexpected times—you will probably get doused. A visit to the gardens is highly recommended: nowhere else can you experience so completely the realm of fantasy that the grand Salzburg archbishops indulged in. The **Monatsschlösschen**, the old hunting lodge, contains an excellent folklore museum. The palace deer park now includes a **zoo** featuring free-flying vultures and Alpine animals that largely roam unhindered. You can get to Hellbrunn by Bus 55, by car on Route 159, or by bike or on foot along the beautiful Hellbrunner Allee past several 17th-century mansions. The restaurant in the castle courtyard serves good food. ✉ *Fürstenweg 37, Hellbrunn,* ☎ *0662/820372.* ☎ *Tour of palace AS30; water gardens AS70; combination ticket AS90.* ☾ *Apr. and Oct., daily 9–4:30; May–Sept., daily 9–5:30; evening tours July–Aug., daily on the hr 6–10.*

DINING

The prices in Salzburg's excellent restaurants are certainly higher than in much of the rest of Austria but, in general, justifiably so: you can experience some truly exquisite cuisine. Many restaurants favor the *neue Küche*—a lighter version of the traditional, somewhat heavy specialties of Austrian cooking, but with more substance than nouvelle cuisine. The only truly indigenous Salzburg dish is *Salzburger Nockerln,* a snowy meringue of sweetened whisked egg whites with just a hint of lemon, but the Salzburgers have a wonderful way with fish—often a fresh catch from the nearby lakes of the Salzkammergut. In the more expensive restaurants, the set menus give you an opportunity to sample the chef's best; in the less expensive ones, they help to keep costs down. Note, however, that some restaurants limit the hours during which the set menu is available. Many restaurants are open all day; otherwise, lunch is served from approximately 11 to 2 and dinner from 6 to 10. In more expensive restaurants it's always best to make a reservation. At festival time, most restaurants are open seven days a week and have generally more flexible late dining hours.

$$$$ ✕ **Bei Bruno.** A short walk from Schloss Mirabell, this intimate restaurant in the Bristol Hotel offers some of the best food in the city. Chef Bruno Plotegher specializes in fresh fish, simply prepared, and the menu changes frequently to showcase what's in season, such as the delicious *Steinpilze* (porcini mushrooms) and potato casserole. Look for sea bass in a champagne sauce with Chinese peas and spaghettini, or monkfish in a saffron sauce with potato ravioli and asparagus. There are also chicken, beef, and vegetarian dishes. Bei Bruno is a perfect choice for after-theater dining. Service is friendly and attentive. The restaurant is sometimes closed in winter months. ✉ *Makartpl. 4,* ☎ *0662/8485–11–861. Reservations essential. AE, DC, MC, V.*

$$$$ ✗ **Paris Lodron.** The restaurant in Schloss Mönchstein is a retreat into Old World elegance, with antique furniture, exquisite porcelain, and heavy, plated cutlery providing a wonderful contrast to the Austrian nouvelle cuisine. The chef specializes in fresh seafood creations and lamb, and the food is among the best Salzburg has to offer, with a frequently changing menu. The sophisticated ambience makes dining here an especially memorable experience. Opt for the tiny terrace in summer. It's very popular, especially at festival time. ⊠ *Mönchsberg 26,* ☎ *0662/ 848555–0. Reservations essential. Jacket and tie. AE, DC, MC, V.*

$$$$ ✗ **Pfefferschiff.** The "Pepper Ship" is the most acclaimed restaurant
★ in the city of Salzburg—even if it is 3 km (2 mi) northeast of the center. It is set in a pretty, renovated rectory adjacent to a pink-and-cream chapel. Klaus Fleishhaker, an award-winning chef, and his wife Petra make sure guests feel pampered in the country-chic atmosphere, which features polished wooden floors, antique hutches, and tables laden with fine bone china and Paloma Picasso silverware. The menu changes seasonally, but look for scampi tempura with asparagus and arugula, lobster crepes, or *Seeteufel* (monkfish) in an olive crust with pesto polenta. Lamb and duck are also offered. For dessert try the sublime rhubarb tartelette with buttermilk ice cream. A taxi is the least stressful way of getting here, but if you have your own car, drive along the north edge of the Kapuzinerberg toward Hallwang and then Söllheim. ⊠ *Söllheim 3, A–5300, Hallwang,* ☎ *0662/661242. Reservations essential. AE.*

$$$ ✗ **Zum Eulenspiegel.** Delicious food matches the unique setting in this
★ house, which is hundreds of years old. Tables, set with white linen, are in wonderful nooks and crannies reached by odd staircases. It's right in the middle of the Old City, and the staff speaks English. Try the potato goulash with chunks of sausage and beef in a creamy paprika sauce, or the house specialty, fish stew Provençal. These are served at lunch, or all day in the bar downstairs. ⊠ *Hagenauerpl. 2,* ☎ *0662/843180– 0. Reservations essential. AE, DC, MC, V. Closed Sun. except during festival, and Jan.–mid-Mar.*

$$ ✗ **Ährlich.** Just because this restaurant is all-organic, it doesn't mean it isn't fun. The dining room has a country casual ambience with cozy booths. Select from a tempting array of dishes such as *Kürbiscremesuppe* (pumpkin cream soup), *Welsfilet* (catfish in a paprika sauce), or lamb in an herb crust with rosemary ravioli. The fresh pumpkin ice cream is a fine way to top off the meal. ⊠ *Wolf-Dietrich-Str. 7,* ☎ *0662/ 871275. AE, DC, MC, V. Closed Sun. No lunch.*

$$ ✗ **Bistro Bio Terra.** Located inside the Rupertinum Galerie, this casual
★ vegetarian restaurant serves tasty dishes entirely free of animal products or preservatives. The chef takes Italian recipes and creates his own vegetarian versions. The blackboard menu changes daily, but look for bruschetta with a variety of toppings or arugula and grilled oyster mushrooms with a Parmesan-paprika puree. You could make an entire meal of the enticing antipasti. Several fresh fruit juices are also offered. The owners sometimes decide not to offer dinner at short notice during the winter months, so between October and March it's best to telephone before setting out. ⊠ *Philharmonikerg. 9,* ☎ *06222/849414. No credit cards. Closed Sun.–Mon.*

$$ ✗ **K+K am Waagplatz.** This upstairs restaurant is particularly pleasant, with white linen tablecloths, candles and flowers, and windows opening onto the street. Menu selections consist of locally caught fish, delicious chicken-breast medallions in a cheese crust with pasta and basil-tomato sauce, and lentil salad with strips of goose breast, as well as traditional Austrian dishes and game in season. Service is friendly. ⊠ *Waagpl. 2,* ☎ *0662/842156. AE, DC, MC, V.*

$$ ✗ **Stiftskeller St. Peter.** In what is said to be Europe's oldest Gasthaus, founded by Benedictine monks in the 9th century, choose between the

242

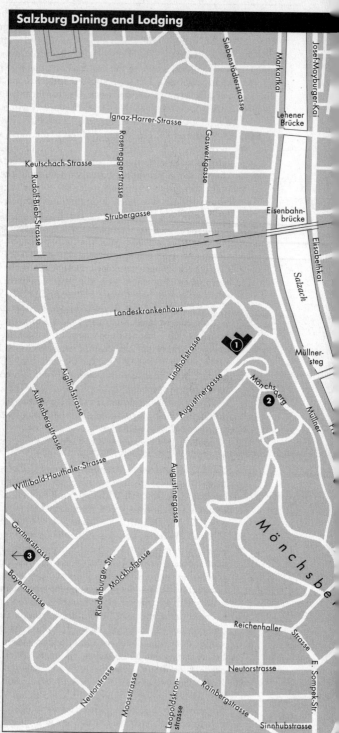

Salzburg Dining and Lodging

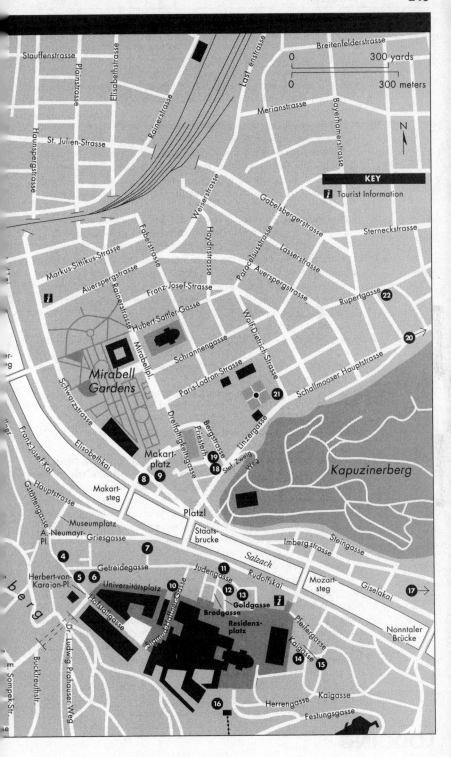

KEY

ℹ️ Tourist Information

0   300 yards

0   300 meters

Stauffenstrasse

Plainstrasse

Elisabethstrasse

Rainerstrasse

St. Julien-Strasse

Haunspergstrasse

Lastenstrasse

Merianstrasse

Breitenfelderstrasse

Bayerhamerstrasse

Weiserstrasse

Gabelsbergerstrasse

Sterneckstrasse

Markus-Sittikus-Strasse

Auerspergstrasse

Rainerstrasse

Fabekstrasse

Haydnstrasse

Paracelsusstrasse

Lasserstrasse

Franz-Josef-Strasse

Auerspergstrasse

ℹ️

Hubert-Sattler-Gasse

Mirabellpl.

Schrannengasse

Wolf-Dietrich-Strasse

Rupertgasse   **22**

20

Schwarzstrasse

Mirabell Gardens

Paris-Lodron-Strasse

Schallmooser Hauptstrasse

21

Kapuzinerberg

Elisabethkai

Franz-Josef-Kai

Dreifaltigkeitsgasse

Bergstrasse

Priesterh

Linzergasse

Stef. Zweig Weg

19

18

Makartplatz   **8**   **9**

Makartsteg

Hauptstrasse

Gstättengasse

Museumplatz

A.-Neumayr-Pl.

Griesgasse

Platzl

Staatsbrucke

Salzach

Steingasse

Imbergstrasse

7

Getreidegasse

Herbert-von-Karajan-Pl.   **5**   **6**

4

Universitätsplatz

Hofstallgasse

Sigmund-Haffner-Gasse

Judengasse

11

Rudolfskai

10

12   **13**

Goldgasse

Brodgasse

Residenzplatz

ℹ️

Mozartsteg

Giselakai

17

Nonntaler Brücke

Buckfreuthstr.

Dr.-Ludwig-Prahauser-Weg

E. Sompek-Str.

Pfeifergasse

Kaigasse

14   **15**

16

Herrengasse

Kaigasse

Festungsgasse

N

fairly elegant, dark wood-paneled Prälatenzimmer (Prelates' Room) or one of the several less formal rooms. Locals claim that Mephistopheles met Faust here. In summer, the dramatic gray-stone courtyard is a favorite. You'll find standards ranging from Wiener schnitzel to the delicate poached St. Peter's fish. Specialties include the *Klostertopf,* thick soup served in a loaf of bread, fish caught in local rivers and lakes, and, of course, Salzburger Nockerl. ⊠ *St. Peter Bezirk 4,* ☎ *0662/ 848481. AE, DC.*

$$ ✕ **Zipfer Bierhaus.** Arched ceilings, brick floors, flowered curtains, and wooden banquettes provide the right setting for good, standard local fare such as roast pork and dumplings, served with Zipfer beer, of course. This is one of Salzburg's oldest Gasthäuser; look down the ancient cistern in the passageway connecting the two main rooms. ⊠ *Sigmund-Haffner-G. 12/Universitätspl. 19,* ☎ *0662/840745. No credit cards. Closed Sun.*

$$ ✕ **Zum Mohren.** Good food, a central location by the river, a welcoming atmosphere, attentive service, and reasonable prices have made Zum Mohren very popular with both Salzburgers and tourists. The restaurant is in the cellar of a 15th-century house with polished copper pots adorning the walls. The menu is not overly adventuresome, but there are always several fish dishes and at least one vegetarian item among a selection of Austrian specialties like sautéed veal liver and roast hare. ⊠ *Judeng. 9/Rudolfskai 20,* ☎ *0662/842387. AE, MC, V. Closed Sun. and mid-June–mid-July.*

$ ✕ **Augustinerbräu.** Salzburg's homegrown version of a Munich beer house is at the north end of the Mönchsberg. You can bring your own food; pick up a stone jug of strong, frothy (not fizzy) beer; and sit down in the gardens or at a dark-wood table in one of the large halls. Shops in the huge monastery complex sell salads that can look a little weary late in the day, as well as sausage and fried chicken, and a little stall has tasty spirals of salted radish. If you don't feel up to cold beer, there's an old copper beer warmer in the main hall. ⊠ *Augustinerg. 4,* ☎ *0662/ 431246. No credit cards.*

$ ✕ **Ristorante Pizzeria al Sole.** Next to the Mönchsberg elevator, this Ital-
★ ian restaurant is owned by two friendly brothers who regularly travel over the border to Italy to bring back the freshest ingredients. Sit upstairs in a pretty room lined with Venetian prints or in the more casual downstairs area, then choose from a wide variety of scrumptious thincrust pizzas, such as Gorgonzola and sage or salmon with fresh mozzarella and basil. Pasta dishes are numerous and delicious, and may include tagliatelle with grilled shrimp or penne with tuna and capers. Be sure to end with *sorbetto di limone*—a refreshing concoction of lemon sorbet, *prosecco* (Italian sparkling wine), and a dash of vodka, served in a champagne glass. ⊠ *Gstätteng. 15,* ☎ *0662/843284. AE, DC, MC, V.*

$ ✕ **Zum Fidelen Affen.** The name means "At the Faithful Ape," which explains the ape motifs in this popular Gasthaus, dominated by a round copper-plated bar and stone pillars under a vaulted ceiling. Besides the beer on tap, the kitchen offers tasty Austrian dishes, such as *Schlutzkrapfen,* Tyrolean cheese ravioli with a light topping of chopped fresh tomatoes and basil, spinach spätzle in a ham and cheese gratiné, or a big salad with strips of fried chicken in a pumpkin-seed-oil dressing. The soft, warm pretzels are especially good. ⊠ *Priesterhausg. 8,* ☎ *0662/877361. Reservations essential. DC, MC, V. Closed Sun. No lunch.*

LODGING

It is difficult for a Salzburg hotel not to have a good location—you can find a room with a stunning view over the Kapuzinerberg or Gaisberg or one that simply overlooks a lovely Old City street. Many hostelries are charmingly decorated in *Bauernstil*—the rustic, peasant-luxe look of Old Austria. Note that many hotels in the Old City have to be accessed via footpower, as cars are not permitted on many streets. If you have a car, of course, you may opt to do what many do—find a hotel or converted castle on the outskirts of the city. Needless to say, if you're planning to come at festival time, you must book as early as possible. If you don't have a reservation, go to one of the tourist information offices or the accommodations service (*Zimmernachweis*) on the main platform of the railway station.

$$$$ 🏨 **Bristol.** No two rooms are alike in this luxurious turn-of the-century hotel, which has great views of the river and fortress. In the last couple of years all rooms have been completely renovated with great care in a unique and sumptuous style and feature marble bathrooms and all the little extras. The staff is especially friendly. Added bonuses are its close proximity to both the Old City and Schloss Mirabell, buffet breakfast, and the excellent restaurant, Bei Bruno (☞ Dining, *above*). ⊠ *Makartpl. 4, A–5020,* ☎ *0662/873557,* ℻ *0662/873557–6. 60 rooms. Restaurant, bar. AE, DC, MC, V. Closed Jan.–Feb.* 🐾

$$$$ 🏨 **Goldener Hirsch.** The "Golden Stag" has the best location of all Salzburg's luxury hotels: just down the street from Mozart's Birthplace. Rooms in this nearly 600-year-old town house have a simple, rustic charm with bright rag rugs; the stag motif is everywhere, even on lamp shades, which were hand-painted by an Austrian countess. Breakfast is not included in the room price. ⊠ *Getreideg. 37, A–5020,* ☎ *0662/8084–0,* ℻ *0662/848511–845. 70 rooms. 2 restaurants, bar, parking (fee). AE, DC, MC, V.* 🐾

$$$$ 🏨 **Österreichischer Hof.** The clientele at this beautiful hotel on the bank
★ of the Salzach River has ranged from the Beatles and the Rolling Stones to, more recently, Hillary and Chelsea Clinton. It's owned by the Gürtler family, who also own the famous Hotel Sacher in Vienna. Each room is different, but all are exquisitely decorated, with care and attention given to every possible whim or need, and the staff is warm and friendly. The danger here is that the rooms are so lovely and comfortable you won't want to leave to explore the city. Room prices include a delicious buffet breakfast, including Sekt (Austrian sparkling wine). In nice weather tables are set outside on the terrace where you can enjoy a salad or hamburger (called a "Salzburger") for lunch while gazing across at the fortress. ⊠ *Schwarzstr. 5–7, A–5020,* ☎ *0662/88977,* ℻ *0662/88977–14. 120 rooms. 3 restaurants, bar, exercise room, meeting rooms. AE, DC, MC, V.* 🐾

$$$$ 🏨 **Schloss Mönchstein.** This palatial mountain retreat is in its own mag-
★ ical world with gardens and hiking trails, yet just minutes from the city center. Within these ancient, ivy-covered walls is a treasure trove of lovely, luxurious rooms, some hung with tapestries and others with views of the woods and Salzburg in the distance. Service is pleasant and discreet, and the Paris Lodron restaurant is the epitome of Old World elegance (☞ Dining, *above*). The castle has its own wedding chapel, which is particularly popular with American and Japanese couples. Getting in and out of town calls for a car or taxi, unless you are willing to negotiate steps or take the nearby Mönchsberg elevator, which is about an eight-minute walk away. ⊠ *Mönchsberg 26, A–5020,* ☎ *0662/848555–0,* ℻ *0662/848559. 17 rooms. Restaurant, bar, café, tennis court, chapel, free parking. AE, DC, MC, V.* 🐾

$$$ 🏨 **Kasererbräu.** A variety of tastes went into designing this hotel, resulting in a mixture of kitsch and elegance. The public rooms are decorated with antiques and Oriental carpets; some of the guest rooms have sleigh beds or pretty carved and handpainted headboards, while others are more plainly decorated. Apart from the friendly staff, the hotel has two big advantages: it's right next to Mozartplatz and it has pleasant sauna and steam-bath facilities included in the price. ⊠ *Kaig. 33, A–5020,* ☎ *0662/842445–0,* FAX *0662/842445–51. 43 rooms. Sauna, parking fee. AE, DC, MC, V. Closed early Feb.–early Mar.*.

$$$ 🏨 **Rosenvilla.** A haven of peace and tranquillity, this upscale bed and breakfast in a suburban villa is located across the Salzach River from the Altstadt. Rooms are a mixture of contemporary furniture and French Empire accents, with pretty fabrics and lots of light; some have balconies overlooking a lawn. A special three-day offer includes dinner at the owners' top-ranked restaurant, Pfefferschiff (☞ Dining, *above*), which is a great value. The Rosenvilla is a 15-minute walk from the center, or you can take Bus 49, which runs every 10 minutes. ⊠ *Höfelg. 4, A–5020,* ☎ *0662/621765,* FAX *0662/6252308. 15 rooms. Parking. AE.* 🐾

$$–$$$ 🏨 **Blaue Gans.** In the past couple of years the "Blue Goose" has un-
★ dergone a total overhaul, and the result couldn't be more appealing. Care has been taken to keep its Old World charm intact, and the ancient wood beams, winding corridors, and low archways add to the fun. Guest rooms are spacious and have contemporary furnishings, whitewashed walls with cheeky framed posters, and cheerful curtains; a few have skylights. The popular restaurant serves local variations of Austrian dishes, such as *Spinatschlutzkrapfen* (spinach and goat cheese ravioli). Stepping straight out onto Getreidegasse, with Mozart's Birth-place just a few houses away, makes this 500-year-old hotel a top choice, so make reservations well in advance. ⊠ *Getreideg. 43, A–5020,* ☎ *0662/841317,* FAX *0662/841317–9. 44 rooms. Restaurant, bar, parking. AE, DC, MC, V.* 🐾

$$–$$$ 🏨 **Weisse Taube.** A traditional family-run hotel, close to the Mozart-platz, the "White Dove" is a good choice and centrally located. The 14th-century house, with its uneven floors and ancient stone archways, is a historic property, though the rooms are furnished plainly, with dark-wood accents. Several no-smoking rooms are available, and the main section of the breakfast room is also no-smoking. The staff is friendly and helpful. ⊠ *Kaig. 9, A–5020,* ☎ *0662/842404,* FAX *0662/841783. 33 rooms. Bar, no-smoking rooms, meeting room. AE, DC, MC, V. Closed 2 wks in Jan.*

$$–$$$ 🏨 **Wolf Dietrich.** Guest rooms in this small, family-owned hotel, set across
★ the river from the Altstadt, are elegantly decorated (some with Laura Ashley fabrics) and have extra amenities, such as VCRs (they stock *The Sound of Music*) and attractive sitting areas. Those in the back look out over the looming Gaisberg and the cemetery of St. Sebastian (☞ Exploring Salzburg, *above*). The staff is exceptionally warm and helpful. ⊠ *Wolf-Dietrich-Str. 7, A-5020,* ☎ *0662/871275,* FAX *0662/882320. 30 rooms. Restaurant, indoor pool, parking. AE, DC, MC, V.* 🐾

$ 🏨 **Bergland.** Just about a 10-minute walk from the train station, this cheer-ful, pleasant family-owned pension offers modern, comfortable rooms with breakfast included in the price. The sitting room features an English library. ⊠ *Rupertg. 15, A–5020,* ☎ *0662/872318.* FAX *0662/872318–8. 17 rooms, 15 with bath. No credit cards. Closed late Oct.–Dec. 20.* 🐾

$ 🏨 **Haus Kernstock.** This modest alpine chalet near the airport is at the end of a cul-de-sac in a pretty setting. Rooms have a cheerful, home-spun touch, and the breakfast is ample, featuring homemade jams. Frau Kernstock has two bikes that she lends for exploring the countryside, and she'll also meet you at the bus stop if you let her know in advance. ⊠ *Karolingerstr. 29, A-5020,* ☎ *0662/827469,* FAX *0662/827469. 5 rooms. MC, V. From city, Bus 27, Kugelhof stop; from train station, Bus 77, Karolingerstr. stop.*

$ 🏨 **Schwarzes Rössl.** Once a favorite with Salzburg regulars, this tradi-tional Gasthof now serves as student quarters for most of the year but is well worth booking when available. Rooms are fresh and immaculate, if not charming, and the location is excellent—close to the night-time action. ⊠ *Priesterhausg. 6, A–5020,* ☎ *0662/874426,* ☎ *01/401–76–20. 51 rooms with bath. AE, DC, MC, V. Closed Oct.–June.*

NIGHTLIFE AND THE ARTS

The Arts

Information and Tickets

Information and tickets for the main Salzburg Festival (late July–August), the Easter Festival (early April), and the Pentecost Concerts (late May) can be obtained from **Salzburger Festspiele** (⊠ Hofstallg. 1, A–5020 Salzburg, ☎ 0662/8045–579; 0662/8045–361 for Easter Festival, FAX 0662/8045–760; 0662/8045–790 for Easter Festival,). You must reserve well in advance. Any office of the Salzburg Tourist Office (☞ Visitor Information *in* Salzburg A to Z, *below*) and most hotel concierge desks can provide schedules for all arts performances, and you can find listings in the daily newspaper *Salzburger Nachrichten.*Tickets can be purchased directly at the box office, at your hotel, via the **Salzburg Ticket Service** (⊠ Mozartpl. 5, ☎ 0662/840310, FAX 0662/842476), or at a ticket agency like **Polzer** (⊠ Residenzpl. 3, ☎ 0662/846500, FAX 0662/840150) or **American Express** (⊠ Mozartpl. 5, ☎ 0662/8080–0, FAX 0662/8080–9).

Music

There is no shortage of concerts in this most musical of cities. The Salzburg Palace Concerts, the Fortress Concerts, and the Mozart Serenades take place year-round. In addition, there are the Easter Festival, the Pentecost Concerts, Mozart Week (January 24–February 2), and the Salzburg Cultural Days (October). Mozart Week is always special; in recent seasons, Nicholas Harnoncourt, Carlo Maria Giulini, and John Eliot Gardiner have conducted the Vienna Philharmonic.

For jazz, check **Jazzclub Live Salzburg** (⊠ Urbankeller, Schallmooser Hauptstr. 50, ☎ 0662/646424) for its Friday events. The **Rockhaus** (⊠ Schallmooser Hauptstr. 46, ☎ 0662/884914) has live music on Monday nights in a 400-year-old cellar.

Opera

The great opera event of the year is, of course, the **Salzburg Festival** (☞ Information and Tickets, *above*). The season at the **Landestheater** (⊠ Schwarzstr. 22, ☎ 0662/871512–21, FAX 0662/871512–70) runs from September to June. New productions in 2001 will include Strauss's *Die Fledermaus,* Puccini's *Tosca,* and the musical *Victor/Victoria.* You may place ticket orders by telephone Monday and Saturday 10–2, Tuesday–Friday 10–5.

The delightful, acclaimed **Marionettentheater** (⊠ Schwarzstr. 24, ☎ 0662/872406–0, FAX 0662/882141) is also devoted to opera, with a particularly renowned production of *Così fan tutte* to its credit, and gives performances during the first week of January, during Mozart Week (late January), from May through September, and after December 25. Tickets usually range from AS250 to AS500. The box office is open Monday to Saturday 9–1 and two hours before the performance.

Theater

The Salzburg Festival famously performs Hugo von Hofmannsthal's morality play *Jedermann* (in German) annually in the forecourt of the city cathedral (⊠ Salzburger Festspiele, Postfach 140, ☎ 0662/8045–579, FAX 0662/8045–579–760,). Customarily, the festival features the Vienna Philharmonic, but other orchestras can be expected to take leading roles as well.

Nightlife

Bars/Nightclubs

Bazillus (✉ Imbergstr. 2a, ☎ 0662/871631) is small, scruffy, and makeshift, but very cool; it's open daily 11 AM–1 AM. **Chez Roland** (✉ Giselakai 15, ☎ 0662/874335) is the haunt of "loden-preppies," or the wealthy and stylish young, and is open Monday–Saturday 6 PM–1 AM. **Seitensprung** (✉ Steing. 11, ☎ 0662/881377), which means "having someone on the side," is an elegant cocktail bar with food, open daily 8 PM–3 AM. **Shamrock Irish Pub** (✉ Rudolfskai 12, ☎ 0662/841610) attracts the young crowd and is always packed. Guinness is on tap. One of Salzburg's most popular bars is **Vis à Vis**, which resembles a '60s nightclub with its cavelike atmosphere (✉ Judeng. 13, ☎ 0662/841290); it's open daily 7 PM–3 AM.

Casino

Salzburg's **Casino** (☎ 0662/854455, FAX 0662/854455–16) is a bit out of the center in the posh Schloss Klessheim. A free shuttle bus will pick you up hourly at Anton-Neumayr-Platz from 2:30 to 11:30 PM or from Mirabellplatz, hourly from 2:40 to 11:40 PM. The return shuttle departs the casino at 3 PM, continuing on the hour until midnight. Admission is free. It's open daily from 3 to 3 AM (except November 1 and 2 and December 24). Men must wear a jacket and tie. Remember to take your passport.

Discos

Jexx (✉ Gstätteng. 7, ☎ 0662/844181) is large, has a youngish crowd, and goes for the American market; it's open daily 9 PM–4 AM. **Half Moon** (✉ Anton-Neumayr-Pl. 5, ☎ 0662/840074) caters to yuppies and beautiful people and is open daily 10 PM–4 AM. The local disco scene has become more volatile, so check with the tourist office for the current best attractions.

OUTDOOR ACTIVITIES AND SPORTS

Bicycling

The Hellbrunner Allee out to Hellbrunn Palace and the Almkanal path out past Leopoldskron Palace are two of the nicest and least strenuous routes. The tourist office has maps of cycle paths, and rentals are available (☞ Getting Around *in* Salzburg A to Z, *below*).

Fishing

There is plenty of fishing around Salzburg, largely for trout, carp, and pike. The season runs from May to December. Day licenses are available for around AS250, depending on season and waters, from **Sport Rehm** (✉ Rudolf-Biebl-Str. 5a, ☎ 0662/435751), **Sporthaus Markus Maier** (✉ Rainerstr. 2, ☎ 0662/871441), or **Starfish** (✉ Auerspergstr. 10, ☎ 0662/877000).

Golf

The **Golf and Country Club Salzburg** (✉ Schloss Klessheim, Salzburg-Klessheim, ☎ 0662/850851), just west of the city, is a 9-hole course at Klessheim castle. Take the A1 freeway to the Klessheim exit.

Skiing

In the immediate vicinity of Salzburg, it is possible to ski down the **Gaisberg** or the **Untersberg,** though these may not be ski runs to please the expert. A cable car from St. Leonhard (about 13 km, or 8 mi, south of Salzburg) takes you up 6,020 ft right to the top of the Untersberg (✉ Untersbergbahn, ☎ 06246/72477). You can ski down, arriving in the village of Fürstenbrunn, where taxis or buses take you back to St. Leonhard. Cross-country skiing is possible on the **Hellbrunner Allee**

(✉ Hellbrunn, ☏ 0662/820372), and around the **Gaisberg** (Rauchen-bühelhütte).

Skis can be rented at **Sporthaus Markus Maier** (✉ Rainerstr. 2, ☏ 0662/871441). For **snow reports** in winter (in German), call ☏ 0662/1584.

Swimming

The **Paracelsus-Kurhaus** (✉ Auerspergstr. 2, ☏ 0662/883544) has a large swimming pool with a sauna and Turkish bath. There are several outdoor pools: try **Freibad Alpenstrasse** (☏ 0662/620832), which you can reach on Bus 3; **Freibad Leopoldskron** (✉ Leopoldskronerstr. 50, ☏ 0662/829265); or **Freibad Volksgarten** (Hermann-Bahr-Promenade 2, ☏ 0662/623183–0), which you can reach via Bus 6 or 49.

Tennis

Salzburg has plenty of courts, although not in the center of town. The best tennis clubs are **Salzburger Tenniscourts-Süd** (✉ Berchtesgadner Str. 35, ☏ 0662/820326), which you can reach via Bus 5; **Tennishalle Liefering** (✉ Unter der Leiten/Lieferinger Spitz, ☏ 0662/432197), which you can reach on Bus 29; and **Tennisklub Salzburg** (✉ Ignaz-Rieder-Kai 3, ☏ 0662/622403), which you can reach on Bus 6 or 49.

SHOPPING

For a small city, Salzburg has a wide range of stores. The specialties are traditional clothing, like lederhosen and loden coats, jewelry, glassware, handicrafts, confectionery, dolls in native costume, Christmas decorations, sports equipment, and silk flowers. A *Gewürzsträussl* is a bundle of whole spices bunched and arranged to look like a bouquet of flowers (try the markets on the Universitätsplatz). At Christmas there is a special Advent market on the Domplatz. Stores are generally open weekdays 8–6 and Saturday 8–noon. Many stores stay open until 5 on the first Saturday of the month and on Saturday during the festival and before Christmas. Some supermarkets stay open until 8 on Thursday or Friday. Only shops in the railway station, the airport, and near the general hospital are open on Sunday.

Shopping Streets

The most fashionable specialty stores and gift shops are to be found along Getreidegasse and Judengasse and around Residenzplatz. Linzergasse, across the river, is less crowded and good for more practical items. There are also interesting antiques shops and jewelry workshops in the medieval buildings along Steingasse and in the Goldgasse.

Specialty Stores

Antiques

Along Gstättengasse you'll find, among others, **Kirchmayer** (✉ Gstätteng. 3, ☏ 0662/842219–0), **Marianne Reuter** (✉ Gstätteng. 9, ☏ 0662/842136), **Peter Paul Burges** (✉ Goldg. 12, ☏ 0662/848115), and **Schöppl** (✉ Gstätteng. 5, ☏ 0662/842154). For an amazing assortment of secondhand curiosities, try **Trödlerstube** (✉ Linzerg. 50, ☏ 0662/871453). An annual antiques fair takes place from Palm Sunday to Easter Monday in the state rooms of the Residenz.

Confectionery

If you're looking for the kind of *Mozartkugeln* (chocolate marzipan confections) you can't buy at home, try the two stores that claim to have discovered them: **Konditorei Fürst** (✉ Brodg. 13, ☏ 0662/843759–0) and **Konditorei Schatz** (✉ Getreideg. 3, Schatz passageway, ☏ 0662/842792).

Crafts

Fritz Kreis (⊠ Sigmund-Haffner-G. 14, ☎ 0662/841768) sells ceramics, wood carvings, handmade glass objects, and so on. **Salzburger Heimatwerk** (⊠ Residenzpl. 9, ☎ 0662/844110–0) has clothing, fabrics, ceramics, and local handicrafts at good prices. **Christmas in Salzburg** (⊠ Judeng. 10, ☎ 0662/846784) has rooms of gorgeous Christmas tree decorations, some hand-painted and hand-carved. **Gehmacher** (⊠ Alter Markt 2, ☎ 0662/846842) offers whimsical home decoration items.

Galleries

Salzburg is a good place to buy modern paintings, and there are several galleries on Sigmund-Haffner-Gasse. One of the best known, which also has an exhibition gallery plus a tiny coffee bar, is **Galerie Welz** (⊠ Sigmund-Haffner-G. 16, ☎ 0662/841771–0).

Jewelry

For exquisite costume jewelry and antique pieces, go to **Anton Koppenwallner** (⊠ Klampfererg. 2, ☎ 0662/841298–0), **Paul Koppenwallner** (⊠ Alter Markt 7, ☎ 0662/842617; ⊠ Universitätspl. 4, ☎ 0662/841449), or **Gerhard Lährm** (⊠ Getreideg. 27, ☎ 0662/843477–0), which is somewhat more expensive. **Franz Moltner** (⊠ Getreideg. 14, ☎ 0662/348116) offers costume jewelry, including lovely Fabergé eggs that can be attached to a necklace. Explore the **Schmuckpassage** (Jeweler's Passageway), which joins buildings between Universitätsplatz and Getreidegasse.

Men's Clothing

Men's outfitters are everywhere; the best are **Adriano** (⊠ Getreideg. 3, ☎ 0662/848774) and **Resmann M Exclusiv** (⊠ Getreideg. 25, ☎ 0662/843214–0).

Traditional Clothing

Dschulnigg (⊠ Griesg. 8, ☎ 0662/842376–0) is a favorite among Salzburgers for lederhosen, dirndls, and *Trachten,* the typical Austrian costume with white blouse, print skirt, and apron. For an enormous range of leather goods, some made to order, try **Jahn-Markl** (⊠ Residenzpl. 3, ☎ 0662/842610). **Lanz** (⊠ Schwarzstr. 4, ☎ 0662/874272) sells a wide selection of long dirndls, silk costumes, and loden coats. **Madl am Grünmarkt** (⊠ Universitätspl. 12, ☎ 0662/845457) has more flair and elegance in its traditional designs. A more specialized place, selling wool and silk shawls and chamois-leather skirts and waistcoats, is **Wacht** (⊠ Griesg. 7, ☎ 0662/841622).

Women's Clothing

If dirndls are not your style, try **Adriano** (⊠ Getreideg. 3, ☎ 0662/848774, **La Femme** (⊠ Griesg. 21, ☎ 0662/845203), or **Resmann Couture** (⊠ Rudolfskai 6, ☎ 0662/841213–0).

SALZBURG A TO Z

Arriving and Departing

By Car

The fastest routes to Salzburg are the autobahns. From Vienna (320 km/198 mi), take A1; from Munich (150 km/93 mi, A8 (in Germany it's also E11); from Italy, A10. The only advantage to having a car in Salzburg is that you can get out of the city for short excursions or for cheaper accommodations. The Old City on both sides of the river is a pedestrian zone (except for taxis), and the rest of the city, with its narrow, one-way streets, is a driver's nightmare. A park-and-ride system covering the major freeway exits is being developed, and there are several underground garages throughout the city.

By Plane

Salzburg airport (✉ Innsbrucker Bundesstr. 96, ☎ 0662/851211), 4 km (2½ mi) west of the city center, is Austria's second-largest international airport. There are direct flights from London and other European cities, but not from the United States.

Americans can fly to Munich and take the 90-minute train ride to Salzburg. Alternatively, you can take a transfer bus from or to the Munich airport; in Salzburg the contact is **Salzburger Mietwagenservice** (✉ Ignaz-Harrer-Str. 79a, ☎ 0622/8161–0, ☒ 0622/436324).

Taxis are the easiest way to get downtown from the Salzburg airport; the ride costs around AS150 to AS170 and takes about 20 minutes. City Bus 77, which goes by the airport every 15 minutes, takes you to the train station (about 20 minutes), where you change to Bus 1, 5, 6, 51, or 55 for the city center. Alternatively, you can take Bus 77 four stops to Aiglhof (look for a Mobil gas station on the corner), cross the road, and take Bus 29 (every 10–15 minutes) to the center of town.

By Train

You can get to Salzburg by rail from most European cities, arriving at **Salzburg Hauptbahnhof** (✉ Südtirolerpl., ☎ 0662/1717, a 20-minute walk from the center of town in the direction of Mirabellplatz. A taxi should take about 10 minutes and cost AS75. **Train information** is available by phone (☎ 0662/1717); don't be put off by the recorded message in German—eventually, you will be put through to a real person who should be able to speak English. You can buy tickets at any travel agency or at the station. The bus station and the suburban railroad station are across the street. Major building works are still in progress in front of the station and hamper access.

Getting Around

The Old City, composed of several interconnecting squares and narrow streets, is best seen on foot. An excellent bus service covers the rest of the city. A tourist map (available for AS10 from tourist offices in Mozartplatz and the train station) shows all bus routes and stops; there's also a color-coded graphic public-transport-network map that's free, so you should have no problem getting around. Virtually all buses and trolleybuses (O-Bus) run via Mirabellplatz and/or Hanuschplatz.

By Bicycle

Salzburg is fast developing a network of bike paths as part of its effort to get cars out of the city. A detailed bicycle map with suggested tours (AS89) will help you get around.

Bikes can be rented year-round at the **Salzburg Hauptbahnhof** (railway station; ✉ Südtirolerpl., Counter 3, ☎ 0662/8887–3163), with savings for holders of that day's train tickets. You can rent a bike by the day or the week from **Shake & Snack** (✉ Kajetanerpl. 3–4, ☎ 0662/ 848168). Also check **VELOactive** (✉ Willibald-Hauthaler-Str. 10, ☎ 0662/435595, ☒ 0662/435595–22). It's best to call and reserve in advance; you will need to leave your passport or a deposit.

By Bus or Trolleybus

Single tickets bought from the driver cost AS20. Special multiple-use tickets, available at tobacconists (*Tabak-Trafik*), ticket offices (main office, ✉ Griesg. 21, ☎ 0662/4480), and tourist offices, are much cheaper. You can buy five single tickets for AS15 each (not available at tourist offices), a single 24-hour ticket for AS40, or five transferrable 24-hour tickets at AS32 each.

By Horse-Drawn Carriage

One of the most delightful ways to tour Salzburg is by horse-drawn carriage. Most of Salzburg's **Fiakers** are stationed in the Residenzplatz. In the Christmas season, large, decorated horse-drawn carts take people around the Christmas markets. ☎ *0662/844772;* ✉ *AS420 per Fiaker (up to 4 people) for 20 min, AS820 for 50 min, AS1,240 for 1 hr, 15 min, and AS1,640 for 1 hr, 40 min.*

By Taxi

There are taxi stands all over the city; for a radio cab, call 0662/8111. Taxi fares start at AS33. Limousines can be hired for AS800 to AS1,000 per hour (three-hour minimum) from **Salzburg Panorama Tours** (☎ 0662/883211, FAX 0662/871628).

Contacts and Resources

Changing Money

Banks are open weekdays 8–12:30 and 2–4:30. You can change money at the railway station in summer daily 7 AM–10 PM and in winter daily 7:30 AM–9 PM.

Consulates

The **U.S. consulate** (✉ Alter Markt 1/3, ☎ 0662/848776, FAX 0662/849777) is open Monday, Wednesday, and Friday 9–noon. The **U.K. consulate** (✉ Alter Markt 4, ☎ 0662/848133) is open weekdays 9–noon.

Doctors and Dentists

If you need a doctor or dentist, call the **Ärtztekammer für Salzburg** (✉ Bergstr. 4, ☎ 0662/871327–0); for emergency service on weekends and holidays, call the **Ärzte-Bereitschaftsdienst Salzburg-Stadt** (✉ Dr.-Karl-Renner-Str. 7, ☎ 0662/141).

The main **hospital** is the St. Johannsspital-Landeskrankenanstalten (✉ Müllner Hauptstr. 48, ☎ 0662/44820), just past the Augustinian Monastery heading out of town.

Emergencies

Police, ☎ 133. **Fire,** ☎ 122. For **ambulance** or medical emergency, ☎ 144.

English-Language Bookstores

American Discount (✉ Waagpl. 6, ☎ 0662/845640), the only English-language bookstore in Salzburg, concentrates on popular paperbacks and magazines. You can, however, find some books in English in most good bookstores. **Hintermayer** (✉ Goldg. 3, ☎ 0662/875754–1), sells discount paperbacks in English.

Guided Tours

Because the Old City is largely a pedestrian zone, bus tours do little more than take you past the major sights. You would do better seeing the city on foot unless your time is really limited.

DAY TOURS FROM VIENNA

American Express (✉ Kärntnerstr. 21–23, A–1010 Vienna, ☎ 01/515–40–0, FAX 01/515–40–70) and **Vienna Sightseeing Tours** (✉ Stelzhammerg. 4/11, A–1030 Vienna, ☎ 01/712–4683-0, FAX 01/714–1141) run one-day bus trips Tuesday and Saturday to Salzburg from Vienna; the AS1,300 fare includes a tour of the city, but not lunch. Also on Tuesday and Saturday, **Cityrama Sightseeing** (✉ Börseg. 1, A–1010 Vienna, ☎ 01/534–130, FAX 01/534–13–16) offers a similar tour.

ORIENTATION

Bob's Special Tours (✉ Kaig. 10, ☎ 0662/849511–0, FAX 0662/849512), **Salzburg Panorama Tours** (✉ Schranneng. 2/2, ☎ 0662/883211, FAX 0662/

871628), and **Albus/Salzburg Sightseeing Tours** (✉ Am Mirabellpl. 2, ☎ 0662/881616, FAX 0662/878776), conduct 1½- to 2-hour city tours. The desk clerks at most hotels will book for you and arrange hotel pickup. Depending on the number of people, the tour will be in either a bus or a minibus; if it's the former, a short walking tour is included, since large buses can't enter the Old City. Tours briefly cover the major sights in Salzburg, including Mozart's Birthplace, the festival halls, the major squares, the churches, and the palaces at Hellbrunn and Leopoldskron.

SOUND OF MUSIC TOURS

The **Sound of Music** tour (☞ Close-Up box, *above*) has been a staple of visits to Salzburg for the past 20 years and is still a special experience. All tour operators conduct one. The bus company actually featured in the film, Albus, offers a 3½-hour tour departing daily, which includes such sights as Anif Castle, Mondsee Church, and the little summerhouse in the gardens of Hellbrun. (✉ Mirabellpl. 2, ☎ 0662/881616, FAX 0662/633790). Some travelers say the most personal approach is found with **Bob's Special Tours** (☞ *above*).

WALKING

The tourist office's folder "Salzburg—The Art of Taking It All In at a Glance" describes a self-guided one-day walking tour that's marked on a map.

Pharmacies

In general, pharmacies are open weekdays 8–12:30 and 2:30–6, Saturday 8–noon. When they're closed, the name and location of a pharmacy that's open are posted on the door.

Travel Agencies

American Express (☎ 0662/8080–0, FAX 0662/8080–9) is next to the tourist office at Mozartplatz 5–7. **Columbus** is near the Mönchsberg (✉ Münzg. 1, ☎ 0662/842755–0, FAX 0662/842755–5) in the Old City.

Visitor Information

The **Salzburg City Tourist Office** (✉ Auerspergstr. 7, A–5024 Salzburg, ☎ 0662/88987–0, FAX 0662/88987–32) handles written and telephone requests for information. You can get maps, brochures, and information in person from **Information Mozartplatz** in the center of the Old City (✉ Mozartpl. 5) and from the **Railway Station** (✉ Platform 2A, ☎ 0662/88987–340).

Don't forget to consider purchasing the Salzburg Card. **SalzburgKarten** are good for 24, 48, or 72 hours at AS225, AS300, and AS390, respectively, and allow no-charge entry to most museums and sights, use of public transport, and special discount offers. Children under 15 pay half.

All the major highways into town have their own well-marked information centers: **Salzburg-Mitte** (✉ Münchner Bundesstr. 1, ☎ 0662/88987–350), open April–October, daily 9–7, and November–March, Monday–Saturday 11–5; **Salzburg-Süd** (✉ Park & Ride-Parkplatz, Alpensiedlung-Süd, Alpenstr. 67, ☎ 0662/88987–360), open November–March, Monday–Saturday 11–5, and April–October, daily 9–7; **Salzburg-West-Airport** (✉ Innsbrucker Bundesstr. 95, ☎ 0662/851211 or 0662/852091), open April–May and September–October, Monday–Saturday 9–6, and June–August, daily 9–7; **Salzburg-Nord** (✉ Autobahn, Kasern service facility, ☎ 0662/88987–370), open June–September, daily 9–7.

6 SALZKAMMERGUT

Remember the first five minutes of *The Sound of Music*? Castles fronting on water, mountains veiled by whipped-cream clouds, and flower-strewn valleys dotted with cool blue lakes: Austria in all its Hollywoodian splendor. Those scenes were filmed here, not far from where the von Trapp children "Do-Re-Mi"-ed. Nearby, visit the delightfully picturesque towns of St. Wolfgang, Bad Ischl, Hallstatt, and Fuschl and feel as though you were in an operetta—then discover Gosau, one of Austria's most beautiful lakes.

T HE TRIPS IN THIS CHAPTER reach heights both physical and spiritual. From the Schafberg, above St. Wolfgang, you can see just about every lake in the entire region, and in the pilgrimage church below, Michael Pacher's great, 16th-century winged altar, 10 years in the making, rises like a prayer. Ready your camera, dust off your supply of *wunderschöns*, and prepare for enchantment as you head into this compact quarter of Austria. The Lake District of Upper Austria, centered on the region called the Salzkammergut (literally, "salt estates"), presents the traveler with many such soaring mountains and needlelike peaks; a glittering necklace of turquoise lakes; forested valleys that are home to the *Rehe* (roe deer) immortalized by Felix Salten in *Bambi*—Austria at its most lush and verdant. Some of these lakes, like the Hallstätter See and Gosauer See, remain quite unspoiled, partly because the mountains act as a buffer from busier, more accessible sections of the country. Another—historic—reason relates to the presence of the salt mines, which date back to the Celtic era; with salt so common and cheap nowadays, we forget it was once a luxury item mined under strict government monopoly. The Salzkammergut was therefore closed to casual visitors for centuries, opening up only after Emperor Franz Josef I made it his official summer residence in 1854 and turned it into the "drawing room" of the Lake District. Lured by idyllic landscapes and cosmopolitanism, a host of prominent people from crowned heads and their ministers to artists of all stamp soon flocked regularly to Bad Ischl.

Updated by Bonnie Dodson

To the west of Bad Ischl are the best known of all the Salzkammergut's 27 lakes—the Wolfgangsee, the Mondsee, and the Attersee (*See* is German for "lake"). Not far beyond these lakes, the traveler will find one of Austria's loveliest spots, Gosau am Dachstein. Here the three Gosau lakes are backdropped by a spectacular sight that acts as a landmark for many leagues: the Dachstein peak. Baron Friedrich von Humboldt, the 19th-century biologist and traveler, called Gosau am Dachstein one of the most beautiful spots in the world, and few persons at that time had seen more of the world than he. It is not surprising that Gosau inspired Wagner while he was writing *Parsifal;* even today, Gosau remains a world's end, a place where people are content simply to drink in the view.

However, many activities beckon nearby. In summer, vacationers head for the lakes, streams, meadows, and woods for boating, fishing, swimming (the taller the lakeside peak, the colder the water), and stimulating pine-needle baths. A favorite passion for Austrians is *Das Wandern*, or hiking. The Lake District has many miles of marked trails, with lovely stretches around Bad Ischl—with more than 100 km (62 mi) of trails alone; the Attersee area, which has one great 35-km (22-mi) course that takes about 7½ hours to complete; the mountains in the Hallstatt and Altaussee/Bad Aussee areas; and Bad Aussee, with more than 150 km (93 mi) of trails. Cycling is also a growing sport and a fine way to see miles of landscape at a human pace and also take care of your fitness requirements. In winter, many come to the region to ski in the mountains of Salzburg Province and Styria. Within this pastoral perfection, you can stay in age-old *Schloss* hotels or modern villas. Many enticing restaurants have sprung up and shoppers come to buy the linens and ceramics, wood carvings, and painted glass of the region.

Pleasures and Pastimes

Dining

Fresh, local lake fish is on nearly every menu in the area, so take advantage of the bounty. The lakes and streams are home to several types of fish, notably trout, carp, and perch. They are prepared in a variety of ways, from plain breaded (*gebacken*), to smoked and served with *Kren* (horseradish), to fried in butter (*gebraten*). Look for *Reinanke,* a mild whitefish straight from the Hallstättersee. Sometimes at country fairs you will find someone charcoaling fresh trout wrapped in aluminum foil with herbs and butter: it's worth every schilling. *Knödel*—bread or potato dumplings usually filled with either meat or jam—are a nice specialty. Desserts are doughy as well, though *Salzburger Nockerl* consists mainly of air, sugar, and beaten egg whites. And finally, keep an eye out for seasonal specialties: in summer, the restaurants often serve chanterelle mushrooms (*Eierschwammerl*) with pasta, and in October it's time for delicious venison and game during the *Wildwochen* (game weeks).

Culinary shrines are to be found around Mondsee. However, in many of the towns of the Salzkammergut you'll find country inns with dining rooms but few independent restaurants, other than the occasional, very simple *Gasthaus*. Prices for meals include taxes and a service charge but not the customary small additional tip.

CATEGORY	COST*
$$$$	over AS500 (€36)
$$$	AS300–AS500 (€22–€36)
$$	AS200–AS300 (€14–€21)
$	under AS200 (€14)

per person for a typical three-course meal, with a glass of house wine

Lodging

In the grand old days, the aristocratic families of the region would take paying guests at their charming castles. Today, most of those castles have been, if you will, degentrified: they are now schools or very fine hotels. But you needn't stay in a castle to enjoy the Salzkammergut—there is a wide range of accommodations, ranging from luxurious lakeside resorts to small country inns or even guest houses without private baths; in most places, the *Herr Wirt,* his smiling wife, and his grown-up children will do everything to make you feel comfortable. While we cover the best in every category, note that every village, however small, has a Gasthaus or village inn. In peak summer season St. Wolfgang is packed, and you may find slightly less crowding and the same magnificent settings 3 km (2 mi) up the lake at Ried or back at Strobl.

Room rates include taxes and service and, almost always, breakfast, except in the most expensive hotels; it is wise to ask beforehand. It is customary to leave a small additional tip (AS20) for the chambermaid. Happily, these hotels do not put their breathtakingly beautiful natural surroundings on the bill.

CATEGORY	COST*
$$$$	over AS1,700 (€123)
$$$	AS1,200–AS1,700 (€87–€123)
$$	AS950–AS1,200 (€69–€86)
$	under AS950 (€69)

All prices are for a standard double room for two, including local taxes (usually 10%) and service (15%).

🕾 *following the text of a review is your signal that the property has a Web site, where you will find details and, usually, images; for a link, visit www.fodors.com/urls.*

Exploring the Salzkammergut

Whether you start out from Salzburg or set up a base in Bad Ischl—the heart of the Lake District—it's best to take in the beauties of the Salzkammergut in two separate courses: first around the Mondsee, the

Wolfgangsee, and Bad Ischl, and then south to the Hallstätter See, Gosau am Dachstein, then east to Bad Aussee and the Altausseer See, returning via the Pötschen mountain pass.

Numbers in the text correspond to numbers in the margin and on the Salzkammergut/Lake District map.

Great Itineraries

IF YOU HAVE 2 DAYS

Setting out early from Salzburg or Vienna, head to the core of the Lake District, **Bad Ischl** ⑤. Franz Lehár—the composer of so many operettas that glorified the region—had a vacation villa here, where he could rub elbows with other notables just as eager to holiday in Franz Josef's favorite getaway. After exploring the emperor's villa, a majestic manor in the warm "imperial" yellow so typical of Austria, created for his empress, Elisabeth—the immortal "Sisi"—stop in at Zauner (just as Franz Josef did) for some of the best pastry in Europe. Delicious, but beware: *two* to a person will be plenty. After quickly taking in this history-rich spa—today, it is one of the best equipped in Austria—head south on Route 145 toward Hallstatt. After Bad Goisern bear right past Au and then turn right over the bridge to cross the River Traun into Steeg (don't worry about the factory smokestack—it's an isolated affair in these parts). Traveling alongside the Hallstätter See, you will think you have made a magical detour into Norway: the lake, surrounded by towering peaks, almost looks like a fjord. Twenty-nine kilometers (18 mi) from Bad Ischl you'll come to a junction with Route 166. Here you should turn right into the ravine of the Gosaubach river. After heading through very scenic territory framed by steep wooded slopes for some 32 km (20 mi), you'll reach ☷ **Gosau am Dachstein** ⑦, which spreads out over a comfortable north–south valley, at the end of which lie the famous Gosau lakes. You have reached one of Austria's most beautiful spots. There are three lakes here, several miles apart from each other and all framed by the craggy heights of the Dachstein range. After taking in the views, spend the night in the village and awaken to a dazzling dawn glistening over the snow-swept Bischofsmütze peak.

Head back to Route 145 and south to **Hallstatt** ⑧, which, in addition to being the "world's prettiest lakeside village," is also the oldest settlement in Austria. After spending quality time with your Nikon (do your photography in the morning when the village is nicely lit), check out one of two natural wonders: the salt mines above Hallstatt (accessible by funicular or by a good one-hour walk) or, continuing around the southern end of the lake for 5 km (3 mi), the **Dachstein Ice Caves** ⑨ at Obertraun. Leaving Upper Austria, head for **Bad Aussee** ⑩ along the romantic old road that follows the Traun River. It is still in part covered with hand-hewn paving stones and has at one point an impressive gradient of 23% (closed in winter). After exploring the town's picturesque 15th- and 16th-century architecture, you should still have time for a stroll around neighboring **Altaussee** ⑪, whose romantic setting inspired so many artists and poets. Return to Bad Aussee, and then catch Route 145 north across the Pötschen pass to Bad Ischl, enjoying spectacular vistas along the way back.

IF YOU HAVE 4 DAYS

If you have a more leisurely schedule, you'll want to explore more of the Lake District, while still encompassing the itinerary outlined above. Start off by taking Route B158 from Salzburg, making a detour left toward Thalgau. After 5 km (3 mi) you'll reach Thalgau, and then a little farther on, the lake, where you'll go left to Route B154 and **Mondsee** ①, the gateway to the Salzkammergut. (You can also take the A1 Autobahn in the direction of Vienna, exiting at Mondsee.) Stroll along the

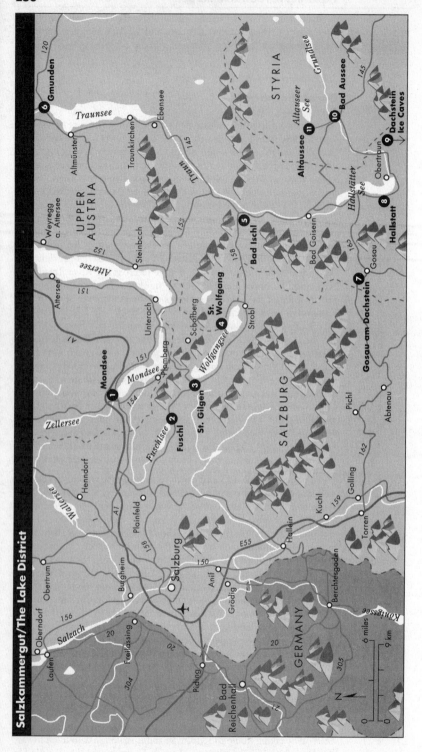

charming Marktplatz square full of lively cafés and restaurants, and the impressive St. Michael Parish Church, where Maria married Captain von Trapp in the *Sound of Music* movie. Back on Route 158, head for **Fuschl** ② and the famous Hotel Schloss Fuschl, overlooking the western tip of the Fuschlsee, former address of the prince-archbishops of Salzburg. This is an ideal spot for lunch (be sure to make reservations), as the dining room and terrace have grand vistas. Then it's back to Route 158 again, where a stop is in order at **St. Gilgen** ③. The town gets very crowded in summer, especially along the shore, which is lined with ice-cream parlors and souvenir shops. But the little house near the dock on Ischler Strasse, where Mozart's mother and sister were born, should be on your itinerary. From St. Gilgen head south on Route 158, bearing left toward Strobl, and then left again to drive along the eastern shore of the Abersee. The road bypasses the bulge of the lake, which consists mainly of campsites and very crowded beaches (one of which offers a beautiful view of St. Wolfgang). ▦ **St. Wolfgang** ④ is a town that all but clicks your camera shutter for you. For centuries it secretly harbored one of Austria's great art treasures, the great altarpiece by the late-Gothic wood-carver Michael Pacher, in the parish church. However, it was the inn—now Hotel Weisses Rössl (White Horse)—which stands near the dock, that spread the fame (and made the fortune) of this little Alpine town: It became the subject of a very popular operetta, *Im Weissen Rössl,* composed for the most part by Ralph Benatzky and premiered in Berlin in 1930. After an enchanting steamer trip on the lake, enjoy the popular excursion by rack rail to the top of the nearby Schafberg mountain; then return to St. Wolfgang for a dinner of trout *blau* (steamed) and an overnight stay. The next morning, backtrack to Strobl and then follow signs for Bad Ischl to join Route 158. **Bad Ischl** ⑤ is the unofficial "capital" of the region and was Emperor Franz Josef's old stomping grounds. Have lunch at one of the excellent recommended restaurants, then take in some of the town's sights. If you are doing a four-day tour of this region, Bad Ischl is the departure point for Gosau am Dachstein, as outlined above in the 2-day itinerary. After spending a day or two exploring the glories of Hallstatt and Altausseerland, return to Bad Ischl and go west to Salzburg—or if Vienna is your destination, take Route B145 north to ▦ **Gmunden** ⑥, at the top of the Traunsee. This is one of the prettiest drives in the Salzkammergut, taking you past many little lakeside villages, most notably tiny Traunkirchen, dramatically perched on a peninsula with a former Benedictine nunnery. In Gmunden take time to shop for local ceramics, board the steam-wheeler *Gisela* for a boat tour, or ride the cable car to the top of the Grünberg. Spend the night in Gmunden or continue north a short distance to the A1 autobahn, which will take you to Vienna or Salzburg.

When to Tour the Salzkammergut

Year-round, vacationers flock to the Lake District; however, late fall is the worst time to visit the region, for it is rainy and cold, and many sights are closed or operate only part-time. By far the best months are July and September. August, of course, sees the countryside overrun with visitors from the nearby Salzburg Music Festival (even so, who can resist a visit on to Bad Ischl on August 18, when Emperor Franz Josef's birthday is still celebrated). Another seasonal highlight is the annual Narcissus Festival held in May or June at Bad Aussee (the town is blanketed with flowers). Bad Aussee also has a special Carnival celebration (in February, with varying dates year to year), with men dressed as women and banging drums (the so-called *Trommelweiber*) on one day, then the *Flinserln* parading in costumes bedecked with silvery paillettes, on the next day. Others like to visit Hallstatt for its annual Corpus Christi procession across the lake.

ON THE ROAD TO ST. WOLFGANG AND BAD ISCHL

The mountains forming Austria's backbone may be less majestic than other Alps at this point, but they are also considerably less stern; glittering blue lakes and villages nestle safely in valleys without being under the constant threatening eye of an avalanche from the huge peaks. Here you'll find what travelers come to the Lake District for: elegant restaurants, Baroque churches, meadows with getaway space and privacy, lakeside cabanas, and forests that could tell a story or two.

Mondsee

❶ *35½ km (22 mi) east of Salzburg, 100 km (62 mi) southwest of Linz.*

Mondsee is the gateway to the Salzkammergut for many tourists and Salzburgers alike. *Mondsee* means "Moon Lake," a name whose origins are the subject of some debate. Some say this body of water (11 km/7 mi long and 2 km/1 mi wide), which vaguely resembles a moon crescent, was named after a prehistoric lunar deity, whereas others say it was named after a person. The Mondsee Monastery has its own story about a Bavarian duke being saved from falling into the lake water by a full moon that showed him a safe passage, after which he vowed to found a monastery. The water is warmer than in any other of the high-placed lakes, which makes it a good place for swimming, and Mondsee has some of the best dining the Salzkammergut has to offer. Most travelers first head for the town square to visit the marvelous Baroque twin-towered **Michaelerkirche** (St. Michael's), built in 1470. This is the largest parish church in Upper Austria, possibly because its original role was as the church of the 8th-century Benedictine monastery. It holds a special place in the hearts of many travelers, as they remember it as the church in which, in *The Sound of Music* film, Maria finally wed her Captain von Trapp.

Dining

$$$$ ✕ **Seehof.** At this lakeside restaurant, the terrace setting is idyllic, the cuisine excellent, and the range of Italian, French, and Austrian wines comprehensive. Dining choices range more toward Austrian standards; specialties include venison on a bed of sauerkraut, spring lamb, and fish fresh from the lake. Located in the huge park of the Seehof Hotel, this restaurant is a favorite of Mondseers in the know. ⊠ *Au 30, Loibichl-Mondsee,* ☎ *06232/5031–0,* ℻ *06232/5031–51. Reservations essential. AE, DC, MC, V. Closed mid-Sept.–mid-May.*

Outdoor Activities and Sports

GOLF
The **Golfclub am Mondsee** (⊠ St. Lorenz 50, ☎ 06232/38350, ℻ 06232/3835–83) has 18 holes and a par-72. Call for information about fees. The course is open March–November.

Fuschl

❷ *20 km (12 mi) south of Mondsee, 30½ km (19 mi) east of Salzburg.*

Fuschl is so close to Salzburg that many visitors to the Salzburger Festspiele choose to stay in a hotel here, enjoying urban comforts while savoring rural pleasures at the same time. Located on Route 158, the town is on the Fuschlsee, a gem of a very clear small lake with bluish-green deep water ideal for swimming, surrounded by a nature preserve. There's not much to do in Fuschl, the beaches being very limited in number—though those willing to hike can reach an extremely narrow strip on the northern shore, which is especially popular with nudists. The town of Fuschl, however, boasts many good places to eat and spend the night, including Schloss Fuschl, one of the finest establishments in the Salzkammergut.

Dining and Lodging

$$$$ ✗ **Brunnwirt.** You'll have to knock to be admitted, but once inside, you'll find elegantly set tables in this atmospheric 15th-century house. Frau Brandstätter presides over a kitchen that turns out good-size portions of excellent Austrian and regional dishes. You might be offered game (in season) or roast lamb, but always with a light touch. Fish fresh from the lake is a regular specialty. ⊠ *Brunn 8,* ☎ *06226/8236,* ⅁⅄ *06226/ 8236. Reservations essential. Jacket and tie. AE, DC, MC, V. Closed Mon. No lunch except Sun. and during Salzburg Festival wks.*

$$$$ 🏨 **Schloss Fuschl.** Just 16 km (10 mi) from Salzburg, this 15th-century
★ castle was built as a hunting lodge for the city's prince-bishops. It was later owned by Joachim von Ribbentrop, Hitler's foreign minister, before it became a hotel in the 1950s. Ringed by mountains and on three sides by the pristine Fuschlsee, it has one of the most magical settings in Austria. Suites and superior rooms are regally splendid, and though the standard rooms are more modern, most have spectacular views of the lake. In fine weather, dining is outdoors on the beautiful stone terrace. The cuisine is given a five-star presentation, but many dishes are instantly forgettable. Opt for the smoked fish or the delicacies just caught from the Fuschlsee, which is unpolluted by motorboats. One of the house specialties is a delicate smoked trout from the smokehouse on the premises. ⊠ *A–5322 Hof bei Salzburg,* ☎ *06229/2253–0,* ⅁⅄ *06229/2253–531. 62 rooms, 22 apartments. Restaurant, pool. AE, DC, MC, V.* 🐾

St. Gilgen

❸ *10 km (6 mi) south of Fuschl, 34 km (21 mi) east of Salzburg.*

Rather overbuilt around the edges and overwhelmed by an invasion of foreign visitors, the center of St. Gilgen remains pleasant enough. All the local color left to St. Gilgen comes from its indirect musical ties: A Mozart fountain in the town square commemorates the fact that Mozart's mother and sister Nannerl were both born here, in a little house near the dock on Ischler Strasse. The town features a nice beach, the northernmost on the Wolfgansee.

Dining and Lodging

$$ ✗ **Grossgasthof Kendler.** St. Gilgen is a rather basic place when it comes to food, and the right place for a homey Salzkammergut experience is the big and friendly Kendler, right in the middle of town. It does its own butchering, so the meat is always fresh (lamb kebabs, venison in season, pork dishes), but the trend is also toward lighter foods, including good salads and spinach dumplings. The Kendler also has a guest house. ⊠ *Kirchenpl. 3, A–5340,* ☎ *06227/2223,* ⅁⅄ *06227/720390. 40 rooms. Restaurant, sauna, steam room, exercise room. DC, MC. Closed early Nov.–mid-Dec.*

$$ ✗🏨 **Hotel Gasthof zur Post.** This house, one of the most attractive in town, dates from 1415. The rooms are contemporary and have modern baths. The restaurant emphasizes regional fare; try the cream of garlic soup or the boiled beef. ⊠ *Mozartpl. 8, A–5340,* ☎ *06227/2157,* ⅁⅄ *06227/2157–600. 15 rooms, some with bath. Restaurant, sauna. AE, DC, MC, V. Closed early Nov.–early Dec.*

$$$–$$$$ 🏨 **Parkhotel Billroth.** This elegant villa, decorated in turn-of-the-century style, is set in a huge park 10 minutes from the town center but close to the lake. The house is pleasantly worn at the edges yet spaciously arranged and luxuriously appointed, with a fine dining room. Sun terraces are particularly inviting. ⊠ *Billrothstr. 2, A–5340,* ☎ *06227/*

2217, FAX 06227/2218–25. *44 rooms. Restaurant, bar, massage, sauna, tennis court, exercise room, beach, boating. AE, V. Closed Oct.–May.*

Outdoor Activities and Sports
SKIING

St. Gilgen/Zwölferhorn (⊠ St. Gilgen, A–5340, ☎ 06227/2348, FAX 06227/72679) has two runs totaling 10 km (7 mi) for ski experts, while **Strobl/Postalm** (⊠ Strobl, A–5350, ☎ 06137/6255, FAX 06137/5958) offers family-style skiing with 12 km (8 mi) of runs. Both Postalm and St. Gilgen also offer a ski school.

St. Wolfgang

④ *19 km (12 mi) east of St. Gilgen, 50 km (31 mi) east of Salzburg.*

A delightful way of entering the picture-book town of St. Wolfgang is to leave your car at Strobl, at the southern end of the Wolfgangsee, and take one of the steamers that ply the waters of the lake. Strobl itself is a delightful setting, but not as fashionable as St. Wolfgang; if you prefer a quiet vacation base, this may be its attraction for you. Between St. Wolfgang and Strobl, the Wolfgangsee still retains its old name of "Abersee." One of the earliest paddleboats on the lake is still in service, a genuine 1873 steamer called the *Kaiser Franz Josef.* Service is regular from May to mid-October. The view of the town against the dramatic mountain backdrop is one you'll see again and again on posters and postcards. If you decide to drive all the way to town, be prepared for a crowd. Unless your hotel offers parking, you'll have to park on the fringes of town and walk a short distance, as the center is a pedestrian-only zone.

The town has everything: swimming and hiking in summer, skiing in winter, and natural feasts for the eye at every turn. Here, you will find yourself in the Austria of operetta. Indeed, St. Wolfgang became known round the world thanks to the inn called **Weisses Rössl** (☞ Dining and Lodging, *below*), which was built right next to the landing stage in 1878. It featured prominently in a late-19th-century play, which achieved fame as an operetta by Benatzky in 1930. Ironically, the two original playwrights, Gustav Kadelburg and Oskar Blumenthal, had another Weisses Rössl in mind.

You shouldn't miss seeing Michael Pacher's great altarpiece in the 16th-century **Wallfahrtskirche** (pilgrimage church) one of the finest examples of late-Gothic woodcarving to be found anywhere. This 36-ft masterpiece took 10 years (1471–81) to complete. The crowning of the Virgin Mary is depicted in detail so exact that you can see the stitches in her garments. Surrounding her are various saints, including the local patron, the hermit St. Wolfgang. Since the 15th century, his namesake town has been a place of pilgrimage. You're in luck if you're at the church on a sunny day, when sunlight off the nearby lake waters dances on the walls in brilliant reflections from the stained-glass windows. ۞ *May–Sept., daily 9–5; Oct.–Apr., daily 10–4; altar closed to view during Lent.*

OFF THE   **SCHAFBERG** – From May to mid-October the rack railway trip from St.
BEATEN PATH   Wolfgang to the 5,800-ft peak of the Schafberg offers a great chance to survey the surrounding countryside from what is acclaimed as the "belvedere of the Salzkammergut lakes." On a clear day, you can almost see forever—at least as far as the Lattengebirge mountain range west of Salzburg. Figure on crowds, so reserve in advance (☎ 06138/2232, FAX 06138/2232–12) or start out early. The train—itself a curiosity dating from 1893—departs hourly: May 1 to July 6 and September 11 to October 26, daily from 9:05 AM to 5:40 PM; July 7 to September 10,

daily from 8:05 AM to 5:40 PM. The train does not run in bad weather. Allow at least a good half day for the outing, which costs AS260.

Dining and Lodging

$$$–$$$$ ✕🏠 **Landhaus zu Appesbach.** Very secluded and quiet and offering excellent service, this old manor hotel set away from the hubbub of the village is the place to get away from it all while at the same time enjoying the activities of the region. Rooms are a mixture of country antiques and modern pieces, with grand overtones. The Duke of Windsor once enjoyed a respite here. It has its own restaurant, for guests only. ✉ *A–5360 St. Wolfgang am See,* ☎ *06138/2209,* ℻ *06138/2209–14. 26 rooms, 9 suites. Restaurant, sauna, steam room, tennis court, beach, dock. AE, DC, MC, V.* 🐾

$$$$ ✕🏠 **Weisses Rössl.** The "White Horse" has been featured in films and
★ theater over the years (thanks to the famous operetta set here), and is now part of the Romantik Hotel group. Despite an extensive, heavy-handed modernization, rooms still retain a bit of country charm. The dining terraces, built to float over the water, are enchanting. Order the *Regenbogenforelle* (rainbow trout), or *Laibchen,* a hearty, delicious vegetable strudel. Keep in mind that this hotel is world famous (busloads come "to have a look"); book well in advance, especially for the summer. ✉ *Markt 74, A–5360,* ☎ *06138/2306–0,* ℻ *06138/2306–41. 72 rooms. Restaurant, bar, indoor pool, lake, sauna, tennis court, exercise room, windsurfing, boating. AE, DC, MC, V. Closed Nov.–mid-Dec.* 🐾

$ ✕🏠 **Gasthof Zimmerbräu.** In this pricey town, it's a pleasant surprise
★ to find a budget Gasthof. The house, which is four centuries old, was once a brewery; for the last hundred years it's been run by the Scharf family. Centrally located, the Zimmerbräu is not near the lake but does feature its own bathing cabana by the water. The decor is appealingly rustic in some rooms, contemporary in others, but all rooms have balconies, and there is a lovely sitting room with Biedermeier furnishings on the first floor. ✉ *Im Stöck 85, A–5360,* ☎ *06138/2204,* ℻ *06138/ 2204–45. 24 rooms. Restaurant. No credit cards. Closed Nov.–Dec. 26.*

Nightlife and the Arts

Free brass band concerts are held in St. Wolfgang in the Marktplatz every Saturday evening at 8:30 in May, and on both Wednesday and Saturday at 8:30 PM from June to September. Folk events are usually well publicized with posters. Not far from St. Wolfgang, the town of Strobl holds a Day of Popular Music and Tradition in early July—"popular" meaning brass band, and "tradition" being local costume. Check with the regional tourist office for details.

Bad Ischl

⑤ *56 km (35 mi) east of Salzburg, 16 km (10 mi) southeast of St. Wolfgang.*

Many travelers used to think of Bad Ischl primarily as the town where Zauner's pastry shop is located, to which connoisseurs drove miles for the sake of a cup of coffee and a slice of *Guglhupf,* a lemon sponge cake studded with raisins and nuts. Pastry continues to be the best-known drawing card of a community that symbolizes, more than any other place except Vienna itself, the Old Austria of uniforms and balls and waltzes and operettas. The town is charmingly laid out on a peninsula between the Rivers Traun and Ischl, whose amazing waters still run crystal clear. Bad Ischl was the place where Emperor Franz Josef chose to establish his summer court (there is a story, too, that his mother, Sophie, had stayed at the spa in 1829, when trying to conceive the future emperor). And it was also here that Franz Josef met and fell in love with his future empress, the troubled Sisi, though his mother had intended him for Sisi's elder sister. Today you can enjoy the same sort of pastries *mit Schlag* that the emperor loved. Afterward, you can hasten off to the town's modern spa, one of the best-known in Austria. The town initially grew up around the curative mineral springs that are still the raison d'être for the classic 19th-century *Kurhaus* (spa building) and the baths in the adjoining new buildings.

You'll want to stroll along the shaded **Esplanade,** where the pampered and privileged of the 19th century loved to take their constitutionals, usually after a quick stop at the spa pavilion of the **Trinkhalle,** still in the middle of town on Ferdinand-Auböck-Platz.

★ The quickest way to travel back in time to the gilded 1880s in Bad Ischl is to head for the **Kaiservilla,** the imperial-yellow (signifying gold and power) residence, which looks rather like a miniature Schönbrunn. Markus von Habsburg, great-grandson of Franz Josef I, still lives here, but you can tour parts of the building to see the ornate reception rooms and the surprisingly modest residential quarters. ✉ *Kaiserpark,* ☎ *06132/23241.* ✉ *Grounds AS35; combined ticket, including tour of villa, AS130.* ⊘ *Easter, Apr. weekends, and May–mid-Oct., daily 9–11:45 and 1–4:15.*

Don't overlook the small but elegant "marble palace" built near the Kaiservilla for Empress Elisabeth, who used it as a teahouse; it is now home to a **photography museum.** (The marriage of Franz Josef and Elisabeth was not an especially happy one; a number of houses in Bad Ischl bearing women's names are said to have been quietly given by the emperor to his various lady friends around town (☞ Schratt, *in* Dining and Lodging, *below*). You'll first need to purchase a ticket to enter the park grounds. ✉ *Kaiserpark,* ☎ *06132/24422.* ✉ *AS15.* ⊘ *Apr.–Oct., daily 9:30–5.*

A steady stream of composers followed the aristocracy and the court to Bad Ischl. Bruckner, Brahms, Johann Strauss the Younger, and Oscar Straus all spent summers here, but it was Franz Lehár, composer of *The Merry Widow,* who left the most lasting musical impression. The operetta festival in summer (☞ Music *in* Nightlife and the Arts, *below*) always includes one Lehár work. **Lehár's villa** is now a museum, open for guided tours. ✉ *Pfarrg. 11,* ☎ *06132/26992.* ✉ *AS55.* ⊘ *Easter and May–Sept., daily 9–noon and 2–5; last tours at 11:30 and 4:30.*

Bad Ischl is accessed easily via various routes. From St. Wolfgang, backtrack south to Strobl and head eastward on Route 158. To get to the town directly from Salzburg, take the A1 to Mondsee, then Routes 151 and 158 along the Wolfgangsee and the Mondsee. There are many buses that depart hourly from Salzburg's main railway station; you can also travel by train via the junction of Attnang-Puchheim or Stainach-Irdning (several transfers are required)—a longer journey than the bus ride, which is usually 90 minutes.

Dining and Lodging

$$–$$$ ★ ✕ **Weinhaus Attwenger.** This inviting restaurant is set in a turn-of-the-century gingerbread villa under massive trees overlooking the river. The tranquil garden is ideal for summer dining, and inside the villa the cozy, wood-paneled rooms are decorated with antique country knickknacks. Order the hearty rack of mildly spicy "dry-rub" spare ribs and baked potato, or ask for seasonal recommendations; the fish and game dishes are particularly good. ✉ *Lehárkai 12,* ☎ 📠 *06132/23327. No credit cards. Closed Mon. and two wks in Mar.*

$ ✕ **Café Zauner.** If you haven't been to Zauner, you've missed a true highlight of Bad Ischl. There are two locations, one along the Esplanade overlooking the River Traun (open only in summer) and the other a few blocks away on Pfarrgasse. The desserts—particularly the house creation, *Zaunerstollen,* a chocolate-covered confection of sugar, hazelnuts, and nougat—have made this one of Austria's best-known pastry shops. Emperor Franz Josef, who was a frequent visitor to Bad Ischl in the early days of his rule, used to visit every day for a Guglhupf, a lemon sponge cake. ⊠ *Pfarrg. 7,* ☎ *06132/23522. MC. Closed Tues.*

$$$$ ✕⊞ **Schratt.** About a mile outside of Bad Ischl on the road to Salzburg
★ is the enchanting, secluded villa where the actress Katharina Schratt once lived. "Kati" was Emperor Franz Josef's mistress in his later years, and during their time together most of European royalty dropped in for a visit. Nowadays it's one of the best places to dine in the area. Choose between two dining rooms—one with a Jugendstil slant, the other country-style with chintz curtains, a ceramic stove, and a hutch displaying homemade jams. Try the *Zanderfilet* (pike perch) on a bed of delicate beets soaked in port wine, or beef tenderloin strips with oyster mushrooms in a cream sauce. For dessert, order the traditional Guglhupf sponge cake, Franz Josef's favorite—it even comes warm out of the oven. Upstairs are four lovely, antiques-filled bedrooms for overnighters. ⊠ *Steinbruch 43,* ☎ 🅵🅰🆇 *06231/27647. Reservations essential. 4 rooms. AE, MC. Closed Tues., Wed., early–mid-Nov., and various wks during spring.*

$$ ✕⊞ **Goldener Ochs.** The "Golden Ox" is in a superb location in the town center with the sparkling River Traun just a few steps away. Rooms are modern with blond-wood furniture; some have balconies, and there are a few large rooms designed for families. The kitchen prides itself on its health-oriented cooking. ⊠ *Grazerstr. 4, A–4820,* ☎ *06132/235290,* 🅵🅰🆇 *06132/235293. 39 rooms. Restaurant, sauna, fitness center. AE, DC, MC, V.*

Nightlife and the Arts

The main musical events of the year in the Salzkammergut are the July and August operetta festivals held in Bad Ischl. In addition, performances of at least two operettas (*The Merry Widow* is a favorite standard) take place every season in the **Kongress and Theaterhaus** (☎ 06132/23420), where tickets are sold. For early booking, contact the Operrettengemeinde (⊠ Kurhausstr. 8, A–4820 Bad Ischl, ☎ 06132/23839, 🅵🅰🆇 06132/23839–39).

Outdoor Activities and Sports

GOLF

Bad Ischl Golfclub (☎ 06132/26340, 🅵🅰🆇 06132/26708), in Aschau, 6 km (4 mi) from the center of town, has 18 holes, par-71, and is open April–November.

TENNIS

The Salzkammergut is great tennis territory, with courts in almost every town. The best is probably the **Tennisclub Bad Ischl,** which has indoor and outdoor courts, ball-throwing machines, and equipment rentals (☎ 06132/24432 or 06132/23926).

Gmunden

❻ *76 km (47 mi) northeast of Salzburg, 40 km (25 mi) southwest of Linz, 32 km (20 mi) northeast of Bad Ischl.*

Gmunden, at the top of the Traunsee, is an attractive town to stroll about in. The tree-lined promenade along the lake is reminiscent of past days of the idle aristocracy and artistic greats—Schubert, Brahms, and the Duke of Württemberg were just some who strolled under the chestnut trees. In the town hall you'll find a famous carillon, with bells made from local clay. The gloriously ornate, arcaded yellow-and-white **town hall,** with its corner towers topped by onion domes, can't be overlooked. You can easily walk to the **Strandbad,** the swimming area, from the center of town. The beaches are good, and you can sail, water ski, or windsurf.

Take time to look at, or visit, two castles: the "lake" castle, **Schloss Orth,** on a peninsula known as Toskana, was originally built in the 15th century. It was once owned by Archduke Johann, who gave up his title after marrying an actress and thereafter called himself Orth. He disappeared with the casket supposedly holding the secret of the Mayerling tragedy after the death of Emperor Franz Josef's son Rudolf. The **Landschloss** on the shore is a simple 17th-century affair now operating as a government school of forestry; you can visit the courtyard, with its coats of arms and rococo fountain, daily 8 AM–dusk.

★ From Gmunden, take a lake trip on the **Gisela,** built in 1872, the oldest coal-fired steam side-wheeler running anywhere. It carried Emperor Franz Josef in the last century and is now restored. For departure times, check with Traunseeschiffahrt Eder (☎ 07612/65215 or 07612/66700, ℻ 07612/66741). The boat route crisscrosses the whole 12-km (7-mi) length of the lake.

From beyond the railroad station, take the 12-minute cable-car ride to the top of the **Grünberg.** From here you will have a superb view over the Traunsee, with the Dachstein glacier forming the backdrop in the south. In the winter, there are good ski runs here. ⊠ *Freyg. 4,* ☎ *07612/64977–0.* ▣ *Round-trip AS115, one-way AS85.* ☉ *May–June and Sept., daily 9–5; July–Aug., daily 9–6; Oct., daily 9–4:30.*

To get to Gmunden from Bad Ischl, take Route 145 along the western shore of the Traunsee—note the Traunstein, Hochkogel, and Erlakogel peaks on the eastern side, the latter nicknamed "die schlafende Griechin" (the slumbering Greek girl)—and then along the Traun River. You can also take a train to the town via Attnang-Puchheim from Salzburg, or from the main station in Linz.

OFF THE
BEATEN PATH

TRAUNKIRCHEN – About 4½ km (3 mi) north of Ebensee on Route 145 you'll come to Traunkirchen; stop for a look at the "fishermen's pulpit" in the parish church. This 17th-century Baroque marvel, carved from wood and burnished with silver and gold, portrays the astonished fishermen of the Sea of Galilee pulling in their suddenly full nets at Jesus' direction.

Dining and Lodging

$$–$$$ ✕ **Grabner.** Behind a rather unprepossessing facade is a culinary trea-
★ sure bearing the name of its innovative owner and award-winning chef, Rudolf Grabner. You can dine either in the *Stuberl,* an informal, cozy tavern with a ceramic oven (and a bar offering several single-malt Scotches), or in the pricier, more elegant room across the hall. Two winners are the local specialty of small spinach dumplings drizzled with browned butter and Parmesan, or the crispy sliced chicken breast on a bed of oyster mushroom risotto. To reach the Grabner, cross the Traun bridge from the town center and continue straight up the road for about 1 km. ⊠ *Scharnsteinerstr. 13,* ☎ *07612/4169,* ℻ *07612/4169–2100. AE, DC, MC, V. Closed Nov. No lunch Mon., Tues.*

$$$ ▣ **Grünberg am See.** This sprawling, multi-level chalet hotel makes a
★ pretty picture along the lakeshore opposite Gmunden's city center. Rooms are spacious with contemporary blond-wood furniture, and many have balconies with stunning views. The popular restaurant serves good local cuisine, emphasizing fish fresh from the lake. The hotel offers superb sports opportunities, from hiking to cycling to swimming. ⊠ *Traunsteinstr. 109, A–4810,* ☎ *07612/777–00,* ℻ *07612/77700–33. 30*

rooms. Restaurant, bar, hiking, beach, bicycles, free parking. AE, DC, MC, V. Closed 2 wks in Feb.

$$$ ☷ **Seehotel Schwan.** Set on the edge of the lake in the center of town, this grand old hotel is part of the Best Western chain. Rooms are standard, but the views make up for what they might be lacking in character. The restaurant, with huge windows overlooking the lake, has a creative menu with lots of fresh fish offerings. ⊠ *Rathauspl. 8, A–4810,* ☎ *07612/63391–0,* FAX *07612/63391–8. 30 rooms. Restaurant, bar. AE, DC, MC, V.*

Shopping

Among the many souvenirs and handicrafts you'll find in Salzkammergut shops, the most famous are the handcrafted ceramics of Gmunden. The green-trimmed, white country ceramics are decorated with blue, yellow, green, and white patterns, including the celebrated 16th-century *Grüngeflammte* design, solid horizontal green stripes on a white background. You'll find them at the **Gmundner Keramik** shop (⊠ Keramikstr. 24, ☎ 07612/5441–0).

GOSAU, HALLSTATT, AND BAD AUSSEE

It is hard to imagine anything prettier than this region of the Salzkammergut, which takes you into the very heart of the Lake District. The great highlight is Gosau am Dachstein—a beauty spot that even the least impressionable find hard to forget. But there are other notable sights, including Hallstatt, the Dachstein Ice Caves, and the spa of Altaussee. Lording over the region is the Dachstein range itself—the backbone of Upper Austria, Styria, Land Salzburg, and a true monarch of all it surveys.

Gosau am Dachstein

★ **❼** *10 km (6 mi) west of the Hallstättersee.*

Lovers of scenic beauty should not leave the Hallstatt region without taking in Gosau am Dachstein, considered the most beautiful spot in Austria by 19th-century travelers but unaccountably often overlooked today. This lovely spot is 10 km (6 mi) west of the Hallstätter See, just before the Geschütt Pass. You travel either by bus, rail, or motorboat as far as Gosaumühle—the village makes a good lunch stop (and, with its many *Gasthöfe* and pensions, could be a base for your excursion)— and from there you must walk, at the most an hour or two, depending on your speed, but you won't regret the hike. Of the three Gosauseen (Gosau lakes), the first—the Vorderer Gosausee—is the crown jewel, located some 8 km (5 mi) to the south of the town itself. Beyond a sparkling, almost fjordlike basin of water rises the amazing Dachstein massif, majestically reflected in the mirrorlike surface of the lake. Other than a restaurant and a gamekeeper's hut, the lake is undefiled by man-made structures. At the right hour—well before 2:30 PM, when, due to the steepness of the mountain slopes, the sun is already withdrawing— the view is superb. Following the path around the lake will clarify some of the greatest passages in Richard Wagner's *Parsifal,* which were composed with these vistas in mind. Then you may choose to endure the stiff walk to the other two lakes (not as spectacularly located), which will take another two hours; take a cable car up to the Gablonzer Hütte on the Zwieselalm (you might consider skiing on the Gosau glacier); or tackle the three-hour hike up to the summit of the Grosser Donnerkogel. At day's end, head back for Gosau am Dachstein, settle in at one of the many Gasthöfe (reserve ahead) overhung with wild gooseberry and rose-bushes (or stay at one of Gosau's charming *Privatzimmer* accommodations). Cap the day off with a dinner of fried *Schwarzrenterl,* a delicious regional lake fish. To get to Gosau, travel north or south on Route 145, turning off at the junction with Route 166, and travel 36 km (20 mi) east through the ravine of the Gosaubach River.

Dining and Lodging

$$$ ×⊡ **Hotel Koller.** One of the most charming hotels in Gosau, the
  ★ Koller was originally the home of famed industrialist Moriz Faber. With peaked gables and weather vanes, the Koller has a fairy-tale aura when seen from its pretty park. Inside are an open fireplace and warm wood-work; guest rooms—many offering breathtaking views—have blond-wood furniture and cheerful curtains. A special feature is the tavern's gala dinners, featuring regional barbecued specialties and health foods supplied fresh by the farmers of Gosau. Live folk music is sometimes offered. Half board is required. ⊠ *A–4824 Gosau am Dachstein,* ☎ *06136/88410,* FAX *06136/884150. 18 rooms, 5 suites. 2 restaurants, bar, pool, sauna, steam room, playground. No credit cards. Closed Nov. and also for month around Easter (dates vary).*

Hallstatt

  ★ ❽ *89 km (55 mi) southeast of Salzburg, 19 km (12 mi) south of Bad Ischl.*

As if rising from Swan Lake itself, the town of Hallstatt is the subject of thousands of travel posters. "The world's prettiest lakeside village" perches precariously on the lakeside on what seems the smallest of toe-holds, one that nevertheless prevents it from tumbling into the dark waters of the Hallstättersee. Down from the steep mountainside above it crashes the Mühlbach waterfall, a sight that can keep you riveted for hours. Today, the town is a thriving tourist center and a bit too modernized, considering that Hallstatt is believed to be the oldest community in Austria. More than a thousand graves of prehistoric men have been found here, and it has been such an important source of relics of the Celtic period that this age is known as the Hallstatt epoch.

Most of the early relics of the Hallstatt era are in Vienna (including the greatest Iron Age totem of them all, the Venus of Willendorf, now a treasure of Vienna's Naturhistorisches Museum, ☞ Chapter 2), but some are here in the **Prähistorisches Museum** (Prehistoric Museum). ⊠ *Seestr. 56,* ☎ *06134/8398.* ⊡ *AS50.* ☉ *Apr. and Oct., daily 10–4; May–Sept., daily 10–6, Nov.–Mar., Wed. 2–4.*

Salt has been mined in the area for at least 4,500 years, and the **Hall-statt mines** are the oldest in the world. Take the cable car up and tour the mines above town; after a 10-minute walk, you enter the mines on a little miner's train (tall people, keep your heads down) and go deep into the mountain, sliding down wooden chutes to an artificial sub-terranean lake, which is used to dissolve the salt. There is also an Iron Age cemetery and a restaurant up here. ⊠ *Salzberg,* ☎ *06134/8400.* ⊡ *Cable car round-trip AS105, one-way AS65; mine and tour AS140.* ☉ *Late Apr.–late Sept., daily 9–4:30, last car up at 4; late Sept.–Oct. 26, daily 9–3, last car up at 2:30.*

About ten years ago the Zentrasport Janu shop's intention to put a new heating system in their cellar unexpectedly turned into a **historical exca-vation** when workmen found the remains of a Celtic dwelling, now open to visitors. ⊠ *Seestr. 50,* ☎ *06134/8298.* ⊡ *Free.* ☉ *Mon.–Sat. 9–6.*

The Hallstatt market square, now a pedestrian area, is bordered by col-
  ★ orful 16th-century houses. Be sure to visit the **parish church of St. Michael,** which is picturesquely sited near the lake. Within the 16th-century Gothic church you'll find a beautiful winged altar, which opens to reveal nine 15th-century paintings. The charnel house beside the church is a rather

morbid but regularly visited spot. Because there was little space to bury the dead over the centuries in Hallstatt, the custom developed of digging up the bodies after 12 or 15 years, piling the bones in the sun, and painting the skulls. Ivy and oak-leaf wreaths were used for the men, Alpine flowers for the women, plus names, dates, and often the cause of death. The myriad bones and skulls are now on view in the charnel house. The lakeside vistas are spectacular, and people love to feed the fish by the shore.

To get to Hallstatt from Bad Ischl, head south on Route 145 to Bad Goisern—which also has curative mineral springs but never achieved the cachet of Bad Ischl. Just south of town, watch for signs for the turnoff to the Hallstättersee. Since the lake is squeezed between two sharply rising mountain ranges, the road parallels the shore, with spectacular views. The Hallstatt railroad station is on the opposite side of the lake; if you arrive by train, a boat (**Hemetsberger,** ✉ Hallstättersee-Schiffahrt, ☎ 06134/8228) will take you across to the town every hour. Boat tours around the lake via Obertraun are available May–September at 1, 2, and 3; July–August also at 11 and 4:15. Boat tours around the lake via Steeg, July–August at 10:30, 1:30, and 3:30. Embark via train for Hallstatt from Bad Ischl or via the Stainach-Irdning junction. From Bad Ischl, you can also take a half-hour bus ride to Hallstatt.

Dining and Lodging

$$$ ✕🍴 **Grüner Baum.** Directly on the shore of the lake and at the foot of a picture-perfect square is this traditional inn dating from 1760. The family pets sit near the reception desk on worn armchairs, giving the hotel a friendly, homey atmosphere. Rooms are simply furnished and in need of sprucing up; try to get one with a balcony facing the lake. ✉ Marktpl. 104, A–4830, ☎ 06134/8263, ℻ 06134/8420. 20 rooms. Restaurant, bar, lake. AE, DC, MC, V. Closed late Oct.–Apr.

$$–$$$ ✕🍴 **Gasthof Zauner.** Located a few steps up the hill from the front
★ entrance of the Grüner Baum, this several-storied wooden chalet offers charming, rustic rooms with carved headboards and balconies overlooking the village and lake. The hotel's upstairs restaurant is well-known in the area for fresh fish, so be sure to book ahead. Try the light cheese soup followed by the delicious grilled Reinanke, a mild, local lake fish. ✉ Marktpl., A–4830, ☎ 06134/8246, ℻ 06134/8246–8. 12 rooms. Restaurant. DC, MC, V. Closed mid-Nov.–mid-Dec.

Outdoor Activities and Sports

BOATING

The lakes of the Salzkammergut are excellent for **canoeing** because most prohibit or limit powerboats. Try canoeing on the Hallstätter See (for information, contact Alois Zopf, ✉ Hauptstr. 237, Bad Goisern, ☎ 06135/8254, ℻ 06135/7409) or white-water **kayaking** on the Traun River (for information, call Fritz Schiefermeyer, ☎ 06134/8338).

HIKING

There are many great hiking paths around Hallstatt; contact the local tourist office for information about the path along the Echerntal to Waldbachstrub past pleasant waterfalls, or the climb to the Tiergartenhütte, continuing on to the Wiesberghaus and, two hours beyond, the Simony-Hütte, spectacularly sited at the foot of the Dachstein glacier. From here mountain climbers begin the ascent of the Hoher Dachstein, the tallest peak of the Dachstein massif.

Dachstein Ice Caves

★ ❾ 5 km (3 mi) east of Hallstatt.

Many travelers to Hallstatt make an excursion to one of the most impressive sights of the eastern Alps, the **Dachstein Ice Caves.** From Hallstatt, take the scenic road around the bottom of the lake to Obertraun; then follow the signs to the cable car, the *Dachsteinseilbahn,* which will ferry you up the mountain (you can hike all the way up to the caves, if you prefer). From the cable-car landing, a 15-minute hike up takes you to the entrance (follow signs to DACHSTEINEISHÖHLE) of the vast ice caverns, many of which are hundreds of years old and aglitter with ice stalactites and stalagmites, illuminated by an eerie light. The most famous sights are the **Rieseneishöhle** (Giant Ice Cave) and the **Mammuthöhle** (Mammoth Cave), but there are other caves and assorted frozen waterfalls. The cave entrance is at about 6,500 ft, still well below the 9,750-ft Dachstein peak farther south. Be sure to wear warm, weatherproof clothing; inside the caves it's cold, and outside, the slopes can be swept by chilly winds. ☎ *06131/362.* 🎫 *Cable car round-trip AS170, Giant Ice Cave AS90, Mammoth Cave AS90, combined ticket for both caves AS150.* ⊙ *Mammoth Cave: May 22–Oct. 15, daily 9:30–5; Giant Ice Cave: May 6–Oct. 15, daily 9:30–5.*

Bad Aussee

⑩ *81 km (50 mi) southeast of Salzburg, 24 km (15 mi) west of Hallstatt.*

Following the bumpy old road westward (often closed in winter) from Hallstatt, you'll find yourself in company with the railroad and the Traun River (watch out for the precipitous 23% gradient at one point) and enter a region dotted with small lakes. The heart of this region is Bad Aussee, a great mecca in the summertime, for the town's towering mountains and glacier-fed lake keep the area cool. Even in midsummer, the waters of the lake are so cold that the presence of the municipal swimming pool is easy to account for. In the town, salt and mineral springs have been developed into a modern spa complex, yet the town retains much of its 15th- and 16th-century character in the narrow streets and older buildings, particularly in the upper reaches. The 1827 marriage of Archduke Johann to the daughter of the local postmaster brought attention and a burst of new construction, including some lovely 19th-century villas. Bad Aussee is a good base for hiking in the surrounding countryside in summer and for excellent skiing in winter. Many travelers come to Bad Aussee via the train from Salzburg, making a connection southward at the Attnang-Puchheim junction.

Dining and Lodging

$ ✕ **Lewandofsky.** This popular café in the center of town is *the* place to meet, especially in summer when tables are spread under the chestnut trees overlooking the main square. Choose from a tempting array of pastries and marzipan-topped gingerbread to go along with the excellent coffee. ⊠ *Kurhauspl. 144, A–8990,* ☎ *03622/53205. No credit cards.* ⊙ *Open Mon.–Sat. 8–8, Sun. 10–8.*

$$$$ ✕🏨 **Erzherzog Johann.** A golden yellow facade identifies this tradi-
★   tional house, which, though in the center of town, is quiet. A direct passageway connects the hotel to a spa next door, with a heated Olympic-size swimming pool and cure facilities. The hotel rooms are large and contemporary in style, and all have balconies. Extras include complimentary coffee and cake in the afternoon and a van that fetches guests at the train station free of charge. The elegant restaurant serves the best creative cooking in the area; look for poached salmon and wild rice or baby lamb with potato strudel. ⊠ *Kurhauspl. 62, A–8990,* ☎ *03622/52507,* 🆂 *03622/52507–680. 62 rooms. Restaurant, bar, indoor pool, sauna, spa, exercise room, free parking. AE, DC, MC, V. Closed late Nov.–mid-Dec.*

$$$ 🏨 **Kristina.** Set in a lovely wooded park, this hotel is decorated with antlers and trophies in the style of a hunting lodge; its rooms are ap-

propriately outfitted with older furniture. ⊠ *Altausseer Str. 54, A–8990,* ☎ *03622/52017,* 🖷 *03622/52017–1. 11 rooms. Restaurant. AE, DC, MC, V. Closed mid- to late Jan. and Nov.–mid-Dec.*

Altaussee

🔟 *4 km (2½ mi) north of Bad Aussee.*

Taking a fairly steep road from Bad Aussee, you'll find Altaussee tucked away at the end of a lake cradled by gentle mountains. This is one of the most magical spots of the Salzkammergut. Over the years, it attracted so many fine musicians and writers who came for inspiration (Johannes Brahms, Arthur Schnitzler, and Hugo von Hofmannsthal, to name just a few) that author Alex Storm famously called the lake "an inkwell into which we all dip our quills." The town is completely unspoiled, perfect for those who simply want an Alpine idyll: to do nothing, hike in the meadows, climb the slopes, or row on the lake. The end of May to the beginning of June is perhaps the best time to visit; the field flowers have burst forth and Bad Aussee holds its famous narcissus festival, which includes a procession to Altaussee.

During World War II, Nazi leaders stored stolen art in underground caverns near Altaussee. In their hurry to get the job done, they skipped a few details; one story has it that a famous painting from Vienna, possibly a Rubens or a Rembrandt, was overlooked and spent the remaining war years on the porch of a house near the entrance to the mines. At the end of the war, Allied forces were directed to the mines by the local populace, and, once unsealed, the caverns released a treasure trove unlikely ever again to be assembled in one place.

Salt is still dug in the nearby Sandling Mountain, and the **mines** are open to visitors. Check with the tourist office or phone for details of guided tours. ☎ *06132/200–2551 or 0664/1034185.* 🎟 *AS150.* ⊙ *Apr. 16–30, daily 10–2; May–Sept., daily 10–4.*

If time allows and you feel fit enough, do the approximately 2½-hour walk up the Loser Mountain that begins at the end of Altaussee (follow the colored marks and occasional signs), where at the top of the Panorama Strasse you can rest and refuel at your choice of two restaurants: the cafeteria-style **Loser-Berg** (at the very top of the mountain) or the **Loserhütte** (☞ Dining, *below*). A much easier way to reach the top of the Panorama Strasse is to drive, but you pay for the privilege— AS40 for your car and AS72 per person.

Dining and Lodging

$ ✕🏠 **Loserhütte.** A short walk down a well-marked path just before the
★ crest of Loser Mountain leads to this chalet restaurant with a wrap-around terrace affording panoramic views of the surrounding mountains and the sparkling lake below. Dishes are local and hearty, such as the *Pfandl,* a mixture of home-fried potatoes, pork and cheese served in a blackened skillet. Don't confuse this restaurant with the Loser-Berg cafeteria which is a little bit farther up the mountain. The Loserhütte also has seven simply furnished bedrooms upstairs for overnighters. ⊠ *Fischerndorf 80, A–8992,* ☎ 🖷 *03622/71202. 7 rooms. Parking. No credit cards. Closed Nov.–mid-Dec. and late Apr.–mid-May.*

$$ 🏠 **Hubertushof.** This stunning former hunting lodge with green shutters is perched on a hillside high above the town. Run by its indomitable owner, Countess Strasoldo, it is a treasure of a home, with gleaming Biedermeier and rococo antiques, wood-beamed ceilings, and brass chandeliers. Bedrooms are either country rustic with carved cedar headboards or furnished with elegant, faux French provincial pieces. Breakfast is served on the terrace overlooking the lake and surrounding mountains.

To reach the Hubertushof, turn off the main road in Altaussee at the Hotel Tyrol and go straight, continuing to your right at the fork. ✉ *Puchen 86, A–8992,* ☎ *03622/71280,* FAX *06322/71280–80. 8 rooms. Bar, hiking. MC, V. Closed mid-Oct.–Dec. 26, Jan. 10–31, and variable weeks Mar.–May 14.*

En Route   To get back to Bad Ischl, your best bet is to return to Bad Aussee and then take Route 145 north. It's only 28 km (18 mi), but a great deal of this consists of precipitous ups and downs, the highest point being at 3,200 ft before you head down through the Pötschen Pass. Not surprisingly, the views are spectacular; don't miss the lookout point at a hairpin turn at Unter, far above the Hallstätter See.

SALZKAMMERGUT A TO Z

Arriving and Departing

By Car

Driving is by far the easiest and most convenient way to reach the Lake District. From **Salzburg,** you can take Route 158 east to Fuschl, St. Gilgen, and Bad Ischl or the A1 autobahn to Mondsee. Coming from **Vienna** or Linz, the A1 passes through the northern part of the Salzkammergut; get off at the Steyrermühl exit or the Regau exit and head south on Route 144/145 to Gmunden, Bad Ischl, Bad Goisern, and Bad Aussee. From the Seewalchen exit, take Route 152 down the east side of the Attersee, instead of the far less scenic Route 151 down the west side.

By Plane

The Lake District is closer to Salzburg than to Linz, but ground transportation is such that there is little preference for one departure point over the other. The **Salzburg** airport is about 53 km (33 mi) from Bad Ischl, heart of the Salzkammergut; the **Linz** airport (Hörsching) is about 75 km (47 mi). Both cities have good connections to European destinations but no flights to or from North America. A number of charter lines fly into Salzburg, including some from the United Kingdom.

By Train

The geography of the area means that rail lines run mainly north–south. Trains run from Vöcklabruck to Seewalchen at the top end of the Attersee and from Attnang-Puchheim to Gmunden, Bad Ischl, Hallstatt, Bad Aussee, and beyond. Both starting points are on the main east–west line between Salzburg and Linz.

Getting Around

By Bus and Train

Railroad service is fairly good, but you won't get off the beaten path. Where the trains don't go, the post office or railroad buses do, so if you allow enough time, you can cover virtually all the area by public transportation. Check at the railroad station in Salzburg or Bad Ischl on the availability of a "Salzkammergut Ticket," good for unlimited travel on all trains within the Salzkammergut region and for a 50% reduction on the lake steamers and Schafbergbahn mountain railway on any four days within a 10-day period from May to the end of October.

By Car

For sheer flexibility—plus being able to stop when you want to admire the view—travel by car is the most satisfactory way to see the Salzkammergut. Roads are good, and traffic is excessive only on weekends (although it can be slow on some narrow lakeside stretches). Just remember that gasoline is expensive in Austria.

Contacts and Resources

Bicycling
Much of the Salzkammergut is rather hilly if you are just a casual cyclist, but you'll find reasonably good cycling country around the lakes, including the Wolfgangsee (though Route 158 can become quite noisy and fume-filled). Sports shops throughout the area rent bikes; local tourist offices can point you to the right place. You can cycle the 14 km (9 mi) from St. Wolfgang to Bad Ischl on back roads.

Canoeing
Helpful firms for the entire Salzkammergut region are **Intersport Steinkogler** (⊠ Salzburger Str. 3, Bad Ischl, ☎ 06132/23655) and **Pro-Travel** (⊠ Markt 94, St. Wolfgang, ☎ 06138/2525, FAX 06138/3054).

Skiing
The Salzkammergut offers challenging runs for experts and gentle slopes for novices. The main ski center is in St. Gilgen (☞ *above*).Great cross-country trails can be found in **Fuschl** (⊠ Fuschl am See, A–5330, ☎ 06226/8250, FAX 06226/8650) and Strobl, and there's a 15-km (9-mi) high-altitude trail in Postalm. In the **Ausseerland** region you'll find powder-perfect skiing lessons in Altaussee at the Helmut Kaiss Ski School (⊠ *Altaussee, A–8992,* ☎ *03622/71310,* FAX *03622/71701*).

Emergencies
The emergency numbers are ☎ 133 for the **police,** ☎ 144 for an **ambulance,** and ☎ 122 for the **fire department.** Call ☎ 120 for the **automobile club ÖAMTC.** If you need a doctor and speak no German, ask your hotel how best to obtain assistance.

Fishing Licenses
The Salzkammergut is superb fishing country for casting or trolling—the main season runs June–September—but you will need a license. Many townships have their own licensing offices. **Attersee:** Matthäus Hollerweger (⊠ Esso station, Nussdorf, ☎ 07666/8063–4). **Bad Ischl:** Ischler Waffen, Manfred Zeitler (⊠ Schröpferpl. 4, ☎ 06132/23351). **Ebensee:** (⊠ Langbathsee 1, Baier/Landgasthof in der Kreh, ☎ 06133/6235). **Gmunden:** Forstverwaltung Gmunden (⊠ Klosterpl. 1, ☎ 07612/64529, FAX 07612/65664); Höller Kammerhof (⊠ Kammerhofg. 6, ☎ 07612/72330); **Gasthof Steinmaurer** (⊠ Traunsteinstr. 23, ☎ 07612/704888). **Hallstatt:** Zentrasport Janu (⊠ Seestr. 50, ☎ 06134/8298–0). **Mondsee:** Family Faber (⊠ Gaisberg 85, ☎ 06232/4238); Radsport Hofer (⊠ Herzog-Odilo-Str. 52, ☎ 06232/3121). **St. Wolfgang:** Fischerhaus Höplinger (⊠ Dr.-Rais-Promenade 79, ☎ 06138/2241).

A number of hotels in the **Altaussee–Bad Aussee** area have packages that combine a week's stay with the fishing license; for details and booking, contact Steirischer Tourismus (⊠ St. Peter–Hauptstr. 243, A–8042 Graz, ☎ 0316/4003, FAX 0316/4003–10).

Guided Tours
Day-long tours of the Salzkammergut whisk you all too quickly from Salzburg to St. Gilgen, St. Wolfgang, and Mondsee: **Albus/Salzburg Sightseeing Tours** (⊠ Mirabellpl. 2, A–5020 Salzburg, ☎ 0662/881616, FAX 0662/878776); **Salzburg Panorama Tours** (⊠ Schranneng. 2/2, A–5020 Salzburg, ☎ 0662/883211, FAX 0662/871628). Full-day tours to Salzburg from Vienna pass through Gmunden and the Traunsee, Bad Ischl, the Wolfgangsee, St. Gilgen, and Fuschlsee, but you can't see much from a bus window: **Cityrama Sightseeing** (⊠ Börseng. 1, A–1010 Vienna, ☎ 01/534–13–0, FAX 01/534–1316); **Vienna Sightseeing Tours** (⊠ Stelzhammerg. 4/11, A–1031 Vienna, ☎ 01/712–4683–0, FAX 01/714–1141).

Swimming and Water Sports

There's every kind of water sport in the Salzkammergut, from windsurfing to sailing. You can water-ski at Strobl and St. Wolfgang on the Wolfgangsee and at most towns on the Attersee and Traunsee. At Ebensee, check with **Diving School Gigl** (⊠ Strandbadstr. 12, ☎ 06133/6381), which also offers skin diving. In Gmunden, contact **Wasserskischule** (⊠ Traunsteinstr., ☎ 07612/63602). A "round" will cost you about AS120.

You can explore the mysterious depths of the Hallstätter See by scuba diving with **Tauchschule und Bergefirma Zauner** (⊠ Markt 113, ☎ 06134/8286).

Visitor Information

The main tourist offices for the provinces and regions covered in this chapter are as follows:

Salzkammergut/Salzburger Land (⊠ Postfach 1, A–5300 Hallwang bei Salzburg, ☎ 0662/6688, FAX 0662/6688–66, ✆). **Styria** (⊠ St. Peter-Hauptstr. 243, A–8042 Graz, ☎ 0316/4003, FAX 0316/4003–10). **Tourismusverband Ausseerland** (⊠ Chlumeckypl. 44, A–8890 Bad Aussee, ☎ 03622/54040, FAX 03622/540407, ✆). **Upper Austria** (⊠ Schillerstr. 50, A–4010 Linz, ☎ 0732/771264, FAX 0732/600220).

Most towns in the Salzkammergut have their own *Fremdenverkehrsamt* (tourist office):

Altaussee (⊠ Fischerndorf 44, A–8992, ☎ 03622/71643, FAX 03622/716437). **Bad Aussee** (⊠ Chlumeckypl. 44, A–8990, ☎ 03622/52323, FAX 03622/52324). **Bad Ischl** (⊠ Bahnhofstr. 6, A–4820, ☎ 06132/27757, FAX 06132/27757–77). **Gmunden** (⊠ Am Graben 2, A–4810, ☎ 07612/64305, FAX 07612/71410). **Gosau am Dachstein** (⊠ Tourismusverband Gosau, A–4824, ☎ 06136/8295, FAX 06136/8255). **Hallstatt** (⊠ Seestr. 169, A–4830, ☎ 06134/8208, FAX 06134/8352). **Mondsee** (⊠ Dr.-Franz-Muller-Str. 3, A–5310, ☎ 06232/2270, FAX 06232/4470). **St. Gilgen** (⊠ Mozartpl. 1, A–5340, ☎ 06227/2348, FAX 06227/7267–9). **St. Wolfgang** (⊠ Au 120, A–5360, ☎ 06138/2239, FAX 06138/2239–81).

7 CARINTHIA

Carinthia could be labeled "Extract of Austria" since it contains a greater variety of Austria's charms than any of the country's other provinces. Routine-burdened Viennese dream of its Austrian Riviera, where waterside gaiety emanates from such resorts as Maria Wörth and Velden; the richly scenic cities of Klagenfurt and Villach beckon; and luminous art treasures await— Spittal's Porcia palace, Gurk's great Romanesque cathedral, and the iconic model for the Gothic castle in Walt Disney's *Snow White*, Hochosterwitz Castle.

N 1877 THE GERMAN COMPOSER Johannes Brahms wrote of an unexpected holiday he spent in Carinthia: ". . . the first day was so lovely that I determined to stay for a second, and the second was so lovely that I have decided to stay here for the time being." Today's travelers will find it just as hard to leave this blessed land.

Updated by
Bonnie Dodson

With the best summer weather in Austria, fine ski resorts, assorted medieval strongholds, and art-filled churches, this geographically compact province offers an array of delights for any visitor. While Carinthia—or Kärnten in German—has Austria's highest peak, the famous Grossglockner (which rises to 12,470 ft), nature's glories are only part of the region's allure. Art lovers will immediately head to architectural landmarks such as the Romanesque Gurk Cathedral, Renaissance gems like Schloss Porcia in Spittal, and Baroque beauties everywhere. And who can resist the 9th-century castle of Hochosterwitz from afar? You almost expect a dragon to appear in a puff of smoke upon its ramparts or to hear troubadours warbling at the entrance. Then there is also the waterside gaiety in such resorts as Maria Wörth and Velden, set within the pleasure-land that is the Austrian Riviera. Of course, The province's summer season is custom-tailored for bicycling, fishing, hiking, and water sports—so reservations usually need to be booked well in advance for its resort towns. Carinthia is is a multiethnic area, whose three nationalities—Austrian (German), Slovene, and Italian—are gradually becoming proud of their common roots. Since post–World War I days, when parts of Carinthia were almost given away to the new Yugoslav state, the spirit in the land has changed. It seems the more Europe grows together, the more a sense of solidarity and regional identity deepens. Klagenfurt is the official seat of the government, but over the course of time Villach, an equally attractive small city, has emerged as the "secret" capital, especially when the spirit of carnival captivates Austria; the Villach Carnival reigns supreme during the week before Lent. Its costume parades, floats, parodies, and cabarets are now televised annually for international consumption. Another popular event is the Carinthian Summer Festival, held here and in various other spots in the region in July and August.

If you approach Carinthia from Vienna not by the official A2 autobahn that passes through Graz but on Route 83 from the Murtal in the north, passing through Bad Einöd and Friesach, you will be taking one of the main gateways into this sunniest of all Austrian provinces. The broad, open countryside you cross from there to the Wörther See—a mecca for sun worshipers—is only one aspect of Carinthia. If you approach the province from any other direction, you will get a very different impression—that of an area walled in by towering mountains, surmountable only through a few, mostly high passes. Whichever route you take, your ultimate Carinthian destinations will surely offer many rewards.

Pleasures and Pastimes

Dining

Thanks to the region's many lakes and rivers, this is fish country: carp, pike, perch, eel, bream, crawfish (when in season, which is rather short), and, best of all, a large variety of trout. Austrian brook trout and rainbow trout are delicious. The most popular way of serving them is "blue," the whole fish boiled in a court bouillon and accompanied by drawn butter. Or try it *Müllerin*—sautéed in butter until a crisp brown. In summer try cold smoked trout with lemon or horseradish for a delicate hors d'oeuvre. Carinthia's basically peasant tradition, however, is also reflected in its culinary specialties, such as *Kärntner Käsnudeln* (giant ravioli stuffed with a ricotta-like local cheese and a whisper of mint), *Sterz* (polenta served either sweet or salty), and *Hauswürste* (smoked or air-cured hams and sausages, available at butcher shops). Through much of Carinthia you'll discover that, other than simple Gasthäuser, pizzerias, and the ubiquitous Chinese restaurants, most dining spots are not independent establishments but belong to country inns. When a hotel dining operation is especially noteworthy, we flag it by including it under the heading of "Dining and Lodging." Prices for meals include taxes and a service charge but not the customary small additional tip of 5%.

CATEGORY	COST*
$$$$	over AS500 (€36)
$$$	AS300–AS500 (€21–€36)
$$	AS200–AS300 (€14–€20)
$	under AS200 (€14)

per person for a typical three-course meal, with a glass of house wine

Lodging

Accommodations range from luxurious lakeside resorts to small country inns and even guest houses without private baths. Room rates include taxes and service and almost always breakfast, except in the most expensive hotels, but it is wise to ask. When comparing prices, note that many hotels in the resort towns require half board (one meal in addition to breakfast). The larger hotels offer a choice of menu. When staying two or three days or longer, it is customary to leave a small additional tip (AS20) for the chambermaid.

CATEGORY	COST*
$$$$	over AS2,200 (€160)
$$$	AS1,600–AS2,200 (€116–€160)
$$	AS1,000–AS1,600 (€72–€115)
$	under AS1,000 (€72)

All prices are for a standard double room for two, including taxes and service charge.

✎ *following the text of a review is your signal that the property has a Web site, where you will find details and, usually, images; for a link, visit www.fodors.com/urls.*

Exploring Carinthia

You can get a taste of Carinthia in a weekend, or savor it all during a week-long stay. For our shortest itinerary, we tackle the Austrian Riviera; for a longer stay, Villach makes a good base.

Great Itineraries

Numbers in the text correspond to numbers in the margin and on the Carinthia map.

IF YOU HAVE 3 DAYS

If your time is limited, head to the Austrian Riviera, balm to travelers who wish simply to sun and soak. Start off with a visit to the provincial capital **Klagenfurt** ① before heading out to the most popular lake, the Wörther See. You can make stops along the way at resorts such as **Krumpendorf** ② and **Pörtschach** ③, before spending the night and next day in ⌦ **Maria Wörth** ④, with its postcard-perfect spired chapel overlooking the lake. For the next night, head to chic ⌦ **Velden** ⑤. On your final day, take in the towns of Maria Gail, **Egg am Faaker See** ⑥, and **Viktring** ⑦, with its Cistercian monastery dating back to 1142.

Carinthia

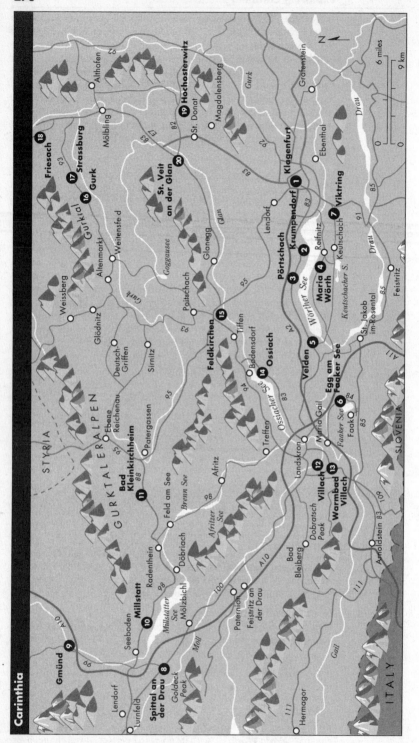

The best way to start your trip is to take a day to explore ⛢ **Spittal an der Drau** ⑧, the principal town in Upper Carinthia. After an overnight stay, head for the medieval walled town of **Gmünd** ⑨ and continue on to the resorts on the Millstätter See, with your next night spent at ⛢ **Millstatt** ⑩. The Roman baths at ⛢ **Bad Kleinkirchheim** ⑪ will soothe tired muscles on the third day; spend your third night at one of the spa's friendly chalet-style hotels. On your fourth day pass the quiet resort town of Feld am See on the Feldsee before pulling into ⛢ **Villach** ⑫—one of Carinthia's most historic cities—for your last night and day.

Start your visit in ⛢ **Villach** ⑫, nestled on the banks of the Drau River, wandering the meandering lanes of the Altstadt (Old Town). Spend the night in the city or head for the nearby spa of **Warmbad Villach** ⑬; the next day, relax with a massage or soak in the soothing hot springs, and then check out the imposing ruins of Landskron Castle. Spend your third day enjoying the resort town of ⛢ **Ossiach** ⑭ and its 11th-century monastery, where the soft sounds of music waft through summer nights during the annual music festival. Stay two nights there, for you'll want to get an early start on the day's full schedule of sightseeing attractions, including the medieval city of **Feldkirchen** ⑮; the massive Romanesque cathedral at **Gurk** ⑯; and a stop in **Strassburg** ⑰, formerly the seat of the bishopric. Pull into ⛢ **Friesach** ⑱, where it's easy to imagine lords and ladies descended from the Middle Ages living in this village, for your fifth evening. Spend your fifth night back in Friesach, a good base for touring. On the sixth day discover **St. Veit an der Glan** ⑳, Carinthia's capital until the 16th century; then move on to the amazing castle-fortress of **Hochosterwitz** ⑲. For your last evening and day, return to ⛢ **Klagenfurt** ①.

When to Tour Carinthia

To see the province in its best festive dress of blue and emerald lakes, framed by wooded hills and rocky peaks, and also do some swimming, come between mid-May and early October. Early spring, when the colors are purest and the crowds not yet in evidence, or fall, is perhaps the best time for quiet sightseeing.

KLAGENFURT AND THE SOUTHERN LAKES

Because of the resorts, the elegant people, the cultural events, and the emphasis on dawn-to-dawn indulgences, the region surrounding Carinthia's pleasure lakes vies with the Salzkammergut for the nickname "Austria's Riviera." The most popular of the Fünf Schwesterseen (Five Sister Lakes) is certainly the central lake, the Wörther See, sprinkled with such resorts as Krumpendorf, Velden, and Maria Wörth—once called the quietest village in all Austria but subsequently overrun by hordes of tourists. The Wörther See is 17 km (10½ mi) long and the warmest of Carinthia's large lakes; people swim here as early as May. A great way to see the lake is from one of the boats that run from end to end, making frequent stops along the way. Try to book passage on the S.S. *Thalia*, built in 1908 and now beautifully restored. You can follow the north shore to Velden by way of Pörtschach, or swing south and take the less traveled scenic route; in any case, you should visit picturesque Maria Wörth on the south shore.

Klagenfurt

❶ *329 km (192 mi) southwest of Vienna, 209 km (130 mi) southeast of Salzburg.*

Klagenfurt became the provincial capital in 1518, so most of what you see today dates from the 16th-century or later. And while Klagenfurt itself may not pulse with excitement, it's an excellent base for excursions to the rest of Carinthia. You can hardly overlook the *Lindwurm,* Klagenfurt's emblematic dragon with a curled tail, which adorns the fountain on Neuer Platz (New Square). The notion of Klagenfurt's dragon became more intriguing when the fossilized cranium of a prehistoric rhinoceros was found nearby. Through the Kramergasse you reach the longish **Alter Platz,** the oldest square of the city and the center of a pleasant pedestrian area with tiny streets and alleys. South of the Neuer Platz (take Karfreitstrasse and turn left on Lidmansky-Gasse) is the **Domkirche** (cathedral), completed as a Protestant church in 1591, given over to the Jesuits and reconsecrated in 1604, and finally declared a cathedral in 1787. The 18th-century side-altar painting of St. Ignatius by Paul Troger, the great Viennese rococo painter and teacher, is a fine example of the transparency and light he introduced to painting.

North of the Neuer Platz (go along Kramergasse for two blocks, then angle left to the Pfarrplatz), is the parish church of **St. Egyd,** with its eye-catching totem-pole bronze carving by Austrian avant-garde artist Ernst Fuchs in the second chapel on the right. In the next chapel is the crypt of Julian Green (1900-98), the noted French-born American novelist whose works include *The Closed Garden* and *The Other One.* On a visit to Klagenfurt several years before his death for the production of one of his plays, he perceived the city to be a sanctuary of peace in the world and decided he wanted to be buried here.

One of the most notable sights of the city is the **Landhaus** (district government headquarters), with its towers and court with arcaded stairways. It was completed in 1591 and at the time formed a corner of the city wall. The only interior on view is the dramatic **Grosser Wappensaal** (Great Hall of Coats of Arms), which contains 665 coats of arms of Carinthia's landed gentry and a stirring rendition of the Fürstenstein investiture ceremony portrayed by Fromiller, the most important Carinthian painter of the Baroque period. ✉ *Alter Pl.,* ☎ *0463/577570.* 🎫 *AS15.* ☉ *Apr.–Sept., weekdays 9–noon and 12:30–5.*

🔄 From Klagenfurt, take Villacher Strasse (Route 83) rather than the autobahn to the Wörther See, Austria's great summer-resort area. You'll pass by the **Minimundus** park, literally meaning "miniature world," with more than 175 models at a 1:25 scale of such structures as the White House, Independence Hall, the Eiffel Tower, and the Gur-Emir Mausoleum from Samarkand (Uzbekistan). ✉ *Villacher Str. 241,* ☎ *0463/21194,* 📠 *0463/21194–60.* 🎫 *AS120.* ☉ *Apr., early Oct., daily 9–5; May–June and Sept., daily 9–6; July–Aug., daily 9–6.*

🔄 Just down the road from Minimundus is the **Reptilien Zoo,** featuring crocodiles, cobras, rattlesnakes, and several kinds of hairy spiders, as well as colorful fish from the nearby Wörther See. ✉ *Villacher Str. 237,* ☎ *0463/23425,* 📠 *0463/23425–14.* 🎫 *AS110.* ☉ *Apr.–Oct., daily 8–6; Nov.–Mar., daily 9–5.*

Located in the house where Robert Musil—author of the award-winning, three-volume novel *The Man Without Qualities*—was born in 1880, the **Robert Musil Museum** displays documents and photographs belonging to him, as well as first editions of his work. Musil's writing focused on the cultural disintegration and spiritual crisis of his day.

He fled Nazi-occupied Austria in the 1930s and died penniless in Switzerland in 1942. ⊠ *Bahnhofstr. 50,* ☎ *0463/501429.* ⛛ *AS40* ☉ *Mon.–Fri. 10–5, Sat. 10–2.* ⋐

OFF THE
BEATEN PATH

PYRAMIDENKOGEL – On the shore of the Keutschacher See, about 8 km (5 mi) west of Klagenfurt, lies the town of Keutschach, with the Romanesque church of St. George, a Baroque castle, and an 800-year-old linden tree. A winding 5-km (3-mi) road ascends to the observation tower atop the 2,790-ft Pyramidenkogel; from here on a clear day you can see out over half of Carinthia.

KLOPEINERSEE – This is the warmest lake in Austria (if not in all Europe), located about a 30-minute drive east of Klagenfurt. With water temperatures averaging 28 degrees Celsius (82 degrees Fahrenheit) from spring to fall, it's a popular spot for sunbathing. Surrounded by gentle mountains, the lake is 1 ½ mi long and ½ mi wide, and motorboats are not allowed. To reach the Klopeinersee, take the west Völkermarkt/Tainach exit from the A2 autobahn and follow signs to the lake. For information on lakeside hotels and pensions, contact Klopeinersee Tourismus (☞ Visitor Information, *below*).

Dining and Lodging

$$$$ ✕ **Maria Loretto.** Gorgeous is the word to describe this spot's setting,
★ which offers a view over the Wörther See and makes a fitting backdrop for some of the area's best seafood. This former villa has several charmingly rustic dining rooms to choose from, or you can sit outdoors on the wraparound terrace overlooking the lake. Don't miss the appetizer of delicate trout caviar and smoked salmon on crispy toast points, then try the grilled calamari or *Seeteufel* medallions (monkfish drizzled with garlic butter). Meat and vegetarian pasta dishes are also offered. You'll need a taxi to get here. ⊠ *Lorettoweg 54,* ☎ *0463/ 24465. Reservations essential. V. Closed Jan.–Feb. and Tues. Sept.–June.*

$$–$$$ ✕ **Oscar.** This bustling, modern restaurant with floor-to-ceiling win-
★ dows, crimson glass chandeliers, and close-set tables mainly offers innovative Italian dishes, and portions are large. Start with spinach crepes in a light cheese sauce or mushroom risotto with chicory, then move on to pork medallions stuffed with local cheese in a sage sauce with vegetables. Pizza is also tempting. For dessert try the creamy coconut tiramisu. ⊠ *St. Veiter Ring 43,* ☎ *0463/5001–77,* ℻ *0463/ 507517. AE, DC, V, MC. Closed Sun.*

$ ✕ **Hamatle.** Dine upstairs or down in this friendly, casual establishment just off the Villacher Ring. This is the place to go for Kärntner Käsnudeln, a Carinthian specialty of large, round ravioli. Here they're light as a feather and stuffed with your choice of spinach, cheese, or minced beef. Schnitzels and other Austrian specialties are also featured. ⊠ *Linseng. 1,* ☎ *0463/555700,* ℻ *0463/555704. AE, DC, MC, V. Closed Mon.*

$$$ 🏨 **Moser-Verdino.** With a facade of dusky rose adorned with wrought-iron balconies, this has been the city's leading hotel for more than a century. Rooms are spacious with soothing tones, imitation Jugendstil accents, pretty drapes with matching bedskirts, and nice castle prints on the walls. The staff is exceptionally warm and helpful. The café is nearly always full and is a good spot for a snack. ⊠ *Domg. 2, A–9020,* ☎ *0463/57878,* ℻ *0463/516765. 71 rooms. Bar, café, sauna, parking (fee). AE, DC, MC, V.* ⋐

$$$ 🏨 **Musil.** Modern amenities have been tastefully incorporated into a 15th-century nobleman's palace in the center of town. The style is personal, intimate, and different in each room, ranging from Baroque to Biedermeier and simple Austrian rural. Rooms open onto a series of

circular interior balconies. The popular café serves cakes from the hotel's own bakery. ⊠ *10-Oktober-Str. 14, A–9010,* ☎ *0463/511660,* FAX *0463/511660–4. 12 rooms. Restaurant, bar, café. AE, DC, MC, V.*

$$–$$$ 🏨 **Sandwirt.** This centrally located hotel, incorporated into a 17th-century town house, has been in the same family for several generations. Rooms are large, with high ceilings and contemporary furnishings, but those on the first floor are the most attractive and have comfortable sitting areas. The hotel is part of the Best Western group. ⊠ *Pernhartg. 9, A–9010,* ☎ *0463/56209,* FAX *0463/514322. 40 rooms. AE, DC, MC, V.*

$$–$$$ 🏨 **Schlosshotel Wörthersee.** At the end of the lake and on its own beach, this pale yellow mansion with fancy woodwork, towers, and balconies will remind you of the era of the grand hotels. The rooms are modern and plainly furnished; the preferred ones overlook the lake. The restaurant serves hearty local cuisine in the atmosphere of an informal Heuriger. ⊠ *Villacher Str. 338, A–9010,* ☎ *0463/21158–0,* FAX *0463/21158–8. 41 rooms. Restaurant, bar, café, sauna, beach, bicycles. AE, DC, MC, V.*

Nightlife and the Arts

Opera and operetta are performed year-round at the Stadttheater in Klagenfurt, a pretty Art Nouveau building designed by the famous theater architects Helmer and Fellner of Vienna and completed in 1910. The schedule here often features overlooked jewels—in 1999 Mozart's *La Clemenza di Tito* and Imre Kálmán's *Csárdásfürstin* were the main productions. For details and tickets, contact **Stadttheater Klagenfurt** (⊠ Theaterpl. 4, A–9020, ☎ 0463/55266). The box office is open Sept.–June, Mon.–Sat. 9–1 and 2–6.

For a true after-hours scene in Klagenfurt, head for the Pfarrplatz-Herrengasse area, where you'll find a number of intimate bars and cafés. In the Old City, the Klagenfurt crowd gathers at any number of jaunty places, such as the **Tapferes Schneiderlein** on Herrengasse, but the **Scotch and Lemon** (⊠ Pfarrpl. 20, ☎ 0463/540972) remains the top dancing venue.

Outdoor Activities and Sports

BICYCLING

You can rent bicycles at the **Klagenfurt main station** (☎ 0463/5811365). Many visitors enjoy biking trips to the nearby Wörther See.

GOLF

Golfplatz Klagenfurt-Wörthersee at Schloss Seltenheim (☎ 0463/40223, FAX 0463/40223–20) recently expanded from 9 holes to a full 36-hole course. The greens fee is AS600 (AS700 on summer weekends) and the club is open March–October.

TENNIS

If you're in the mood to take to the courts, check out **Tenniscenter Allround** (⊠ Welzeneggerstr., ☎ 0463/31571) or **Tennisplätze M. Schoklitsch** (⊠ Feschnigstr. 209, ☎ 0463/41140).

Krumpendorf

❷   *10 km (6 mi) west of Klagenfurt.*

The first town on the north side of the Wörther See is less chic and far less pretentious than the other resorts, but pleasant all the same. The resort's water sports and down-home atmosphere appeal to families., particularly those seeking to escape the higher prices and singles invasions of other areas.

Lodging

$ 🏨 **Schloss Hallegg.** Just east of Krumpendorf, a small road heading
★   north leads to an early 13th-century castle, tucked away on the edge of a nature preserve above the lake. Now adapted as a hotel, it has

rooms that are spacious and comfortable. You'll get breakfast only, but there is a choice of restaurants in town. There's a small lake for swimming and fishing, and ample grounds for hunting and riding. ☒ *Hallegger Str. 131, A–9201,* ☎ *0463/49311. 15 rooms. Lake, tennis court, horseback riding, fishing. No credit cards. Closed mid-Sept.–mid-May.*

Pörtschach

❸ *6 km (4 mi) west of Krumpendorf.*

Midway along the Wörther See is Pörtschach, one of the two top vacation spots on the lake. Here, the water is often warm enough for swimming as early as May, which is early indeed for an Alpine region. You'll find dozens of places to stay and even more things to do under the stars: the nightlife here is as varied as the daytime activities. Elegant villas line the peninsula, which is abloom with flowers and verdant foliage during the summer months. Chicly dressed visitors head for the lakeshore promenade to enjoy the view.

Dining and Lodging

$$$ ✕ **Rainer's.** Make your way through the bar to this "in" restaurant. The most favored tables are on the balcony overlooking the lake, although the two inside rooms have an intimacy of their own. Food choices are limited but good; try the grilled shrimp in herb sauce or the roast hare, or settle for a steak. ☒ *Monte-Carlo-Pl. 1,* ☎ *04272/2300,* 𝙵𝙰𝚇 *0427/2300–17. AE, MC, V. Closed mid-Sept.–mid-May. No lunch.*

$$$ ✕🏨 **Schloss Leonstain.** This appealing 500-year-old castle, complete
★ with tower and antique furnishings, is unfortunately situated between the railroad and the highway (quiet is hard to find). The restaurant is among the best in town and is well worth a visit on its own. In summer, tables are set up in the courtyard as well as in the historic dining rooms. ☒ *Hauptstr. 228, A–9210,* ☎ *04272/2816–0,* 𝙵𝙰𝚇 *04272/2823. 38 rooms. Restaurant, lake, sauna, golf course, tennis court, boating. AE, DC, MC, V. Closed early Oct.–early May.*

$$$–$$$$ 🏨 **Schloss Seefels.** About 3 km (2 mi) west of Pörtschach, this hotel attracts a prominent international clientele. The sprawling, interconnected buildings are set in a huge park on the lake, the staff is friendly, and the elegantly furnished rooms are in the grand-hotel mode. You can go by boat directly to Klagenfurt and to the Kärntner golf course across the lake. Half board is required. ☒ *A–9210 Pörtschach/Töschling,* ☎ *04272/2377,* 𝙵𝙰𝚇 *04272/3704. 73 rooms. Restaurant, bar, indoor-outdoor pool, sauna, golf course, tennis court, exercise room, beach, boating, fishing. AE. Closed Oct.–Apr.*

$$–$$$ 🏨 **Europa.** This modern hotel, uninspiring on the outside, stands directly on the water. Ask for a room on the lake side and enjoy a view of the sunniest corner of the lake. Half board is standard. The view is wonderful from the restaurant. ☒ *Augustenstr. 24, A–9210,* ☎ *04272/2244–0,* 𝙵𝙰𝚇 *04272/2298. 47 rooms. Restaurant, lake, golf course, tennis court, boating, bicycles. No credit cards. Closed Oct.–Apr.*

Outdoor Activities and Sports

GOLF

You can improve your swing at the 18-hole, par-72 **Golfanlage Moosburg-Pörtschach** (☎ 04272/83486, 𝙵𝙰𝚇 04272/82055). The club is open April–early November. Greens fee is AS580 for adults.

HORSEBACK RIDING

Riding is a nice way to see some of the scenic countryside. Contact the **Reitstall Knoll** in Wölfnitz (☎ 0463/49273); special offers include lodging.

WATER SPORTS

Pörtschach is a center of activity for windsurfing, parasurfing, and sailing. Check **Herbert Schweiger** (✉ 10-Oktober-Str. 33, ☎ 04272/2655). Several hotels on the Wörther See offer sailing and surfing packages.

Maria Wörth

❹ *10 km (6 mi) west of Klagenfurt.*

The spire of Maria Wörth's parish church reflected in the waters of the Wörther See is one of Austria's most-photographed sights. This unpretentious little town is situated on a wooded peninsula jutting out toward the center of the lake and almost entirely surrounded by water. It actually has two notable churches, both dating from the 12th century. The smaller **Rosenkranzkirche** (Rosary church) in the town itself is basically Romanesque with later Gothic additions. The interior has a Romanesque choir with fragments of 12th-century frescoes of the apostles, a stained-glass Madonna window from 1420, and Gothic carved-wood figures. The larger **Pfarrkirche** (parish church), despite its Romanesque portal, is mainly Gothic, with a Baroque interior, revealing all the "wrinkles" acquired since the days of its appearance in the 9th century. Skulls and bones can still be seen in the round Romanesque charnel house in the cemetery.

Lodging

$$$ 🏨 **Astoria.** This massive, comfortable villa on the lake is just 2 km (1 mi) from the 18-hole, par-71 Kärntner Golf Club course at Dellach; the hotel offers golf-holiday packages. The rooms are attractively furnished; those overlooking the lake are preferred. You'll have to take half board. ✉ *A–9082,* ☎ *04273/2279,* 🆉 *04273/2279–80. 45 rooms. Restaurant, Weinstube, indoor pool, sauna, tennis court. MC. Closed mid-Oct.–May.*

$$$ 🏨 **Seewirt.** This large, sprawling hotel in Dellach right by the lake has all the amenities to make a stay on the southern shore of the Wörther See pleasant. The hotel's own farm produces some of the food you eat, and the fishing is also done "in-house." Golf players get a 30% discount on the greens fee at the golf course (☞ Outdoor Activities and Sports, *below*). ✉ *Fischerweg 12, A–9082 Dellach,* ☎ *04273/2257,* 🆉 *04273/280572. 19 rooms. Restaurant, sauna, 18-hole golf course, tennis court, exercise room, beach, boating, baby-sitting. No credit cards. Closed Oct.–May.*

Outdoor Activities and Sports

GOLF

Enjoy the scenic view while getting in your 18 holes at the **Kärntner Golf Club,** one of Austria's oldest golf clubs, at Dellach (☎ 04273/2515, 🆉 04273/2606). The club is open April–October. Greens fees are AS600 on weekdays, AS700 on weekends.

Velden

❺ *8 km (5 mi) west of Maria Wörth.*

Velden, the largest resort on the lake, is perched at the west end of the Wörther See. The atmosphere here strives to retain its international chic—classy and lively—and the summer carnival in August adds to the action. The fact that a casino has settled here says a lot about Velden, which has very little in the way of sights otherwise. The town's most famous beauty spot is the lakeside promenade, accented by turn-of-the-century lamps and mansions. However, if you're looking for a tranquil holiday, Velden may be too exuberant. The town gets pricey in the July–August main season.

Dining and Lodging

$$$$ ✕ **Casino-Restaurant.** If you're looking for fine cuisine plus a view, this place offers a wondrous vista over the lake. The cuisine ranges from international to regional and seasonal specialties. Keep an eye out for chanterelles in summer and venison at the end of September. The casino complex (☞ Nightlife, *below*) is limited to those 18 and over, and you'll need your passport for identification. ⊠ *Am Corso 17,* ☎ *04274/2948–57. Jacket and tie. AE, DC, MC, V.*

$$$–$$$$ ✕⊞ **Golf-Park-Hotel Velden.** This exclusive establishment, set in a park amid a stand of huge old trees, has been luxuriously renovated to offer every comfort, attracting tennis stars and Saudi royals. From the spacious lobby to the modern guest rooms, you'll find elegance and attentive service. The gourmet restaurant is particularly noted and, for this region, is distinctively cordon bleu in style and quality. ⊠ *Seecorso 68, A–9220,* ☎ *04274/2298–0,* 𝔽𝔸𝕏 *04274/2298–9. 89 rooms. 2 restaurants, bar, indoor pool, beauty salon, sauna, spa, 3 tennis courts, exercise room. AE, DC, MC, V. Closed late-Sept.–mid-Apr.*

$$–$$$ ✕⊞ **Hubertushof.** Two typical resort houses from the turn of the century comprise this family-run complex directly on the lake. A touch of the original Art Deco carries over into some of the rooms, most of which have balconies. The best rooms face the lake. The Hubertusstuberl restaurant is gaining a reputation for its way with regional specialties, such as lamb. ⊠ *Europapl. 1, A–9220,* ☎ *04274/2676–0,* 𝔽𝔸𝕏 *04274/2657–60. 46 rooms. Restaurant, indoor pool, sauna, exercise room, boating. DC, MC, V. Closed mid-Oct.–mid-Apr.*

Nightlife

The **casino** in the center of Velden is a focal point of the evening, but you must be 18 or over. Along with the gambling tables and slot machines, the complex contains a disco, bars, and a restaurant (☞ Dining and Lodging, *above*), whose terrace overlooks the lake. You'll need your passport to enter the casino. ⊠ *Am Corso 17,* ☎ *04274/ 2064,* 𝔽𝔸𝕏 *04274/2982. Jacket and tie.* ☉ *Daily 3* PM*–3 or 4* AM.

Outdoor Activities and Sports

WATER SPORTS

Velden is another good site for windsurfing, parasurfing, and sailing. Rentals are available at **Segel-und-Surfschule Wörthersee/Berger** (⊠ Seecorso 40, ☎ 04274/2691–0, 𝔽𝔸𝕏 04274/2691–20).

OFF THE BEATEN PATH **MARIA GAIL** –The Romanesque parish church here has an unusually good 14th-century Gothic winged triptych altar. To get to Maria Gail, 15 km (9 mi) west of Velden, take Villacher Strasse, Route 83, out of Velden. If you're heading on to Faaker See, you'll pass, several miles beyond Maria Gail, one of the most famous roadside shrines in Austria: framed by lake and mountain, this *Manterl* is a great photo op.

Egg am Faaker See

❻ *4 km (2½ mi) east of Maria Gail.*

With turquoise-green waters that seem almost Mediterranean, the Faaker See presents an idyllic setting for swimming and boating. Boating aficionados take to the lake in droves with a rainbow array of sails skimming across the horizon (motorboats are not allowed); even so, the round lake—with its tiny island in the middle—remains less crowded than other resort areas here. Watching over all is the mighty pyramid of the Mittagskogel of the Karawanken range.

Dining and Lodging

$$$$ ✕⊞ **Karnerhof.** A huge chalet with a long, low extension is set in a
★   quiet park right on the lake, with the mountain range serving as a scenic
        backdrop. This affiliate of the Silencehotel group offers attractive
        rustic rooms and the excellent Götzelstube restaurant. All dishes are
        freshly prepared, and the fish is particularly fine. ⊠ *Egger-Seeprom-*
        enade 4/Karnerhofweg 10, A–9580, ☎ *04254/2188,* ℻ *04254/3650.*
        105 rooms. Restaurant, café, indoor-outdoor pool, sauna, tennis
        court, exercise room, beach. AE, DC, V. Closed mid-Oct.–Mar.

$$–$$$ ✕⊞ **Sonnblick.** This family-run modern hotel is not especially attrac-
        tive, but it has pleasant sun-drenched balconies, windows festooned with
        bright red geraniums, and a gemütlich atmosphere. Guests are greeted
        with a "welcome" cocktail and evening barbecues are staged on the ter-
        race overlooking the mountains. The hotel justifiably prides itself on
        its extensive wine cellar, featuring regional and European vintages. ⊠
        Dreimühlenweg 23, A–9580, ☎ *04254/21670,* ℻ *04254/216715. 32*
        rooms. Restaurant. AE, DC, MC, V. Closed mid.-Oct.–Apr.

Outdoor Activities and Sports

GOLF

Take in a game of golf at the 18-hole, par-72 **Golfanlagen Velden-Kösten-**
berg (☎ 04274/7045, ℻ 04274/708715). The club is open April–early
November.

Viktring

❼ *17 km (10½ mi) east of Egg am Faaker See, 6½ km (4 mi) southwest*
   of Klagenfurt.

From the west and the Faaker See, you can get to Viktring by following the Rosental valley on Route 85 until you come to the junction with
Route 91 and then turn north toward Klagenfurt. Alternatively, take
the narrow country road along the Pyramidenkogel (☞ Klagenfurt,
above); it begins in Lind and goes by Keutschach and its pretty little
lake. From Viktring it's 6½ km (4 mi) back to Klagenfurt.

You can still see parts of the moat remaining from the **Cistercian con-**
vent established here in 1142. Don't miss the convent's arcaded cloisters, and look for the 14th- to 16th-century stained glass in the choir
of the church, behind the Baroque high altar. Every summer the old
walls are the setting for music learning and performance, modern to
jazz, at **Musikforum Viktring** (⊠ Stift-Viktring-Str. 25, A–9073 Klagenfurt, ☎ 0463/28–22–41, ℻ 0463/28–16–26).

THE DRAU VALLEY

The Drau Valley is a Carinthia for all reasons—there's a little here of the
best of everything you can find in the province. One of the most impressive
Renaissance castles in the country can be found in Spittal an der Drau,
which comes alive with a series of theatrical events and concerts during
the summer months. Take a ride on the wild side with a visit to the Porsche
Museum, which documents the history of the innovative car maker. Or
you can soothe tired muscles at a Roman bath before relaxing away from
the crowds at the quiet lakeside resort on the Feldsee. We begin, however, at the main town in Upper Carinthia, Spittal an der Drau.

Spittal an der Drau

❽ *31 km (20 mi) northwest of Villach.*

The name Spittal, meaning "hospital" or "station," goes back to the
Middle Ages—this little town was an important stop on the north–south

route across the Alps. The ancient building was then used as a basis for the impressive Gothic church (on your left as you enter the town, autobahn exit Spittal-Ost), which was completed in 1311. But the name Spittal an der Drau is synonymous with the architecturally superb **Schloss Porcia,** built in the 16th century by the imperial treasurer Count Gabriel von Salamanca. This castle-palace, in the center of town next to a lovely park, is one of the most beautiful Renaissance buildings in Austria, especially in its gracefully arcaded Italianate courtyard stairways and open corridors, which provide a dreamlike setting for summer performances of classical plays, often by Shakespeare. The upper floors house a museum highlighting regional culture of the past. Otherwise, besides the cozy inner town and its central square, Spittal is unremarkable. By the way, north–south traffic still goes by on the A10 autobahn. ☎ *04762/2890.* ⌨ *AS50.* ☼ *Mid-May–Oct., daily 9–6; Nov.–mid-May, Mon.–Thurs. 1–4.*

☾ The **Goldeckbahn,** the aerial tramway that leaves from behind the tennis hall on Ortenburgerstrasse (☎ 04762/2864–0), will take you up to the 6,960-ft peak of the Goldeck mountain, from which you get splendid panoramic views to the north and east.

Dining and Lodging

$–$$ ✕▥ **Langasthof Tell.** In the village of Paternion, halfway between Villach and Spittal, stands a nicely renovated 700-year-old country inn with a real familial feeling and excellent Carinthian cooking—homemade sausages, liverwurst, and all sorts of so-called *Pfandlgerichte* (dishes fried in a pan). The traditional interior courtyard is very pretty. ⊠ *Marktpl. 14, A–9711 Paternion,* ☎ *04245/2931,* ℻ *04245/3026. 16 rooms. Restaurant, fishing, bicycles. MC. Closed in late fall for 2 wks.*

$$ ▥ **Alte Post.** This traditional, friendly house in the center of town has comfortable modern rooms, a good restaurant, and the bonus of fishing rights on a reserved stretch of the Drau River. ⊠ *Hauptpl. 13, A–9800 Spittal,* ☎ *04762/2217–0,* ℻ *04762/5125–57. 42 rooms. Restaurant, bar. AE, DC, MC, V. Closed Jan.*

$ ▥ **Ertl.** This salmon-fronted, family-run hotel in a beautiful 19th-century building is just steps from the railroad station but away from heavy traffic. It even has a garden of sorts. If you're touring by train it's ideal; the rooms are large and attractively decorated. ⊠ *Bahnhofstr. 26, A–9800 Spittal,* ☎ *04762/2048–0,* ℻ *04762/2048–5. 40 rooms. Restaurant, pool, bicycles. AE, DC, MC, V. Closed Nov.*

Nightlife and the Arts

In Spittal an der Drau, from July through August, the *Komödienspiele,* three plays focusing on human foibles and virtues, are presented with a minimum of pomp in the marvelous setting of Schloss Porcia. The experience is always great fun. Spittal is also the setting for an international **choir festival,** usually held in early July. **Program information** and ticket details for both events are from the same source (☎ 04762/3420; 04762/3161 after July 1, ℻ 04762/3237).

Outdoor Activities and Sports

GOLF

An 18-hole course, a driving range, a pro shop, a nice restaurant, wonderful views of the lake and the mountains—you couldn't ask for more at **Golfclub Millstätter See.** ⊠ *Millstatt,* ☎ *04762/82548,* ℻ *04762/82548–10.* ⌨ *Greens fees range from AS500 to AS600.*

HIKING

There's unusually good hiking starting from Spittal, and even better from Gmünd, Seeboden, Millstatt, Bad Kleinkirchheim, Feld am See, and Afritz. Local visitor information offices will have suggestions for routes and for combining a hike with a return by local bus.

Gmünd

🅨 *19 km (12 mi) north of Spittal an der Drau via Rte. 99 (Gmündner Strasse).*

Not far from where the Malta mountain stream rushes into the Lieser is the colorful town of Gmünd. The warm pastels of the town's building facades on the oval-shape central square stand in contrast to the dark green of the surrounding forested hills. This little 16th-century town with medieval walls has been carefully restored. The "new" **castle** (1651) is watched over by the old castle, in ruin above the town. See the **Pfarrkirche** (parish church) and the ancient fresco on the outside wall, which shows the town as it was in the 17th century—little different from the way it looks today, except that the old castle is now complete. The **Stadtmuseum** (town museum) can be found in the lower gate tower.

The automobile designer Ferry Porsche was born and worked in Gmünd; the informative and fascinating **Porsche Museum** shows a series of the cars and experimental models he designed and built. The museum is directly northwest of the old walled town. ☎ *04732/2471.* 🎟 *AS65.* ☉ *Mid-May–mid-Oct., daily 9–6; mid-Oct.–mid-May, daily 10–1.*

Dining and Lodging

$$ ✕ **Alte Burg.** You might not expect to find a gemütlich setting within the ruins of a 13th-century castle, so you'll be surprised to discover this attractive restaurant, set amid renovated dungeons and battlements, decorated with Carinthian wrought iron and antiques. On the menu, look for regional specialties such as roast lamb and Kärntner Käsnudeln (large, cheese-stuffed ravioli). This food comes with a view, as the castle picturesquely overlooks the town. ✉ *Alte Burg,* ☎ *04732/3639. AE, DC, MC, V. Closed Wed.–Thurs. Sept.–June, and mid-Jan.–wk before Easter.*

$ 🏨 **Kohlmayr.** Behind the pinkish facade of this family-run hotel on the town square you'll find a particularly friendly staff and modern, attractive rooms in rustic decor. Up the stone steps is a large reception room furnished with country antiques (including a spinning wheel). The rooms in front have a stunning view over the square. The whole town gathers in the *Bierstube* in the late afternoon and on Sunday morning. The restaurant offers good standard Austrian country fare. ✉ *Hauptpl. 7, A–9853,* ☎ *04732/2149,* 🖷 *04732/2153. 22 rooms. Restaurant, Weinstube. No credit cards. Closed Nov.*

Outdoor Activities and Sports

HIKING
In summer you can head up the scenic Malta Valley to see the massive hydroelectric dam and lake, and hike at the top.

Millstatt

🅪 *5 km (3 mi) southeast of Gmünd.*

The largest resort on the Millstätter See is crowned by an impressive **Benedictine abbey** and adorned with imposing towers, antique courtyards, and centuries-old linden trees. The abbey was founded in the 11th century but secularized in the 18th. The twin-towered Romanesque church of the abbey complex was partially rebuilt in Gothic style and later given some Baroque ornamentation, but its 12th-century Romanesque portal remains its outstanding feature. Note also the *Kreuzgang,* the arcaded cloister between the church and the monastery, with its complicated pillar ornaments.

There is an old legend that St. Domitian cast 1,000 heathen statues in the lake around the turn of the 8th century. The **statues** along the waterfront promenade here are the beginning of an extensive artistic initiative called "1,000 statues," aimed at foiling old Domitian posthumously.

Dining and Lodging

$$$ ✕🏨 **Alpenrose.** This attractive house, with rustic-style rooms, advertises itself as Austria's first "bio-hotel." It is constructed entirely of natural materials (primarily wood and brick) and uses no plastic. The excellent restaurant continues the theme, featuring only natural ingredients (many of the vegetables are organically grown in the side garden). Half board is required. In winter there's free transport to nearby ski areas. ✉ *Obermillstatt 84, A–9872,* ☎ *04766/2500–0,* FAX *04766/3425. 34 rooms. Restaurant, pool, sauna. No credit cards. Closed late Nov.–mid-Dec.*

$$–$$$ ✕🏨 **See-Villa.** This beautiful old villa in burnt yellow with a splendid garden was once a private mansion belonging to the Counts Tacoli. Count Anton Tacoli still is the master of the house; his guests are many and all are satisfied. The selection for vegetarians is picked from the villa's own vegetable garden, as are the herbs; fish are from the lake. ✉ *Seestr. 68, A–9872,* ☎ *04766/2102,* FAX *04766/2221. 18 rooms. Restaurant, beach, windsurfing. MC. Closed Oct. 16–Apr. 30.*

$$ ✕🏨 **Die Forelle.** This four-story balconied house sprawls along the lake, its tree-shaded terrace directly over the water. The public rooms are elegant but comfortable, the guest rooms bright and welcoming. The hotel has its own stretch of fishing water. Fish is featured at the ambitious and successful restaurant. ✉ *Fischerg. 65, A–9872,* ☎ *04766/2050–0,* FAX *04766/2050–11. 68 rooms. Restaurant, pool, sauna, tennis court, boating, fishing. DC, MC, V. Closed Nov.–Apr.*

Nightlife and the Arts

In Millstatt there's something going on throughout much of the year: Musical Spring runs mid-May–June; International Music Weeks take over during July and August, followed by Musical Autumn in September. Most events take place in the Benedictine abbey. For program details and ticket reservations, contact **Musikwochen Millstatt** (✉ Stiftg. 1, A–9872, ☎ 04766/2022–35, FAX 04766/3479).

Outdoor Activities and Sports

BICYCLING

The Millstätter See is a naturally beautiful area to cycle, with well-tended and -marked paths going all around the lake and over to other places, such as up the Malta Valley from Gmünd (☞ *above*) or over to Seeboden. For information contact the tourist office in Millstatt (☞ Carinthia A to Z, *below*). Bicycles can be rented at the **Spittal-Millstätter See railroad station,** among other places (☎ 04762/356–3181).

Bad Kleinkirchheim

⑪ *6 km (4 mi) north of Radenthein via Rte. 88.*

Barely known 30 years ago, the town of Bad Kleinkirchheim has become a booming and stylish resort thanks to its terrific combination of sports, activities, and the spa, which attracts people seeking a variety of cures. Although it's also popular in summer, the town is unquestionably Carinthia's top ski resort, and Austrians flock to the slopes here in winter for great cross-country skiing, snowboarding, and skating. After a day on the slopes you can plunge into the (re-created) **Roman baths,** fed by thermal mineral springs. Nearby, the **Katharinenkapelle** (St. Catherine's Chapel) marks the location of one of the springs. It has an organ loft with carved-wood reliefs and a late-Gothic winged altar. Stop at **St. Oswald,** north of town, to look at the unusual iron hinges on the doors of the late-Gothic church, and step inside to see its frescoes from 1514 and to admire the groined vaulting on the ceiling.

Lodging

$$$–$$$$ 🏨 **Pulverer.** This friendly hotel, in a group of interconnected chalet-style buildings, is not only in the center of town but is one of the centers of activity. You can take a cure with the medicinal thermal waters, then undo the good work at the enticing buffets: breakfast, salad, strudel, and hors d'oeuvres. The guest rooms are done in elegant country-rustic decor. ✉ *Bach 1, A–9546,* ☎ *04240/744,* 🙰 *04240/793. 40 rooms, 50 apartment-suites. Restaurant, indoor-outdoor pool, sauna, spa, golf privileges, exercise room. No credit cards. Closed late Apr.–mid-May.*

$$$–$$$$ 🏨 **Ronacher.** You can easily spoil yourself at this family-managed combination sports-and-cure facility, with its in-house thermal baths and luxurious balconied rooms in modern-rustic decor. The large hotel is off the main road in the middle of town. It organizes many activities for those who dislike the chore of planning. Half board is required. ✉ *Bach 18, A–9546,* ☎ *04240/282,* 🙰 *04240/282–606. 92 rooms. Restaurant, indoor-outdoor pools, sauna, spa, exercise room. AE, DC, V. Closed Apr. and late Oct.–mid-Dec.*

$$ 🏨 **Putz-Römerbad.** This family-run chalet-style hotel, tucked away behind fir trees, is a bit east of the center. A thermal-mineral spring bath is just down the hall, and sports facilities are a short walk away. Public rooms are spacious, balconied guest rooms slightly less so; the warmth of the rustic decor creates a comfortable atmosphere. Rooms on the south side have a view of the mountains. Half board is required. ✉ *Zirkitzen 69, A–9546,* ☎ *04240/8234–0,* 🙰 *04240/8234–57. 32 rooms. Restaurant, sauna, spa, exercise room. AE, DC, V.* ✎

Outdoor Activities and Sports

GOLF

Golfclub Bad Kleinkirchheim (☎ 04275/594, 🙰 04275/504) is challenging for beginners and advanced golfers alike, thanks to a fine 18-hole, par-72 course. The greens fee is AS400–AS600, depending on the season, and the club is open May–October.

SKIING

Made famous by local ski legend Franz Klammer, the ski resort at **Kleinkirchheim** (✉ A–9546, ☎ 04240/8212, 🙰 04240/8537) has more than 100 km (60 mi) of prepared trails. Less famous and glamorous than the resorts in neighboring Tirol, the region caters to parents and their children. The combination spa is the clincher as far as pure rest and relaxation go. The Römerbad spa, for example, has an outdoor pool open in winter, which is a delightful treat after a long day on the slopes. Local hotels and tourist offices can provide information on lesson and lift packages (in some cases use of the two spas, Römer and St. Kathrein, is included). For information, contact the tourist office (☞ Carinthia A to Z, *below*).

THE GURKTAL REGION

Storybook names, such as Tannhäuser, Snow White, and the Holy Hemma, are encountered throughout the Gurktal region of Carinthia. The region is populated with medieval strongholds, idyllic lakes, and towns reeking with charm down to the last cobblestone.

Villach

⑫ *50 km (30 mi) west of Klagenfurt.*

Carinthia's "other" capital (Klagenfurt is the official one) sits astride the Drau River. The Romans may have been the first to bridge the river here to establish their settlement of Bilachium, from which the present name Villach is derived. The city is compact, with narrow, twisting lanes (restricted to pedestrians) winding through the Old City south of the river. Small, attractive shops are tucked into arcaded buildings, and each corner turned brings a fresh and surprising perspective. Renaissance houses surround the main square, which has a Baroque column honoring the Trinity. The 16th-century alchemist and physician Theophrastus Bombastus Hohenheim—better known as Paracelsus, the inventor of homeopathic medicine—lived at Hauptplatz 14; his father was the town physician.

The late-Gothic 14th-century **St. Jacob** (St. James's) was Protestant during the mid-1500s, making it Austria's first Protestant church. Its marble pulpit dates from 1555; the ornate Baroque high altar contrasts grandly with the Gothic crucifix. If the stair entry is open and you don't mind the rather steep climb, the view from the 310-ft tower is marvelous. Near the river, at the intersection of Ossiacher Zeile and Peraustrasse, the pinkish **Heiligenkreuz** (Holy Cross Church), with two towers and a cupola, is a splendid example of fully integrated Baroque. A good time to visit Villach is around August 1, when the townspeople and those from surrounding villages don traditional clothes and celebrate *Kirtag*—the traditional feast day of each town's patron saint—with music, folk dancing, and general merrymaking.

In the summer, a particularly lovely way to explore the Drau River from Villach is to take a cruise on the **MS Landskron**; watching the sun set over the mountains while you dine on board makes for a memorable evening. For schedule and details, check with the tourist office or Drau-Schiffahrt (✉ Neubaug. 32, ☎ 04242/58071, 🅵🅰🅷 04242/58072).

OFF THE BEATEN PATH	**LANDSKRON –** An interesting stopping point is this ruined castle, which has spectacular views over Villach, the Ossiacher See, and the Karawanken mountain range to the south. The original castle here dated from 1351 and was destroyed by fire in 1861; since then, sections have been rebuilt. It is also a keep for birds of prey, which are trained for shows. To get here, take Route 83 about 4 km (2½ mi) northeast of Villach.

Dining and Lodging

$$$ **✗ Postillion.** Located in the Hotel Post, the Postillion is known among
★ locals as the best restaurant in town (in fact, this is where culinary giant Wolfgang Puck got his start—he worked here as an apprentice chef for three years before heading to Los Angeles to open his own well-known restaurant, Spago). Dine in country-casual comfort on wild duck carpaccio followed by Kärtner Käsnudeln, that favorite Carinthian specialty of large, round ravioli stuffed with cheese. Vegetables and herbs are straight from the bountiful hotel garden. In summer, tables are set outdoors in the Orangerie, where wild roses and ivy climb the courtyard walls. ✉ *Hauptpl. 26.* ☎ *04242/26101–0,* 🅵🅰🅷 *04242/26101–420. Reservations essential. AE, DC, MC, V.*

$$$ **✗🏠 Hotel Post.** This beautifully adapted Renaissance palace, which
★ dates from 1500, is in the pedestrian zone in the heart of the old city. Over the centuries the house has played host to royalty, even empress Maria Theresa way back in the 1700s. Architects have cleverly created an elegant, stylish hotel while preserving the Old World features of the

building, most notably the arcaded inner court. Rooms are attractively furnished with polished mahogany and lovely fabrics, some in tones of pale apricot and mauve; a few have balconies overlooking the pretty courtyard. The Post is a member of the Romantik Hotel group. ⊠ *Hauptpl. 26, A–9500,* ☎ *04242/26101-0,* FAX *04242/26101-420. 77 rooms. Restaurant, bar, sauna, exercise room, free parking. AE, DC, MC, V.*🏊

$$ ✕🖭 **Hotel Mosser.** You won't be able to miss the Hotel Mosser; it's right in the center of town, with faded orange and green candy-stripe columns and a peach exterior. The furnishings are a bit nondescript, but the rooms tend to be spacious; ask for one facing the courtyard to avoid the noise from the street below. The hotel's restaurant serves classic Austrian fare, from schnitzel to sausages. ⊠ *Bahnhofstr. 9, A–9500,* ☎ *04242/24115,* FAX *04242/24115-222. 29 rooms. Restaurant, massage. AE, DC, MC, V.*

Outdoor Activities and Sports

HIKING

Southwest of Villach, the extremely scenic 16-km (10-mi) Villach Alpine highway climbs the mountain ridge to about 5,000 ft. From there, a lift gets you up to Hohenrain; then you can hike the marked trail—or take the train—up to the peak of the **Dobratsch,** towering 7,040 ft into the clouds and providing a spectacular view. Close to parking lot 6, at 4,875 ft, is an Alpine botanical garden, which is open mid-June–August, daily 9–6. The 11 parking and outlook points along the highway offer great panoramas.

TENNIS

In the Villach area, try **Tennisplätze ASKÖ** (⊠ Landskron, Süduferstr., ☎ 04242/41879) or **Tenniscamp Warmbad** (⊠ Villach–Warmbad Villach, ☎ 04242/32564).

Warmbad Villach

⑬ *3 km (2 mi) southwest of Villach.*

On the southern outskirts of Villach lies Warmbad Villach, its name reflecting the hot springs of radioactive water, believed to combat aging, among other unwelcome things. This remains one of the classic spas of Carinthia—one discovered by the Romans—and people come to enjoy its thermal springs and swimming pools for various rheumatic ailments. Many hotels have been built around the *Kurpark,* the wooded grounds of the spa.

Dining and Lodging

$$$ ✕🖭 **Warmbaderhof.** With a tranquil park setting and a comfortable, ★ meandering house seducing you into relaxation, the cure's the thing here. Ask for one of the modern, balconied rooms overlooking "Napoléon's Meadow." The Bürgerstube restaurant offers regional and national specialties, including game in season. Das kleine Restaurant, with wood and brass decor, changes its offerings with the seasons. ⊠ *Kadischenallee 22–24, A–9504,* ☎ *04242/3001-0,* FAX *04242/3001-80. 123 rooms. 2 restaurants, bar, indoor-outdoor pool, sauna, exercise room, horseback riding. AE, DC, MC, V. Closed Nov.–mid-Dec.*

$$–$$$ 🖭 **Josephinenhof.** Modern without being impersonal, this hotel is set in the comfortable isolation of the Kurpark. A unique program is devoted to age control. The hotel will book only full-week packages in the main season. The restaurant here is unexciting, but ample other possibilities are close by. ⊠ *Kadischenallee 8, A–9504,* ☎ *04242/ 3003-0,* FAX *04242/3003-89. 61 rooms. Restaurant, indoor-outdoor pool, sauna, spa, tennis court. AE, DC, MC, V.*

$$–$$$ 🖭 **Karawankenhof.** The larger rooms in this hotel will appeal to those who want to take the cure or to use this as a base for further excur-

sions in Carinthia. Children are particularly welcome. An underground passageway leads to the spa, with its water slide and pools. The glassed-in terrace restaurant is a delight, but the kitchen, alas, does not quite live up to the decor. ⊠ *Kadischenallee 25–27, A-9504,* ☎ *04242/3002–0,* ℻ *04242/3002–61. 80 rooms, 9 apartments. Restaurant, bar, indoor-outdoor pool, sauna, exercise room. AE, DC, V.*

Ossiach

🕦 *19 km (12 mi) northeast of Warmbad Villach via Rte. 83.*

The resort town of Ossiach is now the center of the Carinthian Summer Festival (☞ Nightlife and the Arts, *below*) and is afflicted with wall-to-wall tourists during the high season. The festival, which since its launch in 1969 has expanded to include use of the Congress Center in Villach, covers all styles of music from Baroque to modern, from Gershwin to klezmer. There are also other attractions, including what was originally an 11th-century **monastery,** a typical square building around an inner court, with a chapel at the side. The chapel, despite its stern, conservative exterior, is wonderfully Baroque. The monastery was razed by the Turks in 1484 and promptly rebuilt, though Baroque renovations have left it with its current look. Legend has it that in the 11th century the Polish king Boleslaw II lived incognito in the monastery for eight years, pretending to be mute, in penance for murdering the bishop of Kraków. A tombstone and a fresco on the church wall facing the cemetery commemorate the tale.

Dining and Lodging

$ ✕ **Forellenstation Niederbichler.** This unpretentious, small, dark-stained wood cabin serves some of the freshest fish you're likely to find in Austria. Caught right in the nearby pond, the trout—*blau,* grilled or breaded and fried—makes a memorable meal at a bargain price. Linger outdoors under the brightly colored umbrellas sipping a *Gespritzter* (wine with soda water). ⊠ *Alt Ossiach 76,* ☎ *04243/8225. No credit cards.*

$$$ ⛻ **Stiftshotel Ossiach.** This first-class hotel was once a monastery (dating from the 1620s). Try for one of the high-ceilinged rooms in front overlooking the lake. The rooms (particularly the front corner suites) are spacious, with reproduction period furnishings. The hotel has its own private pier and beach, and the lake boat docks in front. ⊠ *A-9570,* ☎ *04243/8664–0,* ℻ *0222/8664–8. 50 suites. Restaurant, beach, dock. No credit cards. Closed Oct.–Apr.*

$ ⛻ **Seewirt Köllich.** This large rustic house in a quiet corner directly on the lake next to the monastery church offers simple but comfortable rooms with views over the lake (preferred) or of the lush green hills. The hotel has its own lakeside beach and paddle boats and is adjacent to the waterskiing school. The restaurant offers standard fare such as roast pork and goulash. ⊠ *A-9570,* ☎ *04243/2268. 15 rooms. Restaurant, beach, boating. No credit cards. Closed Nov.–mid-May.*

Nightlife and the Arts

Even though Ossiach is a small town (with a population of less than a thousand), it hosts an internationally renowned music event, the **Carinthian Summer Festival,** which has attracted many notable musicians, including the late Leonard Bernstein, the Collegium Musicum Pragense, and soloists from the London Symphony Orchestra. It is held in July and August and emphasizes 20th-century composition; however, along with Benjamin Britten's opera *The Prodigal Son,* you might also hear some Mozart and Vivaldi, plus a little jazz and pop. Chamber concerts are all the more attractive for their setting in the Baroque chapel or the monastery in Ossiach. For a schedule or tickets, contact Carinthischer Sommer, through late May (⊠ Gumpendorfer Str. 76, A–1060 Vienna, ☎ 01/596–8198, ℻ 01/597–1236) or after early June (✉ Stift Ossiach, A–9570 Ossiach, ☎ 04243/2510, ℻ 04243/2353).

In resort centers like Ossiach, you'll find regular evenings of folk music and dancing, some of them organized by the hotels. The local tourist offices will have details, and notices are often posted around the area.

Outdoor Activities and Sports

BICYCLING

The area around the Ossiacher See is excellent for cycling, and many of the main roads have parallel cycling paths. Rental bicycles are in great demand throughout this area, so reserve in advance. You can rent a bicycle at the **Ossiach-Bodensdorf railroad station** (☎ 04243/2218 in summer, or 04243/1717), where there's also a dock; you can put the bike on the boat, get off and cycle to the next boat landing, then return by boat when you run out of energy.

Feldkirchen

⑮ *6 km (4 mi) northeast of Ossiach.*

Feldkirchen is a modest little town that hides well the fact that it is one of Carinthia's oldest communities, having been officially mentioned in a document dating from 888. Some relics of the ancient medieval wall that once surrounded Feldkirchen remain in indistinct form; otherwise the town has a pleasant provincial Baroque look, with pastel facades and a shady central square with a fountain dribbling in the middle and a few cafés and Italian ice-cream parlors occupying space on the sidewalks. The relief of the Virgin Mary over the old pharmacy (*Apotheke*) is the only eye-catcher here. At the north end of town (Kirchgasse) is the parish church, in early Romanesque style with a Gothic choir and Baroque decor. In addition, the town features some Biedermeier-style houses. Though small, Feldkirchen is an important crossroads: one road (Route 93) goes to Gurk, another (Route 94) heads to St. Veit an der Glan, and yet another (Route 95) traverses the remote Nock Mountains up to the Turracher Höhe, a high pass between Carinthia and Styria with a dangerous 23% gradient, a mountain summer resort, and fine skiing center on a pretty lake.

En Route Traveling north along Route 93 out of Feldkirchen are myriad small roads leading to colorful villages. **Goggau** has a small but charming lake; **Sirnitz** (☎ 04279/303, ℻ 04279/3034) has an interesting little castle called Schloss Albeck, with a fine restaurant, Sunday morning concerts (at 11), and an atelier selling clothing made of hand-spun linen. At **Deutsch-Griffen,** with a picturesque defense church accessed by a long covered staircase, an easy hike up the Meisenberg takes you through Carinthia's first bird sanctuary, an initiative by Gottfried Topf, a retired German businessman who moved to the village permanently in 1990. In **Glödnitz** a road leads up to Flattnitz, a solitary but very beautiful spot with a little skiing and a few isolated houses. **Altenmarkt** has another defense church, this one having officially held off the Turks at one time (admittedly it was not the Pasha's main army but rather a marauding gang). **Weitensfeld** was the setting for one of Carinthia's most charming stories. In the 16th century, the plague decimated the population of this tiny town southwest of Gurk. Only three young men and a noblewoman who lived in nearby Thurnhof castle survived. A race was proposed to determine which of them should win her in marriage, and although history failed to record the outcome, the tradition of the race continues every Pentecost weekend. The winner now kisses the noblewoman's statue plus any other attractive female within reach, and the celebration goes on. Thurnhof Castle is up on the left after you leave Weitensfeld.

Gurk

16 *34 km (21 mi) northeast of Feldkirchen.*

Gurk's claim to fame is its massive Romanesque **Dom** (cathedral) surmounted by two onion cupolas and considered the most famous religious landmark in Carinthia. It was founded in the 11th century by
Hemma, Countess of Zeltschach, who after losing her two sons and
husband decided to turn to religious works. She had two oxen tied before a cart and let them walk until they stopped on their own. At that
spot she founded a cloister and gave all her belongings to the church
for building a cathedral. She did not live to see Gurk become a bishopric (in 1072). Construction on the cathedral itself began in 1140 and
ended in 1200. Hemma wasn't canonized until 1938. Her tomb is in
the crypt, whose ceiling, and hence the cathedral itself, is supported
by 100 marble pillars. The Hemma-Stein, a small green-slate chair from
which she personally supervised construction, is also there and alleged
to bring fertility to barren women. In the church itself, the high altar
is one of the most important examples of early Baroque in Austria. Note
the *Pietà* by George Rafael Donner, who is sometimes called the Austrian Michelangelo. The 900-square-ft Lenten altar cloth of 1458
shows 99 scenes from the Old and New Testaments—a beautiful example of a *Biblia Pauperum*, a "poor man's Bible," to teach the Scrip-
tures to those who could not read. It is displayed from Ash Wednesday
to Good Friday. The bishop's chapel includes rare late-Romanesque
frescoes, among the oldest in Europe. The guidebook in English is helpful. At the end of August and in early September a concert series is held
in the cathedral. Tours are restricted by church services or insufficient
participation, but are usually scheduled for 10:30, 1:30 and 3, with
longer tours including the bishop's chapel and the crypt. ☎ 04266/
8236-0, ⚏ 04266/8236-16. ⚏ *Short tour AS35; tour including crypt
AS60; long tour AS95.* ☉ *Daily 9–5; in winter, daily 9–4.*

☼ The **Zwergenpark** is a vast natural setting filled with amusing garden
statuary, consisting largely of typically Austrian-German garden gnomes;
children can traverse the park via a miniature railway. ☎ 04266/8077.
⚏ *AS60, train AS40.* ☉ *Mid-May–mid-June, Mon.–Thurs. 11–4, Fri.–
Sun. 10–6; mid-Jun.–early Sept., daily 10–6; Sept.–mid-Oct., Mon.–
Thurs. 11–4, Fri.–Sun. 10–noon.*

Strassburg

17 *3 km (2 mi) northeast of Gurk.*

The seat of the Gurk bishopric until 1787, the now-restored episcopal palace, which overlooks the Strassburg hamlet houses small museums covering the history of the valley and of the diocese. The Gothic
parish church, one of the most beautiful in Carinthia, has stained-glass
windows dating from 1340. Also of note is the Heilig-Geist-Spital
Church, constructed in the 13th century.

Outside Strassburg, at the intersection of Route 93 and Route 83/E7,
you'll see the 18th-century **Schloss Pöckstein,** belonging to the Carinthian
bishops. In the distance off to the left you'll notice a castle on a hilltop, which you can see close-up by turning left at Mölbling on a road
marked "Treibach/Althofen." The castle is actually in Ober Markt, an
unusually picturesque town with 15th-century decorated houses.

☼ Across the highway from the Pöckstein Castle is the northern terminal of a small narrow-gauge railway, the **Gurktaler Museumbahn.**
Under steam power, the train meanders for 30 minutes down to

Treibach on weekends and holidays, from mid-June to mid-September. For an additional contribution, you can ride in the locomotive alongside the engineer. ☎ *04262/4783.* ☞ *Round-trip AS60.* ☉ *Departures Sat. at 1 and 3, Sun. at 11, 1, and 3.*

En Route At Zwischenwässern and Hirt, Route 93 joins Route 83 coming from Klagenfurt. Heading north (toward Friesach), you'll come to **Brauerei Hirt** (☎ 04268/2050–0), a brewery since 1270. You might have a draft beer under the huge tree in the garden in the shade of a Renaissance arcade or in one of the paneled rooms. The food is good, standard Austrian, and inexpensive.

Friesach

⑱ *16 km (9 mi) northeast of Strassburg via Rte. 83/E7.*

One of the oldest settlements in Carinthia, romantic Friesach is great for wandering. You'll immediately find the **Hauptplatz** (main square), with its old town hall and picturesque 19th-century facades, and as you stroll you'll discover aspects of the medieval-era town: the double wall and the towers, gates, and water-filled moat. Among the medieval tournaments of gallantry that took place here, 600 knights participated in a famous one of May 1224; the Styrian minnesinger Ulrich von Liechtenstein, who appeared dressed and equipped all in green, alone broke 53 lances of his opposing adversaries. Look into the churches. The 12th-century Romanesque **Stadtpfarrkirche** (parish church) on Wiener Strasse has some excellent stained glass in the choir. The 13th-century church in the **Dominican monastery** north of the moat was the first of its order in Austria and contains a wonderful early Gothic choir. If you believe that Tannhäuser was a creation of Wagner's imagination, you will be surprised to learn that descendants of his family were Salzburg administrators in Friesach; a **Tannhäuser Chapel** was erected in 1509 in this church, with a red-marble tomb of Deputy Dean Balthasar Tannhäuser added after his death, in 1516. From a footpath at the upper end of the main square, take a steep 20-minute climb up to the impressive remains of **Schloss Petersberg** to see 12th- and 13th-century frescoes and a museum with beautiful late-Gothic art.

Lodging

$$ ✕⛌ **Metnitztalerhof.** This delightful hotel has overlooked Friesach's medieval town square for more than 400 years. Rooms are furnished with country charm, from the rich, dark-wood pieces to the floral fabrics covering chairs, curtains, and beds. Make sure to ask for a room overlooking the imposing castle ruins. The hotel also hosts gatherings for guests, from wine tastings to medieval-style feasts. ✉ *Hauptpl. 11, A–9360,* ☎ *04268/25100,* ᵮᴬˣ *04268/2510–54. 27 rooms. Restaurant. AE, DC, MC, V. Closed 3 wks in Nov.*

$ ✕⛌ **Friesacherhof.** This comfortable hotel is incorporated into a centuries-old building on the main square. The rooms are rather plain; those in front look out over the square and the Renaissance fountain and can be somewhat noisy. ✉ *Hauptpl. 4, A–9360,* ☎ *04268/2123–0,* ᵮᴬˣ *04268/2123–15. 20 rooms. Restaurant, café. AE, DC, MC, V. Closed mid to late Jan.*

Nightlife and the Arts

From late June to mid-August, there is open-air theater, performed in German, at the outdoor stage of the Dominican Monastery at Friesach. Check with the local tourist office (☞ *Carinthia A to Z, below*) for details and tickets.

Outdoor Activities and Sports

Trails crisscross the hills and mountains near Friesach. Local visitor information offices will have suggestions for routes and for combining a hike with a return by local bus.

Hochosterwitz

⑲   *31 km (19 mi) south of Friesach.*

☾ The dramatic 13th-century castle of **Hochosterwitz** crowns the top of a steep, isolated outcropping, looking just as if it has emerged from the pages of a fairy tale. You can hardly ignore the Disneyland effect, and in fact, this was the inspiration for Walt Disney's *Snow White* castle. Disney and his staff stayed here for many weeks studying it, and you will find Walt's fantasy to be nearly fact. The castle was first mentioned in 860, and after a tumultuous few centuries, ended up in the possession of the Counts of Khevenhüller (1571), where it has remained ever since. It was in this castle that the besieged "Pocket-Mouthed Meg"— Margarethe Maultasch, the original of Feuchtwanger's *Ugly Duchess*— slaughtered the last ox of the starving garrison and dropped it onto the heads of the attacking Tyrolese. The stratagem succeeded, and, dispirited by such apparent proof of abundant supplies, the Tyrolese abandoned the siege. The most recent fortifications were added in the late 1500s against invading Turks; each of the 14 towered gates is a small fortress unto itself. Inside there's an impressive collection of armor and weaponry plus a café-restaurant in the inner courtyard. There's an elevator (which can accommodate wheelchairs), which costs AS40 from a point near the parking-lot ticket office. The hike up the rather steep path to Hochosterwitz, of course, adds to the drama. It's easy to envision yourself as some sort of transplanted knight trying to vanquish the fortress. Your reward at the summit is spectacular vistas from every vantage point. Get to the castle on the back road from Treibach or via Route 83/E7. ⊠ *Laundsdorf-Hochosterwitz,* ☎ *04213/2010 or 04213/2020,* ℻ *04213/202016.* ☞ *AS70.* ☉ *Apr., daily 9–5; May–Sept., daily 8–6.*

St. Veit an der Glan

⑳   *10 km (6 mi) west of Hochosterwitz via Rte. 82.*

The capital of Carinthia until 1518, this old ducal city remains largely unchanged, with the town hall's Baroque facade and ancient patrician houses forming the main square. Be sure to walk into the arcaded Renaissance courtyard of the **Rathaus** (Town Hall), overflowing with flowers in summer; the main state rooms can be seen on guided tours. The 12th-century Romanesque **Pfarrkirche** (parish church) was later given Gothic overtones; note the attractive entry. The ducal palace, **Schloss St. Veit,** located at the north end of town, now houses a small medieval collection; the building itself has a marvelous arcaded stairway in the courtyard.

Dining and Lodging

$$$ ✕ **Pukelsheim.** Despite its enlargement, this restaurant continues to be
★   crowded—which testifies to its good reputation. You'll find regional specialties such as the ravioli-like Kärntner Käsnudeln, *Seeteuful* (monkfish) with olives or stuffed roast chicken. The chef's recommendations are invariably good. Pukelsheim is best known for its desserts: superb cakes and pies made with fruit in season. ⊠ *Erlg. 11,* ☎ *04212/2473. AE, MC, V. Closed Sun.–Mon.*

$$$ ⌂ **Zodiac.** The twelve signs of the zodiac are the theme of this eye-popping hotel designed by Austrian avant-garde artist Ernst Fuchs. The exterior brings to mind a huge, psychedelic candy cane, but rooms are much less startling and are decorated with subdued, pastel fabrics and faux Jugendstil furniture. If you give them your birth date, they'll choose a room for you that is most compatible with your zodiac sign. The Zodiac caused a lot of controversy when it was built in 1998, with many citizens believing it belonged in Las Vegas, not St. Veit. ✉ *Prof.-Ernst-Fuchs-Pl. 1, A–9300,* ☎ *04212/4660–0,* FAX *04212/4660–660. 60 rooms. Restaurant, bar. AE, DC, MC, V.* ✆

CARINTHIA A TO Z

Arriving and Departing

By Car

The most direct route from Vienna is via the Semmering mountain pass through Styria, entering Carinthia on Route 83 just above Friesach and going on to Klagenfurt. From Salzburg, the A10 autobahn tunnels beneath the Tauern range and the Katschberghöhe (the tunnels cost AS70 each) to make a dramatic entry into Carinthia, although the parallel Route 99, which runs "over the top," is the more scenic route. A pretty alternative here that leads you straight into the Nock Mountains or Gurk Valley is to leave the A10 at St. Michael after the Tauern Tunnel, head toward Tamsweg, and then take Route 97 through the Mur Valley; at Predlitz the pass road begins its climb over the steep Turracherhöhe into the Nock Mountains. The fork-off to Flattnitz, the most scenic way into the Gurk Valley, is at Stadl. Several mountain roads cross over from Italy, but the most traveled is Route 83 from Tarvisio.

By Plane

Carinthia is served—mainly by Austrian Airlines and its subsidiary Tyrolean Airways—through the **Klagenfurt–Wörther See airport** (☎ 0463/41500–0), just northeast of Klagenfurt. Several flights daily connect the provincial capital with Vienna. In summer, service is also available from Zürich, Rome, and Frankfurt.

By Train

The main rail line south from Vienna parallels Route 83, entering Carinthia north of Friesach and continuing on to Klagenfurt and Villach. From Salzburg, a line runs south, tunneling under the Tauern mountains and then tracing the Möll and Drau River valleys to Villach. A line from Italy comes into the Drau Valley from Lienz in East Tirol. The main line north from Udine in Italy runs through Tarvisio and up to Villach; other rail lines tie Slovenia with Klagenfurt.

Getting Around

By Bus

As in all of Austria, post office or railroad (*Bundesbahn*) buses go virtually everywhere, but you'll have to allow plenty of time and coordinate schedules carefully so as not to get stranded in some remote location.

By Car

Highways in Carinthia are good, although you can hit some stretches as steep as the 23% gradient on the Turracher Pass road (Route 95), for example. Hauling trailers is not recommended (or is forbidden). The north–south passes are kept open in winter as far as possible, but the tunnels under the Tauern and Katschberg mountains ensure that Route A10 is now passable all year.

By Train

Much of Carinthia's attractive central basin is bypassed by the rail routes. Though you can get into and through Carinthia fairly easily by train, to see the inner province you'll need to rely on a car or the network of buses.

Contacts and Resources

Bicycling

Rental bicycles are in great demand throughout this area, so reserve in advance. The area around the Ossiacher See is excellent for cycling, as are the larger resort towns around the Wörther See along the Austrian Riviera: rent bikes at **Faak am See** (Seeufer Landesstr. 22, ☎ 04254/2149, FAX 04242/202–03127), **Klagenfurt main station** (☎ 0463/5811–359), or **Velden main station** (☎ 04274/2115–0). North of Villach, the area around the Millstätter See is about the only one good for cycling. You can rent bicycles at the **Spittal-Millstätter See railroad station** (☎ 04762/3976–390), or **Millstatt Rad Rentals** (Kaiser-Franz-Joseph-Str. 59, ☎ 0664/3563181). **Central bike reservations** for Carinthia is at ☎ 04242/3109.

Discounts

The **Kärnten Card** costs AS385, lasts for any three consecutive weeks between the first week of May and the first week of October, and allows you free access to 80 museums and other sites of interest. Inquire at the tourist office or call the Carinthia Hot Line (☎ 0463/3000).

Fishing

The Ossiacher See, Wörther See, and Faaker See all have excellent fishing. You'll need a license, issued by the tourist office. Some lakeside hotels offer fishing packages and allow you to fish in reserved waters. The booklet *Kärnten Fischen* from Kärntner Tourismus gives details (in German) about fishing waters, season, possible catch, bait, and local license-issuing authorities. Check also with your hotel or a boat-rental shop (*Bootsverleih*); some can issue licenses.

Hiking

Local visitor information offices will have suggestions for routes and for combining a hike with a return by local bus. You may want to investigate *Hütten,* the refuges up in the mountains where you can spend delightful nights, either in your own room or in a common room. Kärntner Tourismus has information on these huts.

Horseback Riding

Carinthia offers superb riding terrain, from mountains to woodlands, on more than 550 km (340 mi) of riding paths. You'll find stables in nearly 50 towns; an hour's outing will cost you about AS150; day rates are negotiable. A number of hotels offer riding package holidays. The brochure *Reiten* (in German), from Kärntner Tourismus, has details. Or contact **Reit Eldorado Kärnten** (✉ Gerlitzenstr. 11 A–9551, Bodensdorf, ☎ 04243/2322, FAX 04243/2322–20).

Skiing

The best areas for skiing in Carinthia are the **Turracherhöhe** northeast of Bad Kleinkirchheim (✉ A–9565, ☎ 04275/8392, FAX 04275/8392–10), and the **Gerlitzenalpe** (✉ Töbringerstr. 1, Villach, A–9523, ☎ 04242/42000, FAX 04242/42000–42), between Feldkirchen and Villach. A more family-oriented ski resort is **Kleinkirchheim** (✉ A–9546 Bad Kleinkirchheim, ☎ 04240/8212, FAX 04240/8537). Scheduled to open outside Klagenfurt in early 2001 is the **Schleppe Fun Park** (✉ A–9020 Klagenfurt, ☎ 0664/441–4306), offering beginners' slopes and a ski school.

Tennis

Most of the large towns have public courts, but you'll have a wait if you don't book in advance. Many hotels around the southern lakes have their own courts, some of them indoors, and several offer tennis packages.

Visitor Information

The official tourist office for the province is **Kärntner Tourismus** in Velden (⊠ Casinopl. 1, A–9220, ☎ 04274/52100–0; 0463/3000 24-hr hot line, FAX 04274/52100–50).

The following are the leading regional *Fremdenverkehrsämter* (tourist offices): **Bad Kleinkirchheim** (⊠ Bach 120, A–9546, ☎ 04240/8212, FAX 04240/8537). **Friesach** (⊠ Hauptpl. 1, A–9360, ☎ 04268/4300, FAX 04268/4280). **Gmünd** (⊠ Hauptpl. 20, A–9853, ☎ 040732/2222, FAX 04732/3978). **Klagenfurt** (⊠ Neuerpl. 1, A–9010, ☎ 0463/537223, FAX 0463/537295). **Klopeinersee** (⊠ Schulstr. 10, A–9122, ☎ 04239/2222, FAX 04329/3065). **Maria Wörth/Reifnitz** (⊠ A–9081, ☎ 04273/2240–0, FAX 04273/3703). **Millstatt** (⊠ Marktpl. 8, A–9872, ☎ 04766/2022–0, FAX 04766/3479). **Ossiach Lake area** (⊠ A–9520 Sattendorf, ☎ 04248/2336–0, FAX 04248/2336–5). **Pörtschach** (⊠ Hauptstr. 153, A–9210, ☎ 04272/2354, FAX 04272/3770). **Spittal an der Drau** (⊠ Burgpl. 1, A–9800, ☎ 04762/3420, FAX 04762/3237). **Velden** (⊠ Villacherstr. 19, ☎ 04274/2103–0, FAX 04274/2103–50). **Villach** (⊠ Rathauspl. 1, A–9500, ☎ 04242/205–2900, FAX 04242/205–2999).

8   EASTERN ALPS

It's easy to feel on top of the world if you take the Grossglockner High Alpine Highway—the most thrilling pass over the Alps. Nestled in a nearby valley is Heiligenblut, a town commemorated in a thousand postcards. Everywhere, breathtaking Alpine vistas and centuries-old castles polka-dot the landscape. For many travelers the Eastern Alps, concentrated around the Grossglockner peak, represent not only the most fascinating part of Austria's mountainous landscape but its most unspoiled as well.

Y OU CAN GET INTO SERIOUS TROUBLE by judging where to go in Austria on the basis of the alluring photographs found in books and travel brochures. Pictures can be misleading—and, using the sheer joy of nature's (and some of mankind's) creative magnificence as a measure, they can end up endorsing the whole country. One place that truly lives up to its pictures is Heiligenblut. One of the most-photographed places in the country, it remains Austria's most picturesque Alpine village. With the majestic Grossglockner—Austria's highest mountain—for a backdrop, the town cradles the pilgrimage church of St. Vincent. Though every Austrian hamlet seems to have a church, nowhere else does a steeple seem to find such affirmation amid a setting of soaring peaks.

Updated by
Lee Hogan

While this little town is a visual treat, the whole Eastern Alps region is dramatic countryside, with breathtaking scenery and great winter sports equal to those in Switzerland. Here, majestic peaks, many well over 9,750 ft, are home to slow-moving glaciers that give way to sweeping Alpine meadows, ablaze with wildflowers in spring and summer. Long, broad valleys (many names have the suffix -au, meaning "meadow") are basins of rivers that cross the region between mountain ranges, sometimes meandering, sometimes plunging. The land is full of ice caves and salt mines, deep gorges, and hot springs. Today, most tourism is concentrated in relatively few towns, but wherever you go, you'll find good lodging, solid local food, and friendly folk; it is countryside to drive and hike and ski through, where people live simply, close to the land.

Western Carinthia and East Tirol are dotted with quaint villages that have charming churches, lovely mountain scenery, and access to plenty of outdoor action—from hiking and fishing in summer to skiing in winter. Across the southern tier, a series of scenic routes passes from Carinthia to that political anomaly Osttirol (East Tirol). In 1918, after World War I, South Tirol was ceded to Italy, completely cutting East Tirol off from the rest of Tirol and the administrative capital in Innsbruck. The mountains along the Italian border and those of the Hohe Tauern, to the north, also isolate East Tirol, which has consequently been neglected by tourists.

We start out from Villach, in Carinthia, and travel to Lienz, in East Tirol, then into the Defereggental, north to Matrei and back to Lienz. The next itinerary takes you from Heiligenblut over the Grossglockner mountain pass (only in summer), through Salzburg province to the charming Zell am See and beyond. We then head east along the Salzach river valley from Zell am See, with a side trip to Badgastein, then on to Radstadt and Schladming, just over into Styria. Finally, we take in the magnificent Dachstein mountain complex and retrace our steps to go up through the Salzburg Dolomite range, ending about 40 kilometers (25 miles) from Salzburg. You can do it all in a rather full three days, or you could take a leisurely week, exploring the smaller towns and byways.

Pleasures and Pastimes

Dining

While this region contains fine restaurants—in fact, two of the country's top dozen dining establishments are here—most of the dining you'll do in the small towns of the Eastern Alps will take place in *Gasthöfe/Gasthäuser* (country hotels/inns), where the dining rooms are not necessarily separate restaurants. Note that, in many cases, such inns are open only in the peak season. In resort areas, you may be required to take half board (that is, breakfast and one other meal). Prices for meals include taxes and a service charge but not the customary small additional tip of 3%–5%.

CATEGORY	COST*
$$$$	over AS500 (€36)
$$$	AS300–AS500 (€21–€36)
$$	AS200–AS300 (€15–€20)
$	under AS200 (€15)

per person for a three-course meal, including a glass of house wine

Lodging

When you think of Alpine hotels, you probably think of chalet-style inns with flower-decked balconies and overhanging eaves. Not surprisingly, that's mainly what you find in the Eastern Alps, though the range runs from family-run country inns to professionally managed resorts. This part of Austria is relatively inexpensive, except for the top resort towns of Saalbach, Badgastein, and Zell am See. Even there, however, cheaper accommodations are available outside the center of town or in pensions. Prices out of season may be as low as half those of the high season. Room rates include taxes and service and almost always breakfast, except in the most expensive hotels, but it is wise to ask. Half board is required in some lodgings. It is customary to leave a small additional tip (AS20) for the chambermaid.

CATEGORY	TOP RESORTS*	OTHER TOWNS*
$$$$	over AS2,200	over AS1,500
$$$	AS1,500–AS2,200	AS1,000–AS1,500
$$	AS900–AS1,500	AS700–AS1,000
$	under AS900	under AS700

For a standard double room with bath in high season. To compute Euro equivalencies, divide AS amount by 13.76.

🐾 *following the text of a review is your signal that the property has a Web site, where you will find details and, usually, images; for a link, visit www.fodors.com/urls.*

Exploring the Eastern Alps

Austria's Eastern Alps straddle four different provinces: Carinthia, East Tirol, Salzburg, and Styria. Imposing mountain ranges ripple through the region, isolating quaint Alpine villages whose picture-postcard perfection has remained unspoiled through the centuries. The mountainous terrain makes some backtracking necessary if you're interested in visiting the entire area, but driving through the spectacular scenery is part of the appeal of touring the region.

Great Itineraries

Numbers in the text correspond to numbers in the margin and on the Eastern Alps map.

IF YOU HAVE 3 DAYS

Start in the charming villages of **Hermagor** ① and **Kötschach** ②, stopping off at the Geo-Trail, which traces 50 million years of geological history. Then spend the afternoon exploring the East Tirolean capital of 🏛 **Lienz** ③. Castle ruins, picturesque churches, and more spectacular landscapes are in store on your second day as you visit **St. Jakob in Defereggen** ④ and **Matrei in Osttirol** ⑤ before returning to Lienz. On your final day, crown your trip with a visit to that Alpine jewel **Heiligenblut** ⑦, making stops at **Döllach** ⑥ and elsewhere along the imposing Grossglockner highway.

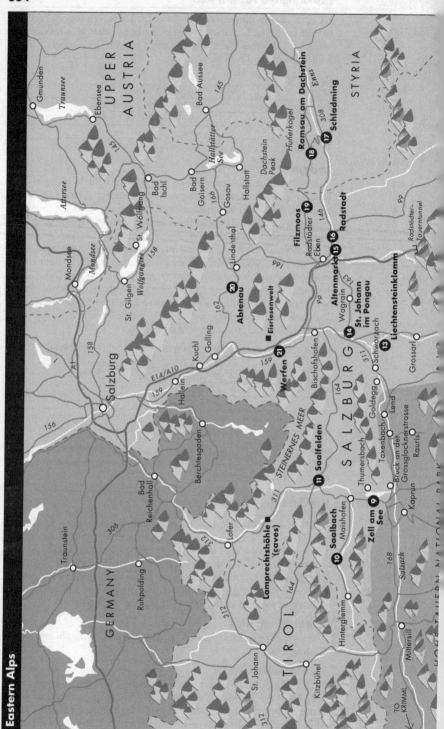

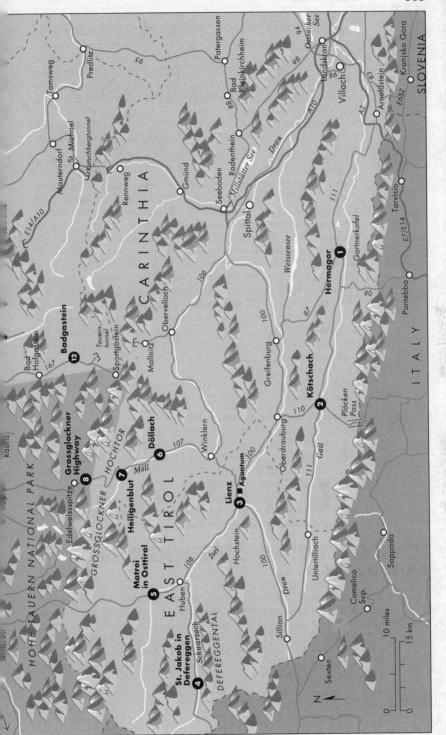

IF YOU HAVE 5 DAYS

Begin your trip in East Tirol's capital, **Lienz** ③, before heading to picture-perfect ☒ **Heiligenblut** ⑦. As long as it's not wintertime, your second day can be spent taking the scenic Grossglockner High Alpine Highway through the Hohe Tauern National Park to the lake resort of ☒ **Zell am See** ⑨. On day three, make a day trip to the mountain resorts of **Saalbach** ⑩ and **Saalfelden** ⑪, and descend into the depths with a tour of the **Lamprechtshöhle** (caves). On your fourth day, travel to ☒ **Badgastein** ⑫ and take the cure. Then use your last day to visit the cathedral in **St. Johann im Pongau** ⑭ and the **Liechtensteinklamm** ⑬, the deepest, most dramatic gorge in the Eastern Alps.

IF YOU HAVE 7 DAYS

With a week at your disposal, you can see even more of the charming Alpine towns that dot the awesome landscape. Explore **Lienz** ③ and the lovely town of ☒ **Heiligenblut** ⑦ on your first day. Then take on the twists and turns of the Grossglockner highway before lingering by the lake at the resort town of ☒ **Zell am See** ⑨. On your third day, see the spectacular **Liechtensteinklamm** ⑬ gorge, and then overnight in ☒ **St. Johann im Pongau** ⑭. Villages seemingly unchanged by the years are on the agenda for the fourth day, with visits to the charming town of **Altenmarkt** ⑮, the medieval haven of **Radstadt** ⑯, and the former silver-mining town of ☒ **Schladming** ⑰. A cable car will whisk you to the top of the Hunerkogel the next day during a stop at **Ramsau am Dachstein** ⑱, and then it's on to the resort town of ☒ **Filzmoos** ⑲. On your sixth day, make an excursion to the dramatic underworld of the **Eisriesenwelt** ice caves near ☒ **Werfen** ㉑, winding up your journey with a trip to the magnificent medieval castle, where birds of prey still swoop over the imposing fortress, and a final evening culinary blowout at Obauer, one of the finest restaurants in Austria.

When to Tour the Eastern Alps

Depending on your interests, the Eastern Alps make a good destination at various times of year. Snowy conditions can make driving a white-knuckle experience, but winter also brings extensive, superb skiing throughout the region—often at a fraction of the cost of the more famous resorts in Tirol. In summer, the craggy mountain peaks provide a challenge to hikers, while caverns head into the bowels of the behemoths. Placid lakes and meandering mountain streams attract anglers for some of the best fishing to be found in the country.

TO LIENZ, UP THE DEFEREGGENTAL, AND BACK

Take Route 86 south out of Villach, through Warmbad Villach, and then Route 83 to Arnoldstein, about 10 km (6 mi) away. You're in the Gail River valley here, with the magnificent Karawanken mountains rising in Yugoslavia on your left. Just beyond Arnoldstein, turn right onto Route 111, marked for Hermagor. On the way up, the views now will be on the right, the dramatic Gailtal Alps in the background as you head west.

Hermagor

❶ *46 km (29 mi) west of Villach.*

The swift Gail flows along the southwest edge of Carinthia through small scattered villages with ancient churches and aged, often wooden, farm houses. The narrow valley is peacefully soft, with many old linden trees, but its fir-treed slopes rise steeply, particularly on the south side, and craggy peaks peer from behind them. The main town in the Gail valley is Hermagor, situated approximately in its center. Hermagor is best known as a summer resort, offering hiking, climbing, and swimming in the nearby Pressegger See, but it also has skiing in winter. During the Middle Ages, villagers believed that the decorated keystones in Hermagor's late-Gothic **parish church** symbolized Jesus Christ's efforts to hold the framework of the church together. Dating from 1484, the church is also notable for its intricately carved and painted winged altar in the south Wolkenstein Chapel.

Did the creation of the world take place in this area? Geologists from all over the world are fascinated by the possible answers that are believed to lie within the nearby Gartnerkogel mountain south of Hermagor off Route 90. Amateur sleuths can join in the experience by

★ following the **Geo-Trail**, along which you can gather fossils and trace 50 million years of geological history. Maps are available from the local tourist office. Botanists are equally intrigued by the blue *Wulfenia*, which blankets the Nassfeld mountain area farther along Route 90 on the Italian border each June. The flower, which is protected under Austrian law, can be found only here and in the Himalayas.

En Route From Hermagor, both Route 87, running northwest to Greifenburg, and Route 111 up to Kötschach offer gorgeous views, and the distances to Lienz on both are about 55 km (35 mi). If you choose Route 87, you can turn right shortly before Greifenburg for a detour to the blue-green **Weissensee,** a virtually undeveloped narrow lake 11 km (7 mi) long, tucked in between high mountain ridges, where there's excellent fishing and boating. Then, at Greifenburg, turn west onto Route 100 up the Drau River valley toward Lienz.

Kötschach

❷ *25 km (16 mi) west of Hermagor.*

Most visitors travel to this town and Mauthen, its twin across Route 111, to enjoy the natural beauty the area has to offer and to pay a call on the Kellerwand, one of Austria's top restaurants. The year-round resort is a good base for excursions via the Plöcken Pass over the border into Italy or up the picturesque Lesach Valley through the Austrian (Lienzer) Dolomites. The early frescoes and unusual decorated arched ceiling that adorn Kötschach's **parish church,** which dates from 1527, make it worth a stop, too.

Dining and Lodging

$$$$ ✕🏨 **Kellerwand.** Elegant tables in a quiet, luxurious atmosphere high-
★ light the superb quality of the food, an uncommonly imaginative treatment of area specialties, including outstanding delicate pasta dishes and roast lamb or venison. (Frau Sonnleitner was named Austrian cook of the year in 1990.) The unpretentious residence includes a small hotel, where rooms and luxury suites are attractively decorated in a country style with tile floors. ✉ *Mauthen 24, A–9640 Mauthen,* ☎ *04715/269-0 or 04715/378-0,* 🖷 *04715/378–16. 12 rooms, 8 suites. Restaurant, bar, sauna. AE, DC, MC, V. Closed 1 wk in mid-Apr., and mid-Nov.–mid-Dec.*

$$$ ✕🏨 **Naturabenteuer Hotel Post.** This interesting house of eccentric design, with odd balconies and a triangular garden, is in the center of town. Excursions, climbing, rafting, and fishing are offered, and rooms are attractively decorated. ✉ *Hauptpl. 66, A–9640 Kötschach-Mauthen,* ☎ *04715/221,* 🖷 *04715/222–53. 24 rooms. Restaurant, bar, café, pool, sauna, exercise room, fishing. No credit cards. Closed end of Oct.–mid-Apr.*

En Route　　The scenic Route 110 north over the Gailberg will bring you, after about 14 km (9 mi) and some dramatic twists and turns, to Route 100 at Oberdrauburg. From here to Lienz (20 km/12 mi) the highway follows the Drau River valley, with splendid views up into the Kreuzeck mountain range on your right. The Romans recognized the strategic importance of the region and about AD 50 established **Aguntum** here to protect the important trade route against possible usurpers. About 4 km (2½ mi) before you reach Lienz, you'll come to the excavations to the right of the road. You can explore the site, where archaeologists have been unearthing remains of this ancient settlement, quite freely.

Lienz

❸ *34 km (21 mi) northwest of Kötschach–Mauthen.*

Tucked in at the confluence of the Drau and Isel rivers, with the Dolomites a dramatic backdrop to the south, Lienz, a summer and winter resort, is now the capital of the region. The awe-inspiring peaks rising around the town might make your first impression one of human insignificance in the face of overwhelming power and glory. Such feelings of reverence may account for the number of notable churches in Lienz; at least five are worth a visit, particularly the parish church of **St. Andrä**, on Patriadorferstrasse, which you can reach by walking up Muchar Gasse and Schweizergasse or by following the Rechter Iselweg along the river. A Romanesque lion decorates the doorway, giving witness to the church's early roots. The present-day Gothic edifice was completed in 1457, while the interior is Baroque, from the winged high altar to the vividly colored ceiling fresco (1761). Note the ornate marble tombstones of the noble Görz family.

Three blocks away from St. Andrä—cross the Pfarrbrücke into Beda Weber-Gasse and turn left into Patriadorferstrasse—you'll find the **War Memorial Chapel,** designed in 1926 by Clemens Holzmeister, the architect responsible for Salzburg's Festspielhaus and Felsenreitschule (the festival theaters). The wall paintings are by Albin Egger-Lienz (1868–1926), who is renowned for his ability to portray human strength and weakness and who is also buried here. Close to the center of town, the **Franciscan Church** on the Muchargasse was originally a Carmelite cloister, founded in 1349 by the Countess Euphemia of Görz. The church was taken over by the Franciscans in 1785 and restored in 1947–48. A Gothic pietà from about 1400 adorns the left side altar at the back; its wall frescoes are from the 15th century.

A wooden statue dedicated to St. Wolfgang can be found on the Schweizergasse in the 1243 **Dominican Church,** which was subsequently rebuilt in late-Gothic style. **St. Michael's** on Michaeler Platz on the north side of the Isel was completed in 1530, but the north tower, with its onion dome, dates only from 1713. Note the fancy ceiling ornamentation, the 1683 high altar, and the gravestones. The rococo **St. Joseph's,** by the Spitalsbrücke, was badly damaged in 1945 and rebuilt in 1957. **St. Antonius** on the Hauptplatz dates from the 16th century. The recently restored 16th-century **Lieburg Palace** on the Hauptplatz, with two towers, now houses provincial government offices.

A massive tower looms over the **Schloss Bruck,** a battlemented residential castle that dates from 1280 and now serves as the city museum. The remarkably well-preserved castle also has a Romanesque chapel with a late-15th-century ceiling and wall frescoes. Works by Egger-Lienz and Franz Defregger (1835–1921), another Tirolean painter, are displayed here, along with Celtic and Roman relics from nearby excavations. ✉ *Iseltaler Str.,* ☎ *04852/62580.* 💷 *AS45.* ⏱ *Mid–May to mid–October, daily 10–6.*

Dining and Lodging

$$$$ X⊡ **Traube.** In summer, the striped awnings of this central hotel (part
★ of the Romantik Hotel group) shade the cafés on the street and balcony. The atmosphere is elegant, thanks to a mix of older furniture and
antiques, and rooms are spacious and comfortable. The historic hotel
has its own fishing waters and a rooftop swimming pool with wonderful views of the surrounding mountains. The restaurant's food is
not quite up to the setting, but take the recommendations and you won't
be unhappy. ⊠ *Hauptpl. 14, A–9900,* ☏ *04852/64444,* FAX *04852/
64184. 51 rooms. 2 restaurants, bar, café, indoor pool, sauna, fishing,
dance club. AE, DC, MC, V.*

$$$ X⊡ **Parkhotel Tristachersee.** A little more than 4 km (2½ mi) southeast
★ of Lienz (take the road via Amlach marked to Tristachersee) is a small
lake hidden away up a hill. It's a magical setting for this diminutive, to-
tally renovated country hotel, whose rooms have dark paneled walls and
lots of fabrics. A lakeside terrace provides opportunity for relaxation,
and an excellent restaurant features regional cuisine, including fresh fish
from the hotel's own ponds. ⊠ *Tristachersee 1, A–9900,* ☏ *04852/67666,*
FAX *04852/67699. 40 rooms, 8 suites. Restaurant, bar, indoor pool, lake,
sauna. No credit cards. Closed Nov.–mid-Dec. and last 2 wks in Apr.*

$ X⊡ **Gasthof Goldener Stern.** If you are watching your budget but would
like to stay in historic surroundings, then this is the place to go: the
"Golden Star" was built around 1400. The interiors are done in sim-
ple peasant style, nothing fancy, everything cozy. Some of the rooms
in the new annex have balconies. There's no restaurant, but coffee and
homemade cake in the afternoon will make you feel right at home. ⊠
Schweizerg. 40, A–9900, ☏ FAX *04852/62192. 20 rooms. No credit cards.*

Outdoor Activities and Sports

HIKING

Lienz and its surrounding area have miles of marked trails, and de-
tailed maps are available from the tourist office that show mountain
lodges where you can spend the night and other facilities. Trails in
Tirol are designated as easy, moderate, or difficult. Just before Schloss
Bruck (☞ *above*), you'll find a chairlift that rises nearly to the crest
of the 6,685-ft **Hochstein** mountain, from which you get a splendid
panoramic view over Lienz and to the east. You'll have to hike the
last kilometer (½ mi) to reach the very top.

If you want to learn to climb, contact Leo Baumgartner at the **Alpin-
schule Lienz** (⊠ Gaimberg, A–9900, ☏ 04852/68770).

WHITE-WATER RAFTING

Stretches of the **Isel River** from Matrei down to Lienz are raftable from
May to mid-October. The Drau, which always has enough water, is used
for easy rides or beginners. If you are a hard-core rafter, you'll enjoy the
Schwarzach in the Defereggental, known as "Ostirol's toughest river."
For outfitters, check with a tourist office, or contact the **Osttiroler Kajak
Club** in Lienz (☏ 04852/67777 or 048542/65811). Several companies offer
tours at prices beginning around AS500 per person and with a minimum
of five people. Try Dieter Messner at the **Raftingzentrum Ainet** (⊠ House
41, A–9951 Ainet, ☏ 04853/5231) or **Osttirol Adventures,** (⊠ Rechter
Drauweg 1B–Dolomitenbad, A–9951 Camp Ainet, ☏ 04852/61861).

St. Jakob in Defereggen

❹ *43 km (27 mi) northwest of Lienz.*

Few tourists venture into the Defereggen mountain range, although its
craggy slopes are sprinkled with unspoiled villages. The small resort of
St. Jakob in Defereggen is one of the most charming and picturesque in

East Tirol. Sports enthusiasts flock to the area for hiking, climbing, rafting, and fishing in summer and skiing in winter. There are also sulfur baths at nearby St. Leonhard and a waterfall at Mariahilf. To reach St. Jakob from Lienz, head northwest on Route 108, following the Isel Valley, and turn left at the village of Huben, about 19 km (12 mi) out of Lienz, onto a scenic side roadway that takes you up the valley, the Defereggental. St. Jakob is 23 km (14 mi) from Huben. The right-hand side of the Defereggental constitutes the beginning of the **Hohe Tauern National Park,** an area of mountains that touches on three states (Salzburg, Carinthia, and Tirol) and includes the Grossglockner group. The more hardy traveler may want to spend a few days hiking and lodging at any one of several refuges, where one is sometimes treated to very rustic, homemade victuals (cheeses and hams). The national park has several offices; the nearest to Lienz is in Matrei (Nationalparkverwaltung Tirol, ⊠ Rauterplatz 1, A–9971 Matrei in Osttirol, ☎ 04875/5161–0, ⅎ𝔸𝕏 04875/5161–20).

Dining and Lodging

$$$$ ✕⊡ **Alpenhof.** A large chalet, set against a velvet-green hillside, is an ideal starting point for summer hiking and for skiing. From the outside it is completely out of style with the modest houses of the Defereggental, but the rooms are comfortable, with flower-decked balconies, and the hotel pays particular attention to families with children. The restaurant features regional dishes; ask for recommendations. ⊠ *Innerrotte 35, A–9963, ☎ 04873/5351–0, ⅎ𝔸𝕏 04873/5351–500. 85 rooms. Restaurant, bar, indoor pool, sauna, nightclub, children's programs. AE, DC, MC, V. Closed May and mid-Oct.–mid-Dec.*

$ ⊡ **Farmhouses.** If you fall in love with the Hohe Tauern mountains (which happens instantly for the most part) and decide you may want to stay for a while, ask at any tourist office about booking rooms at a farmhouse. Some even offer meals. It's a wonderful way of getting close to the land itself. Prices range from about AS150 per person per day to AS 230. The little brochure "Urlaub am Bergbauernhof" will whet your appetite, and you may consider moving to Osttirol at once, for good. For more information contact Hohe Tauern Süd-Werbung (⊠ Rauterplatz 1, A–9971 Matrei in Osttirol, ☎ 04875/5330, ⅎ𝔸𝕏 04875/5331).

Matrei in Osttirol

⑤ *31 km (19 mi) northeast of St. Jakob in Defereggen.*

Because of its strategic location on one of the easier north–south routes over the Alps, Matrei in Osttirol has a long history to look back on, including Celtic and then Roman periods. Every year on the eve of St. Nicholas's Day (December 6), fantastically dressed characters with furs and bells storm through town in an old tradition called *Klaubaufgehen,* a way to frighten off bad spirits. The **Church of St. Alban** in town is definitely worth entering for its rich interior. The real treasure, however, is the Romanesque **Church of St. Nicholas,** which is on the other side of the Isel at the beginning of the Virgen Valley. It contains some simple carvings, such as the 15th-century statue of St. Nicholas, and its late-13th-century frescoes of various biblical scenes elevate it to a high work of art. Remarkably well-preserved 14th-century frescoes decorate the outside walls. Just north of Matrei, standing on a daunting rock, is **Schloss Weissenstein,** a 12th-century castle that underwent substantial rebuilding in the 1800s and is now privately owned.

Dining and Lodging

$$$$ ✕⊡ **Rauter.** With an ultramodern facade, clean lines, and slick surfaces,
★   this fashionable house offers elegant comfort in stark contemporary contrast to the usual rustic Alpine style. Here, too, are many diversions and the best restaurant in East Tirol. The fish comes from the hotel's

own waters, the lamb from the nearby mountains, and the house bakery supplies the café. A hotel bus brings you to and from hiking areas in summer, ski slopes in winter. Fishing is available for guests staying three days or longer, and there is riding nearby. ⊠ *Rauterpl. 3, A–9971,* ☎ *04875/6611,* FAX *04875/6613. 50 rooms. Restaurant, bar, café, indoor and outdoor pools, sauna, exercise room, fishing. No credit cards. Closed Nov.–mid-Dec.*

$ **⛺ Alpengasthof Tauernhaus.** There's quiet comfort in this simple rustic
★ Gasthof, about 14 km (9 mi) up the Tauern Valley at the base of the Felbertauern pass. The hotel began as a rest house, founded in 1207 by the archbishops of Salzburg. It is a good starting point for hiking and skiing. ⊠ *A–9971,* ☎ *04875/8811,* FAX *04875/8812. 41 rooms, 21 with full bath, 12 with shower. Restaurant, sauna. No credit cards. Closed Nov.*

ACROSS THE GROSSGLOCKNER PASS

This is the excursion over the longest and most spectacular highway through the Alps, the Grossglockner High Alpine Highway, an engineering achievement of the first magnitude. There is a thrill every hundred yards along this scenic route, but your first will be sighting Heiligenblut, one of Austria's prettiest towns, at the foot of the Grossglockner. To explore this region, winter travelers have no choice but to drive north out of Lienz on Route 108, arriving in Mittersill in Salzburg Province via the 5-km (3-mi) Felbertauern toll tunnel (winter AS110, summer AS190) under the Tauern mountains, and taking Route 168 east to Zell am See. But if the road is open, go north over the Grossglockner mountain highway. (The trip can be done by car or bus.) Leave Lienz via Route 107, but stop on the way up the hill outside Iselsberg–Stronach for a great panoramic view over the city. As you go over the ridge, you'll be entering Carinthia again. At Winklern the road follows the Möll River valley, and after about 11 km (7 mi) you'll come to Döllach.

Döllach

❻ *28 km (17 mi) northeast of Lienz.*

Prospectors once searched for gold in Döllach (Grosskirchheim), in the Möll River valley. Today, the history of local gold mining is chronicled in a museum in **Schloss Grosskirchheim.** ☎ *04825/226.* 🎫 *AS35.* ⊙ *May–Oct., guided tours available by request.*

Don't overlook the Gothic **St. Maria Cornach church,** with its ornate Baroque interior.

Dining and Lodging

$$$$ ╳⛺ **Schlosswirt.** Rooms range from somewhat spartan to elegant in this appealing chalet hotel at the base of the mountains on the fringe of the Grossglockner. In season you can climb, hike, ski, and ride horseback in the gorgeous "hidden valley" of the Graden brook. The hotel has its own fishing streams and lake, and it organizes alpine programs for guests and groups. The restaurant has slipped since it started serving tour groups but is still worth a try; ask for recommendations. ⊠ *A–9843,* ☎ *04825/211–0 or 04825/411–0,* FAX *04825/211–165. 25 rooms. Restaurant, lake, sauna, steam room, tennis court, horseback riding, fishing. AE, MC, V. Closed 3 wks in Apr. and Nov.*

Heiligenblut

★ **❼** *10 km (6 mi) north of Döllach.*

Some say the best time to experience this little slice of paradise is after a leisurely dinner at one of the many Gasthöfe, gazing out at the starry firmament over the Hohe Tauern range. Others relish standing around an early morning thaw-out fire, used by hikers setting out to conquer the mighty foothills of the Grossglockner peaks, the highest in Austria. This small town nestled in a valley is known for its picturesque church set against an equally picturesque mountain backdrop, but it's the famed mountain-climbing school and climbing and skiing facilities that draw flocks of all-out active types.

According to local legend, St. Briccius, after obtaining a vial of the blood of Jesus, was buried by an avalanche, but when his body was recovered, the tiny vial was miraculously found hidden within one of the saint's open wounds. The town gets its name, Heiligenblut (Holy Blood), from this miraculous event. Today the relic is housed in the Sakramenthäuschen, the chapel of the small but beautiful Gothic **Church of St. Vincent.** Completed in 1490 after more than a century of construction under the toughest conditions, the church is marked by its soaring belfry tower. Sublimely, the sharply pointed spire finds an impressive echo in the conic peak of the Grossglockner. St. Vincent's contains a beautifully carved late-Gothic double altar nearly 36 ft high, and the Coronation of Mary is depicted in the altar wings, richly carved by Wolfgang Hasslinger in 1520. The region's most important altarpiece, it imparts a feeling of quiet power in this spare, high church. The church also has a noble crypt and graveyard, the latter sheltering graves of those lost in climbing the surrounding mountains.

You can get to Heiligenblut by bus from Lienz or Zell am See (note that some buses stop in the tiny hamlet of Winkl, directly below the town). During the winter, buses run from Heiligenblut to nearby ski runs. Heiligenblut loves tourists, and special deals are usually offered, ranging from bargain cards issued to visitors staying more than three days to cut-rate, one-day ski passes.

Dining and Lodging

$$$$ ✕🏨 **Glocknerhof.** This dark-wood chalet in the center of the village fits perfectly into the surroundings. You'll feel comfortable in its cozy, attractive rooms. Close to climbing in summer and skiing in winter, the hotel has its own fishing streams for guests. Tour groups stop here on the way over the Grossglockner road, and the restaurant is good. They serve their own trout and other mountain-stream fish; ask if there is *Gams* (local chamois) on the menu. ⊠ *Hof 3, A–9844,* ☎ *04824/ 2244,* 🖷 *04824/2244–66. 52 rooms. Restaurant, bar, indoor pool, sauna, fishing, children's programs. MC, V. Closed mid-Apr.–mid-June and Oct.–early Dec.*

$$$–$$$$ 🏨 **Hotel Lächenhof.** This charming hotel is a true *Panoramagasthof*— a guest house with spectacular views of the surrounding Alpine scenery from balconied rooms festooned with flowers. The chalet-style building is perched on a mountain slope and surrounded by lush forest, so it's easy to feel you've left civilization behind. Rooms are comfortably appointed with pastel fabrics and sturdy wood furniture. ⊠ *Hof 70, A–9844,* ☎ *04824/2262,* 🖷 *04824/2262–45. 23 rooms. Restaurant, bar, sauna. AE, DC, MC, V.*

$$$–$$$$ 🏨 **Kärntnerhof.** Several chalet-style houses set close together have been combined to make up this intimate, family-run complex on the edge of thick woods about 2 km (1 mi) from the center of town. There's entertainment twice weekly. ⊠ *Winkl 3, A–9844,* ☎ *04824/ 2004,* 🖷 *04824/2004–89. 43 rooms. Restaurant, bar, indoor and outdoor pools, sauna, exercise room. DC. Closed Easter–May and mid-Oct.–mid-Dec.*

$$$–$$$$ 🏨 **Senger.** Weathered wood and flowered balconies highlight this old farmhouse chalet, which has been cleverly enlarged while keeping its

original rustic atmosphere. The rooms and romantic apartments, with lots of pillows and country prints, continue the attractive rural theme. It's a bit outside the center of town. ⊠ *Heiligenblut 23, A–9844,* ☎ *04824/2215,* FAX *04824/2215–9. 14 rooms, 8 apartments. Restaurant, bar, sauna, exercise room. No credit cards. Closed 1 wk after Easter– June and mid-Oct.–mid-Dec.*

Outdoor Activities and Sports

DIGGING FOR GOLD

From mid-June through September, you can pan for gold in the streams around Heiligenblut. Buy a ticket for an excursion in the town at the **"gold-digging office"**—Raimund Granögger (☎ 04824/2109) or the tourist office. The price (AS160) includes the necessary equipment and a permit to take home your finds.

HIKING AND MOUNTAIN CLIMBING

This is a hiker's El Dorado, with (in summer) more than 240 km (150 mi) of marked pathways and trails in all directions. There are relatively easy hikes to the Kalvarienberg (½ hour), Wirtsbauer-Alm (two hours), and the Leiterfall, a 400-ft-high waterfall (two hours). **Guided tours** are available and enjoyable. They cost anywhere from AS650 to AS3,900 per person and can last two days. The National Park Programs Office (☎ 04825/616114) has all the information.

Grossglockner Highway

★ ⑧ *Grossglockner Highway is 46 km (29 mi) long.*

This is the excursion over the longest and most spectacular highway through the Alps, officially named the Grossglockner High Alpine Highway (107)—the Grossglocknerstrasse. You can do it by bus or private car. There is a mystery about the Grossglockner road. Before it was built, there had been no passage anywhere between the Brenner Pass and the Radstädter Tauern Pass (more than 160 km, or 100 mi, apart) leading over these high mountains, nor was it on record that there had ever before been a regularly used route across the barrier at this point. Yet when the engineers who built the High Alpine Highway were blasting for the Hochtor tunnel, through which it passes at one point, they found, deep in the bowels of a mountain, a Roman statuette of, appropriately, Hercules.

From Heiligenblut the climb begins up the Carinthian side of the Grossglockner. You'll be tapped here for a AS350 toll allowing you to use the Grossglockner High Alpine Highway as much as you like on the same day. There's also a ticket for AS480 good on any two days within a calendar year or for AS450 on any eight consecutive days. The peak itself—at 12,470 ft the highest point in Austria—is off to the west. You can get somewhat closer than the main road takes you by following the highly scenic but steep Gletscherstrasse westward up to the Gletscherbahn on the Franz-Josef-Plateau, where you'll be rewarded with absolutely breathtaking views of the Grossglockner peak and surrounding Alps, of the vast glacier in the valley below, and, on a clear day, even into Italy.

The Grossglockner road twists and turns as it struggles to the 8,370-ft Hochtor. At this point you've crossed into Salzburg Province. The road was completed in 1935, after five years of labor by 3,200 workers. You're now on Edelweiss-Strasse. A stop at the **Edelweissspitze** yields an unbelievable view out over East Tirol, Carinthia, and Salzburg, including 19 glaciers and 37 peaks over the 9,600-ft mark. The rare white edelweiss—the von Trapps sang its praises in *The Sound of Music*— grows here. Though the species is protected, don't worry about the plants you get as souvenirs; they are cultivated for this purpose. It is strictly forbidden to pick a wild edelweiss (and several other plant species), should you ever happen to come across one. Be sure to visit the visitor center and the Alpine museum. An excellent short film (in English) tells the story of the area, and computer-driven dioramas show how animals survive the extreme climatic changes atop the mountain range. ⊠ *Grossglockner Hwy., Km 26,* ☎ *0662/873673 road information.* 🎫 *Free.* ⊙ *Early May–late Oct., daily 9–5.*

Zell am See

★ ❾ *8 km (5 mi) northwest of the Grossglockner.*

After the toll station on the north side of the Grossglockner peak, the highway finally exhausts its hairpin turns (more than 30) and continues to Bruck an der Grossglocknerstrasse. From here it's only about 8 km (5 mi) west on Route S11 and then north on Route 311 to Zell am See. This lovely lakeside town got its name from the monks' cells of a monastery founded here in about AD 790.

In the quaint town center, visit the 17th-century Renaissance **Schloss Rosenberg,** now the town hall. The **Kastnerturm,** built around 1300, was originally a fortified tower for an abbey and then a granary. It now houses the city museum, with an eclectic collection of old furnishings and handicrafts, open June–September, Monday, Wednesday, and Friday 2–5. Unusually fine statues of St. George and St. Florian can be found on the west wall of the splendid Romanesque **parish church of St. Hippolyte.** Built in 1217 (the tower came about two centuries later), the church was beautifully renovated in 1975.

Several locations offer up stunning vistas of the town and its environs. On ground level, take a boat ride to the village of **Thumersbach,** on the opposite shore, for a wonderful reflected view of Zell am See. For a bird's-eye view, a cable car leads virtually from the center of Zell am See up to the **Schmittenhöhe** for a 180-degree panorama that takes in the peaks of the Glockner and Tauern granite ranges to the south and west and the very different limestone ranges to the north. This sweep will impress upon you the geology of Austria as no written description ever could. In addition, there are four other cable-car trips up this mountain, offering some of the most spectacular vistas of the Kitzbühel Alps.

🔵 The romantic narrow-gauge **Pinzgauer Railroad** winds its way under steam power on a two-hour trip through the Pinzgau, following the Salzach River valley westward 54 km (34 mi) to Krimml. Nearby are the famous Krimmler waterfalls, with a 1,300-ft drop, which you can see from an observation platform or explore close at hand (if you can manage a hike of about 3½ to four hours). Be sure to take a raincoat and sneakers. ☎ *06542/17000.* 🎫 *Round-trip AS240.* ⊙ *Trains depart July–Aug., Tues., Thurs., and weekends at 9:15; Sept., Sat. at 9:15.*

Dining and Lodging

$$$$ ✕🏨 **Grand.** In the style of the great turn-of-the-century resort hotels, this totally renovated house right on the lake is, as its name implies, probably the grandest (and most charming) place to stay in Zell, even without all the amenities and health facilities other Zell hotels provide. It stands on its own peninsula, is decorated with mansard roofs and whipped-cream stuccowork, and serves up some fine dining. Most of the accommodations are small apartments, complete with kitchenette and fireplace; the best are those farthest out on the small peninsula. ⊠ *Esplanade 4, A–5700,* ☎ *06542/788,* 📠 *06542/788–301. 111 rooms. 2 restaurants, bar, kitchenettes, indoor pool, lake, sauna, golf, squash, boating, dance club. AE, DC, MC, V.*

$$$$ ✕⊞ **Salzburgerhof.** Sophisticated travelers often pick this impressive
★ family-managed chalet, not far from the lake and the ski lift, as the
town's foremost hotel; comfort and personal service are the rule. Each
of the attractive rooms and suites has a flower-bedecked balcony. The
restaurant is truly excellent; try the *Tafelspitz* (boiled beef) or rack
of lamb in an herb pastry crust. The pleasant garden is used for bar-
becues and evenings of folkloric entertainment. Golfer guests get a
30% discount at the local club. Brand new is the little wellness pavilion with an outdoor pool in the park and a program of thalasso therapy, mud packs, Reiki, and yoga courses. ⊠ *Auerspergstr. 11, A–5700,*
☎ *06542/765–0,* 🝙 *06542/76566. 36 rooms, 24 suites. Restaurant,
bar, indoor pool, lake, sauna, spa, exercise room. AE, DC, MC, V.
Closed Nov.*

$$$$ ✕⊞ **Schloss Prielau.** With its turreted towers and striped shutters, this
★ castle looks as if it stepped out of a fairy tale. Elegantly furnished rooms
with sumptuous fabrics and traditional carved-wood furniture can be
a bit dim, however, because of the narrow, old-fashioned windows. But
the service will make you feel as if you are the newest member of royalty to take up residence here. The restaurant serves classic Austrian
dishes like schnitzel but with a lighter, more refined touch than you
find in most other establishments. ⊠ *Hofmannsthalstr., A–5700,* ☎
06542/72609, 🝙 *06542/72609–55. 12 rooms. Restaurant, bar, lake,
sauna. AE, DC, MC, V.*

$$ ✕⊞ **St. Hubertushof.** On the opposite side of the lake from town, this
sprawling hotel complex offers a great view across the water. Panel-
ing and antlers over the fireplace in the lounge add to its rural style.
Golfers get a 30% reduction at the local course. The dance bar draws
a regular crowd, and the restaurant offers a wide range of international
and local dishes. ⊠ *Seeuferstr. 7, A–5705 Thumersbach,* ☎ *06542/767,*
🝙 *06542/767–71. 112 rooms. Restaurant, bar, café, sauna. AE, DC,
MC, V. Closed Nov.*

Nightlife and the Arts

The emphasis in Zell is more on drinking than on dancing, but the scene
does change periodically. At the moment, one of the "in" places is the
Crazy Daisy (☎ 06542/76359), a dance pub near the Kurhaus, where
town events often take place. Also near the Kurhaus and popular is
the pub **Sugarshack** (☎ 06542/4151). A mature crowd gathers at the
Wunderbar (☎ 06542/73059), in the Grand hotel (☞ Dining and
Lodging, *above*). Check out the action in the cellar of the **Sporthotel
Lebzelter** (☎ 06542/766).

Outdoor Activities and Sports

BICYCLING

The area around Zell am See is a gorgeous spot for bicycling. If you
left your wheels at home, you can rent some at the **train station** (☎
06542/73214–310) for AS180 (AS120 if you have a valid rail ticket)
for a normal city bike. Renting by the week is cheaper. From April to
October, bike tours run from south of Zell am See up to St. Johann
and Salzburg via the Tauern cycle route. Check with **Austria Radreisen**
(⊠ Joseph-Haydn-Str. 8, A–4780 Schärding, ☎ 07712/5511–0, 🝙
07712/4811).

FISHING

The lake's tranquil waters offer fine fishing. Many hotels in the area
have packages for avid anglers.

GOLF

Zell am See and Kaprun share two **18-hole courses** (each par-72). ⊠
Golfstr. 25, ☎ *06542/56161,* 🝙 *06542/56035.* ☉ *Apr.–Oct.*

SKIING

Together with nearby Kaprun, Zell am See offers good skiing for beginner to expert, along with a wide variety of terrain. Towering over Zell am See, the Schmittenhöhe has tree-lined runs that will feel familiar to Colorado and New England skiers. The nearby Kitzsteinhorn mountain (3,200 meters, or 1,560 ft), famous throughout Austria, offers year-round glacier skiing and was the first glacier ski area in Austria. Together these mountains offer 56 lifts, with 130 km (80 mi) of prepared slopes. In addition, there are more than 200 km (330 mi) of cross-country trails and 10 ski schools. For full information on skiing facilities, contact the local tourist office (⊠ Brucker Bundesstr., A–5700 Zell am See, ☎ 06542/770–0, ℻ 06542/ 72032, ✆).

WATER SPORTS

Boating—from paddleboating to sailing—and swimming are excellent on the uncrowded Zeller See. Since powerboats are restricted on many Austrian lakes, you won't find much waterskiing, but there is a waterskiing school, **Wasserskischule Thumersbach** (⊠ Strandbad, Thumersbach, ☎ 06542/72355) on the lake.

Saalbach

🔟 *17 km (9 mi) northwest of Zell am See.*

Noted skiing meccas Saalbach and its neighbor Hinterglemm are part of an area, comprising also Kaprun and Zell am See, that becomes a ski circus in winter. A clever layout of lifts and trails enables you to ski slopes without duplication and still get back to your starting point. When the snow melts, the region offers sensational hiking; both towns offer a wide variety of sports. Saalbach and Hinterglemm have each banned cars from their village center. You can drive to your hotel to unload baggage; watch carefully for signs or ask for specific directions— the routes are convoluted and confusing. Take the **Kohlmais cable car** north out of Saalbach to the top of the ridge for a superb 360-degree view of the surrounding mountain ranges.

To get to Saalbach from Zell am See, continue north on Route 311 to Maishofen, where the Glemm Valley opens to the west; then continue about 9 km (5½ mi) to the west. For those traveling by train or bus, head first to Zell am See for transfers up the valley.

Dining and Lodging

$ ✕ **Iglsbergerhof.** This utterly unpretentious family-run Gasthof serves
★   up some of the best authentic regional specialties in the area. Start with beef bouillon with *Pinzgauer Käspressknödel* (cheese dumplings), then have *Speckknödel* (bread dumpling with bacon chunks) with sauerkraut, and finish with a *Pinzgauer Bauernkrapfen* (a delicious filled doughnut). ⊠ *Vorderglemm 340, Saalbach,* ☎ *06541/6491. No credit cards. Closed Wed. and Nov.–mid-Dec.*

$$$–$$$$ 🏨 **Glemmtalerhof.** This massive chalet is surprisingly intimate inside, with pleasant paneled rooms and 20 apartments in Alpine style, most with balconies. It is mainly a winter resort, but there's still plenty to do in summer. Golfers get a 30% reduction on greens fees at Zell am See courses. ⊠ *Glemmtaler Landstr. 150, A–5754 Hinterglemm,* ☎ *06541/7135–0, ℻ 06541/7135–63. 62 rooms. 2 restaurants, 2 bars, café, pool, sauna, exercise room, horseback riding, nightclub, children's programs. AE, DC, MC, V. Closed mid-Apr.–mid-May and mid-Oct.– mid-Dec.*

$$$–$$$$ 🏨 **Saalbacher Hof.** This family-run chalet complex in the center of town is identified by a rustic bell tower and overflowing pots of red geraniums against weathered dark wood. Warm paneling and a large fire-

place welcome you; the rooms are spacious and comfortable. The hotel can make arrangements for golf and tennis. Every guest gets one free tennis hour daily on the hotel's own court. ⊠ *Dorfstr. 27, A–5753,* ☎ *06541/7111–0,* FAX *06541/7111–42. 90 rooms. 2 restaurants, bar, pool, sauna, golf privileges, tennis court, nightclub. AE, DC, MC, V. Closed mid-Apr.–May and Oct.–Nov.*

Outdoor Activities and Sports
SKIING

In addition to offering toboganing, sleigh riding, and curling, Saalbach and Hinterglemm have some of the finest skiing in Land Salzburg and possibly the finest interconnected lift system in Austria. There are 60 lifts, Austria's largest cable car, numerous cross-country ski trails, and, for ski potatoes, races and competitions are often run on the Saalbach–Hinterglemm Slalom. The most popular expert run is on the Schattberg mountain (a cable car takes you there from the center of Saalbach), where, on high, a restaurant offers fine dining. This is an intermediate skiers paradise, especially the north side of the mountain. Numerous ski schools provide the area with more than 200 instructors. For more information on skiing facilities contact the Saalbach Hintertglemm Tourism Association (⊠ A–5753 Saalbach Hinterglemm, ☎ 06541/ 6800–68, FAX 06541/680069, ✍).

Nightlife
BARS

Saalbach has a number of places that crowd up quickly as the slopes are vacated. The tourist office has a list of bars and discos. For dancing and music, try the **Hinterhagalm** disco-bar (☎ 06541/7212) or the **Visage** disco in the Hotel Kristall (☎ 06541/6376–45). The **Alpenhotel** has its Arena Club, with live music (☎ 06541/6666–0), and **Neuhaus** (☎ 06541/7151–0) features small local bands. There's action at the **Almbar** in the Hotel Glemmtalerhof (☎ 06541/7135–0) and at the **Pinzgauer Stüberl** in Hotel Wolf in Hinterglemm (☎ 06541/6346–37). The Londoner and Knappenkeller in the **Hotel Knappenhof** (☎ 06541/ 6497) in Hinterglemm offer disco or live music in winter and are currently among the "in" spots. Among **bars,** Stamperl, Flockerl, Hinterglemm, and Kuhstall in Saalbach and Lumpie's, Bla-Bla, and Rudi's Kneipe in Hinterglemm are current favorites.

Saalfelden

⓫ *25 km (15 mi) northeast of Saalbach.*

Saalfelden nestles at the foot of the **Steinernes Meer** (Sea of Stone), the formidable ridge that divides Austria from Germany. The town, farther up Route 311 from Saalbach, is a climber's mecca, but only for those who are experienced and who can tackle such challenges as the 9,560-ft Hochkönig. At the edge of the Steinernes Meer, signs lead you to a late-Gothic **cave chapel,** containing a winged altarpiece near a stone pulpit and hermit's cell. Saalfelden is a main stop on the Innsbruck–Salzburg train route.

Sights in town include a 19th-century Romanesque parish church with a late-Gothic winged altar (1539); the nearby 14th-century Farmach Castle, which is now a retirement home; and the 13th-century Lichtenberg Castle, which is now privately owned. For many, the most interesting attraction is the **Ritzen Castle** museum, where the Christmas-manger collection of artisan Xandl Schläffer as well as exhibits on minerals, native handicrafts, and local history are on view. ▣ *AS38.* ☉ *Mid-June–mid-Sept., daily 10–noon and 2–5; mid-Sept.– mid-June, Wed. and weekends 2–4.*

Very enjoyable is the 1½-km (1-mi) **summer toboggan run.** With 63 curves and three tunnels, it is the longest such run in Europe. Take the chairlift up the Huggenberg southwest of Saalfelden on the road to Zell. Other well-marked attractions in the area include the **Vorderkaserklamm gorge.** The **Hirschbichl pass** was a strategic route where several battles were fought during the Napoleonic Wars.

OFF THE BEATEN PATH

LAMPRECHTSHÖHLE – About 14 km (8 mi) northwest of Saalfelden on Route 311 heading toward Lofer, you come to Weissbach, whose claim to fame is a system of caves totaling about 35 km (19 mi). An old legend has it that a treasure is buried here, but no one has ever found it, not for lack of trying. ☎ 06582/8343. ⌨ AS38. ⊘ May 15–Oct. 15, daily 9–7; Oct. 16–May 14, daily 9–4.

Dining and Lodging

$$–$$$ ★ ✕ **Schatzbichl.** The reputation of this simple Gasthaus slightly east of Saalfelden draws guests from near and far. The pine-paneled interior is bright and cheerful, as is the usually overworked staff. Regional dishes are simply prepared and presented; try the garlic soup, lamb chops, or any of the fish offered. ⊠ *Ramseiden 82,* ☎ *06582/73281,* FAX *06582/73281–4. Reservations essential. No credit cards. Closed Tues. Mar.–May and Sept.–Oct., 2 wks in Apr., and Nov.*

$$$$ ✕▥ **Hotel Gut Brandlhof.** This sprawling ranch, about 5 km (3 mi) outside town, is perfect for an active vacation. The vast complex provides all manner of sports facilities, including the 18-hole, par-72 Saalfelden golf course, which belongs to the hotel. The comfortable rooms are done in Alpine-country style. In the wood-paneled restaurant, a *Kachelofen* (tiled brick stove) radiates warmth; the cuisine is first class and Austrian, with an eye to healthy light meals, fresh salads, seasonal specialties, and some international fare. ⊠ *Hohlwegen 4, A–5760,* ☎ *06582/7800–0,* FAX *06582/7800–598. 150 rooms. Restaurant, 2 bars, indoor and outdoor pools, sauna, 18-hole golf course, tennis court, bowling, exercise room, horseback riding, squash, fishing, children's programs. AE, DC.*

$$$ ✕▥ **Gasthof Hindenburg.** This 500-year-old inn in the center of town has been newly renovated from top to bottom to provide modern comfort while retaining historic touches. Room colors are warm and inviting, complementing the wood flooring and the combination of antique and modern furnishings. Some suites have a duplex layout. In summer, the garden restaurant is particularly inviting. There are very pleasant spa facilities on its fourth floor. ⊠ *Bahnhofstr. 6, A–5760,* ☎ *06582/793–0,* FAX *06582/793–78. 38 rooms, 6 apartments. 4 restaurants, bar, sauna, steam room. AE, DC, MC, V.*

$ ▥ **Pension Klinglerhof.** This is just one of several modest bed-and-breakfasts in Saalfelden, where things are simple and comfortable and inexpensive, and the service is all by owners (the Hölzls in this case), who enjoy taking care of their guests. The Klinglerhof is quiet, right near the golf course and the cross-country ski trails and the lifts. ⊠ *Schinking 1, A–5760,* ☎ *06584/7713. No credit cards.*

Outdoor Activities and Sports

BICYCLING

The valley leading to Saalfelden is a great place for seeing sights on two wheels. You can rent a bike at the **railroad station** (☎ 06582/2344–0).

HIKING

From Saalfelden, you can head off through the magnificent Saalach Valley on any of three five- or six-day self-guided expeditions called **"Hiking Without Luggage."** Your bags are transported, your choice of accommodation is prebooked, and guidebooks are available in English. The exhilaration can't be described in words. Information is available from Saalfelden's Pinzgau regional tourist office (⊠ Lofererstr. 5, A–5760, ☎ 06582/4017, 🅵🅰🆇 06582/4017–4).

MOUNTAIN SPAS AND ALPINE RAMBLES

Glacier-covered Alps and hot springs, luxurious hotels, and tranquil lakes are the enticing combinations this Austrian region superlatively serves up. Gold and silver mined from the mountains was the source of many local fortunes; today, glittering gold jewelry finds many buyers in the shops of Badgastein's Empress Elisabeth Promenade. To set off on this trip, head south from Salzburg on the A10 and take the Bischofshofen exit toward St. Johann im Pongau, which gets you to Route 311 and, 17 km (11 mi) later, the Route 167 junction. From Zell am See, head east on Route 311 to pass Bruck again, continue through Taxenbach to Lend, and turn south at the intersection of Route 167.

Badgastein

⑫ *54 km (34 mi) southeast of Zell am See.*

Though it traces its roots all the way back to the 15th century, this resort, one of Europe's leading spas, gained renown in the last century, when VIPs from emperors on down to impecunious philosophers flocked to the area to "take the cure." Today, Badgastein retains much of its 19th-century ambience. The stunning setting—a mountain torrent, the Gasteiner Ache, rushes through the unusual town—adds to the attraction. Most attempts at rejuvenating this turn-of-the-century jewel have met with failure, and we can be thankful for it. The old buildings still dominate the townscape, giving it a wonderful feeling of solidity and charm. The baths themselves, however, are state-of-the-art, as evidenced by the Felsenbad baths in the rocks and the **Thermalkurhaus** (Treatment Complex). The most unusual spa is the "healing mine" in **Böckstein,** near the Empress Elisabeth Promenade; it's an abandoned gold mine with very special air. For complete information on the town's main spas, contact the Badgastein tourist office (☞ The Eastern Alps A to Z, *below*).

A very special tradition in Badgastein is the old heathen *Perchtenlaufen* processions in January of every fourth year (the next is scheduled for 2002): people wearing big masks and making lots of noise chase the winter away, bringing good blessings for the new year.

Badgastein is serviced by many rail lines, with many expresses running from Salzberg and Klagenfurt. You can also reach the town by bus from Salzburg.

Dining and Lodging

$$$$ ✕🏨 **Hotel Weismayr.** This grand old hotel in the middle of town is without a doubt the top address in Badgastein—a 66-room palace with a reputation for luxury and service going all the way back to 1832. Everything is done here to make sure your stay will be pleasant, even healthy: It's a typical spa hotel with all the applications local nature can offer. It also organizes such interesting excursions as hunting tours. The expansive dining rooms in Biedermeier style are the setting for luxurious meals including many seasonal dishes (asparagus in May and June, game in autumn), but the menu also reflects the fact that you are at a spa and health club (fresh salads, vegetarian dishes). ⊠ *Kaiser-Franz-Josef-Str. 6, A–5640,* ☎ *06434/2594–0,* 🅵🅰🆇 *06434/2594–14. Restaurant, piano bar, mineral baths, spa, exercise room. AE, DC, MC, V.*

$$$$ ✕🏨 **Villa Solitude.** In this central turn-of-the-century villa overlooking the gorge below, six elegant suites offer every comfort. Rooms are wood-paneled, with furnishings appropriate to the period. The management is the same as at the Grüner Baum (☞ *below*). In the excellent restaurant, the Brasserie, try fish or fillet of beef; if you're here in summer, you can enjoy meals on the terrace. ⊠ *Kaiser-Franz-Josef-Str. 16, A–5640,* ☎ *06434/5101–0,* ℻ *06434/5101–3. 6 suites. Restaurant. AE, DC, MC, V. Closed Nov.*

$$$–$$$$ ✕🏨 **Grüner Baum.** You're out of the center of town here, in a relaxing, friendly hotel village set amid meadows and woodlands. The guest list in this Relais et Châteaux group hotel has included Austrian Empress Elisabeth and Saudi king Saud. Five separate houses have comfortable rustic, wood-paneled rooms, giving the complex a feeling of intimacy and personality. Children are well looked after. The elegant restaurant has an excellent reputation. ⊠ *Kötschachtal, A–564,* ☎ *06434/2516–0,* ℻ *06434/2516–25. 80 rooms. Restaurant, bar, indoor and outdoor pools, sauna, tennis court, exercise room, children's programs. AE, DC, MC, V. Closed Nov.*

$$$$ 🏨 **Elisabethpark.** The dining and drawing rooms and music bars go on and on in this elegant hotel—modern but of the old school—in the center of town. The grand-hotel atmosphere is underscored by Oriental carpets, marble, and crystal chandeliers. Rooms, with period furnishings, are particularly comfortable, and service has a pleasantly personal touch. ⊠ *A–5640,* ☎ *06434/2551–0,* ℻ *06434/2551–10. 109 rooms. Restaurant, bar, café, indoor pool, sauna, spa, exercise room. AE, DC, MC, V. Closed mid-Apr.–early June and Sept.–mid-Dec.*

$$ 🏨 **Krone.** Most of the pleasant, bright rooms in this in-town hotel have balconies, and you're about three minutes from the cable car up the mountain. In addition, the thermal spa is next door. ⊠ *Bahnhofspl. 8, A–5640,* ☎ *06434/2330–0,* ℻ *06434/2330–86. 60 rooms. Restaurant, bar, spa. MC, V. Closed mid-Apr.–mid-May and Oct.–Nov.*

Nightlife and the Arts

The **Grand Hotel de l'Europe casino** (⊠ Kaiser-Franz-Josef-Str. 14, ☎ 06434/2465, ℻ 06434/246525) has baccarat, blackjack, roulette, and slot machines. A passport is required. The casino is open July–mid-September and December 26–March, daily 7 PM–2 AM. Keep an eye out also for concerts, especially at the **Kongresshaus** in the middle of town (New Year's concerts are held here, for example).

Outdoor Activities and Sports

As a good spa town, Badgastein keeps its guests entertained with all sorts of events from snowboarding competitions to dog-sleigh races. You will not be bored.

GOLF

The **Golfclub Gastein** has an attractive 9-hole, par-36 course. The greens fee is AS390 weekdays, AS500 weekends. Inquire at the nearest tourist office about special golfing packages and whether your hotel is a golf partner, which means you might get a 30% reduction. ☎ *06434/2775,* ℻ *06434/2775–4.* ☉ *Late Apr.–Oct.*

HANG GLIDING

Flinging yourself off high places with a few sails is ideal in the Alps. You'll find a school and a **rental company** at the cable car in Dorfgastein 16 km (10 mi) north of Badgastein (☎ 06433/223–0, ℻ 06433/344–10).

SKIING

Although not as well known to outsiders as other resorts, the Gastein ski area is popular with Austrians. The slopes of the four areas—Dorfgastein, Bad Hofgastein, Badgastein, and Sportgastein—are not well connected, so you'll often have to use the free shuttle bus and do some hoofing in your ski boots. Runs are mostly intermediate, with limited advanced and beginner slopes. For information contact the Kur- und Fremdenverkehrsverband tourist office (⊠ Kaiser-Franz-Josef-Str. 1, A–6540 Badgastein, ☎ 06434/2531–0, ℻ 06434/2531–40, ✎).

Though other Austrian winter sports areas are more popular, don't let this discourage you from trying the excellent facilities and good slopes in the nearby areas of Sportgastein, some 9 km (5½ mi) south of Badgastein, Schlossalm, and Stubnerkogel. These last two are linked by chair lifts. The other ski run near Badgastein is the Graukogel peak, which also offers a restaurant and great Alpine hikes.

Liechtensteinklamm

⑬ *38 km (24 mi) north of Badgastein.*

Traveling from Badgastein along Route 311, turn east toward Schwarzach in Pongau, where the road heads north, to find, between Schwarzach and St. Johann, the **Liechtensteinklamm,** the deepest (1,000 ft), narrowest (12½ ft), and most spectacular gorge in the Eastern Alps. At its far end is a 200-ft waterfall. A tour on a wooden walkway criss-crossing the gorge takes about 45 minutes. ☎ 06412/8572. ☞ AS32. ☉ *Early May–Oct., daily 8–5.*

St. Johann im Pongau

★ ⑭ *43 km (27 mi) north of Badgastein.*

St. Johann has developed into a full-fledged, year-round resort. The area is favored by cross-country and intermediate downhill skiers, as the gentle slopes provide an almost endless variety of runs. The huge, twin-spired parish church, built in 1861 in neo-Gothic style, is known locally as the **Pongau Cathedral**—a mammoth structure that rises quite majestically out of the townscape.

Every four years during the first week of January, the people of St. Johann, like the Badgasteiners, celebrate Pongauer Perchtenlauf, which can be poetically translated to mean "away with winter's ghost." Taking to the streets, they ring huge cowbells and wear weird masks and costumes to drive away evil spirits. The next celebration will be in the year 2001; check with the tourist office for the exact date. St. Johann is on the rail lines connecting Munich, Klagenfurt, and Salzburg.

Dining and Lodging

$$$–$$$$ ✕▥ **Sporthotel Alpenland.** This new-ish hotel has a somewhat more commercial approach to innkeeping than do the family-run chalets, but you get an attractive room, efficient service, and plenty of facilities. Three restaurants offer pizza, steaks, and such local specialties as lamb. ⊠ *Hans-Kappacher-Str. 7–9, A–5600,* ☎ *06412/7021–0,* ℻ *06412/7021–51. 137 rooms. 3 restaurants, bar, indoor and outdoor pools, sauna, tennis court, exercise room. AE, DC, MC, V.*

Outdoor Activities and Sports

GOLF

An 18-hole, **par-70 course** near Schwarzach in Pongau is open May–October. ⊠ *Off Rte. 311 (Box 6), Goldegg,* ☎ *06415/8585,* ℻ *06415/8585–4.*

SKIING

Linked by buses and 80 km (50 mi) of ski runs with other towns in the Pongau Valley, St. Johann remains the ski capital of the region called Sportwelt Amadé, which boasts more than 100 lifts and more than 350 km (218 mi) of well-groomed slopes. St. Johann alone has 12 ski lifts plus several cable-car ascents. Along with other Pongau valley runs, the town offers a Drei-Täler-Skischaukel (three-valley) pass. Inquire at the local tourist office what the best deal is, because they are constantly coming up with new commercial ideas. Contact Tourismusverband St. Johann (✉ Alpendorf, A–5600 St. Johann,, ☎ 06412/6036, FAX 06412/6036–74, 🐾).

Altenmarkt

⑮ *22 km (14 mi) east of St. Johann im Pongau.*

You cross over to Altenmarkt by leaving St. Johann im Pongau on Route 163 heading east across Wagrain and Reitdorf. Altenmarkt is small, but the **Church of St. Mary** contains the *Schöne Madonna,* an outstanding statue of the Virgin Mary that dates from before 1384. Nearby streams make the town a prime fishing site in summer, and skiing takes the spotlight during the winter months. The ski mountain here is part of the extensive Sportwelt Amadé, so a lift ticket gives you access to 350 km (210 mi) of mostly interconnected runs.

Dining and Lodging

$$$$ ✕🏨 **Lebzelter.** A luxurious feel permeates this hotel, centrally located
★   on Marktplatz. The excellent, window-filled country restaurant has a wide reputation. Dishes range from steaks to fish to vegetarian meals, but the emphasis is on traditional fare. ✉ *Marktpl. 79, A–5541,* ☎ *06452/6911,* FAX *06452/7823. 29 rooms. Restaurant, bar, sauna, exercise room, fishing, bicycles. AE, DC, MC, V.*

$$$ ✕🏨 **Schartner.** Although close to the center of Altenmarkt, this hotel may make you feel you are at a country inn, thanks to its large garden and the adjacent meadow. Summer visitors especially will enjoy the outdoor *Gastgarten* for a leisurely breakfast or evening meal. Family run, the inn features a noteworthy restaurant serving fish specialties, Highland beef, and vegetarian entrées. ✉ *Hauptstr. 35, A–5541,* ☎ *06452/5469,* FAX *06452/5469–27. 16 rooms, 14 suites. Restaurant, bar, sauna, whirlpool, steam room, children's playground. No credit cards.*

$$–$$$ ✕🏨 **Markterwirt.** This traditional house in the center of town dates back 900 years. The personal style of the family that runs it is reflected in the charming country decor of the comfortable rooms. The main dining room and the informal *Stube* are good, and the bar offers the tastiest pizza in town. Half board is required. The hotel has its own lake for fishing. ✉ *Marktpl. 4, A–5541,* ☎ *06452/5420,* FAX *06452/5420–31. 28 rooms. Restaurant, café, sauna, fishing. MC, V. Closed Nov.*

Radstadt

⑯ *4 km (2½ mi) east of Altenmarkt.*

Despite wars and fires, the picturesque walled town of Radstadt still retains its 12th-century character. Standing guard over a key north–south route, Radstadt was once granted the right to warehouse goods and to trade in iron, wine, and salt, but the town's present prosperity is due to tourism: the area is growing in popularity as a skiing destination and has been a longtime mecca for hiking in the summer. Radstadt's north and west walls, dating from 1534, are well preserved, as are three of the towers that mark the corners of the old town. Most of the buildings around the square are also from the 16th century. The late-Romanesque **parish church,** north of the square, dominates the town, but reconstructions over the ages have destroyed much of its original character. The interior contains several Baroque altars. To get to Radstadt, motorists usually take the A10 from Salzburg. Trains and buses, too, connect Salzburg with Radstadt (occasionally with a change over at Bischofshofen).

Dining and Lodging

$$$ ✕▥ **Sporthotel Gründler.** The emphasis here is on water, and the sport is fishing; the hotel has rights on 16 km (10 mi) of the Enns River. It also has ties to the Radstadt golf club. In summer, huge outdoor pools and a water slide offer great fun for children. The restaurant specializes in trout. ✉ *Schlossstr. 45, A–5550,* ☏ *06452/5590–0,* ℻ *06452/ 5590–28. 10 rooms, 18 apartments. Restaurant, 3 indoor and outdoor pools, sauna, fishing. MC, V. Closed mid-Apr.–mid-May and mid-Oct.–mid-Dec.*

Outdoor Activities and Sports

GOLF

During the April–November season, hills and a 16th-hole island pose challenges on the town's 18-hole, **par-72 course.** ✉ *Römerstr. 18,* ☏ *06452/5111,* ℻ *06452/7336.* ☉ *Apr.–Nov.*

Schladming

🔟 *20 km (13 mi) east of Radstadt.*

In the 14th and 15th centuries, Schladming was a thriving silver-mining town; then in 1525 the town was burned in an uprising by miners and farmers. Most of what you see today dates from 1526, when reconstruction began, but traces of the earlier town wall and the old miners' houses stand as testament to the town's former glory. Dominating the skyline is the Romanesque tower of the **St. Achaz parish church.**

Schladming is popular as a year-round resort. This is an area where sport is taken seriously; not only does it attract the world's best skiers, but it also gives beginners ample scope. And in happy contrast to fashionable resorts in Tirol and Vorarlberg, Schladming and its surroundings are reasonably priced. To get to Schladming from Radstadt, take scenic Route 146 east along the Enns River valley for about 20 km (13 mi) over the provincial border into Styria at Mandling. The town is also accessible by rail via the Salzburg–Graz line.

Dining and Lodging

$$$–$$$$ ✕▥ **Alte Post.** This traditional house in the center of town dates from
★ 1618 and is notable for its particularly attractive *Stube* and the older rooms with vaulted ceilings. Guest rooms are cozy and comfortable. The restaurants offer good regional and Austrian cuisine in an appropriately genuine atmosphere. It's the place to sit outside in summer, watch people go by, and enjoy solid Austrian cooking, cholesterol and all. Golf arrangements can be made for the nearby Dachstein-Tauern club. ✉ *Hauptpl. 10, A–8970,* ☏ *03687/22571,* ℻ *03687/22571–8. 40 rooms. 2 restaurants, bar, golf privileges, tennis court. AE, DC, MC, V. Closed mid- to late Apr. and mid- to late Nov.*

Outdoor Activities and Sports

FISHING

From May to mid-September you can cast a fly for trout in the nearby Enns River. Contact **Walter Dichtl** (✉ Hauptpl. 28, ☏ 03687/23539).

GOLF

Schladming-Haus (Haus is a little village incorporated into Schladming) has an Alpine setting that's reason enough to play the 18-hole, par-71 course at the **Golf & Country Club Dachstein-Tauern.** ☏ *03686/2630–0,* ℻ *03686/2630–15.* ☉ *May–Oct.*

SKIING

Although not well known to North Americans, Schladming and neighboring Ramsau-Dachstein make up one of Austria's most popular ski
destinations. There are a total of nine mountains to ski on, with more
than 160 km (96 mi) of downhill runs. Free ski buses connect the more
remote mountains in the region. The main ski runs here are on the
Hochwurzen and Planai peaks, both offering cable cars, chairlifts, and
expert downhill runs. The Dachstein-Südwand cable car ascends to a
height of almost 9,000 ft, allowing skiing well into June. Another lure
is the bustling après-ski scene. For details contact the Sportregion
Schladming-Ramsau/Dachstein office (⊠ Coburgstr. 52, A–8970
Schladming, ☎ 03687/22042–0, ℻ 03687/22042–60).

Ramsau am Dachstein

⑱ *6 km (4 mi) north of Schladming.*

Heading north out of Schladming, you take a narrow, winding road
that offers increasingly spectacular views of the Enns Valley and ends
in a broad, sun-bathed valley at the foot of the mighty Dachstein
range. After passing through Kulm, take a left at the next intersection
to reach the small resort town of Ramsau am Dachstein. About 4½ km
(3 mi) west of Ramsau, a small toll road (AS40 per adult) forks off to
the north onto the Dachstein itself, a majestic craggy outcrop of 9,826
ft. Take the impressive 20-minute **Hunerkogel cable-car ride** to the top
of the Alps; a round-trip without skis AS265. A phone call to ☎
03687/81315 will tell you in German what the weather's like up there.
To the north lie the lakes of the Salzkammergut; to the west, the Ten-
nen mountain range. South and east lie the lower Tauern mountains.
A snowmobile ride will take you very close to the Dachstein peak, or
you can hike over if you're wearing proper hiking boots. In summer
the south cliff at Hunerkogel is a favorite "jumping-off spot" for
paragliders. To get to Ramsau without a car, you need to take a bus
from Schladming.

Dining and Lodging

$$–$$$ ✕☷ **Pehab-Kirchenwirt.** *Kirchenwirt* means "inn next to the church,"
and that's exactly where this rustic hotel is. It's been family-run for
the past 200 years! Many of the comfortable rooms have balconies;
those in the back have the best mountain view. You're close to hiking
trails in summer and the hotel-operated ski lift and ski runs in winter.
Hotel guests can use the nearby indoor pool, which has a sauna and
solarium. The restaurant serves good Styrian specialties, among other
things, for which it received an accolade. ⊠ *A–8972,* ☎ *03687/81732,*
℻ *03687/81655. 40 rooms, 5 apartments. Restaurant, café, Weinstube.
AE, MC. Closed Nov. and 1 month after Easter.*

$$$ ☷ **Peter Rosegger.** This rustic chalet in a quiet area on the forest's edge
★   is decorated with homey mementos—framed letters and embroidered
mottoes—of the Styrian writer after whom it is named. This is the place
to stay when you've come for climbing, as Fritz Walcher heads the Alpine
school. Rooms are country comfortable, and though the kitchen is the
best in the area, the restaurant is only for hotel guests, who are treated
to such local specialties as house-smoked trout, Styrian corned pork,
and stuffed breast of veal. ⊠ *A–8972,* ☎ *03687/81223–0,* ℻ *03687/
81223–8. 13 rooms. Restaurant, sauna, exercise room. No credit
cards. Closed mid-Apr.–May and Nov.–mid-Dec.*

Outdoor Activities and Sports

HIKING

If you're interested in learning to climb in the difficult Dachstein area,
contact the **Alpinschule Dachstein** (⊠ Ramsau am Dachstein 233, A–

8972, ☎ 03687/81223–0) or **Bergsteigerschule Dachstein** (✉ Ramsau am Dachstein 101, A–8972, ☎ 03687/81424).

The famous **Dachstein Glacier** can be skied year-round, although summer snow conditions require considerable expertise. The altitude, however, guarantees good snow conditions late into the winter season. A lift ticket also gives you access to the larger Sportregion Schladming-Ramsau/Dachstein. The Gletscherbahn Ramsau (glacier cable-car), completed in 1969, is a remarkable technical achievement. A fully suspended steel cable carries up to 70 persons a distance of more than 2,000 m (6,600 ft) in about 10 minutes to the Dachstein glacier, 2,700 m (8,900 ft) high. For details on skiing facilities contact the Tourismusverband (✉ A–8972 Ramsau am Dachstein, ☎ 03687/818–33, FAX 03687/81085, ✇).

Shopping

In the nearby village of Rössing, you'll find Richard Steiner's **Lodenwalker** (☎ 03687/81930), which, since 1434, has been turning out that highly practical feltlike fabric called loden. Here you can find various colors and textures at reasonable prices. It's open weekdays.

Filzmoos

⑲ *14 km (9 mi) west of Ramsau am Dachstein.*

Filzmoos, one of the most romantic villages in Austria, is still a well-kept secret. Though skiing in the nearby Dachstein mountains is excellent, the not terribly expensive winter resort has yet to be discovered by foreign tourists. During the summer months, meandering mountain streams and myriad lakes attract anglers eager for trout, while hikers come to challenge the craggy peaks. Filzmoos calls itself a balloon village, because it relies heavily on hot-air balloons to show its guests the region. Contact **Büro Dachstein-Tauern-Ballons** (☎ 06453/2781).

Dining and Lodging

$$$ ✕🏨 **Hubertus.** In this highly personal hotel in the center of town, every
★ last detail—from romantic furnishings to modern conveniences—is done to perfection. Fishing enthusiasts have 20 km (12 mi) of mountain streams and two small lakes at their disposal. The restaurant is the best in the area: Frau Maier's way with trout (which you might have caught yourself) is exquisite, but don't overlook the game, roast poultry, or veal sweetbreads. Finish with *Topfenknödel* (cream cheese dumpling), a house specialty. ✉ *Am Dorfpl. 1, A–5532,* ☎ *06453/8204,* FAX *06453/82066. 17 rooms. Restaurant, bar, café, sauna, exercise room, fishing. No credit cards. Closed mid-Apr.–mid-May and mid-Oct.–mid-Dec.*

$$–$$$ 🏨 **Alpenkrone.** From the balconies of this chalet complex, you'll have a great view of the surrounding mountains. Rooms are simple and in no particular style, but the friendly management has succeeded in providing four-star comfort at three-star prices even when the customary half board is considered. ✉ *Filzmoos 133, A–5532,* ☎ *06453/8280–0,* FAX *06453/8280–48. 51 rooms. Restaurant, bar, indoor pool, sauna, exercise room. DC, MC, V. Closed Easter–mid-May and mid-Oct.–mid-Dec.*

En Route From Filzmoos, rejoin Route 99/E14 again at Eben im Pongau. Here you can take the A10 autobahn north to Salzburg, if you're in a hurry. But if you have time for more majestic scenery and an interesting detour, continue about 4 km (2½ mi) on Route 99/E14, and turn north on Route 166, the **Salzburger Dolomitenstrasse** (Salzburg Dolomites Highway), for a 43-km (27-mi) swing around the Tennen mountains. Be careful, though, to catch the left turn onto Route 162 at Lindenthal; it will be marked to Golling. Head for Abtenau.

Abtenau

20 *44 km (28 mi) northwest of Filzmoos.*

Abtenau is a charming little town with a pretty old village square flanked by colorful burghers' houses and the 14th-century **St. Blasius Church,** which has late-Gothic frescoes and a Baroque high altar. A **museum** of local history, which documents primarily the life of local farmers, has been set up south of town in the Arlerhof, an ancient house built in 1325. It's open June–mid-September, Tuesday, Thursday, and Sunday 2–5. Nearby, nature has arranged its own museum, the Trickl and Dachser **waterfalls,** with the nearby cave known as the "cold cellar" (der kalte Keller), where beer used to be stored.

Dining and Lodging

$$$ ✕🏠 **Post.** This older, centrally located hotel, decorated in rustic style with natural wood, has comfortable rooms with up-to-date facilities. And transportation is at the door; the Windhofer family also runs the town's taxi and excursion service. The restaurant is good; try the rump steak Tirol or any of the other beef dishes. ✉ *Markt 39, A–5541,* ☎ *06243/2209–0,* FAX *06243/3353. 40 rooms. Restaurant, café, indoor pool, sauna. DC. Closed Apr. and Nov.–mid-Dec.*

$$$$ 🏠 **Moisl.** This group of typical Alpine chalet–style houses in the center of town, with flower-laden balconies and overhanging eaves, dates back to 1764, but its services and facilities are absolutely up-to-date. Rooms are done in country decor. Evening entertainment includes candlelit dinner and wine and grill parties. ✉ *Markt 26, A–5441,* ☎ *06243/22100,* FAX *06243/2232–612. 75 rooms. Restaurant, bar, café, indoor pool, sauna, tennis court, bowling. No credit cards. Closed Apr. and mid-Oct.–mid-Dec.*

Outdoor Activities and Sports

WHITE-WATER RAFTING

From May to the middle of October, you can raft the Salzach and Lammer rivers. The Lammer, with its "Hell's Run," is particularly wild. Runs begin at AS500 per person. For details, call either of Abtenau's two active clubs: **Alpin Sports** (☎ 06243/3088, FAX 06243/30884 or **Club Zwilling** (☎ 06243/3069 or 06243/3339, FAX 06243/3069–17).

Werfen

21 *41 km (26 mi) from Abtenau.*

The small town of Werfen, adorned with 16th-century buildings and a lovely Baroque church, belies its importance for it actually is the base for exploring three extraordinary attractions: the largest and most fabulous ice caverns in the world; one of Austria's most spectacular castles; and a four-star culinary shrine, Obauer. The riches of Werfen, in other words, place it on a par with many larger, much-touted Austrian cities.

★ From miles away, you can see **Burg Hohenwerfen,** one of the most formidable fortresses of Europe (it was never taken in battle), which dates from 1077. Though fires, reconstructions, and renovations, most recently in 1948, have altered the appearance of the formidable fortress, it still maintains its medieval grandeur. Hewn out of the rock on which it stands, the castle was called by Maximilian I a "plume of heraldry radiant against the sky." Inside, it has black-timber beamed state rooms and an enormous frescoed Knights' Hall. It even has a torture chamber. Eagles, falcons, and other birds of prey swoop dramatically above the castle grounds, adding considerably to the medieval feel. The castle harbors Austria's first museum of falconry, and the birds of prey are rigorously trained. Call to confirm the show schedule, which may change. ☎ 06468/7603, ☒ 06468/7603–4. ◻ *Admission, tour, and birds-of-prey performance AS120.* ◷ *Fortress Easter–Oct., daily (may be closed Mon. in Apr. and Oct.); tours Apr. and Oct., Tues.–Sun. 10–4; May and Sept., daily 10–3; July–Aug., daily 11–5. Birds-of-prey performance Apr.–early July and late Aug.–Oct., daily at 11 and 3.*

OFF THE BEATEN PATH	**EISRIESENWELT** – The "World of the Ice Giants," just southwest of Abtenau, houses the largest known complex of ice caves, domes, galleries, and halls in Europe. It extends for some 42 km (26 mi) and contains a fantastic collection of frozen waterfalls and natural statuesque formations. Drive to the rest house, about halfway up the hill, and be prepared for some seriously scenic vistas. Then walk 15 minutes to the cable car, which takes you to a point about 15 minutes on foot from the cave, where you can take a 1¼-hour guided tour. You can also take a bus to the cable car from the Werfen railroad station (☎ 06468/5293), but be sure to leave at least an hour before the start of the next scheduled cave trip. The entire adventure takes about half a day. And remember, no matter how warm it is outside, it's below freezing inside, so bundle up, and wear appropriate shoes. ☎ 06468/5291 or 06468/5248. ◻ *AS180, including cable car.* ◷ *Tours May–Oct., daily 9:30–3:30 hourly; July–Aug., daily 9:30–4:30 hourly.*

Dining and Lodging

$$$$ ✕ **Obauer.** Worth a detour on your way back to Salzburg, this
★ *Landgasthaus* (country inn) is one of Austria's top half dozen restaurants—some would argue the best. The gourmet temple draws people from around the nation, so reserve well in advance and allow plenty of time: this is superlative cuisine. The menu constantly changes to match the imagination of the Obauer brothers, who share responsibilities as chefs. Diners choose a fixed menu or order à la carte, but either way you'll find perfection in every offering. Ask for advice on the appropriate wines. You can also stay overnight here; the house has seven rooms (reserve in advance). ☒ *Markt 46,* ☎ 06468/5212–0, ☒ 06468/5212–12. *Reservations essential. AE. Closed 2 (varying) days per wk; annual holiday closing also varies.*

$$ ▥ **Hotel-Garni Erzherzog Eugen.** You can't miss this hot-pink Gasthaus with window boxes trailing garlands of geraniums. It's smack in the middle of town. Though the decor is basic and a bit bland—traditional white lace curtains and nondescript furniture—the staff extends a warm and hospitable welcome to its guests. The lodging is under the same management as the nearby Obauer (☞ *above*). ☒ *Markt 38, A-5450,* ☎ 06468/5210–0, ☒ 06468/5210–3. *12 rooms. Bar. No credit cards.*

EASTERN ALPS A TO Z

Arriving and Departing

By Car

If you're coming from northern Italy, you can get to Villach on the E55/A13 in Italy, which becomes the A2 and then the A10; from Klagenfurt, farther east in Carinthia, taking the A2 autobahn is quickest. The fastest route from Salzburg is the A10 autobahn, but you will have to take two tunnels into account at a total cost of AS140 (Tauern- and Katschbergtunnel). In summer on certain weekends (when the German federal states have their official vacations), the A10 southbound can become one very long parking lot, with hour-long waits before the tunnels. Taking the normal road over the passes, although long, is very attractive, but you will not be the only person who thought of it. If coming from abroad, don't forget to buy the autobahn sticker for Austria (☞ Driving *in* Smart Travel Tips A to Z).

By Plane
The closest airport is at Klagenfurt, 50 km (31 mi) from Villach. It is served by Austrian Airlines, Tyrolean Airways, and Swissair. Salzburg, too, has its own airport (☞ Salzburg A to Z *in* Chapter 5). Both have frequent connections to other Austrian cities and other points in Europe, but neither has scheduled overseas connections.

By Train
Villach and Salzburg are both served by frequent rail service from Vienna. Villach is also connected to Italy and Salzburg, which in turn is well connected to Germany. For train information, try one of the following: **Salzburg Hauptbahnhof** (☎ 0662/1717), **Villach** (☎ 04242/1717), **Klagenfurt** (☎ 0463/1717).

Getting Around

By Bus
As is typical throughout Austria, where trains don't go, the post office and railroad buses do, though some side routes are less frequently covered. You'll need to coordinate your schedule with that of the buses, which is not as difficult as it sounds. The Austrian travel offices are helpful in this regard, or **bus information** is available (☎ 0660/5188) in **Villach** (☎ 04242/44410 or 04242/2020–4041) and in **Salzburg** (☎ 0662/167 or 0622/872150). You can take a post office bus from the **Zell am See rail station** (☎ 06542/2295) up and over the mountains to the glacier at Kaiser-Franz-Josefs-Höhe, a 2½-hour trip, or from the **Lienz rail station** (☎ 04852/67067) via Heiligenblut to the glacier, about two hours on this route. Buses run from early June to mid-October.

By Car
A car is by far the preferred means of seeing this area; the roads are good, and you can stop to picnic or just to marvel at the scenery. Be aware that the Grossglockner High Alpine Highway is closed from mid-November or possibly earlier (the first heavy snow) to mid-May or early June. Though many of the other high mountain roads are kept open in winter, driving them is nevertheless tricky, and you'll probably need chains. Keep in mind the cost of driving these roads as well: tunnels, passes, and panoramic roads often have tolls.

By Train
You can reach most of the towns in the Eastern Alps by train, but the Grossglockner and Dachstein mountains are reachable in a practical sense only by road. If you do travel by rail, you can go from Villach to Hermagor, to Lienz, and northward (north of Spittal an der Drau) via Mallnitz and Badgastein to the main line at Schwarzach. There you can cut back westward to Zell am See or continue onward to Bischofshofen, connecting there via Radstadt to Schladming or staying on the main line north to Salzburg.

Contacts and Resources

Guided Tours
Bus tours from Salzburg include the Grossglockner mountain highway (☞ Salzburg A to Z *in* Chapter 5).

Visitor Information
For information about Carinthia, contact **Kärntner Tourismus** (⊠ Casinopl. 1, A–9220 Velden, ☎ 04274/52100–0, FAX 04274/52100–50).

The central tourist board for East Tirol is **Tirol-Information** (✉ Wilhelm-Greil-Str. 17, A–6010 Innsbruck, ☎ 0512/5320–170, FAX 0512/5320–174). For information about Salzburg Province, contact **Salzburger Land Tourismus** (✉ Wiener Bundesstr. 23, Postfach 1, A–5300 Hallwang bei Salzburg, ☎ 0662/6688, FAX 0662/6688–0). The main tourist bureau for **Styria** is Steiermark Information (✉ St. Peter–Hauptstr. 243, A–8042 Graz, ☎ 0316/403033–0, FAX 0316/403033–10).

Many individual towns have their own *Fremdenverkehrsamt* (tourist office). **Badgastein:** Kur and Touristikbüro (✉ Kaiser-Franz-Josef-Str. 27, A–5640, ☎ 06434/2531–0, FAX 06434/2531–37). **Grosskirchheim/Döllach:** (✉ A–9843, ☎ 04825/521–0, FAX 04825/522–30). **Heiligenblut:** (✉ Hof 4, A–9844, ☎ 04824/2001–21, FAX 04824/2001–43). **Hermagor:** (✉ Wulfeniapl. 1, A–9620, ☎ 04282/2043–0, FAX 04282/2043–50). **Kötschach–Mauthen** (✉ Kötschach 390, A–9640, ☎ 04715/8516, FAX 04715/8513–30). **Lienz** (✉ Europapl. 1, A–9900, ☎ 04852/65265, FAX 04852/65265–2). **Matrei in Osttirol** (✉ Rauterpl. 1, A–9971, ☎ 04875/5330, FAX 04875/5331). **Radstadt** (✉ Stadtpl. 17, A–5550, ☎ 06452/7472, FAX 06452/6702). **Ramsau am Dachstein** (✉ Kulm 40, A–8972, ☎ 03687/81925 or 03687/81833, FAX 03687/81085). **Saalbach-Hinterglemm** (✉ Saalbach 550, A–5753 Saalbach, ☎ 06541/680068, FAX 06541/680069). **Saalfelden** (✉ Bahnhofstr. 10, A–5760, ☎ 06582/72513, FAX 06582/75398). **St. Jakob in Defereggen** (✉ Unterrotte 75AH, A–9963, ☎ 04873/5483 or 04873/5484, FAX 04873/5265). **St. Johann im Pongau** (✉ Hauptstr. 16, A–5600, ☎ 06412/6036, FAX 06412/6036–74). **Schladming** (✉ Erzherzog-Johann-Str. 213, A–8970, ☎ 03687/22268, FAX 03687/24138). **Werfen** (✉ A–5450, ☎ 06468/388, FAX 06468/7562). **Zell am See:** (✉ A–5700, ☎ 06542/770–0, FAX 06542/72032).

9 INNSBRUCK AND TIROL

Tirol has a great deal, if not everything: the Holy Roman Empire splendors of Innsbruck, Hansel-and-Gretel villages, majestic mountain peaks, masked Carnival revelers, and more—much more. Brush off your best lederhosen and set out to shop for cuckoo clocks; then try out your vibrato on some Jodeln, true Tirolean singing. Then head for the great ski resorts—St. Anton, Kitzbühel, and Innsbruck—where sport und Spiel are always in high gear.

Updated by
Lee Hogan

IROL IS SO DIFFERENT from the rest of Austria that you might think
you've crossed a border. In a way, you have. The frontier between
the provinces of Salzburg and Tirol is defined by mountains; four
passes make traffic possible. The faster trains cut across Germany
rather than agonizing through the Austrian Alps. To the west, Tirol is
separated from neighboring Vorarlberg by the Arlberg Range.

As small, relatively, as the province is, the idea of Tirol remains all-en-
compassing—it is virtually the shop window of Austria. Its very name
conjures up visions of great chains of never-ending snowcapped mountains; remote, winding Alpine valleys; rushing mountain torrents; and
spectacular glaciers that rise out of the depths like brilliant, icy dia-
monds. In winter you'll find masses of deep, sparkling powder snow;
unrivaled skiing and tobogganing; and bizarre winter carnivals with
grotesquely masked mummers. Come summer, you'll find breathtaking picture-postcard Alpine scenery, cool mountain lakes, and rambles
through forests; and throughout the year, there are yodeling and zither
music, villagers in lederhosen and broad-brimmed feathered hats, and,
of course, the sounds of those distinctive cowbells.

As if the sheer physical splendor of Tirol weren't enough, the region
can look back on a history filled with romance. Up to the beginning
of the 16th century, Tirol was a powerful state in its own right, under
a long line of counts and dukes, including personages of such varying
fortunes as Friedl the Penniless and his son Sigmund the Wealthy. (On
the whole, Tirolean rulers were more often wealthy than penniless.)
The province reached the zenith of its power under Emperor Maximilian I (1459–1519), when Innsbruck was the seat of the Holy Roman
Empire. Maximilian's tomb in Innsbruck gives ample evidence of this
onetime far-reaching glory. Over the centuries, the Tiroleans became
fiercely nationalistic. In 1809–10 Andreas Hofer led bands of local patriots against Napoléon in an effort to break free from Bavaria and rejoin Austria. After three successful battles, including the Battle of
Bergisel just outside Innsbruck, Hofer lost the fourth attempt against
combined French and Bavarian forces, was executed in Mantua, and
became a national hero.

Today, Tirol looks to Vienna for political support in its perpetual dispute with Italy over the South Tirol, a large and prosperous wine-growing region that was ceded to Italy after World War I. Many Austrian
Tiroleans still own property in South Tirol and consider it very much
a part of their homeland. Yet even Austria's Tirol is physically divided:
East Tirol, a small enclave of remarkable natural magnificence wedged
between the provinces of Salzburg and Carinthia, belongs to Tirol, but
it can be reached only through Italy or the province of Salzburg.

And what about the Tiroleans themselves? Like most other mountain
peoples, the Tiroleans are very proud and independent—so much so
that for many centuries the natives of one narrow valley fastness had
little communication with their "foreign" neighbors in the next valley. (It's still possible to find short, dark, and slender residents in one
valley and blond, blue-eyed, strapping giants in the next.) But Tirol
can also be very cosmopolitan, as any visitor to Innsbruck will attest.
The city is Tirol's treasure house—historically, culturally, and com-
mercially. It's also sited smack dab in the center of the Tirolean region
and makes a convenient base from which to explore. Even if you are
staying at an area resort, spend a day or two in Innsbruck first: it will
give you a clearer perspective on the rest of the region.

Pleasures and Pastimes

Dining

Tirolean restaurants range from grand-hotel dining salons—favored spots for chic Innsbruckers—to little Tirolean *Bauernstuben*, rustic restaurants where you can enjoy hearty local specialties like *Tiroler Gröstl* (a skillet dish made of beef, potatoes and onions), *Knödel* (dumpling) soup or *Schweinsbraten* (roast pork with sauerkraut) while sitting on highly polished wooden seats (rather hard ones!). Don't forget to enjoy some of the fine Innsbruck coffeehouses, famous for their scrumptious cakes—and remember that some daytime eating places turn into wine taverns late in the evening. Outside of Innsbruck, you'll find country inns that have dining rooms, but there are few, if any, separate restaurants. Prices for meals include taxes and a service charge but not the customary small additional tip of 3%–5%.

CATEGORY	COST*
$$$$	over AS400 (€29)
$$$	AS300–AS400 (€21–€29)
$$	AS200–AS300 (€15–€20)
$	under AS200 (€15)

per person for a typical three-course meal, with a glass of house wine

Hiking

Tirol has a good share of the more than 50,000 km (35,000 mi) of well-maintained mountain paths that ribbon the country. Hiking is one of the best ways truly to experience the awesome Alpine scenery, whether you just want to take a leisurely stroll around one of the crystalline blue lakes reflecting the mountains towering above them or trek to the top of one of the mighty peaks. Mountain-climbing is a highly organized sport in Tirol, a province that contains some of the greatest challenges to lovers of this sport: the Kaisergebirge (base: Kufstein), the Zillertaler and Tuxer Alps (base: Mayrhofen), the Wettersteingebirge and Karwendel ranges (base: Seefeld), the Nordkette range (base: Innsbruck), and the Ötz (base: Obergurgl). The instructors at the Alpine School Innsbruck are the best people to contact if you want to make arrangements for a mountain-climbing holiday or if you wish to attend a mountain-climbing school; if you already know how, contact the Österreichischer Alpenverein (☞ Outdoor Activities and Sports *in* Innsbruck, *below*).

Lodging

For one reason or another, travelers do not stay very long in Innsbruck itself. The rival attractions of the magnificent countryside, the lure of the mountains and countless Alpine valleys perhaps prove too strong—in any case, Innsbruck hotels report the average stay is usually two to three days, so there is a fast turnover and most always a room to be had. Even so, if you travel during the high season, July–August, and in the winter, it's best to book in advance. If you're driving, you may want to seek out a hotel in Innsbruck that has parking, since otherwise cars must be left some distance from the city center. Hotel rates vary widely by season, with the off-peak periods being March–May and September–November. Some travelers opt to set up their base not in Innsbruck but *overlooking* it, on the Hungerburg Plateau, on the top of a hill 3,000 ft above sea level, or in one of the hotels and inns perched still higher up on the Nordkette chain, both reached by funicular. If you choose these lofty aeries, you will have invigorating mountain air and a wonderful view of the Alps with Innsbruck spread at your feet (commuting to the city, of course, will add to your expenses).

In the popular resort towns, many hotels operate on a half-board basis (breakfast and dinner must be taken) during the ski season, and some take no credit cards. Summer prices are often as much as 50% lower than during the ski season. If you're out for savings, it's a good idea to find lodgings in small towns nearby rather than in the resorts themselves; local tourist offices may be able to help you get situated, possibly even with accommodations in private homes. In our listings, Kitzbühel, St. Anton, and Seefeld are the higher-priced resorts. Prices include tax and service.

CATEGORY	RESORTS*	SMALL TOWNS*
$$$$	over AS2,200	over AS1,000
$$$	AS1,500–AS2,200	AS800–AS1,000
$$	AS900–AS1,500	AS550–AS800
$	under AS900	under AS550

Per person for a standard double room with bath, including breakfast (except in $$$$ hotels), generally half board in resorts in winter. To compute Euro equivalencies, divide AS amount by 13.76.

✎ *following the text of a review is your signal that the property has a Web site, where you will find details and, usually, images; for a link, visit www.fodors.com/urls.*

Skiing

Downhill was practically invented in Tirol, which came to the forefront as a prime tourist destination because of the excellence of its skiing. Modern ski techniques were developed here, thanks to the legendary skiing master Hannes Schneider, who took the Norwegian art of cross-country skiing and adapted it to downhill running. No matter where your trip takes you, world-class—and often gut-numbing—skiing is available, from the glamour of Kitzbühel in the east to the imposing peaks of St. Anton am Arlberg in the west.

Close to the Arlberg Pass is **St. Anton**, which, at 4,300 ft, is home to one of the finest ski schools in the world. The specialty at St. Anton is piste skiing—enormously long runs studded with mogels (and few trees), some so steep and challenging that the sport is almost the equal of mountain climbing. In fact, this is the only place you can heli-ski in Austria. It was here in the 1920s that Hannes Schneider started the school that was to become the model for all others. A short bus ride to the top of the pass brings you to **St. Christoph**, at 5,800 ft. Many excellent tours, served by the Galzip cable railway, start here, but the *Skihaserl*, or ski bunny, would do well to stay down at St. Anton where there are better—and gentler—nursery slopes.

Farther along the Inn is the Ötz Valley. From the Ötztal station you can go by bus to **Soelden**, a resort at 4,500 ft that is not as expensive as others, nor as highly organized. The village of **Obergurgl**, at 6,321 ft, lies at the head of the Ötz Valley, where you can ski until early summer. Not far from Innsbruck is **Seefeld**, at 3,870 ft, long the base of one of Austria's best-known aces, Toni Seelos. At the farther end of Tirol lies **Kitzbühel**, chic and *charmant*, perhaps most famous for its "Ski Circus," a system of ski lifts and trails, floodlit at night, whereby skiers can ski for weeks without retracing their steps. The best time for skiing around **Innsbruck** is January to April.

Exploring Innsbruck and Tirol

Innsbruck makes a good introduction and starting point for exploring Tirol, but Tirol's gorgeous geography precludes the convenient loop tour from the capital city. You must go into the valleys to discover the hundreds of charming villages and hotels, and a certain amount of backtracking is necessary. We've outlined four tours over familiar routes, touching on the best of the towns and suggesting side trips and pleasures off the beaten track. "Around the Lower Inn Valley" will take you east of Innsbruck through the lower Inn Valley, then south into the Ziller and Tuxer valleys, with detours to the Achensee and to Gerlos. "From Jenbach to Kitzbühel," also east of Innsbruck, continues up the Inn Valley to Kufstein on the German border and to the ski resorts of St. Johann and Kitzbühel. "West from Innsbruck to Imst and Ötz Valley" explores the Inn Valley west of Innsbruck to Imst, then goes south up the Ötz Valley. "Landeck, Upper Inn Valley, and St. Anton" heads west from Imst, takes in Landeck and the upper Inn Valley, ending with St. Anton and the Arlberg. Whether you mix or match these tours or do them all, they'll allow you to discover a cross section of Tirol's highlights: the old and the new, glossy resorts, medieval castles, and, always, that superlative scenery.

Great Itineraries

Numbers in the text correspond to numbers in the margin and on the Innsbruck, Eastern Tirol, and Western Tirol maps.

IF YOU HAVE 3 DAYS

Head straight to the heart of Tirol to the provincial capital of ▨ **Innsbruck** ①–⑩; the city is conveniently situated for the traveler to Tirol, for it lies almost exactly in the center of the province on the Inn River. Even if you have already settled on a resort for your holiday, you should spend at least a day in the capital first to check out the beautiful buildings built by the Emperor Maximilian I—from the **Goldenes Dachl** ① to the **Hofburg** ⑤—and by Austria's empress Maria Theresa, who gave her name to the principal street of the town, the Maria-Theresien-Strasse; any sightseeing in Innsbruck begins on this street, which runs through the heart of the city from north to south and is the main shopping center. Far from being exhausting to explore, Innsbruck is only a half-hour walk from one end of the old town to the other. The next day, let the funicular whisk you up the **Hungerburg** for the breathtaking views of Innsbruck below. You can take a leisurely hike along the mountain trail and see the flora and fauna at the Alpine zoo. After returning to the capital city, set out on your final day to visit **Schloss Ambras,** with its impressive collections of medieval curiosities—pack a picnic and stay for a concert if you're traveling during the summer season. More ambitious travelers should consider a quick day trip to the seriously scenic **Stubaital Valley,** one of the showpieces of the Tirol—via the narrow-gauge electric Stubaitalbahn.

IF YOU HAVE 5 DAYS

Begin your Tirolean sojourn with two days in attraction-studded ▨ **Innsbruck** ①–⑩—but don't forget to experience your first taste of the region's grand Alpine setting by fitting in some quick excursions to the outlying **Hungerburg** peak, **Schloss Ambras,** or the **Stubaital Valley.** On day three, charming Alpine villages are on the agenda with a visit to the Ötz Valley: head for **Telfs** ㉖, **Ötz** ㉘, and **Sölden** ㉙, ending your journey at Austria's highest mountain town, ▨ **Obergurgl** ㉚. On the fourth day, spend time exploring castle ruins, Baroque churches, and yet more spectacular scenery in **Imst** ㉗, **Landeck** ㉛, and **Ried** ㉜, with an overnight in ▨ **Serfaus** ㉝. For the peak experience of your trip—literally—head to the slopes on your final day at **St. Anton am Arlberg** ㉞. Keep in mind that modern highways can get you to your destination quickly, but often the most beautiful scenic views lie on off-the-beaten-track roads: ask your hotel concierge for advice on finding the best beauty spots.

IF YOU HAVE 7 DAYS

▨ **Innsbruck** ①–⑩ makes a good base for discovering the entire region but is well worth spending two days exploring on its own. After see-

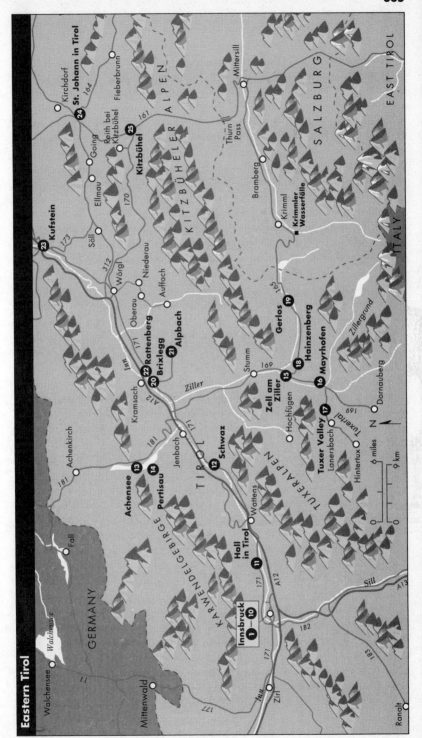

Eastern Tirol

GERMANY

EAST TIROL

ITALY

SALZBURG

KITZBÜHELER ALPEN

KARWENDELGEBIRGE

TUXERALPEN

TIROL

Walchensee
Walchensee
Fall
Mittenwald

Kirchdorf
St. Johann in Tirol
164
Fieberbrunn
Going
Reith bei Kitzbühel
Ellmau
Kitzbühel
161
170
Söll
Kufstein
173
Wörgl
312
Oberau
Niederau
Auffach
Rattenberg
171
Brixlegg
Alpbach
Kramsach
Ziller
Achenkirch
Jenbach
181
181
Achensee
Pertisau
Schwaz
Wattens
Hall in Tirol
171
A12
Innsbruck
1 — 10
171
Inn
177
Zirl
Sill

Mittersill
Thurn Pass
Bramberg
Krimml
Krimmler Wasserfälle
195

Gerlos
Hainzenberg
Stumm
169
Zell am Ziller
Hochfügen
Mayrhofen
18
15
16
Tuxer Valley
17
Tuxertal
Lanersbach
Hintertux
Dornauberg
Zillergrund
169

N

6 miles
6 km
9 km

182
183
Ranalt
Sill
A13

Western Tirol

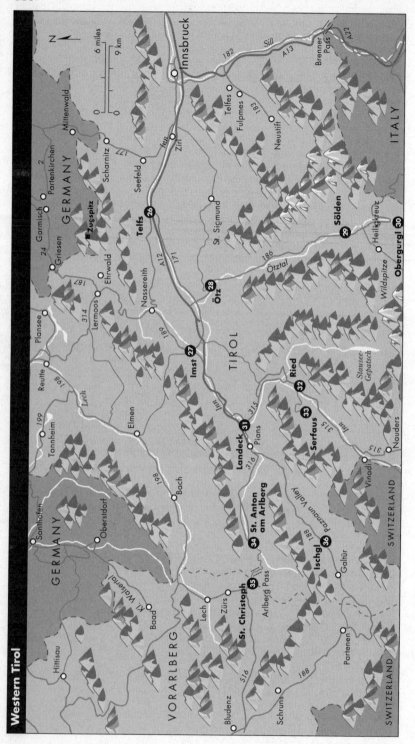

ing the riches of the Old Town of the imperial city and its neighboring attractions, the **Hungerburg** peak and **Schloss Ambras,** set out on the morning of the third day to see how the Habsburgs amassed their vast wealth: visit the mint at **Hall in Tirol** ⑪ and the silver mines at **Schwaz** ⑫. Then spend the night overlooking the pristine ⓣ **Achensee** ⑬ or stay at ⓣ **Pertisau** ⑭. On your fourth day, head south following the Ziller River with stops along the way in **Zell am Ziller** ⑮ and **Mayrhofen** ⑯. From there you can head west to explore the beautiful **Tuxer Valley** ⑰ and the classic Alpine villages of Lanersbach and Hintertux or save your breath and head east to climb the impressive Kreuzjoch mountain in nearby ⓣ **Gerlos** ⑲. On the fifth day, challenge the slopes at either of the world-famous resorts of ⓣ **St. Johann in Tirol** ㉔ or **Kitzbühel** ㉕—two towns that have become almost more fashionable as warm-weather destinations than as skiing meccas. On day six, visit the smaller resorts of **Going, Ellmau,** and **Söll** before visiting Emperor Maximilian's pleasure palace in ⓣ **Kufstein** ㉓. On your final day, visit the medieval town of **Rattenberg** ㉒ and the castles of **Brixlegg** ⑳ on your way back to Innsbruck.

When to Tour Innsbruck and Tirol

The physical geography of the Tirol makes it an especially ideal place in which to enjoy the outdoor life year-round. Ski-crazy travelers descend on the resorts during the winter months; in the summer, when the mountains are awash with wildflowers, camping tents spring up like mushrooms in the valleys as hikers, cavers, and mountain climbers take advantage of the palatial peaks. The annual Tirolean calendar is packed with special events: the famous Schemenlaufen, a procession of picturesque carved wooden masks, held in February in Imst; the Fasching balls, which reach their peak at the end of February in Seefeld; the Hahnenkamm ski race and curling competition held in winter in Kitzbühel; the glacier ski races in April at Obergurgl; the world-famous Gauderfest at Zell am Ziller during the first weekend in May; and the castle concerts at Kufstein and the folk festival in Mayrhofen during July and August.

INNSBRUCK

190 km (118 mi) southwest of Salzburg, 471 km (304 mi) southwest of Vienna, 146 km (91 mi) south of Munich.

The capital of Tirol is one of the most beautiful towns of its size anywhere in the world, owing much of its charm and fame to its unique setting. To the north, the steep, sheer sides of the Alps rise, literally from the edge of the city, like a shimmering blue-and-white wall—an impressive backdrop for the mellowed green domes and red roofs of the Baroque town tucked below. To the south, the peaks of the Tuxer and Stubai ranges undulate in the hazy purple distance.

Innsbruck has been an important crossroads for hundreds of years. When it was chartered in 1239, it was already a key point on the north–south highways between Germany and Italy and the east–west axis tying eastern Austria and the lands beyond to Switzerland. Today Innsbruck is the transit point for road and rail traffic between the bordering countries.

The charming Old World aspect of Innsbruck has remained virtually intact and includes ample evidence of its Baroque lineage. The skyline encircling the center suffers somewhat from high-rises, but the heart, the **Altstadt,** or Old City, remains much as it was 400 years ago. The protective vaulted arcades along main thoroughfares, the tiny passageways giving way to noble squares, and the ornate restored houses all contribute to an unforgettable picture.

Squeezed by the mountains and sharing the valley with the Inn River (Innsbruck means "bridge over the Inn"), the city is compact and very easy to explore on foot. Reminders of three historic figures abound: the local hero Andreas Hofer, whose band of patriots challenged Napoléon in 1809; Emperor Maximilian I (1459–1519); and Empress Maria Theresa (1717–80), the last two of whom were responsible for much of the city's architecture. Maximilian ruled the Holy Roman Empire from Innsbruck, and Maria Theresa, who was particularly fond of the city, spent a lot of time here.

Pick up a free Club Innsbruck card at your hotel for no-charge use of ski buses and reduced-charge ski-lift passes. For big savings, buy the **all-inclusive Innsbruck Card,** which gives you free admission to all the museums, mountain cable cars, the Alpenzoo and Schloss Ambras, plus free bus and tram transportation. Cards are good for 24, 48, and 72 hours at AS230, AS300, and AS370, respectively, and are available at the tourist office, cable cars, and larger museums. (☞ Visitor Information *in* Innsbruck and Tirol A to Z, *below*).

❶ Any walking tour of Innsbruck should start at the **Goldenes Dachl** (Golden Roof), which made famous the late-Gothic mansion whose balcony it covers. In fact, the roof is made of gilded copper tiles, and its recent refurbishment is said to have taken 14 kilograms (nearly 31 pounds) of gold. The house was built in 1420 for Duke Friedrich (otherwise known as Friedl the Penniless), and it is said that the indignant duke had the original roof covered with gold to counter the rumor that he was poor; the balcony was added in 1501 by Maximilian I as a sort of "royal box" for watching street performances in the square below. The structure was altered and expanded at the beginning of the 18th century, and now only the loggia and the alcove are identifiable as original. The magnificent coats of arms representing Austria, Hungary, Burgundy, Milan, the Holy Roman Empire, Styria, Tirol, and royal Germany are copies. You can see the originals (and up close, too) in the Ferdinandeum. The Golden Roof building now houses the **Maximilianeum,** which features memorabilia and paintings from the life of Emperor Maximilian I. ⊠ *Herzog Friedrich-Str. 15,* ☎ *0512/5811–11.* ⊠ *AS50.* ☉ *Mar.–Sept., daily 10–6; Oct.–Apr., Tues.–Sun. 10–12:30 and 2–5.*

❷ Down the street from the Goldenes Dachl is the **Stadtturm,** the 15th-century city tower, with a steep climb of 148 steps to the top. ⊠ *Herzog-Friedrich-Str. 21,* ☎ *0512/5615–003.* ⊠ *AS27.* ☉ *Mar.–June and Sept.–Oct., daily 10–5; July–Aug., daily 10–6.*

❸ Nearby is the dramatic blue-and-white **Helbling House,** originally a Gothic building (1560) to which the obvious, ornate rococo decoration was added in 1730. ⊠ *Herzog-Friedrich-Str. 10.*

❹ The main attraction of the Baroque **Domkirche zu St. Jakob** is the high-altar painting of the Madonna by Lucas Cranach the Elder, dating from about 1520. The cathedral was built in 1722. The ornate Baroque interior also has dramatic painted ceilings. ⊠ *Dompl. 6,* ☎ *0512/5839–02.* ⊠ *Free.* ☉ *Sat.–Thurs. 6–noon and 2–5, Fri. 2–5.*

❺ One of the most historic attractions of Innsbruck is the **Hofburg** imperial palace, which Maximilian I commissioned in the 14th century. (The booklet in English at the ticket office will tell you more interesting tidbits about the palace than the tour guide will.) Center stage is the **Giant's Hall**—designated a marvel of the 18th century as soon as it was topped off with its magnificent trompe-l'oeil ceiling, painted by Franz Anton Maulpertsch in 1775. The rococo decor and the portraits of Habsburg ancestors in the ornate white-and-gold great reception hall

Innsbruck

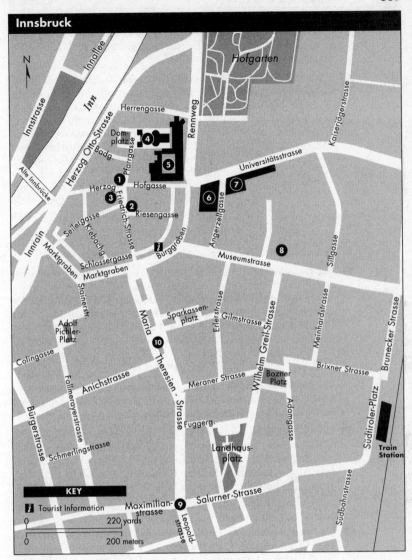

Hofgarten

Innallee

Innstrasse

Innrain

Inn

Alte Innbrücke

Herzog Otto-Strasse

Herrengasse

Rennweg

Kaiserjägerstrasse

Dom platze

Hofgasse

Universitätsstrasse

Hofgraben

Herzog Friedrich-Strasse

Badg.

Riesengasse

Angerzellgasse

Sillgasse

Seilergasse

Krebach g.

Schlossergasse

Burggraben

Museumstrasse

Meinhardstrasse

Brunecker Strasse

Marktgraben

Marktgraben

Stainerstr.

Sparkassen-platz

Erlerstrasse

Gilmstrasse

Wilhelm Greil-Strasse

Brixner Strasse

Adolf Pichler-Platz

Colingasse

Maria

Theresien - Strasse

Meraner Strasse

Bozner Platz

Südtiroler-Platz

Train Station

Fallmerayerstrasse

Anichstrasse

Fuggerg.

Adamgasse

Bürgerstrasse

Schmerlingstrasse

Landhaus-platz

Südbahnstrasse

KEY

i Tourist Information

Maximilian-strasse

Salurner-Strasse

Leopold-strasse

0 ———— 220 yards

0 ———— 200 meters

were added in the 18th century by Maria Theresa; look for the portrait of "Primal" (primrose)—to use the childhood nickname of the empress's daughter, Marie-Antoinette. ⊠ *Rennweg 1,* ☎ *0512/587186.* 🎫 *AS55.* ⊙ *Hourly tours daily 9–5.*

❻ Close by the Hofburg is the **Hofkirche** (Court Church), built as a mausoleum for Maximilian I (although he is actually buried in Wiener Neustadt, south of Vienna). The emperor's ornate black marble tomb is surrounded by 24 marble reliefs portraying his accomplishments, as well as 28 larger-than-life statues of his ancestors, including the legendary King Arthur of England. Andreas Hofer is also buried here. Don't miss the 16th-century **Silver Chapel,** up the stairs opposite the entrance, with its elaborate altar and silver Madonna. The chapel was built in 1578 to be the tomb of Archduke Ferdinand II and his wife, Philippine Welser, the daughter of a rich and powerful merchant family. Visit the chapel in the morning to take pictures; the blinding afternoon sun comes in directly behind the altar. ⊠ *Universitätsstr. 2,* ☎ *0512/ 584302.* 🎫 *AS30; combined ticket with Tiroler Volkskunstmuseum(☞ below) AS75.* ⊙ *July–Aug., daily 9–5:30; Sept.–June, daily 9–5.*

❼ The **Tiroler Volkskunstmuseum** (Tirolean Folk Art Museum), in the same complex as the Hofkirche, exhibits Christmas crèches, costumes, rustic furniture, and entire rooms from old farmhouses and inns, decorated in styles ranging from Gothic to rococo. Displays are somewhat static, and the information cards are in German. The small Christmas Manger Museum, on the other hand, is fascinating. ⊠ *Universitätsstr. 2,* ☎ *0512/ 584302.* 🎫 *AS60; manger museum AS25.* ⊙ *July–Aug., Mon.–Sat. 9– 5:30, Sun. 9–noon; Sept.–June, Mon.–Sat. 9–5, Sun. 9–noon.*

Ⓒ The **Palm House** in a corner of the Hofgarten is home to a fascinating collection of exotic plants. ⊠ *Rennweg 2,* ☎ *0512/584803–27.* 🎫 *Free.* ⊙ *Weekdays 8–noon and 1–5.*

❽ The **Ferdinandeum** (Tirolean State Museum Ferdinandeum) houses Austria's largest collection of Gothic art, 19th- and 20th-century paintings, and medieval arms. Here you'll find the original coats of arms from the Goldenes Dachl balcony. Chamber music concerts are offered at various times throughout the year. ⊠ *Museumstr. 15,* ☎ *0512/ 59489.* 🎫 *AS60.* ⊙ *Oct.–Apr., Tues.–Sat. 10–noon and 2–5, Sun. 10– 1; May–Sept., Fri.–Wed. 10–5, Thurs. 7–9.* 🕭

❾ The **Triumphpforte,** or Triumphal Arch (⊠ Salurner-Str.) was built in 1765 to commemorate both the marriage of emperor-to-be Leopold II and the death of Emperor Franz I, husband of Empress Maria Theresa.

❿ The **Annasäule,** or St. Anne's Column (⊠ Maria-Theresien-Str.), commemorates the withdrawal of Bavarian forces in the war of the Spanish Succession in 1703 on St. Anne's Day. From here you'll have a classic view of Innsbruck, with the glorious Nordkette mountain range in the background.

Ⓒ A visit to the 400-year-old **Grassmayr Bell Foundry** features a surprisingly fascinating little museum, and will give you an idea of how bells are cast and tuned. Take Bus J, K, or S south to Grassmayrstrasse. ⊠ *Leopoldstr. 53,* ☎ *0512/59416–34.* 🎫 *AS40.* ⊙ *Weekdays 9–6, Sat. 9–noon.*

Three Excursions

Hungerburg

Just barely outside the city at the Hungerburg, a combination of funicular and cable car will take you soaring above Innsbruck's skyline.

Ⓒ Take Streetcar 1 or Bus C to the **base station** (⊠ Rennweg 41, ☎ 0512/ 586158). From here you take the funicular up to the Hungerburg

(2,800 ft), then a two-stage cable car to Seegrube at 6,250 ft and Hafelekar at the dizzying height of 7,500 ft. The round-trip to Hungerburg costs AS48 with the Innsbruck Card; the round-trip to Hafelekar is AS230 with the card. At all three stops you'll find hotels and restaurants commanding breathtaking views over the Tirolean Alps and Innsbruck.

If you're staying in Innsbruck for a few days, you may want to break up this excursion into stages. Starting with Hungerburg, visit a different altitude and perspective each day, enjoying a leisurely lunch at each level.

☺ The **Alpenzoo,** a short walk from the Hungerburg station, has an unusual collection of Alpine birds and animals, including endangered species. The zoo alone is worth the trip up the Hungerburg; if you buy your ticket for the zoo at the base station, the trip up and back is free. ⊠ *Weiherburggasse 37A,* ☎ *0512/292323.* ◰ *AS70.* ☉ *Spring–fall, daily 9–6; winter, daily 9–5.*

Schloss Ambras

When Archduke Ferdinand II wanted to marry a commoner for love, the court grudgingly allowed it, but the couple was forced to live outside the city limits. Ferdinand revamped a 10th-century castle for the bride, Philippine Welser, which was completed in 1556 and was every bit as deluxe as what he had been accustomed to in town. Set in acres of gardens and woodland, it is an inviting castle with cheery red-and-white shutters on its many windows, and is, curiously, home to an odd-ball collection of armaments. The upper castle now houses rooms of noble portraits and the lower section has the collection of weaponry and armor. Be sure to inspect Philippine's sunken bath, a luxury for its time. Look around the grounds as well to see the fencing field and a small cemetery containing samples of earth from 18 battlefields around the world. The castle is located 3 km (2 mi) southeast of the city. To reach it without a car, take Tram 3 to Ambras, or the shuttle (AS30 round-trip; leaves on the hour) from Maria-Theresien-Strasse 45. ⊠ *Schloss Str. 20,* ☎ *0512/348446.* ◰ *AS60; tour additional AS25.* ☉ *Tours Apr.– Oct., Wed.–Mon. 10–5; Dec.–Mar., 2–5; closed in Nov.*

The Stubaital Valley

The delightful little Stubaital valley, less than 40 km (25 mi) long, is one of the showpieces of the Tirol, with no fewer than 80 glistening glaciers and more than 40 towering peaks. If you just want to look, you can see the whole Stubaital in a full day's excursion from Innsbruck. The narrow-gauge electric **Stubaitalbahn** (departure from the center of Innsbruck and in front of the main rail station, as well as from the station just below the Bergisel ski jump) goes as far as Fulpmes, partway up the valley. You can take the bus as far as Ranalt and back to Fulpmes, to see more of the valley, then return on the quaint rail line. Buses leave from Gate 1 of the **Autobusbahnhof,** just behind the rail station at Südtiroler Platz, about every hour (⊠ Stubaitalbahn, ☎ 0512/5307–102).

Dining

$$$$ ✕ **Goldener Adler.** This is Innsbruck's most famous hotel (☞ Lodging, *below*), and it also features a very good restaurant. A true rarity, the place is as popular with Austrians as it is with travelers. Two of the rooms are exceptionally beautiful; the others, offering luxe peasant decor, are by no means the poor man's hussar. During the Christmas and Easter holidays and during the summer months, you can listen to live zither music in the Goethe Stube (only open in the evening).

The liveliest crowds favor the Batzenhäusl on the arcade ground-floor level. Start with an Adler-Royal—a glass of *Sekt* (Austrian sparkling wine) with a dash of blackberry liqueur—while perusing the menu, which features a modern slant on traditional dishes. Pork medallions are topped with ham and Gorgonzola, and the *Tiroler Zopfbraten* (veal steak strips with a creamy herb sauce) is accompanied by spinach dumplings and carrots. ⊠ *Herzog-Friedrich-Str. 6, ☎ 0512/5711–11. Reservations essential. AE, DC, MC, V.*

$$$$ ✕ **Schwarzer Adler.** This intimate, romantic restaurant on the ground
★ floor of the Schwarzer Adler Hotel has leaded-pane windows and rustic Tirolean decor, offering the perfect backdrop for a memorable meal. Specialties include lobster ragout with tagliatelle in a red wine sauce and grilled freshwater trout. It's a bit off the beaten track but worth the effort it takes to get there. ⊠ *Kaiserjägerstr. 2, ☎ 0512/587109, ℻ 0512/561697. AE, DC, MC, V. Closed Sun.*

$$$ ✕ **Jörgele.** This flower-bedecked restaurant is in the heart of the Old Quarter near the Goldenes Dachl. Traditional Tirolean classics, such as game stew with mushroom as well as spinach dumplings and liver with bacon and tomatoes, are served in ample portions. The wine list is extensive, with vintages from around the globe, including Argentina, California, and France. ⊠ *Herzog-Friedrich-Str. 13, ☎ 0512/582217. AE, DC, MC, V.*

$$$ ✕ **Sweet Basil.** Passersby often pause to look through the big window of this new, always crowded restaurant next to the Weisses Kreuz hotel, and it's easy to see why. Cozily arranged tables are topped with squat golden candles, made more dramatic because it's the only lighting used. Every month a different style of cuisine is featured, from Tex-Mex to Chinese to Italian, but traditional Austrian dishes are offered as well. Salads are also a big item here. ⊠ *Herzog-Friedrich-Str. 31, ☎ 0512/584996. AE, DC, MC, V.*

$$$ ✕ **Tiroler Stuben.** Highly regarded by locals, the Tiroler Stuben has a
★ broad seasonal menu including lots of vegetarian choices. Try the *Schlutzkrapferln,* Tirolean ravioli stuffed with cheese, potatoes, and spinach, topped with melted butter and Parmesan; the Tirolean braised beef in a bacon and onion cream sauce; or just a simple roast chicken and potato salad. End with profiteroles, vanilla ice cream–filled cream puffs covered with chocolate sauce. Despite the fact that the restaurant is always packed, service is attentive. Ask for help with the wine list, although the open wines, particularly the red St. Laurent, are excellent. ⊠ *Innrain 13 (Ursulinenpassage), ☎ 0512/577931. Reservations essential. AE, DC, MC, V.*

$$ ✕ **Ottoburg.** This Altstadt landmark was superlatively restored to its orig-
★ inal luster in 1999. It's fun just to explore the rabbit warren of paneled rustic rooms upstairs in this red-and-white shuttered house built in 1494. Several of the bay-window alcoves have great views toward the Goldenes Dachl square. The *Gaststube* downstairs is less intimate but offers a lower-cost selection. Try the trout, if it's on the menu, but the chicken and duck dishes are also excellent. ⊠ *Herzog-Friedrich-Str. 1, ☎ 0512/584338. AE, DC, MC, V. Closed Tues. and 2 wks in mid-Nov.*

$$ ✕ **Philippine.** The food here is exclusively vegetarian, with so many tempting items to choose from it's hard to make a decision. You might start with polenta topped with Gorgonzola and ruby-red tomatoes and then go on to cannelloni stuffed with potatoes and smoked tofu, or pumpkin risotto with pumpkin seeds, ginger, and Parmesan. All portions are substantial. The restaurant has a light, cheerful ambience, and tables are candlelit at night. ⊠ *Müllerstr. and Templestr., ☎ 0512/589157. MC, V.*

$$ ✕ **Weisses Rössl.** In the authentically rustic rooms upstairs, an array of antlers and a private art gallery add to the decor. This is the right

Innsbruck Dining and Lodging

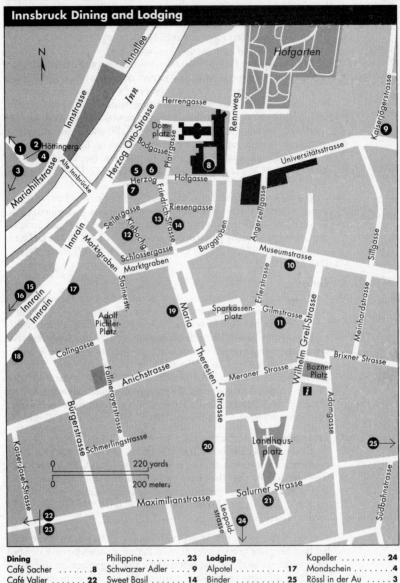

Dining

Café Sacher **8**
Café Valier **22**
Central **11**
Goldener Adler **7**
Jörgele **6**
Katzung **13**
Ottoburg **5**

Philippine **23**
Schwarzer Adler **9**
Sweet Basil **14**
Theresian Brau **20**
Tiroler Stuben **17**
Weisses Rössl **12**
Wienerwald . . . **10, 19**

Lodging

Alpotel **17**
Binder **25**
Goldener Adler **7**
Holiday Inn **21**
Innsbruck **18**
Innsbrücke **2**
Internationales
Studentenhaus **16**

Kapeller **24**
Mondschein **4**
Rössl in der Au **3**
Royal **15**
Tautermann **1**
Weisses Kreuz **14**

place for solid local standards, like *Tiroler Gröstl,* a tasty hash treatment, and Wiener schnitzel (veal cutlet), both of which taste even better on the outside terrace in summer. ⊠ *Kiebachg. 8,* ☎ *0512/583057. AE, MC, V. Closed Sun., early Nov., mid-Apr.*

$ ✕ **Theresian Bräu.** This multilevel brewhouse (erstwhile movie theater) in the center of town is decorated to give the appearance of the inside of a ship, with what looks like a submarine's control panel lining one wall and an assortment of other seafaring items scattered throughout, such as fishnets, steamer trunks, and even rowboats. But the focus here is on beer, brewed right on the premises. They also offer meals and snacks, including zucchini ragout with polenta gratiné, or *Tafelspitz,* a boiled beef dish. People of any age can be found here, but be prepared for loud music. ⊠ *Maria-Theresien-Str. 51–53,* ☎ *0512/587580,* 𝔽𝔸𝕏 *0512/ 587580–5.*

$ ✕ **Wienerwald.** This chain started out with grilled chicken (and very good indeed) but now serves pastas, as well as roast and grilled meats, in a modern rustic environment. In summer, the gardens of both locations are particularly pleasant and are open till 11 PM. ⊠ *Maria-Theresien-Str. 12,* ☎ *0512/584165;* ⊠ *Museumstr. 24,* ☎ *0512/588994. AE, DC, MC, V.*

Cafés

★ **Café Sacher.** The Café Sacher and the celebrated Sacher Torte have until recently been unavailable outside of Vienna. This oh-so-Austrian chocolate layer cake can now be savored in Innsbruck, amidst a turn-of-the-century, plushy atmosphere reflecting the original Sacher in Vienna. The coffee and sweets are, of course, scrumptious, but a full menu is also available, including Eduard Sacher's original recipes for *Tafelspitz* (prime boiled beef) and *Backhendl "Anna Sacher"* (Viennese fried chicken). Open until midnight, this is a good choice following a show at the nearby Kongresshaus or Tiroler Landestheater, but expect higher than average prices. ⊠ *Rennweg 1* ☎ *0512/565626. AE, DC, MC, V.*

★ **Café Valier.** You'll have to walk a few minutes away from the city center to reach this café, but it's worth the effort and the calories you'll consume. The exterior appearance isn't much, but Café Valier's pastries are so good that they have twice been invited to compete in the World Pastry Cup in Lyons, France. The coffee is also excellent, and service is friendly. ⊠ *Maximilianstr. 27,* ☎ *0512/586180. No credit cards. Closed Sun. and Aug.*

Central. Since 1878, this large, traditional café in the Viennese style has been *the* place to relax over a coffee. Recent renovations have stripped away some atmosphere, but newspapers and magazines are still available, as is a variety of food and pastries. On Sunday night enjoy your cappuccino with live piano accompaniment. ⊠ *Gilmstr. 5, in the Central Hotel,* ☎ *0512/5920–0. AE, DC, MC, V. Closed Nov.*

Katzung. This café is just a few doors down from the Goldenes Dachl, and in summer you have a great view from the outdoor terrace. That's the main draw here, though the pastries are very good and they offer a variety of ice-cream sundaes. ⊠ *Herzog-Friedrich-Str. 16,* ☎ *0512/ 586183. No credit cards. Closed Sun.*

Lodging

$$$$ ▣ **Goldener Adler.** There may be grander, more luxurious, better-appointed, quieter hotels in and around Innsbruck—but none could possibly rival the Goldener Adler, or Golden Eagle. Over the centuries the hotel has welcomed nearly every king, emperor, duke, or poet who passed through Innsbruck. Gustav III of Sweden (hero of Verdi's opera *A Masked*

Ball), Metternich, Ludwig I, Goethe, Heine, and Paganini, who cut his name on the window of his room, all stayed here. Centrally placed in the very heart of Old Innsbruck, the hotel is just across the road from the Goldenes Dachl. The outside of the hotel looks suitably ancient, with low arches at street level and typical Tyrolean decoration higher up. Inside, the passages and stairs twist romantically, rooms crop up where you least expect them (beware: readers have complained about closetlike rooms on the upper floors), while the main floor features one of Innsbruck's most popular restaurants (☞ Dining, *above*). ✉ *Herzog-Friedrich-Str. 6, A–6020,* ☎ *0512/586334,* 𝔽𝔸𝕏 *0512/584409. 35 rooms. 2 restaurants. AE, DC, MC, V.*

$$$$ ⊞ **Holiday Inn.** This modern high-rise close to the railroad station looks out of place but offers contemporary comfort in friendly Scandinavian style. The rooms are simply furnished and efficiently modern. Look for Scandinavian specialties in the restaurants; the City Lunch Buffet is justifiably popular. High rollers take note: the hotel features an in-house casino. ✉ *Salurner Str. 15, A–6020,* ☎ *0512/5935–0,* 𝔽𝔸𝕏 *0512/ 5935–220. 172 rooms. 2 restaurants, bar, indoor pool, sauna, free parking. AE, DC, MC, V.*

$$$ ⊞ **Alpotel.** All rooms are quiet in this modern hotel tucked into a small
★ square on the edge of the Old City. The building was designed for apartments, so many of the rooms are almost miniature suites; furnishings throughout are in warm colors and natural wood. Many rooms have balconies overlooking the quiet garden and mountains. The Tiroler Stuben restaurant (☞ Dining, *above*) is outstanding, and the breakfast buffet (included in the room price) features homemade whole-grain bread made from a secret recipe. ✉ *Innrain 13 (Ursulinenpassage), A– 6020,* ☎ *0512/577931,* 𝔽𝔸𝕏 *0512/577931–15. 73 rooms. Restaurant, sauna, free parking. AE, DC, MC, V.*

$$$ ⊞ **Innsbruck.** Here, in one of the city's newest hotels, the mood is modern, from the entry lobby to the efficiently functional guest rooms with their accents of finished wood. With a lobby tastefully refurbished in 1999, a fetching new bar and restaurant, and twenty guest rooms added to meet the demand, this hotel now ranks among one of Innsbruck's finest. From some of the rooms you'll get gorgeous views of the Old City, and, from those on the river side, of the Nordkette mountains directly behind. ✉ *Innrain 3, A–6020,* ☎ *0512/59868–0,* 𝔽𝔸𝕏 *0512/572280. 111 rooms. Restaurant, indoor pool, sauna, free parking. AE, DC, MC, V.*

$$$ ⊞ **Kapeller.** Outside the center in Amras (take Streetcar 3), this friendly Gasthof offers cozy rooms as well as the advantage of a good in-house restaurant. ✉ *Philippine-Welser-Str. 96, A–6020,* ☎ *0512/343106,* 𝔽𝔸𝕏 *0512/343106–68. 36 rooms. Restaurant, free parking. AE, DC, MC, V.*

$$$ ⊞ **Mondschein.** Behind the modest exterior and smallish lobby, you'll find a tastefully renovated and fully modernized hotel, now part of the Best Western chain. Sparkling clean and furnished in rich blue and gold tones, the Mondschein features modern conveniences such as hair-dryers, minibars, safes, and phones in every room. Rooms facing the Inn River are particularly nice, with excellent views of the Old City. A breakfast buffet is included in the price. ✉ *Mariahilfstr. 6, A–6010,* ☎ *0512/22784,* 𝔽𝔸𝕏 *0512/22784–90. 35 rooms. Restaurant, bar, free parking, seminar room. AE, DC, MC, V.*

$$ ⊞ **Royal.** This modern hotel overlooks the river and is only steps from the Old City. Rooms are simple but spacious and comfortable. ✉ *Innrain 16, A–6020,* ☎ *0512/586385,* 𝔽𝔸𝕏 *0512/586385–10. 20 rooms. Breakfast room, free parking. AE, DC, MC, V.*

$$ ⊞ **Tautermann.** This red-shuttered house within walking distance of
★ the city's center has been successfully turned into a friendly family-run hotel with rooms in natural woods and white. Some upper rooms on the west side have bay windows with gorgeous views of the imposing

Hungerburg mountain. Bus A from the main station to Höttinger Kirchenplatz gets you close to the door. ⊠ *Stamser Feld 5/Höttingerg., A–6020,* ☎ *0512/281572,* 🖷 *0512/281572–10. 28 rooms. Breakfast room, free parking. AE, DC, MC, V.*

$$ 🖷 **Weisses Kreuz.** At first encounter, you'll fall in love with this hotel,
★ set over stone arcades in the heart of the Old City. It has seen massive renovations since the first Gasthof stood on this site in 1465, and the rooms are simple but comfortable, with mainly rustic furniture and lots of light wood. The service is friendly and accommodating. There are special rooms on the ground floor in which you can keep your skis; hotel reception and a restaurant are upstairs. ⊠ *Herzog-Friedrich-Str. 31, A–6020,* ☎ *0512/59479,* 🖷 *0512/59479–90. 39 rooms. 2 restaurants. AE, MC, V.*

$ 🖷 **Binder.** A short streetcar trip (Number 3) from the center of town brings you to the less-costly comforts of this small, friendly, family-run hotel. Rooms are modest but modern and attractive. Book well ahead, as Binder has many regular guests. ⊠ *Dr.-Glatz-Str. 20, A–6020,* ☎ *0512/33436–0,* 🖷 *0512/33436–99. 32 rooms. Bar, café, free parking. AE, MC, V.*

$ 🖷 **Innsbrücke.** Rooms at the front of this modest hotel look across the river toward the Old City. You're five minutes from the center on foot or to the railroad station by Bus A or K. Rooms are in beige and light wood, and a few have baths. This place can be somewhat noisy, due to a nightclub, popular with the younger crowd, on the ground floor below. ⊠ *Innstr. 1, A–6020,* ☎ *0512/281934. 30 rooms, 8 with bath. Café. AE, DC, MC, V.*

Summer Hotels

Student accommodations in Innsbruck are turned into hotels from July to October and are extremely good value if you don't require the amenities of a full hotel; you may discover that Austrian university students don't live too badly. Check prices, as these can vary considerably from one hotel to another.

Internationales Studentenhaus. This is not only the best-located but also the cheapest option. ⊠ *Recheng. 7, A–6020,* ☎ *0512/501912,* 🖷 *0512/50115. 275 rooms with bath. Free parking. AE, DC, MC, V.*

Rössl in der Au. Located across the Inn River, it affords a pleasant cityscape view. ⊠ *Höttinger Au 34, A–6020,* ☎ *0512/286846,* 🖷 *0512/ 293850. 125 rooms with bath. Free parking. AE, DC, MC, V.*

Nightlife and the Arts

The Arts

Each year at Pentecost the churches resound with organ music during the annual **International Organ Week** (⊠ Stiftg. 16, A–6020, ☎ 0512/ 5800–23, 🖷 0512/5360–649). **Internationaler Tanzsommer Innsbruck** brings the world's premiere dance companies to Innsbruck between mid-June and mid-July. Momix, the Contemporary American Ballet, Stomp, and the Dance Theatre of Harlem are some of the groups that have recently performed. Tickets are available through the tourist office, or contact the festival (⊠ Burggraben 3, A–6021, ☎ 0512/561–561). The **Festwochen der Alten Musik** (Festival of Early Music) is a good reason to visit Innsbruck between late July and late August, as the annual festival highlights music from the 14th to 18th centuries, performed by many of Europe's finest musicians in dramatic settings such as Innsbruck's beautiful Schloss Ambras, the Hofkirche, and others. Contact the Innsbruck Tourist office or the festival (⊠ Burggraben 3, A–6021, ☎ 0512/5710-32, 🖷 0512/5631–42), and during the summer there are frequent brass-band (Musikkapelle) concerts in the Old Town every weekend. It's said that Tirol has more bandleaders than mayors. Folk shows at the **Gundolf Hotel** and other spots around the city feature authentic Tirolean folk dancing, yodeling, and zither music. The tourist office and hotels have details.

Concerts take place in the modern Saal Tirol of the **Kongresshaus** (✉ Rennweg 3, ☎ 0512/5936–0). Innsbruck's principal theater is the **Tiroler Landestheater** (✉ Rennweg 2, ☎ 0512/52074–4). Both opera and operetta are presented in the main hall, usually starting at 7:30; plays in the Kammerspiele start at 8. Obtain tickets at the box office or at the main tourist office.

Nightlife

The jazzy **casino** adjacent to the Holiday Inn offers blackjack, baccarat, roulette, and plenty of slot machines, as well as a bar and a good restaurant. You must present your passport to enter the casino. ✉ *Salurner Str. 15,* ☎ *0512/587040–0.* ▣ *AS210, exchangeable for AS250 worth of chips; admission free for those not playing.* ☉ *Daily 3 PM–3 AM.*

A popular spot is **Arcos** (✉ Salurner Str., ☎ 0512/582423), next to the arch. The beautiful people gather at **Bellini** (✉ Meranerstr. 5, ☎ 0512/560367). One of the more intriguing bars is the relaxed—or jammed, depending on the hour—**Café Brasil** (✉ Leopoldstr. 7, ☎ 0512/583466), with its fireplace and comfortable, if stylishly shabby, furnishings. The atmosphere is cool modern at **Badgassl** (✉ Dompl. 1, ☎ 0512/575633), by the cathedral.

Currently, the basement **Blue Chip** disco (✉ Wilhelm-Greil-Str. 17, ☎ 0512/565050) and the upstairs **Jimmy's** bar (✉ Wilhelm-Greil-Str. 19, ☎ 0512/570473) are hot spots and packed nightly. Of the classic discos, the best and most enduring is **Kandinsky** (✉ Anichstr. 7, ☎ 0512/582420). If it's a pint of Guinness you're longing for, seek out the **Irish Pub** (✉ Maria-Theresien-Str. 9, ☎ 0512/582011) with authentic Irish ambience.

Along the nightclub circuit, start first at **Filou** (✉ Stiftg. 12, ☎ 0512/580256), where in summer you can sit in an attractive garden until 10 PM, when things move indoors for the sake of neighborhood peace and quiet. **Lady O** (✉ Brunecker Str. 2, ☎ 0512/586432) is the traditional striptease nightclub; you can see a teaser program on the ground floor at 9 PM for an AS20 admission charge, but the first drink costs AS140.

Outdoor Activities and Sports

Golf

Golfclub Innsbruck/Igls in Lans, about 9 km (5½ mi) outside the city, has two 9-hole, par-66 courses (☎ 0512/377165). It is open April–November. **Golfclub Innsbruck/Igls** in Rinn, about 12 km (7½ mi) away, has 18 holes, with a par-71 (☎ 05223/78177). The course is open April–October. Both courses charge a AS460 greens fee on weekdays, AS580 on weekends, but you must be a member of a recognized club to use the courses. Several hotels—Europa-Tyrol in Innsbruck, Sporthotel Igls and Gesundheitszentrum Lanserhof at Lans, and the Geisler at Rinn—have special golfing arrangements.

Health and Fitness Clubs

In Innsbruck, try **City Fitness** (✉ Hunoldstr. 5, ☎ 0512/365696), or for a women-only facility there is **Fame** (✉ Bürgerstr. 2, ☎ 0512/5671-71).

Hiking

Both easy paths and extreme slopes await hikers and climbers. From June to October, holders of the Club Innsbruck card (free from your hotel) can take free, daily, guided mountain hikes. The tourist office has a special hiking brochure. If you want to learn to climb, look to the **Alpine School Innsbruck** (⊠ Natters, In der Stille 1, ☎ 0512/546000–0). If you're already a pro, check in with the **Österreichischer Alpenverein** (⊠ Wilhelm Greil-Str. 15, ☎ 0512/59547–0).

Horseback Riding

Horseback riding can be arranged through **Reitclub Innsbruck** (⊠ Langer Weg, ☎ 0512/347174).

Skiing

In winter, check with the tourist office for information (☎ 0512/59850) on snow conditions and transportation to the main ski areas, which include the Axamer Lizum, Patscherkofel, Seegrube-Nordkette, Glungezer, Schlick 2000, Mutterer Alm, and Stubai Glacier. At press time (summer 2000), the Mutterer Almbahn (lift system) is closed for renovation but should be operative for winter 2001. You'll find a variety of terrains and challenges in Innsbruck, from the beginner slopes of the Glungezer to the good intermediate skiing of the Axamer Lizum and Patscherkofel and the steep runs and off-piste skiing of the Seegrube. Your Club Innsbruck membership card (free with an overnight stay in any Innsbruck hotel) will get you free transportation to the areas and reductions on a number of ski lifts. A Super Ski Pass covers all the ski areas of Innsbruck, the Stubai Glacier, Kitzbühel, and St. Anton, with 520 km (290 mi) of runs, 210 lifts, and all transfers. The Gletscher Ski Pass includes Innsbruck and the Stubai Glacier. If you're a summer skier (and can handle the altitude), there's year-round skiing on the Stubai Glacier, about 40 km (25 mi) from Innsbruck via the free ski shuttle bus (ask at your hotel). You can book with the **Schischule Innsbruck** (☎ 0512/582310) or through the Tourist Office Innsbruck. Hotels have details on winter ski kindergartens.

Swimming

Around Innsbruck there are plenty of lakes, but in town you have little choice other than pools, indoors and out. Outdoors, try the **Freischwimmbad Tivoli** (⊠ Purtschellerstr. 1, ☎ 0512/342344); indoors, try **Hallenbad Amraser Strasse** (⊠ Amraser Str. 3, ☎ 0512/342585), **Hallenbad Höttinger Au** (⊠ Fürstenweg 12, ☎ 0512/282339), or **Hallenbad Olympisches Dorf** (⊠ Kugelfangweg 46, ☎ 0512/261342).

Tennis

Innsbruck has an abundance of courts, although they tend to be scattered and booked well ahead. Your hotel or the tourist office can help.

Try the **Olympia-Eissportzentrum** (⊠ Olympiastr. 10, ☎ 0512/33838) or the **Tennisclub IEV** (⊠ Reichenauer Str. 144, ☎ 0512/346229); your Club Innsbruck card will get you a reduction at both.

Shopping

The best shops are along the arcaded Herzog-Friedrich-Strasse in the heart of the Old City; along its extension, Maria-Theresien-Strasse; and the cross-street Maximilianstrasse in the newer part of town. Innsbruck is *the* place to buy native Tirolean clothing, particularly lederhosen and loden (sturdy combed-wool jackets and vests). Look also for cut crystal and wood carvings; locally handmade, delicate silver-filigree pins make nice gifts. A lively flea market takes place each Saturday from 8 to 1 on Innrain, near St. John's Church (Johanneskirche).

Galerie Thomas Flora (⊠ Herzog-Friedrich-Str. 5, ☎ 0512/577402) sells graphics by the droll Tirolean artist Paul Flora; you'll find much to smile at here, and maybe even to take home. **Rudolf Boschi** (⊠ Kiebachg. 8, ☎ 0512/589224) turns out reproductions of old pewterware, using the original molds when possible. Among other items, he has locally produced, hand-decorated beer mugs with pewter lids. **Swarovski Haus** (⊠ Herzog-Friedrich-Str. 39, ☎ 0512/573100) features almost everything from the world-renowned crystal maker, whose headquarters is located in nearby Wattens, east of Innsbruck (☞ Around the Lower Inn Valley, *below*). **Tiroler Heimatwerk** (⊠ Meraner Str. 2–4, ☎ 0512/582320) is the first place to look for local mementos and souvenirs of good quality. The extremely attractive shop carries textiles and finished clothing, ceramics, carved wooden chests, and some furniture. You can also have clothing made to order. **Lodenhaus Hubertus** (⊠ Sparkassenpl. 3, ☎ 0512/585092) is an outstanding source of dirndls, those attractive country costumes for women, with white blouse, dark skirt, and colorful apron. It also has children's clothing.

AROUND THE LOWER INN VALLEY

Northeast of Innsbruck the Inn River valley broadens out and courses right through Tirol toward Kufstein and the German border. Route 171 along the valley is a much more pleasant route than the autobahn running parallel. Often overlooked by travelers zipping between Innsbruck and Salzburg on the autobahn, this region is nonetheless worth a visit for the well-preserved old towns of Hall and Schwaz and for a trip into the beautiful Zillertal (Ziller Valley), dotted with ski areas and popular as a year-round resort area. Many of the Tirol's finest folk musicians come from this valley, so if you go, ask about live music programs. In summer, a day at the crystal-blue Achensee should be on your program.

Hall in Tirol

⑪ *9 km (5½ mi) east of Innsbruck.*

Hall in Tirol is an old city founded by salt miners. The picturesque old part of the town is made up of narrow lanes running east–west, interrupted by a few short cross alleys. Stop and look around; from the main road, you cannot get a proper perspective of the fine old buildings. The **Rathaus,** built in the mid-15th century, has ornately carved councillors' rooms and beautifully worked mosaics covering the walls. The 17th-century **monastery church,** the oldest Renaissance ecclesiastical building in Tirol, and the **mint tower,** symbol of the town, are both interesting examples of local craftsmanship. The mint was moved to Hall from Meran, and the first coins were struck here in 1477. Legend has it that Duke Sigmund the Wealthy, son of Friedl the Penniless, got his nickname by tossing handfuls of Hall-minted coins to the populace wherever he went. The Inntal (Inn Valley) gave its name to the coin, known as the *Taler,* from which came the word "dollar."

Dining and Lodging

$$$ ✕🏨 **Hotel Restaurant Heiligreuz.** Perched on a hillside shrouded with trees, the Hotel Restaurant Heiligreuz is an intimate home away from home. Dark-wood paneling and comfortable, overstuffed furniture decorate the hotel. Rooms are equally elegant and welcoming, as is the friendly staff. The restaurant offers traditional rib-sticking classics such as *G'röstl,* a concoction of eggs, bacon, and potatoes guaranteed to satisfy the heartiest of appetites. ⊠ *Reimmichlstr. 18, A–6060,* ☎ *05223/57114,* 🖷 *05223/571145. 38 rooms. Restaurant, bar. V.* ❧

Shopping

Traveling east between Hall in Tirol and Schwaz, you'll pass the home of the Swarovski cut-crystal empire, in Wattens. Stop at the **Swarovski Crystal Shop** to browse and perhaps buy some of the famous crystal and glassware, or if you have more time, explore **Crystal World,** an eclectic but fascinating multi-media gallery. ✉ *Kristallweltenstr. 1,* ☎ *05224/51080–0.* ⌸ *AS75.* ◷ *Daily 9–6.* ✥

Schwaz

⑫ *16 km (10 mi) northeast of Hall in Tirol.*

The Habsburg emperors in the 15th and 16th century owed much of their wealth to the silver and copper extracted from the mines here by the Fugger family, bankers and traders who emigrated from Augsburg. First mentioned in the 10th century and founded in the 12th century, Schwaz, on the south bank of the Inn, evolved into a rich and important mining center. The mines of the **Silbergbergwerk Schwaz**—dug deep under the towering Tuxer Alps—indeed may have been the reason for setting up the mint in nearby Hall. ✉ *Alte Landstr. 3a,* ☎ *05242/ 72372–0.* ⌸ *AS150.* ◷ *Jan.–mid-Nov., daily 8:30–5; mid-Nov.–Dec., daily 9:30–4 in winter.*

The 15th- and 16th-century houses built during those prosperous times still stand, and the marketplace has kept its atmosphere. Look at the vast **parish church,** the largest Gothic hall-church in Tirol. The church was expanded in 1490 and divided into two parts (once they were separated by a wooden wall): the southern chancel for the miners and the northern, or "Prince's chancel," for the upper classes.

Another outstanding monument from the 15th and 16th centuries in Schwaz is the treasure-filled **Franciscan Church,** (Franziskanerkirche), founded in the early 16th-century by emperor Maximilian I. This may well be the mendicant order's most beautiful church in the Alpine region.

A fascinating new addition to Schwaz is the **Haus der Völker,** a museum dedicated to ethnography. Displays include ancient Asian sculptures as well as African art. ✉ *Christoph-Anton-Mayr-Weg 7,* ☎ *05242/66090,* ℻ *05242/66091.* ⌸ *AS70.* ◷ *Daily 10–6.*

En Route   **Jenbach,** 8 km (5 mi) north of Schwaz, across the river, is notable mainly as a rail and highway junction; from here Route 169 follows the Ziller River valley (Zillertal) south, past the Gerlos Valley (Route 165) and the Tuxer mountain range to Mayrhofen. The Achensee lies on the plateau to the north, fed by the Achen river rising high in the mountains beyond, on the German border. Both regions have become immensely popular.

Achensee

⑬ *25 km (17 mi) north of Schwaz, 17 km (12 mi) from Jenbach.*

From Jenbach, many travelers head to the Achensee. If you're driving, take Route 181; the initial stretch involves hairpin turns and a steep climb, but the views over the Inn Valley are exquisite.

You could take a bus, too, but the most adventuresome and romantic way to reach the Achensee is on the steam-powered train, the **Achenseebahn** (☎ 05244/62243), built in 1889 as Tirol's first mountain cog railway. The line does its 1,300-ft climb in a nearly straight line more than 7 km (4½ mi) to the lower end of the Achensee (Seespitz), where you can get a lake steamer operated by **Achensee Schiffahrt** (☎ 05243/ 5253) on to Maurach/Buchau, Pertisau, and at the north end, Achenkirch.

The Achen Valley has fine skiing in winter, but the Achensee in summer, with water sports and excellent fishing, is the main attraction. It is the largest and most beautiful lake in Tirol—10 km (6 mi) long— with the great mountains of the Karwendel and Rofan ranges rising from its blue-green waters. The lake steamer connects the villages strung along its length.

Lodging

$$$$ ⊞ **Posthotel Achenkirk.** This comfortable Alpine chalet is also a health center; you'll find every convenience for taking care of fitness, weight loss, and exercise. Horseback riders will find mounts ranging from Haflingers to Shetland ponies. Rooms are in typical Tirolean country style. ✉ *Achenkirch, A–6215,* ☎ *05246/6522–0,* ℻ *05246/6205–468. 97 rooms. Restaurant, indoor and outdoor pools, sauna, tennis court, exercise room, horseback riding, squash. No credit cards. Closed mid-Nov.–mid-Dec.*

Pertisau

❹ *25 km (16 mi) north of Schwaz.*

This small, picturesque village set into the thick pine forest of a nature preserve is the only community on the western shore of the Achensee. It offers excellent swimming, sailing, tennis, fishing, and a golf course, all at budget prices. Although less popular, the eastern side of the lake enjoys at least two more hours of sunshine every day, and the water is consequently warmer. Because this area is so close to Innsbruck, the lake is crowded on summer weekends; try to visit on a weekday.

Dining and Lodging

$$–$$$ ✕⊞ **Kristall.** This chalet lodge set against a wooded mountain offers friendly comfort in ample, elegant public rooms and cheerfully decorated bedrooms. You can take half board or not, and the restaurant is open to the public. ✉ *A–6213,* ☎ *05243/5490,* ℻ *05243/5374–19. 52 rooms. Restaurant, bar, indoor and outdoor pools, sauna, exercise room. No credit cards. Closed Nov.–mid-Dec.*

Outdoor Activities and Sports

GOLF

Golf-Club Achensee in Pertisau is an attractive 9-hole, par-70 Alpine course with 18 tees and many long, straight runs. ☎ *05243/5377.* ☉ *May–Oct.*

En Route Scenic Route 181 leads along the eastern shore of the lake through Buchau to the northern end, passing through Achenseehof and Scholastika, among various small settlements belonging to the community of Achenkirch. Because this area is so close to Innsbruck, the lake is crowded on summer weekends; try to visit on a weekday.

The drive south from Jenbach on Route 169 follows the Ziller River, which rises high in the Alps to the south, in an area of perpetual glacier, then flows north. Route 169 parallels the narrow-gauge Ziller railway,
★ the **Zillertalbahn,** which makes daily runs between Jenbach and Mayrhofen, some under steam power. If your childhood dream was to drive a train, check in Jenbach (☎ 05244/63470, ℻ 05244/63552) about renting this one; you can take a crash course in railroad operations and play engineer of the steam locomotive, all for a modest fee.

The first part of the Zillertal is broad and shallow, and the scenery is not very inspiring. But from Stumm onward, where you pass through some pretty Alpine villages, and particularly the stretch south of Zell am Ziller, the valley starts to live up to its reputation.

Zell am Ziller

❺ *25 km (16 mi) southeast of Jenbach.*

The main town of the Zillertal—the biggest and most famous of the many beautiful Alpine valleys of the Tirol—is noted for its traditional 500-year-old **Gauderfest,** held on the first weekend in May, when thousands of tourists from far and wide pack the little market town of Zell am Ziller for the colorful skits, music, and singing—and great quantities of *Gauderbier,* a strong brew run up for the occasion. You can hear some of the country's best singing, by the valley residents, and listen to expert harp and zither playing, for which the valley is famous throughout Austria. Tradition runs strong here: witness the Perchtenlaufen, processions of colorfully masked well-wishers going the neighborhood rounds on January 5, or the annual Almabtrieb during the last September and first October days, when the cows are hung with wreaths and bells and, amid celebrations, are herded back from the high Alpine pastures into the lower fields and barns. This is a typical Tirolean country town, with Alpine lodges and a round-domed pink village church (note the Baroque painting of the Holy Trinity); in winter it's a center for skiing and sports. Contact the local tourist board, ☎ 05282/2281, ℻ 05282/228180.

Dining and Lodging

$$–$$$ ✕ 🏨 **Bräu.** The core of this thick-walled, five-story, frescoed building
★ in the center of town dates from the 16th century; subsequent renovations and a new wing have brought it quite up to date. The rooms are decorated in warm Alpine style, in beiges, greens, and browns. The hotel can arrange fishing trips. The three-room restaurant complex serves fine food, with emphasis on fish and game. Reserve for the *Bräustübl,* and enjoy the house beer; the house brewery is also the source of the *Gauderbier.* ⌧ *Dorfpl. 1, A–6280,* ☎ *05282/2313,* ℻ *05282/2313–17. 36 rooms. Restaurant, café, sauna. No credit cards. Closed Apr. and mid-Oct.–mid-Dec.*

$$–$$$ ✕ 🏨 **Zellerhof.** This variation on the traditional Alpine chalet is now a hotel school for most of the year, so you'll be looked after by a young and enthusiastic staff. The house is tastefully decorated in the local style, with ample natural wood, and the Tirolean ambience carries over to the comfortable rooms. The intimate restaurant upstairs is excellent. ⌧ *Bahnhofstr. 3, A–6280,* ☎ *05282/2612–0,* ℻ *05282/261265. 40 rooms. Restaurant, bar, café, sauna. AE, DC, MC, V. Closed mid-Oct.–mid-June, except Christmas and Easter.*

Mayrhofen

⓰ *10 km (6 mi) south of Zell am Ziller.*

Down the road you'll come to Mayrhofen, end of the line for the narrow-gauge railway. This is the valley's main tourist base and the favorite summer resort of the British for many years. Mayrhofen is the starting point for summer hiking into the highly scenic valleys that branch off to the southeast, south, and southwest and for excursions into the Ziller glacier areas, at heights of 9,750 ft and more.

At Mayrhofen the valley splits into three *Gründe* (grounds): the Zillergrund, Stillupgrund, and Zemmgrund—prime examples of picture-postcard Alpine areas, swept at the top with glittering, pale-blue glaciers.

Dining and Lodging

$$$ ✕ **Wirtshaus zum Griena.** The restaurant tucked into this 400-year-old farmhouse is about a 10-minute drive north of Mayrhofen. The route is not simple, but everybody knows Griena's—ask at your hotel for directions. Once you get there, you'll find yourself in rustic surroundings of natural-wood paneling. Such local favorites as beer soup, potato-cheese specialties, and schnitzel are tempting. The beer is local and excellent, the wines somewhat disappointing. ⌧ *Dorfhaus 768,* ☎ *05285/62778. No credit cards. Closed June–early July and Nov.–early Dec.*

© 2000 Visa U.S.A. Inc.

When it Comes to Getting Local Currency at an ATM, Same Thing.

Whether you're in Yosemite or Yemen, using your Visa® card or ATM card with the PLUS symbol is the easiest and most convenient way to get local currency. For example, let's say you're in France. When you make a withdrawal, using your secured PIN, it's dispensed in francs, but is debited from your account in U.S. dollars.

This makes it easy to take advantage of favorable exchange rates. And if you need help finding one of Visa's 627,000 ATMs in 127 countries worldwide, visit **visa.com/pd/atm**. We'll make finding an ATM as easy as finding the Eiffel Tower, the Pyramids or even the Grand Canyon.

It's Everywhere You Want To Be®

SEE THE WORLD IN FULL COLOR

Fodor's Exploring Guides bring all the great sights vividly to life with hundreds of photographs, fascinating historical background, and colorful anecdotes. Detailed maps and practical information keep you headed in the right direction.

Pair a **Fodor's** Exploring Guide with your trusted Gold Guide for a complete planning package.

Fodor's EXPLORING GUIDES

At bookstores everywhere.

$$$$ ✕⊞ **Elisabeth.** This newish house, in Tirolean style, radiates elegance
★ without being too formal. The same is true of the well-decorated, luxurious bedrooms, some with ceramic stoves and beautiful wood-carved walls and ceilings. Each room has a balcony overlooking the mountains, and a few have Jacuzzis set in a windowed alcove offering stunning views, plus fireplaces and canopied beds. The hotel has a loyal following, so book ahead. The excellent Gute Stube restaurant, decorated with pretty frescoes, offers international and local specialties such as roast veal or trout. Every Friday evening there is a huge Tirolean buffet and live music. ✉ *Einfahrt Mitte 432, A–6290,* ☎ *05285/6767,* FAX *05285/6767–67. 42 rooms. 2 restaurants, bar, café, indoor pool, sauna, exercise room. AE, DC, MC, V.*

$$–$$$ ⊞ **Kramerwirt.** Here's the center of the action in Mayrhofen, where the crowd gathers. The welcoming warmth of natural wood in the lobby and the Kröll Stube (a small, rustic dining room) is accented by the Tirolean antiques. Still family-run, this hostelry has been around for centuries. You'll feel at home in the comfortable rooms. ✉ *Am Marienbrunnen 346, A–6290,* ☎ *05285/6700,* FAX *05285/6700–502. 85 rooms. Restaurant, bar, sauna, exercise room, dance club, parking. MC, V. Closed 2 wks in Dec.*

Outdoor Activities and Sports
CLIMBING
For the adventuresome, Peter Habeler at the **Alpinschule u. Schischule Mount Everest** (✉ Hauptstr. 458, ☎ 05285/62829, FAX 05285/64260) gives instruction in ice climbing.

Tuxer Valley

⑰ *15 km (9 mi) west of Mayrhofen.*

The fourth arm and highest in altitude of the Inn Valley is the Tuxer Valley, a summer ski region, which ends at the foot of the massive Olperer and Rifflerspitz glaciers, each nearly 11,000 ft high. Frequent buses leave Mayrhofen for **Lanersbach,** a small mountain village, and **Hintertux,** right at the doorway of the great glaciers. Hintertux is also a popular spa, with a small thermal swimming pool, and the center of an ancient wood-carving industry. Rubies (called Tirolean garnets) were once mined in this area, and you might run across local amethyst in the shops as well.

Dining and Lodging
$$$ ✕⊞ **Neu Hintertux.** In the shadow of the nearby mountains, this turreted hotel decorated with frescoes and carved wood exudes traditional Alpine charm. Rooms are delightfully decorated with canopied beds, brocaded fabrics, and tiled stoves. You can enjoy a drink after a day on the slopes around an open hearth in the bar, which is covered in dark, carved wood. Tirolean classics are served in the restaurant. ✉ *A–6294 Hintertux,* ☎ *05287/8580–0,* FAX *05287/8580–409. 54 rooms. Restaurant, bar, sauna, bowling, billiards. No credit cards.*

$$$ ✕⊞ **Rindererhof.** This comfortable Alpine lodge at the end of the line is a good starting point for either climbing or skiing, since you're right at the base station for the cable cars up to the glacier. The outdoor Schirmbar (Umbrella Bar) is the "in" spot for après-ski in Hintertux. ✉ *A–6294 Hintertux,* ☎ *05287/8558–0,* FAX *05287/87502. 30 rooms, 30 suites. Restaurant, bar, sauna. No credit cards.*

$$$ ✕⊞ **Tuxerhof.** The welcoming open fireplace in the lounge sets the relaxed style for this attractive Alpine inn, whose rooms and restaurant are comfortably appointed. In winter, skiing starts literally at the door; in summer, hiking paths will lead you into the surrounding forests and mountains. ✉ *Vorderlanersbach 80, A–6293 Tux,* ☎ *05287/8511–0,*

FAX *05287/851150. 42 rooms, 4 suites. Restaurant, bar, pub, indoor pool, sauna, children's programs, parking. No credit cards.*

$ ✕▥ **Forelle.** This friendly mountain inn offers comfortable rooms in
★ typical Alpine decor and a good restaurant specializing in trout. The hotel has its own fishing stream. ⊠ *Vorderlanersbach 296, A–6293 Tux,* ☎ *05287/87214,* FAX *05287/87543. 34 rooms. Restaurant, bar, indoor pool, sauna, exercise room. No credit cards. Closed mid-Apr.– May and Nov.–mid-Dec.*

Outdoor Activities and Sports

For a complete offering of summer and winter sports programs in and around the Tuxer Valley, contact **Erlebnisclub Tuxertal** (⊠ A-Tux Lanersbach 481, ☎ 05287/87287, FAX 05287/87227).

CLIMBING

Those particularly interested in ice climbing should contact Anton Tomann at the **Hochgebirgs- und Wanderschule Tuxertal** (⊠ Juns 424, A 6293 Lanersbach, ☎ 05287/87372).

Hainzenberg

⑱ *6 km (4 mi) south of Zell am Ziller.*

Hainzenberg was once a gold-mining town. Stop at the **Maria Rast pilgrimage church,** built in 1739 by the prospectors, to see its stuccoes and fine ceiling paintings. Don't look for the western transept wing of the church; it slid down the precipice in 1910.

Gerlos

⑲ *18 km (10 mi) east of Zell am Ziller.*

The sensationally scenic Route 165 climbs east out of Zell am Ziller up to Gerlos, a less glitzy but still splendid choice for a summer or winter holiday, with the 8,300-ft Kreuzjoch mountain looming in the background. Scheduled buses make the run up from Zell am Ziller. The Gerlos ski slopes are varied, and in summer the same slopes offer excellent hiking. Check in advance about hotel arrangements; many of the better houses in Gerlos require a minimum of half board.

Lodging

$$$$ ▥ **Gaspingerhof.** The three Alpine chalets that make up this family-run, rustically furnished complex in the center of town are connected by underground passages. Rooms are done in the bright local custom, with natural woods and colorful fabrics. The nightlife is active. ⊠ *A– 6281,* ☎ *05284/5216,* FAX *05284/533549. 73 rooms. Restaurant, indoor pool, sauna, tennis court. DC. Closed mid-Apr.–mid-May and mid-Oct.–early Dec.*

$$ ▥ **Almhof.** In typical Tirolean style, this Alpine inn about 2 km (1 mi) out of the center offers a friendly reception area and comfortable rooms. ⊠ *Gerlos–Gmünd, A–6281,* ☎ *05284/5323–0,* FAX *05284/ 5323–23. 45 rooms. Restaurant, indoor pool, sauna, tennis court, exercise room, parking. No credit cards. Closed May–early June and mid-Oct.–mid-Dec.*

En Route Beyond Gerlos, the highway climbs the 5,300-ft Gerlos Pass and plunges into the province of Salzburg in a series of double-back hairpins close to the dramatic 1,300-ft **Krimmler Wasserfälle** (waterfalls). You can complete the circuit back into Tirol by continuing east to Mittersill and cutting north to Kitzbühel via the Thurn Pass.

ON THE ROAD TO KITZBÜHEL

In many ways the area between Jenbach and Kitzbühel, north of the Kitzbüheler Alps and south of the German border, is a distillation of all things Tirolean. You'll find perfectly maintained ancient farmhouses with balconies overflowing with flowers, and people who still wear the traditional lederhosen and dirndls as their everyday attire. Here you'll find Alpine villages, medieval castles, and of course wonderfully "kitschi" winter resorts like Kitzbühel and St. Johann. Other delightful destinations here include Brixlegg, which stands at the entrance to the short Alpbach valley and is known for its two famous castles, Schloss Kropfsberg and Schloss Matzen (the latter a beloved schloss hotel recently shuttered); Kufstein, with its brooding Geroldseck fortress and a bevy of warm-water lakes in its vicinity; and Rattenberg, with its glass workshops, founded by Sudeten German refugees from the Czech Republic. Everywhere the people are welcoming, and the scenery is beautiful.

Brixlegg

⓴ *16 km (10 mi) northeast of Jenbach.*

Heading out past Jenbach in the main Inn Valley, continue northeast on Route 171 until you hit Brixlegg, a former copper-mining town. It is the home of Schloss Kropfsberg, built to defend the Ziller Valley from marauding invaders. Another castle from the 12th-century, Schloss Matzen, is perched on a mountainside. For years, sufferers of rheumatism have flocked to Brixlegg to soak in the radioactive sulfur waters of the Mehrn spa.

Dining and Lodging

$$$ ✕ **Herrnhaus.** The wood-paneled rooms lend a rustic, country atmosphere to this simple Gasthaus in the center of town, which is known for its good food. The menu offers regional dishes, including *Speckknödelsuppe* (bacon dumpling soup) and lamb medallions in a potato crust. Service is friendly but can be a little slow. ⊠ *Herrnhauspl. 1, A–6230,* ☎ *05337/62223. No credit cards.*

$$$ ✕ **St. Leonhard.** Located about a 10-minute drive from Brixlegg in Kundl, this excellent restaurant has *das gewisse Etwas,* or that certain something. Along with traditional Tirolean specialties, the roast Muscovy duck with a barley salad in a balsamic dressing is superb, as is the tantalizing dessert *Topfenknödel,* with fresh plum compote. ⊠ *St. Leonhard 2, A–6230,* ☎ *05338/7435,* 𝔽𝔸𝕏 *05338/8607. AE, MC, V.*

Alpbach

⓶⓵ *8 km (5 mi) southeast of Brixlegg.*

From Brixlegg a small side road runs down a valley to the unspoiled picture-book village of Alpbach. The town is nominally a winter-sports center, but it takes the international spotlight once a year in August when world leaders of government and industry gather to discuss global issues at the European Forum.

Dining and Lodging

$$$–$$$$ ✕▥ **Böglerhof.** Much of the original character has been preserved in
★ this beautifully restored old double chalet, with its heavily beamed ceilings and stonework. The rooms are attractively decorated in Tirolean

style. The excellent restaurant, with its small *Stuben* (side rooms), is known for such Austrian specialties as cabbage soup and fillet points in light garlic sauce. The hotel is a member of the Romantik Hotel group. ✉ *A-6236,* ☎ *05336/5227. 50 rooms. Restaurant, bar, indoor and outdoor pools, sauna, tennis court, exercise room. MC, V. Closed late Apr.–mid-May and late Oct.–mid-Dec.*

$$$ 🏨 **Alpbacher Hof.** The massive fireplace sets the keynote in the public rooms of this typical chalet hotel, and the welcoming feeling carries over to the bedrooms. You may be asked to take minimum half board, but the policy is flexible. ✉ *A-6236,* ☎ *05336/5237,* FAX *05336/ 5016. 55 rooms. Restaurant, café, indoor pool, sauna. No credit cards. Closed mid-Apr.–mid-May and late Oct.–mid-Dec.*

Rattenberg

㉒ *2 km (1 mi) northeast of Brixlegg.*

Just up the road from Brixlegg is this quaint medieval town once famous for its silver mines. When the mines were exhausted, Rattenberg lapsed into a deep sleep lasting for centuries. Were it not for the constant procession of cars and trucks (which the residents are trying to ban), you might think you were back in the Middle Ages. Narrow old streets full of relics of its past glory twine around the town, which has remained remarkably unchanged for centuries. Local legend purports that the ruins of Emperor Maximilian's massive castle, which looms above the town, are haunted by ghosts from a bygone era.

Dining

$ ✕ **Hacker.** People come from miles around to sample the scrumptious
★ pastries and excellent coffee in this traditional café, which has been a coffeehouse since 1774. You can also choose from a variety of ice-cream sundaes. Service is especially friendly, and in summer tables are set outside. ✉ *Südtirolerstr. 46, A-6240,* ☎ *05337/62322. No credit cards.*

Shopping

If you're looking for something special and different, go to **Helga Danek** (✉ Inng. 60, 05337/63113), where you'll find beautiful painted glass. There is always a sale section available.

Across the river from Rattenberg lies Kramsach, a glass-production center since the 17th century. At the **glassworks school** (call ☎ 05337/ 62623 to arrange a visit) you can see etching, engraving, and painting on glassware.

En Route Back on Route 171, the road leads to **Wörgl,** a rail junction where the main Austrian east–west line and the shortcut via the "German corner" come together. From Wörgl an extremely scenic road leads south to the small resort villages of Niederau, Oberau, and Auffach.

Kufstein

㉓ *28 km (17 mi) northeast of Brixlegg, 26 km (16 mi) from Rattenberg, 13 km (8 mi) north of Söll.*

Kufstein marks the border with Germany. The town was captured from Bavaria in 1504 by Emperor Maximilian I, who added it to the Habsburg domains. You'll immediately notice that Kufstein is dominated by a magnificent fortress right out of a Dürer etching, **Schloss Geroldseck,** originally built as a "castle for contemplation" in 1200. But Maximilian decided it was better suited for merrymaking and expanded and strengthened it in 1504, rechristening it *Lustschloss,* or "pleasure palace." The fortress, considerably renovated, contains a small **museum** (☎ 05372/67038, 🎫 AS40, ☉ late Apr.–Oct., Tues.–Sun.) and boasts the famed "Heroes' Organ" (said to burst into sound when a national hero dies). With sumptuous rooms and terraced gardens, Geroldseck ranks among the finest of the 1,001 Tirolean castles. The town of Kufstein itself has some beautiful medieval-period streets. ☎ 05372/62207. ⊠ *Free.* ⊙ *May–Oct., daily 9–7, tour Tues.–Sun. at 9:30, 11, 1:30, and 4:30.*

The center of town boasts a remarkable concentration of Art Nouveau buildings, both public and private. The **Burgher's Tower** houses the Heldenorgel, the world's largest outdoor organ, with 26 registers and 1,800 pipes. The instrument is played year-round daily at noon and in summer at noon and 6 PM.

Dining and Lodging

$$–$$$
★
✕🏨 **Alpenrose.** This recently renovated house, on the edge of town in green surroundings, welcomes you immediately with its friendly lobby, which seems to continue the outdoors; the feeling of relaxed comfort carries over into the attractive bedrooms as well. The elegant restaurant is the best in the area; the *Tafelspitz* (boiled beef) and fish, game, and goose in season are particularly recommended, as is the orange soufflé. ⊠ *Weissachstr. 47, A–6330,* ☎ *05372/62122,* 🗏 *05372/ 62122–7. 19 rooms. Restaurant, bar. AE, MC. Closed 1 wk before Easter.*

Shopping

Kufstein is home to the world-famous **Riedel glass works**; a visit to the factory (☎ 05372/64896–0) may be possible. Otherwise you can buy pieces at the **factory outlet** (⊠ Weissach Str. 28–34, ☎ 05372/64896–0), which is open weekdays 9–noon and 1–6, Saturday 9–noon.

En Route
At Wörgl most travelers begin to head east toward the great resorts of St. Johann and Kitzbühel, destinations described below. Route 312 takes you to St. Johann, the noted vacation center, about 30 km (19 mi) away. You can do the circuit of St. Johann and its more famous neighbor, Kitzbühel, by taking Route 161 for 10 km (6 mi) between the two resorts and returning to Wörgl via Route 170. Heading eastward, you first encounter the charming towns of Going, Ellmau, and Söll.

Going, Ellmau, and Söll

10 km (6 mi) to 20 km (13 mi) south of Kufstein.

The villages of Going, Ellmau, and Söll have developed into attractive, small winter and summer resorts. Their altitudes (and their snow) are about the same as those in Kitzbühel and St. Johann, and prices are lower but rising as their popularity grows. Some of the region's finest restaurants and hotels are located around these villages. The Goinger Handwerks-Kunstmarkt, an arts-and-crafts fair, is held one Friday each month from June through September. You can sample local specialties such as *Kässpätzle* (a noodle skillet dish with cheese and onions) and *Prügeltorte* (chocolate layer cake), along with locally distilled schnaps. Farmers and their families demonstrate crafts and skills handed down through the centuries, and if you are there at 8 PM you can hear the Going Musikkapelle (brass band) perform. For details on the Going fair, contact the town's tourist office (☎ 05358/2438).

Dining and Lodging

$$$
✕ **Gasthof Restaurant Lanzenhof.** This festive *Tiroler Wirtshaus*, or traditional Tirolean guest house, serves impeccable traditional Tirolean *Blutwurstgröstl* (sausage) and lamb chops, among other options, with roast pork a particular favorite for many diners. ⊠ *Dorf 23, A–6353 Going,* ☎ *05358/2428,* 🗏 *05358/3592. No credit cards. Closed Sun. and Apr. and Nov.*

$$ ✕ **Schindlhaus.** Original variations on Austrian dishes are served up in a modern setting at this restaurant. Try the lightly braised fillet of venison with red cabbage or one of the fish specialties, served with a delicate sauce. The gemütlich atmosphere and friendly staff provide the perfect finishing touches. ✉ *Dorf 134, Söll,* ☎ *05333/5161. AE, DC, MC, V. Closed Mon.*

$$$$ ✕⌷ **Der Bär.** Within walking distance of the village center, "The Bear," a member of the luxurious Relais & Châteaux group, is known throughout Austria as one of the foremost country inns. An elegant but friendly atmosphere pervades, with relaxed comfort in every respect, attractive bedrooms in Tirolean style included. The kitchen does best with local dishes; try roast lamb, game, or seafood. The wine list also has an extensive choice of Austrian, French, and Italian vintages. ✉ *Kirchbichl 9, A–6352 Ellmau,* ☎ *05358/2395,* ⨑ *05358/2395–56. 45 rooms. Restaurant, indoor and outdoor pools, sauna, exercise room. No credit cards. Closed mid-Apr.–May and early Nov.–mid-Dec.*

$$$$ ⌷ **Stanglwirt.** A 300-year-old coaching inn forms the core of this centrally located health-and-fitness complex, which is also a popular mealtime stop for tour buses. Rooms in the new section are spacious; some are studios with old-fashioned ceramic stoves, in keeping with the Tirolean decor. Guests can ride, swim, hunt, or ski in season or play tennis and squash. This hotel is a great favorite with Germans, who have ranked it among the top 12 resort hotels in Europe. ✉ *Sonnseite 50, A–6353 Going,* ☎ *05358/2000,* ⨑ *05358/2000–31. 62 rooms, 6 apartments. Restaurant, indoor and outdoor pools, sauna, tennis courts, exercise room, horseback riding, squash. AE, DC, MC, V.*

St. Johann in Tirol

㉔ *32 km (24 mi) southeast of Kufstein, 14 km (9 mi) northeast of Kitzbühel.*

For years, St. Johann lived in the shadow of Kitzbühel, but today the town, with its colorfully painted houses, has developed a personality of its own, and for better or worse is equally mobbed, winter and summer. The facilities are similar, but prices are still lower, although climbing. (The dark horse here could be Kirchdorf, 4 km/2½ mi north of St. Johann, where costs appear to be holding, or Fieberbrunn, 12 km, or 7 mi, east on Route 164.) While in St. Johann, don't miss the magnificently decorated Baroque **parish church** or the Gothic **Spitalskirche,** with its fine late-medieval stained glass, just west of town in Weitau.

Dining and Lodging

$$$ ✕ **Das Bräu.** A great place to stop on Highway 312 between Salzburg
★ and Innsbruck is Das Bräu (25 km/15 mi northeast of St. Johann in Tirol), in the pretty village of Lofer. Josef Brüggler was head chef at the Hotel Arlberg in Lech (where he cooked for the late Princess Diana on three skiing visits) before returning to his roots and opening his own restaurant. There are two menus to choose from, one for casual dining and the other for a more elegant meal, and the excellent dishes include locally caught fish, fried chicken, and lamb. The setting is charmingly rustic, with red gingham tablecloths and cowbells, harnesses, and stirrups hanging from the wooden beams. If you don't feel like driving on, you can stay overnight in one of the 28 pleasant bedrooms upstairs. ✉ *Hauptstr. 28, Lofer,* ☎ *06588/82070,* ⨑ *06588/820771. No credit cards. Closed Mon.*

$$$ ✕⌷ **Post.** The painted stucco facade identifies this traditional hotel in the center of town. Natural woods and reds carry over from the public spaces and restaurant into the guest rooms. ✉ *Speckbacherstr. 1, A–6380,* ☎ *05352/62230,* ⨑ *05352/62230–3. 46 rooms. Restaurant, café. AE, DC, MC, V. Closed Apr. and Nov.*

$$$ 🏨 **Alpenapartment Europa.** This apartment hotel next to the recreation center (swimming, sauna, tennis) is attractively furnished in Baroque and regional decor. Many rooms have Tirolean four-posters and furnished kitchenettes. Exhausted skiers delight in knowing that breakfast is served until 11 AM. ✉ *Achenallee 18, A–6380,* ☎ *05352/62285–0,* FAX *05532/62285–5. 16 apartments. No credit cards.*

Kitzbühel ✓

➋➎ *20 km (12 mi) south of St. Johann, 71 km (44 mi) northeast of Gerlos.*

Long before Kitzbühel became one of the fashionable winter resorts, the town had gained a reputation for its summer season. Now, however, the accent is on skiing, with facilities among the finest in the world. The famous Ski Safari (previously known for decades as the Ski Circus)—a carefully planned, clever combination of lifts, cable railways, and runs that lets you ski for more than 80 km (50 mi) without having to exert yourself climbing a single foot—originally put this town on the map. Today, Kitzbühel is in perpetual motion and is always packed in December and again in February. But at any time during the season there's plenty to do, from sleigh rides to fancy-dress balls.

Built in the 16th century with proceeds from copper and silver mining, the town itself is picturesque enough, but take time to also check out the churches: **St. Andrew's parish church** (1435–1506) has a lavishly rococo chapel, the Rosakapelle, and the marvelously ornate tomb (1520) of the Kupferschmid family; the **Church of St. Catherine,** built about 1350, houses a Gothic winged altar dating from 1515.

In summer, you'll be offered a free guest card for substantial reductions on various activities (some of which are then free, like the hiking program), such as tennis, riding, and golf. The best swimming is in the nearby Schwarzsee. To see Alpine flowers in their natural glory, take the cable car up the Kitzbüheler Horn to the **Alpine Flower Garden Kitzbühel** at 6,500 ft; it leaves every half hour.

Dining and Lodging

$$$$ ✕ **Tennerhof.** Located in the Hotel Tennerhof, presently Kitzbühel's
★ leading hotel, this elegant restaurant is known as one of the best in Austria. The proof is in the guest list, which has included the Swedish royal family, Kirk Douglas, Roman Polanski, and Boris Becker. The von Pasquali family has owned and run the hotel and restaurant since 1679, while the restaurant is under the direction of chef Thomas Ritzer—a native Tirolean from Kufstein—who has developed an award-winning cuisine based on classic Austrian cooking with a light Mediterranean-Asian accent. The *Lieblingsmenü der "Hausherren"* (owner's favorite menu) includes a Brennessel cream soup (similar to a spinach cream soup) with sheep-cheese croutons, duck-liver tart with caramelized red-wine pears, fresh-caught local Zander fillet on basil risotto, a superb bouillabaisse, and a dreamy, creamy lemon soufflé. Vegetables and herbs come straight from the hotel garden. In summer, hotel guests can choose to enjoy breakfast with a pot of Earl Gray tea and homemade jam at tables set out on the terrace with the majestic mountains as a backdrop. ✉ *Griesenauweg 26,* ☎ *05356/63181,* FAX *05356/63181–70. Reservations essential. Jacket and tie. AE, DC, MC, V. Closed Apr.–mid-May and mid-Oct.–mid-Dec.*

$$$$ ✕ **Wirtshaus Unterberger Stuben.** In this former residence done up in typical Tirolean fashion with beige and red decor, you may have to reserve weeks ahead to get a table in winter; the place is usually booked solid. The international cuisine is good if not always a match for the prices, offering such temptations as creamed pumpkin soup and stuffed

oxtail. ✉ *Wehrg. 2,* ☎ *05356/66127,* ℻ *05356/66127–6. Reservations essential. No credit cards. Closed mid-May–June and Nov. No lunch Tues.–Wed. except during high season.*

$$ ✕ **Praxmair.** Après-ski can't begin early enough for the casually chic crowds who pile into this famous pastry shop–café, known for its Florentines. ✉ *Vorderstadt 17,* ☎ *05356/62646. AE, DC, MC, V. Closed Apr. and Nov.*

$$$$ ✕🏨 **Romantik Hotel Tennerhof.** Hidden away slightly out of the cen-
★ ter, this is an elegant old country house set in a huge garden near the
golf course, with towering mountains seemingly within reach. Over the years it has attracted celebrities from the Duke of Windsor to Kirk Douglas, but emphasis here is on family, including a special supervised children's room. The pretty bedrooms are done in Tirolean country furnishings, all different, some with ceramic stoves, and most with balconies. This is the kind of place you want to settle into for several days, and the staff is exceptionally warm and accommodating. ✉ *Griesenauweg 26, A–6370,* ☎ *05356/63181,* ℻ *05356/63181–70. 40 rooms. Restaurant, indoor and outdoor pools, sauna, spa. AE, DC, MC, V. Closed Apr.–mid-May and mid-Oct.–mid-Dec.*

$$$$ 🏨 **Weisses Rössl.** Located in the middle of town and now a member of the five-Star Greif Hotel group, the "White Horse" has recently been given a complete makeover, with an elegant but understated reception area, domed glass ceilings, piano bar, and revamped restaurant. The former garden has become a modern wellness facility complete with beauty center and indoor pool. The public salons are warmed with fireplaces ablaze in winter, while the spacious, comfortable guest rooms are adorned in light pine and complemented by modern amenities. ✉ *Bichlstr. 5, A–6370,* ☎ *05356/62541–0,* ℻ *05356/63472. 38 rooms. Restaurant, 2 bars, tennis court, dance club. AE, DC, MC, V. Closed mid-Apr.–mid-May, mid-Oct.–early Dec.* 🐾

$$$ 🏨 **Golf-Hotel Rasmushof.** For an superb Alpine panorama and year-round proximity to outdoor activities, it's difficult to find a better address in Kitzbühel than the Rasmushof, located directly on the 9-hole **Rasmushof** golf course, with a view of the famous Streif downhill ski run, and only steps from the lift. The rooms are drenched in Tirolean antiques, with finishes of barn wood and plush upholstered furnishings. Facilities are fully modern; large family suites are available. ✉ *A–6370 Kitzbühel,* ☎ *05356/65252,* ℻ *05356/65252–49. 30 rooms. Restaurant, fitness center, indoor pool, sauna, steam room, solarium, tennis, golf, meeting facilities, parking. AE, DC, MC, V.*

$$$ 🏨 **Schloss Lebenberg.** A onetime 16th-century castle on a hilltop outside town has been transformed into a wholly modern, owner-managed family hotel. The bedrooms are contemporary in flavor. If the youngsters are too small to go skiing with you, there's a day care center. ✉ *Lebenbergstr. 17, A–6370,* ☎ *05356/6901,* ℻ *05356/64405. 109 rooms. Restaurant, indoor pool, sauna, tennis court, exercise room, nursery. AE, DC, MC, V.*

$$ 🏨 **Goldener Greif.** The original building dates from 1271; renovations in the 1950s gave the house a more contemporary but still traditional Tirolean charm, emphasized by the magnificent vaulted lobby with open fireplaces and antiques. The rooms, too, are charming, some with four-posters, and a few apartments have fireplaces. The hotel houses the Kitzbühel casino. ✉ *Hinterstadt 24, A–6370,* ☎ *05356/64311,* ℻ *05356/65001. 47 rooms. Restaurant, bar, sauna, casino. AE, DC, MC, V. Closed Apr.–mid-June and Oct.–Nov.*

Nightlife and the Arts

Much activity centers on the **casino** in the Goldener Greif hotel, where you'll find baccarat, blackjack, roulette, and one-armed bandits galore.

There's a restaurant and a bar, and no set closing time. You'll need your passport to enter the casino. ⊠ *Hinterstadt 24,* ☎ *05356/62300.* 🆓 *Free.* ⊙ *Dec. 25–Mar. and July–mid-Sept., daily 7 PM.*

The **Tenne** has for generations been *the* evening spot in Kitz. It's partly because of the friendly atmosphere, the capacity, and the music (live), but most of all it's because you can meet people here. There's food, but emphasis is on drink and dance. ⊠ *Hotel zur Tenne,* ☎ *05356/ 64444–0,* FAX *05356/64803–56. AE, DC, MC, V.* ⊙ *Dec. 25–mid-Mar. and Aug., daily 9 PM–3 AM.*

The disco crowd moves from place to place, but check out **Take Five** (⊠ Hinterstadt 22, ☎ 05356/74131), the town's hot spot. Take Five's competition is **Roses** (⊠ Bichlstr. 8, ☎ 05356/63425). Current among "in" spots are the **Stamperl** bar (⊠ Franz-Reisch-Str. 7, ☎ 05356/62555); the **Londoner** (⊠ Franz-Reisch-Str. 4, ☎ 05356/71428); and the **Fünferl** bar in the Kitzbüheler Hof (⊠ Franz-Reisch-Str. 1, ☎ 05356/71300).

Outdoor Activities and Sports
GOLF

The newest place to play is **Golf Eichenheim** (☎ 05356/66615), an 18-hole, PGA-rated course, which opened its fairways in spring 2000. **Golf-club Kitzbühel** (☎ 05356/63007), 9 holes, par-36, is open April–October. **Golf-Club Kitzbühel-Schwarzsee** (☎ 05356/71645), 18 holes, par-72, is open April–October. With the addition of the new Eichenheim course, and 18 other courses within an hour's drive, Kitzbühel may properly lay claim to being the "golf center of the Alps." Golf privileges can be arranged between the Kitzbühel courses and any of the town's top-ranked hotels.

WEST FROM INNSBRUCK

The upper Inn Valley, from Innsbruck stretching down to the Swiss border, is beautiful countryside, particularly the narrow valleys that branch off to the south. Most visitors take Route 171 west from Innsbruck along the banks of the Inn, rather than the autobahn, which hugs the cliffs along the way. This is a region of family-run farms perched on mountainsides and steep granite peaks flanking narrow valleys leading to some of Austria's finest ski areas.

Telfs

㉖ *32 km (20 mi) southeast of Reutte.*

Mythical masked figures invade the streets of Telfs every five years when the town hosts its traditional Carnival celebration of **Schleicherlaufen.** Just before Lent in the year 2000 the whole population celebrated in a festive masked procession. Some of the grotesque masks can be seen in the local museum.

Lodging

$$$$ 🏨 **Interalpen Tyrol.** This resort, outside town at 3,900 ft up the slopes, is simply huge, from the lobby, with its vast expanse of carpet, to the modern rooms. But the lobby's crackling fire is welcoming, and you'll find this a far quieter, more relaxing spot than you might guess from an original impression. ⊠ *A–6410,* ☎ *05262/606,* FAX *05262/606–190. 300 rooms. Restaurant, indoor pool, sauna, spa, tennis courts, exercise room. AE, DC, MC, V. Closed Apr.–early May and Nov.–mid-Dec.*

$ 🏨 **Tirolerhof.** You're within a couple of blocks of the center of town in this comfortable, balconied family-run hotel, convenient also to the indoor and outdoor pools and tennis and squash courts. The restaurant offers standard regional fare. ⊠ *Bahnhofstr. 28, A–6410,* ☎

05262/62237, FAX *05262/62237–9. 37 rooms. Restaurant. AE, DC, MC,*
V. Closed 3 wks before Easter.

En Route From Telfs you have a choice of taking the very scenic Route 189/E6
to Nassereith and down to Imst or following the rail line along the river
on Route 171. Like Telfs, both Nassereith and Imst are attractive for
their richly decorated 15th- and 16th-century buildings and churches.

Imst

㉗ *35 km (22 mi) west of Telfs.*

Imst, a popular summer resort lying a half mile or so back from the
Inn River and the railway line, makes an excellent base from which to
explore the Paznaun Valley and the upper Inn Valley, leading into
Switzerland and Italy.

Here the **Schemenlaufen,** a masked procession depicting the struggle
between good and evil, usually takes place in February. Many of the
magnificently carved masks worn by the mummers—especially those
of the fearsome witches—are very old and works of art. The event is
scheduled every four years and will next occur in the year 2004. The
tradition is ancient, and as in Telfs, you can see many of the 100-year-
old carved masks in the local **museum** (✉ Streleneg. 6); check with the
tourist office for opening times. A great feature of these rustic carnivals is the ringing of cowbells of all shapes, sizes, and tones, and the
resulting noise is quite deafening when the procession hits its stride.
Don't overlook the 15th-century frescoed **parish church** in the upper
part of Imst.

Dining and Lodging

$$ ✕🏠 **Post.** Set in the center of town next to a large park, this 16th-cen-
★   tury former castle, complete with onion-dome towers, belongs to the
Romantik Hotel group. The friendly interior is furnished with an-
tiques, and the modern bedrooms are cheerful. The restaurant is rec-
ommended, particularly for game. ✉ *E.-Wallnöfer-Pl. 3, A–4460,* ☎
05412/66555, FAX *05412/266519–55. 35 rooms. Restaurant, indoor pool.*
AE, DC, MC, V. Closed Nov.–Jan.

$$ 🏠 **Linserhof.** This double-chalet hotel is outside town, set in a lush Alpine
meadow at the base of a wooded hillside. The attractive rooms are in
rustic Tirolean decor, with much natural wood; those on the south side
with balconies are preferable. ✉ *A–6460 Imst/Teilwiesen,* ☎ *05412/
66415,* FAX *05412/66415–133. 42 rooms, 20 apartments. Restaurant,
bar, indoor pool, lake, sauna, tennis court, exercise room, bicycles. AE,
DC, MC, V.*

$ 🏠 **Zum Hirschen.** This comfortable *Gasthof-Pension,* attractively ren-
ovated and close to the center of town, pays particular attention to families with children. ✉ *Th.-Walsch-Str. 3, A–6460,* ☎ *05412/6901–0,*
FAX *05412/69017. 70 rooms. Restaurant, bar, sauna. AE, DC, MC, V.
Closed early–mid-Dec.*

En Route The Ötz Valley climbs in a series of six great natural steps for nearly 42
km (26 mi) from the Inn River to the glaciers around Obergurgl, 6,200
ft above sea level. The entire distance offers stunning scenery, with the
most dramatic part beginning around Sölden, where the final rise begins to the 8,100-ft pass over the Timmel Alps and across the Italian border into South Tirol. It was in this area that Ötzi, the Iceman mummy,
was discovered a few years ago. The body, which is more than 5,000
years old, was found by Austrians who were unaware they had crossed
the Italian border. Ötzi is now in the possession of Italy, who at first wanted

nothing to do with him, thinking he was a recent murder victim. To reach the valley, turn south off Route 171 onto Route 186.

Ötz

㉘ *21 km (12 mi) southeast of Imst, 23 km (14 mi) southwest of Telfs.*

Gothic houses with colorful fresco decorations grace this typically Tirolean mountain village. The parish church of **St. George and St. Nicholas,** whose tower was once a charnel house, sits on a rock promontory above the village. The small St. Michael's Chapel also has a splendid altar dating from 1683.

Lodging
$ ⌂ **Drei Mohren.** You can't miss the roof of this inn, with its wonderful collection of odd towers and onion domes. Fortunately, the interior is less exotic; the comfortable rooms are elegantly paneled, and most have balconies. The restaurant, offering standard local fare, is intended primarily for hotel guests and is tastefully decorated with old etchings. ⊠ *Hauptstr. 54, A–6433,* ☎ *05252/6301,* FAX *05252/2464. 22 rooms. Restaurant, tennis court. AE, DC, MC, V. Closed Nov.–mid-Dec.*

Sölden

㉙ *28 km (18 mi) south of Ötz.*

The highest cable car in Austria moves skiers swiftly from Sölden over the glaciers to a permanent-snow area at almost 9,910 ft on Gaislacher Kogel, where you can ski all year. For the new millennium, the already colossal Sölden ski region has become even more massive with the addition of new lifts, providing faster access to the glaciers, and linking them to the classic ski area at Schwarzkogl. The towering Hochsölden (6,800 ft) ensures excellent snow for the whole season. For information on Sölden's skiing facilities, contact the Tourismusverband Sölden (⊠ Ötztal Arena, A–6450, ☎ 05254/510–0, FAX 05254/3131, ✆).

Dining and Lodging
$$$$ ✕⌂ **Central.** Huge arches and heavy wooden timbers accent the antique furniture and set the atmosphere in this massive riverside hotel where the prominent are said to gather. The bedrooms are spacious and luxuriously furnished. Half board is standard. The intimate Ötztaler Stube restaurant is the best in town; sample the fillet of venison, and don't overlook the excellent desserts. ⊠ *Hochsölden Hof 418, A–6450,* ☎ *05254/2260–0,* FAX *05254/2260–511. 92 rooms. Restaurant, indoor pool, sauna. No credit cards. Closed June–mid-July.*

$$$–$$$$ ⌂ **Liebe Sonne.** You'll be right next to the chairlift to Hochsölden if you stay in this sprawling complex, recently rebuilt to include a new array of amenities. Its atmosphere is rustic, and the paneled rooms are cozy. Half board is required. ⊠ *Rainstadl 85, A–6450,* ☎ *05254/2203–0,* FAX *05254/2423. 59 rooms. Restaurant, bar, indoor pool, sauna, spa, exercise room. No credit cards. Closed May and June.*

Outdoor Activities and Sports
CLIMBING

The nearby Venteral Valley burrows still farther into the Ötztal Alps, ending in the tiny village of Vent, a popular resort center. In summer, the village is transformed into a base for serious mountain climbers, experienced in ice and rock climbing, who want to attempt the formidable **Wildspitze** (12,450 ft) or other, even more difficult neighboring peaks. Hiring a professional local guide is strongly advised. To reach Vent from Sölden, turn off at the road marked to Heiligenkreuz.

Obergurgl

③ *11 km (7 mi) south of Sölden.*

Austria's highest village, tiny Obergurgl, gained its reputation not only for superb winter sports but also as the place where the Swiss physicist Auguste Piccard landed his famous stratospheric balloon in 1931. In winter, a vast expanse of snow and ice shimmers all around you, and the great peaks and glaciers of the Ötztal Alps appear deceptively close all year. A high Alpine road takes you from Obergurgl to the hotel settlement at **Hochgurgl,** another excellent skiing spot, and farther up to the Timmelsjoch Pass (closed in winter) through magnificent mountain scenery. Hochgurgl has since 1988 also become accessible by cable car, bridging the two ski areas. From Hochgurgl, a three-stage chairlift brings you into an area of year-round skiing. For details on Obergurgl's skiing facilities, contact the Tourismusverband Gurgl (⊠ A–6456 Ötztal, ☎ 05256/6466, ℻ 05256/6353, ✒). In summer, also ask at the tourist office about hiking and river-rafting possibilities.

Lodging

$$–$$$$ ⊡ **Bellevue.** This friendly Alpine chalet lives up to its name in every
★   respect: is there another Bellevue among the probable millions in the world with a vista to equal the one here? You can ski right out the front door. Rooms are cozily comfortable, but you'll have to take half board. ⊠ *A–6456,* ☎ *05256/6228. 26 rooms. Restaurant, indoor pool, sauna, exercise room. No credit cards. Closed May–June and Sept.–early Dec.*

$$–$$$$ ⊡ **Edelweiss und Gurgl.** Traditionally, this is *the* place to stay. Reno-
★   vations have turned the massive house into an excellent family-run hotel with a comfortable, relaxed ambience. The cheery rooms have attractive natural-wood touches. Minimum half board is required. ⊠ *A–6456,* ☎ *05256/6223. 100 rooms. Restaurant, bar, indoor pool, sauna. AE, DC, MC, V. Closed May–mid-June and Oct.–Nov.*

LANDECK, UPPER INN VALLEY, AND ST. ANTON

Landeck

③ *24 km (15 mi) southwest of Imst.*

On Route 171 west, Landeck is a popular place in summer and a good base from which to explore the Paznaun Valley and the upper Inn Valley, leading into Switzerland and Italy. Landeck is known for an ancient and awe-inspiring rite that takes place on **"Cheese Sunday,"** the Sunday following Ash Wednesday. At dawn the young men set out to climb to the top of the great rocky crags that overshadow and hem in the old city on three sides. As dusk falls, they light huge bonfires that can be seen for miles around and then set fire to great disks of pinewood dipped in tar, which they roll ablaze down to the valley below. The sight of scores of these fiery wheels bounding down the steep slopes toward town is a fearsome spectacle worthy of Ezekiel.

The 13th-century **Burg Landeck castle** dominates from its position above the town. Climb up and catch the superb views from this vantage point. Also note the 16th-century winged altar in the 15th-century Gothic **parish church of the Assumption.** Downhill and, increasingly, cross-country skiing can be found in Landeck and throughout the Upper Inn Valley. Equipment is available for rent, though the selection and quality will vary from place to place.

Lodging

$ 🏨 **Schrofenstein.** Directly in the middle of town, this older house still shows its original beamed ceilings and marble floors in the public areas. The rooms are comfortably modern, those overlooking the river preferred. ⊠ *Malser Str. 31, A–6500,* ☎ *05442/62395. 54 rooms. Restaurant. AE, DC, MC, V. Closed mid–late Apr. and Nov.–mid-Dec.*

$ 🏨 **Schwarzer Adler.** Virtually in the shadow of the town castle, this traditional, family-run hotel offers solid comfort in typical Tirolean style, with red checks and light wood. ⊠ *Malser Str. 8, A–6500,* ☎ *05442/ 62316,* FAX *05442/62316–50. 32 rooms. Restaurant. No credit cards. Closed Nov.–mid-Dec.*

Outdoor Activities and Sports

HIKING

Would-be climbers can take lessons by contacting Hugo Walter at the **Bergsteigerschule Piz Buin-Silvretta** (⊠ A–6563 Galtür, ☎ 05443/8565).

Ried

🔟 *19 km (12 mi) south of Landeck.*

At Landeck the Inn River turns southward along the edge of the Silvretta mountains. The valley, tucked between two dramatic ranges, climbs toward the Italian border. As you follow Route 315/S15 beside the river, you'll come across **Schloss Sigmundsried,** a small castle built around an earlier tower by Duke Sigmund the Wealthy about 1470; the castle holds intriguing 16th-century coat-of-arms paintings. Today, you can canoe or raft the river along the edge of the Silvretta mountains.

Serfaus

🔟 *8 km (5 mi) southwest of Ried.*

At Ried, turn west off Route 315 for the scenic but steep climb up to Serfaus. This old village, perched on a plateau above the valley, has taken on new class in recent years as an important winter-sports center. There are several ski lifts, and the Komperdell cable car takes you, in summer, too, up to points from which you can either hike or just enjoy the views. For details about Serfaus's skiing facilities, contact the Tourismusverband (☎ 05476/62390, FAX 05476/6813, ✉). The Skischool Serfaus (☎ 05476/6268, FAX 05476/6268–15) features an extensive program for kids, including instruction for all ages and a "Kinder Schneealm," a large playground for kids on skis.

Dining and Lodging

$$$–$$$$ ✕🏨 **Maximilian.** The transformation of a former Serfaus Gasthof into a modern hotel seems to have worked, successfully blending the old and the new, and the house is now a member of the Silence Hotel group. Rooms in the new section, some with open fireplaces, are more spacious, but all are comfortable. A separate, excellent restaurant in a cozy side room is open to the public in the evening, with two fixed menus available. ⊠ *Herrenanger 4, A–6534,* ☎ *05476/6520,* FAX *05476/6520– 52. 36 rooms. Restaurant, indoor pool, sauna, exercise room, children's programs. No credit cards. Closed May–June and Oct.–mid-Dec.*

St. Anton am Arlberg

🔟 *49 km (30 mi) northwest of Serfaus, 22 km (15 mi) west of Landeck.*

Tucked between the entrance to the Arlberg tunnel and the railway (if you're coming from Serfaus, backtrack to Landeck and take Route 316/ S16 west toward Vorarlberg), St. Anton swarms with visitors at the height of the season. The wealthy, the prominent, including, occasionally, the royal, appear regularly to see and be seen—some even to enjoy the winter sports. Their presence boosts prices into the very-expensive-to-outrageous category, but if you shop around, you can find accommodations outside the center of the action at a bearable price. St. Anton is a particularly lovely town in summer—which seems on the verge of becoming the more fashionable season.

Modern skiing techniques were created and nurtured in St. Anton. In 1921, Hannes Schneider (1890–1955), an unknown young ski instructor with innovative ideas, set up a ski school to teach his new technique, at the invitation of the just-founded Kandahar Ski Club. This "Arlberg School" method, developed by Schneider in the '20s and '30s, laid down the basic principles since followed by all skiing courses the world over. St. Anton's remains one of the world's leading ski schools. Thanks to an amazing system of funicular trains, double chairlift, and interconnected T-bars, St. Anton can access skiers to the Arlberg's region's enormous 300-odd km (200-odd mi) of marked runs. If you decide to take to the slopes, remember that skiing remains serious business in St. Anton: Many slopes are so steep you'll be sharing them with mountain climbers.

Dining and Lodging

$$$$ ✕🖾 **Brunnenhof.** Set in the intimate, homey atmosphere of an old farmhouse in nearby St. Jakob is one of the best restaurants in the area. From the excellent Tirolean and international menu you might choose a mushroom, garlic, or cheese soup and follow it with roast rack of lamb in an herb crust. The wine list is good. The 10-room hotel offers cozy comfort at moderate prices from December to April and from June to September. ⊠ *A–6580,* ☎ *05446/2293,* 📠 *05446/2293–5. Restaurant. No credit cards. Closed May–June and Oct.–Nov.*

$–$$$ 🖾 **Schwarzer Adler.** The beautifully frescoed facade of this 420-year-
  ★   old inn in the center of town creates the right setting for the open fireplaces, Tirolean antiques, and colorful Oriental carpets inside. Rooms are tastefully furnished in Alpine style and fully equipped. An annex across the street has somewhat less elegant (and cheaper) rooms. The lively Disco Kartouche is in the basement of the main house. ⊠ *A–6580,* ☎ *05446/2244–0,* 📠 *05446/2244–62. 63 rooms. Restaurant, café, sauna, exercise room, dance club, baby-sitting. AE, DC, MC, V. Closed mid-Apr.–May and Oct.–Nov.*

$–$$ ✕🖾 **Karl Schranz.** Your first impression of this new and spacious Alpine lodge is made by the lobby's welcoming fireplace—a showcase for trophies won by the champion skier and owner-manager, Karl Schranz, from 1957 to 1972. A shuttle bus takes guests to and from the center of town. The rooms are large and modern, with elegant wood paneling. The Jägerstube restaurant features Austrian and Tirolean fare. ⊠ *A–6580,* ☎ *05446/2555–0,* 📠 *05446/2555–5. 23 rooms. Restaurant, bar, sauna, exercise room, baby-sitting. No credit cards. Closed May– June and Oct.–Nov.*

Nightlife and the Arts

For some visitors to St. Anton, the show, not the snow, is the thing. Nobody complains about a lack of action!

Check out these popular après-ski spots: **Drop In** (⊠ Sporthotel St. Anton, ☎ 05446/3131); the **Postkeller** cellar disco (⊠ Hotel Neue Post, ☎ 05446/2213–274); and the **terrace of the Hotel Alte Post** (⊠ Hotel Neue Post, ☎ 05446/2553), which hops in early springtime. In Moos, Gunnar Munthe's **Krazy Kanguruh** bar with its cellar disco is a favorite gathering spot; it opens at 3:30 PM (☎ 05446/2633). Some of the best, original, local Alpine atmosphere for drinking and dining can be found at **Rodelalm** (☎ 0663/858855) and **Sennhütte** (☎ 05446/2048).

Outdoor Activities and Sports

SKIING

The *Skihaserl,* or ski bunny, as the beginner is called, usually joins a class on St. Anton's good "nursery" slopes, where he or she will have plenty of often very distinguished company. The Skischule Arlberg (☎ 05446/3411, FAX 05446/2306, ✍) here is excellent and is considered by some to be the Harvard of ski schools. Once past the Skihaserl stage, skiers go higher in the Arlberg mountains to the superlative runs from the top of the Galzig and the 9,100-ft Valluga above it. Check with your hotel or ski-lift ticket offices about an **Arlberg Skipass,** which is good on cable cars and lifts in St. Anton and St. Christoph on the Tirol side and on those in Zürs, Lech, Oberlech, and Stuben in Vorarlberg— 85 in all. For complete details on St. Anton's skiing facilities, contact the town's tourist office (☎ 05446/22690, FAX 05446/2532, ✍).

St. Christoph

③⑤ *2 km (1 mi) west of St. Anton am Arlberg.*

A hospice to care for imperiled travelers stranded by the snows on the pass was founded in what is now St. Christoph as early as the 15th century. Today, the snow is what attracts visitors to the area. Even the Austrian government has gotten in on the act, holding its exacting courses for aspiring ski instructors here. While St. Christoph hasn't the same social cachet as St. Anton, the skiing facilities are precisely the same (and even closer at hand). If you take your skiing seriously and are willing to forgo the high life as too distracting or too expensive, you may find winter sports per se more fun at St. Christoph.

Dining and Lodging

$$–$$$$ ✕▥ **Arlberg Hospiz.** This huge pink building re-creates much of the
★ legendary ancient hospice that stood here until a fire in the 1950s. Carved-wood paneling and rich Oriental carpets abound. The rooms are luxurious in the extreme; service is attentive but not obtrusive. The associated Hospizalm restaurant has earned a reputation for creative cooking: You might be offered cream of lobster or oyster soup, veal or venison, or fish dishes. The wine list is outstanding. ✉ *A–6580 St. Christoph am Arlberg,* ☎ *05446/2611,* FAX *05446/3545. 102 rooms. Restaurant, bar, indoor pool, sauna, exercise room, dance club, babysitting. No credit cards. Closed May and Oct.–Nov.*

Ischgl

③⑥ *67 km (42 mi) southeast of St. Christoph.*

Ischgl, the largest town in the Paznaun Valley, offers excellent skiing, particularly in the small Fimber Valley to the south, and in summer is a popular high-altitude health resort. You can get to the 7,500-ft Idalpe via the 4-km-long (2½-mi-long) Silvretta cable-car run. The enchanting Paznaun Valley follows the course of the Trisanna River for more than 40 km (25 mi). The valley runs into the heart of the Blue Silvretta mountains, named for the shimmering ice-blue effect created by the great peaks and glaciers. They are dominated by the Fluchthorn (10,462 ft) at the head of the valley near Galtür.

Slightly higher up the valley is **Galtür,** the best-known resort in the Paznaun, equally popular as a winter-sports area, a summer resort, and a base for mountain climbing. Although Galtür is a starting point for practiced mountaineers, many of the climbs up the Blue Silvretta are

very easy and lead to the half dozen mountain huts belonging to the
Alpenverein. Galtür and the Silvretta region inspired Ernest Hemingway's novella *Alpine Idyll*; the author spent the winter of 1925 here,
and the town still remembers him.

Dining and Lodging

$$–$$$$ ✕⛺ **Madlein.** This modern chalet-style hotel not far from the center
is the place to stay for sheer Alpine elegance and to see the town's ac-
tion. The rooms are attractive, but you'll be tempted to spend your time
in such places as the beamed Almbar with its large dance floor and
friendly atmosphere. The restaurant has a fine kitchen. ⊠ *A–6561,* ☎
05444/5266, FAX *05444/5636. 65 rooms. Restaurant, bar, indoor pool,
sauna, nightclub. No credit cards. Closed May–June and Oct.–Nov.*

INNSBRUCK AND TIROL A TO Z

Arriving and Departing

By Bus

Innsbruck is connected by bus to other parts of Tirol, and the termi-
nal (⊠ Südtiroler Platz, ☎ 0512/1717 or 0512/585155) is beside the
railroad station.

By Car

To get to Innsbruck, exit from the east–west autobahn (Route A12/
E60) or from the Brenner autobahn (Route A13/E45) running south
to Italy. Since the Old City is a pedestrian zone and much of the rest
of the downtown area is paid parking only, you'll be best off leaving
the car in a central garage, unless your hotel has parking.

By Plane

The **airport** (☎ 0512/22525 flight information), 3 km (2 mi) west of
Innsbruck, is served principally by **Austrian Airlines** and **Tyrolean. Buses**
(Line F) to the city center (Maria-Theresien-Strasse) take about 20 min-
utes. Get your ticket from the bus driver; it costs AS21. **Taxis** should
take no more than 10 minutes into town, and the fare is about AS100–
AS150. Transfer services operated by **Four Seasons Travel** (⊠ Müller-
str. 14, ☎ 0512/584157, FAX 0512/585767) run to and from the *Zen-
tralbereich* at Munich airport, departing Munich at 7, 9, and 11 AM
and 4 PM. Service from Innsbruck to Munich is on demand; make ar-
rangements in advance, allowing 2½ hours for travel. One-way fare is
AS460, round-trip AS820; reservations are recommended.

By Train

Direct trains (☎ 0512/1717 information and reservations) serve Inns-
bruck from Munich, Vienna, Rome, and Zürich, and all arrive at the
railroad station at Südtiroler Platz.

Getting Around

By Bus and Streetcar

In **Innsbruck,** most bus and streetcar routes begin or end at Maria-There-
sien-Strasse, nearby Bozner Platz, or the main train station (Haupt-
bahnhof). You can get single tickets costing AS21 on the bus or streetcar.
Multiple-ride tickets bought in advance at most tobacconists (*Tabak-
Trafik*), the Verkehrsbetriebe (transportation services) office (⊠ Mu-
seumstr. 23), or the tourist office (☞ Visitor Information, *below*) are
cheaper; a block of four tickets is AS61. A 24-hour ticket good for the
city costs AS35; other 24-hour network tickets cover areas outside the
immediate city. A weekly ticket costs AS123. For information, check
with the tourist office. You can transfer to another line with the same

ticket as long as you continue in more or less the same direction in a single journey. The bus is also the most convenient way to reach the six major ski areas outside the city. A Club Innsbruck pass (free from the tourist office or your hotel if you spend one night or more) gives you free transportation to the ski areas; many hotels provide shuttle service to the special ski bus stop. These are not the regular city buses, but special, deluxe ski buses that leave from the Landestheater on Rennweg, across from the Hofburg. Check with your hotel or the tourist offices for schedules.

In **Tirol,** as throughout Austria, where the train doesn't go, the post office or railroad bus does, and except in the most remote areas, buses are frequent enough so that you can get around. But bus travel requires time and planning. In summer, tour-bus operators run many sightseeing trips through Tirol that often include East and South Tirol. Check with your travel agent or the nearest tourist office.

By Car

Private cars are not allowed in **Innsbruck**'s Old City, and parking anywhere near the center in Innsbruck requires vouchers, which you buy from blue coin-operated dispensers found around parking areas. Each half hour normally costs AS5. Maximum parking time is 1½ hours. Large blue *P* signs direct you to parking garages. The bus is about as convenient as a car for reaching the ski areas if you have to cope with chains and other complications of winter driving.

Driving is the best way to see the rest of **Tirol,** since it allows you to wander off the main routes at your pleasure or to stop and admire the view. Roads are good, but a detailed highway map is recommended. Watch your gas gauge, particularly on Sunday and holidays, when some stations may be closed.

The autobahns are fastest, but for scenery you'll be best off on the byways. One important exception is the 1¾-km (1-mi) Europa Bridge on the Brenner autobahn running south into Italy, although if you follow the parallel route from Patsch to Pfons, you'll have the views without the traffic. Roads with particularly attractive scenery are marked on highway maps with a parallel green line.

By Horse-Drawn Carriage

Horse-drawn cabs, still a feature of Innsbruck life, can be hired at the stand in front of the Landestheater. Set the price before you head off; a half-hour ride will cost around AS320.

By Taxi

In Innsbruck, taxis are not much faster than walking, particularly along the one-way streets and in the Old City. Basic fare is AS52 for the first 1½ km (1 mi). Call to order a **radio cab** (☎ 0512/5311, 0512/45500, or 0512/1718).

By Train

The railroad follows nearly all the main routes in Tirol, with highways and tracks sharing the same narrow valleys. Some of the most fascinating and memorable side trips can be made by rail: two narrow-gauge lines steam out of Jenbach, for example, one up to the Achensee, the other down to Mayrhofen in the Zillertal. From Innsbruck, the narrow-gauge Stubaitalbahn runs south to Telfes and Fulpmes.

The main railway line of Tirol runs east–west, entering Tirol via the Griessen Pass, then heading on to St. Johann and Kitzbühel before wandering over to Wörgl and onward to Jenbach, Hall in Tirol, and Innsbruck. From Innsbruck on, the line follows the Inn Valley to Landeck, then to St. Anton, where it plunges into an 11-km (7-mi) tunnel under the Arlberg range, emerging at Langen in Vorarlberg. From Innsbruck, a line runs north into Germany to Garmish-Partenkirchen and onward back into Austria, to Ehrwald and Reutte in Tirol and beyond, into Germany again. A line from Innsbruck to the south goes over the dramatic Brenner Pass (4,465 ft) into Italy.

Contacts and Resources

Car Rentals

Avis (✉ Tourist Center, Salurner Str. 15, ☎ 0512/571754, FAX 0512/577149). **Budget** (✉ Michael-Gaismayr Str. 7, ☎ 0512/588468, FAX 0512/584580). **Europcar** (✉ Salurner Str. 8, ☎ 0512/582060, FAX 0512/582107).

Currency Exchange

In addition to banks (open weekdays 7:45–12:30 and 2:15–4) and post offices, you can **change money** in Innsbruck at the American Express office (✉ Brixnerstr. 3, ☎ 0512/582491), at the main train station (the office is open daily 7:30–12:30, 12:45–6, and 6:30–8:15) and the city tourist information office (☞ Visitor Information, *below*). But compare rates; you'll probably do best at a post office or bank. **Cash machines** can be found in Innsbruck (✉ Hofg. 2 and Herzog-Friedrich-Str. 7).

Emergencies

Police (☎ 133). **Ambulance** (☎ 144).

Guided Tours

In Innsbruck, bus tours with English-speaking guides cover the city highlights (two hours), leaving daily at noon, year-round, from the hotel information office at the Südtiroler Platz station. In summer, additional buses are scheduled at 10 AM and 2 PM; and a shorter, hour-long tour leaves the Volkskunstmuseum Monday–Saturday at 10:15, noon, 2, and 3:15. Guided 1½-hour walking tours on Saturday and Sunday highlight historic personalities and some offbeat features associated with the city. Your hotel or one of the tourist offices will have tickets and details.

Late-Night Pharmacies

Several pharmacies stay open late in Innsbruck on a rotational basis. The newspaper will give their names, addresses, and phone numbers. Ask your hotel for help.

Lodging

If you arrive in Innsbruck without a hotel room, check with the **Zimmernachweis** (room accommodation service) next to the railroad station (✉ Südtiroler Pl., ☎ 0512/583766–0). The office is open summer, daily 8 AM–10 PM, and winter, daily 9–9. The same organization also has offices on the incoming **west autobahn** (☎ 0512/573543), the **east autobahn** (☎ 0512/346474), the Kranebitter Allee (north) **autobahn exit** (☎ 0512/284991), and the **Brenner (south) autobahn** (☎ 0512/577933). Call for information on **youth hostels** (☎ 0512/346179 or 0512/346180). The booklet "Children's Hotels" (in English, available from the Tirolean tourist office) lists Tirolean hotels that cater particularly to families with children.

Travel Agencies

American Express. ✉ *Brixnerstr. 3,* ☎ *0512/582491–0,* FAX *0512/573385.* ⊙ *Weekdays 9–5:30, Sat. 9–noon.*

Visitor Information

Innsbruck's main tourist office (✉ Burggraben 3 A–6021, ☎ 0512/59850, FAX 0512/59850–7. ✍) is open daily 8–6.

The **Österreichischer Alpenverein** is the place to go for information on Alpine huts and mountaineering advice (✉ Wilhelm-Greil-Str. 15, ☎ 0512/59547–34, FAX 0512/575528). It's open weekdays 8:30–6, Saturday 9–noon.

Most small-town tourist offices have no specific street address and are accommodated in the village hall. Address letters to the Fremdenverkehrsamt (tourist office) and include the postal code of the town. On the Internet, information is available from the Web site of the Tirol Tourist Board at www.tiscover.com.

Achenkirch (✉ A–6215, ☎ 05246/6270, FAX 05246/6780). **Brixlegg** (✉ Marktstr. 6b, A–6230, ☎ 05337/62581, FAX 05337/62581). **Gerlos** (✉ A–6281, ☎ 05284/5244–0, FAX 05284/5244–24). **Imst** (✉ Johannespl. 4, A–6460, ☎ 05412/6910–0, FAX 05412/6910–8). **Ischgl** (✉ A–6561, ☎ 05444/52660, FAX 05444/5636). **Jenbach** (✉ Achenseestr. 37, A–6200, ☎ 05244/63901, FAX 05244/63552). **Kitzbühel** (✉ Hinterstadt 18, A–6370, ☎ 05356/62155, FAX 05356/62307). **Kufstein** (✉ Münchner Str. 2, A–6330, ☎ 05372/62207, FAX 05372/61455). **Landeck** (✉ Malserstr. 10, A–6500, ☎ 05442/62344, FAX 05442/67830). **Mayrhofen** (✉ Dursterstr. 225, A–6290, ☎ 05285/6760, FAX 05285/6760–33). **Obergurgl/Hochgurgl** (✉ A–6456, ☎ 05256/466, FAX 05256/353). **Rattenberg** (✉ Klosterg. 94, A–6240, ☎ 05337/63321, FAX 05337/65417). **St. Anton am Arlberg** (✉ A–6580, ☎ 05446/2269–0, FAX 05446/2532). **St. Johann in Tirol** (✉ Poststr. 2, A–6380, ☎ 05352/63335–0, FAX 05352/65200). **Schwaz** (✉ Franz-Josef-Str. 26, A–6130, ☎ 05242/63240, FAX 05242/65630). **Serfaus** (✉ Unteres Dorf 13, A–6534, ☎ 05476/6239, FAX 05476/6813). **Sölden/Ötztal** (✉ Rettenbach 288, A–6450, ☎ 05254/2212–0, FAX 05254/3131). **Tux/Lanersbach/Hintertux** (✉ A–6293 Lanersbach, ☎ 05287/8506, FAX 05287/8508). **Zell am Ziller** (✉ Dorfpl. 3a, A–6280, ☎ 05282/2281, FAX 05282/2281–80).

10 VORARLBERG

"What God has put asunder by a mountain, let no man join by a tunnel"—so said the Vorarlbergers of old. Once the Arlberg Tunnel linked Austria's westernmost province to the rest of the country, the secret was out: Vorarlberg—nicknamed the "Ländle," the "Little Province"—was really Austria's Switzerland; cheaper in some ways, perhaps less efficient in others. The world at large discovered ski slopes that rival those of Austria's neutral neighbor, gorgeous Lake Constance, and the lush forests of the Bregenzerwald. In colder months, a winter wonderland is the main lure—especially at Lech, where skiing is almost as important as being seen.

THEY SAY YOU CAN LEARN ALL ABOUT AUSTRIA just by going to the Vorarlberg, like studying the ocean in a drop of water. This postage stamp–size province seems to be Austria in miniature—it features a sampling of the best of everything the country has to offer. Music devotees descend every summer on Vorarlberg for its elegant Schubertiade—held in Feldkirch and Schwarzenberg—and on Bregenz for its famed lakeside music festival. Nature lovers head to the Bregenzerwald—a wide area of dense forests, charming valleys, and lush meadows dotted with thick clusters of red, white, and yellow Alpine flowers—a region that remains decidedly private and unostentatiously beautiful. Literature buffs arrive to see the sun set in the village of Schruns, where Hemingway spent several winters writing *The Sun Also Rises*. And merrymakers like to throng Lech and Zürs, two top ski resorts where the fragrances of hot chocolate and *Pfefferrminz Tee* mingle with the expensive perfumes worn by the jet set.

Updated by
Bonnie Dodson

Tiny Vorarlberg covers an area of less than 1,000 square mi and is the smallest (with the exception of Vienna) of Austria's federal states. As its name implies, the state lies "before the Arlberg"—that massive range of Alps, the watershed of Europe, mecca of winter sports—and forms the western tip of Austria. Until the tunnel was cut through, the Arlberg was passable only in summer; in winter, Vorarlberg was effectively cut off from the rest of the country. And while Austrians from the east may go skiing or vacation in neighboring Tirol, and although they may be well traveled, many never make it to Vorarlberg over the course of their lives. The Viennese semi-affectionately refer to Vorarlberg as the "Ländle," or "Little Province."

Nowhere in Austria will you find such determined adherence to old customs as in the villages and towns of the Vorarlberg. You'll see folk costumes on people in the street, not in museums, and your chances are good of running into a local celebration at any time of year. The province has much in common with neighboring Switzerland. Not only are the dialects similar, but the landscape flows across the border with continuity. Both peoples descended from the same ancient Germanic tribes that flourished in the 3rd century BC. Both have the same characteristics of thrift, hard work, and a deep-rooted instinct for democracy and independence. In fact, after the collapse of the Habsburg monarchy following World War I, Vorarlberg came very close to becoming a part of Switzerland. In 1919, 80% of the populace voted in favor of negotiating with the Swiss to join the confederation, but the St. Germain peace conference put an end to such ideas, and Vorarlberg remained Austrian.

Pleasures and Pastimes

Dining
Vorarlberg's cuisine is lighter than those of neighboring Tirol and the rest of Austria. Fresh ingredients from the region's farms, lakes, and forests are the norm, with an emphasis on dairy products from the cows that graze the mountains and meadows of the region. Be sure to try a slab of *Vorarlberg Alpine* from one of the huge rounds, or any of the other 30 different varieties of cheese produced at local farms. Cheese is also added to soups and noodle dishes and fried in fritters. Fresh river trout is caught in the waters of Lake Constance and in the surrounding lakes and streams. You'll see fish fried, broiled, and steamed on restaurant menus throughout Vorarlberg. In small towns throughout the region, restaurants are often the dining rooms of country inns.

CATEGORY	COST*
$$$$	over AS500 (€36)
$$$	AS300–AS500 (€21–€36)
$$	AS150–AS300 (€11–€20)
$	under AS150 (€11)

for a typical three-course meal with a glass of house wine, service, and tax, but excluding 3–5% tip

Lodging

Vorarlberg has loads of accommodation options, from local farmhouses where you share chores to ski chalets high on the slopes of the Western Alps to a converted castle-hotel perched above the Bodensee. In ski resorts in Vorarlberg, hotel rates in season are often well above the range of our chart. At most of those hotels, the price includes a mandatory two meals a day, and often credit cards are not accepted. The tourist offices can usually help lead you to more moderate lodgings in private houses. In summer you can often find bargain rates at 50% of the winter tariff. In some towns, such as Bregenz, summer is the high season and may put the establishment into the next-higher price category.

CATEGORY	LECH/ZÜRS*	OTHER TOWNS*
$$$$	over AS2,200	over AS1,200
$$$	AS1,500–AS2,200	AS900–AS1,200
$$	AS900–AS1,500	AS600–AS900
$	under AS900	under AS600

Per person per night for a standard double room in high season, including breakfast (in resorts, including one additional meal in winter), service charge of 10%, and tax. To compute Euro equivalencies, divide AS amount by 13.76.

✍ *following the text of a review is your signal that the property has a Web site, where you will find details and, usually, images; for a link, visit www.fodors.com/urls.*

Skiing

One of the main attractions of a stay in Vorarlberg is the world-class skiing available in Austria's Western Alps. After all, modern ski techniques were developed in Vorarlberg by local Hannes Schneider, who founded the first ski school in Arlberg in the 1920s. From intimate, rustic resorts to the glamour of Lech and Zürs, the province has slopes to suit all tastes and levels, and fewer crowds than in the rest of the country.

The Sound—and Sights—of Music

Festival fever in the Vorarlberg every summer summons the faithful to some of the finest concerts in Austria. Grand opera is offered lakeside at the **Bregenzer Festspiele** (Bregenz Summer Music Festival), while elegant recitals of the **Schubertiade** take place in the neighboring towns of Feldkirch and Schwarzenberg. The Bregenz festival is famed for its floating stage—in truth, a group of man-made islands mounted on pilings. Now there is a new indoor theater to accommodate the festivities. In Feldkirch, Schubert *Lieder* lovers come to hear fine musicians offer homage to the great Biedermeier-era composer, as well as Mozart, Beethoven, and other composers during a 10-day period in late June. Equally talented performers are in concert in Schwarzenberg in May, August, and September.

Exploring Vorarlberg

This chapter divides Vorarlberg into three sections. Our first exploring tour takes you through Bregenz, the region's historic capital. Then, we head out to the glorious countryside, taking in the legendary Bregenzerwald to Bludenz, following the Ill Valley to Feldkirch, and heading north again to Bregenz. Here, you can relax in a true backwoods atmosphere while enjoying the beautiful, if somewhat hair-raising, country roads as you pass through mountain hamlets, all with an Old World charm and few discovered by the guidebooks. The last excursion takes in the Arlberg ski resorts.

Great Itineraries

Numbers in the text correspond to numbers in the margin and on the Vorarlberg map.

IF YOU HAVE 2 DAYS

If you only have a weekend to visit Vorarlberg, head to the capital of ⊞ **Bregenz** ① on the shore of the Bodensee (Lake Constance). Spend a day wandering around the lakeshore and the lovely, romantic remains of the once-fortified medieval town. The next day take a boat ride into neighboring Switzerland or Germany. Around the lake are extensive hiking and biking trails for those who'd rather see the sights under their own steam.

IF YOU HAVE 5 DAYS

Visit the resorts in the Arlberg and the Montafon Valley, which have attracted such notaries as Ernest Hemingway and the late Princess Diana. Start your trip in ⊞ **Schruns** ⑪, visiting Hemingway's haunts. Now, you're ready for the Arlberg resorts. On your second day, head up north for **Stuben** ⑬, the hometown of skiing pioneer Hannes Schneider, moving on for your next overnight in ⊞ **Zürs** ⑭. After a little hobnobbing with film stars and royalty, spend your final two overnights in Vorarlberg's most famous ski resort, ⊞ **Lech** ⑮.

IF YOU HAVE 7 DAYS

If you have more time in Vorarlberg, begin by exploring the natural marvels of the **Bregenzerwald** and the history-rich sights of ⊞ **Bregenz** ①. After two overnights in Bregenz, you can venture off the beaten track on your third day by stopping for discount shopping in Egg on your way to the picturesque town of **Schwarzenberg** ②. Then, on your fourth day, head to ⊞ **Bezau** ③ to savor the beauty of the surrounding forests and mountains with a hike into the hills. That afternoon, visit breathtaking **Damüls** ④, where flowers blanket the hillsides during the summer and great skiing welcomes visitors in winter. Head for ⊞ **Bludenz** ⑤ to explore one of the five magical valleys surrounding the town. The fifth day, follow the Ill Valley to the medieval town of ⊞ **Feldkirch** ⑦, and spend two days meandering through the narrow, winding streets admiring the burgher homes and castle from an earlier age when lords and ladies peopled the province. Make a stop in **Hohenems** ⑧ on your last day for a visit to the local Jewish Museum and **Dornbirn** ⑨, famous for its textiles, on your way back to the capital.

When to Tour Vorarlberg

Vorarlberg has something to offer visitors during every season. If you're in the province during warm weather, make sure to stop in Bregenz when the city comes to life with the Bregenzer Festspiele (Bregenz Music Festival). Boat excursions to Switzerland and Germany are also a must. History buffs will enjoy the sights in Bregenz, Bludenz, and especially Feldkirch. And sports enthusiasts will love the wealth of hiking, biking, sailing, and fishing that is available around the region. Of course, if you travel to Vorarlberg during the winter months, then fasten on your bindings and head to the slopes.

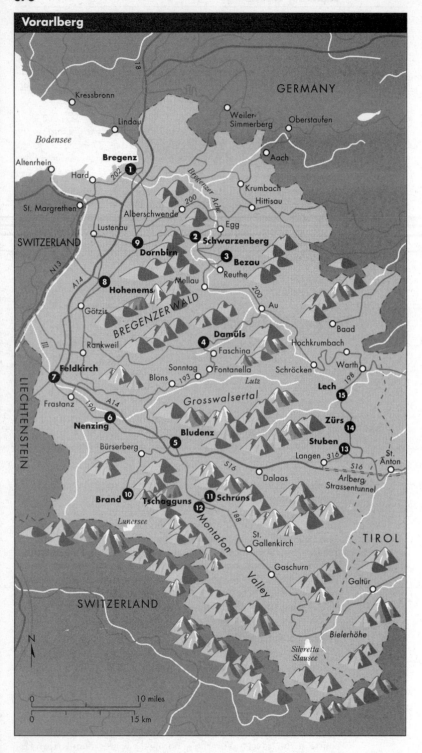

Vorarlberg

BREGENZ

❶ *150 km (90 mi) west of Innsbruck, 660 km (409 mi) west of Vienna, 120 km (75 mi) east of Zürich, 193 km (120 mi) southwest of Munich.*

Lying along the southeastern shore of the Bodensee (Lake Constance) with the majestic Pfänder as its backdrop, Bregenz is where Vorarlbergers come to make merry, especially in summer. Along the lakeside beach and public pool, cabanas and candy floss lure starched collars to let loose, while nearby an enormous floating stage is the site for performances of grand opera and orchestral works (Verdi, Rimski-Korsakov, Wagner, and Strauss are just some of the composers who have recently been featured) under the stars. Bregenz is the capital of Vorarlberg and has been the seat of the provincial government since 1819. The upper town has maintained a charming Old World character, but the lower part of the city fronting the lake's edge is largely unimpressive. Unfortunately, the waterfront is cut off by railroad tracks, though there is a strip of pedestrian walkway that hugs the shoreline.

★ Bregenz is pleasant at any time of year, but the best time to visit is during the **Bregenzer Festspiele** (Bregenz Music Festival; ☞ Nightlife and the Arts, *below*). Acclaimed artists from around the world perform operas, operettas, and musical comedies on the festival's floating stage, part of the Festspiel- und Kongresshaus (Festival Hall and Congress Center) complex. In front of the stage, the orchestra pit is built on a jetty, while the audience of 6,000 is safely accommodated on the 30-tier amphitheater, built on dry land—a unique and memorable setting you are sure to enjoy. Reserve your tickets in advance, as performances sell out early.

The lake itself is a prime attraction, with boat trips available to nearby Switzerland and Germany. Don't forget to bring along your passport. The **Bodensee White Fleet** ferries offer several trip options. You can travel to the "flower isle" of Mainau or make a crossing to Konstanz, Germany, with stops at Lindau, Friedrichshafen, and Meersburg. The longest round-trip excursion is the Drei-Länder Rundfahrt, which includes stops in Germany and Switzerland. The ferries have different operating schedules, but most run only in the summer months. The Mainau excursion is the exception, running from May to mid-September. ⊠ *Bodenseeschiffahrt Ticket Office, Seestr. 4,* ☎ *05574/42868,* FAX *05574/6755–520.*

Most of the important sights of Bregenz can be seen in the course of a walk of about two hours. The town's neoclassical main **Post Office** (⊠ 5 Seestr.) was built in 1893 by Viennese architect Friedrich Setz. Because of the marshy conditions of the land, the post office is built on wood pilings to prevent it from sinking. Behind the post office, the **Nepomuk-Kapelle** (⊠ Kaspar Moosbrugger Pl.) was built in 1757 to serve the city's fishermen and sailors. Today the town's Hungarian community celebrates mass here. To the right of the Nepomuk-Kapelle along Kornmarktstrasse is the **Gasthof Kornmesser,** built in 1720 and a gorgeous example of a Baroque town house. Just after the alley simply marked THEATER along Kornmarktstrasse you'll reach the **Theater am Kornmarkt,** originally constructed in 1838, when Bregenz was still an important commercial port, as a grain storehouse; in 1954, the granary was converted into a 700-seat theater.

Next door to the Theater am Kornmarkt is the **Landesmuseum** (Provincial Museum), where relics from Brigantium, the Roman administrative city that once stood where Bregenz is today, are housed. Gothic and Romanesque ecclesiastical works are also on display in this turn-of-the-century building. ⊠ *Kornmarktpl. 1,* ☎ *05574/46050.* 🎟 *AS20.* ☉ *Sept.–June, Tues.–Sun. 9–noon and 2–5; July–Aug., daily 9–noon and 2–5.*

Originally used as a grain warehouse when it was built in 1685, the **Rathaus,** on Rathausgasse, was turned over to the city in 1720. The ornate facade and tower were added to the city hall in 1898. Next door to the Rathaus is the **Seekapelle** (Lake Chapel), topped with an onion dome. The chapel was put up over the graves of a band of Swiss whose 1408 attempt to incorporate Bregenz into Switzerland was defeated. Behind the Seekapelle is the traditional **Gösser Braugaststätte** (⊠ Anton-Schneider-G. 1). This might be just the moment for a cool beer, a cup of coffee, or the daily vegetarian special. Try to get a table in the Zirbenstüble, with its beautifully carved wood-paneled walls and ceiling.

From Deuringstrasse, which borders on Anton-Schneider-Gasse, take a left on Belrupstrasse, and you'll find the **Pfänderbahn** cable car, which takes you up to the 3,460-ft peak overlooking the city. You can see four countries—and almost 240 Alpine peaks—from here, and the restaurant is open June–mid-September. Children will enjoy a 30-minute circular hike to a small outdoor zoo, with deer, Alpine goats, and wild boar. Admission is free. An added attraction is the **Adlerwarte** (☎ 0663/053040), where eagles and other birds of prey demonstrate their prowess in free flight May–September at 11 and 2:30; admission is AS46. ☎ *05574/42160.* 🎟 *Round-trip AS106 Oct. 14–Mar. 21, AS125 Apr. 1–Oct. 13.* ☉ *Daily 9–7; service on hr and ½ hr. Closed last 2 wks of Nov.*

Off of Belrupstrasse, the **Herz-Jesu Kirche** (Sacred Heart Church) was built in 1908 in brick Gothic style. The stained-glass windows by Martin Hausle are especially bright and colorful. Go left from Belrupstrasse on to Maurachgasse. Walking up Maurachgasse, you'll reach the **Stadtsteig** guarding the entrance to the old city, which bears the emblem of a Celtic-Roman equine goddess (the original is now housed in the Landesmuseum; ☞ *above*). Inside the gate are the coats of arms of the dukes of Bregenz and the dukes of Montfort, the latter crest now the Vorarlberg provincial emblem.

Next to the Stadtsteig, explore the interior of the tiny **Martinskirche** (⊠ Martinspl.) for its fine 14th-century frescoes. The **Martinsturm** (⊠ Martinsg. 3b) boasts the largest onion dome in Central Europe. The tower (1599–1602) has become a symbol of Bregenz and was the first Baroque construction on Lake Constance; it is closed on Monday October–April. Remains of the ancient **city wall** are to the right of the tower on Martinsgasse. The coats of arms of several noble Bregenz families can still be seen on the house standing next to the wall's remains.

Angle on along Martinsgasse to Graf-Wilhelm-Strasse and the brightly shuttered **Altes Rathaus** (Old City Hall). The ornate half-timber construction was completed in 1622. Behind the Altes Rathaus on Eponastrasse stands the former **Gesellenspital** (Journeymen's Hospital); remnants of a fresco still visible on its wall depict St. Christopher, St. Peter, and a kneeling abbot. At the bottom of Eponastrasse is **Ehreguta Square,** named for the legendary woman who saved Bregenz during the Appenzell War of 1407–09. Ehreguta was a maid who overheard the enemy planning an invasion of Bregenz. Discovered listening at the door, she was warned that she would be killed if she breathed a word to anybody. Torn between protecting the city and saving her own life, she decided to tell all to the fire blazing in the kitchen one night, but spoke loud enough for others to overhear and take action to save Bregenz. The **Montfortbrunnen** (fountain) in the center of Ehreguta Square is the scene of a ritual washing of wallets and change purses, when carnival jesters clean out their empty pockets and spin tales about the events of the previous year. The fountain honors the minnesinger Hugo von Montfort, who was born in the city in 1357. The small parallel streets running uphill from the Ehreguta Square roughly outline the boundaries of the town in the Middle Ages. Hidden around the corner of the building at the beginning of Georgen-Schilde-Strasse are the **Meissnerstiege** (Meissner steps), named after a local poet, that lead from the old city to the **parish church of St. Gallus.** At the bottom of the steps follow Schlossbergstrasse up the hill to the church, which combines Romanesque, Gothic, and rococo elements. The interior is decorated simply with pretty pastel colors instead of the usual excessive gilt. Empress Maria Theresa donated the money for the high altarpiece. You'll notice the monarch's features on one of the shepherdesses depicted there. From the hill outside the church there is a wonderful view of the southwestern wall of the Old City, including the **Beckenturm,** the 16th-century tower once used as a prison and named after bakers imprisoned there who had baked rolls that were too small. The **Künstlerhaus Thurn und Taxis** (⊠ Gallusstr. 8) was owned by the regal Thurn und Taxis family until 1915. The building, erected in 1848, now contains a modern gallery. The **Thurn und Taxispark** contains rare trees and plants from around the world.

☺ Children and parents alike will enjoy a ride on the **Hohentwiel,** a restored old-time paddle-wheel steamship that cruises Lake Constance out of Hard, 8 km (5 mi) southwest of Bregenz. Sailings are scheduled irregularly; call for information (☎ 05574/48983, FAX 05574/42467–86).

Dining and Lodging

$$$ ✕ **Ilge-Weinstube.** This cozy, intimate *Keller* (cellar) is Old Bregenz at its best. Rustic decor in the basement of a 300-year-old house close to the oldest section of town draws the youngish "in" crowd. The atmosphere alone makes the Ilge-Weinstube worth a visit. ⊠ *Maurachstr. 6,* ☎ *05574/43609. AE, DC, MC, V. Closed Mon.*

$$ ✕ **Maurachbund.** The elegant furnishings and soft lighting make dining at this restaurant an enjoyable, intimate experience. In summer, diners can choose to eat outside on the back terrace. The menu features a wide variety of fish to choose from as well as traditional Austrian dishes. ⊠ *Maurachg. 11,* ☎ *05574/44020. MC, V.*

$$ ✕ **Wirtshaus am See.** This half-timbered house with a gabled roof is right on the shore of Lake Constance, next to the floating stage used for the Bregenz Festival. The menu has the usual Austrian favorites from schnitzel to *Zwiebelrostbraten* (a skirt steak topped with crispy fried onions). The main attraction here is the spectacular lake view. You can watch the world go by from the restaurant's extensive outdoor terrace. ⊠ *Seeanlagen,* ☎ *05574/42210,* FAX *05574/42210–4. No credit cards. Closed Jan.–Feb.*

$ ✕ **Café Götze.** Locals frequent this small, unpretentious café because it's known to have the best pastries in town. The location halfway between the waterfront and the Old City is convenient. ⊠ *Kaiserstr. 9,* ☎ *05574/44523. Closed Sun.*

$ ✕ **Goldener Hirschen.** Allegedly the oldest tavern in Bregenz and close
★ to the Old City, this rustic restaurant offers delicious traditional fare and drink in a lively atmosphere. The ambitious chef occasionally highlights certain foods, as during the oft-repeated Noodle Week, when diners can choose from a special menu offering a mouthwatering selection of pasta dishes. Particularly good is the spicy spaghetti in a tomato, onion, bacon, and red pepper sauce, or spinach tagliatelle with grilled turkey in a tomato cream sauce with Gorgonzola gratiné. ⊠ *Kirchstr. 8,* ☎ *05574/42815. AE, DC, MC, V. Closed Tues. and 2 wks in Sept.*

$$$$ ✕🏨 **Deuring-Schlössle.** This 400-year-old castle with its Baroque tower
★ has inspired paintings by Turner and Schiele. Rooms are tastefully furnished and have polished wood floors and lovely wainscoting. The owner
is also the chef of the hotel's restaurant (closed Monday lunch), which
is considered to be among the best in Austria. Specialties include beautifully presented pike-perch on a bed of pumpkin puree with baby asparagus. If you want a blow-out meal in a lovely, romantic setting, this
is the place to go. But be prepared for inflated prices, small portions,
and inattentive service. ⊠ *Ehregutapl. 4, A–6900,* ☎ *05574/47800,*
🏿 *05574/47800–80. 13 rooms. Restaurant. AE, DC, MC, V.*

$$–$$$ 🏨 **Mercure.** Adjacent to the Festival Hall and housing the casino, the
house is typical of the chain: functionally modern, all rooms with balconies. Rooms looking out over the lake are best. ⊠ *Pl. der Wiener
Symphoniker, A–6900,* ☎ *05574/46100–0,* 🏿 *05574/47412. 94 rooms.
2 restaurants, bar. AE, DC, MC, V.*

$–$$ 🏨 **Weisses Kreuz.** This traditional, family-run, turn-of-the-century
house has been renovated with care and charm and is now a Best Western hotel. The location on the edge of the pedestrian zone is central,
and the staff is particularly friendly. The rooms are comfortable and
modern; those overlooking the private park out back are quieter. ⊠
Römerstr. 5, A–6900, ☎ *05574/4988–0,* 🏿 *05574/4988–67. 44 rooms.
Restaurant, bar. AE, DC, MC, V. Closed Dec. 25–mid-Jan.*

Nightlife and the Arts

The cultural year starts with the **Bregenzer Frühling,** the spring music
and dance festival that runs from mid-April to mid-May. Information
and tickets are available through the tourist office (⊠ Bahnhofstr. 14,
A–6900, ☎ 05574/4959). The big cultural event in Bregenz is the **Bregenzer Festspiele** (Bregenz Music Festival), held mid-July to mid-Au-
gust. For information and tickets, contact the festival office (⊠ Box
311, A–6901, ☎ 05574/4076, 🏿 05574/407400,✆) Tickets are also
available at the Bregenz tourist office. In the event of rain, the concert
performance is moved indoors to the massive Festival Hall and Congress Center adjacent to the floating stage (it can accommodate at least
1,800 of the 6,900 seats usually available for performances on the floating lake stage). Travel and performance packages are available through
Vorarlberg Landesreisebüro (⊠ A–6850, Dornbirn, ☎ 05572/27762–
14, 🏿 05572/27762–49.)

For the first time in nearly 100 years, a new modern art museum, the
Kunsthaus, has opened in Austria. Designed by Swiss architect Peter
Zumthor, the scaled glass-and-concrete building creates a feeling of space
and light with an innovative feature of 8-ft openings between each story,
which allows sunlight to enter the translucent glass through the ceiling. This marvel of design bathes each gallery in natural light in spite
of concrete walls. ⊠ *Karl-Tizian-Pl., A–6900,* ☎ *05574/485940,* 🏿
05574/485948. ☉ *Open Tues.–Sun. 10–6; Thurs. 10–9.*

The **casino** is the site of much activity (⊠ Pl. der Wiener Symphoniker, A–
6900, ☎ 05574/45127–0). The house opens at 3 PM. Bring your passport.

Outdoor concerts are held during the summer months in the horseshoe-
shape **Music Pavilion** at the end of the promenade on the lake.

Outdoor Activities and Sports

Bicycling

The area around the lake offers superb cycling, and trails have been
laid out to offer varying distances and degrees of difficulty. Maps and
rental bikes are available; ask the tourist office for details.

Skiing

Skiers head for the **Pfänder** mountain, in Bregenz's backyard, which has a cable tramway and two drag lifts. The views are stunning from atop the peak, stretching as far as the Black Forest and the Swiss Alps. The runs (☎ 05572/4216–0) are closed during the second and third weeks of November.

Water Sports

With the vast lake at its doorstep, Bregenz offers a variety of water sports. You can even learn to sail, although a minimum of two weeks is required for a full course at **Segelschule Lochau.** ✉ *Box 7, Alte Fähre,* ☎ *05574/52247.*

THROUGH THE BREGENZERWALD TO BLUDENZ AND FELDKIRCH

Directly behind Bregenz lies the **Bregenzerwald** (Bregenz Forest), a beautiful area studded with densely wooded highlands, sweeping valleys, and lush meadows radiant with wildflowers in summer, all set against a fabulous backdrop of majestic, towering Alps. As you go along, you come across one town after another with *au*—meaning "meadow"—in its name: As the area developed, names were given to the meadows in which settlements were established. Here you will see the Vorarlbergers as they really are. In the little villages, you can spot women still wearing the handsome, stiffly starched folk dress of their ancestors. On festive occasions the girls wear a golden headdress shaped like a small crown, and the married women a black or white pointed cap. Men's costume is worn by musicians in the local bands (which seems to include nearly everyone), with the shape of the cap and the color of various parts of the clothing differing from town to town. Secure in their mountains and, until quite recently, feeling no call to mix with the outside world, Vorarlbergers have remained true to the habits of their forebears.

To reach the Bregenzerwald, travelers can take one of the daily bus services that leave Bregenz or Dornbirn on the main line from Feldkirch to Lindau in Germany—there are no train routes servicing the area. By car, leave Bregenz headed south on Route 190; then make a sharp left after crossing the river on a road marked to Wolfurt and Schwarzach. About 21 km (13 mi) farther, at Alberschwende, you'll come to Route 200; follow the signs for **Egg,** where you should note the old country houses before heading on to Schwarzenberg. If you haven't bought your Alpine hat before you get to Egg, go to the **Capo** hat and cap factory outlet here (✉ Mühle 534, ☎ 05512/2381–0). It's open weekdays 9–noon, 1–5, and sells fashionable headgear as well as Alpine styles.

Schwarzenberg

❷ *31 km (19 mi) southeast of Bregenz.*

One of the region's most colorful villages is Schwarzenberg. The artist Angelika Kauffmann (1741–1807), who spent most of her life in England and Italy, still considered this her home. Even though she became one of the most renowned female artists of the 18th century, few people in Austria east of the Arlberg mountains knew of her until her picture appeared on a new issue of Austrian currency a few years ago. You can see several of her larger works in the Baroque village church, including a painting of the 12 apostles she did at 16, and an altar painting of the Annunciation from about 1800 (the Landesmuseum in Bregenz has her portrait of the Duke of Wellington). The Schwarzenberg **Heimatmuseum** (✉ Hof 765, ☎ 05512/3166) has a room dedicated to Angelika Kauffmann. It's open May–September, Tuesday, Thursday, and Saturday 2–4; October, Thursday and Saturday or by appointment; admission is AS35.

Bezau

③ *4 km (2½ mi) south of Schwarzenberg, 35 km (23 mi) east of Bregenz.*

According to local legend, Bezau's district hall was built on tall columns and was accessible only by ladder. Once the councillors were gathered inside, the ladder was removed until they came to a decision. The **Heimat-museum,** slightly south of the center, contains exhibits on the town's interesting past, including local folk costumes. ✉ *Ellenbogen 181,* ☎ *05514/2559.* ✉ *AS30.* ☉ *June, Tues. and Thurs. 2–4; July–Sept., Tues., Thurs., and Sat. 3:30–5:30, Wed. 10–noon; Oct.–May, Tues. 2–3.*

☞ At the **Bregenzerwald Museumsbahn,** visitors can see all that is left of the onetime narrow-gauge railroad that ran from Bregenz to Bezau and was abandoned in 1980. The museum has managed to preserve more than 6 km (almost 4 mi) of track to Bersbuch, beyond Schwarzenberg, and runs diesel and steam excursions. ✉ *Bahnhof 147,* ☎ *05513/6192,* ℻ *05513/6192–4.* ✉ *Round-trip by steam AS80, by diesel AS60.* ☉ *June–mid-Oct., weekends at 11, 2, and 3:30; hours vary in Nov.–Dec. Closed Jan.–May.*

Dining and Lodging

$$ ✕ **Gasthof Engel.** The Gasthof Engel has some of the best Italian food
★ you'll find in Austria. Fresh regional ingredients are served with elegant simplicity here. A whole page of fresh pasta dishes is featured on the menu as well as traditional meat and fish dishes. The wine list has a fine selection of Austrian and Italian vintages. The service is also exceptional; you'll feel like a long-lost member of the family. ✉ *Pl. 29,* ☎ *05514/2203. No credit cards. Closed Wed. and Nov.*

$$ ☷ **Gasthof Gams.** Dating from the 17th century, this friendly house
★ in the center of town offers every comfort and is a great base for exploring. The rooms have an attractive country-rustic decor, and the hotel welcomes families. ✉ *Pl. 44, A–6870,* ☎ *05514/2220,* ℻ *05514/2220–24. 22 rooms, 5 suites. Restaurant, bar, pool, sauna, tennis court, exercise room. No credit cards. Closed Nov.–mid-Dec.*

Outdoor Activities and Sports

SKIING

Bezau has four regular trails for cross-country skiers and one lift that takes downhill skiers up to the 5,300-ft Baumgartenhöhe. This small area is part of the Bregenzerwald Ski Region. A regional pass gives you access to 135 lifts in Bregenzerwald, Grossen Walsertal, and Lechtal in Tirol, encompassing 282 km (160 mi) of prepared slopes. For details on facilities, contact the Bregenzerwald tourism office (✉ Postfach 29, A–6863 Egg, ☎ 05512/2365, ℻ 05512/3010, ✍).

Damüls

④ *14 km (9 mi) south of Bezau, 59 km (37 mi) southeast of Bregenz.*

If you turn right onto Route 193 at Au, you'll be on the way leading to Damüls—the road is narrow, with a 14% gradient at one point, but when you reach the town you'll agree the climb was worth it. You're at 4,640 ft, the top of the Bregenzerwald. This is great skiing country in winter; for information on facilities, contact the Bregenzerwald tourism office (✉ Postfach 29, A–6863 Egg, ☎ 05512/2365, ℻ 05512/3010, ✍). There are enough slopes and lifts, and the crowds are generally elsewhere. In summer the area is knee-deep in wildflowers, but don't pick them; it's against the law. Check the frescoes in the parish church, which date from 1490, just after the church was built, but were rediscovered under later plaster only about 40 years ago.

En Route   The **Grosswalsertal** (Great Walliser Valley) is extremely scenic. As you start the descent from Damüls heading toward Bludenz along Route 193, look across at the St. Gerold Monastery to your right, but after reaching Blons, keep your eyes on the road: It's full of hairpin turns.

Bludenz

⑤ *22 km (13 mi) southwest of Damüls, 60 km (37 mi) south of Bregenz.*

Bludenz rests in the middle of five mountain valleys, sheltered in part by the Muttersberg peak, nicknamed "the Sun Balcony." The narrow streets of the old city are tightly packed with 17th-century houses and relics of the ancient town defenses, while the mountains present with ski lifts, good slopes, and hiking trails. People here are pleased when you ask for a hot chocolate instead of coffee. Bludenz is a major chocolate-producing center, as you may detect if the wind is coming from the direction of the factories. The town, adorned with houses and pergolas that seem more Italian than Austrian, is a major transportation crossroads, serviced by frequent bus and train routes.

Dining and Lodging

$–$$ ⊞ **Schlosshotel.** Perched on a hill above the castle and overlooking the town, this modern hotel with balconies offers splendid views of the Rätikon mountain range to the south, on the Swiss border; ask for a room in front above the café terrace. The pseudo-rustic decor of the house continues into the guest rooms, whose clean lines and modern furnishings are, in fact, attractive. ⊠ *Schlosspl. 5, A–6700,* ☎ *05552/63016–0,* ℻ *05552/63016–8. 42 rooms. Restaurant, café, miniature golf. AE, DC, MC, V.*

Nenzing

⑥ *12 km (7 mi) northwest of Bludenz.*

Nenzing is the jumping-off spot for the wildly romantic Gamperdonatal, the valley of the Meng river, which rises toward peaks that are 6,500 ft or higher. The valley is hikable, but it's barely passable for cars. The top of the valley is called Nenzinger Himmel, or "Nenzing Heaven."

Feldkirch

⑦ *15 km (9 mi) northwest of Nenzing, 33 km (22 mi) southwest of Bregenz.*

Feldkirch is Vorarlberg's oldest town, with parts dating from the Middle Ages that contribute greatly to the town's romantic character. Picturesque arcades line the narrow main street, and wrought-iron oriels festoon some of the quainter town houses. Marvelous towers and onion domes top some of the buildings, watched over by an assembly of imposing stone blockhouses, which compose the Schattenburg castle complex just above the town.

A number of luminary figures have spent time in Feldkirch. James Joyce stopped for several months en route from Italy to Switzerland, saying later that he formed the basis for *Ulysses* here and that he gathered material for *Finnegan's Wake*. There is a plaque honoring him at the train station, where he spent hours every day observing people and trains for his writing. As a promising student, Sir Arthur Conan Doyle attended the Jesuit boarding school, Stella Matutina, which is now the Provincial Conservatory of Music. He wrote two short stories for the local newspaper, which are stored in the archives. And Thomas Mann used the same boarding school as a setting in *The Magic Mountain*.

Although the composer Schubert had no ties to the town, Feldkirch is now (along with Schwarzenberg) home to the annual **Schubertiade** (☞ Nightlife and the Arts, *below*), a small but elegant music festival that has won world renown for the quality of performers on view—including Jessye Norman and Cecelia Bartoli—with events offered in mid to late June.

An easy walk around the center of Feldkirch will take you to most of the town's highlights. Start at the **St. Nicholas Cathedral** on Domplatz. A mystical light in this church, built in 1478, comes through the stained-glass windows. Walk toward the river, past the district government offices (once a Jesuit monastery) and the bishop's palace, a block back of Herrengasse, to the **Katzenturm** (literally, "cats' tower"; figuratively, "the clergy"), reconstructed by Emperor Maximilian I. This is the most prominent remnant of the town's fortifications and now holds the 7½-ton town bell. Down the Hirschgraben, you'll come to the Chur gate and beside it the **Frauenkirche** (Church of Our Lady), originally dedicated to St. Sebastian in 1473. Now, for the **towers**: Head down Montfortgasse to where the Wasserturm (water tower) and the Diebsturm (thieves' tower) stand guard over the Schillerstrasse bridge. Wander down Vorstadt to the Pulverturm (powder tower) and across to the Mühlenturm (mill tower), whose contrast to the modern Leonhardsplatz is considerable. Turning left, you'll find the St. Johann Church (1218) and, behind it, the **market square** (market days Tuesday and Saturday). The square is the site of the annual wine festival during the second week of July. Across the pedestrian zone you'll come to Liechtenstein Palace, once the administrative center. On your right is the **Rathaus** of 1493, with its frescoes and paneled rooms.

Overlooking Feldkirch, in the Neustadt, is the 12th-century **Schattenburg**, a massive castle that now houses a museum devoted to the decorative arts and armor. Arcades climb up the hill to frame the castle in an intriguing vista. ✉ *Burgg. 1,* ☎ *05522/71982.* ▣ *AS25.* ☉ *Dec.–Oct., Tues.–Sun. 9–noon and 1–5;.*

Dining and Lodging

$$$ **Gasthof Lingg.** Since 1878 this family-run inn has been known for delicious meals. Seasonal specialties, such as wild game, venison, and asparagus, are featured. Located near the Katzenturm in the Old City, the building is notable for the murals on the facade which the Lingg family commissioned in 1888. ✉ *Am Marktpl.,* ☎ *05522/72062,* ℻ *05522/72062–6. AE, DC, MC, V. Closed Mon. and 1 wk. in July, 2 wks. in Feb.*

$$$ ✕ **Schäfle.** Tucked away in the heart of the Old City, this Gasthaus offers atmosphere and food more typical of that in the countryside. The tables are elegantly set, and you can expect such regional fare as tongue, beef fillet, or perch from Lake Constance, all with delicate sauces and a fine touch. ✉ *Naflastr. 3,* ☎ *05522/72203–0,* ℻ *05522/72203–17. No credit cards. Closed Sun. and mid-Dec.–mid-Jan. No lunch Mon.*

$$$ ✕▣ **Central Löwen.** The rooms are large and comfortable but lacking a bit in the charm department. However, the hotel staff is friendly and outgoing. A steam room and sauna are on the premises to help you relax. The hotel's restaurant has a huge selection of Austrian and international favorites. The schnitzel is especially good. ✉ *Schlossgraben 13, A–6800,* ☎ *05522/72070–0,* ℻ *05522/72070–5. 68 rooms. Restaurant, sauna, steam room. DC, MC, V.*

$$ 🏠 **Alpenrose.** This charming old burgher's house in the center of the
★ Old City has been renovated outside and in and offers unusually per-
sonal service. Rooms are tastefully done in period furnishings. The house
is part of the Best Western group. ⊠ *Roseng. 6, A–6800,* ☎ *05522/
72175,* ℻ *05522/72175–5. 24 rooms. AE, DC, MC, V.*

Nightlife and the Arts

The **Schubertiade** presents an impressive series of concerts devoted to
Franz Schubert and his circle, offered in churches, castles, and auditori-
ums in Feldkirch during June, and in nearby Schwarzenberg in May and
September. Everyone from Vladimir Ashkenazy to Dietrich Fischer-
Dieskau has performed here, starring along with members of the Vienna
Philharmonic and Vienna Symphony. ⊠ *Schubertiade GmbH, Schweiz-
erstr. 1, A–6845, Hohenems,* ☎ *05576/72091,* ℻ *05576/75450.* ✑

Hohenems

❽ *9 km (5½ mi) northeast of Feldkirch, 24 km (15 mi) southwest of Bre-
genz.*

"The antiquity of Hohenems is so apparent, so forceful, it looms like
a presence, a mysterious knight, armored cap-a-pie, visor lowered,"
observed James Reynolds in his 1956 book *Panorama of Austria.* Ho-
henems is a town dominated by castles, both ruined (the 12th-century
Alt-Ems citadel atop the Schlossberg) and ravishing, especially the
Schloss Glopper and the castle of Prince-Archbishop Marcus Sitticus
von Hohenems, with its elegantly ornate Rittersaal. Empress Elisabeth
of Austria used to stay in this castle toward the end of her tragically
shortened life and, in fact, used the title of Countess Hohenems when
she traveled "anonymously" around the world. The **parish church,** ded-
icated to St. Carlo Borromeo and rebuilt in 1797, has a noted painted
altarpiece of the Coronation of the Virgin.

In 1617 a decree was signed that welcomed Jews to Hohenems and al-
lowed them to live and work in peace. For the next 300 years a large
Jewish community thrived here, but by 1938 fewer than 20 Jews re-
mained. The **Jüdisches Museum** (Jewish Museum), housed in the Villa
Heimann-Rosenthal, has a large library, as well as photographs and
historical documents on display. ⊠ *Schweizerstr. 5,* ☎ *05576/3989.*
▣ *AS40.* ☉ *Tues., Thurs.–Sun. 10–5, Wed. 10–9.*

Dornbirn

❾ *4 km (2½ mi) northeast of Hohenems, 13 km (8 mi) southwest of
Bregenz.*

Dornbirn, the industrial center of Vorarlberg, is known as the "city of
textiles." The annual Dornbirn Fair, held in early September to tie in
with the Bregenz Music Festival, shows a range of goods and tech-
nologies, but textiles are especially featured.

Dining

$$$ ✗ **Rotes Haus.** The "red" in the name of this 1639 gabled wood house
★ in the center of town refers to bull's blood, originally used as pigment
for the facade, which is still basically red, with decorative panels. Traditional cuisine is served here in a charming series of small rooms. You'll
find lamb, game, and fish on the menu. ⊠ *Marktpl. 13,* ☎ *05572/31555,*
℻ *05572/31625. AE, DC, MC, V. Closed Sun.*

THE ARLBERG AND MONTAFON RESORTS

The Western Alps are a haven for those who love the great outdoors. It's also a region that provides getaway space and privacy—Ernest Hemingway came to Schruns to write *The Sun Also Rises* and, more recently, the late Princess Diana came to Lech with William and Harry to escape from the media. In the spring, summer, and fall, travelers delight in riding, tennis, swimming and, of course, hiking the Montafon Valley, which is dominated by the "Matterhorn of Austria," the Zimba peak, and probably the most attractive of Vorarlberg's many tourist-frequented valleys. When the first snowflakes begin to fall, skiers head to the hills to take advantage of the Arlberg mountain range, the highest in the Lechtal Alps. If you want to avoid the crowds that can clog Austria's other resorts, keep in mind that Lech and Zürs are resorts where the seeing is almost as important as the skiing. If you're traveling by train, Langen is the stop closest to the ski resorts; Route S16/316 takes you by car from Bludenz to Langen and beyond to Route 198 heading north.

Brand

🔟 *70 km (43 mi) south of Bregenz.*

Since it was first settled by Swiss exiles centuries ago, the lush and beautiful Brand Valley has attracted many travelers interested in visiting the enormous glaciers and one of the largest lakes in the Alps, located near the town. Today, Brand is known as a health resort and a winter-sports center. Its hotels lie at the foot of the Scesaplana mountain group (which marks the Swiss border and is the highest range in the Rätikon). There are no rail lines to Brand, so the best way to reach the resort is to take the train to Bludenz and then the bus from there to Brand.

If you are fond of hiking, you can climb by easy stages along the forest paths without much exertion to the famous glacier lake, the **Lünersee.** In winter, the skiing is excellent, and there is a short, modern gondola-type cable railway up the Niggenkopf (5,500 ft) to take you up to the finest ski slopes in just a few minutes. Anyone interested in geology should pay a visit to the tiny village chapel, known as the **"trowel stone" chapel,** built of local rock that can be cut into shape quite easily with an ordinary saw. When exposed to the air, the masonry then shrinks slightly and hardens and becomes rather brittle.

Dining and Lodging

$$–$$$ ✕🏨 **Sporthotel Beck.** The Beck family runs this sports hotel in the shadow of the nearby mountains. Rooms are comfortably furnished and light-filled and have flower-bedecked balconies that look out over spectacular views. The hotel's restaurant features classic Austrian fare like schnitzel, but also lighter dishes for those watching their waistlines. Sports enthusiasts will like the wide range of activities available in the hotel as well as the great mountain-climbing nearby. ⊠ *A–6708,* ☎ *05559/306-0,* 🅵🅰🆇 *05559/306–70. Restaurant, pool, massage, driving range, exercise room, horseback riding. AE, DC, MC, V.*

Outdoor Activities and Sports

GOLF

Golf Club Brand, set in a stunning Alpine valley and Vorarlberg's first course, has 9 holes, par-68. ☎ *05559/450,* 🅵🅰🆇 *05559/450–20.* ⊙ *May–Oct.*

HIKING

From a leisurely stroll to serious mountain trekking, Brand has hiking galore. The most noted trail runs from Brand via Innertal (with a chairlift up to Melkboden) and the Schattenlagant-Alpe to the lower end of the Lünersee. Inquire at the local tourist office for maps.

SKIING

Brand offers 30 km (18 mi) of groomed ski runs served by four chair lifts. It is part of the Alpenregion Bludenz, which also includes Klostertal, Grosses Walsertal, Brandnertal, and Walgau. Rental equipment is available. For details on facilities, contact Alpenregion Bludenz (✉ Rathausg. 12, A-6700 Bludenz, ☎ 05552/30227, FAX 05552/30227-3, ✍). The area immediately around the Brandnertal features ski passes good for 1 to 16 days, with rates for adults, children, and senior citizens varying according to season. The Brandnertal encompasses some 14 lifts and 42 km (25 mi) of prepared runs.

Schruns-Tschagguns

10 km (6 mi) northeast of Brand, 60 km (39 mi) south of Bregenz.

Author Ernest Hemingway spent many winters at the Schruns–Tschagguns skiing area in the Montafon Valley. Today neither of the towns—sited across the Ill River from each other—is as fashionable as the resorts on the Arlberg, but the views over the Ferwall Alps to the east and the mighty Rätikon on the western side of the valley are unsurpassed anywhere in Austria. In winter, the powdery snow provides wonderful skiing. Thanks to an integrated system of ski passes and lifts, the Montafon Valley is considered a "ski stadium" by skiers in the know. They love to head for Hochjoch-Zamang—the main peak at **Schruns**—to have lunch on the spectacularly sited sun terrace of the Kapell restaurant. Then it's on to Grabs-Golm over the river in **Tschagguns.** Others prefer the Silvretta-Nova run at Gaschurn and St. Gallenkirch. In summer, the heights are given over to climbers and hikers, the mountain streams to trout fishermen, and the lowlands to tennis players.

Dining and Lodging

$$$–$$$$ ✕▥ **Löwen.** This central hotel looks huge, but inside, the country style works well, and the rustic dark-wood exterior is carried over elegantly into the modern rooms with balconies. The hotel is set in the center of a grassy garden platform, which forms a greenbelt around the main building and serves as a roof for the ground-floor pool and restaurants. The excellent Edelweiss restaurant, with its graceful table settings (candlelit at night), serves regional specialties done with flair. ✉ *Silvrettastr. 8, A–6780,* ☎ *05556/7141,* FAX *05556/73553. 85 rooms. 4 restaurants, bar, indoor pool, sauna, exercise room, dance club. AE, DC, MC, V. Closed mid-Apr.–mid-May and mid-Oct.–mid-Dec.* ✍

$$–$$$ ✕▥ **Montafoner Hof.** This cozy hotel in Tschagguns is perfect for families. The management is warm and friendly and makes guests feel at home. The hotel is also known for its popular restaurant, which features delicious, traditional Austrian cooking. ✉ *Kreuzg. 9, A–6774 Tschagguns,* ☎ *05556/7100–0,* FAX *05556/7100–6. 48 rooms. Restaurant, indoor and outdoor pool, sauna, solarium, garage. No credit cards.*

$$–$$$ ▥ **Alpenhof Messmer.** Set on a lush green hillside slightly out of the
★ center of town, this oversize double chalet welcomes you with fireplaces and comfortable rustic furnishings. Most of the imaginatively decorated rooms have balconies with a view over the town. It is a member of the Silence Hotel group. The family management is particularly friendly and helpful, and the same goes for the restaurant staff. ✉ *Grappaweg 6, A–6780,* ☎ *05556/72664–0,* FAX *05556/76156. 35 rooms. Restaurant, bar, indoor pool, sauna, exercise room. No credit cards. Closed mid-Apr.–mid-May and mid-Nov.–mid-Dec.* ✍

Outdoor Activities and Sports

FISHING

The local mountain streams and rivers are full of fish. Licenses are available; ask the regional tourist office in Bregenz for detailed information on seasons and locations.

SKIING

Schruns is one of the skiing centers of the Montafon region, which also includes the Bartholomäberg, Gargellen, Gaschurn/Partenen, St. Gallenkirch/Gortipohl, Silbertal, and Vandans ski areas. They are accessible with a Montafon Ski Pass and together have 70 lifts and 320 km (148 mi) of groomed runs. Ski passes are valid for 3 to 14 days or 21 days, with rates for adults, children, and senior citizens varying according to season. Rental equipment is available. For details contact Montafon Tourism (⊠ Montafonerstr. 21, A–6780 Schruns, ☎ 05556/72253–0, ℻ 05556/74856, ✍).

Stuben

🔞 *38 km (23 mi) northeast of Schruns, 29 km (23 mi) east of Bludenz.*

Traveling through the Montafon via Route 316, you'll come to the village of Stuben, hometown of that pioneer of Alpine ski techniques, Hannes Schneider. From December to the end of April, the magnificent skiing, at 4,600 ft, makes Stuben popular among serious skiers who are willing to forgo the stylish resorts such as Lech just up the road. Stuben has skiing links with St. Anton, Lech, and Zürs. For information on its facilities contact the Arlberg region tourist office (⊠ Postfach 54, A–6764 Lech, ☎ 05583/2161–0, ℻ 05583/3155, ✍). The village is poised right above the Arlberg Tunnel, so travelers can't—appearance to the contrary on maps—arrive there via rail from Innsbruck or Bregenz. They must detrain at Langen am Arlberg and then take a bus on to Stuben.

Dining and Lodging

$$$ ✕▥ **Hotel Mondschein.** A welcoming exterior, accented with pink geraniums in flower boxes and dark green shutters, greets visitors as they come down the street from the town church. Inside this traditional Alpine country house, dating back to 1739, the greeting is almost as warm as the fires blazing in the hotel's hearths, while the pricey restaurant prides itself on its fish selections. Unlike other Stuben hostelries, this one is right in the center of town. Depending on the season, rates include half board. ⊠ A–6762, ☎ 05582/511 or 05582/721, ℻ 05582/736. *25 rooms. Restaurant, indoor pool, health club, baby-sitting. No credit cards. May and mid-Sept.–mid-Dec.*

Zürs

🔞 *13 km (8 mi) north of Stuben, 90 km (56 mi) southeast of Bregenz.*

The chosen resort of the rich and fashionable on this side of the Arlberg, Zürs is little more than a collection of large hotels. Perched at 5,600 ft, it is strictly a winter-sports community; when the season is over, the hotels close. But Zürs is more exclusive than Lech and certainly more so than Gstaad or St. Moritz in Switzerland—this is the place wealthy emirs bring their private ski instructors. Zürs is also the place where the first ski lift in Austria was constructed in 1937. In most hotels you'll be asked to take full board, so there are relatively few "public" restaurants in town and little chance to dine around. But the hotel dining rooms are elegant; in many, jacket and tie are de rigueur in the evening.

Dining and Lodging

$$$-$$$$ ✕⊞ **Sporthotel Edelweiss.** This 19th-century house has received an agreeable face-lift, giving it a colorful, contemporary interior, including the guest rooms. The Zürserl disco is *the* place in the evening. The restaurant, Chesa Verde, is the best in town, offering fresh fish, game, and other regional standards, but be sure to reserve. Prices include half board. ⊠ *A–6763,* ☎ *05583/2662,* ℻ *05583/3533. 66 rooms, 5 apartments. Restaurant, sauna, exercise room, dance club. No credit cards. Closed mid-Apr.–Nov.*

$$$$ ⊞ **Lorünser.** The hospitable elegance of this hotel draws royalty, including Prince Albert of Monaco and Queen Beatrix of the Netherlands. In the reception area, carved ceiling beams, open fireplaces, and attractive accessories create a welcoming ambience. Rustic wood is used to good effect in the stylish guest rooms. Prices include full board, half board by arrangement. ⊠ *A–6763,* ☎ *05583/2254–0,* ℻ *05583/2254–44. 74 rooms. Restaurant, bar, sauna, exercise room. No credit cards. Closed mid-Apr.–early Dec.*

$$$$ ⊞ **Zürserhof.** This world-famous hostelry at the north end of town com-
★ prises five chalets—five of the most luxurious and expensive chalets in the world (prices can near $900 a day with board). Many of the accommodations are elegant, spacious apartments or suites with fireplaces; newer ones have Roman baths. The family-run house has nevertheless managed to preserve an intimate atmosphere. Prices include half board. When celebrities want to be private, they come here. ⊠ *A–6763,* ☎ *05583/2513–0,* ℻ *05583/3165. 97 rooms. Restaurant, bar, indoor pool, beauty salon, sauna, driving range, tennis court, exercise room, dance club. No credit cards. Closed mid-Apr.–Nov.*

Outdoor Activities and Sports

SKIING

There are three main lifts: east of Zürs, take the chairlift to Hexenboden (7,600 ft) or the cable-car to Trittkopf (7,800 ft), with a restaurant and sun terrace; to the west, a lift takes you to Seekopf (7,000 ft), where there is another restaurant. This is avalanche country, so skiers need to be particularly alert.

Lech

⓯ *9 km (5½ mi) north of Zürs, 90 km (56 mi) southeast of Bregenz.*

Just up the road from the Zürs resort, Lech is a full-fledged community—which some argue detracts from its fashionableness. But there are more hotels in Lech, better tourist facilities, bigger ski schools, more shops, more nightlife, and prices nearly as high as those in neighboring Zürs. Zürs has the advantage of altitude, but Lech is a less artificial and very pretty Alpine village. And Lech is a favorite winter vacation spot for Princess Caroline of Monaco and also the Belgian royal family. Be sure to check with the hotel of your choice about meal arrangements; some hotels recommend that you take half board, which is usually a good deal. You can't get to Lech via rail; take the train to Langen am Arlberg station stop, and then transfer to a bus for the 15-minute ride to town.

Dining and Lodging

$$$$ ✕ **Brunnenhof.** This cozy dinner restaurant in the hotel of the same name,
★ slightly north of the town center, has gotten increasingly better in recent years, justifying the tag "Gourmet-Hotel." The menu has offered such innovative dishes as fillet of perch over a bed of squash and fillet of beef with artichoke sauce. The wine list includes selections from Austria, France, Italy, Spain, Australia, and California. Be sure to reserve well in advance, for this is one of the best restaurants in town, and it's regularly full. ⊠

House 146, ☎ 05583/2349, FAX 05583/2349–59. *Reservations essential. No credit cards. Closed Sun. and mid-Apr.–mid-Dec.*

$$$–$$$$ ✕🗟 **Gasthof Post.** A gemütlich atmosphere dominates in this green-
★ shuttered chalet hotel, with murals, flower boxes, and a wood-pan-
eled interior. The à la carte restaurant is the best in town; try the
medallions of lamb or grilled salmon, but save space for one of the out-
standing desserts. ⊠ *Dorf 11, A–6764,* ☎ *05583/2206–0,* FAX *05583/
2206–23. 40 rooms. Restaurant, bar, indoor pool, sauna. No credit
cards. Closed mid-Apr.–June and mid-Sept.–Nov.* ✍

$$$–$$$$ ✕🗟 **Montana.** In Oberlech, in the pedestrian zone just above the town,
★ you'll find this easygoing hotel, run by an outgoing expatriate Alsa-
tian. He has installed a *Vinothek* (wine shop), where tastings are held
and wine is sold by the glass or bottle. The bright interior colors con-
trast well with the weathered wood; the rooms are friendly and snug.
The ski slopes are just outside the door. The restaurant, Zur Kanne,
has French overtones and is remarkable for its attention to detail,
both in the kitchen and in the table settings. Ingredients are fresh daily,
and dishes range from lobster hash to beef fillet gratiné. Prices for the
hotel include half board. ⊠ *House 279, A–6764,* ☎ *05583/2460,* FAX
*05583/2460–38. 42 rooms. Restaurant, bar, indoor pool, sauna. No
credit cards. Closed May–Nov.* ✍

$$–$$$$ ✕🗟 **Krone.** Directly across the street from two of the main lifts, this
family-managed hotel grew out of a 250-year-old house and now be-
longs to the Romantik Hotel group. The adaptations and moderniza-
tion have not affected the general ambience of comfort and well-being
that's reflected in the beamed ceilings, tile stoves, and Oriental carpets.
The restaurant, one of the town's three best, is noted for its game and
regional specialties; try the fillet of whitefish on cucumber or the rack
of lamb. ⊠ *House 13, A–6764,* ☎ *05583/2551,* FAX *05583/2551–81.
56 rooms. Restaurant, bar, indoor pool, sauna, exercise room, dance
club. No credit cards. Closed mid-Apr.–mid-June and Oct.–Nov.*

$$ 🗟 **Aurelio.** This hillside chalet, fairly close to the center of town, is not
far from the lower station of two of the lifts, one of which runs in sum-
mer as well. The hotel is family-run and friendly; the rooms are cheer-
ful and cozy. ⊠ *NR 130, A–6764,* ☎ *05583/2214,* FAX *05583/3456.
18 rooms, 4 apartments. Restaurant, bar, children's programs. MC,
V. Closed Apr.–mid-June; Oct.–Nov.*

Nightlife and the Arts

Lech is known almost as much for après-ski and nightlife as for the
snow and the slopes. Ask at the tourist office about the "in" spots, as
the crowd tends to move around. Prices vary from place to place, but
in general you'll pay AS65–AS80 for a mixed drink.

You can join the crowd as early as 11 AM at the outdoor and famed
Red Umbrella bar for snacks and drinks at the Petersboden Sport Hotel
at Oberlech (☎ 05583/3232). Activity continues at the late-afternoon
tea dance at the Tannbergerhof (☎ 05583/2202).

Hot après-ski spots include the bars in the **Goldener Berg** (☎ 05583/
2205) and **Burg** (☎ 05583/2291) hotels in Oberlech, and **Monzabon**
(☎ 05583/2104) in Lech. Among the popular places for a mid-evening
drink (starting at 9:30) are **Pfefferkörndl** in the Pfefferkörn Hotel (☎
05583/2525–429) The **Krone Bar** in the Krone hotel (☞ Dining and
Lodging, *above*) opens at 9 PM and goes on until 2 or 3 AM.

Outdoor Activities and Sports

SKIING

Lech is linked with Oberlech and Zürs with more than 30 ski lifts, all
accessed by the regional ski pass, which allows skiers to take in the
entire region. You can ski right from Zürs to Lech. In addition, there

is a vast network of cross-country trails. For complete information on skiing facilities contact the Arlberg region tourist office (⊠ Postfach 54, A–6764 Lech,, ☎ 05583/2161–0, 🅵🅰🆇 05583/3155, ✍).

VORARLBERG A TO Z

Arriving and Departing

By Car

From Germany, the autobahn (Route A14/E17) takes you into Bregenz; roads from Switzerland lead to Lustenau and Hohenems; from Liechtenstein, Route 16 (Route 191 in Austria) goes to Feldkirch; and Routes A12/E60 from eastern Austria and 315 from Italy meet at Landeck to become Route 316/E60, then head westward through the Arlberg auto tunnel (toll AS130). Alternatively, your car (and you) can get to Vorarlberg on the car train that runs to Feldkirch from Vienna, Graz, or Villach.

By Ferry

From May to October, passenger ships of the Austrian railroad's **Bodensee White Fleet** (☎ 05574/42868, 🅵🅰🆇 05574/67555–20) connect Bregenz with Lindau, Friedrichshafen, Meersburg, and Konstanz on the German side of the lake. The Eurailpass and Austrian rail passes are valid on these ships. You'll need your passport.

By Plane

The closest major airport is in Zürich, 120 km (75 mi) away. Munich is 190 km (119 mi) away, and Innsbruck is 200 km (125 mi) away. Several trains a day serve Bregenz from the **Zürich Kloten airport.** In winter a bus leaves the airport Friday, Saturday, and Sunday at 12:30 PM for resorts in the Arlberg and Montafon regions. You can book through Swissair. On the Austrian side, call **Arlberg Express** (⊠ A–6754 Klösterle, ☎ 05583/2000, 🅵🅰🆇 05582/3155) for information and bookings.

Rheintalflug (☎ 01/7007–36911 in Vienna, 05574/48800 in Vorarlberg; 🅵🅰🆇 01/7007–6915 in Vienna, 05574/48800–8 in Vorarlberg) flies between Vienna and Altenrhein on Lake Constance in Switzerland. A direct bus service takes passengers free of charge to and from the airport and Bregenz, Dornbirn, and Lustenau.

By Train

The main rail line connecting with Vienna and Innsbruck enters Vorarlberg at Langen after coming through the Arlberg Tunnel. Both the *Arlberg* and *Orient Express* trains follow this route, which then swings through Bludenz to Feldkirch. There the line splits, with the *Arlberg* going south into Liechtenstein and Switzerland, the other branch heading through Dornbirn to Bregenz and on to Lindau in Germany.

Getting Around

By Bus

Post office, railroad, and private bus services connect all the towns and villages not served by the railroad, using tracked vehicles when necessary in winter. Even so, some of the highest roads become impassable for a few hours.

By Car

A car is the most flexible way of getting about in Vorarlberg, but the roads can be treacherous in winter. You are not allowed on some mountain roads in the Arlberg without chains, which you can rent from a number of service stations.

By Taxi

Taxis start at AS41, so taking one even a short distance can be expensive. Call to order a **radio cab** (☎ 05574/65400 or 05574/42222).

By Train

The railroads connect the main centers of Vorarlberg remarkably well; besides the lines described above, the Montafon electric (with occasional steam) rail line runs parallel to the highway from Bludenz southeast to Schruns.

Contacts and Resources

Car Rentals

Avis (✉ ÖBB train stations, ☎ 0512/571754) cars are available only with a reservation. **Hertz** (✉ F. M. Felder-Str. 2, Dornbirn, ☎ 05572/27706, FAX 05572/31878).

Discounts

A Bodensee-Pass includes the Swiss and German as well as the Austrian lake steamers, all at half price, plus area trains, buses, and cable-car lifts. The pass comes in 7- and 15-day variations. The Network Vorarlberg ticket makes public transport economical, with daily, weekly, or monthly passes available. You can choose tickets for regions of various sizes, from one urban area to the entire Vorarlberg network. The Family 1-day Runabout is a real bargain, and valid for an entire family irrespective of size; the Vorarlberg information offices in Bregenz and Vienna have details.

Emergencies

In case of an emergency, call ☎ 133 for the **police,** ☎ 144 for an **ambulance,** and ☎ 122 for the **fire department.**

Visitor Information

The headquarters for **tourist information** about Vorarlberg is based in Bregenz (✉ Bahnhofstr. 14, A–6900 Bregenz, ☎ 05574/42525–0, FAX 05574/42525–5 ✑); there is a **branch office** in Vienna (✉ Tuchlaubenstr. 18, A–1010 Vienna, ☎ 01/535–7890, FAX 01/535–7893).

Other regional tourist offices (called either Tourismusbüro, Verkehrsverein, or Fremdenverkehrsamt) are located throughout the province at the following addresses:

Bezau (✉ Pl. 39, A–6870, ☎ 05514/2295, FAX 05514/3129). **Bludenz** (✉ Werdenberger Str. 42, A–6700, ☎ 05552/62170, FAX 05552/67597). **Bregenz** (✉ Bahnhofstr. 14, A–6900, ☎ 05574/4959, FAX 05574/43443–4 ✑). **Feldkirch** (✉ Herreng. 12, A–6800, ☎ 05522/73467, FAX 05522/79867). **Lech** (✉ A–6764, ☎ 05583/2161-0, FAX 05583/3155 ✑). **Montafon Valley** (✉ Montafoner Str. 21, A–6780 Schruns, ☎ 05556/72253–0, FAX 05556/74856 ✑). **Zürs** (✉ A–6763, ☎ 05583/2245, FAX 05583/2982 ✑).

11 BACKGROUND AND ESSENTIALS

Portraits of Austria

Books and Videos

Chronology

Map of Austria

Smart Travel Tips A to Z

Vocabulary

Menu Guide

BEYOND THE SCHLAG

Portrait

Today's Austria—and in particular its capital, Vienna—reminds some observers of a formerly fat man who is now at least as gaunt as the rest of us but still allows himself a lot of room and expects doors to open wide when he goes through them. After losing two world wars and surviving amputation, annexation, and occupation, a nation that once ruled Europe now endures as a tourist mecca and a neutralized, somewhat balkanized republic.

Still, there are oases of perfection, such as those Sunday mornings from September to June when—if you've reserved months in advance—you can hear (but not see) those "voices from heaven," the Vienna Boys Choir, sing mass in the marble-and-velvet royal chapel of the Hofburg. Lads of 8 to 13 in sailor suits, they peal out angelic notes from the topmost gallery, and you might catch a glimpse of them after mass as you cut across the Renaissance courtyard for the 10:45 performance of the Lipizzaner stallions in the Spanish Riding School around the corner. Beneath crystal chandeliers in a lofty white hall, expert riders in brown uniforms with gold buttons and black hats with gold braid put these aristocrats of the equine world through their classic paces.

Just past noon, when the Spanish Riding School lets out, cross the Michaelerplatz and stroll up the Kohlmarkt to No. 14: Demel's, the renowned and lavish pastry shop founded shortly after 1848 by the court confectioner. It was an instant success with those privileged to dine with the emperor, for not only was Franz Josef a notoriously stodgy and paltry eater, but, when he stopped eating, protocol dictated that all others stop, too. Dessert at Demel's became a must for hungry higher-ups. Today's Demel's features a flawless midday buffet offering venison en croûte, chicken in pastry shells, beef Wellington, meat tarts, and frequent warnings to "leave room for the desserts."

Closer to the less costly level of everyday existence, my family and I would lay on a welcoming meal for visitors just off plane or train: a freshly baked slab of *Krusti Brot* to be spread with *Liptauer,* a piquant paprika cream cheese, and *Kräuter Gervais,* Austria's answer to cream cheese and chives, all washed down by a youngish white wine. Such simple pleasures as a jug of wine, a loaf of bread, and a spicy cheese or two are what we treasure as Austrian excellence in democratic days. And if our visitors really carried on about our wine, we would take them on the weekend to the farm it was from, for going to the source is one of the virtues of living in this small, unhomogenized land of 7.5 million people that is modern Austria.

"Is it safe to drink the water?" is still a question I hear sometimes from visitors to Vienna. "It's not only safe," I reply, "it's recommended." Sometimes they call back to thank me for the tip. Piped cold and clean via Roman aqueducts from a couple of Alpine springs, the city's water has been rated the best in the world by connoisseurs as well as by authorities such as the Austrian Academy of Sciences and an international association of solid-waste-management engineers. Often on a summer evening, when our guests looked as though a cognac after dinner might be too heavy, I brought out a pitcher of iced tap water, and even our Viennese visitors smacked their lips upon tasting this refreshing novelty. But don't bother to try it in a tavern; except for a few radical thinkers and the converts I've made, virtually all Viennese drink bottled mineral water, and few waiters will condescend to serve you any other kind.

People say that after two decades in Vienna one must feel very Viennese, and maybe they're right, because here I am chatting about food and drink, which is the principal topic of Viennese conversation. So, before leaving the capital for the provinces, let me call your attention to three major culinary inventions that were all introduced to Western civilization in Vienna in the watershed year of 1683: coffee, the croissant, and the bagel.

That was the year the second Turkish siege of Vienna was at last repelled, when King Jan Sobieski of Poland and Duke Charles of Lorraine rode to the rescue, thereby saving the West for Christianity. The Sultan's armies left behind their silken tents and banners, some 25,000 dead, and hundreds of huge sacks filled with a mysterious brownish bean. The victorious Viennese didn't know what to make of it—whether to bake, boil, or fry it. But one of their spies, Franz George Kolschitzky, a wheeler-dealer merchant who had traveled in Turkey and spoke the language, had sampled in Constantinople the thick black brew of roasted coffee beans that the Turks called *Kahve*. Though he could have had almost as many sacks of gold, he settled for beans—and opened history's first Viennese coffeehouse. Business was bad, however, until Kolschitzky tinkered with the recipe and experimented with milk, thus inventing the *Mélange*: taste sensation of the 1680s and still the most popular local coffee drink of the 1990s.

While Kolschitzky was roasting his reward, Viennese bakers were celebrating with two new creations that enabled their customers truly to taste victory over the Muslims: a bun curved like a crescent, the emblem of Islam (what Charles of Lorraine might have called *croissant* Austrians call *Kipferl*), and a roll shaped like Sobieski's stirrup, for which the German word was *Bügel*. The invention of the bagel, however, proved less significant, for it disappeared swiftly and totally, only to resurface in America centuries later, along with Sunday brunch.

One would be hard put to tell the sometimes smug and self-satisfied Viennese

that Wien (the German name for the capital) is not the navel of the universe, let alone of Austria, but the person who could tell it to him best would be a Vorarlberger. The 305,600 citizens of Austria's westernmost province live as close to Paris as they do to Vienna, which tries to govern them; their capital, Bregenz, is barely an hour's drive from Zürich, but eight or more from Vienna, and the natives sometimes seem more Swiss than Austrian.

The northern reaches of Tirol and the western parts of Upper Austria border on Germany and have a heartier, beerier character than the eastern and southern provinces. (There are nine provinces in all; Vienna, the capital, counts as a state, too, and its mayor is also a governor.) Although the glittering city of Salzburg, capital of rugged Salzburg Province, perches right on the German border, 26 km (16 mi) from Berchtesgaden, Austrian traditions, folk customs and costumes, and the music of native son Mozart flourish there as nowhere else in the country—revered and cherished, revived and embroidered.

Austria borders not just on Germany and Switzerland but also on Liechtenstein, Italy, Slovenia, the Czech Republic, Slovakia, and Hungary. In Austria's greenest province, Styria, one side of the road is sometimes in Slovenia, and you're never far from Hungary or Italy. Styria is so prickly about its independence, even from Austria, that it maintains its own embassies in Vienna and Washington. It is the source of Schilcher, Austria's best rosé wine, which you almost never see in Viennese restaurants. A few years ago, at a farmhouse near Graz, the Styrian capital, I was sipping some Schilcher that went with some wonderful lamb. "Where is this lamb from?" I asked my host.

"Right here," he replied. "Styrian lamb wins all kinds of prizes."

"Then why can't we find it in Vienna?" I wondered. "When we do get lamb, it comes all the way from New Zealand and costs a fortune."

Portrait

"That's because we don't grow lambs or Schilcher for export," he replied, dead serious.

The influx and tastes of Balkan and Turkish workers have made lamb cheaper and plentiful all over Austria, and now, since the crumbling of the Iron Curtain, Austria is reluctantly becoming even more of a melting pot than it was in the days of the Habsburg empire. The province of Burgenland used to be part of Hungary, and it retains much of its Magyar character in villages where you open a door and find, instead of a courtyard, a whole street full of steep-roofed houses, people, and life. Burgenland also boasts a culturally active Croatian minority, while Carinthia, Austria's southernmost province, has a proud Slovenian minority that is still fighting for the legal right not to Germanize the names of its villages.

The ultimate identity problem, however, belonged until recently to the province of Lower Austria, which is neither low nor south but takes its name from the part of the Danube it dominates on the map. Before 1986,

Lower Austria had no capital city; its state offices were scattered around Vienna, the metropolis it envelops with forest. Upon its selection as the provincial seat, the small city of St. Pölten, with a core of lovely churches and cloisters that swirl around you like a Baroque ballet, danced onto the map of tourist destinations.

Any day of the year, you can take an express train at Vienna's Westbahnhof for an eight-hour, 770-km (480-mi) east–west crossing of most of the country, stopping at five of Austria's nine provincial capitals: St. Pölten; Linz, the Upper Austrian seat; Salzburg; Innsbruck, in Tirol; and Bregenz, in Vorarlberg. But you would be well rewarded, as the pages that follow will demonstrate, by disembarking at each one and giving it a day or two or more of your life.

— Alan Levy

A resident of Vienna for more than two decades, Alan Levy recently relocated to Prague, where he has been editor in chief of *The Prague Post*.

POWDER-PERFECT SKIING

Austrian skiing is a fairy tale. Strip away the ski history and the tourist-brochure hype, and it's still a fairy tale. Austria has the same high, treeless bowls and slopes that make skiing all over the Alps so different from skiing in North America, plus something extra—the loveliest mountain villages in Europe. Classic Austrian ski villages look, and feel, like an art director's fantasy of Alpine charm.

It's hard for American skiers who haven't skied in the Alps to imagine the sheer size and scale of Alpine ski resorts, where many individual ski areas are linked together with a common ski pass and a spiderweb network of lifts, spanning and connecting different valleys and multiple mountains. These large, interconnected ski domains add a new dimension to skiing—that of exploration. To take full advantage of the promise of so much snowy terrain, American skiers should consider hiring a ski-instructor/guide for a day or two. Private instructors are much less expensive in Austria than in the United States, and the upper levels of Austrian ski-school classes are more about guiding than actual teaching.

Another surprise for the American skier in Austria will be the degree to which the entire country seems to embrace skiing (and winter sports in general, including cross-country skiing and, more recently, snowboarding). Skiing is deeply woven into the daily patterns of winter life in the Austrian countryside. A far greater percentage of the population skis than in the United States. In Austria skiing isn't just another sport, it's the national sport. Ski racers are national heroes; the sports pages of Austrian newspapers award ski competitions banner headlines. Winter, Austria, and skiing are virtually synonymous.

Packages, Discounts, and Information

Your best source for information about Austrian ski vacations and resorts is the Austrian National Tourist Office (✉ 500 5th Ave., Suite 2009, New York, NY 10110, ☎ 212/944–6880, FAX 212/730–4568). It has a wealth of brochures, with resort, hotel, and ski information for the main Austrian ski regions. Contacting the tourist bureaus at individual resorts for this kind of information is a much slower process. But all of Austria's Alpine resorts do have tourist bureau–central reservation services that can make hotel reservations for you (☞ addresses and phone numbers for individual resorts, *below*).

Skiing is neither more nor less expensive in the Alps—and in Austria—than in the States. Some costs, like those for lift tickets, are lower; others, like those for fine meals, are higher. Some resorts, like Kitzbühel, are very posh indeed, but there are almost always budget alternatives nearby (neighboring ski villages with more modest prices that are nonetheless connected by lifts to the same large ski domain). Some airlines, notably Swissair, offer all-inclusive air-lodging-skiing packages to many Austrian resorts. (One of the easiest ways to reach the great resorts of the Vorarlberg and the Tirol is to fly to Zürich, then take a short and convenient train ride east into the Austrian Alps.)

The Austrian ski season typically runs from late November to April, depending on local snow conditions. Areas with glacier skiing are a better bet in dry snow years. A number of these very high glacier locations offer summer and autumn skiing. But summer ski zones are rather small; the real magic of Austrian skiing involves snow-frosted villages and endless slopes.

Austrians take their snow reports very seriously. In winter, one television channel is devoted exclusively to broadcasting images of snow conditions, captured by remote-control cameras, at ski areas across the country. Americans can check snow conditions by calling the **Austrian National Tourist Office** in New York and listening to its very accurate "snow-phone" survey of all major Austrian resorts (☎ 212/944–6880, ext. 993).

Favorite Destinations

There are so many choices when it comes to Austrian skiing that you're not going to see it all, and ski it all, in one lifetime. Ski areas dot the map of Austria like spots on a Dalmatian. Foreign ski enthusiasts and newcomers to Austrian slopes would do well to focus first on the biggest ski regions of the Arlberg and the Tirol. These mega-ski regions—places that Austrians sometimes call a Skigrossraum (major ski area)—showcase what makes Alpine skiing so special: an astonishing variety of slopes and lifts that allows the visitor to ski, day after day, often from one village to the next, without ever repeating a lift or a piste. True, there are many tiny and delightful ski villages in Austria, real discoveries for adventurous skiers, but it makes more sense to sample the feast of a major Skigebiet (interconnected ski region, and sometimes called a ski arena) first. Here, to get you started, are some of the finest.

The Arlberg

This is a capital of Austrian skiing: a double constellation of ski-resort towns—Zürs, Lech, and Oberlech, in the Vorarlberg; and, just across the Arlberg Pass to the east and thus technically in the Tirol, St. Anton, St. Christoph, and Stuben. These classic Arlberg resorts are interconnected by ski lifts and trails and share more than 200 km (120 mi) of groomed slopes (and limitless off-piste possibilities), nearly 80 ski lifts, and a common ski pass.

A skier in **St. Anton,** where Hannes Schneider started the first real ski school, can feel like a character out of a 1930s Luis Trenker ski film: from en-

joying Jaeger tea after skiing to dinner at the Post Hotel. Neighboring **St. Christoph** is a spartan resort for skiing purists, a handful of handsome hotels lost in a sea of white, high above timberline, and the permanent home of the Austrian National Ski School's training and certification courses. Several valleys farther west, the plaster walls of many of Lech's hotels are painted with folk art and poetry.

The pièce de résistance of Arlberg skiing is the all-day round-trip, on skis, from Zürs to Lech, Oberlech, and back. This ski epic starts with a 5-km (3-mi) off-piste run from the Madloch down to Zug and ends, late in the afternoon, many lifts and many thousands of vertical feet later, high on the opposite side of Zürs, swinging down the slopes of the Trittkopf.

VISITOR INFORMATION
Lech (Verkehrsbüro, ⌗ A–6764 Lech, ☎ 05583/2161–0, FAX 05583/3155); **St. Anton** (Verkehrsbüro, ⌗ A–6580 St. Anton am Arlberg, ☎ 05446/22690, FAX 05446/253215).

The Tirol/Innsbruck

The Tirol is really the heart of Austrian skiing—about a third of all Austrian ski resorts are found in this province. After St. Anton and the Arlberg, **Kitzbühel,** in the heart of the Tirol, is Austria's best-known ski destination and certainly its most elegant. "Kitz" is picture-perfect and posh—all medieval cobbled streets, wrought-iron signs, and candles flickering in the windows of charming restaurants.

But *Achtung!* Kitzbühel's ski slopes are rather low in altitude, and the snow there is sometimes not as good as at higher resorts. Check the snow depth before a trip here. Fortunately, the area served by the Kitzbühel Safari Pass includes nearby Mittersill, a much higher ski area that should have adequate snow even in dry years. A common pass lets you access 63 lifts serving 157 km (97 mi) of groomed slopes—the most celebrated of which is the Hahnenkamm, the course for Europe's toughest downhill race. Deep-snow enthusiasts will gravitate to the ungroomed slopes of the Schwarzkogel.

Ski Areas

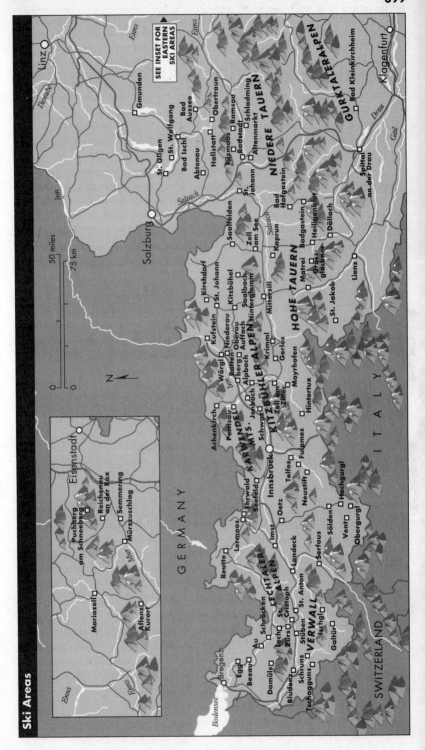

SEE INSET FOR EASTERN SKI AREAS

50 miles

75 km

N

Linz

Danube

Enns

Enns

Gmunden

St. Wolfgang

St. Gilgen

Bad Ischl

Abtenau

Bad Aussee

Obertraun

Hallstatt

Filzmoos

Ramsau

Schladming

Radstadt

Altenmarkt

St. Johann

Salzburg

Inn

Salzach

Salzach

Kirchdorf

St. Johann

Kitzbühel

Saalfelden

Zell am See

Kaprun

Bad Hofgastein

Badgastein

Heiligenblut

Döllach

Spittal an der Drau

Drau

Gail

Klagenfurt

Bad Kleinkirchheim

GURKTALERALPEN

NIEDERE TAUERN

HOHE TAUERN

Mittersill

Krimml

Gerlos

Mayrhofen

Hintertux

Matrei

Gross-glockner

St. Jakob

Lienz

ITALY

Kufstein

Wörgl

Niederau

Oberau

Auffach

Alpbach

Söll

Saalbach

Hinterglemm

KARWENDEL MTS.

KITZBÜHLER ALPEN

Schwaz

Zell am Ziller

Ziller

Achenkirch

Pertisau

Jenbach

Innsbruck

Fulpmes

Neustift

Telfes

Oetz

Ehrwald

Seefeld

Imst

Landeck

Serfaus

Sölden

Vent

Obergurgl

Hochgurgl

Reutte

Lermoos

LECHTALER ALPEN

VERWALL

Galtür

Ischgl

St. Anton

St. Christoph

Stuben

Zürs

Lech

Schröcken

Au

Bezau

Egg

Bregenz

Bodensee

SWITZERLAND

Damüls

Bludenz

Schruns

Tschagguns

GERMANY

Inn

Mur

Inset (Eastern Ski Areas):

Eisenstadt

Semmering

Mürzzuschlag

Reichenau an der Rax

Puchberg am Schneeberg

Mariazell

Aflenz Kurort

Enns

Enns

Mur

In high season, if you want to enjoy the chic atmosphere of Kitz, ski all the celebrated pistes of the Kitzbüheler Ski Safari, and avoid high-end prices, consider staying just down the Brixen Valley in neighboring **Kirchberg.** But if you must be where the action is, with a little looking around you'll find accommodations in all price ranges in Kitzbühel itself.

For an altogether different sort of ski vacation, especially for mixed groups of skiers and nonskiers, consider staying in downtown **Innsbruck** and making day trips to the seven ski areas of the Innsbruck Skigrossraum. Innsbruck has twice hosted the winter Olympics and boasts a stunning collection of medium-size ski areas with grand views: Seegrube-Nordkette, Patscherkofel, Mutterer Alm, Glungezer, Schlick 2000, Stubaier Gletscher, and especially Axamer-Lizum.

In ever-increasing numbers, skiiers are attracted by the excellent snow conditions and après-ski nightlife of **Ischgl,** in the Paznaun (Valley) southwest of Innsbruck, and not far from better-known St. Anton. Although it's not as chic as Kitz or St. Anton, skiiers and snowboarders are drawn to Ischgl and neighboring resorts **Galtur** and **Kappl** by the 265 km (165 mi) of groomed slopes and 67 lifts found here. It is even possible to ski from Ischgl into the village of Samnaun, Switzerland, for some duty-free shopping, before hopping the impressive double-decker Pendlebahn back into Austria.

A favorite Austrian Skigebiet has to be the **Zillertal,** just south and east of Innsbruck. Almost unknown to American skiers, there are 10 different ski areas, strung like pearls up the long Ziller Valley, culminating in the Tux Glacier at the very top (a popular summer-skiing site, too). Mayerhofen, a pretty town full of painted buildings halfway up the Zillertal, is a perfect base for skiing the whole valley. The Ahorn, right above Mayerhofen, is one of the smallest ski areas in this large valley, but it has the finest children's ski school I've ever seen. The Zillertal ski pass includes efficient bus and train transportation up and down the valley from one ski area to

the next. Especially recommended are the slopes of the Königsleiten on a powder morning; the Penken above Mayerhofen for its wide-open slopes; the Eggalm, an intimate, uncrowded balcony of a ski area higher up the valley; and the Tux Glacier for its on-top-of-the-world feeling. The common Ziller Valley ski pass lets you ski 400 km (240 mi) of groomed slopes and use 140 lifts.

VISITOR INFORMATION

✎ *is your signal that the property has a Web site, where you will find details and, usually, images; for a link, visit www.fodors.com/urls.*

Innsbruck (Tourismusverband, ✉ Burggraben 3, A–6020, ☎ 0512/59850, FAX 0512/59850–7 ✎); **Kitzbühel** (Tourismusverband, ✉ Hinterstadt 18, A–6370, ☎ 05356/2155, FAX 05356/2307 ✎); **Ischgl** (Tourist Office, ✉ A–6561, ☎ 05444/5266–0, FAX 05444/5636 ✎); **Zillertal** (Tourismusverband, ✉, A–6280 Zell im Zillertal, ☎ 05282/2281, FAX 05282/2281–80 ✎); **Mayrhofen** (Tourismusverband, ✉ A–6290 Mayrhofen, ☎ 05285/6760, FAX 05285/6760–33 ✎).

Salzburg

Farther east, in the province of Salzburg, there are also a number of stunning integrated ski regions. Despite its grandiose name, the **Europa-Sportregion** is only a grouping together of two—splendid—ski resorts, Kaprun and Zell am See. The skier population here comes from all across Europe, and the large number of British and Scandinavian skiers guarantees that Americans without a word of German will feel at home. Zell am See, a lakeside village, sits beneath the Schmittenhöhe, a wide mountain served by 25 ski lifts, known for its long runs. A few miles away, the village of Kaprun lies under the 10,509-ft Kitzsteinhorn peak, and its glacier skiing makes a winter vacation here very "snow safe." (This is also a major summer-skiing location.) Kaprun has only 16 ski lifts, but they climb quite high.

The **Gasteiner Tal** (Gastein Valley) is the place to combine skiing and spa vacationing. Badgastein and neighboring Bad Hofgastein are better known to Americans for their luxurious thermal and mineral baths. But their ski slopes, linked with those of Grossarl in the next valley over, comprise a beautiful and rather large ski region. Accommodations range from luxury hotels—Badgastein has a distinctly chichi reputation—to traditional Alpine farmhouses. The Gasteiner Tal and nearby Grossarl together offer 53 ski lifts serving 250 km (155 mi) of groomed slopes.

The slopes of **Saalbach-Hinterglemm,** linked with nearby Leogang, are not particularly steep or difficult, but this is a beautifully integrated ski offering with 200 km (120 mi) of groomed pistes and more than 70 lifts, one of which, the Schattbergbahn, is said to be the largest cable car in Austria. It's a good choice for long, aesthetic intermediate ski runs.

The **Salzburger Sportwelt Amadé** Skigebiet drapes over three large valleys and a number of smaller ones. Resorts like Wagrain, Filzmoos, St. Johann im Pongau, Kleinarl, and Radstadt have never been written up in American ski magazines, which invariably stick with the big names like St. Anton and Kitz, but this ski region nonetheless links more than 320 km (200 mi) of groomed slopes with 120 lifts. Lower altitudes make this a recommended destination only in good snow years.

VISITOR INFORMATION
Europa-Sportregion (Kurverwaltung, ✉ Brucker Bundestr. 1, A–5700 Zell am See, ☎ 06547/7700, FAX 06547/720–32 ✆); **Gastein Valley** (Kur- und Fremdenverkehrsverband, ✉ Kaiser-Franz-Josef-Str. 27, A–5640 Badgastein, ☎ 06434/2531, FAX 06434/2531–37 ✆); **Saalbach-Hinterglemm** (Tourism Association, ✉ Saalbach Hinterglemm 550, A–5753 Saalbach, ☎ 06541/

6800–68, FAX 06541/6800–69 ✆); **St. Johann** (Tourismusverband, ✉ A–5600, ☎ 06412/6036, FAX 06412/6036–74 ✆).

Styria

The mountains tend to become lower and the snow conditions less certain as one travels east in the Austrian Alps, so it makes sense for American skiers to concentrate on the more westerly ski destinations. One possible exception is in Styria, the **Dachstein-Tauren Region.** Here the Dachstein Glacier offers a bonus of high-altitude snow. Nine separate villages share a common pass that gives access to 78 lifts, serving 140 km (87 mi) of groomed slopes above the wide Enns river valley. But Dachstein slopes are not as interconnected as those in many other Austrian ski regions and you tend to wind up spending each skiing day above just one of the region's villages: Schladming, Rohrmoos-Untertal, Pichl, Haus im Ennstal, Aich-Assach, Pruggern, Gröbming, Mitterberg, and Ramsau am Dachstein. Cross-country skiing is as popular as downhill skiing in this valley with an amazing 240 km (152 mi) of prepared cross-country trails.

VISITOR INFORMATION
Ramsau am Dachstein (Tourismusverband, ✉ A–8972, ☎ 3687/81925, FAX 3687/82516 ✆); **Schladming** (Sportregion Schladming, ✉ Coburgstr. 52, A–8970, ☎ 3687/22042–0 FAX 3687/22042–60).

–Lito Tejada-Flores

Lito Tejada-Flores has shared his passion for mountain adventure in a series of books, films, and most recently his *Breakthrough on Skis* instructional videos. As a contributing editor to *Skiing* magazine, Lito has skied around the world. He is in love with the Alps and visits Austria every chance he gets.

WHAT TO READ AND WATCH BEFORE YOU GO

Books

Gordon Brook-Shepherd's *The Austrians: A Thousand-Year Odyssey* traces the history of Austria through the postwar years. The 2,000-year history of Vienna is detailed in *The Viennese: Splendor, Twilight and Exile,* by Paul Hofmann. Alan Palmer's *Twilight of the Hapsburgs* covers the years of Emperor Franz Josef's life (1830–1916). For an intriguing portrait of Vienna in the months before and after the murder-suicide of Crown Prince Rudolf and his teenage mistress, read Frederic Morton's *A Nervous Splendor: Vienna 1888/1889. The World of Yesterday,* Stefan Zweig's haunting memoir, begins in what Zweig calls the "Golden Age of Security," the period that was shattered by the First World War. Zweig witnesses the rise of anti-Semitism, which causes him to flee Austria in the 1930s.

Austria has produced many great composers. Recommended as background reading are Maynard Solomon's *Mozart: A Life* and Richard Rickett's *Music and Musicians in Vienna.*

Wittgenstein's Vienna, by Allan Janik and Stephen Toulmin, tells the story of the brilliant young philosopher and his city in the waning days of the Austro-Hungarian Empire. In *Sigmund Freud,* Richard Wollheim provides a concise analysis of the man and his theories.

Robert Musil's most famous work, the sprawling, unfinished, three-volume modernist novel *The Man Without Qualities,* is set in Vienna on the eve of World War I. John Irving's first novel, *Setting Free the Bears,* follows two university students as they conspire to liberate the animals at the Vienna Zoo.

Videos

Vienna and Austria have served as settings for a number of fine films. In *'38: Vienna Before the Fall* (1986), nominated for an Oscar for Best Foreign Language Film, a Gentile and a Jew fall in love just before the Nazi takeover. Postwar Vienna is the backdrop for Graham Greene's suspense classic *The Third Man* (1949), with direction by Carol Reed and zither music by Anton Karas (☞ Box in Chapter 2). Four soldiers—an American, a Russian, a Frenchman, and an Englishman—patrol occupied Vienna in *Four in a Jeep* (1951), arguing politics while helping an Austrian woman whose husband has escaped from a POW camp. Ethan Hawke and Julie Delpy are strangers in Richard Linklater's *Before Sunrise* (1995); they meet on a train and impulsively decide to spend Hawke's last hours in Europe together by wandering through Vienna. *Brother of Sleep* (1995), about a musical genius who is unhappy in love, was filmed in Vorarlberg and was nominated for a Golden Globe for Best Foreign Language Film. The young Dr. Freud (Montgomery Clift) battles with the Viennese medical establishment for acceptance of his beliefs in John Huston's *Freud* (1962). In *The Seven Percent Solution* (1976), a cocaine-addicted Sherlock Holmes (Nicol Williamson) and his sidekick, Dr. Watson (Robert Duvall), team up with Sigmund Freud (Alan Arkin) to rescue a beautiful woman in peril (Vanessa Redgrave). Omar Sharif, Ava Gardner, James Mason and Catherine Deneuve star in *Mayerling* (1968), an account of the murder-suicide of Crown Prince Rudolf and his mistress Marie Vetsera. Rodgers and Hammerstein's *The Sound of Music* (1965) was filmed in Salzburg and the Lake District; it won Oscars for Best Director (Robert Wise) and Best Picture and has become an integral part of tourist promotion for Salzburg (☞ Box in Chapter 6).

A number of films have been set in Austria, although they weren't actually filmed here: F. Murray Abraham won a Best Actor Oscar for his portrayal in *Amadeus* (1984) of Antonio Salieri, a second-rate composer whose jealousy for the first-rate Mozart leads him (the film would have us believe) to attempt to destroy his rival. The film also won Oscars for Best Director (Milos Forman) and Best Picture. Erich von Stroheim directed and stars in the silent classic *The Wedding March* (1928) about an impoverished Austrian nobleman who must choose between marrying for love or for money.

— Keith Besonen

AUSTRIA AT A GLANCE

ca. 800 BC   Celts move into Danube valley.

ca. 100 BC   Earliest fortresses set up at Vindobona, now the inner city of Vienna. Roman legions, and Roman civilization, advance to Danube. Carnuntum (near Petronell, east of Vienna) is established about 30 years later as a provincial capital.

AD 180   Emperor Marcus Aurelius dies at Vindobona. Other Roman settlements include Juvavum (Salzburg) and Valdidena (Innsbruck).

ca. 400–700   Danube Valley is the crossing ground for successive waves of barbarian invaders. Era of the events of the Nibelung saga, written down circa 1100.

ca. 700   Christian bishop established at Salzburg; conversion of pagan tribes begins.

791–99   Charlemagne, king of the Franks, conquers territory now known as Austria.

800   Pope Leo III crowns Charlemagne Emperor of the West.

814   Death of Charlemagne; his empire is divided into three parts.

ca. 800–900   Invasion of Magyars; they eventually settle along the Danube.

962   Pope John XII crowns Otto the Great, of Germany, emperor of the Holy Roman Empire, constituting the eastern portion of Charlemagne's realm. Neither holy, nor Roman, nor an empire, this confederation continued until 1806.

The House of Babenberg

976   Otto II confers the eastern province of the Reich—i.e., Österreich, or Austria—upon the Margrave Leopold of Babenberg.

1095–1136   Reign of Leopold III, later canonized and declared patron saint of Austria.

1156   Austria becomes a duchy. Duke Heinrich II makes Vienna his capital, building a palace in Am Hof.

1192   Leopold V imprisons King Richard the Lion-Hearted of England, who is on his way back from a crusade. Parts of Vienna and several town walls, particularly Wiener Neustadt, south of Vienna, are later built with the ransom money.

1246   Death of Friedrich II (the Quarrelsome), last of the Babenbergs; a long interregnum follows.

The House of Habsburg

1273   Rudolf of Habsburg in Switzerland is chosen duke by the electors of the Rhine; his family rules for 640 years.

1282   Habsburgs absorb the land of Austria.

1365   University of Vienna founded.

1477 Duke Maximilian I marries Maria of Burgundy, whose dowry comprises Burgundy and the Netherlands.

1496 Maximilian's son, Philip, marries Juana of Castile and Aragon, daughter of Ferdinand and Isabella of Spain.

1519 Death of Maximilian; his grandson, Charles I of Spain, inherits Austria, Burgundy, and the Netherlands; he is elected Holy Roman Emperor as Charles V.

1521 Charles V divides his realm with his brother Ferdinand, who becomes archduke of Austria and the first Habsburg to live in the Hofburg in Vienna.

1526 When his brother-in-law, Louis II, king of Hungary and Bohemia, dies fighting the Turks, Ferdinand inherits these crowns and some of their territories; the Turks take the rest.

1529 Turks lay siege to Vienna.

1556 Charles V abdicates; Ferdinand becomes Holy Roman Emperor. A Catholic with many Protestant subjects, he negotiates the Peace of Augsburg, which preserves a truce between theCatholic and Protestant states of his realm until 1618.

1618–48 Thirty Years' War begins as a religious dispute but becomes a dynastic struggle between Habsburgs and Bourbons, fought on German soil by non-Germans. The Peace of Westphalia, 1648, gives Austria no new territory and reestablishes the religious deadlock of the Peace of Augsburg; the Holy Roman Empire remains a loose confederation.

1679 Plague strikes Vienna, leaving 100,000 dead.

1683 Turks besiege Vienna; are routed by combined forces of Emperor Leopold I, the duke of Lorraine, and King Jan Sobieski of Poland. By 1699, armies led by Prince Eugene of Savoy drive the Turks east and south, doubling the area of Habsburg lands. The Turkish legacy: a gold crescent and a sack of coffee beans; Vienna's coffeehouses open for business.

1713 As a result of the War of the Spanish Succession, Austria gains Spanish territories in Italy and Flanders.

1740 Last male Habsburg, Charles VI, dies; succession of his daughter Maria Theresa leads to attack on the Habsburg dominions; long-term rivalry between Austria and Prussia begins.

1740–80 Reign of Maria Theresa, a golden age, when young Mozart entertains at Schönbrunn Palace and Haydn and Gluck establish Vienna as a musical mecca. Fundamental reforms modernize the Austrian monarchy.

1780–90 Reign of Maria Theresa's son Joseph II, who carries her liberalizing tendencies too far by freeing the serfs and reforming the Church. Her daughter, Marie Antoinette, has other problems.

1806 Napoléon forces Emperor Franz II to abdicate, and the Holy Roman Empire is no more; Franz is retitled emperor of Austria and rules until 1835.

1814–15 The Congress of Vienna defines post-Napoleonic Europe; Austria's Prince Metternich (who had arranged the marriage between Napoléon and Franz II's daughter Marie Louise) gains territory and power.

1815–48 Rise of nationalism threatens Austrian Empire; as chief minister, Metternich represses liberal and national movements with censorship, secret police, force.

1848 Revolutions throughout Europe, including Budapest, Prague, Vienna; Emperor Ferdinand I abdicates in favor of his 18-year-old nephew Franz Josef. Under his personal rule (lasting until 1916), national and liberal movements are thwarted.

1856–90 Modern Vienna is created and much of the medieval city torn down; the "waltz kings," Johann Strauss, father and son, dominate popular music. Sigmund Freud (1856–1939) begins his research on the human psyche in Vienna. By 1900, artistic movements include the Wiener Werkstätte and Expressionism.

1866 Bismarck's Prussia defeats Austria in a seven-weeks' war, fatally weakening Austria's position among the German states.

1867 In response to Hungarian clamor for national recognition, the Ausgleich, or compromise, creates the dual monarchy of Austria-Hungary with two parliaments and one monarch.

1882 Austria-Hungary, Germany, Italy join in the Triple Alliance.

1889 Franz Josef's only son, Rudolf, dies mysteriously in an apparent suicide pact with his young mistress, Baroness Marie Vetsera.

1898 Empress Elisabeth is murdered in Geneva by an anarchist.

1907 Universal male suffrage is gained in Austria, but not in Hungary.

1914 June 28: Archduke Franz Ferdinand, nephew and heir of Franz Josef, is assassinated by a Serbian terrorist at Sarajevo in Bosnia–Herzegovina. By August 4, Europe is at war: Germany and Austria-Hungary versus Russia, France, and Britain.

1916 Death of Franz Josef.

The Republic

1918 End of World War I; collapse of Austria-Hungary. Emperor Karl I resigns; Republic of Austria is carved out of Habsburg crown lands, while nation-states of the empire declare autonomy. Kept afloat by loans from the League of Nations, Austria adjusts to its new role with difficulty. Culturally it continues to flourish: Arnold Schoenberg's 12-tone scale recasts musical expression, while the Vienna Circle redefines philosophy.

1927 General strike; antigovernment riots.

1934 Dollfuss suppresses the socialists and creates a one-party state; later in the year he is assassinated by Nazis. His successor, Kurt von Schuschnigg, attempts to accommodate Hitler.

1938 Anschluss: Hitler occupies Austria without resistance.

1945 Austria, postwar, is divided into four zones of occupation by the Allies; free elections are held.

1955 Signing of the Austrian State Treaty officially ends the occupation. Austria declares itself "perpetually" neutral.

1960 Austria joins EFTA, the European Free Trade Association.

1989 Austria becomes the first destination for waves of Eastern European emigrants as the borders are opened.

1990 Austria applies for membership in the European Union.

1992 Austria becomes a member of the European Economic Area.

1999 Spearheaded by Jörg Haider, the anti-immigration and extremist Freedom Party was admitted to Austria's national cabinet, setting the government on a collision course with fellow members of the European Union, who subsequently issued economic and political sanctions against Austria.

2000 With fears of diplomatic isolation from members of the European Union, Austrian leaders continue to circumvent major extreme-right coalitions. Jörg Haider resigns as leader of the Freedom Party but remains governor of Carinthia province. As of summer 2000 he remains a force in Austrian politics, even though he holds no position of national power.

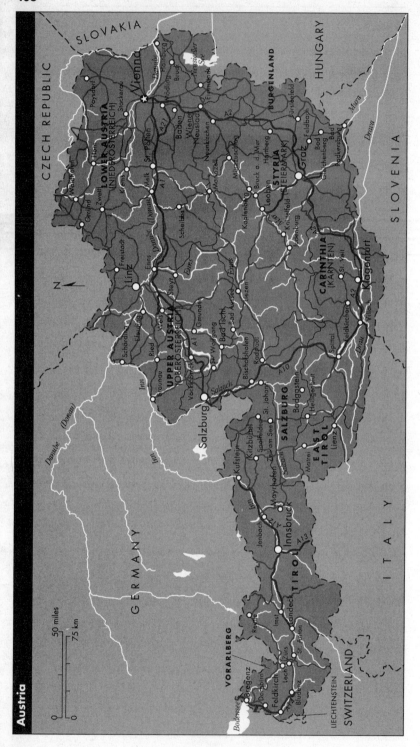

ESSENTIAL INFORMATION

Basic Information on Traveling in Austria, Savvy Tips to Make Your Trip a Breeze, and Companies and Organizations to Contact

AIR TRAVEL

BOOKING

Price is just one factor to consider when booking a flight: frequency of service and even a carrier's safety record are often just as important. Major airlines offer the greatest number of departures. Smaller airlines—including regional and no-frills airlines—usually have a limited number of flights daily. On the other hand, so-called low-cost airlines usually are cheaper, and their fares impose fewer restrictions, such as advance-purchase requirements. Safety-wise, low-cost carriers as a group have a good history—about equal to that of major carriers.

When you book **look for nonstop flights** and **remember that "direct" flights stop at least once.** Try to avoid connecting flights, which require a change of plane. Two airlines may jointly operate a connecting flight, so ask if your airline operates every segment—you may find that your preferred carrier flies you only part of the way. International flights on a country's flag carrier are almost always nonstop; U.S. airlines often fly direct.

Ask your airline if it offers electronic ticketing, which eliminates all paperwork. There's no ticket to pick up or misplace. You go directly to the gate and give the agent your confirmation number—a real blessing if you've lost your ticket or made last-minute changes in travel plans. There's no worry about waiting on line at the airport while precious minutes tick by.

CARRIERS

When flying internationally, you must usually choose between a domestic carrier, the national flag carrier of the country you are visiting, and a foreign carrier from a third country. You may, for example, choose to fly **Austrian Airlines** to Austria. National flag carriers have the greatest number of nonstops. Domestic carriers may have better connections to your home town and serve a greater number of gateway cities. Third-party carriers may have a price advantage.

Austrian Airlines and, with more limited service, **Lauda Air,** are the only air carriers that fly nonstop to Vienna from various points in the United States. There are no longer any American or Canadian air carriers who fly directly to Vienna. Many major American air carriers—such as American, Northwest, and United—do not service Vienna directly; they fly passengers to major European hubs, such as London, Amsterdam, or Frankfurt for transfers to flights with other airlines. Austrian Airlines is currently in partnership with United Airlines. Austrian Airlines also has many routes connecting Vienna with many European capitals, including Paris, London, and Munich.

Travelers from North America should note that many international carriers do service Vienna after stopovers at major European airports. For instance, Lufthansa flies from the U.S. to Frankfurt, Düsseldorf, and Munich, then can offer you connections to Vienna. British Airways (which has 15 gateways from the U.S. alone) offers many direct flights to Vienna from London's Heathrow and Gatwick airports. Note, too, that the western sector of Austria—including Innsbruck, the Tirol, and Vorarlberg—are actually closer by air to Munich than Vienna, so you might consider the option of using an international carrier to Munich, then traveling by train or connecting by air to Innsbruck or even Salzburg.

Within Austria, Austrian Airlines and its subsidiary, **Tyrolean,** offer service from Vienna to Linz and Innsbruck; they also provide routes to and points outside Austria. In addition, Rheintalflug has service between Vienna and Altenrhein (Switzerland, near Bregenz), with bus connections for points in Vorarlberg. Winter schedules on all domestic lines depend on snow conditions.

➤ MAJOR AIRLINES: **Austrian Airlines** (☎ 800/843–0002). **British Airways** (☎ 020/8897–4000; 0345/222–111 outside London). **Lauda Air** (☎ 800/ 951–2645). **Lufthansa** (☎ 800/645– 3880).

➤ FROM THE U.K.: **Austrian Airlines** (☎ 020/7434–7300). **British Airways** (☎ 020/8897–4000; 0345/222–111 outside London). **Lauda Air** (☎ 020/ 7630–5924).

➤ WITHIN AUSTRIA: **Austrian Airlines/Tyrolean** (☎ 01/7007-0, 01/ 1789; main Austrian office at Kärntner Ring 18, A–1010 Vienna). **Rheintalflug** (☎ 01/7007–36911 in Vienna; 05574/48800 in Vorarlberg; 071/ 435120).

CHARTER

Charters usually have the lowest fares but are the least dependable. Departures are infrequent and seldom on time, flights can be delayed for up to 48 hours or can be canceled for any reason up to 10 days before you're scheduled to leave. Itineraries and prices can change after you've booked your flight.

In the U.S., the Department of Transportation's Aviation Consumer Protection Division has jurisdiction over charters and provides a certain degree of protection. The DOT requires that money paid to charter operators be held in escrow, so if you can't pay with a credit card, **always make your check payable to a charter carrier's escrow account.** The name of the bank should be in the charter contract. If you have any problems with a charter operator, contact the DOT (☞ Airline Complaints, *below*). If you buy a charter package that includes both air and land arrangements, remember that the escrow requirement applies only to the air component.

CHECK-IN & BOARDING

Assuming that not everyone with a ticket will show up, airlines routinely overbook planes. When everyone does, airlines ask for volunteers to give up their seats. In return, these volunteers usually get a certificate for a free flight and are rebooked on the next flight out. If there are not enough volunteers, the airline must choose who will be denied boarding. The first to get bumped are passengers who checked in late and those flying on discounted tickets, so **get to the gate and check in as early as possible,** especially during peak periods.

Although the trend on international flights is to drop reconfirmation requirements, many airlines still ask you to reconfirm each leg of your international itinerary. Failure to do so may result in your reservation's being canceled. Always **bring a government-issued photo I.D. to the airport.** You may be asked to show it before you are allowed to check in.

CUTTING COSTS

The least expensive airfares to Austria must usually be purchased in advance and are non-refundable. It's smart to **call a number of airlines, and when you are quoted a good price, book it on the spot**—the same fare may not be available the next day.

Airlines generally allow you to change your return date for a fee. If you don't use your ticket, you can apply the cost toward the purchase of a new ticket, again for a small charge. However, most low-fare tickets are nonrefundable. To get the lowest airfare, **check different routings.** Compare prices of flights to and from different airports if your destination or home city has more than one gateway. Also price off-peak flights, which may be significantly less expensive.

Travel agents, especially those who specialize in finding the lowest fares (☞ Discounts & Deals, *below*), can be especially helpful when booking a plane ticket. When you're quoted a price, **ask your agent if the price is likely to get any lower.** Good agents know the seasonal fluctuations of airfares and can usually anticipate a sale or fare war. However, waiting can be risky: the fare could go *up* as seats become scarce, and you may wait so long that your preferred flight sells out. A wait-and-see strategy works best if your plans are flexible.

If you must arrive and depart on certain dates, don't delay.

If you plan to cover all of Austria, you may fly to Munich, Germany, and rent a car from there or take the train to Salzburg or Innsbruck. Since Germany is a little bit cheaper than Austria, this could prove a good deal, especially if you have a day to spare, and don't mind a very pretty 2-hour ride through Bavaria.

Consolidators are another good source. They buy tickets for scheduled international flights at reduced rates from the airlines, then sell them at prices that beat the best fare available directly from the airlines, usually without restrictions. Sometimes you can even get your money back if you need to return the ticket. Carefully read the fine print detailing penalties for changes and cancellations, and **confirm your consolidator reservation with the airline.**

When you **fly as a courier,** you trade your checked-luggage space for a ticket deeply subsidized by a courier service. There are restrictions on when you can book and how long you can stay.

➤ CONSOLIDATORS: **Cheap Tickets** (☎ 800/377–1000). **Discount Airline Ticket Service** (☎ 800/576–1600). **Unitravel** (☎ 800/325–2222). **Up & Away Travel** (☎ 212/889–2345). **World Travel Network** (☎ 800/409–6753).

ENJOYING THE FLIGHT

For more legroom, **request an emergency-aisle seat.** Don't sit in the row in front of the emergency aisle or in front of a bulkhead, where seats may not recline. If you have dietary concerns, **ask for special meals when booking.** These can be vegetarian, low-cholesterol, or kosher, for example. On long flights, try to maintain a normal routine, to help fight jet lag. At night, **get some sleep.** By day, **eat light meals, drink water** (not alcohol), and **move around the cabin** to stretch your legs.

Austrian Airlines does not permit smoking on board its flights. Meal options include kosher, vegetarian, vegan, and non-dairy.

FLYING TIMES

Flying time is 8 hours to Vienna from New York, 11 hours from Chicago, 13 hours from Los Angeles, and 90 minutes from London.

HOW TO COMPLAIN

If your baggage goes astray or your flight goes awry, complain right away. Most carriers require that you **file a claim immediately.**

➤ AIRLINE COMPLAINTS: U.S. Department of Transportation **Aviation Consumer Protection Division** (✉ C-75, Room 4107, Washington, DC 20590, ☎ 202/366–2220, air consumer@ost.dot.gov, www.dot.gov/airconsumer). **Federal Aviation Administration Consumer Hotline** (☎ 800/322–7873).

RECONFIRMING

It's not necessary to reconfirm flights on Austrian or Lauda, but it's still a good idea to do so by phone a day before departure.

AIRPORTS

The major airport is Vienna's **Schwechat Airport,** about 12 mi southeast of the city. Just south of Graz, in Thalerhof, is the **Graz Airport.** The **Innsbruck Airport** is 2 mi west of Innsbruck, and the **Linz Airport** is 7½ mi southwest of Linz. **Salzburg Airport** is Austria's second largest airport, located about 2½ mi west of the center.

➤ AIRPORT INFORMATION: **Schwechat airport** (Vienna)(☎ 01/7007–0); **Graz airport** (☎ 0316/2902–0); **Innsbruck airport** (☎ 0512/22525–304); **Linz airport** (☎ 07221/600–123); and **Salzburg airport** (☎ 0662/8580).

AIRPORT TRANSFERS

If you are landing in Vienna, the cheapest way to get to the city is the **S7 train** (called the *Schnellbahn*), which shuttles every half hour between the airport basement and the Landstrasse/Wien–Mitte (city center) and Wien–Nord (north Vienna) stations; the fare is AS38 and it takes about 35 minutes. Your ticket is also good for an immediate transfer to your destination within the city on the streetcar, bus, or U-Bahn. Another cheap option is the **bus,** which has two separate lines. One line goes to the City Air Terminal at the Hilton Hotel (near the city's First District) every 20 minutes between 6:30 AM and 11 PM, and less frequently after that; traveling time is 20 minutes. The other line goes to the Southern and Western train stations (Südbahnhof and Westbahnhof) in 20 and 35 minutes respectively. Departure times are every 30 minutes from 8:10 AM to 7:10 PM, hourly thereafter, and not at all 12:10–3:30 AM. Fare is AS70 one-way, AS130 for a round-trip. Another possibility is via taxi with C+K Airport Service, (☎ 01/1731, FAX 01/689–6969), charging a set price of AS270 (don't forget to tip). C+K will also meet your plane at no extra charge if you let them know your flight information in advance.

If you land in **Salzburg,** the bus line No. 77 shuttles every 15 minutes from the airport to the train station, otherwise take a taxi. If you land in **Munich,** the cheapest way of getting to town is with the S8 train that takes about 45 minutes to the main train station (Hauptbahnhof), with stops along the way and connecting rides.

BIKE TRAVEL

Biking is a popular sport in Austria. In central Vienna, special bike lanes make transportation fast, easy and safe. Throughout Austria there are several cycling trails, including the well-known Passau (Germany) to Vienna route, which follows the Danube across the country, passing through the spectacular Danube Valley. There are other cycling trails in the Alps and around lakes in Carinthia and the Salzkammergut (☞ Outdoor Activities and Sports, *below*).

Mountain biking is increasingly popular, with "mountain bike hotels" welcoming enthusiasts, along with rigorous guided tours.

➤ INFORMATION: **Mountain Hotels and Reverie** (✉ Glemmerstr. 21, A–5751 Maishofen, ☎ 06542/804–8022, FAX 06542/804804).

BIKES IN FLIGHT

Most airlines accommodate bikes as luggage, provided they are dismantled and boxed. For bike boxes, often free at bike shops, you'll pay about $5 from airlines (at least $100 for bike bags). International travelers can sometimes substitute a bike for a piece of checked luggage at no charge; otherwise, the cost is about $100. Domestic and Canadian airlines charge $25–$50.

BOAT & FERRY TRAVEL

For leisurely travel between Vienna and Linz or eastward across the border into Slovakia or Hungary, consider taking a Danube boat. More than 300 km (187 mi) of Austria's most beautiful scenery awaits you as you glide past castles and ruins, medieval monasteries and abbeys, and lush vineyards. One of the lovelier sections, particularly in spring, is the *Wachau* (Danube Valley) west of Vienna.

Blue Danube Schiffahrt (☎ 01/588–800, FAX 01/588–8044–0) offers a diverse selection of pleasant cruises, including trips to Melk Abbey and Dürnstein in the Wachau, a grand tour of Vienna's architectural sights from the river, and a dinner cruise, featuring Johann Strauss waltzes as background music.

Most of the immaculate white-painted craft carry about 1,000 passengers each on their three decks. As soon as you get on board, give the steward a good tip for a deck chair and ask him to place it where you will get the best views. Be sure to book cabins in advance. Day trips are also possible on the Danube. You can use boats to move from one riverside community to the next, and along some sections, notably the Wachau, the only way of crossing the river is using the little shuttles (in the Wachau, these are special motorless boats that use the current to cross).

Hydrofoils run daily from Vienna to Bratislava in Slovakia and to Budapest in Hungary from mid-April through October. One-way or round-trip tickets are available. It takes about 90 minutes from Vienna to Bratislava and over six hours from Vienna to Budapest.

At present, no cruise ships are allowed to go along the Danube from Vienna to the Black Sea because two bridges were damaged during the war in Kosovo. Cruise-ship travel is expected to resume sometime in 2001.

➤ BOAT & FERRY INFORMATION: Contact your travel agent or, in Austria, the **Blue Danube Schiffahrt** (✉ Friedrichstr. 7, A–1043 Vienna, ☎ 01/588–800, FAX 01/588–8044–0, www.ddsg-blue-danube.at)

BUS TRAVEL

BUS LINES

Austria features extensive national networks of buses run by post offices and railroads. Where Austrian trains don't go, buses do, and you'll find the railroad and post-office buses (bright yellow for easy recognition) in the remotest regions carrying passengers as well as mail. You can get tickets on the bus, and in the off-season there is no problem getting a seat, but on routes to favored ski areas during holiday periods reservations are essential. Bookings can be handled at the ticket office (there's one in most towns with bus service) or by travel agents. In most communities, bus routes begin and end at or near the railroad station, making transfers easy. Increasingly, coordination of bus service with railroads means that many of the discounts and special tickets available for trains apply to buses as well. There are private bus companies in Austria as well. Buses in Austria run like clockwork, typically departing and arriving on time. Smoking is generally allowed.

➤ PRIVATE BUS LINES: **Columbus** (☎ 01/53411–0). **Blaguss Reisen** (☎ 01/50180-0). **Post und Bahn** (☎ 01/71101). **Dr. Richard** (☎ 01/33100–0).

BUSINESS HOURS

BANKS & OFFICES

In most cities, banks are open weekdays 8–3, Thursday until 5:30 PM. Lunch hour is from 12:30 to 1:30. All banks are closed on Saturday, but you can change money at various locations (such as American Express offices on Saturday morning and major railroad stations around the clock), and changing machines are also found here and there in the larger cities.

GAS STATIONS

Gas stations on the major autobahns are open 24 hours a day, but in smaller towns and villages you can expect them to close early in the evening and on Sundays. You can usually count on at least one station to stay open on Sundays and holidays in most medium-size towns, and it's never a problem to get gas in larger cities.

MUSEUMS & SIGHTS

Museum hours vary from city to city and museum to museum; if museums are closed one day, it is usually Monday. Few Austrian museums are open at night. In summer, the Salzburg Zoo at Hellbrunn has nighttime opening for viewing the nocturnal animals.

PHARMACIES

Pharmacies (called *Apotheken* in German) are usually open from 9 to 6, with a noontime break between 12 and 2. In each area of the city one pharmacy stays open 24 hours; if a pharmacy is closed, a sign on the door will tell you the address of the nearest one that is open. Call ☎ 01/1550 for names and addresses (in German) of the pharmacies open that night.

You may find over-the-counter remedies for headaches and colds much less effective than those sold in the U.S. Austrians are firm believers in natural remedies, such as herbal teas. Vitamins are generally scoffed at, and though available, are very expensive.

SHOPS

In general, you'll find shops open weekdays from 8:30 or 9 until 6, with a lunchtime closing from noon to 1 or 1:30. In smaller villages, the midday break may run until 3. Many food stores, bakeries, and small grocery shops open at 7 or 7:30 and, aside from the noontime break, stay open until 7 or 7:30 PM. Shops in large city centers take no noon break. On Saturday, most shops stay open until 5 or 6 PM, though a few follow the old rules and close by 1 PM. Food stores stay open until 5 on Saturdays. Barbers and hairdressers traditionally take Monday off, but there are exceptions. Fashionable these days is for hairdressers to work evenings and nights on certain "good-for-haircutting" moon days! Also in the country, many shops close on Wednesday afternoon, and in parts of Burgenland close also on Thursday afternoon.

CAMERAS & PHOTOGRAPHY

➤ PHOTO HELP: **Kodak Information Center** (☎ 800/242–2424). *Kodak Guide to Shooting Great Travel Pictures,* available in bookstores or from Fodor's Travel Publications (☎ 800/533–6478; $18 plus $5.50 shipping).

EQUIPMENT PRECAUTIONS

Always **keep your film and tape out of the sun.** Carry an extra supply of batteries, and **be prepared to turn on your camera or camcorder** to prove to security personnel that the device is real. Always **ask for hand inspection of film,** which becomes clouded after repeated exposure to airport X-ray machines, and **keep videotapes away from metal detectors.**

FILM & DEVELOPING

All kinds of film are available for purchase in Austria, with the best prices at grocery and drug stores. Developing is very expensive, especially for one-hour service.

VIDEOS

Austrian video tapes use the PAL system, which is not compatible with NTSC players in the U.S.

CAR RENTAL

Rates in Vienna begin at AS600 a day and AS2,000 a weekend for an economy car with a manual transmission, and unlimited mileage. This includes a 21% tax on car rentals. Renting a car in Germany may be cheaper, but make sure the rental agency knows you are driving into Austria and that the car is equipped with an autobahn sticker (☞ Car Travel, *below*) for Austria. When renting an RV be sure to compare prices and reserve early. It's cheaper to arrange your rental car from the U.S., but **be sure to get a confirmation of your quoted rate in writing.**

➤ MAJOR AGENCIES: **Alamo** (☎ 800/522–9696; 020/8759–6200 in the U.K.). **Avis** (☎ 800/331–1084; 800/331–1084 in Canada; 02/9353–9000 in Australia; 09/525–1982 in New Zealand). **Budget** (☎ 800/527–0700;

0870/607–5000 in the U.K., through Europcar). **Dollar** (☎ 800/800–6000; 0124/622–0111 in the U.K., through Sixt Kenning; 02/9223–1444 in Australia). **Hertz** (☎ 800/654–3001; 800/263–0600 in Canada; 020/8897–2072 in the U.K.; 02/9669–2444 in Australia; 03/358–6777 in New Zealand). **National InterRent** (☎ 800/227–7638; 020/8680–4800 in the U.K., where it is known as National Europe).

➤ LOCAL AGENCIES: **Autoverleih Buchbinder** (✉ Schlachthausg. 38, A–1030 Vienna, ☎ 01/717–50–0, FAX 01/717–5022, with offices throughout Austria).

➤ RVs: **Gebetsroither** (✉ Industriestr. 15, A–2201 Hagenbrunn, ☎ 02246/4150, FAX 02246/4710).

CUTTING COSTS

To get the best deal, **book through a travel agent who will shop around.** Also **ask your travel agent about a company's customer-service record.** How has the company responded to late plane arrivals and vehicle mishaps? Are there often lines at the rental counter? If you're traveling during a holiday period, does a confirmed reservation guarantee you a car?

Do **look into wholesalers,** companies that do not own fleets but rent in bulk from those that do and often offer better rates than traditional car-rental operations. Prices are best during off-peak periods. Payment must be made before you leave home.

➤ WHOLESALERS: **Auto Europe** (☎ 207/842–2000 or 800/223–5555, FAX 800/235–6321, www.autoeurope.com). **Europe by Car** (☎ 212/581–3040 or 800/223–1516, FAX 212/246–1458, www.europebycar.com). **DER Travel Services** (✉ 9501 W. Devon Ave., Rosemont, IL 60018, ☎ 800/782–2424, FAX 800/282–7474 for information; 800/860–9944 for brochures; www.dertravel.com). **Kemwel Holiday Autos** (☎ 800/678–0678, FAX 914/825–3160, www.kemwel.com).

INSURANCE

When driving a rented car you are generally responsible for any damage to or loss of the vehicle. Before you rent, see what coverage your personal auto-insurance policy and credit cards already provide.

Collision policies that car-rental companies sell for European rentals usually do not include stolen-vehicle coverage. Before you buy it, check your existing policies—you may already be covered.

REQUIREMENTS & RESTRICTIONS

In Austria your own driver's license is acceptable. An International Driver's Permit is a good idea; it's available from the American or Canadian automobile association, and, in the United Kingdom, from the Automobile Association or Royal Automobile Club. These international permits are universally recognized, and having one in your wallet may save you a problem with the local authorities.

There is no age limit to renting a car at most agencies in Austria. However, you must have had a valid driver's license for one year. For some of the more expensive car models, drivers must be at least 25 years of age. There is also usually an extra charge to drive over the border into Italy, Slovakia, Slovenia, Hungary, and the Czech Republic, but no extra charge to drive to Germany.

SURCHARGES

Before you pick up a car in one city and leave it in another, **ask about drop-off charges or one-way service fees,** which can be substantial. Note, too, that some rental agencies charge extra if you return the car before the time specified in your contract. To avoid a hefty refueling fee, **fill the tank just before you turn in the car,** but be aware that gas stations near the rental outlet may overcharge.

CAR TRAVEL

Make absolutely sure your car is equipped with the *Autobahnvignette,* as it is called, a little trapezoidal sticker with a highway icon and the Austrian eagle, or with a calendar marked with an M or a W. This sticker allows use of the autobahn. It costs AS550 for a year and is available at gas stations, tobacconists, and automobile-club outlets in neighboring countries or near the border. You

can also purchase a two-month Vignette for AS150, or a ten-day one for AS70. Prices are for vehicles up to 3.5 tons and RVs. For motorcycles it is AS220. Not having a Vignette (which is generally called the *Pickerl*) can lead to high fines. Get your Pickerl before driving to Austria!

Besides the Pickerl, if you are planning to drive around a lot, budget in a great deal of toll money: for example, the tunnels on the A10 autobahn cost AS70 apiece, the Grossglockner Pass road will cost AS350, and passing through the Arlberg Tunnel costs AS130. Driving up some especially beautiful valleys, such as the Kaunertal in Tirol, or up to the Tauplitzalm in Styria, also costs money, around AS120.

The Austrian highway network is excellent, and roads are well maintained and well marked. Secondary roads may be narrow and winding. The main highway routes (autobahns), especially the A2 down to Carinthia and Italy, are packed during both Austrian and German school holidays, as well as on weekends in summer. As a nod to the environment, less salt is being used on highways in winter, but few drivers seem to take heed of the greater hazard. Remember that in winter you will need snow tires and often chains, even on well-traveled roads. It's wise to check with the automobile clubs for weather conditions, since mountain roads are often blocked, and ice and fog are hazards.

AUTO CLUBS

Austria has two automobile clubs, ÖAMTC and ARBÖ, both of which operate motorist service patrols. You'll find emergency (orange-colored) phones along all the highways. If you break down along the autobahn, the nearest phone will be pointed out by a small arrow on the guardrail. Otherwise, if you have problems, call **ARBÖ** (☎ 123) or **ÖAMTC** (☎ 120) from anywhere in the country. No area or other code is needed for either number. Both clubs charge nonmembers for emergency service. Remember to get proper coverage from your home club.

➤ IN AUSTRIA: **Austrian Automobile Club/ÖAMTC** (✉ Schubertring 1–3, A–1010 Vienna, ☎ 01/711–99–55).

➤ IN AUSTRALIA: **Australian Automobile Association** (☎ 06/247–7311).

➤ IN CANADA: **Canadian Automobile Association** (CAA, ☎ 613/247–0117).

➤ IN NEW ZEALAND: **New Zealand Automobile Association** (☎ 09/377–4660).

➤ IN THE U.K.: **Automobile Association** (AA, ☎ 0990/500–600), **Royal Automobile Club** (RAC, ☎ 0990/722–722 for membership; 0345/121–345 for insurance).

➤ IN THE U.S.: **American Automobile Association** (☎ 800/564–6222).

FROM THE U.K.

The best way to reach Austria by car from England is to take North Sea/Cross Channel ferries to Oostende or Zeebrugge in Belgium or Dunkirk in northern France. An alternative is the Channel Tunnel; motoring clubs can give you the best routing to tie into the continental motorway network. Then take the toll-free Belgian motorway (E5) to Aachen, and head via Stuttgart to Innsbruck and the Tirol (A61, A67, A5, E11, A7) or east by way of Nürnberg and Munich, crossing into Austria at Walserberg and then on to Salzburg and Vienna. Total distance to Innsbruck is about 1,100 km (650 mi); to Vienna, about 1,600 km (1,000 mi). The most direct way to Vienna is virtually all on the autobahn via Nürnberg, Regensburg, and Passau, entering Austria at Schärding. In summer, border delays are much shorter at Schärding than at Salzburg. The trip to Innsbruck via this route will take 2–3 days.

If this seems like too much driving, in summer you can **put the car on a train** in s'Hertogenbosch in central southern Netherlands on Thursday, or in Schaerbeek (Brussels) on Friday, for an overnight trip, arriving in Salzburg early the following morning and in Villach three hours later.

➤ AGENCIES: **DER Travel Service** (✉ 18 Conduit St., London W1R 9TD, ☎

020/7290–0111, FAX 020/7629–7442) has details of fares and schedules.

EMERGENCY SERVICES

See Auto Clubs, *above.*

GASOLINE

Gasoline and diesel are readily available, but on Sunday stations in the more out-of-the-way areas may be closed. Stations carry only unleaded (*bleifrei*) gas, both regular and premium (super), and diesel. If you're in the mountains in winter with a diesel, and there is a cold snap (with temperatures threatening to drop below -4°F (-20°C), add a few liters of gasoline to your diesel, about 1:4 parts, to prevent it from freezing. Gasoline prices are the same throughout the country, slightly lower at discount and self-service stations. Expect to pay about AS13 per liter for regular, AS14 for premium. Oil in Austria is expensive, retailing at AS100 upward per liter. If need be, purchase oil, windshield-wipers, and other paraphernalia at big hardware stores.

ROAD CONDITIONS

Roads in Austria are excellent and well-maintained—perhaps a bit too well-maintained judging by the frequently encountered construction zones on the autobahns.

ROAD MAPS

A set of eight excellent, detailed road maps is available from the Austrian Automobile Club/ÖAMTC (☞ *above*), at most service stations, and at many bookstores. The maps supplied without charge by the Austrian National Tourist Office are adequate for most needs, but if you will be covering much territory, the better ÖAMTC maps are a worthwhile investment.

RULES OF THE ROAD

Tourists from EU countries may bring their cars to Austria with no documentation other than the normal registration papers and their regular driver's license. A Green Card, the international certificate of insurance, is recommended for EU drivers and compulsory for others. All cars must carry a first-aid kit (including rubber gloves) and a red warning triangle to use in case of accident or breakdown. These are available at gas stations along the road, or at any automotive supply store or large hardware stores.

The minimum driving age in Austria is 18, and children under 12 years must ride in the back seat; smaller children require a restraining seat. Note that all passengers must wear seat belts.

Drive on the right side of the street in Austria. Vehicles coming from the right have the right of way, except that at unregulated intersections streetcars coming from either direction have the right of way. No turns are allowed on red. In residential areas, the right of way can be switched around; the rule is, be careful at any intersection.

Drinking and driving: since 1998, maximum blood-alcohol content allowed is 0.5 parts per thousand, which in real terms means very little to drink. Remember when driving in Europe, that the police can stop you anywhere at any time for no particular reason.

Unless otherwise marked, the speed limit on autobahns is 130 kph (80 mph), although this is not always strictly enforced. But if you're pulled over for speeding, fines are payable on-the-spot, and can be heavy. On other highways and roads, the limit is 100 kph (62 mph), 80 kph (49 mph) for RVs or cars pulling a trailer weighing more than 750 kilos (about 1,650 lbs). In built-up areas, a 50 kph (31 mph) limit applies and is likely to be taken seriously. In some towns, special 30 kph (20 mph) limits apply. More and more towns have radar cameras to catch speeders. Remember that insurance does not necessarily pay if it can be proved you were going above the limit when involved in an accident.

Sometimes the signs at exits and entrances on the autobahns are not clear—a reason why Austria has a special problem, called the *"Geister-fahrer"*, which means a driver going the wrong way in traffic. Efforts are being made to correct this problem with clearer signage.

CHILDREN IN AUSTRIA

Be sure to plan ahead and **involve your youngsters** as you outline your trip.

When packing, include things to keep them busy en route. On sightseeing days try to schedule activities of special interest to your children. If you are renting a car, don't forget to **arrange for a car seat** when you reserve. Austria is filled with wonders and delights for children, ranging from the performing Lipizzaner horses at the Spanish Riding School in Vienna, the Salzburg Marionettentheater, and the rural delights of farm vacations (☞ Eco-Tourism, *below*).

➤ BABY-SITTING: In Vienna, the central babysitting service is **Kinder-drehscheibe** (✉ Wehrg. 26, A–1050, ☎ 01/581–0660, ℻ 01/585–7432).

DINING

The best restaurants in Vienna do not welcome small children; fine dining is considered an adult pastime. With kids, **you're best off taking them to more casual restaurants and cafés.** *Heurigers* are perfect for family dining, and they usually open by 4 PM. To accommodate flexible meal times look for signs that say *Durchge-hend warme Küche*, which means warm meals are available all afternoon. Cafés offer light meals all day, and you can always get a sausage from a *Würstelstand*.

Several chain restaurants have highchairs (*Hochstuhl*), and a few serve children's portions (*Für den Kleinen Hunger)*, usually *Wienerschnitzel*, a thin slice of veal, breaded and fried.

FLYING

If your children are two or older, **ask about children's airfares.** As a general rule, infants under two not occupying a seat fly at greatly reduced fares or even for free.

In general the adult baggage allowance applies to children paying half or more of the adult fare. When booking, **confirm carry-on allowances** if you're traveling with infants. In general, for babies charged 10% of the adult fare you are allowed one carry-on bag and a collapsible stroller; if the flight is full, the stroller may have to be checked or you may be limited to less.

Experts agree that it's a good idea to use safety seats aloft for children weighing less than 40 pounds. Airlines set their own policies: U.S. carriers usually require that the child be ticketed, even if he or she is young enough to ride free, since the seats must be strapped into regular seats. Do **check your airline's policy about using safety seats during takeoff and landing.** And since safety seats are not allowed just everywhere in the plane, get your seat assignments early.

When reserving, **request children's meals or a freestanding bassinet** if you need them. But note that bulkhead seats, where you must sit to use the bassinet, may lack an overhead bin or storage space on the floor.

GROUP TRAVEL

When planning to take your kids on a tour, look for companies that specialize in family travel.

➤ FAMILY-FRIENDLY TOUR OPERATORS: **Grandtravel** (✉ 6900 Wisconsin Ave., Suite 706, Chevy Chase, MD 20815, ☎ 301/986–0790 or 800/247–7651) for people traveling with grandchildren ages 7–17.

Families Welcome! (✉ 92 N. Main St., Ashland, OR 97520, ☎ 541/482–6121 or 800/326–0724, FAX 541/482–0660).

LODGING

Most hotels in Austria allow children under a certain age to stay in their parents' room at no extra charge, but others charge for them as extra adults; be sure to **find out the cutoff age for children's discounts.**

In Trebesing, Carinthia, parents accompany the babies instead of the other way around; services for the babies are incredible. It began with Austria's first baby hotel, the **Baby und Kinder Hotel.**

SIGHTS & ATTRACTIONS

Places that are especially appealing to children are indicated by a rubber duckie icon in the margin.

SUPPLIES & EQUIPMENT

Supermarkets and drug stores (look for *DM Drogerie* and *Bipa*) carry *Windel* (diapers), universally referred to as Pampers. Remember that weight is given in kilos (2.2 pounds equals 1 kilo). Baby formula is available in grocery stores, drug stores or pharma-

cies. There are two brands of formulas: Milupa and Nestle, for infants and children up to three years old. Austrian formulas come in powder form and can be mixed with tap water.

COMPUTERS ON THE ROAD

If you use a major Internet provider, getting online in Vienna, Innsbruck, Graz, and Salzburg shouldn't be difficult. Call your Internet provider to get the local access number in Austria. Many hotels have business services with Internet access and even in-room modem lines. You may, however, need an adapter for your computer for the European-style plugs. As always, if you're traveling with a laptop, carry a spare battery and adapter. Never plug your computer into any socket before asking about surge protection. IBM sells a pen-size modem tester that plugs into a telephone jack to check if the line is safe to use.

➤ ACCESS NUMBERS IN AUSTRIA: **AOL** (☎ 01/585–8483 or 01/409–3122). For **Compuserve**, you must call Germany (☎ 0049/1805–7040–70).

CONSUMER PROTECTION

Whenever shopping or buying travel services in Austria, **pay with a major credit card** so you can cancel payment or get reimbursed if there's a problem. If you're doing business with a particular company for the first time, **contact your local Better Business Bureau and the attorney general's offices** in your own state and the company's home state, as well. Have any complaints been filed? Finally, if you're buying a package or tour, always **consider travel insurance** that includes default coverage (☞ Insurance, *below*).

➤ BBBs: **Council of Better Business Bureaus** (✉ 4200 Wilson Blvd., Suite 800, Arlington, VA 22203, ☎ 703/276–0100, FAX 703/525–8277 www.bbb.org).

CUSTOMS & DUTIES

When shopping, **keep receipts** for all purchases. Upon reentering the country, **be ready to show customs officials what you've bought.** If you feel a duty is incorrect or object to the way your clearance was handled, note the inspector's badge number and ask to see a supervisor. If the problem isn't resolved, write to the appropriate authorities, beginning with the port director at your point of entry.

IN AUSTRIA

Travelers over 17 who are residents of European countries—regardless of citizenship—may bring in duty-free 200 cigarettes or 50 cigars or 250 grams of tobacco, 2 liters of wine and 2 liters of 22% spirits or 1 liter of over 22% spirits, and 50 milliliters of perfume. These limits may be liberalized or eliminated under terms of the European Union agreement. Travelers from all other countries (such as those coming directly from the United States or Canada) may bring in twice these amounts. All visitors may bring gifts or other purchases valued at up to ECU175 or AS2,300 (about $190), although in practice you'll seldom be asked.

IN AUSTRALIA

Australian residents who are 18 or older may bring home $A400 worth of souvenirs and gifts (including jewelry), 250 cigarettes or 250 grams of tobacco, and 1,125 ml of alcohol (including wine, beer, and spirits). Residents under 18 may bring back $A200 worth of goods. Prohibited items include meat products. Seeds, plants, and fruits need to be declared upon arrival.

➤ INFORMATION: **Australian Customs Service** (Regional Director, ✉ Box 8, Sydney, NSW 2001, ☎ 02/9213–2000, ℻ 02/9213–4000).

IN CANADA

Canadian residents who have been out of Canada for at least 7 days may bring home C$500 worth of goods duty-free. If you've been away less than 7 days but more than 48 hours, the duty-free allowance drops to C$200; if your trip lasts 24–48 hours, the allowance is C$50. You may not pool allowances with family members. Goods claimed under the C$500 exemption may follow you by mail; those claimed under the lesser exemptions must accompany you. Alcohol and tobacco products may be included in the 7-day and 48-hour exemptions but not in the 24-hour

exemption. If you meet the age requirements of the province or territory through which you reenter Canada, you may bring in, duty-free, 1.14 liters (40 imperial ounces) of wine or liquor *or* 24 12-ounce cans or bottles of beer or ale. If you are 16 or older you may bring in, duty-free, 200 cigarettes and 50 cigars. Check ahead of time with Revenue Canada or the Department of Agriculture for policies regarding meat products, seeds, plants, and fruits.

You may send an unlimited number of gifts worth up to C$60 each duty-free to Canada. Label the package UNSOLICITED GIFT—VALUE UNDER $60. Alcohol and tobacco are excluded.

➤ INFORMATION: **Revenue Canada** (✉ 2265 St. Laurent Blvd. S, Ottawa, Ontario K1G 4K3, ☎ 613/993–0534; 800/461–9999 in Canada, ℻ 613/957–8911, www.ccra-adrc.gc.ca).

IN NEW ZEALAND

Homeward-bound residents 17 or older may bring back $700 worth of souvenirs and gifts. Your duty-free allowance also includes 4.5 liters of wine or beer; one 1,125-ml bottle of spirits; and either 200 cigarettes, 250 grams of tobacco, 50 cigars, or a combination of the three up to 250 grams. Prohibited items include meat products, seeds, plants, and fruits.

➤ INFORMATION: **New Zealand Customs** (Custom House, ✉ 50 Anzac Ave., Box 29, Auckland, New Zealand, ☎ 09/359–6655, ℻ 09/359–6732).

IN THE U.K.

If you are a U.K. resident and your journey was wholly within the European Union (EU), you won't have to pass through customs when you return to the United Kingdom. If you plan to bring back large quantities of alcohol or tobacco, check EU limits beforehand.

➤ INFORMATION: **HM Customs and Excise** (✉ Dorset House, Stamford St., Bromley, Kent BR1 1XX, ☎ 020/7202–4227).

IN THE U.S.

U.S. residents who have been out of the country for at least 48 hours (and who have not used the $400 allowance or any part of it in the past 30 days) may bring home $400 worth of foreign goods duty-free.

U.S. residents 21 and older may bring back 1 liter of alcohol duty-free. In addition, regardless of your age, you are allowed 200 cigarettes and 100 non-Cuban cigars. Antiques, which the U.S. Customs Service defines as objects more than 100 years old, enter duty-free, as do original works of art done entirely by hand, including paintings, drawings, and sculptures.

You may also send packages home duty-free: up to $200 worth of goods for personal use, with a limit of one parcel per addressee per day (except alcohol or tobacco products or perfume worth more than $5); label the package PERSONAL USE and attach a list of its contents and their retail value. Do not label the package UNSOLICITED GIFT or your duty-free exemption will drop to $100. Mailed items do not affect your duty-free allowance on your return.

➤ INFORMATION: **U.S. Customs Service** (✉ 1300 Pennsylvania Ave. NW, Washington, DC 20229, www.customs.gov; inquiries ☎ 202/354–1000; complaints c/o ✉ Office of Regulations and Rulings; registration of equipment c/o ✉ Resource Management, ☎ 202/927–0540).

DINING

Austria has the largest number of organic farms in Europe, as well as the most stringent food quality standards. (Finland comes in second, followed by Italy and Sweden, though they all fall far behind Austria; France, Spain, and the U.K. are at the bottom of the list.) An increasing number of restaurants use food and produce from local farmers, ensuring the freshest ingredients for their guests.

When dining out, you'll get the best value at simpler restaurants. Most post menus with prices outside. If you begin with the *Würstelstand* (sausage vendor) on the street, the next category would be the *Imbiss-Stube*, for simple, quick snacks. Many meat stores serve soups and a daily special at noon; a blackboard menu will be posted outside. A number of cafés also offer

lunch, but watch the prices; some can turn out to be more expensive than restaurants. *Gasthäuser* are simple restaurants or country inns. Austrian hotels have some of the best restaurants in the country, often with outstanding chefs. In the past few years, the restaurants along the autobahns have developed into very good places to eat (besides being, in many cases, architecturally interesting to look at).

In all restaurants, be aware that the basket of bread put on your table isn't free. Most of the older-style Viennese restaurants charge AS9–AS13 for each roll that is eaten, but more and more establishments are beginning to charge a per person cover charge—anywhere from AS15 to AS35—which includes all the bread you want, plus usually an herb spread and butter. Tap water (*Leitungswasser*) in Austria comes straight from the Alps and is among the purest in the world.

The restaurants we list are the cream of the crop in each price category.

MEALS & SPECIALTIES

Schnitzels, strudels, and Sacher tortes—with such delights, visitors quickly discover that dining in Austria offers some of the most delicious cuisine in the world. All the gastronomic traditions of the old Habsburg empire have left their mark here, so be prepared for genuine Hungarian *pörkölt* (what we call goulash) and *lecsó* (red pepper and tomato stew), and for heavenly Bohemian desserts. The *Palatschinken* are originally Hungarian as well, thin pancakes that can be stuffed around chocolate, marmalade, or a farmer's-cheese stuffing (*Topfen*). Serb *cevapcici* (kebabs) and *rasnici* also appear on menus with fair frequency, even in Austrian establishments, as does *Serbische Bohnensuppe*, a mighty Serb bean soup.

The national gastronomy itself includes lean spareribs and heavy-caliber bread or potato dumplings (also a Bohemian legacy) mixed with bacon or liver or stuffed with anything from cracklings (*Grammel*) to apricots (*Marillen*). In Carinthia (and to an extent in Burgenland), you should try *Sterz* (also called polenta), filling and healthy cornmeal dishes that have roots in Italy and Slovenia as well. From western Austria comes *Kaiserschmarrn,* the "emperor's nonsense" eaten with cranberry jam. The Styrians have their salads, goat and sheep cheeses, their various soups, garlic soup, pumpkin soup (*Kürbiskremsuppe*), and a basic soup of meat and root vegetables (*Wurzelfleisch*). In some friendly country *Heurige* in Lower Austria, you can try blood sausage, *Blunz'n,* with mashed potatoes, or the standard *Schweinsbraten,* pork roast. And there is more: the famous *Wiener schnitzel* (veal scallop, breaded, deep-fried in fresh oil); *Schinkenfleckerl* (broad flat noodles with ham—a Bohemian recipe), and the cheap but delicious *Beuschl* (lung and heart of beef in a thick sauce always served with a giant Knödel). *Tafelspitz mit Kren* is boiled beef fillet with horseradish.

Venison (*Wild*) is a specialty that crosses restaurant class boundaries. A nice *Rehrücken mit Serviettenknödel* (saddle of deer with a bread dumpling cooked wrapped in cloth) at a four-star establishment is something to write home about. By the same token, you may find a robust *Gamsgulasch* (chamois goulash) in a rustic little hut near the summit of a Styrian mountain, or excellent smoked sausages and hams being offered by a Carinthian *Almbauer* at a few tables outside his summer farm in the mountains.

You need not go thirsty either on your travels. Austria has excellent water, which can be drunk from the tap or straight from the spring at times, and that, good brewers will tell you, makes for excellent beer. Murau in Styria has a top brewery, with a fine restaurant attached. Some swear by Vienna's own Ottakringer. All the orchards in the country also make for terrific fruit juices. The new kid on the block for the past few years is elderberry (*Hollunder*), which comes in dry reds or whites and which—like wine—can be *gespritzt,* mixed with either tap water (*stilles Wasser*) or mineral water (*Mineral*). The *Sommergespritzter* is one-third wine, two-thirds water.

Austria's wines range from good to outstanding. Don't hesitate to ask waiters for advice, even in the simpler restaurants, and as with the food, go for the local wine, if possible. For a light, dry white wine, try the Grüner Veltliner. The Welschriesling is a slightly heavier, fruitier wine. In some areas, the wines have their own special names, for example, Styrians are particularly proud of their Schilcher, a generally dry rosé. The reds, too, are well represented, especially in Burgenland. Blauer Portugieser, Traminer, and Zweigelt tend to be on the lighter side. For a slightly heavier red, select a Blaufränkisch or Blauer Burgunder. A novelty, if you happen to be traveling around Heiligenbrunn in Burgenland, is the powerful Uhudler, made of ungrafted vines that originally came from the United States to make European vines resistant to devastating phylloxera. The Austrian government prohibited making it because of its high alcohol content, but after Austria joined the EU in 1995, the prohibition was lifted for fear other European nations would catch on and turn a good penny making this quintessential Austrian wine.

MEALTIMES

Besides the normal three meals, Austrians sometimes throw in a few snacks in between, or forego one meal for a snack. The day begins with a very early Continental breakfast of rolls and coffee; *Gabelfrühstück,* a slightly more substantial breakfast with eggs or cold meat; a main meal, usually served between noon and 2; afternoon *Jause* (coffee with cake) at teatime; and, unless dining out, a light supper to end the day, between 6 and 9, tending toward the later hour. Many restaurant kitchens close in the afternoon, but some post a notice saying DURCHGEHEND WARME KÜCHE, meaning that hot food is available even between regular mealtimes. In Vienna, some restaurants go on serving until 1 and 2 AM, a tiny number also through the night. The rest of Austria is more conservative.

Unless otherwise noted, the restaurants listed in this guide are open daily for lunch and dinner.

RESERVATIONS & DRESS

Reservations are always a good idea: we mention them only when they're essential or not accepted. Book as far ahead as you can, and reconfirm as soon as you arrive. We mention dress only when men are required to wear a jacket or a jacket and tie.

WINE, BEER & SPIRITS

Austrian wines range from unpretentious *Heurige* whites to world-class varietals. Look for the light, fruity white *Grüner Veltliner,* spicy golden *Traminer,* full-bodied red *Blaufränkisch* and the lighter red *Zweigelt.* Sparkling wine is called *Sekt,* with some of the best coming from the Kamptal region northwest of Vienna. Austrian beer rivals that of Germany for quality. Each area has its own brewery and local beer that people are loyal to. A specialty unique to Austria is the dark, sweet *Dunkles* beer. Look for *Kaiser Doppelmalz* in Vienna. Schnapps is an after-dinner tradition in Austria, with many restaurants offering several varities to choose from.

DISABILITIES & ACCESSIBILITY

The Austrian National Tourist Office in New York has a guide to Vienna for people with disabilities (including hotels with special facilities) and a special map of the city's accessible sights. As a general guideline, the Hilton, InterContinental, and Marriott chain hotels, plus a number of smaller ones, are usually accessible. Once in Austria, check with the Österreichischer Zivilinvalidenverband; the Gesundheitswesen/ Sozialamt der Stadt Wien and the Vienna Tourist Office also have a booklet on Vienna hotels and a city guide for travelers with disabilities.

➤ LOCAL RESOURCES: The **Austrian National Tourist Office** (☞ Visitor Information, *below*). **Österreichischer Zivilinvalidenverband** (✉ Stubenring 2, A–1010 Vienna, ☎ 01/513–1535). The **Gesundheitswesen/Sozialamt der Stadt Wien** (✉ Gonzagag. 23, A–1010, ☎ 01/531–14–0). **Vienna Tourist Office** (✉ Obere Augartenstr. 40, A–1025, ☎ 01/211–14–0).

RESERVATIONS

When discussing accessibility with an operator or reservations agent, **ask hard questions.** Are there any stairs, inside *or* out? Are there grab bars next to the toilet *and* in the shower/tub?

How wide is the doorway to the room? To the bathroom? For the most extensive facilities meeting the latest legal specifications, **opt for newer accommodations** which are more likely to have been designed with access in mind. Older buildings or ships may have more limited facilities. Be sure to **discuss your needs before booking.**

TRANSPORTATION

The railroads are both understanding and helpful. If prior arrangements have been made, taxis and private vehicles are allowed to drive right to the train platform; railway personnel will help with boarding and leaving trains; and with three days' notice, a special wheelchair can be provided for getting around train corridors. If you're traveling by plane, ask in advance for assistance or a wheelchair at your destination. A number of stations in the Vienna subway system have only stairs or escalators, but elevators are being added at major stations.

➤ COMPLAINTS: **Disability Rights Section** (✉ U.S. Department of Justice, Civil Rights Division, Box 66738, Washington, DC 20035-6738, ☎ 202/514–0301 or 800/514–0301; TTY 202/514–0301 or 800/514–0301, FAX 202/307–1198) for general complaints. **Aviation Consumer Protection Division** (☞ Air Travel, *above*) for airline-related problems. **Civil Rights Office** (✉ U.S. Department of Transportation, Departmental Office of Civil Rights, S-30, 400 7th St. SW, Room 10215, Washington, DC 20590, ☎ 202/366–4648, FAX 202/366–9371) for problems with surface transportation.

TRAVEL AGENCIES AND TOUR OPERATORS

As a whole, the travel industry has become more aware of the needs of travelers with disabilities. In the United States, the Americans with Disabilities Act requires that travel firms serve the needs of all travelers. Some agencies specialize in working with people with disabilities.

➤ TRAVELERS WITH MOBILITY PROBLEMS: **Access Adventures** (✉ 206 Chestnut Ridge Rd., Rochester, NY 14624, ☎ 716/889–9096, dltravel@ prodigy.net), run by a former physical-rehabilitation counselor. **CareVaca-**

tions (✉ 5-5110 50th Ave., Leduc, Alberta T9E 6V4, ☎ 780/986–6404 or 877/478–7827, FAX 780/986–8332, www.carevacations.com), for group tours and cruise vacations. **Flying Wheels Travel** (✉ 143 W. Bridge St., Box 382, Owatonna, MN 55060, ☎ 507/451–5005 or 800/535–6790, FAX 507/451–1685, thq@ll.net, www.flyingwheels.com). **Hinsdale Travel Service** (✉ 201 E. Ogden Ave., Suite 100, Hinsdale, IL 60521, ☎ 630/325–1335, FAX 630/325–1342, hinstrvl@interaccess.com).

DISCOUNTS & DEALS

Be a smart shopper and **compare all your options** before making decisions. A plane ticket bought with a promotional coupon from travel clubs, coupon books, and direct-mail offers may not be cheaper than the least expensive fare from a discount ticket agency. And always keep in mind that what you get is just as important as what you save.

CLUBS & COUPONS

Many companies sell discounts in the form of travel clubs and coupon books, but these cost money. You must use participating advertisers to get a deal, and only after you recoup the initial membership cost or book price do you begin to save. If you plan to use the club or coupons frequently, you may save considerably. Before signing up, find out what discounts you get for free.

➤ DISCOUNT CLUBS: **Entertainment Travel Editions** (✉ 2125 Butterfield Rd., Troy, MI 48084, ☎ 800/445–4137; $20–$51, depending on destination). **Great American Traveler** (✉ Box 27965, Salt Lake City, UT 84127, ☎ 801/974–3033 or 800/548–2812; $49.95 per year). **Moment's Notice Discount Travel Club** (✉ 7301 New Utrecht Ave., Brooklyn, NY 11204, ☎ 718/234–6295; $25 per year, single or family). **Privilege Card International** (✉ 237 E. Front St., Youngstown, OH 44503, ☎ 330/746–5211 or 800/236–9732; $74.95 per year). **Sears's Mature Outlook** (✉ Box 9390, Des Moines, IA 50306, ☎ 800/336–6330; $19.95 per year). **Travelers Advantage** (✉ CUC Travel Service, 3033 S. Parker Rd., Suite 1000, Aurora, CO 80014,

☎ 800/548–1116 or 800/648–4037; $59.95 per year, single or family). **Worldwide Discount Travel Club** (✉ 1674 Meridian Ave., Miami Beach, FL 33139, ☎ 305/534–2082; $50 per year family, $40 single).

CREDIT-CARD BENEFITS

When you use your credit card to make travel purchases you may get free travel-accident insurance, collision-damage insurance, and medical or legal assistance, depending on the card and the bank that issued it. American Express, MasterCard, and Visa provide one or more of these services, so **get a copy of your credit card's travel-benefits policy.** If you are a member of an auto club, always **ask hotel and car-rental reservations agents about auto-club discounts.** Some clubs offer additional discounts on tours, cruises, and admission to attractions.

DISCOUNT RESERVATIONS

To save money, **look into discount reservations services** with toll-free numbers, which use their buying power to get a better price on hotels, airline tickets, even car rentals. When booking a room, always **call the hotel's local toll-free number** (if one is available) rather than the central reservations number—you'll often get a better price. Always ask about special packages or corporate rates.

When shopping for the best deal on hotels and car rentals, **look for guaranteed exchange rates,** which protect you against a falling dollar. With your rate locked in, you won't pay more, even if the price goes up in the local currency.

➤ AIRLINE TICKETS: ☎ **800/FLY–4–LESS.** ☎ **800/FLY–ASAP.**

➤ HOTEL ROOMS: **International Marketing & Travel Concepts** (☎ 800/790–4682, imtc@mindspring.com). **Steigenberger Reservation Service** (☎ 800/223–5652, www.srs-worldhotels.com). **Travel Interlink** (☎ 800/888–5898, www.travelinterlink.com).

PACKAGE DEALS

Don't confuse packages and guided tours. When you buy a package, you travel on your own, just as though you had planned the trip yourself. Fly/drive packages, which combine airfare and car rental, are often a good deal. If you **buy a rail/drive pass,** you may save on train tickets and car rentals. All Eurail- and Europass holders get a discount on Eurostar fares through the Channel Tunnel.

ECOTOURISM

Austria is a popular vacation spot for those who want to experience nature—many rural hotels offer idyllic bases for hiking in the mountains or lake areas. There are an increasing number of *Urlaub am Bauernhof* (farm vacations) offered throughout Austria, where families can stay on a working farm and children can help take care of farm animals. Contact the associations below for information on these increasingly popular accommodation options.

➤ GENERAL INFORMATION: **Landidyll-Hotels in Österreich** (✉ Lichthof, A–6135 Stans, ☎ 05242/72109, FAX 05242/711094). **Österreich Werbung Urlaubsinfo** (✉ Margaretenstr. 1, A–1040 Vienna, ☎ 01/587–2000, FAX 01/588–6620).

➤ INFORMATION ON FARM HOLIDAYS: **Kärnten/Das Land der Sonne** (✉ Museumstr. 5, A–9020 Klagenfurt, ☎ 0463/585–0391, FAX 0463/585–0278). **Oberösterreich/Das Land vor den Alpen** (Upper Austria) (✉ Auf der Gugl 3, A–4021 Linz, ☎ 0732/6902–248, FAX 0732/6902–48). **Salzburg/Das Land der Tradition** (✉ Schwarzstr. 19, A–5024 Salzburg, ☎ 0662/870571–26, FAX 0662/870571–89). **Tirol/Das Land der Berge** (✉ Brixnerstr. 1, A–6020 Innsbruck, ☎ 0512/5929–326, FAX 0512/567367).

ELECTRICITY

To use your U.S.-purchased electric-powered equipment, **bring a converter and adapter.** The electrical current in Austria is 220 volts, 50 cycles alternating current (AC); wall outlets take continental-type plugs, with two round prongs.

If your appliances are dual-voltage, you'll need only an adapter. Don't use 110-volt outlets marked FOR SHAVERS ONLY for high-wattage appliances such as blow-dryers. Most laptops operate equally well on 110 and 220 volts and so require only an adapter.

EMBASSIES

➤ AUSTRALIA: **Embassy of Australia** (Mattiellistrasse 2–3, Vienna, ☎ 5128–580).

➤ CANADA: **Embassy of Canada** (Laurenzerberg 2, on the 3rd floor of Hauptpost building complex, Vienna, ☎ 531–38–01).

➤ NEW ZEALAND: **Mission of New Zealand** (Mattiellistrasse 2–4, Vienna, ☎ 505–3021).

➤ UNITED KINGDOM: **Embassy of United Kingdom** (Jauresgasse 10, Vienna, ☎ 01/71613–5151).

➤ UNITED STATES: **Embassy of the U.S.** (Boltzmanng. 16, A–1090, Vienna, ☎ 313–39). **Consulate of the U.S./Passport Division** (Gartenbaupromenade 2–4, A–1010, Vienna, ☎ 313–39).

EMERGENCIES

On the street, the German phrases that may be needed in an emergency are: *Zur Hilfe!* (Help!), *Notfall* (emergency), *Rettungswagen* (ambulance), *Feuerwehrmänner* (firemen), *Polizeiwache* (police station), *Arzt* (doctor), and *Krankenhaus* (hospital).

➤ CONTACTS: **Police** (☎ 133). **Fire** (☎ 122). **Ambulance** (☎ 144).

ENGLISH-LANGUAGE AND LOCAL MEDIA

The *International Herald Tribune, The Wall Street Journal,* and *USA Today* are readily available in most larger cities in Austria. For local Austria-specific information in English, the choice is more limited. Austria's international newspaper, the weekly *Austria Today* is sometimes found at newsstands, but more often available at movie theaters, and gives a general listing of cultural events. For a vast selection of American magazines, go to the bookstore *Morawa* (✉ Wollzeile 11, Vienna). There is no longer an English-language radio station in Austria. You can hear short English news broadcasts at 103.8 Mhz from early morning until 6 PM.

BOOKS

In Vienna, Salzburg, and Graz, it's fairly easy to find English-language bookstores. Bookstores in smaller towns sometimes have an English section or rack.

➤ LOCAL RESOURCES: **Big Ben's** (✉ Serviteng. 4a, Vienna, ☎ 01/319–6412). **British Bookstore** (✉ Weihburgg. 24–26, Vienna, ☎ 01/512–1945–0). **Shakespeare & Co.** (✉ Sterng. 2, Vienna, ☎ 01/535–5053). **American Discount** (✉ Waagpl. 6, Salzburg, ☎ 0662/845640). **The English Bookshop** (✉ Tummelpl. 7, Graz, ☎ 0316/826266–0).

AUSTRIAN NEWSPAPERS & MAGAZINES

The most widely read Austrian German-language newspaper is the *Kronen Zeitung* with a culture section on Fridays, but the most comprehensive section on the culture scene in Vienna can be found in the liberal weekly news magazine, *Falter,* with a new edition every Wednesday. Even though the listings are in German, it's easy to understand. Popular magazines are readily available at Tabak shops and newspaper stands and include the international weekly editions of *Time* and *Newsweek,* European editions of the fashion magazines *Marie-Claire,* and *Elle* (in German), and *Cosmopolitan,* also in German.

RADIO & TELEVISION

For news and weather broadcasts in English from early morning until 6 PM go to the rap music station, *U4* at 103.8 Mhz. For classical music, tune into *Radio Stephansdom* at 107.4 Mhz. *RTL* and *Radio Wien* offer American and British rock music at 92.9 Mhz and 89.9 Mhz respectively. British and Amerian pop can be found at *Energy,* 104.2 Mhz, and *Neue Antenne,* 102.5 Mhz. There are two non-cable television stations in Austria, the state-owned ORF 1 and ORF 2. Service is entirely in German, and American and English movies are dubbed in German. ORF 1 leans more towards sports events and children's shows, while ORF 2 schedules documentaries and Austrian and American TV series and films.

ETIQUETTE & BEHAVIOR

The most common form of greeting in Austria is *Grüss Gott,* which literally means "God greets you." When it comes to table manners, there are some surpising differences from American usage: Austrians eat hamburgers, french fries, and pizza with a knife and fork—and even sometimes ribs. Corn on the cob is seldom found on restaurant menus; it's regarded as animal feed. It's proper to bring flowers to your hostess if you're invited to someone's home for dinner, but never red roses (which are reserved for lovers). Note that if you bring wine to your hostess, it's considered a gift and is usually not served. Austrians are comfortable with nudity, and public and hotel saunas are used by both sexes; in such facilities, people are seldom clothed (though this is an option).

BUSINESS ETIQUETTE

Punctuality is a virtue in Austria. Austrians are very courteous and rather formal in business situations. Business luncheons and dinners are generally paid for by the person who arranges the meeting.

GAY & LESBIAN TRAVEL

Austria is a gay-friendly country in general. In Vienna, the twice-monthly free magazine *Xtra!* runs a calendar of daily events and addresses. Also look for the *Vienna Gay Guide* brochure, which publishes a list of gay-friendly bars, restaurants, hotels and saunas. For additional information, check the Web site www.gayguide.at.

➤ GAY- & LESBIAN-FRIENDLY TRAVEL AGENCIES: **Different Roads Travel** (✉ 8383 Wilshire Blvd., Suite 902, Beverly Hills, CA 90211, ☎ 323/651–5557 or 800/429–8747, ℻ 323/651–3678, leigh@west.tzell.com). **Kennedy Travel** (✉ 314 Jericho Turnpike, Floral Park, NY 11001, ☎ 516/352–4888 or 800/237–7433, ℻ 516/354–8849, main@kennedytravel.com, www.kennedytravel.com). **Now Voyager** (✉ 4406 18th St., San Francisco, CA 94114, ☎ 415/626–1169 or 800/255–6951, ℻ 415/626–8626, www.now voyager.com). **Skylink Travel and Tour** (✉ 1006 Mendocino Ave., Santa Rosa,

CA 95401, ☎ 707/546–9888 or 800/ 225–5759, FAX 707/546–9891, skylink-tvl@aol.com, www.skylinktravel.com), serving lesbian travelers.

➤ LOCAL RESOURCES: **Homosexuelle Initiative (HOSI)** (✉ Novarag. 40, A–1020 Vienna, ☎ 01/216–6604; ✉ Schubertstr. 36, A–4020 Linz, ☎ 0732/609898; ✉ Müllner Haupstr. 11, A–5020 Salzburg, ☎ 0662/465927; (✉ Innrain 100/1, A–6020 Innsbruck, ☎ 0512/562403).**Rosa Lila Villa** (✉ Linke Wienzeile 102, A–1060 Vienna, ☎ 01/586–8150, FAX 01/587–1778). **Referat für gleichgeschlechtliche Lebensweisen** (✉ Technikerstr. 4/ Zahnzubau 1. Stock, A–8010 Graz, ☎ 0316/873–5122). **Homosexuellen Aktion Voralberg (HAV)** (✉ Postfach 868, A–6854, Dornbirn, ☎ 0699/100–20–995).

HEALTH

MEDICAL PLANS

No one plans to get sick while traveling, but it happens, so **consider signing up with a medical-assistance company.** Members get doctor referrals, emergency evacuation or repatriation, 24-hour telephone hot lines for medical consultation, cash for emergencies, and other personal and legal assistance. Coverage varies by plan, so **review the benefits of each carefully.**

English-speaking doctors are readily available, and health care in Austria is usually excellent.

OVER-THE-COUNTER REMEDIES

You must buy over-the-counter remedies in an *Apotheke,* and most personnel speak enough English to understand what you need. Pain relievers are much milder than those available in the U.S.

SHOTS & MEDICATIONS

No special shots are required before visiting Austria, but if you will be cycling or hiking through the eastern or southeastern parts of the country, get inoculated against encephalitis; it can be carried by ticks.

HOLIDAYS

All banks and shops are closed on national holidays: New Year's Day; Jan. 6, Epiphany; Easter Sunday and Monday; May 1, May Day; Ascension Day; Pentecost Sunday and Monday; Corpus Christi; Aug. 15, Assumption; Oct. 26, National Holiday; Nov. 1, All Saints' Day; Dec. 8, Immaculate Conception; Dec. 25–26, Christmas. Museums are open on most holidays but closed on Good Friday, Dec. 24 and 25, and New Year's Day. Banks and offices are closed on Dec. 8, but most shops are open.

INSURANCE

Travel insurance is the best way to **protect yourself against financial loss.** The most useful travel insurance plan is a comprehensive policy that includes coverage for trip cancellation and interruption, default, trip delay, and medical expenses (with a waiver for preexisting conditions).

Without insurance you will lose all or most of your money if you cancel your trip, regardless of the reason. Default insurance covers you if your tour operator, airline, or cruise line goes out of business. Trip-delay covers expenses that arise because of bad weather or mechanical delays. Study the fine print when comparing policies.

For overseas travel, one of the most important components of travel insurance is its medical coverage. Supplemental health insurance will pick up the cost of your medical bills should you get sick or injured while traveling. U.S. residents should note that Medicare generally does not cover health-care costs outside the United States, nor do many privately issued policies. Residents of the United Kingdom can buy an annual travel-insurance policy valid for most vacations taken during the year in which the coverage is purchased. If you are pregnant or have a preexisting condition, make sure you're covered. British citizens should buy extra medical coverage when traveling overseas, according to the Association of British Insurers. Australian travelers should buy travel insurance, including extra medical coverage, whenever they go abroad, according to the Insurance Council of Australia.

Always **buy travel policies directly from the insurance company**; if you buy them from a cruise line, airline, or tour operator that goes out of business you probably will not be covered for the agency or operator's default, a major risk. Before making any purchase, **review your existing health and home-owner's policies** to find what they cover away from home.

➤ TRAVEL INSURERS: In the U.S.: **Access America** (✉ 6600 W. Broad St., Richmond, VA 23230, ☎ 804/285–3300 or 800/284–8300, FAX 804/673–1583, www.previewtravel.com), **Travel Guard International** (✉ 1145 Clark St., Stevens Point, WI 54481, ☎ 715/345–0505 or 800/826–1300, FAX 800/955–8785, www.noelgroup.com). In Canada: **Voyager Insurance** (✉ 44 Peel Center Dr., Brampton, Ontario L6T 4M8, ☎ 905/791–8700; 800/668–4342 in Canada).

➤ INSURANCE INFORMATION: In the U.K.: **Association of British Insurers** (✉ 51–55 Gresham St., London EC2V 7HQ, ☎ 020/7600–3333, FAX 020/7696–8999, info@abi.org.uk, www.abi.org.uk). In Australia: **Insurance Council of Australia** (☎ 03/9614–1077, FAX 03/9614–7924).

LANGUAGE

German is the official national language in Austria. In larger cities and in most resort areas, you will usually have no problem finding people who speak English; hotel staffs in particular speak it reasonably well, and many young Austrians speak it at least passably. However, travelers do report that they often find themselves in stores, restaurants, and railway and bus stations where it's hard to find someone who speaks English—so it's best to have some native phrases up your sleeve (☞ Chapter 11). Note that all public announcements on trams, subways, and buses are in German. Train announcements usually are given in English as well, but if you have any questions, try to get answers before boarding.

LANGUAGES FOR TRAVELERS

A phrase book and language-tape set can help get you started.

➤ PHRASE BOOK & LANGUAGE-TAPE SET: *Fodor's German for Travelers* (☎ 800/733–3000 in the U.S.; 800/668–4247 in Canada; $7 for phrasebook, $16.95 for audio set).

LODGING

You can live like a king in a real castle in Austria or get by on a modest budget. Starting at the lower end, you can find a room in a private house or on a farm, or dormitory space in a youth hostel. Next up the line come the simpler pensions, many of them identified as *Frühstückspension* (bed-and-breakfast). Then come the Gasthäuser, the simpler country inns. The fancier pensions in the cities can often cost as much as hotels; the difference lies in the services they offer. Most pensions, for example, do not staff the front desk around the clock. Among the hotels, you can find accommodations ranging from the most modest, with a shower and toilet down the hall, to the most elegant, with every possible amenity.

Austria has few very expensive ($$$$) hotels outside Vienna, Salzburg, and the major resorts, but has numerous expensive ($$$) ones, usually with swimming pools—sometimes indoor and outdoor—saunas, fitness rooms, and other amenities. The moderate ($$) accommodations in country areas or smaller cities and towns are generally more than adequate: food, service, and cleanliness are of high standards. The newer inexpensive ($) seasonal hotels have private showers. *See* Lodging *in* Pleasures and Pastimes in individual chapters for prices, which vary widely among large cities, resorts, and small country towns, as well as between peak and low seasons. Outside of the largest cities, Austria remains a country of smaller innkeepers and family operations. This fact opens the way for a warm relationship with owners and staff, adding to the pleasures of a vacation.

The Austrian National Tourist offices (☞ Visitor Information, *below*) have detailed brochures (in German) on farm and village holidays, on family apartments, and on hotels specializing in families with small children.

The lodgings we list are the cream of the crop in each price category. We always list the facilities that are available—but we don't specify whether they cost extra: when pricing accommodations, always ask what's included and what costs extra (two items that occasionally fall into the latter category are parking and breakfast). Properties marked ✕⌦ are lodging establishments whose restaurants warrant a special trip.

Assume that hotels operate on the **European Plan** (EP, with no meals) unless we specify otherwise. Increasingly, more and more hotels are including breakfast with the basic room charge, but check. In addition, many hotels (often set in the rural countryside) offer half- or full-pension—this price scale includes two or all daily meals in the basic rate package. If you are interested in the convenience of taking many, if not all, of your meals at your home-base hotel, inquire when making reservations if the hotels offer such plans.

Faxing is the easiest way to contact the hotel (the staff is probably more likely to read English than to understand it over the phone long-distance), though calling also works, and using e-mail messages is increasingly popular. In your fax (or over the phone), specify the exact dates that you want to stay at the hotel (when you will arrive and when you will check out); the size of the room you want and how many people will be sleeping there; what kind of bed you want (single or double, twin beds or double, etc.); and whether you want a bathroom with a shower or bathtub (or both). You might also ask if a deposit (or your credit card number) is required and, if so, what happens if you cancel. Request that the hotel fax you back so that you have a written confirmation of your reservation in hand when you arrive at the hotel.

Here is a list of German words that can come in handy when booking a room: air-conditioning (*Klimaanlage*); private bath (*privat Bad*); bathtub (*Badewanne*); shower (*Dusche*); double bed (*Doppelbett*); twin beds (*Einzelbetten*).

APARTMENT & CHALET RENTALS

If you want a home base that's roomy enough for a family and comes with cooking facilities, **consider a furnished rental.** These can save you money, especially if you're traveling with a large group of people. Home-exchange directories list rentals (often second homes owned by prospective house swappers), and some services search for a house or apartment for you (even a castle if that's your fancy) and handle the paperwork. Some send an illustrated catalog; others send photographs only of specific properties, sometimes at a charge. Up-front registration fees may apply.

➤ INTERNATIONAL AGENTS: **Drawbridge to Europe** (✉ 5456 Adams Rd., Talent, OR 97540, ☎ 541/512–8927 or 888/268–1148, ℻ 541/512–0978, requests@drawbridgetoeurope.com, www.drawbridgetoeurope.com). **Hometours International** (✉ Box 11503, Knoxville, TN 37939, ☎ 865/690–8484 or 800/367–4668, hometours@aol.com, http://thor.he.net/åhometour/). **Interhome** (✉ 1990 N.E. 163rd St., Suite 110, N. Miami Beach, FL 33162, ☎ 305/940–2299 or 800/882–6864, ℻ 305/940–2911, interhomeu@aol.com, www.interhome.com).

CASTLES

➤ INFORMATION: **Schlosshotels und Herrenhäuser in Österreich** (✉ Ferdinand-Hanusch-Pl. 1, A–5020 Salzburg, ☎ 0662/8306–8141, ℻ 0662/8307–86).

FARM HOLIDAYS

Farmhouse Holidays in Austria provides information on basic as well as specialty farms, such as organic farms or farms for children, for the disabled, for horseback riders

➤ INFORMATION: **Farmhouse Holidays in Austria** (✉ Gabelsbergerstr. 19, A–5020 Salzburg, ☎ 0662/880202, ℻ 0662/880202–3).

HOME EXCHANGES

If you would like to exchange your home for someone else's, **join a home-exchange organization,** which will send you its updated listings of available exchanges for a year and will include your own listing in at least one of them. It's up to you to make specific arrangements.

➤ EXCHANGE CLUBS: **HomeLink International** (✉ Box 650, Key West, FL 33041, ☎ 305/294–7766 or 800/638–3841, ℻ 305/294–1448, usa@homelink.org, www.homelink.org; $98 per year). **Intervac U.S.** (✉ Box 590504,

San Francisco, CA 94159, ☎ 800/756–4663, FAX 415/435–7440, www.inter-vac.com; $89 per year includes two catalogues).

HOSTELS

No matter what your age, you can **save on lodging costs by staying at hostels.** In some 5,000 locations in more than 70 countries around the world, Hostelling International (HI), the umbrella group for a number of national youth-hostel associations, offers single-sex, dorm-style beds and, at many hostels, rooms for couples and family accommodations. Membership in any HI national hostel association, open to travelers of all ages, allows you to stay in HI-affiliated hostels at member rates; one-year membership is about $25 for adults (C$26.75 in Canada, £9.30 in the U.K., $30 in Australia, and $30 in New Zealand); hostels run about $10–$25 per night. Members have priority if the hostel is full; they're also eligible for discounts around the world, even on rail and bus travel in some countries.

Austria has more than a hundred government-sponsored youth hostels, for which you need an International Youth Hostel Federation membership card. Inexpensively priced, these hostels are run by the Österreichischer Jugendherbergsveband and are popular with the back-pack crowd, so be sure to reserve in advance.

➤ IN AUSTRIA: **Österreichischer Jugendherbergsverband** (Schottenring 28, A-1010, Vienna, ☎ 01/533–53–53).

➤ ORGANIZATIONS: **Hostelling International—American Youth Hostels** (✉ 733 15th St. NW, Suite 840, Washington, DC 20005, ☎ 202/783–6161, FAX 202/783–6171). **Hostelling International—Canada** (✉ 400-205 Catherine St., Ottawa, Ontario K2P 1C3, ☎ 613/237–7884, FAX 613/237–7868). **Youth Hostel Association of England and Wales** (✉ Trevelyan House, 8 St. Stephen's Hill, Hertfordshire, Hertfordshire AL1 2DY, ☎ 01727/855215 or 01727/845047, FAX 01727/844126); membership in the U.S. $25, in Canada C$26.75, in the U.K. £9.30).

HOTELS

All hotels listed have private bath unless otherwise noted.

➤ TOLL-FREE NUMBERS: **Best Western** (☎ 800/528–1234, www.bestwestern.com). **Choice** (☎ 800/221–2222, www.hotelchoice.com). **Hilton** (☎ 800/445–8667, www.hiltons.com). **Holiday Inn** (☎ 800/465–4329, www.holiday-inn.com). **Inter-Continental** (☎ 800/327–0200, www.inter-conti.com). **Marriott** (☎ 800/228–9290, www.marriott.com). **Ramada** (☎ 800/228–2828. www.ramada.com), **Renaissance Hotels & Resorts** (☎ 800/468–3571, www.hotels.com). **Sheraton** (☎ 800/325–3535, www.sheraton.com).

ROMANTIK HOTELS

For the coziest, most personal accommodations in elegant surroundings, some say the best options are the Romantik Hotels & Restaurants found throughout Austria.

➤ RESERVATIONS: **DER Travel Services** (9501 W. Devon Ave., Rosemont, IL 60018, ☎ 800/782–2424). **Euro-Connection** (✉ Box 2397, 1819 207th Place SW, Lynwood, WA 98036, 206/670–1140 or 800/645–3876). **MLT Vacations** (✉ 5130 Highway 101, Minnetonka, MN 55345, 612/474–2540 or 800/362–3520). **Romantik Travel and Tours** (✉ 16932 Wood-inville-Redmond Rd., Suite A107, Box 1278, Woodinville, WA 98072, 206/486–9394 or 800/826–0015).

MAIL & SHIPPING

Post offices are scattered throughout every district in Vienna and are recognizable by a "square yellow sign that says "Post." They are usually open weekdays from 9–12 and 2–6, Saturday 8–10 AM. The main post office near Schwedenplatz (Fleischmarkt 19, A–1010 Vienna), is open 24 hours daily. For overnight services, Federal Express, DHL, and UPS service Vienna and Austria; check with hotel concierge for nearest address and telephone number.

POSTAL RATES

Within Europe, all mail goes by air, so there's no supplement on letters or postcards. A letter of up to 20 grams (about ¾ ounce) takes AS7, a postcard AS6. To the United States or Canada, a letter of up to 20 grams takes AS13 for airmail. If in doubt, mail your letters from a post office and have the weight checked. The Austrian post office also adheres strictly to a size standard; if your letter or card is outside the norm, you'll have to pay a surcharge. Postcards via airmail to the United States or Canada need AS13. Always place an airmail sticker on your letters or cards. Shipping packages from Austria to destinations outside the country is extremely expensive.

RECEIVING MAIL

When you don't know where you'll be staying, **American Express** mail service is a great convenience, with no charge to anyone either holding an American Express credit card or carrying American Express traveler's checks. Pick up your mail at the local offices (✉ Kärntnerstr. 21–23, A–1015 Vienna, ☎ 01/ 515–40–0; ✉ Mozartpl. 5, A–5020 Salzburg, ☎ 0662/8080–0; ✉ Brixner Str. 3, A–6020 Innsbruck, ☎ 0512/ 58249; and ✉ Bürgerstr. 14, A–4021 Linz, ☎ 0732/669013). You can also have mail held at any **Austrian post office;** letters should be marked *Poste Restante* or *Postlagernd.* You will be asked for identification when you collect mail. In Vienna, if not addressed to a specific district post office, this service is handled through the main post office (✉ Fleischmarkt 19, A– 1010 Vienna, ☎ 01/515–09–0).

MONEY MATTERS

Prices throughout this guide are given for adults. Substantially reduced fees are almost always available for children, students, and senior citizens. For information on taxes, *see* Taxes, *below.*

ATMS

➤ ATM LOCATIONS: **Cirrus** (☎ 800/ 424–7787). **Plus** (☎ 800/843–7587) for locations in the U.S. and Canada, or visit your local bank.

Fairly common throughout Austria, **ATMs are one of the easiest ways to get Schillings.** Although ATM transaction fees may be higher abroad than at home, banks usually offer excellent, wholesale exchange rates through ATMs. Cirrus and Plus locations are easily found throughout large city centers, and even in small towns. If you have any trouble finding one, ask your hotel concierge. Note, too, that you may have better luck with ATMs if you're using a credit card or debit card that is also a Visa or MasterCard, rather than just your bank card.

To get cash at ATMs in Austria, **your personal identification number (PIN) must be four digits long.** Note, too, that you may be charged by your bank for using ATMs overseas; inquire at your bank about charges.

COSTS

A cup of coffee in a café will cost about AS40; a half-liter of draft beer, AS40– AS48; a glass of wine, AS40; a Coca-Cola, AS28; an open-face sandwich, AS36; a mid-range theater ticket AS250; a concert ticket AS400–AS600; an opera ticket AS600 upwards; a 1-mi taxi ride, AS40. Outside the hotels, laundering a shirt costs about AS50; dry cleaning a suit costs around AS160–AS200; a dress, AS120–AS160. A shampoo and set for a woman will cost around AS350–AS450, a manicure about AS180–AS220; a man's haircut about AS250–AS350.

CREDIT AND DEBIT CARDS

Credit cards are coming into widespread use, but figure on using travelers checks and having cash available. Most Austrian travel agencies still take only Diner's Club cards, but Visa and MasterCard are quickly gaining broad acceptance. The multiuse Eurocheck card can be used to pay in many gas stations and restaurants. Some establishments have a minimum sum for use of credit cards; others may accept cards grudgingly.

Should you use a credit card or a debit card when traveling? Both have benefits. A credit card allows you to delay payment and gives you certain rights as a consumer (☞ Consumer Protection, *above*). A debit card, also known as a check card, deducts funds directly from your checking account and helps you stay within your budget. When you want to rent a car, though, you may still need an old-fashioned credit card. Although you can always *pay* for your car with a debit card, some agencies will not allow you to *reserve* a car with a debit card.

Otherwise, the two types of plastic are virtually the same. Both will get you cash advances at ATMs worldwide if your card is properly programmed with your personal identification number (PIN). Both offer excellent, wholesale exchange rates. And both protect you against unauthorized use if the card is lost or stolen. Your liability is limited to $50, as long as you report the card missing.

Throughout this guide, the following abbreviations are used: **AE,** American Express; **DC,** Diner's Club; **MC,** Master Card; and **V,** Visa.

➤ REPORTING LOST CARDS: : **American Express** (336/939–1111 or 336/668–5309) call collect. **Diner's Club** (303/799–1504) call collect. **Mastercard** (0800/90–1387). **Visa** (0800/90–1179; collect: 410/581–9994).

CURRENCY

Up to January 1st, 2002, the Austrian Schilling (AS)—subdivided into 100 groschen—will remain the main unit of currency in Austria but after that date, the new single European Union (EU) currency, the euro, will take over. Until then, people will use the Schilling in their day-to-day transactions and travelers will continue to exchange their money for its colorful 1,000, 500, 100, 50, and 20 banknotes; 20, 10, 5, and 1 Schilling coins; and tiny 10 groschen coins. At press time (summer 2000), the exchange rate was about 14.50 Schillings to the U.S. dollar, 9.91 to the Canadian dollar, 22 to the pound sterling, 8.37 to the Australian dollar, 6.37 to the New Zealand dollar, and 17.47 to the Irish punt. As of 1999 the Euro (ECU) began to be quoted; at press time, 1 ECU equaled about 13.76 Austrian Schillings. For the euro denomination, the exchange rate (summer 2000) was about 1.12 euros to the U.S dollar, 0.74 to the Canadian dollar, 0.63 to the Australian dollar, 0.51 to the New Zealand dollar, and 1.26 to the Irish punt. These rates can and will vary. The schilling is pegged to the German mark at a constant 7-to-1 ratio.

Up to the euro changeover, there will be Austrian coins for 10 and 50 groschen and for 1, 5, 10, and 20 schillings. The paper notes have AS20, AS50, AS100, AS500, AS1,000, and AS5,000 face value. Legally, foreign exchange is limited to licensed offices (banks and exchange offices); in practice, the rule is universally ignored. You can sometimes pay with Deutschmarks, especially in regions near the border, in Salzburg, and in Tirol.

At this point, any transaction not involving cash may currently be transacted in euros. Schillings will stay in circulation up to July 1, 2002, the date of their final demise. After January 1st, 2002, participating European national currencies will no longer be listed on foreign exchange markets. The rates of conversion between the euro and local currencies have already been irrevocably fixed (1 euro = 13.7603 Schillings), eliminating commission charges in currency exchange. Please note that prices in euros correspond generally to the U.S. dollar as their exchange rates are relatively close.

Slowly but surely, the euro is becoming a part of daily European life; for every item purchased—be it a candy bar or a car—the price in both Schillings and euros has to be, by law, listed to familiarize people to this monumental change. Under the euro system, there are eight coins: 1 and 2 euros, plus 1, 2, 5, 10, 20, and 50 euro cent, or cents of the euro. All coins have one side that has the value of the euro on it and the other side with each country's own unique national symbol. There are seven banknotes: 5, 10, 20, 50, 100, 200, and 500 euros. Banknotes are the same for all EU countries.

CURRENCY EXCHANGE

Generally, exchange rates are far less favorable outside of Austria, and there is no need to exchange money prior to your arrival. ATMs are conveniently located in the city centers. Although fees charged for ATM transactions may be higher abroad than at home, Cirrus and Plus exchange rates are excellent, because they are based on wholesale rates offered only by major banks. Otherwise, the most favorable rates are through a bank. You won't do as well at exchange booths in airports or rail and bus stations, in hotels, in restaurants, or in stores, although you may find their hours more convenient than at a bank. Watch for changing developments as the Euro becomes accepted as a standard of exchange.

➤ EXCHANGE SERVICES: **Chase *Currency To Go*** (☎ 800/935–9935; 935–9935 in NY; NJ; and CT). **International Currency Express** (☎ 888/278–6628 for orders, www.foreignmoney. com). **Thomas Cook Currency Services** (☎ 800/287–7362 for telephone orders and retail locations, www.us. thomascook.com).

TRAVELER'S CHECKS

Do you need traveler's checks? It depends on where you're headed. If you're going to rural areas and small towns, go with cash; traveler's checks are best used in cities. Lost or stolen checks can usually be replaced within 24 hours. To ensure a speedy refund, buy your own traveler's checks—don't let someone else pay for them: irregularities like this can cause delays. The person who bought the checks should make the call to request a refund.

OUTDOORS & SPORTS

The Austrians are great sports lovers and go in for a greater variety of sports than any other European nation.

BALLOONING

Filzmoos in the Salzburg province near the Styrian border is one of several ballooning centers.

➤ CONTACTS: **Austrian Aero-Club** (✉ Prinz Eugen-Str. 12, A–1040 Vienna, ☎ 01/505–1028, FAX 01/505–7923). **Österreichischer Ballonfahrer Club** (✉ Endresstr. 79/4, A–1238 Vienna, ☎ 01/888–5888 or 01/889-8222, FAX 01/889–2626).

BICYCLING

Cyclists couldn't ask for much more than the cycle track that runs the length of the Danube or the many cycling routes that crisscross the country, major cities included. Just about every lake is surrounded by bike paths, and there are other rivers, too, such as the Drau, that have trails. You can rent a city bike (21-gear) for AS180 per day (AS120, if you have a rail ticket in your hand) at any of about 130 railroad stations throughout the country

and return it to another. With an all-day ticket (AS90), you can take your bike on the train with you anywhere in the country and leave it at another station with freight facilities for an AS90 return fee. If you have a *Vorteilscard* (☞ Discounts *in* Train Travel, *below*) it's all half price.

Tourist offices have details (in German), including maps and hints for trip planning and mealtime and overnight stops that cater especially to cyclists. Ask for the booklet "Radtouren in Österreich." There's also a brochure in English: "Biking Austria—On the Trail of Mozart" that provides details in English on the cycle route through the High Tauern mountains in Salzburg Province.

➤ CONTACT: **Austria Radreisen** (✉ Joseph-Haydn-Str. 8, A–4780 Schärding, ☎ 07712/5511–0, FAX 07712/4811). **Pedal Power** (✉ Ausstellungsstr. 3, A–1020 Vienna, ☎ 01/729–7234, FAX 01/729–7235).

BOATING AND SAILING

Small boats can be rented on all the lakes of the Salzkammergut region and on the large lakes in Carinthia. You can rent a rowboat on almost all of Austria's lakes and on the side arms of the Danube (Alte Donau and the Donauinsel) in Vienna.

Windsurfing (*Windsegeln*) is extremely popular, particularly on the Neusiedler See in Burgenland, on the Attersee in Upper Austria, and on the side arms of the Danube in Vienna. There are schools at all these locations with lessons and rentals.

➤ CONTACT: **Österreichischer Segel-Verband, the Austrian Yachting Club** (✉ Zetschg. 21, A–1230 Vienna, ☎ 01/662–4462, FAX 01/662–1558).

CAMPING

If your idea of a good holiday is the "great outdoors" and if your purse is a slender one, a camping holiday may be just the thing for you. Austrians love the idea and there are practically as many tourists under canvas as in the hotels and Gasthäuser. You'll find more than 450 campsites throughout the country, usually run by regional organizations, a few private. Most have full facilities, often including swimming pools and snack bars or grocery shops. Charges average about AS230 per day for a family of three, depending on the location and the range and quality of services offered. Many campsites have a fixed basic fee for three adults and one child, parking included. Camping is not restricted to the summer season; some sites are open year-round, with about 155 specifically set up for winter camping. For details, check with the tourist offices of the individual Austrian provinces.

➤ CONTACT: Österreichischer Camping Club (✉ Schubertring 1–3, A–1010 Vienna, ☎ 01/71199–1272).

FISHING

Among Austria's well-stocked lakes are the Traunsee, Attersee, Hallstätter See, and Mondsee in Upper Austria; the Danube, Steyr, Traun, Enns, Krems, and Alm rivers also provide good fishing. Tirol is another good region; try the Achensee, Traualpsee, Walchsee, Plansee, and nearby streams. Also try the Inn and Drau in East Tirol and the Ziller in the Zillertal. Styria provides some of the best trout fishing in Austria, as do the lakes in the Styrian Salzkammergut. Carinthian lakes and the streams in Lower Austria also abound in fish. Ask the Austrian National Tourist Office for the guidebook "Austrian Fishing Waters"; it includes licensing details. The separate provinces also have detailed brochures on waters and licensing. Unfortunately, the rights along many of the best streams have been given, meaning that no additional licenses will be issued, but ask at the local tourist office. Some hotels have fishing rights; we note these throughout the book.

GLIDING

From May to September you can glide solo or learn to glide at one of Austria's schools, at Zell am See (Salzburg province); Niederöblarn and Graz-Thalerhof (Styria); in Wiener Neustadt and Spitzberg bei Hainberg (Lower Austria). In Zell am See and at Wien-Donauwiese (Vienna) there are two-seater gliders, for instructor and passenger; at the other airfields you're on your own.

➤ CONTACT: **Austrian Aero-Club** (✉ Prinz Eugen-Str. 12, A–1040 Vienna, ☎ 01/505–1028–74, FAX 01/505–7923).

GOLF

Austria now has more than 50 courses. Most are private, but for a greens fee you can arrange a temporary membership. Many courses are associated with hotels, so package arrangements can be made. Austrian National Tourist Offices have golfing brochures.

➤ CONTACTS: **Hotelnetzwerk Betriebsführung** (✉ Bräuhausstr. 1a, A–5020 Salzburg, ☎ 0662/827852, FAX 0662/822098). **Österreichischer Golfverband** (✉ Prinz Eugen-Str. 12, A–1040 Vienna, ☎ 01/505–3245–0, FAX 01/505–4962).

HIKING AND CLIMBING

With more than 50,000 km (about 35,000 mi) of well-maintained mountain paths through Europe's largest reserve of unspoiled landscape, the country is a hiker's paradise. Three long-distance routes traverse Austria: E-4, the Pyrenees–Jura–Neusiedler See route, ending in Burgenland on the Hungarian border; E-5 from Lake Constance in Vorarlberg to the Adriatic; and E-6 from the Baltic, cutting across mid-Austria via the Wachau valley region of the Danube and on to the Adriatic. Wherever you are in Austria, you will find shorter hiking trails requiring varying degrees of ability. Routes are well marked, and maps are readily available from bookstores, the Österreichische Alpenverein/ÖAV, and the automobile clubs.

Of the more than 700 refuges in Austria, about a quarter are at altitudes of between 8,200 and 9,800 ft. Mountain guides typically charge AS2,250 a day for glacier tours and easy-to-moderate climbs, with the guides responsible for their own food. For more strenuous climbing and longer periods, you can arrange a fixed fee in advance. A tip is usual at the end of the climb.

If you're a newcomer to mountain climbing or want to improve your skill, schools in Tirol, Carinthia, Styria, and Salzburg province will take you on. Ask the ÖAV for addresses. All organize courses and guided tours for beginners and more advanced climbers.

Tourist offices have details on hiking holidays; serious climbers can write directly to **Österreichischer Alpenverein/ÖAV** (Austrian Alpine Club, ☞ *below*) for more information. Membership in the club (AS560, about $40) will give you a 50% reduction from the regular fees for overnights in the 275 mountain refuges it operates. Senior memberships have a reduced price.

➤ CONTACT: **Österreichischer Alpenverein** (✉ Wilhelm-Greil-Str. 15, A–6020 Innsbruck, ☎ 0512/59547–19, FAX 0512/575528; in the U.K., ✉ 13 Longcroft House, Fretherne Rd., Welwyn Garden City, Hertfordshire AL8 6PQ, ☎ 01707/324835).

HORSEBACK RIDING

Whether you want to head off cross-country or just canter around a paddock, Austria offers many kinds of equestrian holidays, and some hotels have their own riding schools. Ask for the booklet "Riding Arena Austria" from the tourist office. The provinces of Styria, Burgenland, and Upper and Lower Austria are particularly popular with riders.

SKIING

Skiing is without doubt the emperor of winter sports, and Austria is one of the finest places—if not the finest—in which to learn or practice the far-from-gentle art of skiing. For information about skiing centers and facilities in Austria, check the destination name as listed in the regional chapters of this book; also see "Powder-Perfect Skiing" in Chapter 11.

SNOWBOARDING

Snowboarders will find halfpipes and ample challenges in all major winter resorts. You can rent boards and take lessons in many Salzburg Province, Tirol, Carinthia, and Vorarlberg ski areas.

SPECTATOR SPORTS

Soccer is a national favorite. Every town has at least one team, and rivalries are fierce; matches are held regularly in Vienna and Innsbruck. When Austrians aren't skiing, they like to watch the national sport; downhill and slalom races are held regularly in Innsbruck, Kitzbühel, Seefeld, and St. Anton. There's horse racing with parimutuel betting at the track in the Prater in Vienna. Tennis matches are held in Vienna, Linz, and Innsbruck.

WATER SPORTS AND SWIMMING

Waterskiing and sail skiing are popular on the Wörther See (where there's also spectacular night waterskiing with torches) and Millstätter See in Carinthia; on the Traunsee, Attersee, and Wolfgangsee in Salzkammergut; in Zell am See in Salzburg Province; and on the Bodensee (Lake Constance) in Vorarlberg. Waterskiing is not permitted on many of the smaller Austrian lakes, so check first. There are hundreds of places to swim throughout Austria, and with very few exceptions the water is unpolluted. All the lakes in the Salzkammergut, Carinthia, and Tirol have excellent swimming, but are crowded in the peak season. In the Vienna area, the Alte Donau and Donauinsel arms of the Danube are accessible by public transportation and are suitable for families. It's best to go early to avoid the crowds on hot summer weekends. The Alte Donau beaches have changing rooms and checkrooms. Swimming in the Neusiedler See in Burgenland is an experience; you can touch bottom at virtually any place in this vast brackish lake. Swimming naked or at least partly so is fairly common.

PACKING

CHECKING LUGGAGE

How many carry-on bags you can bring with you is up to the airline. Most allow two, but not always, so make sure that everything you carry aboard will fit under your seat or in the overhead bin, and get to the gate early. Note that if you have a seat at the back of the plane, you'll probably board first, while the overhead bins are still empty.

If you are flying internationally, note that baggage allowances may be determined not by piece but by weight—generally 88 pounds (40 kilograms) in first class, 66 pounds (30 kilograms) in business class, and 44 pounds (20 kilograms) in economy.

Airline liability for baggage is limited to $1,250 per person on flights within the United States. On international flights it amounts to $9.07 per pound or $20 per kilogram for checked baggage (roughly $640 per 70-pound bag) and $400 per passenger for unchecked baggage. You can buy additional coverage at check-in for about $10 per $1,000 of coverage, but it excludes a rather extensive list of items, shown on your airline ticket.

Before departure, **itemize your bags' contents** and their worth, and label the bags with your name, address, and phone number. (If you use your home address, cover it so potential thieves can't see it readily.) Inside each bag, **pack a copy of your itinerary.** At check-in, **make sure that each bag is correctly tagged** with the destination airport's three-letter code. If your bags arrive damaged or fail to arrive at all, file a written report with the airline before leaving the airport.

PACKING LIST

Dressing in Austria ranges from conservative to casual, and is somewhat dependent on age. Older people tend to dress solidly, slacks on women are as rare as loud sport shirts are on men. Young people tend to be very trendy, and the trend is basically U.S., with kids in baseball caps, baggy trousers, loud shirts with all kinds of things written on them in (sometimes poor) English. In the country or more rural areas of, say, Styria or Burgenland, things are a little less loud. Jeans are ubiquitous in Austria as everywhere, but are considered inappropriate at concerts (other than pop) or formal restaurants. For concerts and opera, women may want a skirt or dress, and men a jacket; even in summer, gala performances at small festivals tend to be dressy. And since an evening outside at a Heuriger (wine garden) may be on your agenda, be sure to take a sweater or light wrap. Unless you're staying in an expensive hotel or will be in one place for more than a day or two, take hand-washables; laundry service gets compli-

cated. Austria is a walking country, in cities and mountains alike. If intending to hike in the mountains, bring boots with sturdy soles and that rise above the ankle. For lots of city walking a good pair of sports shoes is needed.

Mountainous areas are bright, so bring sunscreen lotion, even in winter. Consider packing a small folding umbrella for the odd deluge, or a waterproof windbreaker of sorts. Sunglasses are a must as well, and if you intend to go high up in the mountains, make sure your sunglasses are good and prevent lateral rays. Mosquitoes can become quite a bother in summer around the lakes and along the rivers, especially the Danube and the swampy regions created by its old arms. Bring some good repellent.

In your carry-on luggage, **pack an extra pair of eyeglasses or contact lenses** and **enough of any medication you take** to last the entire trip. You may also ask your doctor to write a spare prescription using the drug's generic name, since brand names may vary from country to country. In luggage to be checked, **never pack prescription drugs or valuables.** To avoid customs delays, carry medications in their original packaging. And don't forget to carry with you the addresses of offices that handle refunds of lost traveler's checks.

PASSPORTS & VISAS

When traveling internationally, **carry your passport even if you don't need one** (it's always the best form of I.D.) and **make two photocopies of the data page** (one for someone at home and another for you, carried separately from your passport). If you lose your passport, promptly call the nearest embassy or consulate and the local police.

ENTERING AUSTRIA

U.S., Australian, Canadian, New Zealand, and U.K. citizens need only a valid passport to enter Austria for stays of up to three months.

PASSPORT OFFICES

The best time to apply for a passport or to renew is in fall and winter. Before any trip, check your passport's expiration date, and, if necessary, renew it as soon as possible. (Some countries won't allow you to enter on a passport that's due to expire in six months or less.)

➤ AUSTRALIAN CITIZENS: **Australian Passport Office** (☎ 131–232, www.dfat.gov.au/passports).

➤ CANADIAN CITIZENS: **Passport Office** (☎ 819/994–3500 or 800/567–6868, www.dfait-maeci.gc.ca/passport).

➤ NEW ZEALAND CITIZENS: **New Zealand Passport Office** (☎ 04/494–0700, www.passports.govt.nz).

➤ U.K. CITIZENS: **London Passport Office** (☎ 0990/210–410) for fees and documentation requirements and to request an emergency passport.

➤ U.S. CITIZENS: **National Passport Information Center** (☎ 900/225–5674; calls are 35¢ per minute for automated service, $1.05 per minute for operator service).

SENIOR-CITIZEN TRAVEL

To qualify for age-related discounts, **mention your senior-citizen status up front** when booking hotel reservations (not when checking out) and before you're seated in restaurants (not when paying the bill). When renting a car, ask about promotional car-rental discounts, which can be cheaper than senior-citizen rates.

Austria has so many senior citizens that facilities almost everywhere cater to the needs of older travelers, with discounts for rail travel and museum entry. Check with the Austrian National Tourist Office to find what form of identification is required, but generally if you're 65 or over (women 62), once you're in Austria the railroads will issue you a *Seniorenpass* (you'll need a passport photo and passport or other proof of age) entitling you to the senior citizen discounts regardless of nationality.

➤ EDUCATIONAL PROGRAMS: Elderhostel (✉ 75 Federal St., 3rd floor, Boston, MA 02110, ☎ 877/426–8056, FAX 877/426–2166, www.elderhostel.org). **Interhostel** (✉ University of New Hampshire, 6 Garrison Ave., Durham, NH 03824, ☎ 603/862–

1147 or 800/733–9753, FAX 603/862–1113, www.learn.unh.edu).

SHOPPING

SMART SOUVENIRS

Not so long ago, almost any store on Vienna's Kärntnerstrasse could boast that it once created its exquisite jewelry, fine leather goods, or petit-point handbags (as Viennese as St. Stephen's Cathedral) for the imperial Habsburgs. The court has vanished, but the *Hoflieferanten* (court suppliers) still maintain their name and at times the old-fashioned grace, slightly fawning touch, and lots of *Gnä Frau* and *der Herr* thrown in for good measure.

There are various types of souvenirs to take home and enjoy, of course: fine glassware from Riedel's in Kufstein (founded 1756); Swarovski crystal; ceramics from a variety of manufacturers, including Gmundner ware from Gmunden, near Salzburg; and Augarten porcelain, Europe's oldest china after Meissen. These wares are distributed throughout the country in large and loud shops in the pedestrian zones of Vienna, Salzburg, Graz, Innsbruck, Klagenfurt, and so on. The same applies to traditional clothing: lederhosen, dirndls, and the like can be purchased at such places as Lanz (Vienna and Salzburg), Geiger (in Salzburg), Giesswein (in Vienna) or by keeping a sharp eye out for the magic word *Trachten* while driving about. You may accidentally stumble over some treasures in small towns such as Tamsweg or Feldkirchen in Carinthia, or run across a farmer's market where honest-to-goodness handmade traditional clothing and ornamentations are being sold alongside sheep, boar, or deer skins, leatherware of all sorts, the best plum schnapps, and elderberry and wild raspberry syrups. As for pottery and crockery, you may prefer to take home some of the cottage-industry ware from Stoob in Burgenland or a set of wooden plates that simply get better by the year. Sipping a cooled Schilcher on a warm summer evening on your porch at home may be the best way of remembering a terrific trip to Austria (but don't forget customs restrictions).

STUDENTS IN AUSTRIA

To save money, **look into deals available through student-oriented travel agencies.** To qualify you'll need a bona fide student ID card. Members of international student groups are also eligible. Information on student tickets, fares, and lodgings is available from Jugend Info Wien (Youth Information Center) in Vienna.

➤ LOCAL RESOURCES: **Jugend Info Wien** (Youth Information Center; ✉ Dr. Karl-Renner-Ring/Bellaria-Passage, Vienna, ☎ 01/1799), open Monday–Saturday, noon–7 PM.

➤ I.D.S & SERVICES: **Council Travel** (CIEE; ✉ 205 E. 42nd St., 14th floor, New York, NY 10017, ☎ 212/822–2700 or 888/268–6245, FAX 212/822–2699, info@councilexchanges.org, www.councilexchanges.org) for mail orders only, in the U.S. **Travel Cuts** (✉ 187 College St., Toronto, Ontario M5T 1P7, ☎ 416/979–2406 or 800/667–2887, www.travelcuts.com) in Canada.

➤ STUDENT TOURS: **AESU Travel** (✉ 2 Hamill Rd., Suite 248, Baltimore, MD 21210-1807, ☎ 410/323–4416 or 800/638–7640, FAX 410/323–4498), **Contiki Holidays** (✉ 300 Plaza Alicante, Suite 900, Garden Grove, CA 92840, ☎ 714/740–0808 or 800/266–8454, FAX 714/740–2034).

TAXES

VALUE-ADDED TAX

The Value Added Tax (VAT) in Austria is 20% generally but only 10% on food and clothing. If you are planning to take your purchases with you when you leave Austria (export them) you can get a refund. The shop will give you a form or a receipt, which must be presented at the border, where the wares are inspected. The Austrian government will send you your refund, minus a processing fee.

Wine and spirits are heavily taxed— nearly half of the sale price goes to taxes. For every contract signed in Austria (for example, car-rental agreements), you pay an extra 1% tax to the government, so tax on a rental car is 21%.

Global Refund is a V.A.T. refund service that makes getting your money back hassle-free. The service is available Europe-wide at 130,000 affiliated stores. In participating stores, **ask for the Global Refund form** (called a Shopping Cheque). Have it stamped like any customs form by customs officials when you leave the European Union. Then take the form to one of the more than 700 Global Refund counters— conveniently located at every major airport and border crossing—and your money will be refunded on the spot in the form of cash, check, or a refund to your credit-card account (minus a small percentage for processing).

Global Refund (✉ 707 Summer St., Stamford, CT 06901, ☎ 800/566–9828, FAX 203/674–8709, taxfree@ us.globalrefund.com, www.global refund.com).

TELEPHONES

AREA & COUNTRY CODES

The country code for Austria for 43. When dialing an Austrian number from abroad, drop the initial 0 from the local area code.

Austria's telephone service is in a state of change as the country converts to a digital system. We make every effort to keep numbers up to date, but do recheck the number— particularly in Innsbruck, Linz, and Vienna—if you have problems getting the connection you want (a sharp tone indicates no connection or that the number has been changed). All numbers given in this guide include the city or town area code; if you are calling within that city or town, dial the local number only.

DIRECTORY & OPERATOR INFORMATION

For international information dial 11812 for numbers in Germany, 11813 for numbers in other European countries, and 11814 for overseas numbers. Most operators speak English; if yours doesn't, you'll be passed along to one who does.

INTERNATIONAL CALLS

You can dial direct to almost any point on the globe from Austria. However, it costs more to telephone from Austria than it does to telephone to Austria. Calls from post offices are always the least expensive and you can get helpful assistance in placing a long-distance call; in large cities, these centers at main post offices are open around the clock.

To make a collect call—you can't do this from pay phones—dial the operator and ask for an *R-Gespräch* (pronounced air-ga-*shprayk*). Most operators speak English; if yours doesn't, you'll be passed to one who does.

The international access code for the United States and Canada is 001, followed by the area code and number. For Great Britain, first dial 0044, then the city code without the usual "0" (171 or 181 for London), and the number. Other country and many city codes are given in the front of telephone books (in Vienna, in the A-H book).

LOCAL CALLS

When making a local call in Vienna, **dial the number without the city prefix.** A local call costs 2 Schillings for every three minutes.

LONG-DISTANCE CALLS

When placing a long-distance call to a destination within Austria, you'll need to know the local area codes, which can be found by consulting the telephone numbers that are listed in this guide's regional chapters. The following are area codes for Austria's major cities: Vienna, 01; Graz, 0316; Salzburg, 0662; Innsbruck, 0512; Linz, 0732. When dialing from outside Austria, the 0 should be left out. Note that calls within Austria are one-third cheaper between 6 PM and 8 AM on weekdays and from 1 PM on Saturday to 8 AM on Monday.

LONG-DISTANCE SERVICES

AT&T, MCI, and Sprint access codes make calling long distance relatively convenient, but you may find the local access number blocked in many hotel rooms. First ask the hotel operator to connect you. If the hotel operator balks, ask for an international operator, or dial the international operator yourself. One way to improve your odds of getting connected to your long-distance carrier is to travel with more than one company's calling card (a hotel may block Sprint, for example, but not MCI). If all else fails, call from a pay phone.

➤ ACCESS CODES: **AT&T Direct** (☎ 0800/200–288; 800/435–0812 for other areas). **MCI WorldPhone** (☎ 022–903–012; 800/444–4141 for other areas). **Sprint International Access** (☎ 0800/659–0043; 800/877–4646 for other areas).

PHONE CARDS

If you plan to make calls from pay phones, a *Wertkarte* is a convenience. You can buy this electronic phone card at any post office for AS200, AS100, or AS50, which allows you to use the card at any *Wertkartentelephon*. You simply insert the card and dial; the cost of the call is automatically deducted from the card, and a digital window on the phone tells you how many units you have left (these are not minutes.). A few public phones in the cities also take American Express, Diners, Mastercard, and Visa credit cards.

PUBLIC PHONES

Coin-operated pay telephones are dwindling in number. They take AS1, 5, 10, and 20 coins. A three-minute local call costs AS2. At the oldest coin-operated machines (they are huge and grey) drop in at least three one-schilling pieces, pick up the receiver and dial; when the party answers, push the indicated button and the connection will be made. If there is no response, your coin will be returned into the bin to the lower left. The smaller machines are more recent and don't have the button to connect. If your party has an answering machine you'll have to pay a little something. Most pay phones have instructions in English on them. Add AS1 when time is up to continue the connection.

Faxes can be sent from post offices and received as well, but neither service is very cheap.

TIME

The time difference between New York and Austria is 6 hours (so when it's 1 PM in New York, it's 7 PM in Vienna). The time difference between London and Vienna is 1 hour; between Sydney and Vienna, 14 hours; and between Auckland and Vienna, 13 hours.

TIPPING

Although virtually all hotels and restaurants include service charges in their rates, tipping is still customary, but at a level lower than in the United States. Tip the hotel doorman AS10–AS15 per bag, and the porter who brings your bags to the room another AS10 per bag. In very small country inns, such tips are not expected but are appreciated. In family-run establishments, tips are generally not given to immediate family members, only to employees. Tip the hotel concierge only for special services or in response to special requests. Room service gets AS10–AS20 for snacks or ice, AS20 for full meals. Maids normally get no tip unless your stay is a week or more or service has been special.

In restaurants, round up the bill by AS5 to AS50 or about 5%. You can tip a little more if you've received exceptional service. Big tips are not usual in Austrian restaurants, since 10% has already been included in the prices. Hat-check attendants get AS10–AS20, depending on the locale. Washroom attendants get about AS5. Wandering musicians and the piano player get AS20, AS50 if they've filled a number of requests.

Round up taxi fares to the next AS5 or AS10; a minimum AS5 tip is customary. If the driver offers (or you ask for) special assistance, such as carrying your bags beyond the curb, an added tip of AS5–AS10 is in order.

TOURS & PACKAGES

Buying a prepackaged tour or independent vacation can make your trip to Austria less expensive and more hassle-free. Because everything is prearranged, you'll spend less time planning.

Operators that handle several hundred thousand travelers per year can use their purchasing power to give you a good price. Their high volume may also indicate financial stability. But some small companies provide more personalized service; because they tend to specialize, they may also be more knowledgeable about a given area.

BOOKING WITH AN AGENT

Travel agents are excellent resources. But it's a good idea to collect brochures from several agencies as some agents' suggestions may be influenced by relationships with tour and package firms that reward them for volume sales. If you have a special interest, **find an agent with expertise in that area;** ASTA (☞ Travel Agencies, *below*) has a database of specialists worldwide.

Make sure your travel agent knows the accommodations and other services of the place they're recommending. Ask about the hotel's location, room size, beds, and whether it has a pool, room service, or programs for children, if you care about these. Has your agent been there in person or sent others whom you can contact?

Do some homework on your own, too: local tourism boards can provide information about lesser-known and small-niche operators, some of which may sell only direct.

BUYER BEWARE

Each year consumers are stranded or lose their money when tour operators—even large ones with excellent reputations—go out of business. So **check out the operator.** Ask several travel agents about its reputation, and try to **book with a company that has a consumer-protection program.** (Look for information in the company's brochure.)

In the United States, members of the National Tour Association and the United States Tour Operators Association are required to set aside funds to cover your payments and travel arrangements in the event that the company defaults. It's also a good idea to choose a company that participates in the American Society of Travel Agents' Tour Operator Program (TOP); ASTA will act as mediator in any disputes between you and your tour operator.

➤ TOUR-OPERATOR RECOMMENDATIONS: **American Society of Travel Agents** (☞ Travel Agencies, *below*). **National Tour Association** (NTA; ✉ 546 E. Main St., Lexington, KY 40508, ☎ 606/226–4444 or 800/682–8886, www.ntaonline.com). **United States Tour Operators Associa-**

tion (USTOA; ✉ 342 Madison Ave., Suite 1522, New York, NY 10173, ☎ 212/599–6599 or 800/468–7862, FAX 212/599–6744, ustoa@aol.com, www.ustoa.com).

COSTS

The more your package or tour includes, the better you can predict the ultimate cost of your vacation. Make sure you know exactly what is covered, and **beware of hidden costs.** Are taxes, tips, and service charges included? Transfers and baggage handling? Entertainment and excursions? These can add up.

Prices for packages and tours are usually quoted per person, based on two sharing a room. If traveling solo, you may be required to pay the full double-occupancy rate. Some operators eliminate this surcharge if you agree to be matched with a roommate of the same sex, even if one is not found by departure time.

GROUP TOURS

Among companies that sell tours to Austria, the following are nationally known, have a proven reputation, and offer plenty of options. The classifications used below represent different price categories, and you'll probably encounter these terms when talking to a travel agent or tour operator. The key difference is usually in accommodations, which run from budget to better, and better-yet to best. Note that each company doesn't schedule tours to Austria every year; check by calling.

➤ SUPER-DELUXE: **Abercrombie & Kent** (✉ 1520 Kensington Rd., Oak Brook, IL 60521-2141, ☎ 630/954–2944 or 800/323–7308, FAX 630/954–3324). **Travcoa** (✉ Box 2630, 2350 S.E. Bristol St., Newport Beach, CA 92660, ☎ 714/476–2800 or 800/992–2003, FAX 714/476–2538).

➤ DELUXE: **Globus** (✉ 5301 S. Federal Circle, Littleton, CO 80123-2980, ☎ 303/797–2800 or 800/221–0090, FAX 303/347–2080). **Maupintour** (✉ 1515 St. Andrews Dr., Lawrence, KS 66047, ☎ 785/843–1211 or 800/255–4266, FAX 785/843–8351). **Tauck Tours** (✉ Box 5027, 276 Post Rd. W, Westport, CT 06881-5027, ☎ 203/226–6911 or 800/468–2825, FAX 203/221–6866).

➤ FIRST-CLASS: **Brendan Tours** (✉ 15137 Califa St., Van Nuys, CA 91411, ☎ 818/785–9696 or 800/421–8446, FAX 818/902–9876). **Caravan Tours** (✉ 401 N. Michigan Ave., Chicago, IL 60611, ☎ 312/321–9800 or 800/227–2826, FAX 312/321–9845). **Collette Tours** (✉ 162 Middle St., Pawtucket, RI 02860, ☎ 401/728–3805 or 800/340–5158, FAX 401/728–4745). **DER Travel Services** (✉ 9501 W. Devon Ave., Rosemont, IL 60018, ☎ 800/937–1235, FAX 847/692–4141; 800/282–7474; 800/860–9944 for brochures). **Gadabout Tours** (✉ 700 E. Tahquitz Canyon Way, Palm Springs, CA 92262-6767, ☎ 619/325–5556 or 800/952–5068). **Trafalgar Tours** (✉ 11 E. 26th St., New York, NY 10010, ☎ 212/689–8977 or 800/854–0103, FAX 800/457–6644).

➤ BUDGET: **Cosmos** (☞ Globus, *above*). **Trafalgar Tours** (☞ *above*).

THEME TRIPS

➤ BARGE/RIVER CRUISES: **Abercrombie & Kent** (☞ Group Tours, *above*). **KD River Cruises of Europe** (✉ 2500 Westchester Ave., Purchase, NY 10577, ☎ 914/696–3600 or 800/346–6525, FAX 914/696–0833).

➤ BICYCLING: **Backroads** (✉ 801 Cedar St., Berkeley, CA 94710-1800, ☎ 510/527–1555 or 800/462–2848, FAX 510-527–1444). **Butterfield & Robinson** (✉ 70 Bond St., Toronto, Ontario, Canada M5B 1X3, ☎ 416/864–1354 or 800/678–1147, FAX 416/864–0541). **Euro-Bike Tours** (✉ Box 990, De Kalb, IL 60115, ☎ 800/321–6060, FAX 815/758–8851).

➤ CHRISTMAS/NEW YEAR'S: **Annemarie Victory Organization** (✉ 136 E. 64th St., New York, NY 10021, ☎ 212/486–0353, FAX 212/751–3149) is known for their spectacular "New Year's Eve Ball in Vienna" excursion. This highly respected organization has been selling out this tour—which includes deluxe rooms at the Bristol, the Imperial Palace Ball, and a Konzerthaus New Year's Day concert—for ten years running. In 1996, Annemarie Victory premiered a "Christmas in Salzburg" trip, with rooms at the Goldener Hirsch and a side trip to the Silent Night Chapel in Oberndorf. **Smolka**

Tours (⊠ 82 Riveredge Rd., Tinton Falls, NJ 07724, ☎ 732/576–8813 or 800/722–0057) has also conducted festive holiday-season tours that included concerts and gala balls.

➤ HIKING/WALKING: **Alpine Adventure Trails Tours** (⊠ 322 Pio Nono Ave., Macon, GA 31204, ☎ 912/478–4007). **Mountain Travel-Sobek** (⊠ 6420 Fairmount Ave., El Cerrito, CA 94530, ☎ 510/527–8100 or 800/227–2384, FAX 510/525–7710).

➤ MOUNTAIN CLIMBING: **Mountain Travel-Sobek** (☞ Hiking/Walking, *above*).

➤ MUSIC: **Dailey-Thorp Travel** (⊠ 330 W. 58th St., #610, New York, NY 10019-1817, ☎ 212/307–1555 or 800/998–4677, FAX 212/974–1420). **Smolka Tours** (☞ Christmas/New Year's, *above*).

➤ TRAIN TOURS: **Abercrombie & Kent** (☞ Group Tours, *above*). For a special treat, hire your own private rail car once used by kings and heads of state. For details, contact **Le Majestic Nostalgie-Reisen** (⊠ Nordbahnstr. 50, A–1020 Vienna, ☎ 01/214–9490, FAX 01/930–003-6800).

TRAIN TRAVEL

Austrian train service is excellent: it's fast and, for Western Europe, relatively inexpensive, particularly if you take advantage of the discount fares. Trains on the mountainous routes are slow, but no slower than driving, and the scenery is gorgeous! Many of the remote rail routes will give you a look at traditional Austria, complete with Alpine cabins tacked onto mountainsides and a backdrop of snowcapped peaks.

Austrian Federal Railways trains are identifiable by the letters that precede the train number on the timetables and posters. The IC (InterCity) or EC (EuroCity) trains are fastest, but a supplement of AS50 is included in the price of the ticket. EN trains have sleeping facilities. All tickets are valid without supplement on D (express), E (*Eilzug;* semi-fast), and local trains. The EC or IC supplement should be bought in the station with your ticket, in the train it will cost a few schillings

more. Seat reservations are required on some trains; on most others you can reserve for AS40 up until a few hours before departure. Be sure to do this on the main-line trains (Vienna–Innsbruck, Salzburg–Klagenfurt, Vienna–Graz, for example) at peak holiday times. The EC trains usually have a dining car with fairly good food. The trains originating in Budapest have good Hungarian cooking. Otherwise there is usually a fellow with a cart serving snacks and hot and cold drinks. Most trains are equipped with a card telephone in or near the restaurant car. Smoking is now forbidden on all Austrian trains.

Make certain that you inquire about possible supplements payable on-board trains traveling to destinations outside Austria **when you are purchasing your ticket.** Austrians are not generally forthcoming with information, and you might be required to pay a supplement in cash to the conductor while you are on the train.

Railroad enthusiasts and those with plenty of time can treat themselves to rides on narrow-gauge lines found all over Austria that amble through Alpine meadows; some even make flower-picking stops in season. A few lines still run under steam power, and steam excursions are increasingly easy to find. Local stations have descriptive brochures with dates, points of origin, and fares.

CLASSES

The difference between first and second class on Austrian trains is mainly a matter of space. First- and second-class sleepers, and couchettes (six to a compartment), are available on international runs, as well as on long trips within Austria. If you're driving and would rather watch the scenery than the traffic, you can put your car on a train in Vienna and take it to Salzburg, Innsbruck, Feldkirch, or Villach. You relax in a compartment or sleeper for the trip, and the car is unloaded when you arrive.

DISCOUNT PASSES

To save money, **look into rail passes.** But be aware that if you don't plan to cover many miles you may come out ahead by buying individual tickets.

Austria is one of 17 countries in which you can **use Eurailpasses,** which provide unlimited first-class rail travel, in all of the participating countries, for the duration of the pass. If you plan to rack up the miles, get a standard pass. These are available for 15 days ($554), 21 days ($718), one month ($890), two months ($1,260), and three months ($1,558).

In addition to standard Eurailpasses, **ask about special rail-pass plans.** Among these are the Eurail Youthpass (for those under age 26), the Eurail Saverpass (which gives a discount for two or more people traveling together), a Eurail Flexipass (which allows a certain number of travel days within a set period), the Euraildrive Pass, and the Europass Drive (which combines travel by train and rental car). Whichever pass you choose, remember that you must **purchase your pass before you leave** for Europe.

Many travelers assume that rail passes guarantee them seats on the trains they wish to ride. Not so. You need to **book seats ahead even if you are using a rail pass**; seat reservations are required on some European trains, particularly high-speed trains, and are a good idea on trains that may be crowded—particularly in summer on popular routes. You will also need a reservation if you purchase sleeping accommodations.

Another option that gives you discount travel through various countries is the European East Pass, good for travel within Austria, the Czech Republic, Hungary, Poland, and Slovakia: cost is about $240 for any 5 days unlimited travel within a one-month period.

The ÖBB, the Austrian rail service, offers a large number of discounts for various travel constellations. If you are traveling with a group of people, even small, there are percentages taken off for each member. Families can also get discounts. School children and students also get good deals. The Vorteilscard is valid for a year and costs AS1190, allowing 50% fare reduction on all rail travel. If you are planning lots of travel in Austria, it could be a good deal. Ask for other special deals, and check travel agencies. Children between 6 and 15

travel at half price, under 6 years of age for free.

You can buy an Austrian Rail Pass in the United States for travel within Austria for 15 days ($154 first class, $104 second class). It's available for purchase in Austria also, but only at travel agencies.

For AS350 and a passport photo, women over 60 and men over 65 can obtain a Seniorenpass, which carries discounts up to 50% on rail tickets. The pass also has a host of other benefits, including reduced-price entry into museums. Most rail stations can give you information.

Travelers under 26 should inquire about discount fares under the Billet International Jeune (BIJ). The special one-trip tickets are sold by Eurotrain International, travel agents, and youth-travel specialists, and at rail stations.

➤ INFORMATION AND PASSES: **CIT Tours Corp.** (15 West 44th Street, 10th Floor, New York, NY 10036, ☎ 212/730–2400; 800/248–7245 in the U.S.; 800/387–0711; 800/361–7799 in Canada). **DER Travel Services** (✉ 9501 W. Devon Ave., Rosemont, IL 60018, ☎ 800/782–2424, ℻ 800/ 282–7474 for information). **Rail Europe** (500 Mamaroneck Ave., Harrison, NY 10528, ☎ 914/682– 5172 or 800/438–7245, ℻ 800/432– 1329; 2087 Dundas E, Suite 106, Mississauga, Ontario L4X 1M2, ☎ 800/361–7245, ℻ 905/602–4198).

FARES & SCHEDULES

For train schedules, ask at your hotel or stop in at the train station and look for large posters labeled ABFAHRT (departures) and ANKUNFT (arrivals). In the Abfahrt listing you'll find the departure time in the main left-hand block of the listing and, under the train name, details of where it stops en route and the time of each arrival. There is also information about connecting trains and buses, with departure details. Workdays are symbolized by two crossed hammers, which means that the same might not be running on weekends or holidays. A little rocking horse means that a special playpen has been set up for children in the train. Women traveling alone may book special compartments on the night trains or long distance rides (ask for a *Damenabteilung*).

FROM THE U.K.

There's a choice of rail routes to Austria, but check services first; long-distance passenger service across the Continent is undergoing considerable reduction. There is daily service from London to Vienna via the *Austria Nachtexpress*. Check other services such as the *Orient Express*. If you don't mind changing trains, you can travel via Paris, where you change stations to board the overnight *Arlberg Express* via Innsbruck and Salzburg to Vienna. First- and second-class sleepers and second-class couchettes are available as far as Innsbruck.

When you have the time, a strikingly scenic route to Austria is via Cologne and Munich; after an overnight stop in Cologne, you take the *EuroCity Express Johann Strauss* to Vienna.

➤ INFORMATION AND RESERVATIONS: Contact **Eurotrain** (✉ 52 Grosvenor Gardens, London SW1W OAG, ☎ 020/7730–3402), which offers excellent deals for those under 26, or **British Rail Travel Centers** (☎ 020/ 7834–2345). For additional information, call **DER Travel Service** (☎ 020/ 7408–0111) or the **Austrian National Tourist Office** (☞ Visitor Information, *below*).

TRAVEL AGENCIES

A good travel agent puts your needs first. Look for an agency that has been in business at least five years, emphasizes customer service, and has someone on staff who specializes in your destination. In addition, **make sure the agency belongs to a professional trade organization.** The American Society of Travel Agents (ASTA), with 27,000 agents in some 170 countries, is the largest and most influential in the field. Operating under the motto "Integrity in Travel," it maintains and enforces a strict code of ethics and will step in to help mediate any agent-client disputes if necessary. ASTA also maintains a Web site that includes a directory of agents. (If a travel agency is also acting as your tour operator, *see* Buyer Beware *in* Tours & Packages, *above*.)

➤ LOCAL AGENT REFERRALS: **American Society of Travel Agents** (ASTA; ☎ 800/965–2782 24-hr hot line, FAX 703/ 684–8319, www.astanet.com). **Association of British Travel Agents** (✉ 68– 71 Newman St., London W1P 4AH, ☎ 020/7637–2444, FAX 020/7637– 0713, information@abta.co.uk, www.abtanet.com). **Association of Canadian Travel Agents** (✉ 1729 Bank St., Suite 201, Ottawa, Ontario K1V 7Z5, ☎ 613/521–0474, FAX 613/ 521–0805, acta.ntl@sympatico.ca). **Australian Federation of Travel Agents** (✉ Level 3, 309 Pitt St., Sydney 2000, ☎ 02/9264–3299, FAX 02/9264–1085, www.afta.com.au). **Travel Agents' Association of New Zealand** (✉ Box 1888, Wellington 10033, ☎ 04/499– 0104, FAX 04/499–0827, taanz@tias-net.co.nz).

VISITOR INFORMATION

➤ AUSTRIAN NATIONAL TOURIST OFFICE: **In the U.S.:** ✉ 500 5th Ave., 20th floor, New York, NY 10110, ☎ 212/944–6880, FAX 212/730–4568, or write to Box 1142, New York, NY 10108. **In Canada:** ✉ 2 Bloor St. E, Suite 3330, Toronto, Ontario M4W 1A8, ☎ 416/967–3381, FAX 416/967– 4101; ✉ 1010 Sherbrooke St. W, Suite 1410, Montréal, Québec H3A 2R7, ☎ 514/849–3709, FAX 514/849– 9577; ✉ 200 Granville St., Suite 1380, Granville Sq., Vancouver, BC V6C 1S4, ☎ 604/683–5808 or 604/ 683–8695, FAX 604/662–8528. **In the U.K.:** ✉ 30 St. George St., London W1R 0AL, ☎ 020/7629–0461. **Web site:** www.anto.com.

➤ U.S. GOVERNMENT ADVISORIES: **U.S. Department of State** (✉ Overseas Citizens Services Office, Room 4811 N.S., 2201 C St. NW, Washington, DC 20520, ☎ 202/647–5225 for interactive hot line, 301/946–4400 for computer bulletin board, FAX 202/ 647–3000 for interactive hot line); enclose a self-addressed, stamped, business-size envelope.

WEB SITES

Do check out the World Wide Web when you're planning. You'll find everything from up-to-date weather forecasts to virtual tours of famous cities. Fodor's Web site, www.fodors. com, is a great place to start your online travels—just search for the Vienna miniguide, then search for "Links." For basic information: **Vienna** (info.wien.at); **Burgenland** (www.burgenland-tourism.co.at); **Carinthia** (www.tiscover.com/carinthia); **Upper Austria** (www.tiscover.com/upperaustria); **Salzburg** (www.salzburginfo.or.at); **Tirol** (www.www.tiscover.com/tirol); **Voralberg** (www.voralberg-tourism.at); and **Styria** (www.steiermark.com). For **train information**: (www.oebb.at).

For Vienna, here are some top web sites: **Wien Online**—the city's official Web site (www.magwien.gv.at/); **Vienna Scene**—the Vienna Tourist Board Web site (info.wien.at/e/index/html); **Wienerzeitung**—the city's leading newspaper Web site (www.wienerzeitung.at/); **Time Out Vienna** (www.timeout.com/vienna/index.html); **Austria Today**—the country's leading English-language newspaper Web site (www.proteus.at/austria-today/); two **Vienna tickets** Web sites (www.allevent.com/english.html; www.viennaticket.at/english/).

WHEN TO GO

Austria has two main tourist seasons. The weather usually turns glorious around Easter to mark the start of the summer season and holds until about mid-October, often later. Because much of the country remains "undiscovered," you will usually find crowds only in the major cities and resorts. May and early June, September, and October are the most pleasant months for travel; there is less demand for restaurant tables, and hotel prices tend to be lower.

A foreign invasion takes place between Christmas and New Year's Day, at which time many Viennese are already on the slopes of western Austria, and over the long Easter weekend, and hotel rooms in Vienna

are at a premium. July and August and the main festivals (☞ Festivals and Seasonal Events *in* Chapter 1) are crowded times, but again, the Viennese head out for their vacations, so the city itself is relatively calm.

The winter-sports season starts in December, snow conditions permitting, and runs through April. You can ski as late as mid-June on the high glaciers, at altitudes of 8,000 feet or more. Although reservations are essential in the major ski resorts in season, travelers can frequently find rooms in private houses or small pensions if they're prepared to take a slight detour from the beaten path.

CLIMATE

Austria has four distinct seasons, all fairly mild. But because of altitudes and the Alpine divide, temperatures and dampness vary considerably from one part of the country to another; for example, northern Austria's winter is often overcast and dreary, while the southern half of the country basks in sunshine. The eastern part of the country, especially Vienna and the areas near the Czech border, can become bitterly cold in winter thanks to Continental influence.

The *Föhn* is a wind that makes the country as a whole go haywire. It comes from the south, is warm, and announces itself by very clear air, blue skies, and long wisps of cloud. Whatever the reason, the Alpine people (all the way to Vienna) begin acting up; some become obnoxiously aggressive, others depressive, many people have headaches, and (allegedly) accident rates rise. The Föhn breaks with clouds and rain.

The following are average monthly maximum and minimum temperatures for three cities in Austria:

VIENNA

Jan.	34F	1C	May	66F	19C	Sept.	68F	20C
	25	− 4		50	10		52	11
Feb.	37F	3C	June	73F	23C	Oct.	57F	14C
	27	− 3		57	14		45	7
Mar.	46F	8C	July	77F	25C	Nov.	45F	7C
	34	1		59	15		37	3
Apr.	59F	15C	Aug.	75F	24C	Dec.	37F	3C
	43	6		59	15		30	− 1

SALZBURG

Jan.	36F	2C	May	66F	19C	Sept.	68F	20C
	21	− 6		46	8		50	10
Feb.	39F	4C	June	72F	22C	Oct.	57F	14C
	23	− 5		52	11		41	5
Mar.	48F	9C	July	75F	24C	Nov.	46F	8C
	30	− 1		55	13		32	0
Apr.	57F	14C	Aug.	73F	23C	Dec.	37F	3C
	39	4		55	13		25	− 4

INNSBRUCK

Jan.	34F	1C	May	68F	20C	Sept.	70F	21C
	19	− 7		46	8		50	10
Feb.	39F	4C	June	75F	24C	Oct.	59F	15C
	23	− 5		52	11		41	5
Mar.	52F	11C	July	77F	25C	Nov.	46F	8C
	32	0		55	13		32	0
Apr.	61F	16C	Aug.	75F	24C	Dec.	36F	2C
	39	4		54	12		25	− 4

➤ FORECASTS: **Weather Channel Connection** (☎ 900/932–8437), 95¢ per minute from a Touch-Tone phone.

WORDS AND PHRASES

Austrian German is not entirely the same as the German spoken in Germany. Several food names are different, as well as a few basic phrases.

Umlauts have no similar sound in English. An ä is pronounced as "eh." An äu or eu is pronounced as "oy". An ö is pronounced by making your lips like an "O" while trying to say "E" and a ü is pronounced by making your lips like a "U" and trying to say "E".

Consonants are pronounced as follows:

CH is like a hard H, almost like a soft clearing of the throat.

J is pronounced as Y.

Rs are rolled.

ß, which is written "ss" in this book, is pronouced as double S.

S is pronounced as Z.

V is pronounced as F.

W is pronounced as V.

Z is pronounced as TS.

An asterisk (*) denotes common usage in Austria.

English	German	Pronunciation
Basics		
Yes/no	Ja/nein	yah/nine
Please	Bitte	**bit**-uh
May I?	Darf ich?	darf isch?
Thank you (very much)	Danke (vielen Dank)	**dahn**-kuh (**fee**-len dahnk)
You're welcome	Bitte, gern geschehen	**bit**-uh, gairn ge**shay**-un
Excuse me	Entschuldigen Sie	ent-**shool**-di-gen zee
What? (What did you say?)	Wie, bitte?	vee, **bit**-uh?
Can you tell me?	Können Sie mir sagen?	kunnen zee meer **sah**-gen?
Do you know _____?	Wissen Sie _____?	**viss**-en zee
I'm sorry	Es tut mir leid.	es toot meer lite
Good day	Guten Tag	**goo**-ten tahk
Goodbye	Auf Wiedersehen	owf **vee**-der-zane
Good morning	Guten Morgen	**goo**-ten **mor**-gen
Good evening	Guten Abend	**goo**-ten **ah**-bend
Good night	Gute Nacht	**goo**-tuh nahkt
Mr./Mrs.	Herr/Frau	hair/frow
Miss	Fräulein	**froy**-line

Pleased to meet you	Sehr erfreut.	zair air-**froyt**
How are you?	Wie geht es Ihnen?	vee **gate** es **ee**-nen?
Very well, thanks.	Sehr gut, danke.	sair goot, **dahn**-kuh
And you?	Und Ihnen?	oont **ee**-nen?
Hi!	*Servus!	**sair**-voos

Days of the Week

Sunday	Sonntag	**zohn**-tahk
Monday	Montag	**moan**-tahk
Tuesday	Dienstag	**deens**-tahk
Wednesday	Mittwoch	**mitt**-voak
Thursday	Donnerstag	**doe**-ners-tahk
Friday	Freitag	**fry**-tahk
Saturday	Samstag	**zahm**-stahk

Useful Phrases

Do you speak English?	Sprechen Sie Englisch?	**shprek**-hun zee **eng**-glisch?
I don't speak German.	Ich spreche kein Deutsch.	isch **shprek**-uh kine doych
Please speak slowly.	Bitte sprechen Sie langsam.	**bit**-uh **shprek**-en zee **lahng**-zahm
I don't understand	Ich verstehe nicht	isch fair-**shtay**-uh nicht
I understand	Ich verstehe	isch fair-**shtay**-uh
I don't know	Ich weiss nicht	isch vice nicht
Excuse me/sorry	Entschuldigen Sie	ent-**shool**-di-gen zee
I am American/ British	Ich bin Ameri-kaner(in)/Eng-länder(in)	isch bin a-mer-i-**kahn**-er(in)/**eng**-len-der(in)
What is your name?	Wie heissen Sie?	vee **high**-sen zee
My name is . . .	ich heiße . . .	isch **high**-suh
What time is it?	Wieviel Uhr ist es? *Wie spät ist es?	**vee**-feel oor ist es **vee** shpate ist es
It is one, two, three . . . o'clock.	Es ist ein, zwei, drei . . . Uhr.	es ist ine, tsvy, dry . . . oor
Yes, please/	Ja, bitte/	yah **bi**-tuh/
No, thank you	Nein, danke	**nine** dahng-kuh
How?	Wie?	vee
When?	Wann? (as conjunction, als)	vahn (ahls)
This/next week	Diese/nächste Woche	**dee**-zuh/**nehks**-tuh **vo**-kuh
This/next year	Dieses/nächstes Jahr	**dee**-zuz/**nehks**-tuhs yahr
Yesterday/today/ tomorrow	Gestern/heute/ morgen	**geh**-stern/**hoy**-tuh/**mor**-gen

This morning/ afternoon	Heute morgen/ nachmittag	**hoy**-tuh **mor**-gen/ **nahk**-mit-tahk
Tonight	Heute Nacht	**hoy**-tuh nahkt
What is it?	Was ist es?	**vahss** ist es
Why?	Warum?	vah-**rum**
Who/whom?	Wer/wen?	vair/vehn
Who is it?	Wer ist da?	vair ist dah
I'd like to have . . .	Ich hätte gerne . . .	isch **het**-uh gairn
a room	ein Zimmer	ine **tsim**-er
the key	den Schlüssel	den **shluh**-sul
a newspaper	eine Zeitung	i-nuh **tsy**-toong
a stamp	eine Briefmarke	i-nuh **breef**-mark-uh
a map	eine Karte	i-nuh **cart**-uh
I'd like to buy . . .	ich möchte . . . kaufen	isch **merhk**-tuh **cow**-fen
cigarettes	Zigaretten	tzig-ah-**ret**-ten
I'd like to exchange . . .	Ich möchte . . . wechseln	isch **merhk**-tuh . . . **vex**-eln/
dollars to schillings	Dollars in Schillinge	dohl-lars in **shil**-ling-uh
pounds to schillings	Pfunde in Schillinge	pfoonde in **shil**-ling-uh
How much is it?	Wieviel kostet das?	**vee**-feel **cost**-et dahss?
It's expensive/ cheap	Es ist teuer/billig	es ist **toy**-uh/**bill**-ig
A little/a lot	ein wenig/sehr	ine **vay**-nig/zair
More/less	mehr/weniger	mair/**vay**-nig-er
Enough/too much/ too little	genug/zuviel/ zu wenig	geh-**noog**/tsoo-**feel**/ tsoo **vay**-nig
I am ill/sick	Ich bin krank	isch bin krahnk
I need . . .	Ich brauche . . .	isch **brow**-khuh
a doctor	einen Arzt	I-nen artst
the police	die Polizei	dee po-lee-**tsai**
help	Hilfe	**hilf**-uh
Fire!	Feuer!	**foy**-er
Caution/Look out!	Achtung!/Vorsicht!	**ahk**-tung/**for**-zicht
Is this bus/train/ subway going to . . . ?	Fährt dieser Bus/ dieser Zug/ diese U-Bahn nach . . . ?	fayrt **deez**er buhs/ **deez**-er tsook/ **deez**-uh **oo**-bahn nahk . . .
Where is . . .	Wo ist . . .	**vo** ist
the train station?	der Bahnhof?	dare **bahn**-hof
the subway station?	die U-Bahn- Station?	dee **oo**-bahn- **staht**-sion
the bus stop?	die Bushaltestelle?	dee **booss**-hahlt-uh- **shtel**-uh
the airport?	der Flugplatz? *der Flughafen?	dare **floog**-plats dare **floog**-hafen
the hospital?	das Krankenhaus?	dahs **krahnk**-en- house

the elevator?	der Aufzug?	dare **owf**-tsoog
the telephone?	das Telefon?	dahs te-le-**fone**
the rest room?	die Toilette?	dee twah-**let**-uh
open/closed	offen/geschlossen	**off**-en/ge-**schloss**-en
left/right	links/rechts	links/recktz
straight ahead	geradeaus	geh-**rah**-day-owws
is it near/far?	ist es in der Nähe/ist es weit?	ist es in dare **nay**-uh? ist es vite?

MENU GUIDE

English	German
Entrées	Hauptspeisen
Homemade	Hausgemacht
Lunch	Mittagsessen
Dinner	Abendessen
Dessert	Nachspeisen
At your choice	Önach Wahl
Soup of the day	Tagessuppe
Appetizers	Vorspeisen

Breakfast

Bread	Brot
Butter	Butter
Eggs	Eier
Hot	Heiss
Cold	Kalt
Caffeine-free coffee	Café Hag
Jam	Marmelade
Milk	Milch
Juice	Saft
Bacon	Speck
Lemon	Zitrone
Sugar	Zucker

Soups

Stew	Eintopf
Goulash soup	Gulaschsuppe
Chicken soup	Hühnersuppe
Potato soup	Kartoffelsuppe
Liver dumpling soup	Leberknödelsuppe
Onion soup	Zwiebelsuppe

Fish and Seafood

Trout	Forelle
Prawns	Garnele
Halibut	Heilbutt
Lobster	Hummer
Crab	Krabbe
Salmon	Lachs
Squid	Tintenfisch
Tuna	Thunfisch
Turbot	Steinbutt

Meats

Veal	Kalb
Lamb	Lamm
Beef	Rindfleisch
Pork	Schwein

Game and Poultry

Duck	Ente
Pheasant	Fasan
Goose	Gans
Chicken	Hühner
Rabbit	Kaninchen
Venison	Reh
Turkey	Truthahn
Quail	Wachtel

Vegetables and Side Dishes

Red cabbage	Rotkraut
Cauliflower	Karfiol
Beans	Bohnen
Button mushrooms	Champignons
Peas	Erbsen
Cucumber	Gurke
Cabbage	Kohl
Lettuce	Blattsalat
Potatoes	Kartoffeln
Dumplings	Knödel
French fries	Pommes frites

Fruits

Apple	Apfel
Orange	Orangen
Apricot	Marillen
Blueberry	Heidelbeere
Strawberry	Erdbeere
Raspberry	Himbeere
Cherry	Kirsche
Cranberry	Preiselbeere
Grapes	Trauben
Pear	Birne
Peach	Pfirsich

Desserts

Cheese	Käse
Crepes	Palatschinken
Soufflé	Auflauf
Ice cream	Eis
Cake	Torte

Drinks

Tap water	Leitungswasser
With/without water	Mit/ohne wasser
Straight	Pur
Non-alcoholic	Alkoholfrei
A large/small dark beer	Ein Krügel/Seidel Dunkles
A large/small light beer	Ein Krügel/Seidel Helles
Draft beer	Vom Fass
Sparkling wine	Sekt
White wine	Weisswein
Red wine	Rotwein
Wine with mineral water	Gespritz

INDEX

NOTES

FODOR'S AUSTRIA

EDITOR: Robert I. C. Fisher

Editorial Contributors: Bonnie Dodson, Lee Hogan, Alan Levy, Earl Steinbicker, George Sullivan, Lito Tejada-Flores

Editorial Production: Linda K. Schmidt

Maps: David Lindroth, *cartographer;* Rebecca Baer, *map editor*

Design: Fabrizio La Rocca, *creative director;* Guido Caroti, *art director;* Jolie Novak, *photo editor;* Melanie Marin, *photo researcher*

Cover Design: Pentagram

Production/Manufacturing: Robert B. Shields

COPYRIGHT

Copyright © 2001 by Fodor's Travel Publications

Fodor's is a registered trademark of Random House, Inc. All rights reserved under International and Pan-American Copyright Conventions. Published in the United States by Fodor's Travel Publications, a division of Random House, Inc., New York, and simultaneously in Canada by Random House of Canada Limited, Toronto. Distributed by Random House, Inc., New York.

No maps, illustrations, or other portions of this book may be reproduced in any form without written permission from the publisher.

ISBN 0-679-00665-6

ISSN 0071-6340

Ninth Edition

SPECIAL SALES

Fodor's Travel Publications are available at special discounts for bulk purchases for sales promotions or premiums. Special editions, including personalized covers, excerpts of existing guides, and corporate imprints, can be created in large quantities for special needs. For more information, contact your local bookseller or write to Special Markets, Fodor's Travel Publications, 280 Park Avenue, New York, NY 10017. Inquiries from Canada should be directed to your local Canadian bookseller or sent to Random House of Canada, Ltd., Marketing Department, 2775 Matheson Boulevard East, Mississauga, Ontario L4W 4P7. Inquiries from the United Kingdom should be sent to Fodor's Travel Publications, 20 Vauxhall Bridge Road, London SW1V 2SA, England.

PRINTED IN THE UNITED STATES OF AMERICA

10 9 8 7 6 5 4 3 2 1

IMPORTANT TIP

Although all prices, opening times, and other details in this book are based on information supplied to us at press time, changes occur all the time in the travel world, and Fodor's cannot accept responsibility for facts that become outdated or for inadvertent errors or omissions. So **always confirm information when it matters**, especially if you're making a detour to visit a specific place.

PHOTOGRAPHY

Paul Trummer/The Image Bank, *cover (city nestled in mountains, Salzburg).*

Archiv Vorarlberg Tourismus: *Richard Hörmann, 25A. Lech Tourismus, 25B. Dietmar Walser, 2 bottom center.*

Austrian National Tourist Office: *Ascher, 28E. Bartl, 10N, 13D, 16B. Bohnacker, 3 bottom left, 11P. Herzberger, 27B. Kluppenegger, 21B. B. Krobath, 15D. Lamm, 13B. J. Mallaun, 23F. L. Mallaun, 25C. Markowitsch, 10L. W. Mayer, 27C, 30H. Niederstrasser, 23D. Pigneter, 26 top. Trumler, 9I, 10M, 22C, 26A, 29F. W. Weinhaeupl, 16C, 19D. Wiesenhofer, 13A, 18A, 29 top, 30B, 30F.*

Bundesgestüt Piber, *30D.*

Carinthian Tourist Office, *24A, 24B.*

Corbis: *Dave Bartruff, 1. Dennis Degnan, 17D. Ric Ergenbright, 16A. Owen Franken, 6B. Dallas and John Heaton, 11Q. Bob Krist, 32. Adam Woolfitt, 7E.*

Dachstein Eishöhle, *19C.*

Hallstatt Tourist Office, *28D.*

Blaine Harrington III, *6C, 7D, 9K, 22B.*

Liaison International: *Buenos Dias Blldagentur, 9J.*

Lipizzaner Museum, *8G.*

Niederösterreich-Werbung: *Anton Bayr, 12A. Peter Hämmerle, 12C. Karl Korab, 2 top left. Lois Lammerhuber, 14C, 30C. K.M. Westermann, 3 top right, 12B.*

Österreichische Galerie, Belvedere, *8H.*

Restaurant Artner, *30E.*

Rust Tourist Office: *Bryan Reinhart, 13C.*

Salzburg City Tourist Office, *2 top right, 2 bottom left, 2 bottom right, 3 bottom right, 17E, 30A.*

Stift St. Florian, *15E, 30G.*

Stone: *David Ball, 4–5. Paula Bronstein, 21D. Shaun Egan, 7F. Sylvain Grandadam, 6A, 11O, 17F. Michele and Tom Grimm, 19E. John Lawrence, 22A. Steve Vidler, 18B.*

Tim Thompson, *14B, 20 top, 20A, 21C, 23E.*

Tourismusverband Gosau, *3 top left, 30I.*

Tourismusverband Steyr, *14A.*

Thomas Winkler, *30J.*

ABOUT OUR WRITERS

Every trip is a significant trip. Acutely aware of that fact, we've pulled out all stops in preparing *Fodor's Austria*. To help you zero in on what to see in Austria, we've gathered some great color photos of the key sights in every region. To show you how to put it all together, we've created great itineraries and neighborhood walks. And to direct you to the places that are truly worth your time and money, we've rallied the team of endearingly picky know-it-alls we're pleased to call our writers. Having seen all corners of the regions they cover for us, they're real experts. If you knew them, you'd poll them for tips yourself.

The author of our books and video selection, **Keith Besonen**, has written for the on-line magazines *Paper Daily*, *CuisineNet*, and *Salon*. He's fond of Austrian beer, and his favorite place to drink it is Brauhaus Nussdorf in Vienna.

Just when **Bonnie Dodson** thinks she's seen everything Austria has to offer, she makes another discovery. That's one of the happy end results of her work on several editions of this book (for this edition, she updated the Vienna, Side Trips from Vienna, Danube Valley, Eastern Austria, Salzburg, Salzkammergut, and Carinthia chapters). A native of Minneapolis with a graduate degree in writing, Bonnie moved to Vienna eight years ago with her husband and still gets a thrill every time she walks around the cobblestone streets of the historic First District. Like a true Viennese, she believes that coffee-drinking is a life's work. Updating our section on Vienna's cafés, she rarely could resist stopping into her favorite coffeehouses for a Mazagran—a melange with a dollop of whipped cream—and, of course, for the latest city news and gossip. Doing research for this edition also involved lots of driving, making the best of snowy mountain roads, and lots of good eating. Bonnie's husband, **Gary Dodson**, has worked around the globe and speaks five languages. His passions are travel, wine, movies, and Mozart (he wrote our Close-Up box on the great composer), and he enjoys partaking of all four in Austria.

It was the siren song of the mountains that drew **Lee Hogan** to the Austrian Alps. An amateur bicycle racer since the early 1970s, Lee was spellbound by scenes of professional cyclists challenging the high Alpine passes in Europe. Since arriving in Innsbruck two years ago, he has been busy discovering the mountain roads in Austria, northern Italy, and Bavaria. "Seeing things from the seat of a bicycle has always been my favorite way to travel," says Lee. "The pace is slow enough that you can really see where you are, and it is always fun to stop for coffee and strudel and talk with the locals." Talking comes easy for Lee, who stateside was a radio broadcaster since getting a graduate degree in journalism two decades ago. In addition to his work on this edition (he updated our chapters on the Eastern Alps, Innsbruck and Tirol, and Vorarlberg), he writes for the Innsbruck Tourist Office, Tirol Werbung, and the Austrian National Tourist Office. He continues to work in the studio, doing voice-overs for clients including Swarovski Crystal and other Tirolean-based companies.

"To the age, its art; to art, its freedom" was the motto of the famous Vienna Secession group, and **George Sullivan** firmly believes in this maxim, as any reader of our magisterial Vienna Exploring tours (in Chapter 1) can vouch. The history, art, and architecture of European cities have been his favorite subjects since he spent a college summer in London many years ago. A native of Virginia, he gets to Europe as often as he can (he's also written about Florence for Fodor's) and is currently working on an architectural guide to Rome. Austria—the country that gave us *Silent Night, Holy Night*—is never too far from his thoughts: in addition to his writing assignments, he helps run his family's Christmas tree farm.

Robert I.C. Fisher—editor of *Fodor's Austria*, art history buff, and Mozart-worshipper—toasts the Austria team with a hearty *"Prosit"* (cheers). Robert comes to Austria via the legends of Hollywood—such films as Disney's *Miracle of the White Stallions* (the famed Lippizaners) and *Al-*

most *Angels* (on the Vienna Boys Choir), and, of course, *The Sound of Music.* He urges readers to discover the perfect antidote for the high sugar content of the Rodgers and Hammerstein musical: the inspiring book, written by Baroness von Trapp (the real Maria) that served as the basis for the film. The *Story of the Trapp Family Singers,* first published in the 1950s, is filled with great good nature and wit, and for travelers there could be no better introduction to the endearing qualities of the Austrian people.

Danke, vielen Danke (many thanks) to the directors of the Austrian National Tourist Offices in Vienna and in New York and the individual tourist offices in each of the provinces for their generous and considerable assistance in preparing this new edition. Ulrike Weichselbaum of the Upper Austria Tourist Office in Linz and Susanne Bedits and Eva Oswald of the Graz Tourist Office were particularly helpful.

Don't Forget to Write

We love feedback—positive and negative—and follow up on all suggestions. So contact the Austria editor at editors@fodors.com or c/o Fodor's, 280 Park Avenue, New York, NY 10017. Have a wonderful trip!

Karen Cure
Editorial Director